AT ANY COST

AT ANY COST

*Jack Welch, General Electric,
and the Pursuit of Profit*

THOMAS F. O'BOYLE

ALFRED A. KNOPF

NEW YORK

1998

THIS IS A BORZOI BOOK
PUBLISHED BY ALFRED A. KNOPF, INC.

Copyright © 1998 by Thomas F. O'Boyle

www.randomhouse.com

Library of Congress Cataloging-in-Publication Data
O'Boyle, Thomas F.
At any cost: Jack Welch, General Electric, and the pursuit of profit / Thomas F. O'Boyle.
p.   cm.
Includes bibliographical references and index.
ISBN 0-679-42132-7 (alk. paper)
1. General Electric Company—Management. 2. Electric industries—United States—
Management—Case studies. 3. Welch, Jack (John Francis), 1935–   . I. Title.
HD9697.A3U555   1999
338.7′62138′0973—dc21   98-15011
CIP

Manufactured in the United States of America
First Edition

For Mae and Louise,

and in memory of Thomas E. O'Boyle

Turning and turning in the widening gyre
The falcon cannot hear the falconer;
Things fall apart; the centre cannot hold;
Mere anarchy is loosed upon the world,
The blood-dimmed tide is loosed, and everywhere
The ceremony of innocence is drowned;
The best lack all conviction, while the worst
Are full of passionate intensity.

William Butler Yeats,
The Second Coming

CONTENTS

8 pages of illustrations will be found following page 244

AUTHOR'S NOTE

The General Electric Company is without doubt one of the most fascinating and important institutions in twentieth-century American society, and I have been fortunate to have had the cooperation of hundreds of people in my investigation of it. Regrettably, however, Jack Welch and a number of other company executives were unwilling to be interviewed. I have made a serious effort to gain Mr. Welch's input, to give him and those others an opportunity to respond regarding the issues and concerns raised in this book, but my requests have been unavailing. Instead, I was referred to GE's Corporate Public Relations office, which to a responsible journalist is not the same as conducting an in-depth interview. Regardless, I have continued to refine the book's content and to investigate and verify the facts. I have done everything in my power to write a balanced and fair account of General Electric, gathering information and viewpoints from as many sources as possible. I have spoken to those who are fans of GE and Mr. Welch, and those who are not.

AT ANY COST

PROLOGUE

JEFF DEPEW HAD THE JOB of a lifetime. The General Electric Company, America's most prestigious and profitable corporation, had sent Depew to Japan as its overseas emissary to run a subsidiary that sold $100 million worth of electrical goods annually in Asia and the South Pacific. He was a thirty-something executive, president of GE Electrical Distribution and Control Asia/Pacific Limited, negotiating deals with people twice his age. A fast-track workaholic in a corporation with hundreds of fast-track workaholics, he was in the express lane, having raced through eleven jobs in nine years. Each new job had brought more money, more status, more responsibility, more deals to be done.

Depew's personal and professional lives had blended into a big blur. He could no longer tell where one began and the other ended; his ex-wife had said more times than he cared to recall, "Jeff, you're married to GE, not to me." Depew couldn't disagree because he was devoted to his job and because he loved it. He got a jolt out of working for General Electric, and the man reputed to be the greatest dealmaker in American business, Jack Welch. Depew loved the shooting highs he got from making deals. It may be hard to imagine anything less glamorous than the prosaic electrical products that Electrical Distribution and Control made, but ED&C, as it was called, had the same deep appeal common to all of GE's businesses—the opportunity to execute bold strategies and global alliances. Depew was a geopoliticist, and making deals appealed to his sense of international intrigue and high adventure. He loved the strategizing, the finessing, the give-and-take. To him, doing deals was an art form, like kabuki or bonsai, and doing them in Japan was even more artful.

Depew was the type of executive who made Jack Welch smile: smart, aggressive, confident, young. He had been hired in 1981, the same year Welch was elevated to CEO and began the most systematic program of change ever attempted in corporate America. Depew was anointed as an acolyte, a high achiever, and a survivor as well. He went through management boot camp with five other MBAs, all graduates of Harvard, Stanford, Northwestern, or other top business schools. The other five were gone from GE within a few years, leaving only Depew, who personified the youth movement that Welch had initiated. Old-timers, those presumed incapable of change, were sacked in favor of upstarts like Depew, who were handed unheard-of opportunities to reshape GE. Depew climbed to the executive rung in just five years, then to the senior executive rung in four more, winning Welch's praise and approval with each successive promotion. The next rungs, vice president and then corporate officer, were inevitable. Welch made the climb worthwhile—as president of a GE subsidiary, Depew had a salary of $123,000 a year, and with the performance bonuses, deferred compensation, stock option plans and other perks, his annual compensation easily surpassed $500,000, putting him among the four hundred or so most highly compensated executives in the company. The amenities weren't bad either: membership in the exclusive Tokyo Birdie Club, a chauffeured Lexus LS400, and housing in a fully subsidized, fully furnished apartment. But an even bigger reward was the ability to exercise power, at a much earlier age than was typical in the best companies of corporate America.

The deal that consumed Depew in the spring and summer of 1991 was the biggest of his ten-year career at GE. It was very important to General Electric because its Electrical Distribution and Control division was in trouble. For more than a century GE had been the leading manufacturer of basic electrical goods like control panels and circuit breakers, the dominant player in the dominant market, America. By the late 1980s, however, the business was changing. Global dominance was now the ticket to success, and ED&C had very little global presence. The number-one player in the world, France's Groupe Schneider, had bought out several American players to establish a pre-eminent position in the U.S. market, while GE flailed about trying to find a coherent strategy that would fend off its French rival. GE had executed several small transactions in Europe, and it had also established a joint sales venture with Fuji to sell products in Japan. Neither initiative had been successful. Larry Bossidy, the then vice chairman, had given Depew specific instructions to cultivate a relationship with Mitsubishi Electric, one of Japan's premier electrical equipment manufacturers and a Fuji rival. Depew's mission was clear: to improve radically GE's position in Japan. "Success in this assignment will position you well for continued career growth when you return to the U.S.," ED&C president Stephen Rabinowitz had written in the August 1990 letter offering Depew the promotion. And Mitsubishi seemed to be the path to success.

In a society where business relationships were feudal, Mitsubishi was a leading *samurai*. Although Mitsubishi Electric was only about half the size of General Electric, whose $60 billion in annual revenue at that time equaled the entire economic output of the state of Israel, the Mitsubishi "family" in its totality dwarfed GE. Mitsubishi was one of the giant *keiretsu* that controlled Japan, Inc. Through its cross-holdings in other companies, the Mitsubishi family held stakes in about fifty other enterprises, a diverse collection of businesses that included Mitsubishi Bank, Nikon cameras, and Kirin beer. Depew had successfully navigated the treacherous waters of the Mitsubishi *keiretsu*, and had met with his counterparts dozens of times, making great strides in winning their trust. After only six months in Japan, Depew was told by one Mitsubishi associate that he ought to find a Japanese wife. It was a high compliment, a sign that he had won a level of acceptance accorded to few *gaijin*.

What Depew envisioned was a "quantum leap," GE jargon for the type of deal that typically gets Welch excited. The proposed merger would take the better part of a year to consummate and would combine GE's and Mitsubishi's ED&C businesses into one entity, a dominating world player with combined annual sales of $3.5 billion. As the discussions with Mitsubishi progressed, Depew became convinced the deal made strategic and economic sense, and that both companies had enormous incentive to make it work. The combined company could be the world leader in six of the eight product lines Depew and his colleagues evaluated, and the deal would also allow GE to establish a relationship with the Mitsubishi *keiretsu*. Tapping into that powerful network could spawn lucrative relationships elsewhere. Depew saw the potential synergy, and he convinced Paolo Fresco, Welch's right-hand man on international matters (now chairman of the Italian automaker Fiat), that the initial gambit should involve ED&C, with many GE divisions to follow once the alliance had been established. Rabinowitz, Depew's boss, visited Japan several times for talks with Mitsubishi counterparts, as did several other division vice presidents. Rabinowitz, Depew, and Fresco agreed that sufficient progress had been made; it was now time to bring together the two top men, Welch of GE and Moriya Shiiki of Mitsubishi, for a brief get-acquainted session during Welch's trip to Japan in September 1991.

The day before their get-together, Welch met with the presidents of each of GE's Japanese subsidiaries for an operations review at the Okura Hotel in Tokyo. A presentation by Depew lasted forty minutes, and dealt exclusively with the Mitsubishi talks. He gave Welch a detailed analysis of how they had progressed, and what still needed to be done. While all the details hadn't been agreed upon yet, and wouldn't be for at least five months, everything looked great, Depew told Welch, who was excited, and anxious to proceed. Depew left the Okura confident that he and Welch were at one in their thinking.

The envisioned meeting was a standard protocol session, part of the mating dance that preceded every big merger. Welch knew the protocol of mergers and acquisitions. Back in November 1985, during his first meeting with RCA chairman Thornton Bradshaw, Welch had studiously avoided discussion of the matter that was uppermost in his mind—his desire to buy RCA. It was bad form to appear too eager. The forty-five-minute session at the Park Avenue apartment of matchmaker Felix Rohatyn, the prominent New York investment banker and now U.S. Ambassador to France, was kept strictly to a general discussion of consumer electronics, U.S. competitiveness, and the Japanese. At their next session a month later, Welch popped the question, and the historic marriage of RCA and GE was officially consummated shortly thereafter.

The meeting of Welch and Shiiki was supposed to proceed the same way—exchange a few pleasantries, pronounce their mutual respect and admiration for each other, and exit. It was still too early to get into details; those would be ironed out in subsequent sessions by the due-diligence teams that were being assembled. The only hint Depew had that Welch intended to advance a different agenda came during the limo ride to Mitsubishi headquarters in central Tokyo. Welch said cryptically, "We can do this faster." Depew dismissed the comment, not understanding the portent it represented for the deal, and, ultimately, for himself.

Arriving at the Mitsubishi building, the GE contingent—Welch, Fresco, Depew, and two other executives, one of whom served as interpreter—was escorted to a seventh-floor meeting room, where Shiiki and a complement of five associates were waiting. Depew had met Shiiki once before but had forgotten how tall he was for a Japanese. Towering over Welch, who stands five feet eight inches tall, Shiiki was the epitome of the Japanese executive persona— dignified, elegant, smooth, very much in control. Welch was also looking good. Depew always admired his spit-and-polish on appropriate occasions. There was a certain elegance about Welch: the solid silk handkerchief that perfectly matched his tie, the slim, elegant black watchband and face with white minute hands, distinctive yet subtle. There was a sleek exterior covering a cauldron of fiery emotions that stirred within his compact yet powerful frame. As Welch and Shiiki exchanged business cards, the setting seemed perfect. All systems were go. They began with a profuse exchange of thanks and the expected expressions of mutual admiration. Seated directly across from Shiiki, Welch quickly concluded the pleasantries and moved to the end of his chair. "It looks like we have a great opportunity here," he began, speaking through an interpreter. "We've seen your facilities, and we've been very impressed with them."

Welch reviewed for Shiiki why the deal looked so attractive—the product lines looked good, the cultures looked good, everything seemed to be a perfect fit. It would be an important combination, one that would allow both GE and Mitsubishi to smash Schneider. Shiiki nodded his head in agreement. "In the past," Welch continued, "we've tried to do deals with big Japanese companies—Hitachi, Toshiba—and we've had troubles. Maybe in this instance we can make two elephants dance. But you have a big bureaucracy, and we have a big bureaucracy. So let's not let the bureaucracies get in the way. Let's agree to do this deal right now."

Depew's jaw dropped. The full significance of the limo comment suddenly became clear to him, like a baseball bat across his forehead. He tried to keep cool, not allowing the Japanese to see the rush of emotions that were exploding inside him. Welch had crossed the protocol line. Maybe he could have gotten away with it in America, but not in Japan, where protocol is religiously observed. You didn't ignore a business card when it was offered, and you didn't push for an immediate commitment when negotiating with the Japanese—and especially not in a case like the present one, since Mitsubishi had already agreed to a five-month timetable that Welch had seemed comfortable with before the meeting began. Welch had thrown a curveball Shiiki wasn't the least bit prepared to hit. Depew watched helplessly as Shiiki and the Mitsubishi contingent recoiled, pressing their spines to the back of their chairs. They shot looks at Depew as if to say, "What's going on here?" Depew didn't have the slightest idea.

Shiiki reiterated his desire to go ahead with the plan, which under the circumstances Depew considered a victory, a subtle yet significant sign of how badly Mitsubishi wanted to do the deal; but Shiiki was not going to make a formal commitment on the spur of the moment. Mitsubishi had a long-standing relationship, dating back more than eighty years, with Westinghouse Electric Corporation, GE's traditional rival. Shiiki was willing to walk away from that relationship—the GE deal under consideration was bigger and bolder than anything Mitsubishi had with Westinghouse, and Shiiki was convinced that Westinghouse intended to abandon the business (which it later did). Shiiki needed a partner of stature to prepare for that eventuality, which was why he had been eager to talk to Welch. At the same time, Japanese etiquette required that Mitsubishi tell Westinghouse of its intentions before the latter heard about it from GE. Depew knew the Westinghouse aspect was sensitive; he had spent six months massaging this issue in negotiations with Mitsubishi, and had explained its sensitivity to Welch at the Okura meeting, but when Shiiki, in his reply to Welch, mentioned his obligation to inform Westinghouse before making a formal commitment to GE, Welch got testy.

"What do you mean, you have to tell Westinghouse?" he demanded. Shiiki tried to explain the nature of the relationship, but no explanation would suffice. Welch, who felt he had been embarrassed by someone who was trying to play off GE against Westinghouse, reiterated his concern that he didn't want to move forward unless Mitsubishi was unequivocally committed to doing the deal with GE. Shiiki assured him that was the case, and the deal would get done. On that note the get-together ended.

Welch had violated protocol because he believed the deal had to be done fast or it wouldn't be done at all, and he left convinced that Shiiki's reluctance to do it in speedier fashion was in fact a sign that they weren't eager after all. "This smells bad," he said to Depew and Fresco on the way out. "I don't think they want to do it." Welch went on to a meeting at the Ministry of Trade and Industry, while Depew and Fresco ducked into another session with Mitsubishi that appeared to go better than the first. A consensus was reached on how the negotiations ought to proceed, and ideas were exchanged on how the deal might be structured.

Several weeks later, however, Depew got a call from Rabinowitz. The deal, his boss told him, was hanging by a thread. Welch was very angry about how things had gone. He felt he had been sandbagged and embarrassed before one of the most prominent members of the Japanese business community. The only thing that would salvage the negotiations was a personal letter of apology from Shiiki, in which he stated his full commitment to do the deal. As far as Depew was concerned, it was Welch who ought to do the apologizing. Still, a letter seemed to be in the offing when Depew got a second call from Rabinowitz, who had again talked to Welch. Depew was now ordered to terminate immediately all discussions with Mitsubishi and instead focus on repairing the broken relationship with Fuji. Depew reluctantly followed orders and told his Mitsubishi counterparts what he had been directed to do. He apologized for not being able to deliver his management.

It didn't end there, however. Someone had to take the fall, and in December Rabinowitz was fired. Two weeks later, in January 1992, at the annual GE senior management conclave in Boca Raton, Florida, Welch had a private session with the dozen or so top executives of ED&C, which Depew attended, as did James McNerney Jr., Rabinowitz's replacement and a rising star within GE. Welch ran through the changes he wanted to see: better productivity, more growth, a coherent strategy. No more fiascoes like what had happened in Europe—or with Mitsubishi. Welch lingered on Mitsubishi, citing it as a supreme example of business failure, a poor strategy poorly executed.

All eyes were glued on Depew, who interjected calmly but emphatically,

"They still want to do the deal, and it still makes sense, economically and strategically." Welch jabbed back, then Depew returned the volley. Four times Welch made a statement, and four times Depew replied. The people seated around the table were clearly unaccustomed to seeing and hearing a public confrontation between Welch and a subordinate. They edged away from the table and from Depew, as if a leper were suddenly in their midst. Welch was also on unfamiliar territory. Rarely did anyone challenge him, and he grew slightly more agitated and redder in the face with each successive response from the obstreperous Depew, whose colleagues looked at him as if to say, "Are you nuts?" Finally, the exchange ended. "I never want to hear about Mitsubishi again," Welch said.

Two months later, Depew, who had flown from Tokyo to GE headquarters in Fairfield, Connecticut, for a meeting, was told afterward not to return to Tokyo. McNerney "needs to see you" was the message. Depew waited around several days before McNerney, who was in Europe, phoned in. "We're taking a different approach to the Asia/Pacific region. We want more of a sales orientation rather than business development. We're eliminating your position. I'm sorry," McNerney said. Depew's stellar career at GE had ended.

He never challenged GE's right to fire him. "It's a feudal society. Jack demands fealty from his subordinates," says Depew, who now works for General Motors. Later that year McNerney, as a reward for his allegiance to Welch, was promoted to senior vice president, stationed in Hong Kong. He was promoted in 1995 to head GE's lighting unit, and again in 1997 to head the aircraft-engine unit, and is now considered a front-runner in the race to succeed Welch when he retires in the near future. In May 1993, Depew filed suit against GE over the terms of his severance, a complaint that named Welch as a defendant. It was a fitting end to their relationship: Depew, whose sole existence at GE had been defined by the deals he had struck and the money he had made, wanted a better deal. The substance of his suit was that GE had reneged on more than $500,000, the difference between the severance package McNerney had promised and the one the company eventually offered and Depew reluctantly accepted.*

A BLOWN DEAL, a broken promise, a messy lawsuit—that's certainly not the image American business has come to associate with Jack Welch. Since taking

---

* In September 1997, a federal judge dismissed Depew's suit. The judge ruled he had failed to substantiate his claim that GE's executive severance plan represented an employee-benefit plan protected by federal labor law. Depew and his attorney have appealed the decision.

the reins of power at GE in 1981, he has been hailed as the wunderkind of Big Business, the man who revived an American institution. He is, according to reputation, America's premier corporate changemaster, our most prominent and successful big businessman. His methods and methodology are extolled in business schools, praised by the media, and copied by other CEOs.

He is the most recent in a long line of GE stars, a proud lineage that traces its origins to the most famous inventor in American history. Ever since Thomas Edison gazed upon the first flicker of incandescent light, GE, its scientists, and its executives have been at the forefront of the American century. The forerunner of GE that Edison founded in 1878 to support his endeavors evolved in the twentieth century into the prototypical corporate conglomerate, a powerful multinational whose reach today, to say the least, extends well beyond lightbulbs. GE manufacturing plants are located in thirty states, Puerto Rico, and twenty-five other countries around the globe. Nearly two million Americans own shares in GE, not counting the millions more who own shares indirectly through stock mutual funds, making it one of the most widely held stocks on Wall Street. With annual revenue greater than the gross domestic product of all but forty-eight of the 185 countries in the United Nations, GE is a corporate leviathan the likes of which not even Thomas Hobbes could have envisioned. Nine of its twelve business divisions are big enough to be listed on the Fortune 500. Besides electrical and lighting products, it makes plastics, aircraft engines, 400,000-pound locomotives, motors, appliances, giant turbines that generate electricity, and medical diagnostic equipment. Service operations, where most of the growth has been during the Welch era, include an information services group; a television network, NBC, with more than two hundred affiliate stations; and GE Capital, the nation's largest finance operation. More than three hundred retailers, from Montgomery Ward (which GE owns) to Levitz Furniture, use credit card systems run by GE Capital, which manages more credit cards than American Express and owns more commercial aircraft than American Airlines.

General Electric's influence extends well beyond its products. As one of the titans of American capitalism in the twentieth century, it has been respected by its peers and envied for its success, and has greatly influenced how governments and other corporations conduct their affairs. When the concept of decentralization swept corporate boardrooms in the 1950s or strategic planning in the 1970s, GE set the pace. GE gave us the first industrial research-and-development lab; the first industrial park; a price-fixing culture that for a long time was nearly impervious to government control; the take-it-

or-leave-it bargaining strategy of Lemuel Boulware, GE's top labor negotiator in the 1950s; and Ronald Reagan, host of *General Electric Theater.*

Each of the eight men who have run GE has captured the spirit of his times. In the thirties, it was Gerald Swope, the New Deal Democrat who gave capitalism a kindly face; in the forties, Charles Wilson, who headed the War Production Board and captained GE's immense contributions to the arsenal of democracy; in the fifties, Ralph Cordiner, a former Schick razor salesman who hired Reagan to sell the nation on conspicuous consumption, and "living better . . . electrically"; in the sixties, Fred Borch, whose hands-off approach to management nurtured many infant businesses; in the seventies, Reg Jones, the finance specialist and portfolio manager who advanced the concept of scientific management; and in the eighties, Jack Welch, who built the proto-typical global company, and in the process created immense wealth. General Electric under Welch is the world's most profitable and most valuable company, and the rewards to investors have been significant indeed—continuation of twenty-two consecutive years of dividend increases, a near perfect progression of ever higher profit, quarter after quarter and year after year, a 1,155 percent increase in the value of its shares from 1982 to 1997. In the summer of 1997, General Electric became the first corporation to be valued at more than $200 billion, up from $57 billion a decade earlier, and by July 1998 its shares had risen in value by yet another $100 billion.

That Welch has changed General Electric—and that shareholders have benefited enormously—is undeniable. Long before most chief executives had heard of corporate restructuring—and long before "downsizing" became a word heard daily in American life—Welch was practicing it. During his seventeen-year tenure, he has eliminated hundreds of thousands of jobs, bought and sold hundreds of businesses, removed entire echelons from the corporate hierarchy, and shifted assets from mature manufacturing businesses into entertainment and financial services. His approach to personnel cuts earned him the nickname "Neutron Jack." In some circles—including the Reagan White House, where he was a regular guest—it has been an epithet of honor.

Welch has wrought great change, but whether General Electric and the nation are better off because of it is open to question. His record as the man who saved General Electric is riddled with inconsistencies and seeming deception. Welch is impetuous, inclined to make lightning strikes and wage blitzkrieg. His decisions on people, assets, and strategies can be made in a heartbeat; one bad review with Jack may be the end of a long career. And the record shows that many of Welch's snap decisions have turned out to be stupendous blunders.

Although Jeff Depew's story presents a picture of Welch different from the one we're accustomed to reading, it is representative. Welch has many strengths, to be sure. One need look no further than Westinghouse, for more than a century GE's chief rival in the U.S. electrical-equipment industry and a corporation that has effectively ceased to exist, to understand that even great companies can be extinguished by mediocre management. In Westinghouse's case, its two CEOs from 1983 to 1990, Douglas Danforth and John Marous, eager to please Wall Street and to pump up earnings as quickly as possible, followed a strategy that was a virtual clone of Welch's. It was in the execution of the strategy that Welch succeeded where Danforth and Marous failed. Calamity has not befallen GE, partly because its position was always superior to Westinghouse's, and partly because Welch was a superior leader. He has been a proactive catalyst of change, anticipating events rather than reacting to them, and he ruthlessly excises the cancer that has killed many large institutions, including Westinghouse—complacency.

At the same time, Welch is a person of glaring weaknesses. His way of doing business carries with it a heavy penalty, not necessarily for him or stockholders, but for the people who do his bidding and for government and society, which must often clean up his mess. There have been many fiascoes, but one of the biggest was the ill-fated rotary compressor, a refinement of the mass-produced home refrigerator GE invented in the 1920s. The rotary was supposed to be a revolutionary breakthrough, a project Welch championed as a "quantum" technological leap. Instead, testing of the new compressor was cut short to meet the deadline that had been imposed, and when the new product failed, it did so in massive numbers. GE replaced defective compressors in millions of refrigerators, and in 1988 it took a $450 million charge to offset its costs. As job losses go at GE, the compressor debacle was relatively insignificant—all told, about five hundred people had lost employment by the time the plant closed for good in 1993—but the event was near-catastrophic in that it almost cost GE its refrigerator business.

General Electric has compiled a record during Welch's tenure that speaks for itself in both the severity of the miscues and the scope of the offenses:

• In one of Wall Street's biggest scandals of the nineties, GE's Kidder, Peabody securities firm lost $1 billion before the remains were sold to Paine Webber in 1994. The Securities and Exchange Commission subsequently sanctioned three of Kidder's former senior bond executives, one for books-and-records violations and the other two for failing to supervise adequately.

• *Dateline NBC,* the signature newsmagazine of GE's television network, rigged GM pickup trucks with rockets so they would explode in catastrophic fashion for viewers, which caused General Motors to sue NBC for libel. (GM dropped the suit after *Dateline* issued an on-the-air apology.)

• GE's Aircraft Engine division pleaded guilty in 1992 to stealing $42 million from Uncle Sam and diverting the money to an Israeli general to win orders for jet engines.

• The same division paid $7.2 million to the federal government in 1995 to settle a whistleblower lawsuit brought by a young GE engineer who had charged his company with selling to the United States Air Force jet engines that didn't comply with contract terms.

• GE was involved in more instances of Pentagon fraud (before it sold its arms business in 1993) than any other military contractor, with fifteen criminal convictions and civil judgments between 1985 and 1992, compared with seven for Teledyne, which had the second most in the eleven-year period covered by the General Accounting Office report.

In addition, GE has been the defendant in many lawsuits during the Welch era. Among the more noteworthy allegations are these:

• Kidder, Peabody was sued by the Equal Employment Opportunity Commission and accused of illegally forcing out seventeen investment bankers because of age—to that date, the largest age-discrimination case ever filed by the federal government against a Wall Street brokerage house. (Some five years later, the trial court dismissed the case because the employees had signed arbitration agreements with Kidder, Peabody, and, the court said, they could pursue their claims through arbitration if they chose to do so. That decision is now on appeal.)

• GE's nuclear businesses were the object of several lawsuits based on alleged retaliation against employees who sought to expose illegal and unsafe practices at commercial and federal nuclear facilities. (GE has managed to avoid civil liability in all but one instance. In the case of Vera English, described in Chapter 11, the Nuclear Regulatory Commission fined GE $24,000.)

• GE's synthetic diamond business and the De Beers cartel were indicted, along with two executives, in February 1994 for conspiring to fix prices, capping a two-year Justice Department probe that led to a lawsuit which was later dismissed.

• GE's medical and plastics businesses were accused in separate suits filed in 1997 of having hired away key senior executives from Bayer of Germany and Dow Chemical, respectively. The suits alleged that GE had sought through the hirings to improperly obtain confidential trade secrets. Moreover, Bayer alleged that its departing executive met privately with senior GE executives, including Welch, then returned to his job, where he requested special briefings on confidential matters in his final days at Bayer. Both suits were quickly settled.

  • GE's Mutual Liability Insurance Company has been accused of deceiving Massachusetts insurance regulators in applying for permission to relocate to Bermuda four months before it declared insolvency in 1995, a move that the state's highest court later reversed, saying it should not have been allowed. In another case involving Massachusetts, the state attorney general is investigating allegations that GE covered up internal memos that might have revealed the presence of banned chemicals on residential property in Pittsfield; eighteen homeowners have sued the company for damages from diminished property values.

  In many companies, scandals like these would have been more than enough for the board of directors to send the CEO packing. In the 1970s, illicit campaign contributions to the Nixon White House toppled Robert Dorsey, CEO of Gulf Oil. But at General Electric, this pattern of wrongdoing doesn't seem to have inspired even introspection on the part of directors or shareholders about the regularity and persistence of its manifestations. Moreover, Welch distances himself from the taint of scandal, usually by hiring a prominent, well-connected lawyer whose investigation of the matter purports to be "independent" while he himself sidesteps any personal responsibility. "Let's not kid ourselves," Welch told the *Wall Street Journal* immediately following disclosure of the Kidder scandal, "this is a kick in the teeth for those guys." But not for him. "Those guys"—the Kidder executives who were fired—included Welch's close associate Mike Carpenter, who ran Kidder, Peabody and reported directly to him.

  Why hasn't there been a more candid examination of GE's ethical problem? Because the man at the top doesn't think there is one, and directors, who have profited enormously in the Welch era, no doubt concur. When Welch took over GE, it ranked eleventh among American corporations in the total value of its stock. He made it number one. General Electric now earns more profit in a single quarter than it did the entire year before Welch took over, and most people nowadays, Welch included, would argue that's the bottom line for judging a CEO's performance. He's paid to make the shareholders wealthier, and on that score Welch has delivered. If a few miscreants at GE don't follow the rules, what's that got to do with him? The common element in all these transgressions is the business credo championed by Welch. He's intimidating, tough, and unrelenting in his pursuit of ever higher profits, as are the people who report to him. That's why GE racked up earnings gains quarter after quarter for more than twelve years, a string that wasn't broken until the Kidder scandal and subsequent writeoffs. It's also why the company has broken so many rules: Strength pushed too far becomes weakness.

More than any other large corporation in America, General Electric has assumed the personality of its general. It is a company where greed plays a powerful role. Consider the value of the GE shares Welch owns, which appreciated by $83 million in 1996 alone, bringing the value of his holdings then to $316 million. And that's not counting his unexercised stock options, which were worth another $107 million. With sums such as those at stake, is it any wonder why he would be anxious to please Wall Street? Or consider the fortunes being made, and, on occasion, fought over, in divorce proceedings. One lawsuit that received national attention in 1997 pitted Gary Wendt, the chief executive of GE Capital, against his wife, Lorna, and ignited a national debate over the role of corporate wives. The decision, by a state court judge in Connecticut, awarded the former Mrs. Wendt far less than the $50 million she had demanded—half of what she contended was Mr. Wendt's net worth—but far more than the $8 million, plus alimony, he had offered. As a GE wife who had furthered her husband's career, she was, the judge ruled, entitled to at least a share of Mr. Wendt's stock options and stock dividends.

General Electric is also a company managed by threat and intimidation rather than encouragement. "People at GE don't go off to work every morning. They go off to war," says one former battle-weary executive. Drawing an analogy with World War II, he adds: "The basic problem is this—we have Patton, he thinks he's Eisenhower, we need Bradley." Welch needs to win the way other people need to breathe, and he defines winning very narrowly: being number one or number two in your business and getting the numbers, achieving your profit goals. The bottom line is always that you had better make your bottom line. The constant pressure to "go get the numbers" has led, inevitably, to aberrant behavior. The impact this Darwinian mentality has had on General Electric is huge; the impact it has had on America is more complex, and one of the primary concerns of this book.

WELCH HAS DEFINED the landscape in which dramatic change has occurred not only at GE but elsewhere in American business. As CEOs have sought to emulate his success, they have also adopted his tactics, and in this sense he is the father of a bare-knuckle approach to business that has won more and more believers. What mergers and acquisitions were to the 1980s, productivity—extracting more work out of ever fewer people—has been to the 1990s. It is a manic quick-fix done at the behest of Wall Street in which businessmen have become desensitized to the damage they do to society, just as they were oblivious to the excesses of buying and selling in the 1980s. Businessmen have crafted their own euphemistic terms for extracting more out of less. It's called "reengineering" or "rightsizing," and consultants are paid princely sums to design and facilitate the process. There are of course occasions when downsizing is inevitable, a necessary response to a fast-changing, globally competitive economy. All too often, however, it has become the option of first rather than last resort. "Don't we have a responsibility," asked Gerald Greenwald, the CEO of UAL Corporation, the employee-owned parent of United Airlines, "to use attrition long before we think of buyouts and certainly before we think of layoffs?" Chiding his fellow CEOs at the same forum on corporate responsibility, Donald Hastings, the head of Cleveland-based Lincoln Electric Company, added: "Everyone is assuming that layoffs are inevitable. Thinking ahead and having creative solutions for when there is a downturn is what management is all about." Both United and Lincoln Electric have no-layoff policies.

Unfortunately, opinions such as these have not been the consensus among the captains of industry in our era. And, equally unfortunate, companies, like GE, that regard layoffs as a course of first resort have jettisoned more than people. They've also abandoned the old-fashioned business values that made this the American century—loyalty, trust, respect, teamwork, hard work, compassion—in a feverish pursuit of the quick buck. Today, these values, with rare exceptions, aren't even a part of the American business lexicon, except as meaningless rhetoric. What a society loses when these values are jettisoned is the glue that holds it together. "What I'm concerned about is the idolatry of the market," William Bennett, the conservative intellectual and former cabinet member in the Reagan and Bush administrations, recently told the *Wall Street Journal*, in an article which raised the prospect of a backlash against capitalism because of its excesses. "Unbridled capitalism . . . may not be a problem for production and for expansion of the economic pie, but it's a problem for human beings. It's a problem for . . . the realm of values and human relationships because it distorts things."

While American businessmen may not view downsizing as representative of the "values" crisis that Bennett and others have spoken of, clearly there are connections. Workers simply disposed of inevitably must call into question everything they have come to believe in. Is it any wonder that pollsters who track the extent to which Americans trust each other have found that trust has declined steadily in the last twenty years? Or that the Conference Board, in one recent survey of five thousand households across the nation, found that only 45 percent judged their own family's economic situation better than in the recession year of 1990, while 21 percent felt they were worse off?

Corporate restructurings such as the one Welch has engineered—and others now underway at many corporations large and small—are more fraught with peril, more damaging to individuals and to society than we understand or care to believe. The price that is paid in keeping shareholders content is staggering. And eventually the shareholders, too, end up paying a price, assuming they continue to hold the stock, as the consequences of a disregard for people damage the corporation in many ways.

Consider the case of Robert E. Allen, a Welch disciple and the former chairman of AT&T. In the summer of 1995, Allen told the company's 300,000 employees, via satellite, that "no one should get their stomach in a knot over press stories about massive layoffs." Four months later, on the first workday of 1996, he announced that the company would lay off forty thousand employees over three years. Allen had miscalculated badly. In February, he was pictured on the cover of *Newsweek* as a "Corporate Killer," the poster boy for greedy executives who collected millions—his own $16 million salary and stock-option deal by then had been disclosed—while throwing others out of work. Allen's mishandling of the AT&T downsizing eroded his credibility, triggering a cascade of events that undermined investor confidence in his leadership. Soon, the stock price was falling and by the fall of 1997, Allen was out. Contrast his fate with that of Henry Schacht, Allen's counterpart at the AT&T spinoff Lucent Technologies. Of the forty thousand AT&T layoffs, twenty-three thousand were to come from Lucent. But Schacht, formerly the CEO of Cummins Engine, where he had built a reputation as an executive who valued loyalty and teamwork, took steps even amid this traumatic downsizing to win the trust of his work force. He closed the executive dining room to bring the top rung and the bottom together at mealtime. He gave every worker one hundred shares of Lucent stock at a discounted price. He met with employees to listen to their concerns and address them. Employees have been rewarded for the faith they showed; their shares are now worth more than three times what they paid for them. And the nineteen thousand jobs that were ultimately eliminated have all been regained.

The negative effects of downsizing are becoming more and more apparent. One recent survey of sixty-two major U.S. companies found that more than 70 percent reported serious problems with low morale and mistrust of management caused by years of upheaval and restructuring. Another survey revealed that companies that had downsized since 1990 had experienced a greater increase in disability claims than those that hadn't downsized. And some companies where managerial machismo once ruled have decided to reverse course. One example is Delta Air Lines, where the new CEO, Leo F. Mullin, has gained a reputation for nurturing employees, in sharp contrast to his predecessor, Ronald W. Allen, who in the early 1990s slashed jobs by the thousands and was feared for his autocratic behavior. But Delta, an airline long noted in the industry for the exuberance and loyalty of its workforce, found that as employee morale sagged, customer complaints soared. So when Delta's board of directors decided it was time for a change, they wanted a leader who would "be a great listener and capture the imagination of Delta employees," Dayton Ogden, president of the executive search firm that the board retained and that found Mullin, told the *Washington Post*. "People skills were very important to them."

To be sure, businesses must be run efficiently, and Welch is brilliant at extracting more work out of ever fewer people. But as the directors at Delta discovered, efficiency can be pushed too far. Cost-cutting has become a grotesque addiction within GE, so much so that it has undermined the creativity and risk-taking Welch always hopes to engender. This book is about the Welch revolution: how it took place, who is responsible for it, what has gone right and wrong, and the achievements and consequences. The story of Jack Welch and what he has done at GE raises questions that have serious implications for this nation.

Perhaps the most serious of those is this: Do companies have obligations beyond the bottom line? Polls show that as much as 95 percent of the American public reject the view that corporations' only role is to make money. Businessmen, however, have for the most part responded to that question with a resounding "no," discarding employees at a rate of about three million a year since 1991. This downsizing takes an enormous social toll in widening income inequality and the most acute job insecurity since the Depression. Out-of-work people—and people fearful of losing their jobs—suffer, as do their families. The burdens come in many forms: broken marriages; unemployment or, when a job is found, often lower-paying employment; no medical care; counseling to counteract anger, diminished self-esteem, and heightened anxiety; depletion of savings or retirement money; alcoholism; suicide; and increasing cost to government and social agencies.

Unemployment may be low, but so many people seem anxious about their jobs and the future. Federal Reserve Chairman Alan Greenspan noted as much in testimony to Congress in February 1997. Job insecurity had become such a pervasive and powerful force in today's economy, Greenspan said, that it explained a paradox which had to be factored into the Fed's thinking on interest rates: why inflation hasn't risen as expected this far into an economic expansion. Workers have been too worried about keeping their jobs to demand higher wages, Greenspan said, and as evidence he cited a survey of employees at more than four hundred large corporations in the U.S. Between 1979 and 1990, according to the survey, no more than 24 percent of those polled ever answered yes to the question "I am frequently concerned about being laid off." In the 1990s, the number shot up, hitting 46 percent in 1995 and 1996.

But does it have to be this way? Will society have to suffer as people like Welch squeeze every last cent of profit out of their businesses to satisfy stockholders? Should Welch be extolled for this—lionized in the business press as a national hero, touted on talk shows as the kind of take-charge leader who should be in the White House? Or should he be seen as the leader of a money-making machine who exhibits little concern for his fellow man or, in many ways, his country? Are we not at a crossroads where the needs of the country and the needs of shareholders have to be addressed together? What is the bottom line on what Welch contributes to public wealth and what he adds to government's burden?

While no one has come up with broadly agreed-upon solutions, a consensus is emerging that the private sector must take better care of its employees and communities. "We're edging back toward sanity," James B. Miller, a former CEO himself and author of *Best Boss, Worst Boss*, told the *Washington Post*. "I think the pendulum is starting to swing toward more humane, more sensitive bosses." Consider the White House–sponsored Corporate Citizen Conference, an event hosted by President Clinton in May 1996. The President showcased companies that had adopted family-friendly policies and challenged the one hundred CEOs who attended to "show how [humane employment practices] are consistent with making money and succeeding in the free enterprise system." Or consider the gospel according to Mark—Mark Albion, that is, a former Harvard marketing professor who now delivers forty speeches a year to business schools on the importance of values and integrity and who founded a firm that links MBAs with socially responsible employers. Albion wasn't always so altruistic. But after six years at Harvard Business School, where he became disillusioned with the school's "money, power, fame" culture, he found his new calling.

Jack Welch, on the other hand, is the epitome of what the so-called free market system—a stunning oxymoron—has led to. So as we stand at a crossroads, and as we consider what our economic landscape is to look like if we are to compete and prevent civic unrest and domestic hardship, it's useful to look at Jack Welch. In examining this classic example of a CEO at the end of this century, let us see what our business world has become, and whether that world is a model for building our future. Or whether, instead, it is a warning sign that we must change that world—even if it means enforced change—to serve the public good.

We begin more than a century ago, with a founding father of General Electric, the wizard of Menlo Park, Thomas Alva Edison.

CHAPTER ONE

MADE IN AMERICA

EVERYTHING THAT WE IDENTIFY today as the General Electric Company—the products, profits, dividends, services, assets, and people that make up one of the world's most powerful corporations—has its origin in a single idea. The idea wasn't a new product per se; the products, thousands of them, would come later. Rather, it was a way of marshaling Yankee ingenuity to create a truly revolutionary concept: the industrial research laboratory.

Before 1876, only the cultivated devotees of pure science possessed laboratories, and they used them either as teaching instruments or to add to the sum of human knowledge, not to make things. The laboratory of plant physiology, established in Paris at the Museum of Natural History in 1873, was created so that plants could be studied through means of modern chemical analysis. At the same time, Louis Pasteur was exploring human disease at his Parisian lab, while the HMS *Challenger*, the world's foremost oceanographic vessel, left the harbor in Plymouth, England, with passengers on the most ambitious scientific exploration yet planned—to map the depths of the seas and to report on the flora and fauna encountered.

Thomas Edison, just twenty-nine years old and already a prolific inventor with more than one hundred patents, brought a new approach to the endeavor of scientific research. The lab he founded in 1876, a modest wood-frame structure in the quiet countryside of Menlo Park, New Jersey, would be the world's first to unite practical engineering with theoretical science. Edison was obsessed with inventing not just devices but whole systems, and it was in the lab that he began inquiries into the phenomenon he called "the electric light problem." Two years later he founded the Edison Electric Light Company to support his incandescent light research with a staff of "twenty earnest men," as he called his Menlo Park colleagues, among whom were several distinguished mathematicians, physicists, and university-trained engineers, as well as clockmakers and machinists. Their goal was simply to *make things* in the facility that Edison called his little "invention factory." "We've got to keep coming up with something useful," he told his associates. "We can't be like those old German professors who spend their whole lives studying the fuzz on a bee."

Edison never showed much interest in profit—he railed against wealth and declared that "interest is an invention of Satan," while repeatedly losing whole fortunes—yet the Edison laboratory held true to its mission. It was prodigious in its inventive creativity: At Menlo Park the first cries of the infant phonograph were heard, the brilliant light of the Edison lamp shone forth, America's first full-scale electric locomotive rumbled over a small track outside, and the mysterious vacuum tube also appeared, hinting at the future of electronics and radio. "There is no similar institution in existence to this one," Edison wrote. "We do our own castings, forgings, and can build anything from a lady's watch to a locomotive. . . . Inventions that formerly took months and cost large sums can now be done [in] two or three days with very small expense, as I carry a stock of almost every conceivable material."

Asked on his eightieth birthday what he considered his greatest invention, Edison replied, "The research laboratory." Inventions were merely the byproduct of the invention factory, which brought forth a new way of focusing the talents and energies of his team. Edison had "made a business out of invention itself," German economist Werner Sombart later wrote. Among the people who recognized their indebtedness to Edison and his revolutionary idea of industrial research was Henry Ford, who attributed much of his success in the mass production of automobiles to his friend and camping buddy, and built an exact replica of the invention factory at his Henry Ford Museum in Dearborn, Michigan. When the museum was dedicated in 1929, on the fiftieth anniversary of the electric light breakthrough, Edison reenacted his triumphant moment as hundreds of dignitaries, including Ford, Orville Wright, Madame Curie, Will Rogers, Harvey Firestone, and President Herbert Hoover, looked on. When Edison—the most important person of the millennium, according to one 1997 ranking by the editors of *Life* magazine—died in 1931, Americans dimmed their lights on the night after his funeral.

Since that time a deluge of technological invention has transformed the world we live in, activity that derives its essential form and character from the invention factory Edison pioneered in 1876. Menlo Park was the birthplace of modern American technology, the beginning of science and industry working side by side in the pursuit of innovation, and the ushering in of a new era of American commercial supremacy. It also signaled the birth of the General

Electric Company, and of the spirit of creative innovation that would propel its growth in the next century.

The electrification of America was soon in full swing. Edison's discovery of incandescent light was the seminal event representing the end of one era and the beginning of another—the steam age was dead, and the electrical age had begun. But what set Edison apart from his inventive peers of that era was that he was not content merely to invent the lightbulb; he created an entire electrical infrastructure, manufacturing and installing everything that was required to deliver electrical light. The new age took a giant step forward on September 4, 1882, when, at 3:00 in the afternoon, Edison and his team of engineers lighted up four city blocks on the southern tip of Manhattan, including the offices of his financial backer J. P. Morgan and the *New York Times*, with electricity generated by the first American power station, on Pearl Street, using huge coal-fired generators known as dynamos to generate the current that illuminated the light bulbs. The early Edison Electric Light Company was consolidated with other Edison interests in 1889 to form the Edison General Electric Company. Three years later, Charles Coffin, president of the Thomson-Houston Company of Lynn, Massachusetts, and a rival of Edison's, merged his company with Edison General Electric to form GE, breaking a stalemate in patent disputes between the two. The new company was the leader in nearly everything electric, a manufacturer of fans, dynamos, light-bulbs, trolley cars and locomotives, motors, and heaters.

By 1893, the new General Electric Company proudly proclaimed that its lamps extended "in an unbroken line around the earth; they shine in the palace of the Mikado as well as in the Opera House of Paris." Talk of electricity was everywhere. H. L. Mencken later nicknamed the 1890s "the Electric Decade," while Andrew Carnegie declared electricity "the most spiritual, most ethereal of all departments in which man has produced great triumphs." In 1899, an advertisement in the *Times* proclaimed:

ELECTRICITY lights our city.
ELECTRICITY runs our street cars.
ELECTRICITY causes wagons without horses to go.
ELECTRICITY permits us to talk great distances.
ELECTRICITY will do our cooking and heating.
ELECTRICITY will soon do everything.

In the early years of the new century, a few large industrial concerns, among them GE, the Bell System, and Eastman Kodak, established laboratories of their own. The scope of their activities broadened beyond those of Edison's inaugural lab to include basic scientific research as an adjunct to practical inventive work. In 1922, Edison, by that time an American icon, visited, after an absence of twenty-five years, General Electric's huge plant and industrial research laboratory in Schenectady, New York. The factories that had grown up out of the old Edison Machine Works he had established there in 1886 encompassed most of the downtown area and employed eighteen thousand workers who, at the order of President Gerald Swope, assembled to welcome and cheer Edison. A bronze plaque was unveiled in his honor at the door of the laboratory he had initiated, the successor to Menlo Park. Staffed with hundreds of technicians, among them the nation's leading scientists and engineers working in fields of technology that Edison had only dimly imagined, the lab turned out inventions in such a torrent of creativity it had been dubbed "the House of Magic." Edison beheld devices that even he could scarcely have imagined: a lightning machine that discharged 120,000 volts of electricity in a single bolt, lamps thousands of times more powerful than the incandescent bulb he had invented, vacuum tubes for long-distance radio transmission, and photoelectric mechanisms that reproduced sound on tape for motion pictures and phonographs.

In the intervening quarter century the men who had succeeded Edison had worn the inventive mantle well. The most significant of them was Charles Proteus Steinmetz, who joined the company in its second year. He was a German émigré, a dwarfed hunchback with a salt-and-pepper beard and a domed forehead, a cigar-chomping mathematics-professor-in-residence, a patent-winning engineer, a textbook author, and a peripatetic luminary on topics ranging from the behavior of alternating current to management theory. In 1900, Steinmetz proposed that GE should respond to Westinghouse's advances in electric lighting by setting up a research lab to pursue work in the field. In December of that year, the company hired Willis Whitney to be the first director of the research lab, which was then a barn in back of Steinmetz's house. The barn burned down the following spring, and the lab was relocated to a small building with the GE facilities. Soon thereafter Whitney, who would guide the lab's efforts for thirty-two years, and Steinmetz began attracting some of the brightest scientific minds of this or any other century. There was Ernst Alexanderson, the Swedish émigré whose high-frequency alternator made the first, historic radio broadcast possible; William Coolidge, who perfected the modern X-ray tube and whose discovery of how to make tungsten ductile revolutionized many products, including the Edison lamp; and Irving

Langmuir, who greatly enhanced the efficiency of lightbulbs by putting gas in them, and whose work measuring the sizes and shapes of atoms and molecules received international recognition in 1932 when he became the first industrial scientist to receive a Nobel Prize. These men were the technological giants of their time, and their bequest to GE, and to the nation, was enormous.

The General Electric breakthroughs in the first half of the twentieth century were at the leading edge of modern technology, fundamentally changing American life, and representing a rich legacy. Indeed, it is not overstatement to say that GE was the world's most significant company technologically in the first half of this century. As engineer John Broderick wrote in his 1929 memoir *Forty Years with General Electric*: "The General Electric Company is not a manufacturer in the sense in which manufacturing is commonly understood, but is that and something more. It originates the products which it supplies to the public. In addition to executives, salesmen, and manual workers, its organization is made up of scientists, research and designing engineers, and inventors—men who contribute in one way or another to the development of apparatus and devices for the generation, distribution, control, and use of electric energy."

GE made things that stood the test of time. Anyone who has an old GE appliance that still functions after fifty years can attest to that. The inventions weren't merely durable; they also endured because they were unique. Seven of the nine manufacturing businesses in which GE remains had their genesis in products created by Edison, Steinmetz, Alexanderson, Coolidge, Langmuir, and other contemporaries: the electric light (1879), the electric meter (1882), the electric motor (1887), the steam turbine (1901), the X-ray machine (1913), the diesel-electric locomotive (1924), and the refrigerator (1925). The two other businesses, plastics and aircraft engines, also reflect breakthrough technology, though of 1950s origin. Engineering, research, and manufacturing were the elements that defined GE and made it a significant force in American life. The list of achievements and inventions seems improbable by today's standards. GE research gave us products as diverse as the first motion picture with talking sound, the first jet engine, the first synthetic diamond—and the first children's Silly Putty. GE products were fixtures in nearly every sphere of American life: in the home, in the factory, in space, aboard trains, planes, and ships, in communications, in sports arenas, even in the Panama Canal. The GE system that runs the canal, including more than one thousand electric motors and countless relays, switches, and control devices, has operated continuously since the canal opened in 1914.

No decade better exemplified the old General Electric than the 1950s. A 1955 article in *Fortune* magazine summed up the company's scope in manufacturing this way: "One measure of GE's vast diversification is the fact that the company is presently engaged in manufacturing in twelve of the twenty-one major industries. Looked at this way, a share in General Electric might be called a share in an investment trust engaged in manufacturing." In 1956, *Reader's Digest* described "that factory of the future you've been reading about." The factory was Appliance Park, which when it opened four years earlier had represented an investment of $156 million, a white-goods colossus spread out over ninety-three acres of buildings in Louisville, Kentucky. In one day, more than 3,000 job applicants lined up in response to a GE announcement of additional hiring at the park.

Appliance Park was the vision of Ralph Cordiner, the then CEO, who hired Ronald Reagan. The future president was just what Cordiner wanted: Tall, handsome, and well spoken, he would project a presence that the public would soon come to associate with the GE way of life. The company furnished the Reagans' "all-electric home," which was featured in GE advertisements of that time: "Ronald and Nancy Reagan, circa 1954, relax in the living room of their GE all-electric home," proclaimed one ad, with Nancy gazing upon Ron while he sat and read. The home had gadgets not yet on the market, including a dishwasher with built-in garbage disposal. Reagan became America's most conspicuous consumer, fulfilling Cordiner's vision of a pitchman who would literally create demand. The future president also spent two of the eight years he was under contract to GE on the road, visiting each of the company's more than 130 manufacturing facilities in the United States and addressing all of its 250,000 employees. Reagan of course was best known as the host of *GE Theater*, the weekly Sunday night television drama that ran on CBS from 1954 to 1962. "In engineering, in research, in manufacturing skill, in the values that bring a better, more satisfying life," each segment began with a crescendo, "at General Electric, progress is our most important product."

It is impossible to tour the Hall of Electrical History in Schenectady—its name is simply the Hall of Electrical History, with no reference to GE—and not see truth in those words. The evidence is literally right before you, in the artifacts, photographs, and papers that the Hall preserves, a treasure trove of GE memorabilia that provides insight into the products that made GE great and the men who made them.

One of the most significant inventions that GE contributed to twentieth-century society was radio, which, contrary to popular misconception, wasn't invented by Guglielmo Marconi. Marconi's invention, "wireless telegraphy," was a means of sending Morse code through the air, and though it was an unqualified breakthrough, the next step of transmitting the human voice without wires wouldn't have been accomplished without the ingenuity of Steinmetz and his brilliant associates. GE's involvement with radio began in 1901, when Reginald Fessenden, a thirty-three-year-old university professor in Pittsburgh and former chief chemist to Edison, wrote Steinmetz a letter. Fessenden, an early radio pioneer and student of Marconi's wireless telegraph, asked Steinmetz to assist in the creation of a device that would generate electromagnetic waves strong enough to broadcast voices and music over long distances. The machine Fessenden envisioned would have to spin at tremendous velocity, a machine capable of spitting out one hundred thousand wave cycles per second. He had tried himself to build the elusive generator but had failed; it was an engineering feat that everyone Fessenden consulted said was impossible.

A generator capable of producing 100,000 cycles per second would have to operate at a speed of twenty thousand revolutions per minute. Steinmetz, whom the American writer John Dos Passos later called the most valuable apparatus General Electric had, accepted the challenge. A man of immense creativity and brainpower, Steinmetz had already formulated the law of hysteresis, a formula that put the properties of alternating current into mathematical form, and made electrification of the nation practical. Yet not even Steinmetz could produce the generator Fessenden wanted. Its speed was limited to four thousand revolutions per minute—beyond that the armature began to fly apart—and the waves of ten thousand cycles per second it generated were incapable of carrying sounds properly. Steinmetz gave up. But in 1904 Fessenden renewed his request, and Steinmetz gave the task to Ernst Alexanderson, a recently hired immigrant from Sweden. "The alternator was one of the inventions I had to make in order to hold my job," he later quipped. Within two years, Alexanderson's new alternator had arrived at Fessenden's radio station at Brant Rock, Massachusetts. The tapered disc that generated the waves rotated on a stationary armature at an incredible speed of seven hundred miles an hour at its periphery, yet because of its ingenious design wobbled no more than three one-hundredths of an inch. By Christmas Eve 1906, a few telegraph operators on ships in the North Atlantic heard not the usual dots and dashes but Fessenden reading from St. Luke's Gospel. As an encore, he played "O Holy Night" on his violin—music that reached listeners as far away as Norfolk, Virginia. Soon, amateur radio operators in the United States and elsewhere were using Alexanderson's invention to chat with each other, hurling the sounds of a human voice across continents and oceans. Nor was he finished inventing: On a January afternoon in 1928, he transmitted from the lab to his home in Schenectady a video image three inches square. The image—of a man removing his glasses, putting them back on, and blowing a smoke ring—wasn't much to look at, but it marked the beginning of a device that would become even more powerful and influential than radio. It was the world's first television broadcast, and within four months of Alexanderson's demonstration, GE was broadcasting images three times a week.

The Alexanderson alternator was the most powerful generator of radio waves then known, and hence had tremendous commercial significance. In 1915, Marconi, whose American Marconi Company had already purchased one alternator for broadcasting purposes, agreed to pay $4 million for several more after touring the Schenectady General Electric plant. GE was about to install a huge two-hundred-kilowatt machine when the United States entered the First World War. Completed in 1918, the two-hundred-kilowatt alternator broadcast news of the armistice across the Atlantic, but the war had convinced many people in government that radio was more than merely a communications tool; it was a vital national interest. Franklin Delano Roosevelt, then assistant naval secretary, did not want control of this equipment to pass into foreign hands. Bowing to pressure from Roosevelt and others in government, GE subsequently refused to sell American Marconi any additional alternators. It was a devastating blow in that Marconi was convinced that the Alexanderson alternator was the only means by which he could span the globe with wireless communications, an opinion seconded by David Sarnoff, a young Russian émigré and technical genius who had been asked by Marconi, his boss, to evaluate the machine.

The leaders of American Marconi subsequently accepted GE's proposal to combine their interests in a new American company, Radio Corporation of America, which when founded in 1919 was immediately a powerhouse in radio and, eventually, in television. Ironically, thirteen years later, in November 1932, government trustbusters declared the radio monopoly anticompetitive, and forced GE to give up its ownership of RCA just three days after FDR swept to victory and four days before the case was set for trial. History would again reverse itself in 1986, when less aggressive enforcement of antitrust law, this time under the administration of former GE pitchman Ronald Reagan, would allow GE to reacquire RCA.

A discussion of GE's technological achievements wouldn't be complete without some mention of the lightbulb, of which there are dozens, of varied vintage, on display in the Hall of Electrical History. In solving the "electric light problem," Edison, who had only a grade-school education, and his chief assistant, Charles Bachelor, had methodically tested dozens of carbonized materials, including cedar, coconut hair, and fishing line, before hitting upon the one that worked—cotton sewing thread. But the carbon in Edison-type lightbulbs evaporated readily. These bulbs also wasted electricity, making them costly to use, because they radiated much of their energy as heat rather than as visible light. At the turn of the century, there was considerable interest in other forms of electric lighting that might rely on new physical principles or employ new filament materials. Tungsten, an intractable, brittle metal, offered great promise; hard to work with, costly to fabricate, it nonetheless had unique physical properties, among them a very high melting point, which made it the ideal metal as a substitute for metallized carbon filament. In 1905, Willis Whitney, director of the GE Research Laboratory and a onetime chemistry professor at the Massachusetts Institute of Technology, hired William Coolidge, a former MIT colleague, who immediately took up the task that had confounded Whitney—the taming of tungsten.

Each day, as the buoyant Whitney greeted researchers at the lab with his characteristic "Having good fun today?," Coolidge toiled to find a way that would render tungsten pliable. After two years of heating, hammering, squeezing, rolling, and pressing the metal, Coolidge finally found that by drawing tungsten through hot diamond dies, it could be fabricated into wire thinner than a human hair yet stronger than any other substance known to man. The conquest of tungsten was a breakthrough as significant as Edison's own discovery, for it represented a giant leap forward in incandescent lamp technology. Introduced in 1911, Coolidge's lamp had a rugged tungsten filament that could withstand the vibrations of automobiles, railroad cars, and trolleys. It also yielded seven times more light per watt than Edison's first carbon lamps, while consuming just a fraction of the energy. The Coolidge process, which GE still uses today with only slight modifications, saved the nation $200 million in 1914 alone.

The next big breakthrough came just two years later. Irving Langmuir, the chemist who would go on to win the Nobel Prize, was curious as to why the bulbs of incandescent lamps blackened, dimming severely after only a few hundred hours of use. Following extensive inquiries into the gases inside the lamp, Langmuir found that a new coiled-helix filament sealed inside a globe of inert gas—first nitrogen, and later argon—would greatly enhance its efficiency and reduce bulb-blackening. He had arrived at the electric lightbulb in the form we use today. Protected by patents, it regained for GE the unassailable position that the company had previously held with its Edison-type bulbs. Langmuir's curiosity had a dual benefit as well: As part of his inquiry into gases inside the bulb, he had invented an exhaust pump that produced a higher vacuum than ever before achieved. Langmuir's mercury condensation pump left only one molecule of air in ten billion, a quantum leap from the one in a hundred thousand that was previously thought to be a vacuum. The breakthrough allowed Langmuir to patent a new type of vacuum tube, one that would succeed the Alexanderson alternator in the next generation of radio transmission technology. Langmuir's achievement would also aid Coolidge in his next breakthrough—the modern X-ray tube. Introduced in 1913, the "Coolidge tube," as it was known, combined his knowledge of tungsten with Langmuir's vacuum achievements to create a device that has been the basis for all X-ray tubes manufactured since.

THE NUMBER AND QUALITY of products that GE scientists and engineers invented and manufactured in the first half of this century leave one awestruck, as does the ideology that guided the creators' endeavors. It was a unique time in American history, a time when technologists everywhere were imbued with a sense of "civic religion." They believed that their inventions were advancing the "American way of life" and that they were building a better tomorrow. In the thirties, American engineers built the Hoover Dam, the Golden Gate Bridge, the Empire State Building. Engineers were heroes, and the confidence of that age in technology was perhaps best represented in the 1939 New York World's Fair. Regular commercial television broadcasts began in New York on April 30, 1939, the fair's opening day.

At the General Electric pavilion—one of the most popular sites at the fair, situated on the Plaza of Light just beyond the fair's theme structure, the towering, blazing-white Trylon and the squat Perisphere—visitors gaped at lightning bolt demonstrations in Steinmetz Hall (which did not disrupt the FM broadcast signal they were also demonstrating). New gadgets were on display in the Hall of Electrical Living, such as an automatic electric dishwasher and a TV picture tube.

The ideology of that era is captured in a GE advertisement from 1939 that extols the virtues of electricity and the industrial progress it had wrought:

> Fifty years ago, there were only 4,000,000 factory jobs in this country—today there are twice as many. Because industry devised machines to make products at low cost, more millions of people could buy them.
>
>   General Electric scientists and engineers, by applying electricity to the machines of industry, have been responsible for much of this

progress. Their efforts today are creating not only MORE GOODS FOR MORE PEOPLE AT LESS COST, but also MORE AND BETTER JOBS AT HIGHER WAGES.

TODAY, research, engineering, and manufacturing are not the priorities they once were to the company that virtually invented them. Now, GE makes more money in financial services, and finds the opportunities more exciting there, than in the gritty business of making things.

An exchange in 1995 between Jack Welch and Roberto C. Goizueta, then chief executive of Coca-Cola, was a reminder that Welch's aversion to manufacturing strikes even fellow CEOs as peculiar. The occasion was a discussion between the two, moderated by the editors of *Fortune* magazine. When the editors asked, "What's on the agenda for the rest of the decade?," Goizueta made it clear he was sticking with the soft-drink business, but Welch hedged. "I think, without question, that financial services, because of the opportunities available, will become an increasing mix of our business. That is absolutely going to happen." To which Goizueta replied, "That's interesting. I would never find excitement in the financial services. I would like to produce something that I could touch." It was an odd juxtaposition: Goizueta, the consummate marketing man, hardly a nuts-and-bolts guy, reminding the head of what was once the nation's preeminent manufacturer about the satisfaction that comes from making a product.

Manufacturing fell out of favor at General Electric more than a decade ago, which is unfortunate for the United States because manufacturing jobs pay better wages than service jobs and generally have more economic and intellectual spinoffs associated with them. And for the communities that have depended upon GE—or any other company that has abandoned manufacturing—for much of this century, that has meant anguish and chronic uncertainty. In contrast with the abiding belief, in 1939, that the future held great promise, and that "more and better jobs at higher wages" were laudable contributions to society, the nineties are characterized by diminishing jobs, and a diminished faith in the future. Companies move jobs all the time, to be sure. But seldom do they move them with as little consideration given to the human and societal consequences as does GE. Consider Welch's announcement in January 1998 of another year of record profit. Buried in that proclamation was a $2.3 billion charge to cover, among other things, the costs of eliminating more than four thousand manufacturing jobs. Fifteen hundred of them would move from Louisville to Georgia and Mexico, another nine hundred from

Schenectady to a suburb of Atlanta and points overseas, and still another six hundred from Fitchburg, Massachusetts, also to points overseas. In all three cities, union and government officials had engaged in months of negotiations, offering wage concessions, tax breaks, anything, so that their locals and communities would be allowed to keep the jobs. In the case of Schenectady, the lobbying effort enlisted two of the most prominent Republicans in the state, Governor George Pataki and Senator Alphonse D'Amato, both of whom made personal appeals to Welch on behalf of the city—to no avail.*

No city has been hit harder by the continual contraction of GE's manufacturing presence than Schenectady, where GE now employs a tenth of the forty thousand people who once worked there, in a town only twice that size. While Detroit made cars, Akron made tires, and Pittsburgh made steel, Schenectady was identified with a single industry, that of electrical equipment. Edison had intended to give that distinction to Buffalo, New York, but the vacant broom factories in Schenectady that he spied from his train in 1886 would be ideal, he thought, as the new home for his Edison Machine Works. A century later, Schenectady has become the casualty of an ethos far different from what drove Edison. In the process, Schenectady, which has twenty-two thousand fewer GE jobs than it did in 1978, has gone the way of many older "tank towns" that were once pillars of the GE empire: Erie, Pennsylvania, six thousand fewer; Pittsfield, Massachusetts, eight thousand fewer; Lynn, Massachusetts, seven thousand fewer; Fort Wayne, Indiana, four thousand fewer; Louisville, Kentucky, thirteen thousand fewer; Evendale, Ohio, twelve thousand fewer. All of these communities have the same worn, dazed look, that puts one in mind of a losing prizefighter about to answer the bell for the fifteenth round. Jobs have vanished and buildings have been torn down. It's a story that has been repeated a thousand times in cities across the once vibrant industrial heartland, repeated with such frequency that America has become inured to it, much like stepping over a drunk in the street. Cities that once offered good wages and stable employment to generations of workers don't anymore. If the contentious debate over the North American Free Trade Agreement of 1993 represented anything, it was this: Good jobs have gone away, and only the disenfranchised who have lost them—and the self-styled populists courting their votes, politicians like Pat Buchanan and Ross Perot—seem to care.

The subject of the vanishing job has special poignancy when considering

---

* "You can't be happy," Senator D'Amato was quoted as saying in the *Schenectady Gazette* on December 18, 1997, after his meeting with Welch. "We're downright annoyed. We would have hoped GE would want to be a part of the economic re-growth of this state."

General Electric, partly because GE jobs were so plentiful in another era and partly because the company has earned record profits while eliminating them. Throughout its history, GE had engendered loyalty through a paternalistic employment philosophy that eschewed layoffs, even during the Great Depression, when sacrifice was shared as workers cut the length of their workweek to keep as many people working as possible. When Charles Coffin, the first chairman, retired in 1922, GE employed 82,000 people; by 1980, the year before Jack Welch took over, the GE payroll had swelled to 402,000 people, 285,000 of them in the United States, and the company had a net profit of $1.5 billion on revenue of $25 billion. What was the nation's fourth-largest employer then—it is the tenth-largest now—has made a great deal of money since. Its $90.8 billion in revenue in 1997 generated $8.2 billion in net income, but with vastly fewer people: GE now employs 276,000—165,000 of whom work in the United States—for a net job loss of 128,000 over the seventeen-year period.* There are 120,000 fewer Americans on the GE payroll than in 1980, and that number understates the magnitude of the job loss in manufacturing, since it includes employment gains from financial services, which has grown fivefold as a proportion of GE's whole. GE has either closed or sold ninety-eight plants in the United States during the Welch era, 43 percent of the 228 it operated in 1980. That's a larger reduction, percentage-wise, than in companies the public typically associates with retrenchment strategies, such as General Motors.

Did it have to be so Malthusian? Certainly the days of eschewing layoffs are long gone; even the Japanese (and IBM) have long ago capitulated on that. And certainly, outlawing layoffs would not be the appropriate answer. That's what Germany has effectively done, but the result is a cosseted economy that lacks vitality, which employers are fleeing to escape the onerous employment rules and restrictions. Earlier in this century, Austrian economist Joseph Schumpeter likened the process of decay and renewal in modern economies to "the winds of creative destruction," but in Germany and, to a lesser extent, Japan, inefficiency is not swept away. This was true when the United States government, in the sixties and seventies, protected the grossly inefficient U.S. steel industry from greater foreign efficiency, which only made the cataclysm that much more wrenching when the protection was removed in the eighties. The role of government should not be to outlaw change but rather to soften the blow to those affected by it. Layoffs are an important part of the creative-

---

* As recently as 1995, GE's employment had dipped as low as 222,000. The 54,000-person increase in recent years reflects the addition of new businesses, including $17.2 billion worth of acquisitions in 1997 alone, mostly in financial services.

destructive dynamic Schumpeter spoke of, in that they can enhance efficiency and promote greater productivity, which fuel the engine of any economy.

The problem with General Electric—and, for that matter, most large American corporations recently—is that the emphasis has been placed too heavily on destruction and too little on creation. Welch's defenders—and there are many, among them Robert Allen, AT&T's former CEO, who in January 1996 announced plans to dismiss forty thousand people as part of its breakup into three companies—assert that he did exactly the right thing for GE's shareholders and for the health of the company. They argue that had GM executives been more courageous and taken the bold steps that Welch took, the company would now be more competitive in the world auto industry and would have rewarded shareholders with fatter dividends and heftier stock gains, which is, after all, the sole responsibility of a CEO. "The job of industry is to become competitive—not to be a social experiment. God help us if we pass legislation to make American companies less productive and compromise our global competitiveness," argues Albert Dunlap, the former CEO of Scott Paper, known to detractors as "Chain Saw Al," after engineering the merger of Scott with Kimberly-Clark and pocketing more than $100 million in the process. Welch himself argues that his greatest mistake, in hindsight, was that he did not move fast enough, that he was too cautious and evolutionary in executing his strategy of change.

But this argument overlooks the fact that all too often (and certainly in the case of GE, as we will see), downsizing is not done to improve the health of the organization and keep it from being overrun by third-world rivals; it's done to satisfy the immediate demands of Wall Street. As such, it represents the chief flaw of American business: its fixation on the short term. Firing people is now trendy in American business, and it is a quick and dirty way to appease investors, who twenty years ago viewed layoffs with disdain but now consider them a sign of management's mettle, its willingness to get the job done. But very often, downsizing is not in a company's long-term best interests. Companies can become so fixated on cutting back and cutting costs that they forget how to grow, and how to nurture new opportunities. That's exactly what has happened in GE's manufacturing businesses. Adjusted for inflation, its sales of manufactured goods in 1995 were about 10 percent *less* than they were in 1980.

Downsizing also wrecks morale among those who survive. People come to feel that the organization doesn't care about their welfare, and they respond by becoming nine-to-fivers, unwilling to put forth extra effort, certainly unwilling to take risks, and in some instances embracing a work ethic and practices that are openly disloyal. The American Management Association found in a survey of one thousand companies that fewer than half had laid off people and managed to increase their operating profits afterward. That would seem to explain why the U.S. economy's productivity gains have been relatively modest considering the extent of recent personnel cutbacks.

"The conventional economic wisdom has it that the prime job of management is to maximize profits. But through my research and that of others, one message rings clear: Don't put profits first!" argues business theorist and consultant Robert H. Waterman Jr., in his latest book, *What America Does Right*. "Today's top enterprise does the best job for its shareholders by treating them as only one of the three main constituent groups essential to their success. The other two are quite clearly their people and their customers. This doesn't mean that shareholders get ignored. The point is that shareholder interests sit on the same plane as those of others who have a stake in the company."

An example of a company that doesn't put profits first—and a useful counterpoint to General Electric—is Motorola, which in recent years has established itself as one of America's preeminent high-technology manufacturing concerns. Motorola's origins were hardly the stuff of lightbulb legend. It was founded in 1928 by Paul Galvin, who began his business career making "battery eliminators" for Sears radios. At that time, radios ran only on batteries, but thanks to Galvin's product, people could plug their radios into wall sockets. Galvin knew the battery eliminator would become obsolete when radios were made to run off household current, and he had prepared for that eventuality by developing a successor product, the car radio. By the 1930s, Galvin had recast his enterprise as a maker of car radios and had changed its name to Motorola. Walkie-talkies and televisions would follow.

Despite its humble beginnings, the Schaumburg, Illinois, company has proven that an old-line manufacturer can transform itself into a high-growth enterprise by investing in new technology and new manufacturing. As recently as the mid-1980s, for instance, Motorola was being driven out of the paging business by Japanese rivals, and its situation in the nascent cell-phone business was so desperate that it was close to withdrawing from it altogether. But rather than quitting, as GE did in consumer electronics, Motorola fought back against the Japanese with radical designs that set new standards in miniaturization and highly automated, high-precision manufacturing. The numbers tell the story. In 1992, Motorola invested $1.4 billion in new plant and equipment, the same amount spent by General Electric, which had about three times more revenue from manufacturing. Despite the enormous size disparity, Motorola spent the same amount on research and development, $1.3 billion. And in 1993, its spending was $224 million, or 17 percent, more than GE's, marking the first time in Motorola's history that it outspent General Electric in R&D, a difference that has widened since to almost $1 billion. GE has slipped to sixteenth place among corporate R&D spenders, even though it's first in profit.

As the global leader in a new generation of electronically based products—cellular phones, pagers, two-way radios, and microchips, businesses in which GE no longer competes—Motorola has added 43,000 manufacturing jobs since 1992. Though market shares have slipped recently, as it bungled the move from analog to digital wireless phone technology, Motorola still has a commanding 85 percent share of the global market for pagers, and 40 percent of the world market for cellular phones. While Motorola has hitched its star to electronics, GE has withdrawn from the manufacture of electronic components, as well as many products that contain them. Ironically, forty years ago General Electric invented and patented many of the solid-state components that opened up the electronic age, and made pagers, cellular phones, and countless other products possible.

For several years in the early nineties, Motorola was a darling of Wall Street. Its shares appreciated 62 percent, 77 percent, and 26 percent, respectively, in 1992, 1993, and 1994, while GE registered gains in the first two years of 15 percent and 23 percent and a loss in the third of 2.7 percent. But in 1995 the market soured on Motorola when its profits came in a hair or two below expectations. Its shares were down 1.7 percent, during a year in which the Dow Jones industrial average soared 33.5 percent, while GE shares registered a 41 percent gain. But Motorola—which has done some restructuring of its own recently, announcing plans to eliminate 15,000 jobs in response to weak Asian markets, overcapacity, and generally weak prices—didn't respond to Wall Street's disfavor by slashing R&D (likely the reason its shares were shunned). On the contrary, it is plowing ahead with such futuristic ideas as Iridium, a satellite-based telecommunications project that will span the globe, enabling users to place calls from anywhere on the earth's surface with a small handheld phone. Most of today's communications satellites move in sync with the Earth above a fixed point 22,300 miles up. Iridium's sixty-six satellites are instead being placed between four hundred and one thousand miles up. This lower-orbit network, which began service in September 1998, will permit the use of smaller, lower-powered gear, such as pocket-size phones, and will transmit signals without the intervention of ground stations, and hence without delays.

And on the human front, at the very time that Wall Street was pounding its stock, Motorola rolled out a new series of courses designed to teach its employees how to be better parents. The company already requires every employee to take forty hours of job-related training each year. The parenting classes, which count toward the forty-hour requirement and were designed by a team of consultants to be specific to a variety of family situations, reflect the company's belief that it must address the needs of its people.

Motorola has also sought to promote loyalty and create a sense of belonging among its work force. In 1975, when the company was struggling to find an identity and had reduced its payroll by 30 percent, CEO Robert Galvin, son of Paul Galvin, decreed that no member of the Service Club (for employees who have worked at Motorola for ten years or more) could be dismissed. Some had been, and when Galvin discovered it, he demanded that they be rehired. Today, according to Motorola's recruiting booklet: "Employees with ten or more years of service cannot be released without the explicit concurrence of the Chairman of the Board." About 47,000 of Motorola's 150,000 employees are Service Club members.

Motorola's commitment to on-the-job education is widely considered the strongest of any corporation in America. Symbolic of this commitment is Motorola University, which has headquarters in Schaumburg, a budget of $120 million, and fourteen branch campuses stretching from Tokyo to Honolulu. Unlike GE, where only the elite receive classroom instruction at its Management Development Institute in Crotonville, New York, Motorola training embraces everyone in the corporation, from the lowliest mill hand to the CEO. Motorola U. also lends assistance to public school districts in Florida, Illinois, and Massachusetts, where the company has large concentrations of employees.

This commitment to education isn't born out of a 1960s-era desire to change the world but reflects instead hard-headed business decisions from a company that views education as a competitive weapon. It has learned to harvest the knowledge of its workforce, with stunning results, achieving quality standards in manufacturing that even the Japanese envy. Since 1987, it has lowered its defect rate per million parts from six thousand to about 20, a level of near-perfection known in engineering parlance as "six sigma quality," saving the company $11 billion from 1987 to 1996. The savings so intrigued Welch that GE in 1996 adopted a six sigma program amid the usual huzzahs in the business press, which is curious because he was actually about a decade late in discovering "quality." In any event, GE has a lot of catching up to do: Its defect rate per million of twenty-three thousand, two years after adopting the program, is still significantly higher than Motorola's was when it began six sigma in 1987.

Motorola's investments in quality, new products, and people reflect the same sort of confidence about the future that GE scientists at the 1939 World's Fair exhibited. R&D is the basis for new products, and when a nation or a company rein in that investment, its future is imperiled. Although cutting back on research saves money, a huge price is paid in lost opportunities. Unfortunately for the United States, corporations and government are increasingly, and shortsightedly, unwilling to fund cutting-edge research. And while Motorola has been bucking that trend, GE has been leading it.

The diminished importance of research to General Electric, once the pre-eminent American R&D corporation along with IBM and Bell Labs, is such that it no longer ranks among the top ten corporate spenders in America. GE reinvests 1.9 cents of every sales dollar in R&D, about half the average for all U.S. industry and significantly less than its two main world rivals, Hitachi of Japan and Siemens of Germany, with 7 cents and 8 cents, respectively. Even excluding from this measure GE's revenue from financial services, whose only interest in R&D is improved methods of debt-collecting, doesn't help GE's standing: It reinvests 3 cents of each manufacturing-derived dollar.

Patents, a measure of technological output, tell another important aspect of this story. For decades, GE was the undisputed and unchallenged king of the hill, garnering more U.S. patents each year for its innovations than any other company, foreign or domestic. GE hit its peak patent year in 1965, when the United States Patent Office issued it 1,063, while Hitachi had fourteen patents (it had only two in 1960). By 1980, Hitachi had 391 to GE's 770; six years later Hitachi overtook GE for the first time and has patented more inventions than its American rival every year since. Hitachi in fact has been the top U.S. patent recipient in three of the last ten years, and its challengers for the top spot have been mostly Japanese, including Canon, NEC, Mitsubishi Electric, and Toshiba, and more recently IBM and Motorola, which has tripled its annual patent output in the last decade and was issued 40 percent more patents in 1997 than GE.

Siemens, meanwhile, has spent billions of dollars in the past decade investing in microelectronics, trying to pull equal with the Japanese in technology after having fallen far behind. In December 1993, it announced spending of more than $1 billion to build a new semiconductor production facility in Dresden, Germany, which is now making the latest generation of micro-electronic wizardry—the 64-megabit D-Ram memory chip. The memory chips are key parts in computers and satellite television and are regarded as vital for the development of increasingly sophisticated multimedia products that will be invented in the years to come. Siemens could have abandoned the chip business and improved its overall profitability, which is about half that of General Electric. The semiconductor business continues to be unprofitable primarily because of the heavy instruments required to build new production facilities, and there's little doubt that Welch, had he been calling the shots, would have jettisoned it long ago. That's exactly what he did in the late 1980s, even though GE's market position then was superior to Siemens's, which was the equivalent of a mile behind its Japanese and American rivals in the middle of a ten-mile race. But to Siemens, which caught up, immediate profits are not the sole consideration.

The same was true in November 1997, when Siemens announced plans to buy Westinghouse Electric's power-generation division for $1.53 billion. Westinghouse had decided that it could no longer tolerate a business characterized by excess capacity, slow demand, and price-cutting, particularly in light of its new, more profitable profile as the nation's largest owner of radio stations, as well as CBS. When the *Wall Street Journal* asked Albert Hoser, CEO of Siemens's U.S. unit and the executive who had negotiated the deal, why his company would expand its presence in an industry Westinghouse was abandoning, even though the market shares of the two companies were roughly equivalent, he replied: It would be "unthinkable" for Siemens to abandon a business so basic to electricity. Siemens management has an ideology that guides their thinking, one that is product- rather than profit-driven, and they view a continued presence in everything involved in electricity—from the turbine that generates it to the microchip that exploits it—as crucial to their corporate mission to be "one of the most competitive companies in the field of electrical and electronic engineering and [to] set the pace for advances in technology." To underscore that point, Hoser, during his encounter with the *Journal,* reached for a 150th-anniversary book about Siemens, pointing to a section on Werner von Siemens, whose invention of the dynamo laid the basis for modern power generation.

While manufacturing has become increasingly less important to General Electric, services have become increasingly more so, as GE has mirrored, and perhaps led, a similar evolution of the American economy. As recently as 1969, GE's own ideology, according to the mission statement then in force, sounded remarkably similar to Siemens's—"to carry on a diversified, growing, and profitable world-wide manufacturing business in electrical apparatus, appliances and supplies." Now, as opposed to Siemens, which has identified electrical and electronic engineering as a core field where it believes it is poised to lead globally because of its unique history and expertise, GE's values statement cites the personality attributes that the dynamic GE manager should exhibit: He or she is, among other things, "decisive," "reality-based," "self-confident," "aggressive," has a "passion for excellence" and "enormous energy," "hates bureaucracy" and "relishes change." Because Welch believes that a manager can manage anything, General Electric added a television network, NBC, to its portfolio, even though it knew nothing about broadcasting, while greatly expanding its participation in financial services, buying and later selling the once venerable Kidder, Peabody, even though it knew nothing about running a Wall Street securities firm. Today, financial services, which contributed 8 percent of corporate earnings in 1980, generate about 40 percent.* The company Thomas Edison began generates more revenue from selling insurance, lending money, servicing residential mortgages, managing credit cards, leasing jet aircraft and railcars, and a myriad of other financial activities than it does from its five largest manufacturing businesses *combined.* And while GE spent $1.5 billion in 1997 to continue the activities of Edison's greatest invention, the research lab, NBC spent $1.75 billion that same year to continue broadcasting pro basketball.

From a corporate perspective, the metamorphosis from manufacturing to services might seem sensible. Manufacturing can be a tough way to make money, and services offer several advantages: There are generally fewer unions to deal with, fewer liabilities to incur, lower capital outlays for new products and new equipment, and often higher profit margins (the earnings of GE Capital Services have grown an average of about 20 percent annually since 1978). But as GE has retreated from manufacturing, the consequences have been profound, for there are few American companies of the size and clout of a GE to step into the breach. While many American companies know how to lend money, and have a long tradition doing just that, and while many know how to run a television network, and understand the creative dynamics of the entertainment business, GE was unrivaled as the nation's top manufacturer of highly engineered electrical and electronic products. But rather than reinvesting heavily to fully exploit its historic skills, as Hitachi and Siemens have

---

* Some credit analysts see the 40 percent ratio as a threshold that should not be breached because it puts the parent company in the position of being too reliant on GE Credit, possibly threatening GE's cherished triple-A credit rating. "The forty percent [of profits] is about as much as we want to see it get to," Dick Schmidt, an analyst at Standard & Poor's, the credit-rating agency, said in the *Financial Times* on October 9, 1997. His concern is that because GE Capital has the implicit backing of its parent, and hence its triple-A rating, it borrows more cheaply in the capital markets while also bearing a heavier debt burden than many of its rivals. But at some point, as GE Capital becomes an increasingly larger part of GE, the situation could become a case of the tail wagging the dog.

done, an American icon has chosen to quit business after business because the money to be made lending money or producing television shows was greater than the Edisonian mission of *making things*. In the process, the importance of a significant American institution has been diminished.

To see the national consequences in this shift from manufacturing to services, one need look no further than the consumer electronics industry. Once GE had sold out to France's Thomson, abdicating its role as the U.S. standard-bearer in consumer electronics, only Zenith, a company whose resources pale in comparison to GE, was left to fight the war with the Japanese. It surrendered in 1995, selling out to a South Korean company. Thus, we have increased our reliance on foreign companies and thereby weakened our international trade position in a very significant industry, one that is likely to become increasingly so in the years to come. When politicians like Pat Buchanan call for tariffs on Asian imports to encourage Americans to buy goods made in America, that proposal ignores business reality, at least in consumer electronics—*all* the products are manufactured by foreign entities. Welch denounced the criticism he received at the time for selling out to a foreign company as "ludicrous, absolutely ludicrous." Yet when Westinghouse agreed to sell its power-generation division to Siemens, leaving GE as the only American player left in that industry, GE lobbyists in Washington immediately voiced opposition to the sale. It should not be permitted, they and others, most notably South Carolina Senator Ernest Hollings, argued, on the grounds that it jeopardized America's national interests.

The contrast between the philosophy of GE and that of Hitachi, which almost never lets go of a business, couldn't be more striking. Back in the 1960s and early 1970s, when Matsushita Electric, RCA, and GE quit the computer field, Hitachi stuck it out, enduring high R&D outlays while the division lost money. But Hitachi top management, by tradition engineers rather than M.B.A.'s and financial types, continued to subsidize computers with cash from heavy-equipment and consumer-products businesses. Within a decade the computer business had evolved into Hitachi's biggest cash generator, and today computers and the chips that run them account for about one-third of its sales. Hitachi and Japanese rival NEC have already built prototypes of the first chips capable of storing more than one billion pieces of information, sixteen times more storage capacity than the 64-megabit version that Siemens, Hitachi, and others have begun producing, and the equivalent of ten copies of the complete works of Shakespeare on a thumbnail-size sliver of silicon.

The man who founded Hitachi in 1910 was Namihei Odaira, whose founding invention—a five-horsepower induction motor—is enshrined in a museum that tour guides call "the holy place," where visitors must remove their shoes. Odaira's statement of his credo is still inscribed on walls throughout Hitachi City. "Though we cannot live one hundred years, we should be concerned about one thousand years hence," he wrote. It's not empty rhetoric. The size and scope of Hitachi's research effort make General Electric's look lilliputian in comparison. Hitachi's R&D expenditures exceed $5 billion a year, about 6 percent of all corporate research spending in Japan and nearly four times what GE spends, even though the two companies are of comparable size. Hitachi maintains nine separate research centers in and around Tokyo, each with a different focus, that employ more than five thousand scientists and engineers, including sixteen hundred Ph.D.'s (GE has five hundred).

If Hitachi's preservation of continuity sounds odd to American ears, GE's lack of it sounds just as odd to the Japanese. One has to go back to Welch's predecessor, Reg Jones, to find a CEO of General Electric who paid public tribute to GE's founding fathers,* much less the daily ritual that people at Hitachi relish in Odaira. In 1978, Jones presided over festivities commemorating the one-hundredth anniversary of the founding of the Edison Electric Light Company, which included a two-hour prime time television special that GE sponsored on ABC, hosted by John Wayne. As part of the celebration, Jones, then nearing the end of his tenure as steward of the Edison legacy, gave a speech in which he defined what he called "the spirit of General Electric."

Standing between portraits of Edison and Steinmetz, Jones said, "We have roots. We are not merely a 'bundle of assets hastily thrown together in a feverish search for profits,' as somebody once said about one of our competitors. Rather, we are a product of history, shaped and tempered by time. We have our legendary people, places and events, our famous firsts and our famous failures. Out of all these and many other nameless, long-forgotten events we have forged a distinctive set of traditions, values and beliefs that we call 'the spirit of General Electric.' It inspires great loyalty, it encourages moral integrity, and it honors innovation. In my view it is one of our most valuable assets."

Neither Jones nor the people who had come to pay their respects to Steinmetz and Edison foresaw the change that would soon engulf not only their beloved General Electric but all of American business.

Jones's speech marked the final expression of the ethos that had guided

* On July 14, 1998, Welch paid rare public tribute to Edison's achievements, announcing on the *Today* show that GE would donate $5 million toward preserving the "invention factory," a cause championed and brought to Welch's attention by Hillary Clinton. "I didn't understand until recently the breadth and depth of what [Edison did]. It's remarkable," Welch told Mrs. Clinton and viewers. "He really did design the process of invention . . . almost every product General Electric has something to do with was invented around here in this laboratory."

business in America in the twentieth century. For decades the men who had steered the giant enterprises had held true to the axiomatic belief that the job of management wasn't just to maximize profits and satisfy shareholders but also to satisfy two other constituencies that had to be given equal weight in a corporation's considerations—employees and communities. When Jones invoked the "spirit of General Electric," defining as its hallmarks loyalty, morality, and innovation, he was echoing a values-based theme that had been invoked many times before by prominent American businessmen and perhaps was best articulated in a series of lectures in 1962 at the Columbia University Graduate School of Business. Those lectures were delivered by Thomas Watson Jr., who by then had succeeded his father as chairman and chief executive officer of International Business Machines Corporation. The lectures, later published under the title *A Business and Its Beliefs*, advanced the thesis that "the most important single factor in corporate success" was not technology, not strategy, but the corporation's commitment to "a sound set of beliefs."

"Beliefs," Watson said, "must always come before policies, practices and goals. The latter must always be altered if they are seen to violate fundamental beliefs. The only sacred cow in an organization should be its basic philosophy of doing business." This was the "final and most important lesson" to be learned from the history of IBM. The first belief, Watson said, was "respect for the individual," the second "to give the best customer service of any company in the world," and the third "the force that makes the other two effective. We believe that an organization should pursue all tasks with the idea that they can be accomplished in a superior fashion."

By the late 1970s, however, Watson's values-based thesis had given way to a new philosophy that in the 1980s and 1990s would come to be accepted in the business world as dogma. This philosophy was perhaps best stated in the late-1970s best-seller *Looking Out for #1*. "Clear your mind," Robert J. Ringer advised his readers, ". . . Forget foundationless traditions, forget the 'moral' standards others may have tried to cram down your throat, forget the beliefs people may have tried to intimidate you into accepting as 'right.' Allow yourself to take control as you read, and, most important, think of yourself— Number One—as a unique individual. . . . You and you alone will be responsible for your success or failure." The philosophy was hardly new— Niccolo Machiavelli's *The Prince* had laid the intellectual groundwork as early as 1513—but what made it seem new was its widespread acceptance in the American business community.

Ringer's Darwinian vision of the future came to fruition in the events that followed, as the 1980s and 1990s brought unprecedented change and trauma to corporate America. Between January 1981 and January 1986, 10.8 million Americans lost their jobs because of plant shutdowns and corporate restructurings. CEOs swapped assets like baseball cards in the greatest flurry of merger and acquisition activity in the history of American business, which peaked in 1988, a record surpassed in 1994 and eclipsed in every year since. But there were consequences to the "screwor-screwee" theory that Ringer advanced in his book ("The screwor is always the other guy; the screwee is always you"). The demise of values-based thinking brought with it significant curtailments in research and investment. It brought with it great scandals and unprecedented litigation, a me-first ethic that was put on vivid display as the largest insider-trading scandal in American business history slowly unfolded. Yet for all the media attention that Ivan Boesky and Michael Milken received, there were indictments galore against many companies in the mainstream of American business, many of them against General Electric.

Above all, the new zeitgeist brought with it the notion that "gamesmanship" was superior to "industrial enterprise," and the values of frugality, industry, hard work, and perseverance. Those values had no place, it was decided, in a more competitive business environment. Maximizing profits was management's sole objective, and some people represented fat that had to be trimmed if the objective was to be met. As people became increasingly irrelevant to the corporate game plan, American business laid the groundwork for a cynicism that soon spread to politics, sports, the arts, education, law, science, medicine, religion. Only winning mattered, only money mattered, only enhancing the wealth of shareholders mattered. If that meant extraordinary measures, well, then, why not, for these were extraordinary times, uncharted in the history of American business and, for that matter, American society. Being first, being the biggest, that was the only way to succeed, the only way to ensure one's survival, the only way to keep predators from your doorstep. Businessmen began to redefine themselves as citizens of a global economy, with a corresponding decline in the loyalty and responsibility they felt to communities under their control. The notion that business could serve society in ways other than measured by money and profits—through promoting quality of life, jobs, stability, values, ethics, the beliefs that Watson, Jones and countless other businessmen spoke in favor of for generations—was suddenly considered as old-fashioned as Henry Ford's Model T or Thomas Edison's carbon filament lightbulb. Even Watson's own IBM cut its payroll by 180,000 people.

There were, to be sure, a handful of big companies that still clung to traditional business values. Hallmark Cards and its CEO, Irv Hockaday, continued a tradition, begun when the greeting card company was founded by the

Hall family in 1910, of keeping people on the payroll during periods of slack demand to do community service work while they were retrained for new jobs; when Hallmark closed two plants in 1992, it offered all affected employees a chance to relocate to other work sites, and many did. Cooper Tire & Rubber, the world's ninth-largest tire-maker, which for thirty years had occupied the same spartan headquarters in Findlay, Ohio, didn't let the phenomenal 6,800 percent increase in the value of its shares in the 1980s alter the company creed of valuing people. And Levi Strauss adopted the most rigorous ethics policy in corporate America, an "Aspiration Statement" written by top management that commits the apparel maker to "responsible commercial success," "leadership in satisfying our responsibilities to our communities and to society," and creating a work environment in which employees "feel respected, treated fairly, listened to" and achieve "balanced personal and professional lives." Under the program, the company has doubled the percentage of women and minorities in its managerial ranks since 1984, when Robert D. Haas, the great-great-grandnephew of founder Levi Strauss, became CEO.

Even when Levi Strauss announced plans to close eleven of its thirty-seven apparel factories in North America, as it did in November 1997, it distinguished itself with a generous severance package that treated hourly and salaried employees alike. All of the 6,395 affected workers were paid full salary for eight months beyond their last working day, and an additional three weeks of pay for each year worked. They received company-paid health benefits for eighteen months, incentives to take early retirement, up to $6,000 each for education, moving, or job training, and a $500 bonus check as soon as they had found new work. In addition, the Levi Strauss Foundation granted $8 million over three years to the eight communities where the factories were situated. One union official, with whom Levi Strauss negotiated the severance terms, called the package "by far the best severance settlement apparel workers have ever gotten, which will enable the affected workers to move forward with their lives."

Companies like Hallmark, Cooper Tire & Rubber, and Levi Strauss were, however, marching to the beat of a different drummer. Most CEOs were dancing to the tune of the profit rhumba, with Jack Welch playing his theme song: *Control Your Destiny or Someone Else Will* (the title of his authorized hagiography). For better or worse, he would be the man of our times, the quintessential business leader of the 1980s and 1990s, and he would take General Electric and this nation on one wild ride.

CHAPTER TWO

PASSING THE BATON

THE BRAVE, new world that GE was about to enter began on December 19, 1980, when the courtly, British-born Reginald Harold Jones, the seventh chief executive in GE's eighty-eight years, announced selection of the eighth. In the forty-seventh-floor boardroom of the New York offices, Jones read from a typed statement, making public a decision directors had made earlier that day. There were no puffs of white smoke and no coronation wreaths, but Jones and the board had chosen a new king, one who would soon seize the company by the throat and shake it until it was dizzy.

It is hard to imagine two men more different than Reg (rhymes with "leg") Jones and the man who would succeed him the following April, John Francis Welch Jr. Jones was the epitome of the GE system, not the lab and factory traditions, but rather the managerial class, which had come to rival and eclipse the engineering and technology culture that dominated the company in its first half century. An accomplished bureaucrat and skilled practitioner of scientific management, Jones had joined the company's prestigious Financial Management Program in 1939. After twenty years in finance and having distinguished himself as a "traveling auditor," the crème de la crème of the financial staff, Jones had a tour of duty in line assignments. In 1968 he became chief financial officer and catapulted from there five years later into the CEO's job, the first executive from the finance ranks in GE history to head the company. Though Jones had spent all but eight of his sixty-three years in the United States, he still retained the mannerisms and speech of the proper English gentleman, born in Staffordshire, England, in 1917, and looking and acting more like an Anglican priest than America's most admired businessman.

Welch, on the other hand, was as profane as Jones was urbane. The *Wall Street Journal* reported that GE had replaced "a legend with a live wire," an understatement of seismic proportions. The CEO-designate's roots were working-class Irish Catholic, and he didn't fit GE's staid, buttoned-down, Ivy League traditions. "Kinetic" would have been a more appropriate description of the new CEO, who as a younger man had nervously bitten his nails, a habit he had learned to control somewhat as he climbed the corporate ladder. He still had peculiar habits: Colleagues had watched in amazement while Welch consumed five sticks of gum at once, or whole buckets of ice. Welch stammered and cussed like a longshoreman, but what he lacked in polish he offset with raw energy, typifying Samuel Johnson's definition of the well-balanced Irishman—a man with chips on both shoulders. Always scratching and clawing for more, Welch was an iconoclast in a company that was itself an icon.

He was the atypical CEO in other ways as well. As a group, CEOs tend to come from the upper strata of society; studies have shown the rich and upper-middle class to be overrepresented among American CEOs by a considerable margin. Roberto C. Goizueta, the son of a wealthy Cuban sugar magnate, received his secondary education at private boarding schools in Connecticut, then attended Yale University. Some CEOs, such as August Busch III of Anheuser-Busch, J. Peter Grace of W. R. Grace, and Arthur O. Sulzberger of the *New York Times*, were formally groomed to take over positions held by their fathers. Whereas if Welch had followed in his father's footsteps, he would have gone to work taking tickets for the Boston & Maine Railroad. John Francis Welch Sr. was a committed union man, a quiet train conductor who left for work before sunrise, returned home after sunset, and had relatively little influence on his son.

For Welch, it was his other parent who mattered. Like both Henry Ford and Andrew Carnegie, he was greatly influenced by the upbringing he received from a deeply religious mother. Grace Welch, a devout Roman Catholic, had been trying to have a child for sixteen years before she finally gave birth to Jack in 1935; she never had another. Jack spent a great deal of time with his mother—they attended baseball games together, sitting in the bleachers to watch the Red Sox or the old Boston Braves, and played cards, usually gin rummy. Grace also insisted that her son go to church every day. She would sit in the front pew during morning Lenten mass while Jack went through the daily rituals of a Catholic altar boy (Welch quit Catholicism after his mother's death in 1966). Grace Welch instilled in her son not just ambition and independence but tremendous self-confidence, which aided him immeasurably once he reached General Electric.

Young Jack at times pitied his passive father. In 1953, during Jack's senior year in high school, he was one of three students nominated for Navy ROTC scholarships. The winners would receive free room, board, and tuition at the college of their choice, no small thing for working-class parents seeking a way to pay for their only son's higher education. Jack Sr. decided to try and pull strings to ensure his son's selection, with devastating consequences for Jack Jr., as he later recalled. Not only was he not selected, he also despaired as his parents scrounged around helplessly for contacts they simply didn't have. The two successful nominees went to prestigious private schools—one to Columbia, the other to Tufts—while Jack, who had had his heart set on Dartmouth, enrolled at the state University of Massachusetts at Amherst.

The incident reinforced in Welch's mind his working-class status, his sense of himself, he later recalled, as someone who "always had my nose pressed against the glass." As a child, Welch grew up poorer than he wanted to be; as an adolescent, he earned pocket money caddying for the wealthy (he listed "to make a million" as his "repressed desire" in the high school literary magazine); as a teenager, he failed to win the elite scholarship to an Ivy League school that he felt, based on his academic achievement, was rightfully his. Welch would enter adulthood with an overarching need to prove himself. By winning, he hoped to open the doors that had been closed to him, and gain entry to a club he had been excluded from his entire life.

From the very first day he drove into Pittsfield, Massachusetts, in October 1960 after accepting his first job there, with GE—driving a brand-new Volkswagen Beetle, a graduation gift from his father—Welch's need to succeed was apparent to colleagues, who noticed how competitive he was. Welch confided to a colleague soon after his arrival that he had quit playing weekend softball with his office mates because they seemed to resent his aggressive play. If he knocked them down sliding hard into second, they would hold a grudge. On another occasion, he came upon three colleagues who were playing golf at the Berkshire Hills Country Club. Playing alone, Welch, a scratch golfer who had captained his high school golf team, asked if he could join them. "No," they said. The incident bothered Welch, who felt slighted and couldn't understand why he had been treated so shabbily.

For the next seventeen years, Welch was a fixture in Pittsfield, either working in, running, or supervising the plastics business. Plastics had gotten its start in 1912, when Charles Steinmetz, the modern "Jove," recommended a major strengthening of staff in research chemistry to explore new directions in "artificial resins." Many patents followed, but the plastics department, which was officially formed in 1931, had been a bust commercially. By 1960, GE employed 10,300 people in Pittsfield, ten thousand of whom made the company's mainstay electrical and ordnance product. The other three hundred were chemists and chemical engineers in the plastics business. In Pittsfield in those days, according to GE's rigid social hierarchy of that time, the denizens of Plastics were considered second-class citizens.

Welch's arrival brought a new era. When, as a Ph.D. chemical engineer fresh out of the University of Illinois, he joined GE, he found a business distinctly unlike the rest of the company, a business perfectly suited to his brash, aggressive personality. He became its spiritual godfather, and the culture of plastics became an extension of its chief. "It was Jack Welch plastics in those days. If he could have, he would have printed his business cards that way," recalls former colleague Charles Carson. Although Welch didn't fit the typical GE mold, there was one hallowed tradition he upheld splendidly: He got results. Moreover, Welch's tendency to rattle cages and shake things up was exactly what Jones wanted, convinced as he was that the more than four hundred thousand GE employees needed a wake-up call. They would get one.

Outwardly, the numbers didn't suggest a problem. The company Welch inherited was, financially at least, one of the strongest in America: Its triple-A debt rating, $2.2 billion in cash and marketable securities, and a 19.5 percent return on equity attested to GE's position as a pillar of financial integrity. It had never had an unprofitable year in its history, had paid a dividend every year since 1900, and had virtually no debt. General Electric was America's most admired corporation, and Jones, whom President Jimmy Carter had twice offered a cabinet-level job, was the most admired CEO. "Probably no single company has made such a singular contribution to the arts and wiles, the viewpoints and the techniques of large-scale corporate management as GE," *Management Today* wrote in a 1978 story. But where others saw invincibility, Jones saw vulnerability. Although himself the product of a hidebound management culture, Jones had come to realize that the bureaucracy it imposed on the company was in fact a serious flaw rather than a strength. GE wasn't alone in its tendency toward wasteful sloth. As a director of the Bethlehem Steel Corporation, Jones had had a ringside view of the sleepy inertia that was a way of life throughout Big Steel and much of industrial America.

The elements of decline that would hit the steel industry with hurricane force in the 1980s were already in place and had been festering since the salad days of the 1950s, as wages climbed, productivity fell, and international competition intensified. What was worse, foreign rivals, be they Hitachi or Nippon Steel, were gaining an edge technologically. Companies like Bethlehem and GE, Jones feared, were falling behind. That was the pattern in industry after industry—autos, electrical machinery, tires, textiles—and although the signs were clear, the organizations themselves had grown so sluggish and complacent that they were unwilling or unable to adopt a different mentality. Jones, who had seen at Bethlehem the difficult task management faced when it tried to shake a lumbering giant out of its lethargy, worried that GE was succumbing to the same tendencies. In his letter to General Electric shareholders in 1980, Jones addressed the issue: "U.S. business finds itself challenged by aggressive overseas competitors. National productivity has been declining and, in industry after industry, product leadership is moving to other nations. Companies that refuse to renew themselves, that fail to cast off the old and embrace new technologies, could well find themselves in serious decline in the 1980s. We are determined that this shall not happen to General Electric."

The bureaucracy Jones feared was strangling the company had its genesis in the 1950s. At that time, GE was greatly admired and technologically unassailable, holding the same status in American industry as IBM did in the 1960s and 1970s. Yet the history of great institutions teaches one paradoxical lesson that Jones understood: When the institution is most admired, it is in all likelihood at greatest risk. It was in the midst of one of General Electric's greatest growth spurts, the early 1950s, that CEO Ralph Cordiner, seeking to correct what he perceived as a fundamental problem, would end up creating an even bigger one. General Electric's organizational structure hadn't changed since the days of Edison. A relatively small group of executives at headquarters oversaw the activities of eleven divisions, each of which was responsible for a certain territory and certain products, effectively operating as independent fiefdoms. Each site had full authority for production, sales, and distribution of the products it was assigned to produce, and particular divisions took the lead for particular products. Schenectady, for instance, was responsible for turbines; Fort Wayne, Indiana, motors; Louisville, Kentucky, appliances; Nela Park, Ohio, lighting; Erie, Pennsylvania, locomotives; and so on. The Works factory complexes evolved into small cities, with their own schools, parks, radio stations, and housing, while the Works manager became a sort of lord mayor, who typically resisted the attempts of corporate headquarters to rein him in or otherwise impose control.

Cordiner, who was as revolutionary in his time as Welch would be in his, was convinced that the Works had to be broken up into smaller, more focused units, each with a narrower product agenda. Marketing had never been GE's forte, and it was this lack of a marketing focus that contributed to Cordiner's determination to recast the company. On many occasions, GE had breakthroughs it had failed to seize upon, only to have a rival exploit the invention:

The engineer who dreamed up the first diesel-electric locomotive in 1924, for instance, later defected to rival General Motors, which took the concept, gave it the support GE hadn't, and dominated the locomotive market for decades; similarly, the promising commercial advantage GE had in jet engines, based on its invention of the first jet engine in the early 1940s, slipped away to Pratt & Whitney, and wasn't recovered until the 1980s.

At his first board meeting in January 1951, Cordiner—five feet two inches tall, with a cold and aloof personality, Napoleonic in appearance and demeanor—proposed a radical reorganization of GE, based on the nouveau concept of decentralization, to counteract the company's tendency toward what he called "security, complacency, and mediocrity." His message, similar to Welch's three decades later, was that GE would be transformed from a stodgy enterprise into a dynamic one by basing rewards on performance and by giving managers more responsibility for the products they were charged with. While the company's operations were broken up into product departments that were small enough, in his words, "for a man to get his arms around," Cordiner also had an unstated purpose—he wanted ultimate authority. The only way to achieve that goal was to wrest control from the Works managers, the traditional power brokers, who were emasculated by the creation of hundreds of separate product departments. Instead of just one giant motors business, for instance, with one Works manager at the apex, motors was subdivided into nine departments, each with a discrete focus—lamps, turbines, switchgear, appliances. The entire corporation was reorganized following this same pattern, on the theory that the sum of the departments would be greater than the former whole.

The changes Cordiner wrought were revolutionary. Over a twenty-month period he changed the jobs of two thousand senior executives, as managers who had spent their entire careers in old General Electric towns like Schenectady, Pittsfield, Erie, and Bridgeport were told to pick up and move their families to places like New York City, Louisville, and Rome, Georgia. Cordiner embraced the concept of interchangeable "professional managers" as a rationale for moving his loyalists into jobs they were unfamiliar with. Many old traditions were unilaterally abolished. In their place, Cordiner in 1956 established the GE Management Development Institute, its Harvard-on-the-Hudson business school in Crotonville, New York, a kind of boot camp where managers were indoctrinated in the new principles and quickly learned to spout the new rhetoric.

Cordiner's revolution was carried out by two trusted lieutenants who would leave an indelible mark on the character of GE. The first, Lemuel Boulware, his top labor strategist, forged the company's take-it-or-leave-it bargaining strategy, which meant that GE's first offer on any contract was its final offer, and labor could either accept or strike. "Boulwarism" came to represent for that generation of organized labor what Pinkerton guards were for an earlier one, while GE embraced union avoidance on a grand scale. Managers who had a union petition in a nonunion plant lost their jobs. "If management is doing its job, you don't need unions," Boulware was fond of saying. The second assistant, Harold Smiddy, a management specialist and Cordiner's chief of staff, installed the administrative apparatus that allowed Cordiner to assert authority over the more than one hundred separate product departments, a complex system of rules and procedures, set forth in eight Blue Books, the General Electric bible of that time. The "speed, simplicity, self-confidence" mantra Welch would chant years later was a version of the commandments Cordiner and Smiddy decreed, and serves as testimony to the cyclic convulsions of the modern General Electric. Consider this sample of the Cordiner credo from the Blue Books, which sounds just like a Welch quotation from the pages of *Fortune*: "A minimum of supervision, a minimum of time delays in decision making, a maximum of competitive agility, and thus maximum service to customers and profits to the company."

The Blue Books applied the principles of scientific management to every conceivable situation a manager might face, and, in turn, dictated the proper response, spelling out in infinite detail the four key Cordiner dictums: plan; organize; integrate; and, last but by no means least, *measure*. "Measure" meant that the correct response to the question, "What is it we make in Louisville?" eventually wasn't "refrigerators"; it was "money." Cordiner's regimen in this regard, as in all matters, was harsh: Every department general manager had to produce a net profit margin of at least 7 percent every quarter.

The changes Cordiner put in place had many unintended consequences, one being that the finance function grew tremendously in stature and influence. Decentralization required more financial controls to keep tabs on the separate departments, and the finance staff, which was charged with policing Smiddy's system, exercised ultimate control over money and personnel. Rather than simply keeping track of the cash, finance evolved into a domain unto itself—to this day, a General Electric line manager cannot select, hire, or fire his financial subordinate without approval of the chief financial officer. The tyranny of numbers meant that businesses that didn't meet their minimum operating requirements were jettisoned, often with little regard to potential for future growth. Others were "harvested," GE parlance for using the cash one business generated to finance the growth of another. As finance gained more power, technology and engineering had less, and GE evolved from a company whose heroes were inventors into one where the upwardly mobile and admired were financial types. The result was the creation of a corporate culture that was risk-averse, very short term in its thinking, and more focused on maintaining profits than on investing in new products and new technologies.

The Cordiner era also spawned gridlock of truly monumental proportions. The bureaucratic overlay of a new departmental structure atop an existing one eventually became mind-boggling in its complexity, and within two decades the Cordiner initiative had mushroomed into some two hundred separate product departments, which reported to forty-six divisions, which reported to ten groups, which reported to the CEO. In 1969, Fred Borch, Cordiner's successor, commissioned a study of the company by the consulting firm McKinsey & Company. Once the recommendations had been implemented, it only added more girth to the bureaucracy. By the end of Jones's tenure, when *nine* layers separated him from the lowly foot soldier in the factory, General Electric had become a suffocatingly ossified place. The Cordiner era was rife with irony: It had given rise to the very things it was supposed to eradicate. Not surprisingly, growth had sputtered—GE's 1981 revenues, in constant inflation-adjusted dollars, were only double those of 1958—stifled by the sheer number of rules, procedures, and hierarchies that dictated everything. Employees were assigned to one of twenty-eight civil service style levels of rank, which determined office size even down to a standardized number of ceiling tiles. Subordinates fawned over their bosses, spoke only when spoken to, kept their ties knotted and their shirtsleeves clean, and, above all, followed orders, whether they made sense or not.

The Cordiner era had one more unintended consequence. The unrelenting demands placed on managers to "make their numbers," even when the numbers were clearly unachievable, led to one of the great business scandals of modern times. From 1959 until 1961, General Electric was indicted again and again as the lead conspirator in the biggest antitrust conspiracy of this century, a scandal summed up by a headline in *Fortune* magazine: "The Incredible Electrical Conspiracy." It was the darkest period in General Electric's history, a time when the Justice Department pondered breaking up the company, so manifold and wanton were the transgressions. More than a dozen General Electric executives had conspired with managers at twenty-eight other manufacturers of electrical equipment to fix prices, rig bids, and divide markets. The twenty indictments charged that GE and its accomplices had colluded during an eight-year period on electrical equipment valued at nearly $2 billion a year, everything from $2 insulators to multimillion-dollar turbine generators.

The scandal was reminiscent of the early days of the steel industry, when Elbert Gary, a former judge and the first chairman of the United States Steel Corporation, which had been created by J. P. Morgan in 1901, would allocate market share among the steel chieftains who attended his infamous "Gary dinners." That practice culminated in the government's 1911 monopoly charge against Judge Gary and United States Steel. Fifty years later, the collusion in the electrical industry was just as bold. Executives would gather two or three times monthly to divvy up business, typically in hotel encounters the conspirators referred to as "choir practice," swapping confidential pricing information, agreeing in advance on winning bids, and invariably allocating the highest share to GE. "The Incredible Electrical Conspiracy" brought many careers to an abrupt end.

The price-fixing scandal had its roots not only in the pressure put on GE executives to perform but in their belief that it wasn't wrong to fix prices. "Sure, collusion was illegal," one veteran executive said at the time, "but it wasn't *unethical*. Those competitor meetings were just attended by a group of distressed individuals who wanted to know where they were going." At the time, General Electric was being subjected to the most virulent competition in its history. Before World War II, the electrical equipment industry, which accounted for some 25 percent of corporate sales, was an oligopoly; customers would order products, and GE would in turn tell them the price they were to pay. But the market dynamics changed after the war as smaller companies jumped into the fray. Customers had a wider choice of heavy electrical equipment, and price was becoming a key selling point. The electric utilities turned the situation to their advantage, instituting a new practice: the competitive bid. The specter of competition rankled many executives in the corporate suite, who saw it as a threat to corporate profits as well as their careers. Thus was born the collusion.

Throughout its history, the men who had run GE had taken a dim view of competition. The first was Charles Albert Coffin, General Electric's founder, who for thirty years served as its most senior executive. Coffin had orchestrated the merger of the two entities that created GE to sidestep the competition that was hurting the early electrical industry. In 1881, two years after Edison's discovery of incandescent light, Coffin, a gifted administrator and descendant of Benjamin Franklin, bought controlling interest in a company that had been founded in Philadelphia by Elihu Thomson and Edwin J. Houston, two high school teachers. Coffin renamed the enterprise Thomson-Houston Electric Company and moved it to Lynn, Massachusetts, where he manufactured shoes, a business he gave up once electricity began to flourish. By 1888, the annual volume of Thomson-Houston had grown more than tenfold, from $300,000 five years before to $3.5 million. But the feverish pace of invention had ushered in a period of vigorous patent conflicts, and the thicket of lawsuits sapped the strength of the major competitors as they fought infringement actions or tried to skirt each other's patents.

With the patent situation growing more litigious and the combatants growing more weary, Henry Villard, president of Edison General Electric, sought a truce. When he suggested to Thomas Edison a union of Edison General Electric with Coffin's company, Edison did not protest, for his own company was in a bind. Although Edison held the all-important patent to the incandescent lamp, which had withstood a vigorous legal challenge, the Edison company was desperately in need of cash, its reserves depleted by Edison's expensive quest, begun the decade before, for perfect iron ore. Edison was also growing weary of the fratricide within the electrical business. The early electrical industry was more than simply a rivalry between competing companies; as is the case with most new technologies, it was also a rivalry between competing systems. Edison had stubbornly stuck with direct current long after George Westinghouse's alternating-current networks had carried the day, while Coffin had chosen alternating current, which was increasingly the system of choice for most products, including incandescent lamps. It took more than a year before the negotiations had concluded, but on April 15, 1892, an alliance was reached with the formation of a company that was christened, simply, General Electric. Edison and his allies lost out: Not only did the new company not bear his name, but Villard was ousted by J. P. Morgan, financier of the deal and the loudest voice on the new board of directors. Although Edison remained a director of the new company for more than a decade, he never attended another meeting after the first.

The concentration of the two leading companies in the infant electrical industry, together employing ten thousand workers and having combined revenues of more than $20 million, was widely attacked as a menacing monopoly at a time when the public was alarmed about anticompetitive "trusts." A muckraking magazine called *Electricity* made accusations against GE's bookkeeping methods, and Coffin's integrity. Moreover, Congress had just passed the Sherman Antitrust Act, an outgrowth of public opinion, which viewed monopolies as decidedly un-American. Within a decade thereafter, President Theodore Roosevelt, the great trustbuster, began busily dismantling the giant corporations that threatened to stifle competition; Roosevelt's successor, William Howard Taft, went after Standard Oil, the American Tobacco Company, and United States Steel. Coffin, however, was undeterred, striking a rapprochement with Washington that allowed GE to go virtually unchallenged, either by the federal government or by rival concerns, in the early electrification of America. The patent suit Edison won forced other light bulb manufacturers to license GE technology, and the result was a monolith in lighting and electricity that was unassailable as GE and Westinghouse effectively created a duopoly in electrical products. Rival inventors were either bought out or driven away through litigation, and the patent protection gave Coffin the leverage to negotiate cross-licensing agreements, even overseas, that further shielded GE from its rivals.

The men who succeeded Coffin shared his disdain for competition. Gerard Swope, a political liberal who became president in 1922, was a champion of workers' rights, continuing the traditions of "welfare capitalism" begun by socialist Charles Steinmetz. Swope believed that the company should treat its workers like family, and during his tenure, which lasted until 1940, General Electric became one of the nation's most paternalistic and progressive employers, acquiring the nickname "Generous Electric." Generous it was: Swope saw to it that people in the GE "family" had insurance, a mortgage assistance program, company-sponsored unemployment compensation, pensions, bonuses, profit sharing, and many other benefits unheard of at that time. As an adviser to Franklin Roosevelt, Swope made his ideas instrumental in the New Deal, and he was also an outspoken opponent of "excessive competition" in business, which he believed had been the cause of the Great Depression. At the same time, Swope extended the company's market dominance around the globe: By 1935, GE owned 40 percent of Tokyo Electric, 29 percent of Germany's Osram, 44 percent of France's Compagnie des Lampes, 34 percent of Britain's General Electric Company, 10 percent of Philips in Holland, 100 percent of China's Edison Electric, and more.

Nor was competition a concern to Charles Wilson, Swope's successor. World War II flooded GE with orders; as a critical cog in the arsenal of democracy, the company sold all it could produce. GE's contributions to the war effort were substantial and included everything from gears and turbines for ship propulsion to radar systems, howitzers, aircraft engines, and machinegun turrets. Wilson, who took a leave from the GE presidency at President Roosevelt's request to head the War Mobilization Board, floated on the rising tide of American industrial preeminence. It was the beginning of the military-industrial complex, and a half-century alliance between the military and General Electric. The Pentagon would soon become GE's biggest customer, accounting for as much as 25 percent of corporate sales.

But the 1940s brought some challenges to GE's hegemony, as Washington's laissez-faire attitude toward antitrust ended. Between 1940 and 1948 the government sued GE thirteen times for antitrust violations, charging price-fixing and other anticompetitive practices. The resulting consent decrees, though, did little to reduce GE's clout in lighting. Its share of the U.S. light-bulb market remained around 80 percent until the 1950s, and to this day GE manufactures more than half of the lightbulbs sold in America.

HAD JACK WELCH LANDED in any business other than plastics, it is a virtual certainty that the future CEO of General Electric would have left in a matter of months. The system would have chewed him up and spit him out. Welch was the antithesis of everything GE represented at that time, a young man in a hurry who had no tolerance whatsoever for bureaucracy or delays of any kind, someone who wanted things done *fast*. Speed was the very essence of the man. He rushed ahead, sometimes impetuously, and flouted convention.

Welch was domineering, immature, abrasive, and competitive to a fault but, at the same time, likeable in an unvarnished way. One of his charms was that he didn't try to sublimate his personality or his passion; what you saw was what you got. What you saw was a man whose forceful personality made him appear somewhat bigger than he was. He talked in machine-gun-like bursts, throwing out ideas in a verbal torrent so strong—in high school, his class had voted him the "most talkative and noisiest boy"—that it often came out in a stutter, which had dogged him since childhood. Although Welch could have grown up emotionally crippled by his speech impediment, which was quite severe, his mother convinced him that his wasn't a defect but merely a sign that his mind was racing faster than he could speak.

Welch's cocksure attitude was behavior appropriate to the career opportunities that lay before him. In 1960, GE Plastics was on the threshold of a new era. Plastics of all kinds, not just GE's, were the material of the future (as Dustin Hoffman was so famously advised in *The Graduate*). Growth came as new laboratory concoctions supplanted metal and glass in automobiles and packaging. It was the perfect opportunity for an ambitious young man who had selected chemical engineering as his academic specialty, rather than becoming a priest or doctor as his mother had wanted, and Welch soon proved that he wasn't one to let opportunity slip by. The business Welch had joined was also striving to make something of itself, and overcome its second-class status. GE had come to Pittsfield in 1903 not because of plastics but electrical transformers. That year, as part of the consolidation of the early electrical industry, General Electric purchased the Stanley Electric Manufacturing Company, whose founder William Stanley had developed the first high-voltage, alternating-current transformer. Plastics was a skunk works with some promising ideas and only one going business, silicones, a water-resistant sealant, which made it the perfect place for a renegade like Welch—a business so insignificant it went unnoticed and hence was unusually tolerant of new ideas and unusual behavior.

Even so, Welch was barely one year into his job as a junior engineer when he suddenly quit. He had accepted a position at International Minerals & Chemicals in Chicago because his GE boss had only given him the standard $1,000 annual raise on a salary of $10,500. Welch, who was perpetually dissatisfied and needed fairly regular stroking, felt he deserved more. By the time Reuben Gutoff, who was in charge of the chemical development operation, as it was called in those days, heard about Welch's imminent departure, it was almost too late. The Thursday evening before Welch's last day, Gutoff took him and his wife, Carolyn, to dinner. Welch was vacillating about his decision to leave, and Gutoff called from a phone booth after they had parted to tell Welch again what a terrific future he had at General Electric. From that moment on, Welch, who held off telling colleagues he was staying until his going-away party Friday night, would get heftier raises than his peer group.

By 1963, Welch, a rising star, had been given his first management responsibility, and it was an important one: finding a market for a new type of plastic, polyphenoline oxide (PPO), another breakthrough for the Schenectady research lab. Although GE chemists had discovered PPO in 1956, it had been shelved while the plastics business focused its limited resources on commercial development of another new compound, Lexan. By May 1964, when Welch's group had sold their first PPO, he had convinced Gutoff and Charlie Reed, Gutoff's boss, to build a $10 million factory in Selkirk, New York, to manufacture the polymer. Colleagues marveled at Welch's relentlessness, his ability to buck the system and make it work for him. But it was soon discovered that PPO didn't work. Plastics formed from it were cracking and turning brown, while complaints from customers began pouring in. Some in the group thought that GE should admit failure and fold its tent, but Welch persevered. He counted on his research team to find a solution, which they did.

Blending polystyrene, the plastic used in foam coffee cups, and PPO yielded a new compound, dubbed Noryl, which was patented in 1966. It didn't crack or turn brown and was easy to mold. Welch had won his first big wager, but his persistence also seemed to court disaster. A pilot plant was quickly established in Pittsfield to test a manufacturing process for the new plastic, which was brought along too quickly at Welch's urging, resulting in a catastrophic explosion that reduced the plant to rubble. Fortunately, no one was hurt. Although Reed, the group executive in charge of plastics, felt Welch had been reckless—a tendency he had observed before—he also admired his ability to get things done and thought that even egregious mistakes should be forgiven, a courtesy Welch didn't always extend to his own subordinates.

Welch faced a marketing challenge with Noryl, because it didn't have the unique properties of Lexan, a transparent, virtually unbreakable plastic that was an ideal substitute for glass. The helmet visors of the astronauts who landed on the moon in 1969 were made from Lexan. Noryl, on the other hand, had no clear-cut market, so one had to be created, and Welch was determined to do so. GE's own appliance division was the first beachhead. After much persuasion, he convinced division managers to sheathe electric can openers in Noryl rather than metal. One colleague who didn't accede to his entreaties was Stanley Gault, a GE manager who went on to become CEO of Rubbermaid and Goodyear Tire & Rubber Company, and whose long-standing feud with Welch began during this period, associates say. Years later, the rivalry intensified when Gault and Welch were competing against each other for the CEO's job, but it began in the late 1960s, when Welch pitched Noryl as a housing for room air-conditioners. Gault, who ran the business then, didn't want to spend money retooling machinery to adapt to plastic. Gault also wanted a six-month moratorium before Welch took the idea outside GE. The concession was granted after much wrangling, but Welch wasn't happy about it.

As Noryl grew—it was a $50 million business by 1973—so did the legend of Jack Welch. He was a kind of Billy the Kid, the enfant terrible whose exploits became even more legendary because he broke the rules and never seemed to get caught. Welch attracted attention to himself not so much because of the results he achieved but because of the way he got them. Like a speeding boat in a narrow canal, he left a big wake behind him. In nearly everything he did, he caused a stir. He was the proverbial bull in a china shop, a metaphor Welch evidently liked: In 1968, he commissioned a television commercial that had a bull breaking everything in a china shop that wasn't made of GE plastic. In addition to a flair for sales, Welch had now revealed himself to be nakedly ambitious, and very political. Tom Morton, a retired newspaper editor in Pittsfield who wrote the first profile of Welch in the mid-1960s, recalls how Welch's ambition was readily apparent even then. In the aftermath of the price-fixing scandal, GE was trying to repair its damaged reputation. "All of the top managers were very active in community affairs," Morton recalls, "except Welch. His eye was on the prize. The prize wasn't to get a reward from the United Way."

Even at this early stage, Welch was sizing up his likely adversaries for the CEO's job. One colleague remembers being in his office when Welch got word that Thomas Vanderslice, a rival Welch was already tracking, had been promoted. Welch immediately called a friend to assess what the promotion meant. As it turned out, Welch's instincts were good: Vanderslice would be among the finalists vying for the CEO's job in the horse race Reg Jones organized a decade later.

Although a Ph.D. chemical engineer, Welch appeared to have little interest in engineering or science. Management—controlling assets and people— was what really excited him. More instinctual in his decision making than studious, he prided himself on his ability to size up a situation quickly and make the right decision immediately. He would do the same with people. One encounter and he would usually have a person pegged as a winner or a loser. Sometimes his opinion might be formed simply on the way a person looked, for appearance and style mattered a great deal to Welch: looking good was an important part of the total package. If Welch once judged a person to be a winner, he would often stick with his judgment even as evidence to the contrary mounted. Conversely, a person classified as a "dink," the term he commonly used to put down people who weren't the guerrilla warriors he admired, would find it difficult to overcome that status.

The young man had a volcanic temper. One visitor to Pittsfield recalls a scene when Welch and a subordinate, standing just outside Welch's office, were shouting at each other. "Why don't you go in there so we don't have to listen to you?" the visitor asked. "If I do, the son of a bitch will kill me," came the subordinate's reply. Welch loved rough-and-tumble repartee, and the locker room camaraderie that went with it. An ex-jock, he took an approach to business that was reminiscent of the way he had captained hockey teams as a high school senior in Salem, Massachusetts—confrontational, fast-paced, and free-flowing. In the business arena, net income was the analogue for goals scored: Winners made their profit goals, losers didn't—and got dropped from the team. How well you scored last year didn't matter. Why you weren't making the numbers this year was also irrelevant. What mattered, all that mattered, was performance. "Jack doesn't allow people to deviate from the performance they're assigned for the year," says one GE manager. "You either deliver what you committed to or you're in a world of hurt. There's no absolution."

Like the fisticuffs of hockey, Welch's business confrontations could also get out of hand. He would get so angry at times he would literally tremble. On occasion, his outbursts reduced grown men to tears. The angrier he got, the more he would stammer, particularly on expletives, which made for some Porky Pig–like imitations when he wasn't within earshot. Mimicking Welch behind his back became a way of relieving the omnipresent stress in Plastics, which was as highly charged as some of GE's other businesses were somnolent.

Plastics was a fraternity of loud, boisterous, young men mostly in their twenties who were each trying to outgun the others, comradeship rooted in performance. Salesmen were the top guns. Their job was to go get the pounds—to sell, sell, sell, while maintaining a respectable golf handicap. A five-thousand-pound order was cause for celebration; everyone feasted on pizza and beer. Soon the plastics division was growing 60 percent a year. Welch was their leader, the godfather of the "family" business, as he affectionately called Plastics. And the members of his gang were well rewarded. "Jack always took care of his people," recalls John Thoma, a top salesman.

Welch now was a man on the move. In 1968, after five years running the Noryl business and just thirty-two years old, he became the youngest general manager in the corporation, responsible not only for Noryl but for Lexan. He kept the rivalry going between the two products by keeping the two departments separate, a violation of Blue Book dogma and one that encouraged ferocious competition. "We fought more with the Noryl guys than with the competition outside GE," Lexan salesman Thoma recalls. "You had to have the killer instinct or you wouldn't survive." Having the killer instinct meant maintaining a fearsome work schedule, staying up until 5 a.m. some nights partying, and looking sharp for the morning meeting three hours later. The hours were long, the demands frightful—it was considered normal to leave on a trip Monday morning, come home Friday night, work all day Saturday, only to start the cycle again Monday morning. Families and spouses weren't part of the equation.

Success forged a very definite culture, defined by a set of unwritten beliefs and values distinct from the rest of GE. It was here, in Plastics, that Welch would formulate the basic business principles and ideas he would later seek to imprint on all of GE. It was here that the "speed, simplicity, self-confidence" credo was born and had its clearest manifestation. The way business was done at Plastics would become, in Welch's mind, the only way to do business, the model that every GE division should seek to emulate: A business that had a bias toward action, that was agile, lean, and fast, that could outrun its competitors. The people of Plastics had the cocky self-assurance of their leader, a swagger that set them apart. Accustomed to luxury and extravagance, Plastics' salesmen hired yachts to entertain their customers, while GE Lighting gave out coffee mugs to theirs. It was not unusual for a sales manager to charter a plane, buy up a block of Super Bowl tickets on the fifty-yard line, and treat his customers to an all-expenses-paid weekend of football, food, and drink. It was a culture that put a premium on lavishness, on being loud, on making a statement.

John McLaughlin, a GE manager who purchased materials used to make GE appliances, once discovered just how determined Welch could be in accomplishing his objectives. In the early 1970s, when McLaughlin paid GE Plastics forty-six cents a pound for phenolic resin, a low-grade plastic used in toaster ovens, iron handles, and other appliances, he found another supplier outside GE that would sell its phenolic for thirty-eight cents a pound. Because the appliance division consumed huge quantities of phenolic, the eight-cent price differential meant big savings, and McLaughlin got authorization to switch to the cheaper source. When Welch heard about the pending switch, he met with McLaughlin, who refused to back down. Later, at GE's annual managers' gathering in Florida, Welch cornered his adversary after dinner. From about 10:30 p.m. until 2 a.m. (the bar closed at midnight), Welch, never one to duck a fight, pressed his point. " 'You'll never buy it for thirty-eight cents,' he kept saying," McLaughlin recalls. "At one point he turned to me and said, 'I'm going to offer you a two-level promotion in my group so I can fire you.' " McLaughlin held his ground.

Sometime later, GE's top brass got involved. Welch had asked Herman Weiss, his boss, to nix the purchase. Weiss reviewed it with vice chairman Walter Dance, who years later would oppose Welch's candidacy for CEO. Dance conferred with Robert Frederick, Welch's counterpart in consumer products, McLaughlin's boss two levels up, and another eventual candidate for CEO. Frederick told McLaughlin he would support him, which he did. Plastics bought large quantities of tungsten from GE's lamp division (in Frederick's group), and Welch threatened to find another supplier if McLaughlin did not back down. Eventually, McLaughlin, deciding that discretion was the better part of valor, went back to GE Plastics. Once Welch had won, though, he was gracious: He sent McLaughlin a free truckload of Noryl.

Welch caused a commotion, too, with his personal conduct. There were public scenes at GE parties and social occasions. In the mid-1970s, while Welch headed the Components and Materials Group, of which Plastics was then a division, Alison Pfeister met him for the first time. She was a consultant at Booz, Allen and had accompanied her husband, Ed Russell, at that time a GE strategic planner, to a party in Fairfield, Connecticut, to celebrate the promotions of two executives, Tom Thorsen and Mike Allen, who worked for Welch and had been named vice presidents. At one point in the evening, Welch came over to their table. He was loud and crude, Pfeister recalls. "He behaved as if he could do just what he wanted, almost as if the rules didn't count for him," she says. "He was very different from all the staid kind of GE guys."

Incidents such as these contributed to the controversy that surrounded Welch. Some colleagues considered him a wild man. Welch himself acknowledged, in a 1973 self-appraisal, that he needed "improvement in handling socio-political relationships."

Reg Jones, who had heard the unflattering stories that emanated from Pittsfield, was in the CEO's job less than two years when he set in motion the process of choosing his successor. The decision to begin the search so soon into his own term of office reflected Jones's meticulous nature. Jones was a temperate man who did not like to make decisions in a frenetic way. Speed had its place, but so did planning. Jones wanted time to study, to consider at length all the leading candidates, and to apply the new management science of strategic planning, which he had championed. What better place to execute it than in the search for his successor? The process Jones initiated was exacting in its thoroughness, dragging on for six years through many successive stages, and proved, in the end, highly divisive. It began in 1974, when Jones asked Theodore LeVino, a trusted aide who ran GE's Executive Management Staff, to prepare a list of possible successors. The nineteen candidates (culled from an initial pool of ninety-six) that LeVino submitted the following year, didn't include Welch, who was then just thirty-nine years old, still in Pittsfield, and running the Components and Materials Group. When Jones asked why he hadn't been included, the response was that Welch was too young, was too much of a maverick, and had too much of a tendency to operate outside bureaucratic norms. But Jones, who was then fighting none too successfully against those same bureaucratic norms, wanted Welch included, and as CEO he got his wish.

By early 1977, the LeVino list of twenty candidates had been whittled down to seven. Jones's initial favorite was Alva Way, who as chief financial officer occupied the same office Jones had had before becoming CEO, but Way had no operating experience and had refused Jones's pleas to get it, effectively disqualifying himself. Of the six remaining candidates, Welch was the definite dark horse and had little enthusiastic support at the very top of the corporation. The two men who were second in command, vice chairmen Walter Dance and Jack Parker, were outspoken opponents of Welch. They had favorites of their own: Dance supported Stan Gault, the executive Welch had sparred with years before; Parker favored John Burlingame, a GE career man who was thirteen years older than Welch.

Jones also had some reservations about the young man in Pittsfield. One former director who was on the board at the time recalls that "Reg Jones was a very straight man. . . . Jack, on the other hand, wouldn't fall into the deeply religious school. He's brash and enthusiastic, loves to play and have a good time." But in the end Jones overcame his reservations and became an enthusiastic Welch supporter, convinced that his strengths—energy, intensity, intellect, and an absolute determination to get the job done—far outweighed his weaknesses. However, the board, which included Parker and Dance, appeared to favor Burlingame, who was more of a known quantity than Welch, and hence represented less risk. In addition, the CEO stew included three other choice candidates: Tom Vanderslice, who like Gault was a long-standing rival of Welch's; Robert Frederick, Jones's corporate planning chief; and Edward Hood Jr., a nuclear engineer who was considered the least political of the group.

In 1977, Jones devised another plan for distinguishing among the various candidates, reorganizing the entire corporation into six so-called sectors, and five of the six candidates—Welch, Gault, Vanderslice, Burlingame, and Hood—were made "sector executives," each with responsibility for the multibillion-dollar portfolio of businesses in one "sector." Frederick, the sixth candidate, remained in a staff planning job. As a further test, Jones made each man responsible for a business he was unfamiliar with, and the sector Welch drew included a collection of GE's oldest, most hidebound businesses: Lighting, Major Appliances, Housewares, and Consumer Electronics. Determined to show Jones and the board that he could achieve high growth as he had at Plastics, Welch seized on several technology initiatives to get his businesses going. Major Appliances took up a washing machine code-named L-7, which was to wash clothes using harmonic vibrations; Lighting championed the "Halarc lamp," which was supposed to be a leap forward in lighting technology. Although both projects were eventually outright fiascoes, they wouldn't be deemed so until well after Welch was already CEO.

Oddly, the performance of the individual sectors to which each candidate had been assigned had little influence on the outcome. More critical were the "airplane interviews" Jones initiated in 1978. Seizing on a concept Jones's predecessor Fred Borch had used in picking him, Jones subjected each of the candidates to a set of interviews during which he posed a hypothetical question: "Suppose you and I are flying in the company plane, it crashes and we both die. Who should be chairman of the General Electric Company?" The purpose of the exercise was to enable Jones to get a sense of the candidates' strategic thinking and give him insight into who might work well with whom.

Jones interviewed each candidate twice. The first time Jones posed his hypothetical question, the candidates were caught off guard and blurted out revealing answers. Some tried to climb out of the wreckage, or, like Welch, forgot that they were supposed to be dead. When Jones asked Welch who was the best candidate, he responded: "Why, me, of course." Jones countered: "No, no, Jack, you and I are killed." Jones was impressed with Welch's thinking after the first round. Instead of evaluating the other candidates, Welch had focused on the attributes the future CEO of GE would need to succeed. The company was far too bureaucratic, he told Jones in carefully chosen words, and needed to become more entrepreneurial and less stodgy, themes that resonated with Jones. The second airplane interview, conducted three months later, solidified Jones's thinking that Welch was the right man for the job. This time, the candidates were forewarned and had time to prepare their responses. Jones came away convinced that Welch was the only leader tough enough to bring about the changes he believed were necessary—a leveling of the GE bureaucracy.

The interviews also revealed the matrix of relationships among the CEO candidates. By the second round it was clear to the participants that Jones was trying to define feasible teams, and Welch, Hood, and Burlingame had included each other on their lists. The selection process, which by then was in its fifth year, had become highly politicized and divisive; three or four of the contenders had told Jones in no uncertain terms that they would depart if they weren't selected. The process became even more heated in August 1979, when Jones, for the first time, revealed to selected board members that he favored Welch. Dance and Parker, who were to retire at the end of the year, weren't advocates of Welch and expressed strong opposition to Jones's decision. A lengthy dialogue ensued.

The compromise Jones offered was this: He would nominate Welch, Burlingame, and Hood—the three consensus candidates who had indicated a willingness to work together—as vice chairmen and directors, giving the board another year to evaluate the relative strengths and weaknesses of each. Jones had handled the process shrewdly. Although nothing unique happened in that year, it gave Jones additional time to sell Welch to the board. Dance and Parker, his two main opponents, had left; so would the four candidates who had lost out—Way, Gault, Frederick, and Vanderslice. The selection process had been a bruising contest, as Darwinian as the events that would follow.

CHAPTER THREE

TOTAL WAR

ONE DAY IN THE FALL OF 1981, Jack Welch, having assumed the reins of General Electric in April, came across a letter in *Fortune* that commented on a series the publication had run on strategic planning and on the parallels between contemporary business strategy and nineteenth-century military strategy. Karl von Clausewitz and Helmuth von Moltke, two Prussian military men who advanced the concept of "total war," had demonstrated that effective strategy, be it in the business or military realm, "was not a lengthy action plan. It was the evolution of a central idea through continually changing circumstances," an executive in Ohio had written. "Men could not reduce strategy to a formula. Detailed planning necessarily failed."

The letter struck a resonant chord with Welch, who at that time was struggling to formulate and articulate a strategy that would guide his endeavors at General Electric, and he incorporated the letter and the theories of Clausewitz and Moltke into a speech he gave to Wall Street securities analysts on December 8, 1981, at the Pierre Hotel in New York City. Though it was not fully appreciated at the time, the speech would have enormous consequences for General Electric, and for the business world at large. It was Welch's declaration of "total war." While Welch had been CEO just eight months, and the ideas he would embrace hadn't been publicly revealed, his early rhetoric was already accelerating heartbeats within GE. It was clear, from day one, that Welch meant business, for the message he had delivered internally was an ominous one: GE was a damned troubled company.

Convincing people that conditions were indeed as grave as Welch said was the first obstacle he confronted. After all, the company had sailed through several recessions, recording twenty-six straight quarters of improved earnings. At esteemed bastions of corporate capitalism like the Harvard Business School, General Electric was widely acclaimed as America's best-managed company. But to naysayers who challenged his assessment, Welch would irately declare there was a war on, and GE was losing. The enemy wasn't just Westinghouse, Siemens, or Hitachi; the enemy was GE *itself,* and Welch left little doubt that the enemy would be defeated. The speech laid out how. Welch had already identified the most pressing problem GE faced: the lowly value of its shares. While Jones was much praised at business school forums, Wall Street had found his company decidedly unelectric. GE shares, which had traded at a lofty premium of twenty-two times per share earnings a decade earlier, now sold at a lackluster multiple of eight. An investor who in 1971 had bought $1,000 worth of GE stock would have seen the value of his investment cut in half in constant dollars, and even including GE's generous dividends, the shareholder wouldn't have beaten inflation.

Welch, who shared Wall Street's disdain, was particularly critical of the extensive strategic planning apparatus Jones had put in place. Planning under Jones had evolved into a bureaucratic system in which the central planners spent more time talking to themselves than they did to managers out in the field who were running the businesses. As head of Plastics and later a sector executive, Welch had come to despise the formality of Jones's planning, and the rigidity and corporate paralysis that he felt it inspired. Welch wanted to run the show, to do what he wanted to, without the advice and consent of others. "Take a look around you," he told a roomful of alarmed corporate planners the first time he addressed them in 1981, "because you won't be seeing each other anymore." All but about a dozen of the two hundred positions in corporate planning were eliminated.

Welch preferred a more straightforward approach to planning, akin to the military theories Clausewitz and Moltke had advocated. A business "plan" had to be more strategic in nature—this was war, after all—and had to advance general principles and goals that were appropriate to the battlefield conditions a manager faced. Welch dropped the inviolate rule of the Jones era that every business had to have a strategy approved each year. If conditions in a business were static, said Welch, then the strategy would only be reviewed every two or three years. But if conditions were dynamic, the strategy might be under constant review, and changed at a moment's notice.

His disdain for planning notwithstanding, Welch knew he needed some sort of central concept, which he presented to analysts that fateful day in December 1981, his first public explanation of what he hoped to accomplish. "If I could, this would be the appropriate moment for me to withdraw from my pocket a sealed envelope containing the grand strategy for the General Electric Company over the next decade," he said. "But I can't, and I am not going to attempt, for the sake of intellectual neatness, to tie a bow around the many diverse initiatives of General Electric." Instead of a central strategy, Welch offered a central idea, "a simple core concept that will guide General Electric in the eighties and govern our diverse plans and strategies. In trying to find a way to express these ideas and to share them with you, I found a powerful letter written by a Bendix planning manager to the editor of *Fortune* magazine. I want to share it with you because it captures, in words I find difficult to improve on, much of my own thinking about strategic planning for a company like General Electric."

After reading the letter, Welch explained his concept, which he called "Number One, Number Two." Although market dominance had been a top priority of General Electric ever since the days of Charles Coffin, Welch would give new urgency to an old theme. Each of GE's businesses, which numbered in the hundreds, had to achieve market leadership, defined as a Number One or Number Two ranking. The concept was a perfect extension of Welch's rough hewn, win-at-all-costs personality, forged in the hardscrabble schoolyards of Salem, Massachusetts. There was a basic insecurity inside Welch that drove him and had always driven him. He needed to win every game he played, and Welch brought that same warlike truculence to business.

"Where we are not Number One or Number Two," Welch continued, "we have got to ask ourselves that very tough Peter Drucker [the prominent management theorist] question: 'If you weren't already in the business, would you enter it today?' And if the answer is no, face that second difficult question: 'What are you going to do about it?' The managements and companies in the eighties that don't do this, that hang on to losers for whatever reason— tradition, sentiment, their own management weakness—won't be around in 1990." People inside GE immediately grasped the significance of what Welch had said. Sam Egbert, a senior public relations official, distributed copies of the speech to his staff with the foreboding note: "This contains things each of us needs to know, by heart."

The analysts, though, didn't get it. The speech was deemed a flop, and Welch was crushed. He had disclosed his grand strategy and had expected a standing ovation, but what he got instead was a series of rudimentary questions about the future course of earnings. Welch fumed. Hadn't they heard anything? Didn't they understand the significance of what he had said? Apparently not, for the analysts didn't care about philosophies or military strategy. They wanted fatter profits, and they wanted them immediately. Welch did too; that's why he had come to the Hotel Pierre that day, to show Wall Street how determined he was to get them, but his frustration over his failure to captivate an audience he knew would be crucial to his success as CEO spilled out in the open. Growing increasingly angry, he began yelling at the securities analysts. "What the hell difference will that make?" he shouted at one questioner who asked what impact the price of copper would have on next year's earnings. Welch left the Pierre Hotel that day even more determined to win the respect and admiration of Wall Street.

Some months after the speech, Welch took another step toward that goal, scribbling three interlocking circles on the back of an envelope, the three categories of businesses he intended to keep: Services, Technology and "Core," made up of GE's oldest manufacturing operations. "Anything outside the circles," he decreed, "we will fix, sell or close." Welch might as well have said "sell, close or sell," for that is what he ultimately did to all the businesses that weren't inside the circles. Other executives running those businesses outside the circles may have labored long and hard to fix them and save them from divestiture, but fixing took time, and Welch was an impatient man. When he was unhappy—with employees or with the performance of a business that was not Number One or Number Two, and even some that were—he cut the cord and moved on. One four-panel cartoon strip that made its way around Schenectady said it all: the first panel, under the caption "THE PROBLEM," showed a horse and buggy stuck in mud; in panel two, "THE ENGINEERING SOLUTION," there were two horses and one driver laboring to pull the buggy out; panel three, "THE MANAGEMENT SOLUTION," depicted one horse and two drivers; and in panel four, "THE WELCH SOLUTION," the horse and driver were gone, and the abandoned buggy was for sale.

The "Number One, Number Two" concept underscored how Welch's blitzkrieg-like attitude would come to dominate to an unhealthy degree decision making within General Electric. The company, which had effectively originated strategic planning, was effectively abandoning it in favor of a more indiscriminate approach that was a proxy of Welch's personality. Even businesses that were Number One but had been placed outside the circles were ultimately sold in a blizzard of more than one hundred divestitures. "Number One, Number Two" became shorthand for getting rid of that which didn't suit the chairman, and for those businesses outside the circles, Welch's designation was like being sent to a leper colony. When customers learned that a business was no longer on Welch's favored list, they began shunning it for obvious reasons; who wanted to order products from a business that wasn't thought of as a viable, long-term supplier?

The Pierre Hotel speech had set the tone for the harsh actions that were to follow. The earnings goals that Welch had set meant that costs had to be cut, and the most identifiable cost was the one that walked on two legs, as Henry Ford had been fond of saying. Because employee compensation was the second-largest cost item on every manager's budget, cutting costs meant one thing—layoffs, big ones. By the end of 1982, only a year after the speech, the 404,000 employees that Welch had taken command of had been chopped by thirty-five thousand, and just one year later another thirty-seven thousand were gone. By today's standards, that may not sound too harsh—AT&T announced plans to eliminate forty thousand jobs in one fell swoop on the first workday of 1996—but seen in the context of the early eighties, Welch's actions were indeed extraordinary. At that time, "downsizing" was still in its infancy; the word's first usage, as something done to people rather than to cars, had only been coined in January 1982, in a story in *Fortune*. And the companies that did it then were for the most part steel, rubber, and auto makers sustaining heavy losses in the midst of the worst recession since the Great Depression. What made Welch's reductions notable was that his actions had been taken not to curtail losses but to enhance profitability, and in that regard they presaged a change in philosophy that would become the prevailing attitude in the 1990s. Welch had savaged the GE workforce, exhibiting a brutality that communicated a clear, unequivocal message to upper management: either get results or get out. Understandably, managers were preoccupied with their own survival, for the choice they confronted in this environment was Darwinian—it was either their head or someone else's.

Most opted for the latter, and those senior executives who didn't share Welch's vision of how a business ought to be run were gone in a hurry. Some, like Ralph Ketchum, a universally respected and well-liked executive who ran GE Lighting, were sacked so abruptly that their dismissals gave rise to Welch's nickname of "Neutron Jack," after the bomb which killed people but left buildings standing. A surge of black humor swept through the company. Ketchum's dismissal was cast as a Mafia hit, and, according to a story that circulated through offices, Lawrence Bossidy, then Welch's top deputy and now chief executive of conglomerate Allied Signal, had told his driver parked outside GE's Nela Park lighting complex in Cleveland to "keep the motor running."

Even executives who thought their friendship with Welch would buy them protection, such as Chief Financial Officer Tom Thorsen, discovered that they were sorely mistaken. Welch wanted allegiance, and if he didn't get it, he would find someone else to give it to him. Dismissed in 1984, Thorsen, whose bond with Welch was thought to be brotherlike from their days together at GE Plastics, left the company after the two clashed over the degree of autonomy the finance function would have. In a May 16, 1984, memorandum to Thorsen's successor, Dennis Dammerman, Welch gave his reflections "about Finance—where it is and where I think it has to go." "There is no place that quantum change is needed more than in Finance," Welch wrote. "Finance is not an institution—it has to be . . . the driving force behind making General Electric 'the most competitive enterprise on earth.' "

That Welch would not be the status quo CEO that most of his predecessors had been was clear, for the change he had in mind was a much more encompassing makeover of a corporation than a corporate leader had ever before attempted. His was a revolution, a kind of business evangelism. Welch insisted that his subordinates conform to his way of thinking. If they didn't, they would have to leave.

The people placed in positions of authority were devoted disciples of Jack Welch: results-oriented, no-nonsense executives who shared his philosophy of how business ought to be conducted. Welch took three additional steps to solidify his control: He did away with the sector structure, established by Jones in 1977, which acted as a buffer between him and the heads of GE's operating divisions; following the lead of onetime Chicago Mayor Richard Daley, who personally approved every promotion in the Chicago police department above the rank of sergeant, Welch would cast the decisive ballot on every promotion to the level of manager and above; and he consolidated the number of operating divisions that had profit-and-loss responsibility, from about 150 business units in 1981 to less than fifty.

Like Henry Ford's Ford Motor or Tom Watson's IBM, Jack Welch's GE would become an extension of his personality, a kind of cult where even people who weren't told what to do would infer what they thought their leader wanted and act accordingly. Discipleship was a definite aim of the Welch revolution. In this regard, GE's Management Development Institute at Crotonville, New York, a remote site overlooking the Hudson River near Sing Sing prison, became a podium for promoting discipleship, mimicking what Ralph Cordiner had done in the 1950s. First Welch had to persuade the town fathers of Crotonville to change a city ordinance that had prohibited him from landing his helicopter on the site. Welch would fly to a site nearby and limo in, which he considered a waste of time. The town fathers refused to grant the landing rights he demanded until Welch gave them an ultimatum—either I get my heliport, or we take the institute elsewhere. They capitulated.

Soon Welch was choppering in with great regularly, for "visioning" exercises and other interaction with subordinates. Although Crotonville is renowned as one of the finest corporate centers of its kind, Welch's heavy hand has prompted much cynicism over what some GE employees regard as little more than brainwashing. Some call it "Scrotumville," for all the males who have been emasculated in places like "the Pit," the 110-seat amphitheater where Welch does his most forceful preaching. A bit of cynicism does indeed seem justified because Welch had very definite ideas about how he wanted his senior managers to behave and think and act. Welch wanted more than mere allegiance to his orders. He wanted the GE executive corps to execute them with enthusiasm and gusto, to carry them out as if they were their own, to "own" them, in Welch parlance.

Getting people to adopt his values meant getting rid of the values he disapproved of, one of which was loyalty. From the vantage point of today's ever-turbulent workplace where jobs vanish by the thousands, loyalty seems terribly old-fashioned. The concept itself became so passé, after a decade's worth of massive downsizing, that the unthinkable has happened: Some CEOs and business consultants now concede that loyalty wasn't such a bad idea after all. U.S. companies now lose half their employees every four years, half their customers in five, and half their investors in less than twelve months. In *The Loyalty Effect*, business consultant Frederick F. Riechheld argues that by failing to promote loyalty, American businessmen opened a Pandora's box for themselves in that they increasingly face harsh demands from "short-term investors" who immediately want higher profits. And by appeasing these investors, businessmen take actions—reducing product quality, raising prices too rapidly, laying off key personnel—that undercut future growth. "It is management's over-attentiveness to the demands of these short-term investors that is stalling growth at many companies," he asserts. "This hurts not only customers and employees, but is equally detrimental to long-term investors."

In the early eighties, however, Welch felt loyalty was strangling GE. Like IBM, GM, U.S. Steel, and other corporate titans of this century, General Electric had been a place of cradle-to-grave employment. Corporate loyalty was not just some fuzzy concept; to the people who worked for GE, it had real meaning. On the hundredth anniversary of the founding of the Edison Electric Light Company in 1978, when Reg Jones spoke of the "spirit of General Electric," loyalty—along with moral integrity, and innovation—were the defining elements he cited. General Electric was a society unto itself. "There are three great experiences available on earth," it was said at one 1972 meeting of the GE Alumni Club in New York City. "The Roman Catholic Church, the Mafia, and General Electric." Members of this society referred to themselves as "solid citizens," a phrase GE expatriates still use to describe the ties that bind them, and they had the monogram stamped squarely on their backsides, as was commonly said. People joined GE right out of college, worked forty-year careers, retired in General Electric communities, and even in retirement regularly attended events and meetings of the Elfun society and other GE social clubs.

With the arrival of Welch, mass layoffs were suddenly in vogue, and the concept of loyalty had to be repudiated. Loyalty smacked of sentimentality, · which was naive and inappropriate for the competitive realities of the eighties. Welch felt that loyalty bred complacency, and complacent workers were not productive; insecure workers were. Welch wanted everyone in General Electric to prove their worth every day, and if they thought they were facing a firing squad, they might be more inclined to work harder and faster.

In 1982, Welch had initiated a series of breakfast meetings with employees, forums he used to communicate his vision of the values he wanted the new GE to embrace, as the layoffs, divestitures, and executive firings cut through GE like a scythe. At one session, where about twenty headquarters employees were seated around a conference table amid urns of coffee and plates of Danish, Welch began by saying that he wouldn't tolerate autocratic, tyrannical managers. "People who treat people poorly will find themselves leaving the General Electric Company," one person who attended the session recalls Welch saying. The reaction around the room was universal. Welch's legendary reputation for cruel and callous behavior had preceded him. "Everyone sat there with their mouths wide open. They couldn't believe what he had said, because he was the leading intimidator," the executive recalls.

What Welch said next disturbed him even more. Loyalty to a company was, he declared, a nonsensical concept that had no place at General Electric anymore. Returning to his office, the executive, reflecting further upon what Welch had said, decided to write him a note of rebuttal. Some days after the chairman received the note, he summoned the executive, which led to a spirited discussion between the two over the value of loyalty, an encounter that illustrated why Welch felt compelled to denounce loyalty. The new CEO complained that he was getting stacks of mail from the wives of men who had been laid off, and they always started out the same way: "After so and so many years of loyal, devoted service, how could you treat my husband this way?" Welch hated the mail and hated the thought that people regarded him as unfeeling and inhuman. The public perception of him as some sort of mass murderer ate away at him. Underneath the tough exterior was a conflicted man, who thought the "Neutron Jack" moniker grossly unfair, given the courageous restructuring he was undertaking, and who resented the attention being focused on the casualties, as he resented anything that put him in an unfavorable light. Several years later, the executive again sparred with Welch—this time over an advertisement IBM had run trumpeting its policy of retraining employees rather than dismissing them—but to Welch's credit, the executive was not punished, though he did elect to take early retirement when the company later offered it. "I wasn't his favorite person; I knew that," the executive says.

Welch had distanced himself, intellectually, from the human consequences of his policies, from what they were doing to people; but the letters reminded him that there was pain and suffering, and it was substantial. "That's why the word 'loyal' became a bad word to him," the executive explains. "His feeling was you have a contract for that day. We pay you to perform, and the moment we don't think you're performing to our satisfaction, we have the right to fire you. We don't owe you a thing."

Nor was Welch content with merely assailing loyalty as a concept—the very word had to be expunged from GE's lexicon. What ensued was something akin to the Cultural Revolution under Mao; people at corporate headquarters in Fairfield, Connecticut, referred to it as the "campaign against loyalty." The headquarters staff was instructed not to use the word "loyalty," and to excise it from press releases and the like, which for years had commended an executive upon retirement for his years of "loyal, dedicated service." Frank Doyle, a GE spinmeister who eventually became executive vice president, was a spokesman for the campaign. He would meet with employees to explain why loyalty was no longer an important corporate value. During one particularly contentious meeting with a group of attorneys, "Frank made it quite clear that the word 'loyalty' was not what Jack wanted to hear," one attorney in attendance recalls. "We really tore into him. He felt it was necessary to beat loyalty over the head as an obsolete concept. It struck us as such a strange idea to advocate."

Like "Number One, Number Two," the values Welch advocated were an extension of his personality. Loyalty, tradition, convention—values Welch had little regard for—were deemed outmoded concepts; in their place was a rugged, bare-knuckle approach to business that had as its mantra "speed, simplicity, self-confidence," the hallmarks of Welch's personality. The Pierre Hotel speech had given a preview of Welch's values, including one he outlined that day, what he called "reality"-based thinking: "We have to permeate every corner, every mind in the businesses of this company with an attitude, with an atmosphere that allows people, in fact, encourages people to see things as they are, to deal with the way it is."

To some people, however, the values policy had a hollow ring because they had seen how Welch had behaved over the years: the unkind remarks, the cruel behavior, the stories that circulated about his conduct, the way he seemed to go out of his way to ridicule others and put them down. Richard Sim, a former executive at Med Systems, a GE division, recalls that Welch had some very strong likes and dislikes—and one of his strongest dislikes was obesity. "Jack had this idea that fat people were undisciplined slobs," Sim says. Nor was Welch shy about expressing his feelings. One obese executive who worked under Welch in the early 1970s underwent an operation at a Florida clinic in a futile attempt to control his weight, which had climbed to more than three hundred pounds. The clinic had been recommended to him by others who had undergone the procedure, which involved a surgical stapling of the lower bowel. The executive says he had the procedure reversed after several years because the diarrhea it induced was life-threatening. "It was a foolish thing to have done," he says. "Nobody in GE told me to do it, but it was clear by what people said that executives shouldn't look like I did."

Med Systems had one particular manager, recalls Sim, a valued employee who was obese. Because Welch had uttered disparaging comments about fat people, it was feared that if he saw the fat manager he would fire him. So whenever Welch came to Milwaukee to visit Med Systems, the employee would be hidden. "It was idiotic, but it was done," Sim says. "I used to wonder, What happens if he doesn't like bald people, or people who wear yellow ties with blue dots."

Sim ran the ultrasound business and was considered a rising star at Med Systems. He was so good at what he did that when he announced his intention to leave, Welch requested a meeting to talk him out of it. Every one of GE's then thirteen operating divisions, each of which would have ranked among the nation's biggest businesses, was larger than Applied Power, a smallish, privately held maker of hydraulics equipment based in Milwaukee that had offered Sim a job as chief operating officer. "Jack kept saying, 'If you want to play the big game, stay here.' It was pure Jack. He wants to be perceived as the biggest gorilla in the jungle." Rather than changing Sim's mind, the meeting only reinforced his determination to leave. He had become progressively disenchanted with Welch, and distressed at how his personality had come to dominate Medical Systems. "I didn't respect him as a human being," Sim recalls. "Jack is a guy who uses and abuses people. That troubled me. I didn't want to be one of Jack's boys."

As with many bright and overbearing business executives, Welch's greatest strengths—his leadership and decisiveness—were also his most glaring weakness. Bud Rukeyser, who had been NBC's chief of communications for more than twenty years when GE bought the television network in 1986 as part of its acquisition of RCA, experienced firsthand the destructive impact Welch could have. As communications chief, Rukeyser, an institution at NBC, was charged with an important task—maintaining NBC's relations with the media that covered it. Reporters trusted Rukeyser; he had great credibility, something General Electric, a newcomer to broadcasting, desperately needed. Robert Wright, a Welch buddy from their days together in Plastics, who despite scant knowledge of broadcasting was made network president, also realized that Rukeyser was a valuable asset and wanted him to stay. Rukeyser resigned in the spring of 1988, having decided he could no longer brook Welch's policies.

A genial man who bears an extremely close resemblance to brother Louis, host of the PBS investment show *Wall Street Week*, Rukeyser genuinely likes Welch as a person. "He's a classic man's man," Rukeyser says. "He's funny, charismatic, recalls names, puts his arm around you, the kind of guy other guys like to hang around." Put Welch in a bar, Rukeyser explains, and other men will gravitate to him. As a businessman, however, Welch has a dark side that soon became apparent at NBC. To Rukeyser, a broadcasting network was a public trust, with special obligations to the public and special characteristics. It was, after all, show business and hence tended to be very relationship-oriented; big stars had big egos, which had to be stroked the right way (a lesson Welch and Wright both belatedly learned when David Letterman bolted to CBS). Television was also an enormously powerful medium, and with that special access, Rukeyser believed, came special responsibilities. Welch and Wright were astonished to learn that NBC had a department of more than fifty people called broadcast standards, which monitored network telecasts. When Rukeyser tried to explain the rationale for keeping the standards staff— the department was an ombudsman of sorts, monitoring not only the content of NBC programs but the advertising it aired, and hence performed an important function in maintaining the public's trust—he was greeted with blank stares.

To Welch, broadcasting was a business, no different than any other, and he regarded claims of uniqueness, advanced not just by Rukeyser but by many others, as nonsense. And, as in any business, lowering costs and firing people would make it more profitable. "What they did was systematically clean the place out of anyone who knew anything about broadcasting," Rukeyser recalls. His job ceased to be fun, a not uncommon occurrence within NBC under General Electric. In a survey conducted in February and March of 1988 among

NBC's seven thousand employees, three-quarters of the fifty-four hundred respondents said the network was a "worse" place to work since GE had taken over, while only 2 percent said it was "better."

Rukeyser had seen the handwriting on the wall two years before he resigned. In his very first meeting with Welch in August 1986, Rukeyser, having spent his entire adult life at NBC, more than thirty years, tried to educate Welch, who had all of two months' experience in broadcasting. "I went through my brilliant litany of why broadcasting was special," he recalls, tongue in cheek. After a few minutes, Welch stopped Rukeyser and said, "I don't believe a word of it. What you've just described is exactly the same as the securities business." Welch, who trusted his instincts far more than the protestations of underlings, had already fit NBC into a neat little box he was familiar with, and would make his decisions accordingly. Yet he would have benefited from Rukeyser's counsel: Running NBC was clearly a more complicated task than Welch had assumed. The top-ranked network when GE bought it, NBC fell to third place under GE ownership, in violation of the "Number One, Number Two" dictum.

By 1991, with NBC's ratings collapsing and its losses mounting, Welch employed a favorite formula from the past, that of cutting costs. Arthur Kent, who had gained notoriety covering the Gulf War for NBC News, recalled in a speech to the Commonwealth Club of California the reception he received upon his return to New York: "We walked into NBC's headquarters and we heard, 'Fifty-five million bucks. That's how much you guys cost us out there, running around with your satellite dishes, charging around the desert with the First Cavalry Division, interrupting football, interrupting soap operas, sitcoms, drama, all over the schedule.' And we said, 'Wait a second, before the war, General Electric told us they were going to foot the bill.' . . . No, GE wanted us to make up that slack. . . . NBC News lost 40 percent of its international news-gathering capability within three months of the end of the Gulf War. Bureaus were closed, staff were fired, and in the beginning of 1992, when our bureau, the Rome bureau, was encouraged to join *Dateline NBC* with the pledge that if we did not join this new prime-time newsmagazine show our bureau would be closed, we discovered what the future of NBC television was going to be. Within five weeks of starting, our international news stories were taken off the agenda. We pressed for an explanation why. We were told the entertainment division in Burbank did not believe that international news had a place in prime-time viewing."

Welch was convinced that television had been a bad investment, and a deal was almost completed in 1992 to sell the network to Paramount. Additional talks were subsequently held with Time-Warner, Disney, and Sony. But, illustrating the old adage that it is better to be lucky than to be good, the deals were either too complicated or the price too paltry. Welch rejected them and hung on to NBC, which is now back in first place. The turning point came in 1993, when Welch announced that NBC was not for sale. Although people on the outside still doubted him—everything at General Electric is for sale at the right price—the decision did represent a new beginning in one important regard: It focused Wright's attention on fixing the network rather than abandoning it. At that time, NBC's pipeline of new shows was empty, and its programming operation had fallen into disrepair. NBC's only hit show, *Cheers*, was ending production. Wright hired Don Ohlmeyer, a legendary figure in the sports television business, to run the West Coast programming operation, and within three seasons NBC was back on top on the strength of such hits as *Seinfeld*, *E.R.*, and *Frasier*. By 1998, even though NBC's profit and prime time ratings had begun to slip and comedian Jerry Seinfeld had "Seined off," the network was still highly profitable—profit that permitted Wright to spend freely on such ventures as MSNBC, a new cable-news rival to CNN, or in bidding to retain broadcast rights for the National Basketball Association, for talk-show host Geraldo Rivera, or for keeping *E.R.* (NBC paid a record $13 million per episode for three more seasons of the hospital drama). But now that NBC appears on the verge of another downward cycle, Wright is again seeking to sell at least part of the network, evincing the sparse tolerance shown within GE for lower profits, even for a business as prominent as NBC.

The turnaround at NBC illustrated the positive aspects of Welch's management style: his ability to inspire and win the enthusiasm of people; his willingness to take chances in support of their efforts; and his penchant, zeal even, for fast-paced, action-based decision-making. One coup that NBC scored in December 1995 was directly attributable to Welch: He put up $4 billion of GE's money for the broadcast and cable rights to the 2004 and 2008 Summer Olympics and the 2006 Winter Olympics, even though where those games would be held, and hence the times they would be televised, had not been decided. NBC Sports president Dick Ebersol had persuaded the International Olympic Committee to abandon its past practice of selling the rights through competitive bidding—and it took Welch "maybe a minute" to commit the money, Ebersol told the *New York Times*, even though the sum amounted to about two-thirds of what GE had paid for RCA.

Ebersol didn't mention it, but there was likely another reason Welch had snapped up the Olympics rights. Welch liked glitz, which subordinates speculated was the real reason he had hung on to NBC years before, even when it was the third-place network. He loved hobnobbing with the stars, hosting

Manhattan dinner parties attended by the likes of Tom Brokaw, Jane Pauley, and Bryant Gumbel, holding court before an entourage of well-wishers who fawned over him at the sporting events his company televised. NBC was Welch's entree into the world of glamor and celebrity, and he loved it. He loved wooing them as well, and he came to Wright's aid in successfully negotiating new contracts with Brokaw, Rivera, and Jerry Seinfeld, though not with Gumbel, a golf partner of Welch's who nonetheless bolted for bigger money at CBS.

The glitz of financial services also appealed to Welch, though for different reasons. It was fast-paced wheeling and dealing, completely unlike most of General Electric. Before becoming CEO, when he was the sector executive in charge of a group of businesses that included Financial Services, Consumer Electronics, and Lighting and Appliances, Welch had developed a clear preference for Financial Services. The Credit Corporation, as it was called in those days, was a stark contrast to Lighting, which was headquartered in Cleveland on a leafy campus of Georgian buildings and placid lawns that had changed little since the days of Edison. Financial Services, on the other hand, which was headquartered in Stamford, Connecticut, near the corporate headquarters in Fairfield, was like a weight lifter on steroids. It was muscle-bound, and it knew how to flex its pecs, doing big deals, doing them fast, and making tons of money. In 1995, for instance, GE spent more than $4 billion in a succession of lightning-fast transactions, snapping up two German companies involved in reinsurance, a French consumer-finance company, banks in Poland and Germany, a British commercial-financial group, as well as additional annuity and life insurance businesses in the United States.

Welch found routine manufacturing dull, unable to provide the "quantum leaps" that kept his interest, but the bulk of what General Electric did was routine manufacturing. Although Welch tolerated Lighting because it provided plenty of cash, Appliances and Consumer Electronics were a different matter, which he referred to collectively as the "cesspool." They were too erratic, too cyclical in nature, too competitive. Welch may have enjoyed the rough-and-tumble of competitive athletics, but he understood that competition was bad business. It tended to depress prices, which might be good for consumers but was not good for a CEO who wanted to dominate markets, earn fat profits, and get the stock rocketing skyward.

One of the businesses Welch disliked most was Appliances, and his sessions with appliance managers in Louisville, Kentucky, were intense affairs. James West, a former executive in Louisville, recalls witnessing one browbeating that he felt went beyond the bounds of decency. When it was through,

West recalls, the recipient left the room, called a cab, and, fearing he was having a mental breakdown, checked himself into Our Lady of Peace, a local hospital.

When word came that Welch would be visiting a GE Appliances factory, the news was greeted with a mix of anguish and terror, as if the National Weather Service had just reported that a tornado was on its way. His trip to Tyler, Texas, in 1978, where GE made central air-conditioning units, was preceded by a whirlwind of activity. The plant was spruced up, and management cautioned workers to be on their best behavior; repairs that had been put off got done; floors were scrubbed, while a fresh coat of paint was applied; the sunny skies and citizenry of Tyler greeted Welch on the appointed day. But the tour didn't go well, one executive who accompanied Welch recalls. At one point, a forklift almost backed over him as his entourage recoiled in horror. After about an hour in the plant, Welch, like a judge at a sentencing hearing, reached a verdict. "This is a product where you're at the mercy of an installer-dealer," he said. The executive says he knew at that moment the business would be jettisoned, even though General Electric was a leading manufacturer of central air-conditioners. Sure enough, it was one of the first businesses to go several years later, after the Hotel Pierre speech.

The speed with which some businesses left the GE "family" was stunning. Even executives charged with running the businesses often hadn't been consulted and didn't know that a sale was imminent. John Harnden, a Schenectady inventor and GE retiree, has bitter memories of how he learned the Housewares business had been sold.

Housewares was a General Electric institution. When the sale was announced, the *New York Times* said it was "as if GM had suddenly abandoned car making." The GE monogram—the familiar corporate insignia, the "meatball," as GE employees affectionately referred to it—had first appeared in 1899 on an electric fan. By 1983, General Electric was still the market leader in toasters, coffeemakers, clocks, irons, hair dryers, and many other home appliances. Profits had slipped, however, as competition intensified and the Japanese introduced more high-tech gadgets featuring microelectronics. Harnden was put to work on a special task force that was seeking to save housewares by rewiring small appliances with solid-state circuitry. A man on a mission, Harnden felt it was crucial that General Electric, with its proud heritage of manufacturing and product innovation, stay in consumer electronics and not capitulate to the Japanese. He also shared the belief, which had been GE doctrine since at least the 1920s, that the appliance business was more important than just its contribution to the bottom line. General Electric reaped an incalculable benefit through the omnipresence of its name in the American home; the GE name, which the American public had come to associate with durability and reliability, engendered goodwill that extended to other GE products.

As a result, Harnden attached special significance to the work he began in 1983. Maybe, just maybe, the business could be saved. In November, as he was in the midst of a presentation to Housewares management, explaining how GE could fight back against the Japanese by rolling out a new line of solid-state irons, bathroom scales, and thermometers, a phone call interrupted the meeting. "We might as well adjourn," someone said. "The business has been sold to Black & Decker." Unaware that Welch had been negotiating a sale, the room fell silent. Harnden, whose anger lingers to this day, wept.

A storm of protest erupted throughout General Electric—many employees felt Welch had betrayed company tradition—fueled by Welch's failure to cushion the blow. That lack of compassion and sensitivity to people's feelings has become the hallmark of General Electric during the Welch era. Employees often feel like deer caught in the headlights of an oncoming car, ambushed by unforeseen events. While Welch talks often of "controlling one's destiny"— one of his favorite catchphrases—they feel helpless to control their own.

CHAPTER FOUR

THE BIG SWING

THE RUTHLESS DOWNSIZING of an American institution that employees felt was in no need of ruthless downsizing inspired tremendous antipathy toward Jack Welch, who in the summer of 1984 was designated America's toughest boss in a poll by *Fortune* magazine. He received more than twice as many votes as the second-place finisher. The magazine wrote: "According to former employees, Welch conducts meetings so aggressively that people tremble. He attacks almost physically with his intellect—criticizing, demeaning, ridiculing, humiliating." *Fortune* offered this trenchant observation from one anonymous foot soldier: "Working for him is like a war. A lot of people get shot up; the survivors go on to the next battle."

That was one view, but there was another. By the fall of 1983, while Welch was solidifying his reputation as the toughest boss in America, he was also winning praise as one of the most decisive leaders in American business—a man whose passion and sheer enthusiasm for life could be infectious, at times inspirational. The power and intensity of Welch's personality was indeed overwhelming. No matter what he did—whether it was making friendly inquiries, comparing golf scores, or closing a billion-dollar deal—Welch did it in a manner that conveyed urgency. Yet his personality embodied two very distinct characters: one was coldhearted and calculating, the epitome of the flinty-eyed CEO who viewed people as chess pieces on his board; the other funny, cheerful, charming, someone whose spirited, personable disposition could win people over.

To the people who came to like and admire him, Welch was the Babe Ruth of CEOs, the business Bambino, nothing less than the most awesome and challenging leader ever to suit up in pinstripes. They marveled at his swagger, his cocksureness, his lightning-quick, stilettolike mind, his winning ways, and his absolute refusal to accept defeat. Welch's ability to inspire was rare indeed in the often uninspiring, sometimes downright dull business world, where most CEOs were a bland, timid, colorless lot. Welch, in contrast, was a dynamo—a person of courage and determination who through sheer force of will could control events and towered over his peers. Even a few former subordinates whom Welch had fired still yearned, years later, to get back into his good graces; he was a kind of father figure who, invariably, had given them their first big break. The loyalists' devotion to Welch bordered on idolatry—for them, it was impossible to see their leader in anything other than positive terms, even when confronted with evidence to the contrary. One such loyalist was Kevin Sharer, who in December 1983 met Welch for the first time.

Sharer was a thirty-three-year-old consultant at that time whose employer, McKinsey & Company, was one of the two most prestigious consulting firms in America. (The other was Boston Consulting Group.) A graduate of the United States Naval Academy, Sharer had done work for GE, impressing Mike Carpenter, whom Welch had hired away from Boston Consulting that same year to head up his scaled-down office of strategic planning. Welch had made five runs at Carpenter to induce him to leave a successful career as a BCG vice president and join General Electric, finally persuading him on the fifth try.

Carpenter, who reported directly to Welch and whose title was vice president of corporate planning, performed a role that wasn't planning in the way Reg Jones would have understood the term. The staff Carpenter began assembling late in 1983 was the business equivalent of Navy Seals and their mission was to grow General Electric via acquisition. It would be strategic planning in the form and function that suited Welch—a nimble cadre who would ferret out every possible acquisition, seize every opportunity to grow, making GE bigger and more powerful, and earning Welch the acclaim of investors, business school professors, and other CEOs. Welch wanted a staff that was quick on its feet as well as street-smart, men who could take the pounding that he dished out, even enjoy the combat their commander relished. Welch and Carpenter wanted business commandos, and Sharer, a young man who was ready to go to war, wanted to be part of their team.

Just minutes after meeting Welch for the first time, Sharer knew this was the kind of man he longed to work for. Sharer had had an eventful morning, driving a rental car from New York City that had conked out on the Merritt Parkway in Connecticut on his way to an early-morning appointment with Welch in Fairfield. Sharer stumbled into a diner with what must have been a wild-eyed and panicky look; one patron, a good Samaritan who took pity on Sharer and his plight, offered to drive him the rest of the way to GE headquarters, where he arrived with twenty minutes to spare. When Welch strolled into the office, fresh from his morning workout (as was his ritual then) and gym bag in hand, he gave Sharer a firm handshake and began questioning him in his signature style, a pugnacious cross-examination akin to how F. Lee Bailey might question a witness.

"I know a lot of guys from military school. They're not very bright. What about you?" Welch asked, with a twinkle in his blue eyes that a person who wasn't intimidated could warm to.

Sharer immediately thought he was back in the Navy, and his mind flashed to similar encounters he'd had with Admiral Hyman Rickover, which had prepared him well for this moment. After his graduation from Annapolis, Sharer had chosen duty as a nuclear submarine officer and was Lieutenant Commander of the USS *Memphis*, a Class 688 nuclear attack sub, when it was commissioned in 1977. Rickover had a policy of accompanying the crew on the inaugural cruise of every new nuclear sub, and the *Memphis*, which embarked from Newport News shipyard in Virginia, was no exception. Rickover's style was direct, up-front, and in-your-face. He would challenge you on points just to see how you would defend yourself, and if he sensed weakness or the slightest hint that you were trying to bullshit your way through, he would blow you out of the water.

Welch's style was similar. You had to be ready to tussle and joust—quickly and clearly articulate the facts, and defend yourself at a high rate of exchange. "Jack can be intimidating to people who lack confidence, but for me it was the most fun I ever had," Sharer recalls. Though Welch was a tough questioner— as tough as Rickover had been—Sharer evidently held up well. A month later, in January 1984, he joined Carpenter's staff, accepting a $110,000-a-year position along with Vincenzo Morelli and Gregory Vereschagin, the two other senior members of Carpenter's planning staff.

At the time, the business world was in great turmoil. The court-ordered mitosis of American Telephone & Telegraph, the severing of Ma Bell from its "babies," had just taken effect. On the West Coast, a small company few people knew of, Apple, introduced its Macintosh personal computer, which would challenge IBM's growing control over the market for personal computers. More important to General Electric, however, were two pace-setting trends that had their origins in the steel and oil industries, and would dominate headlines for years to come. The first—downsizing, as it came to be called— was represented in United States Steel's announcement, made public two days after Christmas 1983, to cut in one whack 20 percent of its primary steel-making capacity, the largest one-day reduction in the long and often troubled history of the company. More than fifteen thousand people lost their jobs that day as the nation's largest steelmaker, and first billion-dollar corporation, slashed its payroll. Before the decade was out, U.S. Steel's mill employment, 106,500 in 1979, fell to around twenty thousand, and its annual steelmaking capacity, thirty-six million tons in 1979, was lowered to twelve million in a rapid-fire succession of cutbacks that cut a wide swath through the Rust Belt.

The second trend—the mega-merger—was witnessed just two weeks later when Texaco, the nation's third-largest oil company, bought Getty Oil Corporation for the then stunning sum of $10 billion (the folly of this acquisition wasn't apparent until several years later, when a Texas jury ordered Texaco to pay Pennzoil a like amount for preempting a prior agreement with Getty, which was later reduced to $3 billion in a negotiated settlement). At the same time, a renegade Texas oil man, T. Boone Pickens, was making a name for himself as the gunslinger who shot down another complacent industry. What cheap steel imports and overcapacity did to Big Steel—shake an industry out of its lethargic cocoon—Pickens did to Big Oil. He had cast his eye on Pittsburgh's unsuspecting Gulf Oil Corporation, which was ripe for the picking. As one of the industry's fabled "Seven Sisters," Gulf had hubris and a rich legacy, born from the fabled Spindletop gusher in Texas at the turn of the century, a well that had been drilled with Mellon money. Gulf CEO Jimmy Lee considered the company invincible, and T. Boone a crackpot who did not deserve serious consideration. Lee was wrong: by March, Gulf had been pushed into the open arms of Standard Oil of California (Socal), which offered $80 a share for Gulf, or $13.5 billion. It was at the time the biggest merger in U.S. history, but even the Gulf-Socal deal was surpassed in the dealmaking frenzy that would soon engulf corporate America—and General Electric as well.

Welch's priorities in his first three years had been divesting businesses rather than acquiring them. The more than one hundred operations he had sold off between 1981 and 1983 had left GE with more than $3.5 billion in cash, including $2.4 billion from the sale of one single asset—Utah International, an Australian coal property that Reg Jones had acquired.

Welch had also made some sizable investments in the future, which seemed to suggest that the hallowed traditions of Edisonian invention would be well protected in the new era, and that General Electric was renewing its commitment to its historic mission of manufacturing, engineering, and research excellence. By the spring of 1984, however, Welch had grown impatient with the incremental improvements that a flood of spending had brought, and he initiated a new program called "Taking a Swing." The General Electric Company would begin swinging for the fences, as he explained in *General Electric Monogram*, the company's in-house magazine:

Aaron. Ruth. Mays. Robinson. Killebrew. Mantle. The top six home run hitters in baseball history. Hall of Famers all.

But fame comes in many guises. For these baseball immortals, it comes not only in slugging records but also from being among the leaders in career strikeouts.

One reason, of course, is that the fiercer the swing a batter takes, the higher the risk of walking back to the dugout with his head down rather than circling the bases, doffing his cap, and collecting applause. The cautious hitters, the bunters, may not strike out as often, but their names and faces don't show up on bronze plaques with the same frequency as those who take the big swing.

If GE is to continue to put distance between itself and the bunters of the business world, it *must* take the big swing with increasing frequency. That may mean some strikeouts along the way. But the prospects of hitting a home run make the risks worthwhile.

The task of hitting home runs fell to Mike Carpenter and his handpicked team of all-star strategists, Morelli, Sharer, and Vereschagin, whose mission was clear: find acquisition candidates that would put runs on the earnings scoreboard. Welch wasn't particularly concerned with what GE bought as long as it was a home run, and he was willing to consider just about any industry except pharmaceuticals, for which he showed a clear distaste. Large liabilities scared Welch, and, although he didn't mind being in the medical diagnostic business, the prospect of making drugs that people ingested raised the specter in his mind of staggering liabilities if anything went wrong. Welch also wasn't enthusiastic about any industries in which the Japanese were significant players; he regarded them as virtually invincible in high repetition, precision manufacturing. Welch was basically a duopolist at heart, for obvious reasons—a company that was the industry leader in a two-rival field would make a lot more money than the leader in a twenty-rival race. With those criteria in mind, Carpenter's staff began sifting through data on more than six thousand acquisition candidates.

Carpenter and his team in short order recommended to Welch the purchase of Employers Reinsurance Corporation, which GE subsequently bought in the spring of 1984 for just over $1 billion. It was the first of many unglamorous but largely successful acquisitions in which General Electric would stray from its historic manufacturing mission into the arcane field of financial services. Over the next decade, Welch would acquire financial service concerns by the dozens—in computer leasing, aircraft leasing, container leasing, portable building leasing, truck leasing, credit cards—growing the nonmanufacturing side of General Electric so aggressively that by 1992 Capital Services would be America's largest finance company, having surpassed General Motors Acceptance Corporation; with more than $200 billion in assets, it was only slightly smaller than America's largest banks.

Although Welch was somewhat leery of Employers Re—its principal business was reinsurance, meaning that it insured liabilities on policies that someone else had already written—it was also managed risk, and he had every confidence that in financial services at least, General Electric was savvy at risk analysis. Carpenter's staff had analyzed data on about 250 of the nation's largest financial service companies and liked what they saw in Employers Re, but in the end it was the tumult of the times that made the deal possible. Employers Re had been owned by Getty Oil, and after Texaco acquired Getty, Texaco wanted out of insurance so it could concentrate on its historic businesses in oil and gas. Welch, on the other hand, was rewriting GE's history, and if financial services were the path to higher earnings, so be it.

Possible acquisitions were presented to the team from a variety of sources, including Welch himself, who is an avid reader of newspapers and business periodicals and was greatly influenced by what he read. He would get an idea out of *Business Week, Fortune,* or the *Wall Street Journal* and ask the staff to consider it. The executives who ran the individual businesses were a source as well, as possible deals came their way through a network of industry contacts and associations. Then there were the omnipresent investment bankers who hovered over Carpenter's staff; they knew Welch was on the prowl, that he had money, and that he was eager to spend.

Despite all these conduits, however, more than a year and a half passed before Welch and Carpenter took another big swing. During that time many acquisition possibilities were considered—a few very seriously, including Raychem and E Systems, two defense companies, as well as CBS, which Ted Turner had made a run at (and was purchased years later by Westinghouse)—but nothing came to fruition. Welch wanted action, but he was at the same time uncharacteristically timid; some deals collapsed because he was unwilling to pay what the sellers wanted, others because the chemistry didn't seem right. Moreover, the deal that most interested him, one Carpenter's staff had investigated and heartily endorsed, the acquisition of RCA, was beyond Welch's reach. General Electric was hamstrung by consent decrees left over from the days when antitrust law was more vigorously enforced, and one of the most infuriating, from Welch's perspective, proscribed GE's relationship with RCA.

To avoid antitrust prosecution in 1932, General Electric President Owen Young had signed a consent decree with the Justice Department in which the company agreed to divest its interest in RCA, and under which it was still prohibited (along with Westinghouse and AT&T, which also divested their stakes) from owning any portion of RCA.

With merger and acquisition activity exploding and companies being bought and sold in an unprecedented orgy of dealmaking, Welch watched passively from the sidelines as some of the biggest deals in the history of business were concocted. Meanwhile, GE's earnings growth had ground to a halt. He was frustrated, and growing increasingly jittery at his company's inactivity in the M&A game. His frustration was apparent in his response to a question posed to him in the fall of 1985 during a presentation at Harvard Business School. Asked his greatest regret in his four and half years at the helm of GE, Welch replied: "I don't think I've moved fast enough." He also believed that his managers were likewise much too timid. Of the senior managers who reported to him, only Robert Wright, who ran GE Capital Services and was advancing a plethora of acquisition ideas, seemed to have grasped the concept of "the big swing." The others clung to the traditional GE mold, the one Welch had great disdain for, which favored growing opportunities internally through careful investment in research and technology rather than gobbling up other entities.

Welch's impatience was clearly in step with the times. The year 1985 was a watershed in the history of corporate control, as the ownership of venerable companies changed hands with stunning frequency, facilitated in part by the discount financing of "junk bond" king Michael Milken, head of high-yield securities at Drexel Burnham Lambert. Wall Street that year witnessed a series of hostile takeovers that left investors reeling: Pickens's bid first for Philips Petroleum, then Unocal, Carl Icahn's acquisition of Trans World Airlines, Rupert Murdoch's purchase of Metromedia, Ronald Perelman's conquest of Revlon, Sir James Goldsmith's victory over Crown Zellerbach, and Kohlberg Kravis & Roberts's assaults on Storer, then Beatrice. Nor was this acquisition activity limited to just the predators; established companies also got into the act. In the month of June alone, R.J. Reynolds bought Nabisco; General Motors acquired Hughes Aircraft, and Baxter Travenol bid for American Hospital Supply. In July, Monsanto acquired G.D. Searle; and in September, Philip Morris acquired General Foods. In the midst of this chaos, Welch desperately wanted to be a participant. The pressure to do a deal, any deal, began to build, and Carpenter's staff was enthused and somewhat relieved when Welch, who in the fall had begun breakfasting regularly with New York investment banker

Felix Rohatyn, brought them news on November 7 that he had met the night before with RCA Chairman Thornton Bradshaw and Rohatyn over cocktails at a Park Avenue apartment in Manhattan.

The consent decree that for fifty-three years had prevented GE from owning RCA had been suddenly, and without apparent prodding from GE, dropped some months before by the Reagan Justice Department as part of what Carpenter's staff were told was a "business as usual" departmental review of obsolete rules. Although the confluence of the Justice Department decision and RCA's desire to auction itself off struck the planning staff as too coincidental to be believed—after all, Welch was a frequent guest at the Reagan White House, and GE's Washington operation was as slick as any corporate office operating inside the Beltway—still it was a gift that, no matter where it had come from, Carpenter and his men were quite willing to accept. Of the trio of strategic planners, Kevin Sharer was most enthusiastic about the acquisition, code-named project "Island," and he was selected to summarize the sixty-page report the staff had prepared on RCA.

It was a heady experience for Sharer, who at thirty-five years old was recommending that the General Electric Company undertake the biggest acquisition in its ninety-three-year history, as well as the biggest nonoil merger in the history of American business. Sharer gave a strong endorsement of the deal to GE's senior management, including Welch, Carpenter, finance chief Dennis Dammerman, and vice chairman Larry Bossidy. A week later Welch met with Bradshaw for a second time, and a week after that—on Thursday, December 12, 1985, at a press conference in midtown Manhattan—Welch proudly announced to the world that GE and RCA had come to terms under which his company would acquire Bradshaw's for $6.28 billion. Welch was positively giddy. "This is going to be one dynamite company," he boasted.

The RCA acquisition was a watershed in many ways. Rohatyn, the man who had played matchmaker, would later sour on the eighties. "We have just seen the end of the greatest decade of speculation and financial irresponsibility since the twenties," he said in a speech at Northwestern University in 1991. "The junk-bond peddlers and the raiders, the speculators and the savings-and-loan hustlers, have turned this country into a vast casino."

All four men who had helped Welch hit his home run subsequently received choice jobs running GE operations around the world. For Kevin Sharer, that meant a position as general manager of GE's Americom satellite services operation in Rockville, Maryland; Gregory Vereschagin became head of a Japanese subsidiary in Tokyo; boss Mike Carpenter became vice president at General Electric Capital Services in Stamford, Connecticut; Vincenzo Morelli ran the European operations of GE's Medical Systems division out of London. Later, Morelli would be just one of the victims of the winds of "creative destruction"—Schumpeter's metaphor for the process of decay and renewal in modern economies—that swept through the venerable Radio Corporation of America in the years following Welch's purchase of it.

JACK WELCH IS THE CHAMPION of his age, just as David Sarnoff was the champion of his, and each age has had its acceptable norms of how business ought to be done. In Welch's age the buying, selling, and restructuring of giant corporations has become so commonplace that the human dimension has been lost. In just five years, from 1981 to 1986, Welch eliminated 130,000 jobs from General Electric, generating savings of about $6.5 billion. Welch was on to something too compelling to ignore; the savings he generated from those dismissals *exceeded* the entire price he paid for RCA in June 1986. Those five years were hugely rewarding for GE's shareholders, and Welch finally won the universal acclaim of Wall Street. Now the market was panting over his latest conquest, which would be another opportunity for him to do the thing he did best: to "delayer" a business, the then popular term for hacking off the limbs.

Sarnoff's age had been different. In 1900, at the age of nine, he had emigrated to New York City with his family, leaving the Russian shtetl of Uzlian, where his father worked as a house painter. In 1906, at the age of fifteen and with his father's death imminent, he abandoned school and took a job at the New York City offices of the Marconi Company, the predecessor of RCA, where he was offered work not as a telegraph operator, his ultimate ambition, but as an office boy sweeping floors and running errands. When Sarnoff retired fifty-nine years later, in 1965, from the position of chief executive officer at RCA, he received a letter from Konosuki Matsushita, the founder and director of the huge Japanese electronics concern that bore his name. "You are," Matsushita wrote, "the bravest man of our generation."

By "bravest," Matsushita was referring to Sarnoff's willingness to take risks—and at times take on shareholders—to forgo immediate gain. Throughout his career, Sarnoff had a vision of the future, funneling vast sums into research and development, and passing up immediate gain for greater profits later on. In the 1920s, he delayed production of radios to perfect the superheterodyne model; in the 1930s, he diverted profits from radio into the development of black-and-white television; and in the late 1940s and early 1950s, he diverted black-and-white profits into color television sets, which RCA began making in 1954 at its factory in Bloomington, Indiana.

Sarnoff combined an intense interest in new technology with a flair for marketing. On April 20, 1939, ten days before the New York World's Fair opened, he strode to the podium of the RCA Pavilion—shaped to resemble a giant vacuum tube and located on the "Avenue of Patriots"—to declare, "Now we add radio sight to sound. It is with a feeling of humbleness that I come to this moment of announcing the birth of a new art so important in its implications that it is bound to affect all society . . . an art which shines like a torch in a troubled world . . . a creative force we must learn to utilize for the benefit of all mankind."

An RCA camera then broadcast the image of the Trylon and Perisphere to a few hundred sets. That same year, he established NBC, the first television broadcasting network, to create demand for his new invention; and two years after that he broke ground for a new research laboratory in Princeton to take the place of smaller laboratories at RCA plants in Camden, New Jersey. Sarnoff envisioned inventors and engineers working together in the campus setting, a major university nearby and close as well to his offices at 30 Rockefeller Center, which would allow him to come down for the day and see firsthand the progress his researchers were making. That vision became reality: In its Princeton laboratory, RCA developed and patented hundreds of advances in radio and television technology. Even so, shareholders weren't always happy, and Sarnoff faced down the most contentious of them, who complained that their dividends lagged behind those of other large corporations.

The men who succeeded Sarnoff as RCA's CEO, however, had neither his success nor his conviction. His son Robert was dismissed by directors in 1975, less than four years after the "General's" death, beginning a succession of ruinous leadership. The first successor, Anthony Conrad, lasted just ten months, dismissed after the Internal Revenue Service revealed he hadn't filed income tax returns for the previous five years. Then Edgar H. Griffiths, known internally by the nickname "bottom line Ed" and at first loved by Wall Street, was forced out in 1981 when directors tired of his tendency to fire anyone whom he considered disloyal. Next came Thornton Bradshaw, recruited from the presidency of the Atlantic Refining Company, who vowed to return RCA to its roots, and get it out of the car-leasing, real-estate-renting, carpet-weaving, and chicken pot pie–selling businesses it had strayed into in the sixteen years since Sarnoff's departure. But except for revitalizing NBC, which climbed from its traditional third-place ratings position to first thanks to

Grant Tinker's brilliance, Bradshaw was no more effective than his two predecessors had been.

He was also quite naive. He apparently believed Welch's assurances,
which had been made to him as well as to the board, that RCA wouldn't be dismembered willy-nilly. At the December 1985 press conference where Bradshaw
announced to the world the end of RCA, he asserted that the takeover "gives us
the financial capacity to do what we have to do," implying that RCA would
remain intact and would be stronger than ever. Little did he know that the
empire David Sarnoff had built over a lifetime would soon be dismembered.

AT FIRST, Welch was intrigued by the competitive synergies of combining
under one roof the consumer electronics businesses of GE and RCA. Although
Welch had never been a fan of consumer electronics—five years before, he had
placed it outside the circles—the addition of RCA gave GE a commanding 25
percent share of the domestic TV-set business. The merger seemed an ideal fit
in that it would combine two of the most famous names in corporate
America, creating a manufacturing and technology colossus, one that would
be better positioned to take on the Japanese in the important field of consumer electronics. The joint GE-RCA press release, which wrapped the merger
in the American flag, called the alliance "an excellent opportunity for both
companies to create a combined company that will improve America's competitiveness in world markets."

Welch chose Rick Miller, a hotshot executive and rising star at RCA who
had caught his eye, to head up the new combined Consumer Electronics
group. Although Miller had little background in manufacturing—he had been
RCA's chief financial officer—he relished the challenge of what Welch called
"the toughest job in GE." A challenge it was, for the Japanese owned the world
consumer electronics industry. But Miller and consultant Ira Magaziner, a
brainy former Brown University student activist whom GE kept on retainer as
a manufacturing guru, were convinced that with pluck and a little patience
America could manufacture television sets as cheaply and efficiently as Asian
rivals.

Miller knew he would need time, and before accepting the job he convinced Welch to accept three conditions: an office at GE headquarters in Fairfield, Connecticut, in addition to one in Bloomington, allowing Miller to
monitor the feedback Welch would get on the business; a waiver, until 1989, of
the earnings target Welch had set, a minimum of 15 percent profit yearly on

the $1 billion of assets GE had in the business (three points lower than the standard minimum threshold); and lastly, a commitment from Welch that he show his support for the business in a public way.

In the months that followed, Miller, with the input of Magaziner, threw himself into the job of saving America's last best hope in consumer electronics. In a show of bonhomie, Miller and his managers served hot dogs and cake to assembly-line workers in Bloomington, who had reluctantly accepted concessions to support the campaign. The televisions got a facelift, complete with a redesigning of their electronic innards. Miller slashed more than a quarter of the salaried workforce, and also steamlined RCA's massive sales and distribution system. At first, Welch appeared to be holding up his end of the bargain, expressing public support for Consumer Electronics, and he went out of his way to squelch rumors that he intended to divest it. In an interview published in the *Monogram*, Welch said General Electric was committed to keeping the business for at least three years. Welch "has given the business until 1989 to show it can earn its way," *Fortune* magazine wrote in a July 1987 story. Publicly reclassified as a support business for the core circles, Consumer Electronics was also given prominent display in the 1986 annual report.

But by early 1987, a little less than a year after the merger, while Miller had made significant strides in reducing costs, Welch was beginning to lose faith. Profit margins were slipping as two Korean producers, Lucky-Goldstar and Samsung, cut prices for their sets; sales in the first quarter fell 6 percent. Miller spent more time in Fairfield, assuring Welch that remedial actions were being taken to offset these setbacks. By April and May, Miller was proven correct: Market conditions had improved, and sales were back on track. Welch, though, could be a fickle taskmaster, whose behavior followed fairly predictable patterns. He tended to get infatuated with people, and in the early infatuation stage would smother a business with affection. At first Welch had shown his supportive side to Miller, who had been given the title of senior vice president; he encouraged Miller to recruit the best team possible, and told him that money was no object. But a young executive could fall out of favor just as quickly, and such was the case with Miller, who suddenly couldn't do anything right in Welch's eyes.

About the same time Welch was having second thoughts, he was becoming increasingly smitten with Vincenzo Morelli, the suave, sophisticated strategic planner who had been the apple of Welch's eye from almost the day he had joined General Electric in 1983. Morelli was the new kid on the block, at a time when Welch favored new kids. Part of the Welch revolution, after all, had been generational. Older entrenched executives—people too old, in

Welch's view, to change their ways—were dispensed with.* The system seldom made allowances for individuals. If you had been hired prior to 1981, before Welch took over, you were suspect, and presumed to be averse to "change," a favorite word in the new GE vocabulary. Experience—having occupied the same job or been in the same business for any length of time—became a decided detriment.

Morelli, on the other hand, represented everything that Welch found appealing. An Italian national, he was cosmopolitan, young, smart, and spoke English with a thick British accent that Welch found captivating. Morelli not only had looks and breeding; he had the proper CV, having worked previously at the Boston Consulting Group, a farm team for General Electric from which Welch plucked the most promising talent and elevated them to the big time. The drill was always the same: Once hired in, the new recruit would do a short boot camp in some corporate function at headquarters, in Morelli's case on the planning staff Carpenter, another BCG alum, headed. If the recruit performed satisfactorily, he would be given a plum job running a GE operation somewhere in the empire, commanding people twice his age, and putting the techniques Welch had taught into practice.

Morelli was named head of the European operations of GE Medical Systems, one of Welch's favorite businesses. Once a sleepy maker of X-ray machines, Med Systems became a powerful player in the emerging field of diagnostic imaging technologies after it began reporting to Welch in 1973, when he took charge of the Components and Materials Group. Welch liked the business for its growth and also the public relations opportunities it gave General Electric as the provider of cutting-edge health care technology that saved lives. Although GE was the dominant maker of CAT scanners and magnetic resonance machines in America and was beginning to build a presence in Japan, its European operations were minimal; Siemens and Philips owned the market. In the middle eighties, Welch was getting more exposure to the global marketplace—during a twelve-day world tour in 1985, Paolo Fresco, a debonair Italian and senior GE executive, had arranged for him to meet top CEOs in Japan, Korea, and Europe—and increasingly was seeking global solu-

---

* One of the more intriguing age-discrimination cases against GE was brought by Richard Hannye, whose thirty-four-year career in GE's finance ranks came to an end in 1988 when he was forced to take early retirement. In connection with the case, GE was court ordered to produce documents revealing the age of all high-level finance executives (level sixteen and above) in the ten-year period prior to Hannye's termination, together with the candidate slates for all openings during that period. These documents seemed to show that when Welch downsized the financial executive ranks from 287 to 192 in the mid-eighties, the percentage below age forty jumped 71 percent while the percentage above age forty declined by almost 12 percent.

tions to problems. In September 1985, three months before the RCA acquisition, Morelli pitched himself as the savior of Med Systems in Europe, which was losing $25 million a year on sales that were only slightly larger. Although Walt Robb, Med Systems president, wanted to get out of Europe altogether, Morelli had a plan for reversing the situation, and Welch went for it.

Now, at age thirty, Morelli would have his big chance. Over the next two years, losses were eliminated and sales doubled, but Morelli and Welch were frustrated that the "quantum leap" they both sought still eluded them. While market share had improved, from 2 percent to 6 percent, that was incrementalism, not the kind of performance that brought promotions. Morelli felt he needed something dramatic to make a bigger mark, and in June 1987, he invited Welch to Lisbon, Portugal, where the European Congress of Radiology was having its annual meeting. There, Morelli arranged a series of meetings for Welch with European radiologists, hoping to pique his interest in an idea he had broached before—an alliance with France's Cie. Générale de Radiologie (CGR), one of Europe's biggest makers of X-ray machines.

Welch seemed enthused when he left Portugal for Paris, but just how enthused wasn't apparent until several days later. While attending the French Open tennis tournament in Paris along with the NBC entourage that televised the event, Welch had dinner with Alain Gomez, one of the CEOs Fresco had introduced him to on the world tour two years before. Gomez, chairman of Thomson SA, France's largest electronics company and the owner of CGR, was also looking to make a deal, and it took him and Welch all of a half hour to reach agreement. When Morelli heard the news via a phone call from Paolo Fresco, he was ecstatic.

Like two kids swapping baseball cards, Welch had traded one company, GE's Consumer Electronics business, for another, Gomez's CGR. In the book *Control Your Destiny or Someone Else Will,* Welch summarized his thinking: "We didn't need to go back to headquarters for a strategic analysis and a bunch of reports. Conceptually, it took us about thirty minutes to decide that the deal made sense, and then a meeting of maybe two hours with the Thomson people to work out the basic terms. We signed a letter of intent in five days."

Some members of the RCA board felt they had been misled—they had accepted the GE offer because they felt the company would not be dismantled haphazardly. From Welch's perspective, he hadn't promised to keep RCA intact. In any event, Consumer Electronics was the sixth RCA business GE had sold or closed since the merger was announced. In the span of just eighteen months, GE had cut the number of RCA employees from 87,577 before the merger to 35,900, through layoffs or the sale of RCA's assets. RCA Records, the label of Elvis Presley and Nat King Cole, had been sold to Bertelsmann; the Sarnoff Research Center in Princeton was given to the Stanford Research Institute as a tax writeoff; satellite operations were sold to private investors; even the famous RCA logo at 30 Rockefeller Center in Manhattan was replaced by a huge orange "GE." Today, the only former RCA business GE still owns is NBC.

Returning from his trip to Europe, Welch called on Miller, who listened quietly as he was told of the deal that had been struck. Miller told Welch he couldn't disagree with his decision—what good would that have done?—but the turn of events was nonetheless shocking. Miller, who resigned once Thomson took over, wasn't the only one who was surprised; so were readers of *Fortune.* The magazine's July 6 edition, which hit the newsstands just before Welch announced that he was divesting Consumer Electronics, contained an article, "GE's Gamble on American-Made TVs," in which readers were told that General Electric had reaffirmed its commitment to American manufacturing. Welch explained his flip-flop, saying he couldn't pass up the opportunity to buy CGR, which he called "the chance of a lifetime."

Welch agreed to the swap because Med Systems was one of his favorite businesses and Consumer Electronics was not. Buying CGR seemed to make strategic sense as well, because Med Systems needed to expand its presence in Europe, following the strategic course Morelli had advocated. Yet had Welch investigated CGR more thoroughly—and relied less on Morelli—he would have discovered why Gomez was so anxious to get rid of it. A sedate, state-owned maker of medical diagnostic equipment that had been run much like a government ministry, CGR was a mess. Prior to 1982, it had been a failing independent company; the French Socialist government, fearing that left on its own CGR would fail, had forced Thomson to take it. Gomez, a former paratrooper whose approach to business was as steely-eyed as Welch's, had tried in vain to return it to the government.

After GE's acquisition, Morelli was given the assignment of proving that it was, indeed, the "brilliant masterstroke" he had proclaimed it to be. At just thirty-three, Morelli was made a vice president. "You're the youngest vice president in this corporation since Thomas Edison," Welch, the proud father, told Morelli, the adoring son.

An audit conducted just before the deal closed suggested that Morelli's optimism wasn't justified. CGR's financial condition was mediocre at best—its only profitable year in recent history was 1986, and that, as GE soon discovered, was an aberration—but rather than backing out, Welch got Gomez to pony up more cash. Because the businesses to be swapped were of unequal size—Consumer Electronics had annual sales of $3 billion, while CGR was selling about $800 million of X-ray and other diagnostic machines in Europe—Gomez had agreed to pay cash to offset the difference. The cash payment was eventually settled at $800 million once the audit indicated less favorable financials.

How unfavorable wasn't clear until about two years later, and by then CGR had sucked up about $300 million in cash from parent General Electric just to keep it solvent. CGR's problems were legion. It had invested big sums in Germany, where it was fighting an uphill battle against entrenched rival Siemens, which was making more inroads in the French market, along with Philips. For years the French government, which purchased nearly all of the big-ticket medical diagnostic equipment in the country, had bought exclusively from CGR; the government accounted for 40 percent of the company's sales, and even paid a premium of as much as 15 percent on its purchases. Welch had wanted to clean house initially the way he would have in the United States, firing people and immediately lowering costs, but Morelli had counseled caution. This was Europe, not the United States, where it was more difficult to do such things. Besides, Morelli argued, it was not smart to alienate the French government, your largest customer.

But in 1988, as CGR lived off a still relatively robust order backlog, the Socialists regained full control of parliament, and orders soon evaporated as the new government changed health-care procurement policies. Faced with yawning social security deficits, the government, which could no longer afford to pay more for machines that were at best comparable to Siemens and Philips equipment, began asking CGR's rivals to submit competing bids. In the ensuing price war, CGR went from being a protected preferred supplier to an underbidder. The Socialists also sharply curtailed government purchases of big-ticket medical equipment.

Although CGR faced a financial crisis of significant proportions, it wasn't immediately apparent to either Morelli or Welch. The severity of the situation was masked by poor accounting controls that didn't reveal the true financial status. In the late summer of 1989, Morelli and CGR were still the apples of Welch's eye. Proud of the coup he believed he had scored and wanting to show it off to the board—CGR was the largest acquisition outside the United States that General Electric had ever made, and it highlighted a theme Welch had recently been preaching to directors and subordinates, that of globalization—Welch gave directors and their spouses a whirlwind tour of Paris and his pet Plastics and Med Systems projects in Europe. After a board meeting in Holland, at GE Plastics' Bergen op Zoom complex, a visit to Morelli was next on the itinerary, with a presentation at Buc, CGR's technical center near Versailles. To further celebrate the occasion, Welch had asked Reg Jones to join in the festivities, the first board meeting Jones had attended since his retirement, in accordance with strict GE custom, which required that the outgoing CEO sever all ties with the company.

Public performance was a skill Welch admired greatly, and few were better at it than Morelli. On this day he was at the top of his game. At one point in the presentation, a lightbulb on the overhead projector he was using burned out. Without missing a beat, he reached for a second projector nearby and continued on. "That's pretty impressive," one director quipped. "No better than a Goodyear tire change at Indy," Morelli ad-libbed, in deference to director Robert Mercer, retired chairman of Goodyear. Even more remarkable, Morelli was able to convince the General Electric board—a who's who of business luminaries, including former Citicorp Chairman Walter Wriston and billionaire financier Henry Hillman of Pittsburgh—that the situation at CGR was decidedly upbeat. Welch wrote Morelli a note afterward, commending him for his superb performance.

Just weeks later, however, Welch was forced to retract his praise when he learned that CGR appeared headed for disaster. During an operations review in Phoenix, John Trani, president of Med Systems and a frequent Morelli adversary, gave Welch a view that didn't square with what Morelli had told the board. CGR had missed its cash flow target by a wide margin in the third quarter, which had just ended, Trani told Welch. "I have no idea where they are financially," he pronounced somberly. Neither did Morelli, who disliked Trani as much as Trani disliked him. Welch gave Morelli a sorrowful look and said, "Vincenzo, how could you give such a glowing report to the board?" Morelli said he was having great difficulty getting accurate numbers out of his financial staff, which had struggled converting CGR's previous accounting and financial-controls system to the GE system. Welch immediately dispatched Alberto Cerruti, a GE vice president, to do a thorough audit, and Cerruti returned with a bombshell: CGR was posting huge losses, much larger than anyone had previously understood. The "chance of a lifetime" was effectively bankrupt.

A few months later, in the spring of 1990, Trani flew to Paris, and in the crowded breakfast room of the Intercontinental Hotel told Morelli he was fired. Morelli, ever the European, couldn't fathom what he had done to be treated in such a discourteous way—in the Intercontinental Hotel, amid all the tourists. "Couldn't we have done this in private?" he asked, but that was not Trani's way. Trani, though, did offer him an audience with Welch, and the next day Morelli flew the Concorde to John F. Kennedy Airport in New York, hopped on a commuter flight to Bridgeport, Connecticut, and then accompanied Welch on a flight to Washington.

As bad as his encounter with Trani had been, the one with Welch was worse. Welch's reaction was that of the betrayed father. Morelli, whose father had died suddenly when he was an adolescent, had never received anything but praise from the man he regarded as a surrogate father figure. On this day, however, Welch ridiculed and demeaned Morelli, throwing insults at him in a torrent so violent that Morelli could scarcely believe Welch was the same man who had formerly been so supportive. After an hour-long diatribe, during which Welch told Morelli that he was not fit to run any General Electric business, Welch reversed himself and said Morelli could run the European lighting business if he wanted to. Morelli, who left the plane shaken, rejected the offer weeks later—which provoked another eruption from Welch—and left General Electric altogether.

Morelli may have been gone, but the problems at CGR weren't. Trani, who was given full authority over the French operation, made turning CGR around his top priority. The stakes were huge: Not only were large sums of money imperiled, but Welch's prestige was also at risk. An army of financial types descended on Paris to fix the problem. Some stayed for years.

CGR encountered additional problems that were beyond its control. In 1991, it was sued after X-ray equipment used in the treatment of cancer gave radiation overdoses to twenty-seven patients at a Spanish state hospital. Of the twenty patients who subsequently died, the deaths of at least ten could be traced to the excess radiation. Although the problem stemmed largely from hospital employees' errors in calibrating the machines rather than from the equipment itself, the incident badly damaged CGR's reputation.

Costs had to be cut—CGR had a huge bureaucracy—but in France convention dictated that large layoffs had to win government approval. CGR needed lower labor costs to survive, but the French government had dragged its feet in giving GE the authorization it needed to lower employment, and Welch, a captive of the French system, was tearing his hair out. He would pound tables in government ministries, which accomplished little and mostly amused the French, who seemed convinced he was some sort of madman. Trani selected Steven Riedel, a native of Indiana, whose chief qualification for Morelli's job was his loyalty to Trani; he, too, failed to lead CGR out of its morass.

Welch was at his wits' end. Trani had instructed Riedel to develop a plan for making CGR profitable by 1995, which came to be called "Vision '95." When Welch learned during one of his frequent trips to Paris that they were now deferring a turnaround until 1995, he exploded. "I can't understand why you're talking about 1995?" he asked. "Don't you realize you're a bankrupt organization?" Months later, Riedel was gone. Welch was now visiting Paris about three times a year to probe the depths of what had become a seemingly bottomless pit. In June 1992, just before Riedel resigned, Welch opened one session with a simple question: "Can anyone tell me why we are in this fix?" No one, of course, had the courage to tell him, for Welch had done it to himself, trading a sound business for an unsound one.

Subsequent events have shown how misguided his suppositions in buying CGR were. The medical imaging business ground to a halt, as public and private health care providers around the world balked at paying exorbitant prices for fancy, multimillion-dollar diagnostic tools. RCA's prospects, meanwhile, brightened considerably. After several lean years in which no one in the world made a profit making television sets, Thomson included, the company has begun to reap the benefits of the more than $400 million it has invested in RCA since the acquisition. Thomson thrived with the introduction of its Digital Satellite System in June 1994, a pizza-size dish that allows purchasers to receive crystal-clear television signals via satellite and bypass cable television. The dish—the fastest-selling consumer electronics product in history—was so popular that Thomson, which sold nearly two million units in the first year, couldn't build them fast enough to keep up with demand. Operating profits jumped fourfold, and Thomson added two hundred people to its research staff to investigate new opportunities. In 1995, Thomson introduced another new electronic innovation, "smart" VCRs that skip past recorded commercials, bolstering its position as the leading seller of VCRs in the United States. And other new technology is in the pipeline that promises even bigger profits in the years to come, including the most dramatic development in television technology since Sarnoff's historic broadcast in 1939—the shift from analog to digital television. America lost its last, best hope in consumer electronics, while Thomson has opportunities galore.

The purchase and dismemberment of RCA was a watershed in another respect. The thirty-minute swap of Consumer Electronics for CGR signaled clearly that Jack Welch was not about to subdue his personality to accommodate General Electric; on the contrary, his values and his way of doing business would be assimilated by GE. The company and its senior executives would have to learn to accommodate him. Welch had dictated the terms of warfare, but like any war it would have unintended consequences.

CHAPTER FIVE

A CULT OF PERSONALITY

THE STRONG-WILLED, domineering business executive has played a major role in shaping the giant enterprises that have dominated American business in the twentieth century. John D. Rockefeller created Standard Oil; J. P. Morgan and Andrew Carnegie collaborated in the birth of U.S. Steel; Henry Ford built a machine that would consume vast quantities of oil and steel. Ford's vision of a mass-produced automobile, within the reach of the masses, revolutionized twentieth-century commerce. When the first Ford automobile, the "quadricycle," rattled onto the road in 1896, the typical car of that time had a price tag of $9,000 and was exclusively a plaything of the rich. Automobiles were limited-edition novelties; the several thousand or so that existed were mostly powered by steam or electricity, and prices were inevitably high because each one was a hand-designed and handmade work of art.

Ford's grandparents and their seven children had emigrated from Ireland during the first Potato Famine in 1847, settling near Detroit, in Dearborn, Michigan, where their eldest son, William, eventually became a prosperous farmer. His son Henry, born in 1863, hated the drudgery of farm life and instead spent most of his time tinkering with machinery and taking apart watches and putting them back together. In 1880, after the death of his beloved mother, he ran away to Detroit, taking a job as an apprentice in a machine shop at $2.50 a week while moonlighting in a jewelry store, repairing watches. By 1888, his passion for tinkering had led him to a job at the Detroit Edison Company, and within five years Ford was the chief engineer there, making $1,000 a year. In his off-hours, Henry fiddled with gasoline engines in a backyard workshop, hoping to perfect a workable motor for a self-propelled gasoline vehicle. By 1899, his experimental automobile had gained enough recognition that William C. Maybury, the mayor of Detroit, and a few friends put up $15,000 to establish the Detroit Automobile Company, with Ford as the "chief engineer" and partner. Ford's boss at Detroit Edison offered him a promotion to stay but on the condition that he abandon his crazy experiment; Ford quit. Although Detroit Automotive folded the following year, Ford's third and last company, the Ford Motor Company, was founded in 1903; by the time World War I drew to a close in 1918, Ford Motor supplied 60 percent of the automobiles built in America.

Henry marched through the alphabet, developing and selling Models A, B, C, F, K, N, R, and S, but the most successful was his Model T, introduced on October 1, 1908. The original Model T sold for $850; by 1926, when Ford Motor had produced the fifteen-millionth, the price had dropped to $284. As with Edison, however, Ford's greatest contribution wasn't a specific invention but rather a new way of structuring effort to make things. Edison had created the "invention factory," and with it the concept of science and industry working together to produce new discoveries; Ford had introduced the concept of mass production. "The way to make automobiles," Ford had said as early as 1903, "is to make one automobile like another, to make them all alike, to make them come through the factory just alike." By 1913 Ford had his first continuously moving assembly line, which reduced the average assembly time for a Model T from 12.5 hours to 1.5, and boosted production from 82,388 cars in 1912 to 585,388 in 1916.

Workers, however, didn't like the constant demands of assembly-line work, so Ford, to combat chronic absenteeism and high turnover, reduced the shift time from nine hours to eight—and doubled a skilled worker's wage to the then-unheard-of sum of five dollars a day. It made Henry Ford a national hero, and the higher wages were also beneficial in a way he hadn't foreseen, as he himself later acknowledged: "Our own sales depend in a measure upon the wages we pay. If we can distribute high wages, then that money is going to be spent and it will serve to make storekeepers and distributors and manufacturers and workers in other lines more prosperous and their prosperity will be reflected in our sales." By the 1920s, Ford was acclaimed as a genius who epitomized the American ideals of hard work, perseverance, and fair play.

But there was a second Henry Ford, who had little in common with public perceptions of the first. This Ford was an ignorant, practically illiterate man who seldom read books because "they mess up my mind," and who disclosed in one newspaper interview his view of history as "more or less bunk." He was cruel, unforgiving, intolerant, a bigot, and a virulent anti-Semite. This Ford established a "Sociological Department," a Gestapo-like agency with a corps of investigators who visited employees in their homes, inspecting them to make sure that standards of cleanliness were met, and demanding to see marriage licenses and bankbooks to check compliance with Ford Motor rules as set forth in Henry's pamphlet titled *Rules of Living.* Paranoia and ruthlessness were the distinctive marks of Ford in his latter years. He drove off many executives who had played key roles in the company's development, and fought constantly with minority shareholders until eventually winning complete control of Ford Motor in 1919. "First came the elimination of constitutional checks and balances," Ford family historians Peter Collier and David Horowitz later wrote, "in the putsch by which Henry got rid of all minority stockholders; next there were purges of those who had helped make the company; and finally a dictator emerged, supported by a few tough lieutenants and a cult of personality."

Ultimately, Ford was his own worst enemy. A libel lawsuit he filed against the *Chicago Tribune,* seeking $1 million in damages, exposed him to a brutal cross-examination by the *Tribune*'s attorney, Elliott Stevenson, that proved highly embarrassing to Ford. While the jury eventually found the *Tribune* guilty of libel, it awarded Ford just six cents in damages. Despite growing senility, Ford maintained a steadfast belief in his own invincibility, refusing the pleas of his family, including his son Edsel, to relinquish control of the company. Instead of giving power to Edsel, he gave it to a thug, Harry Bennett, a champion boxer, and friend of mobsters and ex-cons, who in 1927 was made chief personnel officer over the seventy-five thousand people who labored in Ford's Rouge Works, an industrial colossus of ninety-three buildings spread over a two-thousand-acre tract of land near the Rouge River in Detroit. Bennett was responsible not only for all hiring and firing but for security as well, and he built an army that the *New York Times* in 1937 described as "the largest private quasi-military organization in existence." There were many violent confrontations with labor, as Bennett's rule poisoned the company's labor relations for generations to come.

In the factory, Ford ignored important marketing considerations, which rivals quickly capitalized on, such as his refusal to add new technology to the Model T—hydraulic brakes and a six-cylinder engine—enabling General Motors and Chrysler to make major inroads on Ford's share of the U.S. automobile market, which by the start of World War II had fallen to less than 20 percent, one-third of its peak of twenty years before. Ironically, when Henry Ford died in 1947 at the age of eighty-three, his greatest legacy was that in almost destroying the company he had built, he provided an invaluable lesson: Nowhere in the history of American business have the dangers of one-man rule been more vividly demonstrated than in the calamitous decline of Ford Motor.

JACK WELCH IS A THROWBACK to the era of the great business titans. The generations that succeeded men like Ford, Carnegie, Morgan, and Rockefeller were part of a new aristocracy in the United States, the heads of America's largest corporations, but they were largely different from that first generation. As a group, they tended to be a rather bland and colorless lot, and General Electric was no exception. Charles Wilson, Fred Borch, and Reg Jones—three of the four men who preceded Welch as CEO in the period following World War II—were relatively indistinguishable, the proverbial men in gray flannel suits. They were career bureaucrats, largely unknown to the American public, consensus and status quo managers who had little real impact on the institution and culture of General Electric. Welch, on the other hand, was cut from the same cloth as Ford and Carnegie. "You've got to be live action all day," Welch told the *Washington Post* in 1997, explaining his philosophy of how a CEO ought to manage. "And you've got to be able to energize others. You cannot be this thoughtful, in-the-corner office guru . . . you cannot be a moderate, balanced, careful articulator of policy. You've got to be on the lunatic fringe." He has been a man on a mission, and his mission in the years following the acquisition of RCA, in the latter half of the 1980s, was to grow GE via acquisition.

In that regard, Welch also differs from his predecessors. He is closer in temperament to a Wall Street tycoon or real estate mogul, a Henry Kravis or a Donald Trump, than a captain of industry, because Welch loves to do deals, and he takes pride in his ability to do them fast. Building a better mousetrap or sponsoring laboratory research is not what gets Welch's adrenaline pumping; making deals does. While the purchase of RCA had whetted his appetite to hit more home runs, the CGR experience had clearly shown that his zeal to do deals could also cloud his judgment. Yet in the aftermath of the RCA actions, Welch became convinced of his own invincibility, certain he would hit a home run every time he stepped to the plate. As a result, he became reckless. And, like Henry Ford, once Welch had resolved to do something, he was an unstoppable force—the deal would be done, whether it made sense or not.

In 1986, Welch bought Kidder, Peabody, a venerable Wall Street securities firm, at the urging of Robert Wright, who a few months later replaced Grant Tinker as president of the NBC television network, once RCA had been swallowed. Certain that Kidder was a fantastic opportunity, Wright convinced Welch, though at least one GE board member demurred, objecting to the purchase on the grounds that Kidder was involved in the financing and shaping of hostile takeovers, an unsavory business that the director believed GE should avoid. Although the board sided with Welch, the director's objection was prescient—Kidder turned out to be quite dirty, and a horrendous mistake as well, for Welch but even more for Mike Carpenter, who later ran Kidder and whose GE career ultimately ended there. In fairness to Welch, no CEO could possibly do his job without taking chances. Moreover, it could be argued that many of the chances he took in the late eighties were appropriate risks. At the same time, a CEO's performance is judged on outcomes, and there is no doubt that the succession of deals Welch orchestrated in this period did not, to say the least, have favorable outcomes. In 1989, just days after the fall of the Berlin Wall, Welch thought he had scored another coup, going behind the former Iron Curtain to snap up the Hungarian lightbulb maker Tungsram. But years of losses followed, a fiasco rivaling CGR that required General Electric to inject fresh capital into Tungsram to keep the troubled company from going under. And in 1988, Welch stumbled again when he acquired the chemical operations of Borg-Warner Corporation, an act that nearly wrecked Welch's most cherished business, GE Plastics.

EXTRAVAGANCE WAS A WAY OF LIFE at GE Plastics, so it stood to reason that at some point, after years of riotous living, there would be a day of reckoning. Like Welch's Phi Sigma Kappa college fraternity, which threw the wildest parties at the University of Massachusetts, Jack's boys at Plastics were a wild fraternity. Aggressive behavior wasn't just condoned; it was considered part of the culture, the way one ought to behave. Anyone who ever worked there— and even some who didn't—has a story to tell. One attractive woman who interviewed for a job at Plastics in 1973 recalls being asked: "Would you fuck a customer for a million-dollar order?" She walked out of the interview.

Certain incidents became cultural icons, talked about and embellished years later. January 1973 was the year of "Katanga," a muscular looking Jamaican who intended to provide entertainment at a GE sales retreat by wrestling a crocodile—before someone from Plastics beat him to it. Folks cheered as their hero, clad in a bathing suit, swam out to the drugged crocodile on a dock, mounted the reptile, and pretended to hump it. The sales meetings were an annual ritual within GE Plastics, a time of high jinks and debauchery, an escape from the unrelenting stress at the most performance-driven business of a company obsessed with performance. Trashing hotels was considered being one of the boys; so was playing demolition derby with rental cars. At the annual meeting one year in Montreal, the German sales contingent heaved a grand piano out the hotel window (fortunately, it was on the ground floor). The damage done at some hotels was so great that GE Plastics was asked not to return; at a Caribbean gathering in the mid-1970s, one manager stood up and implored: "You better behave here. This is the last island that will accept us."

Jack's boys took their cues from Jack, who epitomized the swaggering extravagance of Plastics, and whose love of outrageousness also meant looking the other way when Welch protégés did outrageous things. A case in point was Uwe Wascher, a GE vice president and gonzo marketer whose exploits are almost as legendary as Welch's. Wascher's flamboyance and cocky, self-confident swagger epitomized the Plastics culture; he spoke often of "giga-markets" and vowed to take the business to heights where no man, no company, had gone before. No stunt was too overstated. After arriving for their annual confab in the Dominican Republic, just beyond the shanties and slums of downtown Santo Domingo, the General Electric Plastics contingent of about five hundred marketing managers was driven by bus to a secluded site. Evening was approaching, the weather was warm. Arriving at their destination, a stone amphitheater, people buzzed in anticipation. It was a surreal setting—the sound of Handel's *Water Music* filled the theater, a laser show flashed light onto the stage and into the dusk, the music crescendoed as natives gathered on the verdant hillsides to peer down at the spectacle below while the crowd began chanting, "Ooo-veh, Ooo-veh." Then Uwe Wascher, his profile barely visible and shrouded in mist at the end of a long tunnel, ran forward out of the tunnel and onto the stage, an entrance worthy of Michael Jackson, greeting a crowd that was awestruck.

A controversial character in GE, Wascher acquired the nickname *Der Führer* because of his German nationality and blitzkrieglike behavior. When Wascher encountered a problem, he ran over it—literally. On one occasion, according to a most likely apocryphal story, when a GE security guard in Pittsfield was blocking Wascher from moving in the direction he wanted to go, he shoved the guard out of the way—with his Porsche. Although his antics weren't universally applauded within GE—he had his detractors, among them vice chairman Larry Bossidy—Welch liked Wascher's flamboyance and ruthless aggression. "There was a rapport and comfort level between the two of them," one former executive of GE Plastics says. "It was very clear through their interaction that Jack liked the way Uwe shook things up."

Wascher certainly did that early in 1986, as the national sales staff gathered in Phoenix, Arizona, for their annual confab. Part of the entertainment that year was "Casino Night," when one floor of the Camelback Marriott Hotel was transformed into a gambling casino for GE's use. The evening was a rude awakening for Rebecca Deitz, who just two months before had joined Plastics in the Boston sales office. Wascher strode around the casino, playfully toting a bullwhip and periodically hitting women on the backside, among them Deitz, who was stunned.

"I didn't even know who Uwe Wascher was," she recalls. "He said, 'It's all in good fun.' But he only did it to the women." Deitz never lodged a formal complaint, but in the frat boy mentality of GE Plastics, her failure to see the humor quickly branded her a troublemaker.

Several months later, while visiting friends in Montreal during Easter weekend, she developed a kidney infection and had to be hospitalized. She was supposed to be in Pittsfield that Monday for a training session, but when Deitz called her boss to explain, he insisted that she leave the hospital and drive back. Deitz, who had a high fever, refused. After that incident, relations with her boss went downhill fast. She was seen as having an insufficient commitment to her job, and, a year later, Deitz and GE Plastics parted company. It was a mutually desired separation. Deitz, who now works for a rival company, says she was fed up with the slap-and-tickle games that went on at Plastics. Sexual harassment was a common event. The culture was a macho one that condoned lewd comments from male coworkers, ranging from "I can see your nipples with that bra on" to "Your ass is getting a little big, Becky. You better hit the gym."

During social hours at sales meetings, it was not uncommon for superiors to make forceful advances on female subordinates. Newcomers were typically the first to be approached, with some men slipping their room key into the pocket of the woman they had chosen, a practice known in Plastics as the "force fuck." The men seemed to feel such behavior was acceptable, Deitz says, because of the stories that circulated—but were never verified—about Welch's past exploits when he had been at Plastics.

Acting like him also meant having big ambitions, and in 1988 those ambitions led Welch and his colleagues at Plastics to bid the outrageous sum of $2.3 billion for the chemical operations of Borg-Warner. A Midwestern company, virtually invisible in its hometown of Chicago save for a neon sign that emblazoned the Chicago skyline along the lakefront, Borg-Warner was at once a victim and a symbol of the cannibalistic chaos of the 1980s. As prosaic as the products it made, principally auto parts and garden variety plastics and chemicals, its one distinguishing characteristic was an underperforming stock, and in that regard Borg-Warner epitomized the type of company that attracted attention from raiders like T. Boone Pickens and Carl Icahn who specialized in finding the stocks of undervalued companies and bidding up their shares. The predator who preyed upon Borg-Warner was Sam Heyman. In December 1985, just two days before Welch disclosed his purchase of RCA, Heyman's GAF Corporation had launched a $6 billion hostile bid for another venerable but underperforming company, Union Carbide, for which Michael Milken raised $5 billion in financing in a matter of days.

Heyman figured that the sum of Union Carbide's parts was worth considerably more than what the shares were selling for and that the stench hanging over the company from its poison gas leak in Bhopal, India, which had killed thirty-eight hundred people and injured twenty thousand more the year before, was unwarranted. One of America's blue-chip companies and a component of the Dow Jones industrial average, Union Carbide evaded capture but was nearly destroyed in the process. As a defense, Carbide sold its profitable consumer products group, which made such products as Glad garbage bags, Eveready batteries, and Prestone antifreeze, and bought back 56 percent of its stock to boost the value of its shares. Heyman and other shareholders were temporarily rewarded, but the $3.3 billion in new debt Union Carbide had added to its balance sheet buckled the company. In 1990, Carbide announced a plan to cut its annual operating costs by $200 million, a goal that was raised to $400 million the following year and $575 million the year after that. Wall Street took notice of its efforts—Carbide shares appreciated 35 percent in 1993, the fifth-best performance for the year among the thirty companies on the Dow Jones industrial list—but at a cost that was staggering in its human proportions. Carbide's workforce, which was 98,400 in 1984 before Heyman had cast his eye on the company, had shrunk to twelve thousand by 1994. Although such human misery might prompt rational questions about what price success, Heyman had neither the philosophical bent nor the historical orientation to ask them. Indeed, from his perspective, even though his prey had evaded capture, going after Carbide had been an unqualified success, and he next turned his attention to Borg-Warner, of which he owned 20 percent by the spring of 1987.

To maintain independence and evade Heyman, Borg-Warner invoked many of the dodge-and-swerve tactics that Carbide had employed, even though management undoubtedly knew they would likely prove ruinous. The most aggressive of these was taking the company private, buying up shares through the ubiquitous leveraged buyouts that fee-happy Wall Street investment bankers such as, in this case, Merrill Lynch, were anxious to orchestrate. Borg-Warner's nearly $4 billion bid for 90 percent of its stock topped GAF's offer, allowing the company to remain independent, but the transaction had been horribly conceived. Less than a year later, by the spring of 1988, it was already clear that Borg-Warner's cash flow from operations was insufficient to service the debt it had incurred in buying back its shares and that the company would suffocate without a rapid cash infusion. At that point Borg-Warner's management had no choice but to dismember itself to repay its debts—casting off employees and auctioning off the business that was most likely to fetch top dollar, the chemical division, which accounted for more than a third of its sales.

Although General Electric is generally regarded as one of the few companies that tend to be proficient at acquiring other companies, its purchase of Borg-Warner chemical was a textbook example of why mergers almost never yield the kind of financial and strategic returns the acquiring company anticipates. That's a lesson scores of companies have learned in the nineties—in banking, health care, entertainment, communications, computer software, insurance—and they have paid dearly for it by ruining not only the businesses they acquire but sometimes their existing franchise. Invariably, mergers don't work for several reasons: inadequate understanding by the acquirer of the company it is acquiring; no truly compelling strategic rationale; unrealistic expectations of the synergies that will be achieved; paying too much; conflict over differing corporate cultures; or failing to meld the two companies quickly. GE did move quickly in acquiring Borg-Warner chemical, but the acquisition illustrated another theme common to many mergers: that the priciest deals are motivated at least in part by CEO hubris and that multibillion-dollar decisions about the future of companies are frequently made in seat-of-the-pants fashion.

In hindsight, there's little doubt that the enormous sum GE paid in buying Borg-Warner chemical would have been better spent keeping a few more researchers on the payroll, from both a societal and shareholder perspective. Ironically, buying Borg-Warner was an alternative that Mike Carpenter's staff had considered—and rejected—several times, as had the staff of Glen Hiner, who in 1978 assumed the toughest job in General Electric as head of GE Plastics. The strategic planners had decided against Borg-Warner not so much because it was a poorly run company—it wasn't—but because the profit margins on the commodity grade products it made were a fraction of GE's.

Hiner's thinking reflected the mentality of the times. Mergers were undertaken not because they made sense—many smart people had already concluded that it would be a mistake for GE to buy Borg-Warner—but as a defensive reflex: If we don't do it, someone else will. In Hiner's mind, the risk of acquiring Borg-Warner was much less than the career risk of *not* acquiring it. Allowing a rival company in the plastics business to snap it up wouldn't sit well with the man Hiner lived in fear of and who wanted subordinates to take big swings. He had to endure substantial second-guessing given Welch's commanding knowledge of every aspect of the plastics business. Welch had never really given up running Plastics, and people in Pittsfield still talked about "Jack" as if he had an office down the hall. The stress of having to deal with Welch was readily evident to members of Hiner's staff when the two men were together. Hiner, normally a person of great polish and panache, whose political skills were unrivaled, changed his demeanor in the presence of Welch—he would exhibit a slight twitch or quiver that wasn't visible on other occasions, and he didn't have the same air of comfort, style, and confidence.

Ignoring the advice he had been given by his own staff, Hiner convinced himself and Welch, who needed little convincing, that it made perfect sense for GE to buy Borg-Warner, the market leader in a family of common plastic resins, known scientifically as acrylonitrile-butadiene-styrene (ABS), that were molded to make telephones, refrigerator liners, sporting goods, and other household products. ABS was produced in greater volumes and sold at lower prices than Lexan or Noryl, GE's high-tech flagship plastics, and hence represented a totally different market for GE, with different market dynamics and characteristics. But the differentiation between Noryl, Welch's marketing conquest of the 1960s and traditionally a higher-priced product, and ABS had been eroding, and Hiner was convinced that the only way to stop the erosion was by devouring Borg-Warner, a company Welch regarded highly, before someone else did. As a result, there was almost no price Hiner and Welch weren't willing to pay to keep Borg-Warner out of a rival's hands.

That kind of thinking propelled GE to pay an outrageous sum in the auction that followed, in which three other companies—Dow Chemical, Bayer of Germany, and Exxon Corporation—were active bidders. Dow dropped out of the bidding when the price went beyond $1.75 billion, and Bayer quit at $2 billion. People on Hiner's staff were flabbergasted when they heard that GE's winning bid was $2.3 billion, about $1.5 billion more than the book value of the Borg-Warner assets.

The purchase of Borg-Warner represented the conquest of euphoric thinking over reality-based thinking, which was the mantra that, according to Welch, GE managers were supposed to live by. A realistic look at Plastics and its prospects would have yielded far different conclusions than the assumptions under which Hiner and Welch had bought Borg-Warner. Although GE Plastics had grown phenomenally over the prior two decades, it had been propelled by some unusual factors that were unlikely to continue. Plastics had enjoyed phenomenal growth in the 1960s and 1970s, supplanting traditional materials like steel, wood and glass, but by the late 1980s it was itself a material that had hit middle age, which made further market inroads increasingly difficult to attain and eroded growth. In addition, GE for years had faced relatively little competition—its products were unique, and customers paid top dollar as a result—but as its patent protections expired, more rivals were climbing into the ring.

But Hiner, who in 1988 was acclaimed one of the six best managers in corporate America by *Business Week* and whose leadership of GE Plastics had won the grudging respect of Welch, got swept up in the boundless euphoria of the times, a euphoria that had always been part of the Plastics culture. With the addition of Borg-Warner, GE Plastics was now a $5 billion-a-year business and would have ranked among the one hundred largest industrial concerns in the United States had it been an independent entity. The very idea that growth wouldn't continue was akin to blasphemy in the go-go mentality of Plastics; nor was Borg-Warner the only big swing Hiner had made. After completing the acquisition in September 1988, he unveiled plans in October to construct a $1.7 billion plastics and silicones complex on the Mediterranean coast in Spain; the following year the estimate rose to $2.5 billion for an even larger facility. That was in addition to the $325 million GE had already spent in 1987 to build a new Lexan plant in Alabama, the largest construction project in GE history.

As the top brass of GE Plastics gathered at the Princess Hotel in San Diego early in 1989 to digest this frenzy of activity, it was projected that GE Plastics' sales would reach $10 billion in five years, and $15 billion in another five, estimates that some people in attendance said were too conservative once the "gigamarkets" Wascher promised—housing and packaging—kicked in. The potential demand was unlimited, or so the thinking went; all GE had to do was keep adding production capacity to keep ahead of demand. "There were some pretty big figures tossed around," recalls one of the three hundred or so managers who attended the meeting. "The assumption was that just about anything that would be made would have GE plastics in it."

A few months before, however, Hiner and about a dozen of his staff had met with their Borg-Warner counterparts at a management retreat in Santa Fe, New Mexico, where it was immediately apparent that the melding of the two cultures represented a bigger task than either Hiner or Welch had counted on. In that regard, the problems GE encountered with Borg-Warner weren't any different than those with the typical acquisition of the 1980s, most of which failed, typically because of the inability to assimilate two organizations. Although most of the Borg-Warner people had favored GE over Exxon as the lesser of two evils—they thought they might receive more benevolent treatment from GE, which had a reputation for managerial excellence—such illusions were quickly shattered.

Richard Smith, Borg-Warner's chief of finance, was stunned by the behavior he observed at the meeting. Borg-Warner was a conservatively run, Midwestern company; people were collegial and courteous to one another, and its culture stressed values like teamwork and cooperation. The way the GE people acted not so much toward them but *each other* was a shock to Smith and his colleagues. It was an unbelievably brazen and confrontational display, an every-man-for-himself environment in which Hiner's staff behaved as they usually did—verbally assaulting each other in a very demeaning way. Smith and his colleagues later discussed among themselves how unproductive, immature, and unprofessional such behavior had been. "I couldn't believe what I had heard," Smith recalls. "I wondered if it was possible to work in that kind of environment."

There were substantive differences as well, for GE was also aggressive in its financial and accounting practices, too aggressive in Smith's opinion. Miscellaneous expenses incurred in the acquisition, such as travel, meals, and lodging, were rolled into the purchase price, Smith says, and amortized over a long period rather than being booked as an immediate operating expense, as he advocated; this GE practice had the effect of lowering current expenses and raising net income. There were other "income plays" that Smith considered inappropriate. One way GE Plastics generated "instant" earnings was through the sale of fixed assets such as machinery or even entire plants to a third-party intermediary, which then leased the asset back, yielding an immediate capital gain on the sale that GE could book as income. Smith objected to some of the things he saw, although not too vigorously, because he knew his days were numbered and any protest would prove futile, so great were the differences in philosophy. By February, Smith and about half of his financial staff in Parkersburg, West Virginia, where Borg-Warner Chemicals was headquartered, were gone.

It was one thing to dispose of redundant financial staffs, but GE also ordered cutbacks in areas where they made little strategic sense. About two-thirds of Borg-Warner's sales-and-marketing staff, for instance, was eliminated almost immediately, and the treatment many people received was absurdly harsh. They were herded into interviews that opened: "You've got five minutes to tell us why you'd be a good member of GE Plastics." That proved to be a grave error in that it reflected a fundamental misconception on Hiner's part of what he had bought. The main asset General Electric had acquired was an ABS resin called Cycolac. The product itself was unremarkable—there were many alternatives to Cycolac—but customers bought it rather than rival products chiefly because of the relationship they had with a sales force that was almost immutable. Customers buying from GE, on the other hand, often never saw the same salesman twice. That didn't matter as much with Lexan or Noryl, which were unique products. As the Borg-Warner sales force departed en masse, they took their relationships and market knowledge with them, and GE's rivals, such as Bayer, Dow and Exxon, which had lost out in the bidding, were only too happy to welcome them aboard. That's not an unusual occurrence with acquisitions—years later, Paine Webber would unsuccessfully sue two rival brokerage firms to prevent them from snatching Kidder, Peabody brokers after it had bought what was left of Kidder from GE—but Hiner and Welch had failed to anticipate the impact this exodus would have on Borg-Warner. Soon Hiner was losing the market share he had paid so dearly to acquire, as the former Borg-Warner sales force snatched away customers.

By July 1989, when GE broke ground in Spain for its massive manufacturing complex, the cumulative effect of a weakening economy, aggressive expansions in Spain and Alabama, and the Borg-Warner debacle was hitting Hiner full force as the Plastics steamroller ground to a halt. Finance chief Robert Brust reported at the July staff meeting that net income for the year was now projected at $466 million, more than $50 million below the operating plan of $519 million, and the following months brought a cascade of increasingly bad news. In October, Brust reported that the division had missed its third-quarter sales target by $115 million, which by December had mushroomed to a $600 million miss for the full year. Net income was now projected to be just $384 million—$135 million below budget. Hiner was getting nervous, and he and Brust began casting about for ways to generate whatever earnings they could—"earnings management," as it was called in GE parlance.

Few corporations in the world are as preoccupied with meeting net income targets as General Electric, and few manage their earnings with more skill, which is not surprising, given the importance Welch places on earnings. As Gary Wendt, the man who succeeded Robert Wright as head of GE Capital Services—the financial juggernaut where annual earnings gains over the last decade have been triple the pace of GE's industrial businesses—stated in a speech once, "Net income isn't the only thing in business, but as Vince Lombardi said, I don't know what the second one is."

Because of GE's enormous size and diversity, managers have at their disposal ways to manage the flow of earnings, and in particular, bolster them at times of slack demand. They can tap any number of hidden reserves to get income as needed, and under generally accepted accounting principles have considerable discretion in assigning value to assets, which greatly influences the earnings they report. For instance, when GE acquired RCA, the decision was made to allocate most of the goodwill—the cost of the acquisition above the book value of RCA's assets—to NBC, which had the effect of increasing the television network's book value and, at the same time, increasing the profits GE booked when other RCA assets were sold.

Another way earnings could be "managed" was through the movement of inventory, which could at times promote operations that were quite elaborate. One of the most infamous examples occurred in the Electrical Distribution & Control business, where the managers of one facility in Connecticut conceived of what came to be known as the "midnight flight." A cargo plane was filled with inventory before a year-end count, flown to Puerto Rico and then flown back the following day so that the inventory valuation would be lower and earnings would be correspondingly higher. Another technique would be to close the receiving dock at a factory several days before the end of a quarter or year to avoid the addition of inventory, even though items in the shipment were sometimes needed for current production.

GE Plastics had a well-earned reputation within the corporation as one of the most aggressive practitioners of "earnings management." But the plan Hiner and Brust executed in the fall of 1989, when they took advantage of a "hidden reserve"—selling the company's interest in Japan's Asahi Diamond Industrial Company—went beyond even GE's own liberal standards of what constituted acceptable behavior.

General Electric's involvement in diamonds was yet another example of a business being spawned through a momentous laboratory breakthrough, in this instance the discovery in 1954 of a process to make diamonds, the hardest substance known to man. Following in the footsteps of Edison, GE researchers cracked a code of modern alchemy, allowing the world of science to invade what had formerly been the exclusive domain of nature. The manufacture of synthetic diamonds soon evolved into a highly lucrative business as GE sold its diamonds to customers like Asahi that fashioned the man-made stones into cutting tools used mostly in construction and oil drilling. To cement its relationship with Asahi, GE in the early 1970s purchased 10 percent of its stock, and as the industrial diamond business grew and prospered, so did the market value of GE's holding, which was worth $80 million by 1989.

Asahi also was GE's most important customer, accounting for about 13 percent of its sales, and in recognition of its growing importance Edward Russell, the GE vice president who headed the synthetic diamond division (GE

Superabrasives), which was part of GE Plastics and hence reported to Hiner, traveled frequently to Japan and executed a joint venture with Asahi to manufacture diamond films. When Russell learned in October that Brust and Hiner were considering selling the Asahi holding merely to offset lower operating income, he objected on the grounds that Arihisa Tanaka, the Asahi chairman, would take it amiss. Brust had already asked his financial representative in Tokyo, Dennis Daigneault, to broach the topic with Tanaka, who considered it a breach of faith and told Daigneault that if the stock were sold, his company might have to rethink its commercial relationship with GE. That message had been relayed back to Pittsfield, but Hiner was adamant that the stock be sold; although he didn't want to jeopardize the Asahi relationship, the $67 million gain Plastics could claim if the shares were sold would go a long way toward helping Hiner out of his earnings jam. Eventually a complicated compromise was forged that Hiner and Brust thought would provide the income they needed without alienating Asahi: GE would "sell" the stock to a third party, Mitsui, GE's distributor in Japan, but only temporarily, agreeing to buy the stock back in three installments, starting in 1991.

Ironing out the details of this arrangement occupied much of management's time in October and November—Russell traveled to Japan twice to explain the transaction to Tanaka and get his reluctant approval—but in late December the transaction hit a major snag. There were three agreements that had to be signed to execute the sale and subsequent buyback, and corporate accounting in Fairfield had no problems with the first two, but the third, which committed GE to buying back the shares from Mitsui, didn't pass muster. Accounting contended that any agreement, even a verbal one, to repurchase the shares might draw unfavorable notice from the Securities and Exchange Commission, which would construe GE as having "parked" the stock, which is illegal under securities law. Stock parking was nothing to trifle with; it was one of the reasons Ivan Boesky was serving a prison term, and why Michael Milken would later go to jail.

Corporate accounting issued a firm edict: Do not under any circumstances sign the third agreement. But instead of abandoning the idea, Daigneault and Herb Rammrath, a Plastics vice president in Tokyo, were instructed to revisit Mitsui and see if some understanding could be struck without GE committing to the buyback in writing. The two parties huddled, and on December 26, 1989, Toshio Chonan, a Mitsui general manager, wrote a two-page letter to Daigneault, outlining Mitsui's understanding of the implied "spiritual" aspects of their arrangement, which stipulated that GE had a "strong desire to buy back shares of Asahi Diamond" but was not allowed to express such "intention in the contract." GE also agreed to pay Mitsui a fee of about $3 million annually for holding the stock. Given that accounting had overruled the transaction, it raised a few eyebrows when the sale came back again as a done deal. "There must have been a hundred people who knew what had gone down," one person in Fairfield recalls, though no one put a stop to it.

The Asahi stock sale provided earnings when Hiner needed them most, contributing to GE Plastics' ability to transform an earnings performance that was in reality subpar into what was proclaimed as its best year ever. Readers of GE's 1989 annual report were told that the Materials Group, made up of the Plastics, Superabrasives, Silicones, and Laminates businesses, recorded a 44 percent improvement in operating profit, the most profitable of GE's nine operating segments that year. There was no mention of the Asahi stock sale, the buyback provision with Mitsui, or the income the transaction had generated—under accounting rules, it wasn't material and therefore needn't be disclosed.

The arrangement may have helped Hiner, but it ended up causing GE untold grief. When Asahi shares lost half their value in the Japanese stock market collapse that followed shortly thereafter, Mitsui, which wasn't about to be left holding the bag, contended that GE was obliged to repurchase the shares in accordance with the Chonan letter. After reading the letter, some senior finance executives in Fairfield reluctantly agreed, and a vigorous internal debate broke out about whether GE needed to take a writeoff on the stock; the debate became even more vigorous once Welch was informed about the possible charge in January 1991. GE ultimately avoided a writeoff, but the whole affair proved costly: Mitsui received concessions from GE worth about $30 million in exchange for agreeing to keep the stock. In addition, the transaction was scrutinized by the Justice Department and the FBI as part of a subsequent investigation into the diamond business, and, adding insult to injury, failed to mollify Tanaka, who subsequently reduced Asahi's purchases of GE diamonds.

As it would turn out, Asahi was the least of Hiner's troubles. Borg-Warner had been purchased at exactly the wrong time, just as the economy was entering its first recession since the early 1980s. Worst of all, Welch had begun to take notice. In March 1990, when the heads of GE's thirteen major businesses met in Fairfield for their semiannual operations review, Welch singled out Plastics as the only business that had experienced negative sales growth in the prior year and at a similar gathering six months later, he lambasted Plastics as the poorest-performing business.

The last two years of Hiner's command were unlike anything GE Plastics had ever experienced. The project in Spain was put on hold, after more than $100 million had already been spent on it; and in December 1990, Hiner told his staff that the $400 million in net income that year included $160 million in nonoperational gains, meaning that the Plastics group had achieved net income from operations of $240 million, a number that included $112 million in net contributed by Superabrasives and Silicones. In other words, the core plastics business, including Borg-Warner but excluding Superabrasives and Silicones, had had net income of just $128 million on sales of $4.4 billion—or less than three cents profit for every dollar of goods sold, a margin that the local Kmart might find acceptable but a shocking decline from the lofty heights of 25 percent profit margins that Plastics once enjoyed. Hiner concluded the meeting by asking his staff to do whatever they could to generate more earnings.

Soon the tyranny of numbers descended with a vengeance. Employment was slashed in reductions that GE euphemistically called "reorganizations," cutbacks that reached deep into the organization and cut almost 40 percent of the salaried workforce in Pittsfield, or about two hundred and fifty people. Many were long-time employees who had worked for Plastics more than twenty years, earned six-figure salaries, and couldn't believe they had become casualties. After receiving his termination notice on November 4, 1991, Jan Vestergaard, a twenty-eight-year veteran of the business, was stunned. "Why me?" he asked Welch in a letter. "You're a terrific guy," Welch answered in a phone call, "but we just can't afford you anymore."

Hiner's staff was pretty much obliterated, with more than half of the department heads who reported to him in 1990 gone less than a year later. As the months passed and conditions worsened, it was increasingly apparent that Hiner, who had agreed to a $500 million net income target for 1991, himself was getting squeezed. The target, which was clearly unachievable but nevertheless was the goal Welch would grade him against, had been lowered to $375 million by July and $310 million by September. Welch was hopping mad, and people began wondering how many misses he would tolerate. The beating Hiner took was severe, with Welch getting so angry on occasion that he trembled. "You fuckin' guys don't know what the fuck you're doing," he would bellow during meetings with Hiner and his staff, while Hiner appeared to be buckling under the strain. "He looked like he was eighty years old," one colleague recalls. A persistent lower back problem recurred, and he began to complain of a buzzing in his ears.

Just how desperate the situation had become was apparent on July 11, 1991, when Hiner and his staff met with Welch in Fairfield for their semi-annual operations review, which seldom went according to plan. Welch disliked the formality of sticking to the prepared text and preferred instead to flip through the summary notebook that accompanied every review at GE, stopping the presenter in midsentence and posing the question he most wanted answered. Failure to stay with him at his lightning pace could be fatal.

Welch clearly wasn't pleased with what Hiner reported that afternoon; not only hadn't the earnings picture improved, it hadn't even stabilized. Borg-Warner had been an unmitigated disaster and was barely breaking even, a far cry from the $300 million in yearly profit contributions that Welch and Hiner had anticipated before the acquisition. Yet Hiner, unwilling to declare Borg-Warner the failure Welch was convinced it was, tried to give it a positive spin, repeating one statement from the summary book: "In hindsight, we would do the acquisition again!" It was an assessment that enraged Welch. "You're fuckin' crazy," he replied, staring at Hiner from across the conference table. Welch then had a private session with Hiner, which commenced after the main meeting had ended. They met for about a half hour, while Ed Russell, the GE vice president who was traveling with Hiner, waited outside. At the conclusion his boss emerged looking shaken.

"Rough meeting?" Russell inquired as the two hopped into the waiting limousine that would whisk them to their corporate jet.

"Very rough."

Hiner didn't elaborate. Five months later Hiner, who at that time had already begun looking for another job, informed Welch he would be leaving to become CEO of Owens Corning in Toledo, Ohio, a company half the size of GE Plastics. It was an opportunity to be one's own boss, to be free from tyranny, an opportunity that had come along just in the nick of time. Hiner had done all he could to improve a bad situation, but the business creed under which he and others operated demanded more. A sagging economy was no excuse for not making one's profit commitments. Outcomes, after all, are what matter.

CHAPTER SIX

THE DEATH OF THOMAS EDISON

THE ERA OF FINANCIAL MANIPULATION that began in the mid-1980s had a lasting impact on the way American business would be conducted in the future at General Electric, and at every other large corporation in America. Boiled down to its essence, financial manipulation represented the conquest of an ethos whose consequences were much more profound than simply the ill-advised acquisition of companies. The frenzy of buying and selling represented the acceptance of expedience, the popularization of the idea that it was better to buy something rather than invest time, money, and energy doing it yourself. Inventing things, creating things, growing things took far too much time in this new results-obsessed, gotta-have-it-now environment. Taking the long view, which might have meant a five-year horizon at the end of the 1970s, became a quarterly horizon by the end of the 1980s.

At the same time, doing the right thing became an increasingly antiquated notion and was replaced by doing the expedient thing. And, to some extent, who could blame the CEOs? It was the "me" decade in American society, and the rallying cry of the business community might have been: "I want what I want and the hell with everyone else." Large shareholders and pension funds like Fidelity and the California Public Employees Retirement System were in effect singing the same refrain, demanding more returns to keep their customers happy and well endowed—for longer retirements, for Ivy League educations, for yachts and travel and vacation homes. As a result, Wall Street would mete out unmerciful punishment upon companies whose earnings were even a fraction below "expectations," and there was always a raider ready to pounce, dismantle, or otherwise prey upon companies that only a few years earlier had thought they were invincible. Keeping shareholders happy had become the full-time preoccupation of American business, and no CEO was more practiced at keeping them content than Jack Welch.

One unforeseen consequence of the ascendance of financial manipulation, however, was the impact it would have on investment in research and development. Investments in R&D had been the backbone of American industrial preeminence in the twentieth century, leading to DuPont's discoveries of Nylon, Orlon, and Teflon; Bell Laboratories' invention of many electronic wonders, including the transistor; RCA's creation of black-and-white and later color television; Kodak's discovery of Kodacolor film; General Motors' creation of freon refrigerants and antiknock gasoline that made possible high-compression engines; and GE's breakthroughs in a plethora of fields, ranging from ductile tungsten, the modern X-ray tube, and manmade diamond to electrical and mechanical devices as big as railroad locomotives and as small as dime-size diodes and rectifiers. The silicon chip, cellular phones, the laser, modern gene technology, and fiber optics all had been nurtured in corporate research labs.

But corporate America's attitudes toward R&D changed dramatically in the 1980s. Over the ten-year period from 1976 to 1985, for example, U.S. industry increased its R&D funding at an annual, inflation-adjusted pace of 6.7 percent, a level that, even though it represented an improvement from the decade that preceded it, was still only half that of Japanese industry. But in 1986, a new era began with real R&D increases in the eight years through 1993 averaging just 1.2 percent, less than one-fifth the rate of increase in the prior decade. As more and more dollars flowed into buying, selling, and financial gimmickry, fewer dollars were available for "pie-in-the-sky" endeavors like research and development.

R&D was decidedly out of favor, viewed by the vast majority of CEOs as an unnecessary extravagance, yielding too few benefits and consuming too much time and energy for them to support. The trend was perhaps best evidenced in 1993, when despite robust profits and the end of recessionary times, the real R&D spending of U.S. industry increased by only 0.7 percent. Real spending declined in 1994, 1995, and 1996, even as profits accelerated. Indeed, winnowing rather than augmenting research budgets was now the practice of many American corporations, including such leading lights as IBM, AT&T, and Kodak, all of which laid off research personnel. According to one survey of 253 of America's biggest companies by the Industrial Research Institute, 41 percent planned to reduce their already paltry R&D budgets in 1994, outnumbering those that planned increases by more than two to one. It was a trend with ominous implications for the future of American industry—and, once again, it was a trend in which General Electric had been the leader.

At the outset of his administration, Welch had a grand plan to grow new technologies into blockbuster businesses, as each of the seven CEOs who had preceded him had done. Upon taking office on April 1, 1981, Welch had described his vision for the company he was going to lead: "A decade from now I would like General Electric to be perceived as a unique, high-spirited, entrepreneurial enterprise." Welch was just twenty-four hours into the job when, in a dramatic public announcement on April 2, he unveiled plans to tap "the emerging megamarket of factory automation," a $500 million investment dubbed "Factory of the Future," GE's attempt to become the leading supplier of factory automation systems, including computerized gear and industrial robots, to American industry. Money was spent lavishly to innovate and improve age-old manufacturing businesses: $300 million to automate the seventy-year-old locomotive facilities in Erie; $500 million to modernize Appliance Park in Louisville; $135 million to produce a revolutionary new compressor for use in GE refrigerators; and $100 million to develop a new medical diagnostic tool, magnetic resonance imaging, that would use powerful magnets to produce cross-sectional photos of the body's tissue (most large hospitals have them today, though GE in 1997 paid $103 million to Raymond Damadian, the man generally credited with inventing the technology, after a jury found it had infringed the basic patent held by Damadian's Fonor Corporation). GE had also spent $235 million to buy Intersil, a producer of metal oxide semiconductors, and $150 million to buy Calma, a fast-growing Silicon Valley maker of computer-aided-design equipment that would support its foray into factory automation.

Welch's ambition to build a high-spirited, technologically innovative enterprise was perhaps best illustrated in October 1982, when he dedicated a new two-story building at the R&D center that would house advanced laboratories in electronics and computer science and, at a cost of more than $130 million, represented the largest expansion in the R&D center's eighty-two-year history. "Nearly half of this investment is aimed at positioning GE at the leading edge of the electronics revolution, letting us apply the tremendous potential of the microelectronic chip to every possible product, service, and process," Welch declared during a ceremony attended by local leaders from business, academia, and government. "These chips are changing the way we live, work, and play, making possible everything from industrial robots and other 'intelligent' machines that will revolutionize the factory, to advanced medical scanners that will let physicians see into the body without X-rays, to smart home appliances, to highly sophisticated home entertainment centers."

As the years passed, however, it became increasingly clear that Welch's vision of building a new blockbuster, high-technology business was hopelessly blurred. Calma floundered, as did Intersil, free-wheeling California-style businesses that were unable to adapt to Welch's management-by-the-numbers regimen. They were among the ventures that failed, following a predictable pattern. In Act One, Welch, charged up about the fantastic market opportunity he believed he had discovered, would smother the business with resources and affection and dispatch a flamboyant, fast-talking executive to lead the business. Act Two was the belated discovery that the business plan he had been sold on was outrageously out of whack and based on wild assumptions. In the case of the Factory of the Future, the numbers were so inflated that GE had boldly predicted in 1981 it would have 20 percent of what would be a $25 billion market by 1990, a prediction that was off by a factor of at least ten. Actually, it's difficult to say with certainty how far off the prediction was, because the market for factory automation systems never did materialize. But Welch didn't wait around for postmortems; his ardor for a business—and the executives who ran it—could cool as quickly as it had seized him once the projections didn't pan out. That was Act Three, as Welch called for the heads of those who had disappointed him. The denouement followed, as the business limped along until the final axe, its dissolution.

Ceramics was another high-tech venture—the phrase seems so dated now—General Electric saw as a megamarket for the future. Convinced that ceramics in the 1980s would be what plastics were in the 1960s—a futuristic material with unlimited growth potential—Welch bought the precision ceramics division of Minnesota Mining and Manufacturing. Eight months later, the entire management team except for the two top executives was fired. Once again, Welch had bought into a flawed vision, in this case presented by Gary Carlson, whose impassioned pleas had convinced Welch that a "quantum leap" could break the hammerlock of Japan's Kyocera, the world's dominant player in ceramics. But Carlson, who upon his appointment as president of GE Ceramics in 1983 predicted that worldwide sales of the material would grow tenfold by 1990 and that GE's share of the market would be as much as 50 percent, had promised too much too soon. GE sold off what was left of it in 1987.

The most spectacular GE failure in technology was yet to come. It would be judged one of the greatest fiascoes in modern engineering, a catastrophe that threatened GE's entire refrigerator business and sapped Welch's confidence in his company's ability to execute "quantum" technological leaps. Previously, GE scientists and engineers had made great contributions to the march of technology in the twentieth century, notably including the Monitor Top refrigerator, a product conceived in 1925, and without a doubt the most significant kitchen appliance of this century, the model upon which all subsequent home refrigerators were patterned.

Like the Model T Ford, the Monitor Top was an absolute breakthrough, a product so unique in conception that it fundamentally changed the American way of life. By 1928, more than one million American households had traded their icebox for a GE hermetically sealed refrigerator, and by 1950 the refrigerator was a fixture in more than 90 percent of American homes. Although GE engineers in Fort Wayne, Indiana, had begun making home refrigerators in 1911, borrowing the idea of a French monk, Marcel Audiffren, the early models couldn't be mass-produced. The compressor, which cooled the icebox and contained noxious gases, had to be airtight, and ordinary welding didn't provide the proper seal. When Willis Whitney became the first director of the GE research lab in 1900, he had insisted that everyone keep detailed lab notebooks, which could prove essential in patent disputes. They also provided possible solutions to scientific conundrums, and engineers found a solution to their welding dilemma in the lab notebooks of William Coolidge. As part of his experiments with tungsten a decade earlier, he had discovered that copper, when melted in hydrogen, sealed cracks, crevices, and holes so small that even a microscope scarcely detected them. This copper brazing, as it was called, sealed the compressor welds, which made possible the previously unheard-of mass production of a moving mechanism sealed in steel which ran for years. Thus was born the Monitor Top (so named because the compressor, sitting atop the refrigerator, looked to one wag like a turret from the *Monitor*, the Civil War ironclad battleship). The Monitor Top's overwhelming popularity convinced management that a viable market existed for "white goods" and led General Electric to fame and fortune as it became the world's leading producer of household appliances. The Monitor Top was also the beginning of GE's participation in the money-lending business, which began during the Depression as a way of enabling cash-strapped customers to buy refrigerators.

By 1979, however, just as GE was commencing its new "We Bring Good Things to Life" ad campaign that trumpeted the company's commitment to serving the major appliance market, the appliance business had fallen into disrepair. So had Appliance Park in Louisville, the white-goods colossus Ralph Cordiner had founded, where GE employed more than twelve thousand people engaged in the manufacture of refrigerators, washing machines, and dishwashers. Although GE was still America's leading maker of refrigerators, its market share and profits were falling. To make matters worse, GE made its refrigerator compressors in Building Four on the massive Appliance Park complex, a 1950s' vintage factory that relied on production methods that

hadn't changed since Cordiner broke ground. As a result, compressor manufacture was very labor-intensive—making a single piston took 220 steps and
even simple grinding operations were done by hand, which meant that it took
GE sixty-five minutes of labor to make a compressor, compared with twenty-
five minutes for rivals in Japan and Italy. Ira Magaziner, the same consultant
who later crafted GE's strategy of fighting back against the Japanese in consumer electronics as well as the Clinton administration's ill-fated plan for
reforming the American health care system, studied Appliance Park and delivered a somber verdict: Either buy compressors abroad or find a way to
leapfrog the competition by building better ones.

Ultimately, the route GE chose was in effect preordained because capitu-
lating to the Japanese would have been suicidal for Roger Schipke, president of
the Appliances division. Welch, after all, was urging subordinates to take "big
swing, quantum leaps," and he was also championing GE's prowess in factory
automation, the envisioned multibillion-dollar business he hoped to create.
What better way for GE to demonstrate its commitment to the "Factory of the
Future" than by building one of its own, where it would make a new space-age
refrigerator compressor called the "rotary," employing a design that seemed to
hold great promise because the new compressor weighed less and was more
energy efficient than the traditional piston-driven reciprocating compressor,
which had three times as many parts.

Actually, the idea of using a rotary compressor to cool a refrigerator
wasn't new at all; it had first been suggested in Louisville more than twenty
years earlier. Rotaries were used extensively in air-conditioners and had even
been tried on an experimental basis in refrigerators without success. Even so,
the rotary offered a way to satisfy Welch's demands and lead the appliance
business out of its predicament. With fewer moving parts, it would be cheaper
to build, and hence more profitable, at a time when Schipke was desperate to
find more profit. On September 1, 1983, Welch approved the plan for the rotary
presented by Schipke and his two top technologists, John Truscott and Tom
Blunt, but with one proviso—it had to be done quickly. Truscott, a Welch
favorite who had made his name doing work on computed tomography scanners and on the breaking of the sound barrier, was responsible for the design
of the new compressor; Blunt, a manufacturing expert who had come to GE
from Ford Motor, was in charge of the $120 million factory in Tennessee, fifty
miles south of Nashville, where the compressor would be manufactured.

Over the next two and a half years, Truscott and Blunt raced to meet the
deadline that had been imposed. By March 1986 the new factory, in Columbia,
Tennessee, was up and running, turning out rotary compressors at a rate of

one every six seconds, a phenomenal feat given the manufacturing tolerances. The design that Truscott's team had come up with required the key parts to work together at a friction point of fifty-millionths of an inch—about one-hundredth the width of a human hair. Nothing had ever been mass-produced at such an extreme tolerance, but Blunt and his team, hotshots in their field, were confident they could do it. Because of the time constraints, however, shortcuts were taken in testing the new compressor. Rather than phasing in the product gradually and supplementing simulated "life" testing with extensive field testing, as GE had done in the past, the field testing was cut back from two years to nine months as managers raced to keep up with their schedules. The limited testing that was done turned up evidence that the compressors weren't performing well, but Louisville technicians who voiced their suspicions, such as Robert Derman, were ignored. "The pressure to get this project done was enormous," Derman recalls. "It was an awfully big task, and there just wasn't enough time to do it right." A colleague adds: "It would have taken a lot of courage to tell Welch that we had slipped off schedule."

Not nearly as much courage, though, as was required about a year and a half later, when Schipke had to give Welch the terrible news. Reports about failed compressors trickled in. The initial failure had been in Philadelphia in July 1987. But by Labor Day, four years after Welch had approved the project, Schipke knew from the deluge of failures that he had a nightmare on his hands. Thousands of refrigerators were failing, and soon it was clear that they would all fail in time because of a design flaw that led to the disintegration of two powdered-metal parts in the compressor. General Electric had brought a grossly defective product to market and, in the process, had put at risk its multibillion-dollar refrigerator business. Soon lawsuits alleged that the defective refrigerators, through their excessive heat and inadequate refrigeration, had caused fires, injuries, and food poisoning. A man in Indiana filed a complaint that contended he had suffered a heart infection that led to a stroke, the result of eating contaminated food. Only quick work by Schipke saved GE Appliances, as he and his management team worked around the clock to stave off total ruin. Schipke immediately dispatched a service task force to replace the compressors in millions of large-capacity GE and Hotpoint refrigerators, at a cost of hundreds of dollars per service call, and in 1988 GE took a $450 million charge to offset its costs. Smaller-capacity models also failed but, to save money, weren't extended the same free compressor replacement offer.

Although Schipke took the blame for the failure, in the final analysis it was Welch's doctrine of "speed, simplicity, self-confidence" that had proved to be the project's undoing. As was the case in ceramics, in Factory of the Future, in Calma, in Intersil, the mission hadn't been simple at all; people who knew that building a reliable rotary compressor was a risky proposition were shunted aside by supervisors who wanted above all to please Welch, some out of fear, others driven by ambition.

The refrigerator debacle would have enormous consequences for General Electric in the years to come. For many people involved in the project, it represented the end of their careers at GE: Schipke, Truscott, and Blunt all subsequently left the company, along with dozens of other senior managers whom Welch deemed responsible for the failure. Rather than demonstrating America's and GE's preeminence in world-class manufacturing, the project was a world-class capitulation. The same managers who had defiantly rejected Magaziner's alternative to purchase compressors from overseas rivals ended up doing just that, and the plant in Tennessee, truly an industrial masterpiece, was discarded in 1993.

Welch's attitude toward technology now changed. He recognized and privately acknowledged the damage that had been done; some years later, when asked about the compressor failure during the filming of a video for employee viewing, he asked that the camera be turned off and said: "On that one, we nearly broke the company." In the aftermath, GE Appliances, which had been built upon the ingenuity of the Monitor Top, would retreat from innovation into a technological cocoon. It didn't even place among the finalists in a 1993 competition sponsored by the federal government, won by archrival Whirlpool Corporation, to find a new environmentally friendly and energy-efficient refrigerator, one that wouldn't emit ozone-depleting chemicals. The chilling spread beyond Appliances. Welch would be less supportive of technology in the future. As a result, GE's involvement and commitment to technology in manufactured products would diminish, while its participation in financial services would expand, as Welch pursued the one field that to him seemed like a sure way to make money. It was a choice that kept the shareholders content, but one that undoubtedly would have appalled Edison.

WHILE JACK WELCH'S EMBRACE OF TECHNOLOGY was best characterized by his dedication in October 1982 of the new two-story, $130 million building at the Research and Development Center, his retreat was symbolized in an event that took place seven years later. To the plaudits of Wall Street securities analysts, Welch declared his intention on November 17, 1989, to purchase up to $10 billion of GE stock over a five-year-period, at that time the largest gesture of its kind in corporate history. Buying the stock, Welch declared, was a better way to generate value for shareholders than taking a "wild swing" investing in new technology or on another acquisition. In the years since that decision, U.S. corporations have followed GE's lead, engaging in unprecedented stock repurchasing. It has become such a commonplace method of financial engineering that there's little controversy about the act anymore, although it is rare in both Germany and Japan, where shareholders don't demand short-term earnings increases but focus on long-term goals, a more productive use of their money. The prior generation of American CEOs, who were less attuned to financial manipulation and faced less pressure to submit to it, were as doubtful of stock buybacks as the Japanese continue to be. They would have regarded the staggering sums U.S. corporations have spent in recent years buying back their shares—$65 billion alone in 1994—as a form of chicanery, as well as a shameful waste of corporate assets. David M. Roderick, U.S. Steel's chairman and chief executive in the 1980s, scornfully dismissed share repurchases as an act he likened to "eating your own mother."

Actually, Welch had said during a meeting in Miami only a year and a half before he announced the buyback that he was against doing it, to the disappointment of securities analysts, who had touted GE shares and were getting increasingly jittery over the lack of upward movement. There were good reasons to reject the stock purchase alternative. By buying up shares, management can boost a stock's price because with fewer shares in circulation, there are more earnings to spread over the fewer shares, yielding a better earnings-per-share ratio. But economists and experts on American industrial policy, such as Robert Reich and Michael Porter, have been critical of share buybacks because rather than boosting the price of the stock in the short term, CEOs should be plowing money back into their businesses to reap investment-derived gains in the long term.

In 1984, the recent failures took a toll on GE's market performance, as the value of its shares fell 3.4 percent after sizable gains in 1982 and 1983. In 1985, GE shares resumed their upward trend, powered by the acquisition of RCA, which the market regarded as an unqualified success (and which demonstrated Welch's lack of confidence in his ability to generate internal growth through investment in new technology). "My real deep sadness is that a company that was once as vital as General Electric can't find internal areas to invest in," said Tom Peters, co-author of *In Search of Excellence*, commenting on GE's purchase of RCA. But investors wanted higher earnings per share, and the purchase of RCA allowed Welch to deliver it immediately, which sent the stock spiraling upward from the high sixties when the acquisition was announced in December 1985 to above one hundred by early 1987, the second time in the Welch era that that barrier had been broken. Welch had once again won the universal acclaim of Wall Street, but the grand prize of "market cap" champion still eluded him, as the total value of GE's stock was third, behind IBM and Exxon.

On March 22, 1987, Welch addressed a meeting of NBC's executives at the Sheraton Bonaventure Hotel in Fort Lauderdale, Florida, while GE shares were surging beyond 107. Many CEOs might have been content to savor this accomplishment and pass out words of encouragement to the people who had helped make it possible, but not Welch, who wore an open-necked shirt and sports jacket but whose demeanor was hardly relaxed. As usual, he had winning on his mind that day, and he desperately wanted to surpass Exxon and IBM. If the NBC executives could keep the network's ratings up and generate more earnings, Welch would be the leader of the most valuable company in America. "We are $4 billion behind Exxon," Welch said, exhorting his charges. "If you guys can still get ratings, then every portfolio manager in the world will have to bet on IBM—a one-product company—or GE. If we can get in that No. 2 position, every portfolio manager in the world will have to choose between IBM and us."

After listening to Welch, the NBC executives were demoralized; under Grant Tinker, the network president who had left NBC when GE purchased it the year before, NBC was already the most profitable network in television history. The 1986–87 season had been a smashing success, with the network scoring victories in the morning time slot with *Today*, in late night with Johnny Carson and David Letterman, in news with Tom Brokaw's *Nightly News*, and in prime time, where NBC had a two-ratings-point lead over CBS and was four points ahead of ABC. But Welch wanted more—Bob Wright, Tinker's successor as network president, was pressuring NBC News president Larry Grossman to reduce head count and drastically cut costs in the news division—and his speech that day confirmed to his listeners how unrelenting the new boss was. The few compliments he offered in the course of his lengthy presentation were overshadowed by his stern recriminations. Asked at one point whether NBC was better off under RCA or GE, Welch replied: "I'd say for the good people, it's a dynamite deal. For the turkeys, it's only marginal." Unlike RCA, GE didn't tolerate "turkeys. . . . Those of you who aren't good, who aren't winners . . . don't get on the NBC boat."

Although NBC did contribute more earnings in 1987 than it had in 1986, its improved performance didn't help Welch achieve the stock market gains he had hoped for that year. The quick succession of wheeling and dealing that had followed the RCA acquisition—the purchase in 1986 of Kidder, Peabody and the swap a year later of GE's Consumer Electronics business for the X-ray maker CGR—had evoked the dreaded word "conglomerate" among investors. Once again, GE was being viewed as a GNP company, one that was too unwieldy to understand and whose earnings would rise and fall in lockstep with the growth of the economy.

The stock market crash on Monday, October 19, 1987, didn't help matters. GE shares fell 8⅞ that day, on top of a three-point decline the Friday before, two days in which the total value of GE stock declined by $11 billion; to put that number in perspective, the total value of GE stock was $12 billion when Welch became CEO in 1981. Watching NBC *Nightly News*'s coverage of the crash that night, Welch thought Brokaw and his colleagues had been too negative and were whipping the public into hysteria. Enraged, he called Grossman, who after the little more than a year GE owned NBC was already on the outs with Welch. "You're killing all the stocks," Welch testily told Grossman over the phone. To which Grossman, an urbane former president of the Public Broadcasting System whom Tinker had hired in 1984 and who considered the news division a public trust, replied: "This is not an appropriate discussion to be having." Grossman never received another critique of the network's news content from Welch; he was fired the following year, as the differences between himself and Wright, as much philosophical as anything else, became irreconcilable.

By May 1988, the crash was a distant memory, and while the market had recovered and resumed its upward course, GE shares were lagging badly, trading below the October lows. Welch was doing all he could to bolster confidence in the stock, meeting with securities analysts as well as buying shares himself as a sign of his confidence. Still, nothing seemed to work, and Welch went public with his exasperation over a share price that was 27 percent lower than it had been a year earlier when he spoke to the NBC executives in Florida. "I cannot understand it for the world," Welch told the *Wall Street Journal.* "As far as our earnings outlook and our performance, it couldn't be better."

The stock, however, continued to languish through 1988 and into 1989, while Welch's goal of becoming the "market cap" leader and overtaking IBM, which had held that title for decades, seemed less and less likely. In his letter to shareholders in March 1989, Welch asserted that 1988 had been "a great year" except for two "thorns . . . among the roses." The first was the failed refrigerator compressor, and the second was the "price of our stock," which rose just 1.4 percent during a year when the Dow Jones industrial average and the Standard & Poor's index of 500 stocks both gained 12 percent. "We're not sure why this is the case," Welch confided, "but it occurs to us that perhaps the pace and variety of our activity appear unfocused to those who view it from the outside." In 1988 "we began hearing: GE is 'too difficult to understand' and 'portfolio managing.' "

Eight months later, when Welch announced the stock buyback in November 1989, GE shares soared to new heights, climbing from the mid-fifties before the buyback to the mid-seventies by July 1990. More important, Welch was now challenging IBM as the stock market king of the hill. He would achieve that status in 1991, and GE has retained it ever since (though the company now faces a challenge from software giant Microsoft). Clearly, investing in new technologies and enhanced research endeavors were out, financial engineering to generate immediate value for shareholders was in.

In truth, Welch was merely confirming a trend that had been well established by 1989 and had begun as early as the 1950s. The need to make a profit and the need to invest in the future is seldom in balance in major corporations and has been a source of great friction in twentieth-century industry. Indeed, Henry Ford's first attempt to manufacture automobiles, the Detroit Automobile Company, failed in 1900 largely because Ford's backers wanted him to focus on increasing sales, while he wanted to refine the production process; Ford refused to capitulate and resigned.

Companies like Intel, which in 1992 replaced Japan's NEC as the world's leading producer of semiconductors, and Motorola, whose CEO Christopher Galvin is the founder's grandson, have an engineering bias because the technologists are in charge, which can at times be a weakness; indeed, it could be argued that Intel's belated recognition of consumer complaints about the Pentium microprocessor in the fall of 1994 was a direct result of the arrogance of their engineers, who despite mounting evidence refused to believe that a chip with the "Intel inside" label could possibly be flawed.

For the first seventy-five or so years of GE's existence—from, say, the invention of the lightbulb in 1879 until Ralph Cordiner's tenure in the 1950s— the technologists called the shots. Engineering was a domain unto itself, and for the people who populated GE's Central Research lab, CR&D, as insiders called it, invention was the raison d'être. Willis Whitney, the Massachusetts Institute of Technology chemistry professor who in 1900 was selected as the lab's first director and for thirty-two years guided its endeavors, always managed to retain a professorial enthusiasm for the work of his researchers.

In the golden years, the days of Edison, Steinmetz, and Whitney, GE's research activities had been product-driven. Product engineering and research were concurrent, housed in buildings in downtown Schenectady in which physicists, chemists, and mathematicians worked side by side with product engineers and tinkerers, whose orientation was toward the practical solution of problems. As the research organization grew in stature and reputation, however, a bigger and grander home was established in 1950 in the suburbs of Schenectady, a physical separation from the product engineers that became more profound as the years passed. The new R&D lab in Niskayuna fostered an approach that was a departure from the Edisonian model of practical invention. One of the reasons the early labs had succeeded, aside from the brilliant minds that occupied them, was that scientists and engineers had worked together, solving common problems and seizing on each other's ideas. The new lab was populated mostly with Ph.D.'s, rather than a mix of scientists and engineers, and the money that supported their endeavors came exclusively from a separate corporate R&D budget, not from the operating divisions themselves, further distancing the activities of CR&D from the divisions that manufactured the actual products. The pace of product-relevant inventions slowed.

On the other hand, a certain amount of distance was beneficial in that it shielded corporate research activities from the vagaries of falling profits. Even if the results of a business unit turned down, product development could continue over many years and not be threatened. Indeed, many of General Electric's biggest and most profitable businesses—Aircraft Engines, Plastics, Medical Systems—were the product of patience and had been nurtured and nursed for years, even decades. In that regard, GE Plastics had become successful not so much because of the skills of Jack Welch but because his employers had the foresight and courage to endure more than a decade of continuing losses until newly patented polymers found commercial acceptance.

With the ascendance of Cordiner, GE's institutional patience began to evaporate. Although skunk works like Plastics were still tolerated, they were often supported in surreptitious ways to keep them hidden from senior management. As early as 1945, GE's prescient engineers and scientists saw that the electrical age, which had overtaken the steam age, was itself about to be eclipsed by the coming electronics age. That year GE began construction of Electronics Park, a 155-acre complex near Syracuse, New York, where many of the basic building blocks of electronics originated—diodes, rectifiers, the essential elements of every electronic product made today. Nor was that the sole site of GE's electronics research. In Schenectady, Ernst Alexanderson, by then an elderly man but still working in "the House of Magic" where he had made his earlier breakthroughs in radio and television, continued to invent. In the late 1940s, he demonstrated an early fax machine; the first electronic oven, the advent of microwave cooking, was developed a few years later.

Cordiner, though, installed harsh profit quotas, which had a particularly pernicious impact on many of GE's nascent technology-based businesses. GE became infamous for its manipulation of a "portfolio" of businesses, some of which would be "harvested" by drawing off the cash flow to support growth in areas that strategists had deemed more attractive or viable. This concept of portfolio management was a disaster, however, for small electronics initiatives, many of which were abandoned because of insufficient profits. Skilled scientists and engineers left General Electric, and many joined Motorola.

As profits became more imperative than technology, a power shift began. The upwardly mobile GE manager was no longer an engineer who understood the physical properties of electricity but someone who had mastered the Harold Smiddy managerial Blue Books. The technologist lost stature, and the modern *manager* gained it, not just at General Electric but at just about every leading American corporation. A legion of consultants sprang up to advise the ruling class, the managers, on how to better manage and reap more profit, not on how to make better products. It was the complete opposite of the Edisonian model upon which GE had been founded and was a concept that our chief foreign rivals didn't buy into to the same degree. While Germany and Japan remained focused on the old-fashioned notion of building better mousetraps, American companies were busy perfecting the new science of management and developing better mousetrap *strategies.* Manipulation became the name of the game, and companies—not just GE, though it was a leader—were busily enhancing their "portfolios." Probably the most zealous follower of the portfolio management strategy was ITT Corporation, whose CEO Harold Geneen in 1959 embarked on a decade-long buying binge, building a sprawling empire that rented cars through Avis, baked Wonder Bread and Hostess Twinkies at Continental Baking, and built homes through Levitt & Sons, but had little focus.

At GE, the ascendance of the managerial culture, which reached its apex under Reg Jones, brought with it a devaluing of the engineers and technical types, "grunts" whose ingenuity had given the managers something to manage. When Welch first came on board, it was widely presumed that as a technologist, he would bring GE back to its roots. Indeed, if anyone should have been an unabashed supporter of research and development, it was Welch. Not only was he well educated in science, but he also owed his entire career to advances that had come out of the lab.

Although GE had begun its involvement in the plastics business in 1928, when it established a plant in Pittsfield to make phenolic resin, it wasn't until 1953 that a Schenectady researcher named Daniel W. Fox made the accidental breakthrough that put Plastics on the map. While trying to find a better material for insulating wire, Fox mixed a concoction that created a big chunk of brown acrylic, a substance that was so hard he couldn't extract his laboratory stirring rod from it. This chunk was kept around the lab as a sort of mascot, defying the efforts of Fox and others who sought, with knives, hammers, even by throwing it down stairwells, to break the mysterious substance. Fox convinced his superiors that the material might have commercial value, and they allowed him to engage in clandestine work that several years later led to the patenting of Lexan polycarbonate plastic. The discoveries of Lexan and Noryl, a derivative of another laboratory breakthrough, polyphenoline oxide (PPO), invented in 1956 by GE scientist Allen Hay, were the single most important events that rocketed Jack Welch up the GE corporate ladder.

Curiously, though, Welch had long showed disdain for "blue sky" research. One of his most scornful expressions, "dink," frequently meant a chemist working in the lab with test tubes. Welch's antipathy toward scientists in white frock coats was so pronounced that when Bob Wentorf, a distinguished GE research physicist and a member of the team that had synthesized the first synthetic diamond in 1954, encountered a former professor of Welch's from the University of Illinois at a scientific conference just after Welch had become CEO, the professor, Harry Drickamer, advised Wentorf to hunker down, get ready for some lean years, and investigate other career alternatives. "He said that Welch wasn't much interested in technology as a student, and he predicted that GE would veer away from technology and innovation under Welch's leadership," Wentorf recalls. Drickamer's observation would prove prophetic.

It wasn't that Welch didn't think technology had value—his experience at Plastics had taught him otherwise—but his attitude toward it reflected the two main impulses of his personality: his purposeful nature and his impatience. He felt research had to have a specific purpose, and it had to yield quick results. Welch regarded technology no differently than any other corporate activity: He would only support it as long as it was yielding discernible results. When CR&D didn't, in 1986 he replaced Roland Schmitt, a GE technologist who had spent his entire career at CR&D and who resisted Welch's attempts to change hallowed technology traditions, as the head of the lab with Walt Robb, a Welch associate from their days together in Med Systems who had more of a marketing and managerial bias. Robb shared Welch's belief that CR&D was an

ivory tower, living too sheltered an existence. They couldn't help but notice
the phenomenal success of Japan Inc., which had overtaken American rivals in
many fields the United States had originally pioneered, including microelectronics and semiconductors. For decades more patents had been granted to
General Electric than any other company. As late as 1985 GE was still the patent
leader. But by 1987 it ranked fourth, behind three Japanese companies—
Hitachi, Canon, and Toshiba. Robb and Welch were convinced that GE was
falling behind because CR&D researchers didn't have nearly enough interaction with the operating divisions and needed to be more product-driven in
their thinking.

The ascendancy in importance of the priorities of the manager as
opposed to those of the technologist would have profound implications in the
changes that Robb implemented after Schmitt's departure and would ultimately lead to a significant contraction of GE's research efforts. Robb decreed
that henceforth the funding for research projects wouldn't come exclusively
from corporate, as it had in the past. Instead, the bulk of the money would
come from the specific businesses themselves. Researchers would be compelled to work on things that were product relevant; otherwise, they wouldn't
have the resources to fund their research, and they would be out of business.
Tying research more closely to the product wouldn't have been a bad solution
per se, but there were four businesses that sponsored the bulk of research
at CR&D—Aerospace, Aircraft Engines, Plastics, and Medical Systems—and
when business turned down, as it did for all four in the early 1990s, earnings
still had to be maintained. And at GE, maintaining earnings when business
erodes means one thing—layoffs, from which research would no longer be
exempt. As a result, in the space of seven years, the staff at CR&D was cut by
about 30 percent; the twenty-one hundred people who worked there under
Schmitt had been reduced to about fifteen hundred by the time Robb retired
in 1993, and that is the number of employees today.

The axe fell hard at GE Plastics. One senior manager, Joe Wirth, the vice
president for technology, quit rather than proceed with the 20 percent reduction Glen Hiner ordered him to implement in the fall of 1990. As the inventor
of Ultem, another trademarked plastics resin that had brought GE a fortune,
Wirth couldn't stomach what he believed was a virtual abandonment of technology. Other renowned technologists, such as Allen Hay, the man who had
invented the forerunner of Noryl, found safe havens in academia. Hay kept on
good terms with his former employer and managed to obtain money from GE
to support his search for new polymers at McGill University in Montreal.
Years later, GE eliminated that as well. Hay points out how much GE's philoso-

phy has changed from the early 1950s when as a Ph.D. in polymer chemistry fresh out of the University of Illinois, he was given a set of keys, escorted to a room at CR&D, and told, "Here's your laboratory. Invent something." Irving Langmuir, the Nobel laureate, noted the same upon his retirement from the research lab in 1950. "There was more academic freedom [at GE] than I had ever encountered in any university," Langmuir said. Forty-odd years later, the letter Hay received from a much wealthier GE informing him that the company intended to discontinue support of his research was a stunner. "They said, 'We don't have any interest in anything new,' " Hay recalls, somewhat bitterly. "A new product for them is a modification of an existing material."

New product development was also given a lower priority at GE's Transportation Systems division in Erie, which for much of this century had been the world leader in locomotive technology. In 1924, GE introduced the locomotive design that would eventually eclipse the steam engine and become the railroad propulsion standard in this century—the diesel-electric, which used a diesel engine to drive a generator that turned the wheels via direct current. In 1968, it introduced another breakthrough, alternating current (AC) locomotives, which at that time was a technology before its time. Although ACs had the potential of better traction, lower maintenance costs, and less fuel consumption, railroads had little incentive to switch over from the reliable DC. Twenty-five years later, however, they did, and early in 1993, Burlington Northern announced the biggest locomotive order in the history of railroading, $675 million for 380 new AC locomotives that went not to GE but to its chief rival, the Electro-Motive Division (EMD) of General Motors. Welch tried mightily to snag the order—he took part in a video conference call with Burlington Northern executives—but in the end they chose EMD because it already had tested prototypes, developed with technical assistance from Siemens of Germany, while GE was about two years behind, offering only a "paper locomotive." To become more competitive, GE Transportation Systems president Bob Nardelli immediately turned to another German partner, Deutz, from which it purchased an AC design. Nardelli did not have the confidence that his own depleted engineering staff could catch up without Deutz's help.

A fateful decision on this subject had been made several years before by Nardelli's predecessor, Michael Lockhart, thirty-nine years old when he took over as president of Transportation Systems in 1989. Lockhart was a Welch favorite, a no-nonsense, by-the-numbers, financial whiz who always got results. The contrast between Lockhart and his predecessor, Carl Schlemmer, epitomized the differences between the old GE and the new. Although Schlemmer and Lockhart were both rock-hard businessmen, Schlemmer was old-school GE—tough and demanding, but at the same time respected and well liked, a man who had deep ties to the community and time to talk to even the lowliest mill hand. Even during the darkest days of the Schlemmer era in the 1980s, when demand for locomotives shriveled and he ordered the layoffs of thousands of people, the people who worked for Schlemmer had confidence that he would try to do the right thing.

Lockhart's orientation, on the other hand, was to numbers rather than people. He spent little time in Erie and kept his contacts with the community to a minimum. As a young, upwardly mobile senior executive, Lockhart knew what had to be delivered to get ahead; awards from the local Red Cross meant little to Welch. And on some level he did deliver—GE overtook EMD during Lockhart's tenure, capturing the No. 1 market share position and posting sizable profits as well. But Lockhart also cut costs so aggressively, particularly in engineering, that his actions led inevitably to GE falling behind on AC technology, the further development of which had been shelved along with such futuristic technologies as magnetic levitation trains, which the Japanese and Germans have pursued feverishly. In one celebrated confrontation early in 1992, John Grisik, a senior executive who reported to Lockhart, took his complaints about the paucity of funds for locomotive development directly to Welch, pleading with him to free up money for more engineers and more engineering. Welch sided with Lockhart, and Grisik left the company shortly thereafter. "General Electric has changed its orientation from manufacturing to investment banking," concludes Tom Johnson, a recently departed locomotive engineer, who estimates that the number of degreed engineers in GE Erie dropped from about two hundred when he arrived there in 1981 to fifteen when he left to join another company in 1994.

Nor were the cutbacks in engineering the only signs of a changed orientation under Welch. In December 1993, Nardelli, continuing the shortsighted thinking of his predecessor Lockhart, ended the Apprentice Program, which since its inception in 1910 had graduated more than nineteen hundred apprentices who received classroom instruction and on-the-job training to elevate their skills. Even the GE spokeswoman charged with breaking the news to the community of Erie acknowledged the obvious—that the program had, for eighty-three years, been dollars wisely spent: "It provided us with highly trained people in the work force." Why, then, get rid of it? It wasn't cost-effective, was her explanation; $1 million a year was an extravagance the General Electric Company (which had a net profit of $4.3 *billion* in 1993) could no longer afford.

Nor was it cost-effective for GE Erie to continue manufacturing its own

propulsion and control systems, even though they represent the guts of a locomotive. GE has been steadily whittling away at the number of parts it manufactures and buying more from outside suppliers all over the world. This
practice, which the union calls "farm-out" and the company refers to as "outsourcing," is standard operating procedure for every manufacturer in America
these days. One survey of major corporations found that 86 percent outsourced at least some activity in 1995, up from 58 percent in 1992. It means less
work being done in Erie and hence fewer jobs there; less use of the $300 mil-
lion "factory of the future" that *Newsweek* in 1982 hailed as the epitome
of world-class manufacturing—and ultimately, perhaps, the end of GE Erie
altogether. As more elements of the process of manufacturing a locomotive
get "outsourced" to lower-wage workers in Mexico, Canada, and beyond—
and more parts of the factory are abandoned—GE's days in Erie look to be
dwindling.

That same "cut, cut, chop, chop" mentality isn't evident at Siemens, the
German company that EMD turned to for its new AC locomotive. While GE
has been cutting back on its research endeavors, Siemens has been augmenting its efforts, particularly at its flagship R&D facility in Princeton, New Jersey,
which has added as much staff in the last several years as GE has eliminated in
Schenectady. The German giant struggles with the same issues that every corporation in the world involved in technology does—how to get the most bang
from their research buck—but unlike GE it hasn't decided that the solution is
to commit fewer bucks. To the contrary, it now employs some forty-six thousand scientists and engineers worldwide, more than three times the number
GE does, even though the two companies' sales are roughly equal.

By contrast, Welch's short-term philosophy can be seen in a diminished
interest in nurturing new technology. "We feel that we can grow within a business, but we are not interested in incubating new businesses," Welch told *Business Week* in a 1993 interview, articulating the company's new philosophy. The
cost of nurturing technology is simply too high, which raises the obvious
question: If a $90 billion enterprise can't afford to do it, who can?

General Electric has lessened its involvement in many emerging technologies, including cellular communications—it holds preferred stock in a
business it sold to Ericsson, a Swedish telecommunications concern, which
participates in an industry that will service half a billion users worldwide by
the year 2000, up from virtually none in 1985—and optoelectronics, the marriage of light and electricity, a field GE would presumably be well positioned
to lead but one that rival Hitachi dominates. Ironically, although General
Electric pioneered the field in 1961 with its invention of a tiny device that when

tweaked with an electric current emitted light, it didn't have the patience to wait out the losses while a market developed, but Hitachi, which snapped up the licensing rights, did. Admittedly, Hitachi is better able to wait because of a variety of societal factors, not the least of which is the protection Japanese multinationals receive from their government. Whatever the reason, Hitachi's optoelectronics business is flourishing. The company now makes semiconductor lasers, the successor to the light emitting diode, technology that found its first mass market as the guts of a compact disc. An even bigger market awaits in telecommunications—already Hitachi has a 60 percent share of the world market for special laser devices that zip voice signals down fiber-optic phone lines—and the field could prove even more significant if beams of light ever replace the etched circuitry on computer chips.

The funds that GE once might have devoted to research or incubating new businesses now are spent augmenting its financial services empire. In the early and mid-1990s, GE Capital implemented a strategy that continues to this day, making opportunistic acquisitions and spending tens of billions of dollars to: snap up distressed property taken over by the federal government from failed savings and loans; acquire stakes in financial service concerns around the globe; increase its interests in consumer finance, auto, and aircraft leasing; become the nation's largest servicer of mortgages; and buy up the portfolios of other companies that have decided to quit the leasing business, including Eastman Kodak.

Even with all this activity, however, the stock wasn't responding as Welch thought it should in 1994. After eclipsing the one hundred barrier for the third time in his fourteen years as CEO—and implementing a two-for-one stock split, also for the third time, in the spring of 1994—GE shares were down 7 percent for the year when, on December 16, Welch announced his second stock buyback in five years, a $5 billion program—since raised by an additional $12 billion—to get the share price moving upward and to maintain his position as America's stock market king.

Wall Street reacted favorably to the news that day as GE shares rose $1^1/_4$ in heavy trading.

CHAPTER SEVEN

DEADLY DECEPTION I

PLEASING WALL STREET wasn't the only thing consuming Jack Welch's energies in the latter half of the 1980s. Keeping problems at bay was also a prime activity, as it is for most CEOs, particularly those atop the companies that have a long history of manufacturing. One such company was GE's longtime rival, Westinghouse.

In the seventies and eighties, Westinghouse followed a strategic course patterned after GE, abandoning many of the products that were synonymous with its name—lightbulbs, refrigerators, household appliances, the products that pitchman Frank Gifford once said "you could be sure" of—to pursue profit outside of manufacturing, in services, especially the field of financial services. Between 1986 and 1990, Westinghouse was caught up in the intemperate real estate speculation that swept the country, doubling its loan portfolio in what appeared to be easy money, but ultimately exposed the company to grave risk when the real estate and leveraged-deal lending markets cratered in the early 1990s. Westinghouse had adopted Welch's strategy but had executed it poorly. Bad loans in excess of $5 billion were written off, the CEO was dismissed, and in the summer of 1993 directors named a successor, Michael Jordan, to lead the company out of its morass.

But even though Westinghouse had turned away from its manufacturing traditions, the legacy of manufacturing lived on. Jordan, whose background was consulting and the soft-drink and snack-food businesses, having spent his career at Pepsi and at consultancy at McKinsey & Company, discovered as much early on in his tenure. Reflecting on his first year in office during an interview in the summer of 1994—one year before he acquired the CBS television network, a transaction that would trigger the divestiture of all of Westinghouse's industrial businesses, a renaming of the corporation to CBS, and a move of its headquarters to New York from Pittsburgh—Jordan said what he least expected and most underestimated wasn't the restructuring of the loan portfolio or bank debt or any of the financial problems Wall Street was focused on but rather "the legacy of problems from the past."

Because of the kind of products General Electric had made—as well as the company's sprawling size and scope, with hundreds of factory sites throughout the world—the magnitude of *its* manufacturing legacy was enormous, and Welch had to devote an inordinate amount of his time to resulting problems. They came in many forms: environmental damage done to former industrial sites; PCBs, the chemicals and suspected carcinogens contained in just about every electrical product manufactured in the United States for nearly half a century; the post–Cold War collapse of defense contracting; and nuclear power, which for Jack Welch was one of the most problematic businesses in the 1980s.

GENERAL ELECTRIC'S INVOLVEMENT in the nuclear business had been a long and tortured one. It began at the close of World War II, when many were anxious to exploit the untapped potential of the atom. To President Truman, who reviewed fifty warships in New York harbor on Navy Day, October 27, 1945, while aboard the victorious USS *Missouri*, the atom represented a possible means of controlling "the ocean approaches to our country." To General Electric, which had helped unleash what J. Robert Oppenheimer called the "radiance of a thousand suns," the atom represented a new and emerging industry, a business it was determined to lead. To Hyman Rickover, then a captain with twenty-three years of naval service who was mothballing ships in the South Pacific, the atom represented a technology that could propel submarines as well as his ambition.

For four decades, Rickover was czar of the U.S. Navy's nuclear program, supervised by the federal edifice he created, the Department of Energy's Office of Naval Reactors, headquartered near the Pentagon in Crystal City, Virginia. In addition, Rickover, a man who understood the intricacies of science as well as government, was one of the founding fathers of a laboratory in upstate New York near Schenectady, the Knolls Atomic Power Laboratory, that would guide the Navy's quest of nuclear propulsion, and became a critical cog in the military-industrial complex. Almost since the dawn of the nuclear age in 1942, when Enrico Fermi's reactor in Chicago sustained the first atomic chain reaction, the United States and the Soviet Union had tried to better the other in nuclear submarine technology, a decisive battleground between the superpowers. Born in 1947 of an alliance between the federal government and Gen-

eral Electric, the Knolls lab designed the reactors that propelled an armada of
Navy submarines and surface vessels and kept the United States on an equal
footing with the "evil empire."

Although Rickover weighed just 125 pounds and stood five feet six inches
tall, his diminutive stature was no measure of the power he would eventually
wield with the United States Congress. "I am a creature of Congress," he said
often, and after his appointment in July 1948 as the Naval liaison to the Atomic
Energy Commission, the civilian agency that succeeded the Army as overseer
of the Manhattan Project, Rickover began building a power base in Washington, attacking that task with characteristic zeal. Rickover soon became a fixture on Capitol Hill, testifying before Congress more than 150 times during a
career that survived seven presidents, the last being Jimmy Carter, who as a
young sailor trained at Knolls. The admiral was second only to J. Edgar
Hoover as the most entrenched federal bureaucrat of his time, and his influence was such that when he retired in 1981 at the age of eighty-one, President
Reagan signed an executive order that would ensure autonomy to the Naval
Nuclear Propulsion Program even though Rickover was gone.

To Congress, Rickover was a man to be feared and respected; feared because
of the powerful allies who embraced him on Capitol Hill, respected because of
his engineering insights. Rickover had recognized the speed and stealth
advantages that nuclear-powered submarines offered over the diesel-powered
varieties used during the war. Unlike diesel subs, which needed to surface
periodically to draw air for engine combustion, the nuclear sub could remain
underwater for weeks at a time. Today, nuclear-powered vessels comprise
about 40 percent of the Navy's fleet, including the entire sea-based strategic
deterrent, the cornerstone of America's nuclear triad.

Rickover's friends in Congress saw him as a brilliant nonconformist bat-
tling a calcified institution that was the epitome of conformity, an image he
reinforced through an appearance, style, and demeanor that was decidedly
non-Navy. He rarely wore a uniform, which the brass interpreted as a show of
contempt for the service (it was). When hostility between the Navy and Rickover reached the flash point, as it did in 1954 and again in 1958, when he was
passed over for promotion, Congress intervened on his behalf. In the second
instance, not only did Congress authorize the promotion, to vice admiral, it
also gave him a special commendation, a congressional gold medal; prior
recipients included such luminaries as George Washington, who received the
first in 1776, the Wright brothers, Thomas Edison, Charles Lindbergh, General
George Marshall, and Jonas Salk.

Congressmen sympathized with Rickover, and he skillfully manipulated their sympathies. On March 20, 1955, the powerful Joint Committee on Atomic Energy held the first congressional committee session undersea as the legislators rode the world's first nuclear-powered sub, the *Nautilus*, launched just two months earlier. The *Nautilus* was powered by a Westinghouse water-cooled reactor, which Rickover had dubbed Project Wizard. Project Genie was the sodium-cooled GE reactor designed at Knolls, which propelled the second nuclear sub, the *Seawolf*. The Rickover Navy, the nuclear Navy, had been born, and so had the Knolls Atomic Power Laboratory.

Throughout its history, Knolls was a typical outpost of the Cold War, shrouded in secrecy and virtually invisible even in the community it called home. Few people in upstate New York knew it existed, and fewer still knew much about its mission. Headquartered in the Schenectady suburb of Niskayuna, the lab consisted of three separate installations, the most closely guarded of which was the Kenneth A. Kesselring site, named after the General Electric manager who oversaw the company's early participation in the nuclear Navy. Located in rural West Milton, New York, about twenty miles north of Schenectady and ten miles west of Saratoga Springs, the Kesselring site sits at the end of a dead-end street, Atomic Project Road. Signs along the road warn intruders that the area is a Restricted U.S. Government Property. The road winds through the dense forest of Saratoga County and leads to a compound of buildings and barbed wire, once home to four nuclear reactors. Here, within a twenty-five-mile radius encompassing more than one million people, the laboratory carried out the bulk of its atomic agenda.

When the Knolls Atomic Power Laboratory was established in 1947, its priority wasn't nuclear submarines but rather the pursuit of a breeder reactor that would generate or "breed" plutonium, the deadly man-made material the military needed for nuclear weapons. The lab extracted this plutonium from a nuclear reactor it operated on Peek Street, near downtown Schenectady. The facility, which was operated until 1955 while a permanent home for Knolls was under construction in Niskayuna, handled large amounts of radioactive materials. Although the federal government and GE both claimed for more than three decades that Peek Street had been perfectly safe throughout its history, those claims now appear dubious. A report issued in November 1988 by the New York State departments of Health and Environment Conservation concluded that on at least two occasions in 1947, plutonium had been incinerated at the site and released into the atmosphere, while two explosions, in 1948 and 1949, had also resulted in the accidental release of an undetermined amount of radioactivity. The findings were supported in interviews with former Peek Street workers, one of whom recalled cleaning up after a large explosion that had razed about six feet of wall. Radiation procedures were lax then: record-keeping in the early days was virtually nonexistent; workers didn't wear protective gear of any kind; old-timers removed their radiation badges when they had reached safety thresholds, placing them in lead boxes to shield them from tipping the scale. Decontamination procedures were also lax. "You just washed yourself off and went right back to work," one worker recalled.

Although the Peek Street site was officially proclaimed radiation free on October 31, 1955, when it was "decommissioned," an assessment by General Electric twenty-four years later, in 1979, concluded that the radioactive material hadn't been entirely removed. Unfortunately, the facility had been used as a *food warehouse* in the meantime—from 1955 to 1979, the new occupant of the building, Buy-Rite Foods, had used it to house groceries, including produce, that were distributed to about eighty Buy-Rite stores in and around Schenectady. As recently as February 1993, thirty-eight years after Peek Street had been declared officially safe for human habitation, the U.S. Department of Energy was still removing residual radiation from the site. Workers wearing respirators and clad in protective garments excavated several tons of soil and cleaned surfaces inside the building, chipping away at walls, floors, and ceiling beams.

The Joint Committee on Atomic Energy, controlled by pro-nuclear Congressmen from pro-nuclear districts, had its first warning about conditions at Knolls in 1959. In March of that year, two representatives of the International Union of Electrical Workers appeared before the subcommittee on research and development to complain about unsafe conditions and practices at Knolls. Jack Suarez, president of Local 301 AE (for atomic energy), and business agent William Hoffman said employees' radiation exposure records were poorly maintained and hadn't been provided to several hundred workers who had left Knolls and had requested them. The two men felt that decontamination and radiation monitoring were so inadequate as to pose a health risk. In addition, GE had cut the staff dedicated to health physics monitoring from forty a decade earlier to ten. The two union representatives expressed concern about radioactive waste that had been released into the Mohawk River, and they also recommended that a qualified and disinterested agency, such as the U.S. Public Health Service, assume responsibility for monitoring health and safety at Knolls. "We have no confidence that the General Electric Company's system of self-monitoring by unqualified or indifferent employees provides adequate protection," the two asserted in their testimony.

That the Congressmen on the committee even asked Rickover about the union's allegations is doubtful; such concerns would have been considered inconsequential, even unpatriotic, at the time. The primary task of the Naval

Nuclear Propulsion Program was keeping ahead of the Soviets, who were also building nuclear subs, and Rickover's stature was such that his assurances alone would have been enough to satisfy congressional queries, had any existed. "I do not believe there is a man in existence who has the composite knowledge which is embodied in Admiral Rickover," Representative Chet Holifield, author of the original atomic energy act, said during debate in 1958 before Congress approved Rickover's second promotion. During another hearing on June 25, 1959, Representative Clarence Cannon, chairman of the House Committee on Appropriations, introduced Rickover as "the most valuable, the most effective man who has ever been honored with the exalted title [of admiral] since John Paul Jones."

It was a time before Three Mile Island and Chernobyl, a time when General Electric envisioned as many as two thousand nuclear reactors electrifying America's factories and homes. The military's appetite for anything atomic was insatiable, and even ludicrous ideas were given serious study. One of the more outrageous government funded research projects pursued by GE was the atomic-powered aircraft engine, which began in the early 1950s and continued for nearly a decade before the project was abandoned as impractical. By 1959, when CEO Ralph Cordiner appeared on the cover of *Time* pitching atomic energy as "a weapon for industrial progress," General Electric had initiated "Citizen Atom," a multimillion-dollar public relations program to extol the benefits of atomic power and to overcome public fears of an energy source that had leveled two Japanese cities. GE scientists regularly showered the public with statistics that purported to show the safety of atomic energy—a family living next door to an atomic power plant supposedly got less radiation than they would living in a brick home—while one scientist went so far as to drink the waste water at one reactor site to demonstrate the safety of nuclear fuel.

When Jack Shannon arrived at Knolls in 1959 at the height of the Cold War, the nuclear business was brimming with promise. Cordiner had orders in hand for dozens of commercial reactors, and the future of nuclear power looked as bright as one thousand suns. GE was assigning its best and brightest engineers to the task of harnessing the power of the atom, and Shannon's assignment put him among the nation's elite engineering minds. The technical challenge appealed to him; so, too, did the status and prestige of what he considered a plum job.

Shannon's association with General Electric spanned his entire life. Born in 1934, he grew up in hardscrabble Schenectady, a realm of smoke and sweat and a fairly typical outpost of the industrial America of that era. The hillside where he played as a youth offered a sweeping panorama of the old GE. Sirens would sound before the smokestacks were blown to clear them of dirt, a warning to the women of Schenectady to retrieve their wash lest it be soiled. As a crane operator in an iron foundry, Shannon's father, Bernard, was exposed daily to noxious fumes. There were no protective masks in those days, and periodically the old man would clear out his sinuses which had become clogged with soot, a routine that young Jack came to know well. His father would boil water and Vicks Vaporub on the kitchen stove, put his head over the pot, and inhale deeply, a process that after much hacking and snorting extracted a yellowish phlegm. Bernard Shannon retired in 1966 and died several years later of pancreatic cancer. The younger Shannon was determined to avoid life in the foundry.

If you were to nominate a person for the role of whistleblower and adversary against General Electric and the federal government, Jack Shannon would seem a very unlikely choice. Besides holding two degrees in nuclear physics and working as a physicist at Knolls, a job that required security clearance, Shannon had enlisted in the Marines toward the end of the Korean War, rose to the rank of major in the Marine reserves, and had won awards as the top United States Naval Academy recruiter in upstate New York. At five foot eight and 165 pounds, Shannon was about the same size as Welch, had a similar background—Irish Catholic, working-class, educated as an engineer—and a similar outlook on life. Shannon still had the lean physique and steely gaze of a prizefighter, which he had been in his youth. He was small but tough and not one to duck a fight.

A devoted disciple of the Naval Nuclear Propulsion Program, Shannon was intensely patriotic and utterly naive about it. As time passed, however, he began questioning Knolls's commitment to health and safety. For years, he had been assured by supervisors that the pint-sized prototype reactors Kesselring operated—smaller than a standard nuclear power plant but nevertheless lethal in the event of an accident—conformed to the highest safety standards. That was incorrect, as Shannon would later discover. The reactors at Kesselring did not have emergency core cooling systems, which would quench a runaway reactor with an infinite quantity of water, and they also did not have containment vessels to keep accidental radiation releases from escaping to the environment. They still don't today.

There were other events that contributed to Shannon's distrust. All Knolls workers had been required to wear dosimeters, a badge worn on the lapel that detected exposure to radiation, but in 1975, Shannon's dosimeter was taken away, along with those of some two thousand other workers at Knolls. Only the four hundred or so employees who actually worked with the reactors and radioactive material would retain them. Although Shannon objected—he didn't feel comfortable working in a radiation-laden environment without a dosimeter—he was overruled. Exposure to radiation wasn't a danger for most employees, he was told, and the omnipresent dosimeters only contributed to unfounded radiation fears and increased operating costs. Years later, Shannon learned that under federal regulations, the urine of workers who worked in close proximity to nuclear reactors and radioactive material was supposed to be checked every six months for radiation, but his urine had never been sampled, not once in the eleven years he worked in critical assemblies and near radioactive materials.

In the early 1970s, Shannon struck up an association with George Fountain, who had run a building at Niskayuna known by its designation as "H2," which was charged with the handling and disposal of liquid radioactive waste and sat atop a hillside overlooking the Mohawk River. Disposal of liquid waste—mostly water laced with nuclear contaminants, including plutonium, uranium, cesium, and strontium—had always been a problem. Until 1964, it had been routinely dumped into the Mohawk, which empties into the Hudson River. Dumping radioactive waste was permitted even though the Mohawk was a source of drinking water and recreation for communities downstream. The state set limits on the permissible discharge each year, and GE always claimed to be well within the thresholds.

The stories Fountain told cast doubt on those claims. Fountain recalled one occasion in the late 1950s when the state had called to say that the radiation monitors downstream weren't functioning and *not* to release any radioactivity that day, but because H2 had a big backlog of waste to unload, Dominic Manieri, who worked for Fountain, decided to release a huge quantity of radioactivity all at once, six hundred curies. By contrast, the federal government estimates that *fifteen* curies of radioactive iodine were released into the atmosphere in 1979 at Three Mile Island. Six hundred curies was four times the amount GE had officially claimed were dumped into the Mohawk in all discharges prior to 1964. In addition, Fountain said other river dumpings went undetected and unreported. The state of New York later dredged the Mohawk to clear it of radioactivity that hadn't been washed out to the Atlantic Ocean, as was thought by chemists at the lab, but instead had settled on the river bottom.

Loyal and conscientious, Shannon had a distinguished career at General Electric. In 1982, Albert Kakretz, the general manager of Knolls, had promoted Shannon to head the Nuclear Criticality Safety, Industrial Safety and Industrial Hygiene department, which monitored health and safety procedures at the Department of Energy facility. It was in this job that Shannon got his first introduction to another problem, that of "tombstones," hot radioactive waste that had been buried. A huge one had been excavated that year from a hillside at the Kesselring site. Since the 1950s the hillside had been the resting place for a 120-ton reactor vessel, about the size of a mobile home, that had been extracted from the *Seawolf.* The highly radioactive hunk of metal, buried in dirt and, it was feared, contaminating groundwater, was dug up and shipped to Idaho for burial.

There were many other tombstones. A few months after taking his new job, Don Belouin, a concerned colleague, escorted Shannon around the grounds at Knolls to show him the sites of buried radioactive waste, including one spot where they found about a dozen metal drums partially sticking out of the ground. Alarmed, Shannon then spent several months combing through the lab's records. He discovered that Knolls had been the burial ground for an estimated 389 tons of toxic and radioactive wastes, held in steel drums that numbered in the thousands and buried at dozens of sites near the lab. Even more alarming, accurate records didn't exist, and there was no way of knowing exactly what was buried, and where.

After three years as head of nuclear safety, Shannon's career suddenly took a turn for the worse with a report he issued, in November 1985, that was highly critical of the lab. The report said that managers at one Knolls site had violated numerous regulations, including the deliberate falsification of records on worker exposure to asbestos. Few health issues were as sensitive to the Navy as asbestos—it was a problem that extended well beyond Knolls. Reactors, laboratories, and ships were loaded with it. Despite years of exemplary performance, Shannon was stripped of his management job. The following September he was demoted again. He claimed this was retaliation. Bob Stater, a fellow physicist who had worked at Knolls for thirty-three years, resigned in protest over Shannon's treatment. "The whole thing was such a farce," Stater later recalled. "There was so much management corruption I didn't feel I should be wasting time in a place like that." Shannon's allegations have never been proven.

Demoted and humiliated, Shannon was returned to the physics department, doing work he hadn't done in twenty years. Although considered one of the top physicists at the lab, he had little background in computers, and his new tasks were exclusively computer-dependent. It was Kakretz's way of meting out punishment to a worker he considered disloyal. "They didn't make any effort to train Jack, and show him how to do the computations. They just put him in there and let him sweat. He was really downcast. What they did to him you wouldn't do to a dog," recalls George Fountain, who worked in an adjacent office.

Early in 1988, Shannon sought help. Although he still held the naive belief that the government would do the right thing, the rules of conduct of the military-industrial complex virtually ensured that it couldn't. Once Kakretz learned that Shannon had gone to the Department of Energy with his complaints, the retaliation against him only intensified. Superiors recommended that he seek psychiatric counseling; one former boss, who in 1979 had told security personnel that Shannon was "a person of unquestioned honesty and integrity," suddenly changed his assessment. The supervisor characterized him as a malcontent who had failed to perform his managerial functions effectively.

In November 1989, four years after his first demotion, Shannon went public, telling his story to a congressional subcommittee and to Sam Donaldson on ABC's *Prime Time Live*. Shannon was on the verge of a nervous breakdown. He was working at the lab during the day and at night poring over a cellar full of documents he had obtained through Freedom of Information Act filings. The documents included his own personnel and security files, which he claimed his superiors at Knolls had falsified in a failed attempt to get his security clearance revoked.*

In January 1990, he took what was to have been a temporary leave of absence from the lab for health reasons, and never returned. Six months later, he was awarded the Cavallo Prize for Moral Courage in Business and Government, a recognition given annually to outstanding whistleblowers. A year later, in April 1991, Shannon confronted Jack Welch for the first and only time, at that year's shareholders meeting. Welch was primed for another bout with antinuclear activists in what had become an annual ritual. The meeting was held in a theater in Decatur, Alabama, near Huntsville, the same city where some forty years before, GE and government scientists had done much of their pioneering work building rockets in the early days of America's space program.

Several hundred people made the trek to Decatur and cast their eyes on Shannon as he approached the microphone to address the assembly. Welch introduced him as a former employee on disability pension. He spared his audience the details of how Shannon had come to be disabled, and how General Electric had treated him. Nor did Shannon choose to talk about

---

* The lawsuit that Shannon subsequently filed on these claims is discussed on p. 179.

himself. Instead, he had come to Decatur to inform the public about conditions at the Knolls Atomic Power Laboratory, conditions he felt posed a threat to their safety. As a nuclear engineer and former officer of Knolls, Shannon knew exactly what the deficiencies were—documenting them had gotten him demoted—and he began with what he considered the most serious offenses. "Why has the General Electric Company allowed Knolls to run nuclear reactors all these years without emergency core cooling systems or containment vessels?" Shannon asked Welch.

To most listeners, it was meaningless jargon, but Welch, who had studied nuclear physics in graduate school, should have known what Shannon meant. Because Knolls was a Department of Energy facility, run according to protocols established during the Cold War, it was not required to have containment vessels and emergency core cooling systems, safety features that the Nuclear Regulatory Commission required of every licensed commercial nuclear power plant in the United States. That was just one of the safety deficiencies, and Shannon began to list more. After about a minute, with Shannon discussing the third of fifteen deficiencies he planned to cite, Welch ended the dialogue. Shannon's attempt to inform shareholders had been as futile as his pleas to the government. Yet the brief encounter foreshadowed great events: Shannon's dogged determination to tell the story of Knolls would contribute years later to Welch's decision to get out of the business of making nuclear arms.

ALTHOUGH THE WORST of GE's activities in the nuclear business had predated Welch, as CEO he was now showered with the fallout. The nuclear business had never been a favorite of Welch's, who had cast a disapproving eye on it almost from the day he assumed control of General Electric in 1981. One of his first exercises as the new CEO had been to ask the leaders of each of GE's businesses to formulate a business plan for the 1980s, and the one he received from Nuclear Power enraged him. Their strategy anticipated that GE would build three new reactors a year. "You can't believe that!" Welch cried to the assembled Ph.D.s from Nuclear. There hadn't been an order for a new nuclear reactor since 1975, nor did it appear likely there would be an order anytime soon.

The business, whose commercial division alone employed more than nine thousand people, not counting thousands more who did government work maintaining and augmenting America's nuclear arsenal, was staffed on the assumption that nuclear power had merely suffered a temporary setback two years before. GE engineers had rationalized the accident that had occurred in Pennsylvania at Three Mile Island on the morning of March 28, 1979. After all, it hadn't even been a GE reactor. The culprit, Babcock & Wilcox, was a relative newcomer to nuclear engineering and had sold only eight of the seventy nuclear-power plants operating in the United States. Westinghouse and General Electric were still the nation's atomic heavyweights. These nuclear scientists, the finest engineering minds of their generation, couldn't believe that the industry they had nurtured from its infancy for more than thirty years was on the verge of extinction.

Welch wasn't so sentimental. He told them to rethink their assumptions, and they returned with a revised plan that assumed no new plant sales, and instead called for a strategy that would focus on providing nuclear fuel and services to existing plants. More than half the jobs in the commercial nuclear division were eliminated, but the strategy worked: The business, which was profitable throughout the 1980s, ended up generating nearly $1 billion in earnings in the decade.

The problems, though, were not financial.

GE's involvement in nuclear arms was extensive. Its ties to the military dated back to World War I and took a quantum leap in World War II. As GE grew in size and stature in the defense industry, eventually becoming the second-greatest provider of armaments and supplies to the Pentagon, it became a prime target for peace activists, who routinely submitted ballot resolutions at shareholder meetings calling for GE to quit the nuclear weapons business. There were also skeletons tucked away in GE's nuclear closet. As a participant in the Manhattan Project, General Electric had garnered opportunity as well as responsibility; the opportunity was gaining a foothold in the early nuclear business, which in the 1950s went beyond the charter of national defense with the construction of the first commercial reactors, while the responsibility was handling the government's nuclear affairs at two federal facilities. One was the Knolls Atomic Power Laboratory, the other the Hanford Nuclear Reservation in Richland, Washington, a parcel of arid federal land about half the size of Rhode Island in the middle of the state that supplied the plutonium that powered America's atomic arsenal, including material for the bomb dropped on Nagasaki in August 1945.

The business of making atomic weapons had been extraordinarily secretive. This secrecy contributed to the magnitude of the misdeeds that were committed in the pursuit of nuclear hegemony, as the government and its activities were shielded from public scrutiny under the protective blanket of national defense. It's now clear that maintaining the peace through nuclear means carried an extraordinary price. Defense contractors, under the auspices of the government, had conducted experiments on human guinea pigs, including injecting some subjects with plutonium. In addition, the Cold War had generated a pulsating wasteland of lethal atomic debris, stretching from the Pacific Northwest to Siberia. Removing radioactive waste from federal weapons facilities has already triggered what is likely to become the largest public works project in U.S. history, an effort expected to exceed the $160 billion estimated for the government bailout of the savings and loan industry. The final cost could be higher than $200 billion over the next thirty years, experts predict; cleaning up Hanford alone is estimated at more than $60 billion by the Department of Energy.

For years, Hanford's mission and GE's role in it were kept secret—people who worked for GE during the years it ran Hanford often didn't know what was going on. "More than once I had the feeling someone knew something I should know but they weren't telling me," says Clayton Crandall, a retired General Electric attorney who was stationed at Hanford from 1960 to 1965, when GE turned management of the facility over to other defense contractors. By the 1980s, bits and pieces of what went on at Hanford began leaking out in the press, in scientific studies, and in congressional hearings, as the legacy of Cold War secrecy and superpower competition slowly came to light.

In 1986, formerly classified documents disclosed that Hanford had regularly showered its neighbors with radioactivity, and one memo described an experiment, called Green Run, in which government and GE managers in 1949 had deliberately released a huge cloud of radioactive iodine 131 and xenon, to see how far downwind it could be traced. The cloud drifted four hundred miles, all the way to the California-Oregon border, carrying hundreds, perhaps thousands, of times more radiation than that emitted at Three Mile Island. Also in 1986, a congressional subcommittee chaired by Representative Edward Markey of Massachusetts made an even more startling disclosure. The subcommittee's report, written by Markey and entitled *American Nuclear Guinea Pigs*, disclosed thirty-one experiments, dating back to 1945, in which some six hundred U.S. citizens had become "nuclear calibration devices for experimenters run amok." "Too many of these experiments used human subjects that were captive audiences or populations . . . considered 'expendable,' " Markey wrote, "the elderly, prisoners, hospital patients, who might not have retained their full faculties for informed consent." Not until 1995, with the establishment by President Clinton of a presidential advisory committee, would the full extent of government-sponsored human radiation experiments become known: nearly four thousand subjects between 1944 and 1974, eighteen of whom were hospital patients injected with plutonium, in most instances without their consent. Those eighteen subjects, or surviving families, received $400,000 each in compensation, as well as an in-person apology from Department of Energy officials.

Seen through the prism of more modern sensibilities, the science of the early nuclear age seems barbaric, but unfortunately for Welch, it was barbarism his company had been involved in and therefore had to keep at bay. One of the more extensive and gruesome experiments disclosed in the Markey report had been performed on inmates at a prison in Walla Walla, Washington, near Hanford. Starting in 1963, sixty-four prisoners had had their scrotums and testes irradiated to determine the effects of radiation on human reproductive organs. Each volunteer was paid $5 plus cigarettes for each radiation exposure and had to sign a consent form, which said in part, "I hereby agree to submit to X-ray radiation of my scrotum and testes." Although the inmates were warned about the possibility of sterility and radiation burns, the forms said nothing about the risk of testicular cancer.

Four months after GE began the prisoner studies, Carlos Newton Jr., a manager in the radiation protection department at Hanford, wrote a memo referring to past experiments the company had conducted at Hanford, where the subjects' consent apparently hadn't been obtained. "The records on the past experiments are inadequate," he said. "The experiments do not appear to have been in compliance with the criminal codes of the State of Washington and there is some question as to whether or not the experiments were conducted in compliance with federal laws." (One former Hanford employee claims he was fired after refusing to submit to a test injection of radioactive material.) The nature of the experiments described in the Newton memo, dated December 12, 1963, was never ascertained.

For Welch, the disclosures of GE's misdeeds at Hanford represented a black eye of the most unseemly sort. Welch dislikes negative publicity, particularly any that might have a financial liability attached to it, and he was beginning to get substantial negative publicity in the nuclear business. GE had taken a leap forward as a defense contractor with the 1986 acquisition of RCA, which was a significant supplier of weaponry of its own. That same year, Infact, a little-known activist organization working out of the same second-floor office in Boston's historic North End that anarchists Sacco and Vanzetti once rented, began a boycott against GE. It was an improbable match: in one corner Infact, supported with a shoestring $700,000 budget from hundreds of individual donors, and in the other GE, one of the world's most powerful multinational corporations with a full-time legal and lobbying staff of more than five hundred.

Infact already had one corporate scalp under its belt. It had been founded in 1977 by three students at the University of Minnesota to wage a campaign against Nestlé and its marketing of infant formula in Third World countries. The formula wasn't the problem per se; the dirty water it was mixed with was. By 1984, Nestlé had grown weary of being labeled a baby killer, and the Swiss food giant finally agreed in writing to implement the World Health Organization's code for marketing breast milk substitutes to underdeveloped nations.

In 1984, when Infact chose GE as its next target, the United States was building five new nuclear bombs every day, and GE played an important role in the construction of every one. It was the sole manufacturer of the detonators that triggered the explosive force of the neutron bombs, devices manufactured since 1956 at a plant in Largo, Florida, just north of St. Petersburg. Infact hoped that by heaping negative publicity on an image-sensitive industry leader and perhaps persuading GE consumers to join the boycott, it might be able to coerce Welch to quit the business. The first public confrontation occurred in 1987, at the GE shareholders' meeting in Montgomery, Alabama, when June Stark Casey rose to tell her story to Welch and company directors, the first of three appearances she would make at GE annual meetings.

Casey was nineteen years old in December 1949, when, as a sophomore at Whitman College in Walla Walla, Washington, fifty miles downwind from the Hanford nuclear reservation, she began losing her hair permanently and was diagnosed with an extreme case of hypothyroidism. She has worn a wig ever since, and her subsequent medical problems—miscarriage, stillbirth, thyroid nodules—were maladies associated with overexposure to radiation. For years Casey assumed that her condition stemmed from some unknown exposure to radiation, and it wasn't until 1986, in a newspaper article that preceded the Markey report, that she finally got an inkling of how she might have been exposed. The secret documents that disclosed the Green Run test established that it had occurred on December 2, 1949, just weeks before her hair began falling out. After telling her story, Casey asked Welch for help in ascertaining what she might have been exposed to.

"Mrs. Casey," she recalls Welch responding, "we called Hanford and they said they knew nothing about this radiation experiment. And besides, we were not in the nuclear weapons business at that time."

"But, Mr. Welch," Casey responded, "my research reveals that following management by DuPont, General Electric managed Hanford from 1946 to 1964, before turning it over to Westinghouse."*

Casey's appearance was the first salvo in a six-year war between Infact and General Electric. The Infact boycott was unique in that it attracted support not just from left-wing, antinuclear zealots but from mainstream America as well. In July 1991, for instance, the United Methodist Church, America's third-largest religious denomination and hardly a bastion of radical politics, took action against GE when the church's Board of Pensions decided to divest its $23 million holding in GE stock. The following May, delegates to the church's annual general conference in Louisville, Kentucky, voted sixty-four to fourteen in favor of a resolution urging General Electric to "cease nuclear-weapons production and promotion and to convert to peace-oriented manufacture." The resolution also asked all United Methodist–related institutions, including its seventy-eight hospitals, to "consider GE's role in nuclear-weapons production" when weighing the purchase of a GE product.

The hospital connection ultimately proved to be a point of vulnerability. Many hospitals, particularly those with a religious affiliation, found an inherent contradiction between, on the one hand, GE's manufacture of such life-saving diagnostic equipment as magnetic resonance and computed tomography scanners and, on the other hand, its role in nuclear weaponry. The leading American producer of medical imaging equipment, GE lost perhaps as much as $50 million in orders from hospitals fed up with its pronuclear policies. Dealing with disaffected customers also proved enormously distracting for upper management. GE executives, including John Trani, Med Systems president, made dozens of calls on hospital administrators who were refusing to buy GE equipment because of the boycott, and Welch himself intervened on several occasions to try to quell the uprising.

In October 1990, for example, the Sisters of Charity of the Incarnate Word, a Roman Catholic order that runs fifteen health care facilities in five southwestern states, informed Trani that it would no longer buy GE medical equipment. Trani sent one contingent to Texas to deal with the problem, then

* Casey followed up her comments with a four-page letter requesting additional information. In reply, GE spokesman Ford Slater said the company had left its records behind at Hanford, and that all they knew was what had been published in the newspapers.

In the years since, Casey has undergone two breast surgeries to combat cancer diagnosed in July 1997, one of which was a partial mastectomy. A benign esophageal tumor was removed. She has taken a prescription pain medication the past five years for unremitting pain in her spine. In addition, her dentist has noticed a massive loss of teeth in the past two years, and has speculated that it might be due to radiation exposure.

went himself. Finally, Welch had five nuns flown to Fairfield on a GE corporate jet for their meeting with the chairman. It was an odd spectacle: the nuns, several dressed in habit and sitting in a corporate dining room, listening over lunch to Welch recount his Irish Catholic upbringing in Salem, and his days as a devout altar boy. At the outset, Welch announced that the company would not renew its contract to produce neutron triggers in Largo, Florida, a decision made after the government, for the first time, had demanded that GE be held liable for any future environmental remediation. "I think he thought that would stop the conversation," says Sister Susan Mika, who attended the meeting. It didn't. The nuns, who gave Welch a paperweight inscribed with an admonition from the prophet Isaiah about turning the instruments of war into plowshares, held their ground. So did Welch. "He's a very intense person," Sister Mika adds. "That's his personality, but he didn't go off the wall."

Infact still wasn't satisfied. In 1990, it decided to turn up the flame a notch by making the film *Deadly Deception*, which was released in June 1991. Welch now had a full-scale public relations nightmare on his hands. The film, made in nine months for just $65,000, was testament to what could be done with a little elbow grease, a few Freedom of Information Act requests, and some videotape. Debra Chasnoff, the film's producer, who knew Infact from her days as an antinuke organizer at Wellesley College, had made only one film previously and had assisted on another. Hers was seat-of-the-pants filmmaking, but it worked.

The twenty-nine-minute documentary told in lurid detail the chilling tales of Hanford and the Knolls Atomic Power Laboratory. Juxtaposing GE's "people helping people" commercials with tragic tales of GE employees and neighbors exposed to radiation, the film highlighted General Electric's involvement in nuclear weaponry.

Infact sent copies of *Deadly Deception* to GE managers, institutional investors, stock analysts, and customers. It gave several GE nuclear whistleblowers the vindication they had sought for many years, and publicized their cause. Among those who benefited were Jack Shannon, and the family of another former Knolls engineer, Richard Frederic Cole, who had been deceased for fifteen years.

THE DEATH OF DICK COLE on July 26, 1976, was one of those events that at the time seemed to signify nothing other than a profound personal tragedy. It would take years for the broader significance to enter the consciousness of the men who knew Cole and who were suspicious about his untimely, inexplicable death. All that lived on, initially, was the grief Cole's passing had brought to the Cole family, a grief that is apparent even to this day—Don Cole, an economics professor at Drew University in Madison, New Jersey, still weeps over the loss of his brother. He cries partly in sadness, partly in anger: sadness over the passing of a good and gentle man who left behind a widow and two small children, a son aged seven and a daughter aged four; anger over the "profound lies" that were told by General Electric and the federal government in an attempt to evade the tough questions Dick Cole posed to his managers before he died. Why didn't you protect me with safer equipment? Why didn't you use better methods for measuring and recording radiation exposures? Why didn't you educate your workers in the health risks associated with radioactive materials?

Those questions to this day remain unanswered, for there has never been a thorough, independent investigation into Cole's death. The government and GE have taken refuge behind their official statement that Cole received a "small" amount of occupational radiation exposure, a dosage roughly equal to what he would have been exposed to in the environment. In its review of Cole's records, the company did not find excessive exposure, or any evidence that the cancer that claimed his life was linked to his employment at the Kesselring site at Knolls.

Dick Cole was just thirty-two years old when he died. He had not been a drinker or a smoker. According to the postmortem of Dr. Robert S. Martin, Cole's oncologist, the malignant melanoma discovered ten months before had invaded nearly every organ of Cole's body, including his liver, kidneys, adrenals, lungs, spine, and bowel.

The atomic activities at Knolls produced two common radioactive byproducts of nuclear fission, cobalt 58 and cobalt 60, which are known to cause cancer, and traces of which, GE acknowledged, were detected in Cole's body. Once ingested, cobalt decays in the lung and spleen, causing cell irregularities. The progression of Cole's cancer was consistent with internal exposure to cobalt: The largest tumors were found on the left lung and in the spleen. The tumors, however, were melanomas, skin cancers typically associated with ultraviolet radiation. Melanoma usually starts on the outside, the skin, and works its way in, spreading to internal organs and tissue. But in Cole's case, the cancer apparently started on the inside. No evidence of skin melanoma was ever found, nor was any point of external entry through which the cancer might have entered his system.

Cole's death was all the more poignant because he had been relentlessly upbeat and well liked, had had many friends at Knolls, and had thought the world of General Electric. "I'm gonna be a big shot in that company someday," he would tell colleagues and relatives. He took evening classes to learn about business and to supplement his engineering education. Cole, a 1965 graduate of the United States Merchant Marine Academy on Long Island, was also a flag-waving patriot. "This country is the best one around," Cole was quoted in the *Hartford Courant*, even as he was dying. Clearly, he believed the system would work if people tried to make it work.

Cole was convinced that his illness stemmed from repeated over-exposure to radiation, and he spent his final months preparing an affidavit "to set the record straight," which might serve as the basis for a lawsuit after his death. The thirty-five-page document—with three addendums and twelve exhibits—summarized, in chilling detail, the many occasions he believed he had been exposed to radiation. Those exposures weren't part of his official health record, he concluded, because the laboratory was grossly negligent in its procedures for monitoring radiation. Indeed, the affidavit served as a broad commentary on Knolls, indicting not only unsafe and unconscientious health and safety practices but the callous attitudes of management that promoted such policies. "In the nearly nine years of my employment at Knolls Atomic Power Laboratory, I have seen numerous instances where the health and safety of employees and the general public have been disregarded to the benefit of the laboratory due to priorities established by upper management," Cole wrote.

One such instance had occurred in April 1975, when Cole wanted to include in a public report the disclosure that more than twenty million gallons of radioactive liquid waste had been discharged from another Knoll installation in Windsor, Connecticut, into the Farmington River between 1960 and 1975. The disclosure was deleted from the report, Cole alleged, at the request of higher-ups in the Office of Naval Reactors.

Cole's duties as a refueling engineer put him in close contact with the nuclear reactors at the Kesselring site in West Milton. During the thirty-nine months he worked there, from December 1967 to February 1971, Cole performed among the most lethal work at the facility, supervising the refueling of one reactor, the shutdown of another, and the disassembly of a third. On one occasion, Cole recalled, he sat on top of the pressure vessel head of a reactor for four hours while guiding a new fuel cell into place, but as his affidavit spells out in great detail, Cole wasn't given a respirator to wear or any form of self-contained breathing apparatus. Samples weren't taken to monitor radiation in the air being breathed. The only monitoring that Cole and his colleagues received was dosimetry badges—and no testing was done to verify their accuracy. More sophisticated methods of detecting internal exposure to radiation, such as whole body scans, weren't employed either. Cole had begun calling these shortcomings to the attention of his supervisors before transferring, in 1971, from the Kesselring site to Windsor.

While at Windsor, Cole received his first whole body scan, a radiation monitoring technique. The scan results showed his system had traces of cobalt 58 and cobalt 60. Even though his supervisors said the positive results were well within permissible levels and that a followup investigation of his exposure was not necessary, Cole persisted. "As I acquired more knowledge in the field of radiation health and dosimetry, I came to the conclusion that all internal exposure is unacceptable and that all positive reported results of internal monitoring should be investigated," Cole wrote in his affidavit.

In the spring of 1975, Cole developed severe back pains, the result, he thought, of a fall he had taken. The pain intensified during the following months, and subsequent X-rays located a slight shadow beside the left lung. Exploratory surgery was recommended. When the surgeons opened him up in September 1975, it was discovered that he had a malignant tumor and that his cancer was far more extensive than initially thought: In addition to the egg-sized melanoma on the lung, four other tumors of the same variety were diagnosed during an eighteen-day stay in the hospital. Cole was told that at best, he would live a few years.

While Cole was in the hospital, he and his doctors demanded an investigation of his radiation exposures and GE complied. Cole knew of many hazardous exposures during his nine years with GE, but the report he received, dated October 8, 1975, covered only one. Robert Zendle, the manager of radiological health and environmental surveillance, who prepared the report, concluded that Cole had received in this one exposure "only about twice" what the general public would have in "natural radiation exposure." Cole then asked to examine his radiation records. At first, GE declined to provide them—they were classified, he was told. Eventually, after Cole threatened to sue, the records were released. After he reviewed them, he stated in his affidavit: "I can not categorically state that radiation exposure caused my malignant melanoma because I am not qualified to do so. I can only point out the negligence on the part of Knolls Atomic Power Laboratory and state that at the age of thirty-two my family and I are faced with the agony of knowing that I have a terminal disease with a statistically poor prognosis."

Although Cole had prepared the affidavit partly to assist his wife in pressing a lawsuit, none was filed. Following Cole's death, Joe Thompson, his father-in-law, gave the affidavit to several attorneys, who judged Dick's case to be eminently winnable. But the family soon discovered the harsh reality of employment at a federal nuclear installation. According to the laws in effect at that time, the family could recover damages limited only to basic workers' compensation. As a result, the family had no leverage with which to extract a settlement from GE—and none was offered. Cole's widow "didn't get a bloody penny, not one plugged nickel," Thompson says bitterly. To this day, his daughter refuses to discuss the case, even with family members. "She has tried to erase it from her memory," Thompson says.

In the end, Dick Cole's life and death were preserved for future generations in some memorable correspondence. Cole wrote love letters to his children, son Ricky and daughter Becky, to be opened after his death. Writing those letters "was the hardest thing I ever had to do," he wrote in his final letter to his brother Don. He also wrote:

> If people ask why I wrote [the affidavit] tell them to look at my young wife and two kids and think what they have gone through. I have been in pain now for nearly a year and the thought of not being with them much longer tears at my heart whenever I look at them. I bear no one ill will at Knolls; I think I have made some fine friends there. I do think that it is through their negligent policies that I was unnecessarily exposed to internal and external doses of radiation of unknown quantities and that this is why I am now dying of cancer.

Less than a month before he died, Cole received a letter from the president of the United States. Although Gerald Ford knew that Cole had a fatal disease, he didn't know that Cole felt the United States government might have contributed in some way to his death. The letter from the White House, in which Ford expressed his "sincere regret that things could not have worked out differently," was written to explain the scheduling conflict that prevented him from attending the Merchant Marine Academy's commencement ceremony, which Cole had asked him to do. Cole undoubtedly felt a tearful irony while reading President Ford's closing words: "I also want to tell you how very much I admire your spirit and personal courage. The example you have set for your family and friends is an inspiring one. You have my deepest respect and warmest regards."

BY 1988, Dick Cole had been dead twelve years. His children were grown, his widow remarried. His death had driven a wedge in the Cole family. The former Mrs. Cole wanted to forget the past; his grieving brother Don couldn't. Cole was long forgotten by everyone at the Knolls Atomic Power Laboratory, everyone except Frank Bordell. Bordell, a nationally respected health physicist, was charged with assessing and interpreting the radiation exposures of Knolls workers. As such, he was a gatekeeper of science as well as morality, and Bordell was exactly the kind of person you'd want to be doing a job like that. His academic credentials were impeccable. He had an undergraduate degree and two graduate degrees in atomic and nuclear physics, radiological health, and dosimetry; he was American Board of Health Physics certified and had served two terms on the national governing body that set standards for the health physics profession; he had been at the prestigious Argonne National Laboratory before joining GE in 1968, and he had worked in the field of radiological health for twenty-eight years, twenty of them with General Electric.

Bordell was also a man of great conscience, which at times had proven problematic at a place like Knolls. As a young man, he felt the Lord's calling, and had studied for the priesthood. Although he had left the seminary, in adulthood he carried rosary beads that he clutched on the job. Bordell was a brooder, and often what he brooded over was the accuracy of his measurements and the integrity of his mathematical computations. He considered scientific precision absolutely essential to what he did. Although measuring radiation exposures was a task few people at Knolls understood, Bordell knew his was a science that had to be above reproach, for lives hung in the balance. When he would share with colleagues his burdens about the accuracy of his radiation computations, they would find his constant consternation amusing. "You know what your problem is, Frank?" they'd say to him. "You're incapable of telling a lie."

As a health physicist, Bordell practiced an arcane profession. The health consequences of exposure to low levels of radiation is one of the most controversial issues in the nuclear community. Some experts argue that any amount of radiation poses a threat to humans, while others maintain there is no evidence to support such concern. Even measuring how much radiation the body has been exposed to is an inexact science. There were two types of exposure Knolls workers received. The first, external radiation, bombarded the body and was supposedly detected by external monitors such as dosimeters or film badges. Radiation could also be swallowed or inhaled, subjecting organs and tissue to internal exposure. Detecting and measuring internal exposures, Bordell's specialty, was a challenging task—if someone tested positive to internal radiation exposure as Dick Cole had, either through a urine sample or a body scan, complicated computations were performed to estimate the most probable date of intake. Once this date was established mathematically by applying standard decay rates of radiation, the dose a worker had been exposed to could be calculated.

Cole's death had laid a heavy burden on Bordell's conscience. Dose calculations were not routinely performed for all workers at Knolls because they had to be done manually, and the staff simply wasn't sufficient to calculate dose exposures for every worker. Bordell had gone back over the Cole file again and again, trying to determine if something had been overlooked or miscalculated. Cole's death was suspicious—thirty-two-year-old men don't die the way he had without probable cause—but the official record didn't show that cause. The calculations had been done accurately, and although they indicated a cobalt level in Cole's system that was well below federal thresholds, Bordell was nevertheless troubled. He was beginning to wonder if the way Knolls measured and calculated radiation uptakes was an accurate method, or if the federal standards had any meaning at all.

Contributing to his suspicions were other deaths he knew of. Bordell had visited several Knolls workers in their final hours; years before, he had sat clutching his rosary beads in the sweltering hospital room of Dominic Manieri, whose skin had the same yellowish cast that Bordell had witnessed in previous bedside visits with other people. Manieri, suffering intense pain from intestinal and colon cancer, pleaded with Bordell to throw him out the fourth-floor window of Schenectady's Ellis Hospital. Bordell knew Manieri's work history, and he knew it was more than happenstance that he was dying of cancer. When Manieri retired in 1977, he had accumulated the second-highest lifetime radiation exposure ever recorded at the lab. Bordell had heard stories from Ernie Phoenix, a colleague of Manieri's who had also died of cancer, about radiation-contaminated water overflowing from storage tanks in the building where they worked and running down the ceiling and walls like a waterfall. Manieri and Phoenix had been part of a cleanup crew that mopped up the radioactive sludge, on that occasion and others.

Bordell's bedside vigils made an indelible mark on him, and he vowed to do everything he could to be more diligent in the future.

CHAPTER EIGHT

DEADLY DECEPTION II

AT THE TIME OF FRANK BORDELL'S EPIPHANY, Jack Welch was having one of his own. Welch was growing tired of hearing the complaints of a war-weary officer corps suffering from extreme battle fatigue, and in 1988 his rhetoric took on a decidedly more humane tone. Understandably, there was great skepticism inside General Electric about the legitimacy of his transformation, and while Welch was articulating his new vision of empowerment and shared values to a Crotonville audience, one listener summoned up the courage to express doubt. "How will you know your new philosophies are working and are being accepted?" Welch was asked. "When my style of leadership is no longer accepted," he replied, without missing a beat.

Unfortunately, command and control was the entrenched way of doing things at GE. Total warfare had brought a kind of martial law, a take-no-prisoners mentality that was utterly lacking in compassion. Welch, who had heard words of anger, frustration, even rage about the way the company treated people, realized that battle fatigue could undermine his entire revolution if something wasn't done to counteract it, and the cynicism it spread. The program he initiated to move from Welch the Terminator to Welch the Facilitator was called Work-Out.

The concept of empowering employees was not new. One of the first champions of greater workplace democracy had been, ironically, Charles Steinmetz, a Socialist who besides being a scientific genius had also dabbled in worker-management theory. Steinmetz's concepts were advanced in the 1950s by the late W. Edwards Deming, arguably the most seminal thinker on management theory of the late twentieth century. Deming distilled his theory into fourteen points, which were rejected by American corporations but were embraced, with great success, by the Japanese, who each year award the Deming Prize to reward outstanding achievement in product quality and to commemorate his contributions to the rebuilding of postwar Japan. To this day, Deming's portrait is one of three that hang in the headquarters foyer of Toyota Motor Corporation in Toyota City, Japan, the other two being Japanese Emperor Akihito and Toyota founder Shoichiro Toyoda. As the Japanese seized an ever increasing share of world markets in the 1980s, American corporations took another look at Deming and his theories. They began to embrace the man they had repudiated earlier.

Deming believed that continuous improvement, *kaizen* as the Japanese called it, could be achieved only by redefining the relationship between boss and subordinate. Quality couldn't be inspected into products, it had to be built in, and he advocated the elimination of production quotas, slogans, exhortations, targets, and other traditional practices that robbed workers of pride in their work. Deming also believed that fear was a terrible motivator of people because it worked against continuous improvement. Instead, an institution had to create constancy of purpose (point one of his famous fourteen points), and layoffs only diminished this sense of purpose and heightened fear, which was an enemy of quality.

Welch wasn't about to eschew layoffs. That would jeopardize what he cherished above all else, earnings. Still, much of the rhetoric he embraced in his Work-Out program was pure Deming. The program began in 1988 as a series of local gatherings patterned after New England town meetings. In groups of thirty to one hundred, hourly and salaried employees would spend several days at a site away from the business discussing common problems. A facilitator, typically an academic from Harvard Business School or a consultant from a prominent consultancy, would serve as referee for the discussions, with the objective being to define problems openly and reach a consensus on solutions. Employees would be listened to and empowered, trust would be built. "Ultimately," Welch said at the time, "we're talking about redefining the relationship between boss and subordinate."

Welch's decision to embrace Work-Out was immediately praised in the business press. The appellation "Neutron Jack" was replaced with a characterization of Welch as nothing less than the great emancipator. "GE's chairman is pushing ideas that could transform the art of management," *Fortune* proclaimed early in 1989, in a cover story that purported to reveal the new Welch. The *Washington Post* enthusiastically described Work-Out as Welch's most unusual effort to remake the company, "because it strikes right at the heart of GE's corporate culture and represents a significant rethinking in the way companies are managed."

It was great copy, portraying a makeover Welch himself wanted to convey—the man who had reinvented General Electric was now seen as re-inventing himself, and the old Welch, the one *Fortune* in 1984 had declared hands down "the toughest boss in America," was gone. In his place was a kinder, gentler Jack, the elder statesman of American business, seen with a broad smile on the cover of *Fortune*, which seemingly affirmed the rebirth of a new man. Yet in their rush to proclaim the new Welch, the business media forgot to ask the most obvious and crucial question: Was the transformation legitimate? Just because he said it was, didn't mean it was so. Could he really "walk the talk," to use his favorite phrase? Would he be willing to sacrifice earnings to empower "associates" and achieve greater workplace democracy? Even if the transformation were legitimate, could he now convince people within GE that it was? Or would he be in their minds, forever, the feared, menacing boss known mostly to the General Electric masses through reputation only? And was it even possible to soften a culture that for eight years had answered Welch's determined call to arms?

The answers could be found in events that began to unfold at the Knolls Atomic Power Laboratory in 1988. At the same time that Welch was claiming to have embraced a new definition of boss-subordinate relationships, the showdown between Frank Bordell, the rosary-bead-clutching health physicist, and his boss, Albert Kakretz, showed how deeply entrenched warfare was in the GE managerial psyche and also cast doubt on the legitimacy of Welch's rebirth.

Of the hundred or so general managers who ran the divisions of General Electric in 1988, none was a more devoted disciple of Welch than Kakretz. A take-charge, no-nonsense executive, he was the very model of the command-and-control managerial mold, taking no prisoners, steamrolling anyone who got in his way, flattening his enemies, and cultivating his allies. Kakretz had begun that process of identifying enemies and eliminating them from the first day he had arrived at Knolls in 1977. One of his first acts had been to install as his top deputy Gerald Sabian, who had an excellent relationship with Rickover, and he took pride in his reputation as a stone-hard, results-oriented businessman. The sign on his office wall, a distinctive twist on a verse of the Twenty-third Psalm, said it all: "I fear no evil because I'm the meanest son of a bitch in the valley."

Kakretz and Sabian tried to surpass each other in meanness, and Jack Shannon early on had a hint of the methodical nature of the purge they had begun. Shannon had received a promotion, and his boss had taken him to the exclusive Mohawk Club in Schenectady to celebrate. Scrawled on the back of Shannon's menu were the names of people on Kakretz's staff, and next to each name were check marks. More than a dozen marks were next to the name of Joe Bulmer, who had just been dismissed. The menu had been left over from a prior personnel session Kakretz had had at the club with Sabian and the other members of his inner circle. Although Shannon dismissed the incident at the time as trivial, almost comical, years later he would come to better understand the significance.

In assembling his "team," Kakretz dealt harshly with the "old guard," defined as anyone who was in a management job prior to his arrival. These people were removed, often abruptly and ruthlessly. Like Welch, Kakretz was dedicated to an agenda of change, and he also shared Welch's belief that there wasn't anything intrinsically special about any business, be it lightbulbs or nuclear reactors—a manager could manage anything. A former Navy officer, Kakretz felt Knolls was desperately in need of the kind of professional management he would employ. Past management had been much too complacent. General Electric was in the business of making money, and in Kakretz's view previous COs had given that goal too little attention; Knolls, in his view, was a ship taking on water and listing badly.

Even under optimal conditions, however, there was little real money to be made at Knolls. It was a quid pro quo in GE's relationship with the Pentagon, a tradeoff to please the admiralty, which didn't want to be saddled with the headache of running the lab. General Electric did that, and the military returned the favor by buying more bombs, the real moneymaker. Because there was little in the way of profit contribution that Knolls could make to the GE coffers, there were few accolades to be had, few kudos that could attract the attention of Welch. Kakretz, though, was an ambitious man. Before coming to Knolls, he had spent time as a strategic planner in Fairfield, where he had rubbed elbows with the power elite. Although Knolls was a backwater, it could also be used as a springboard to greater heights—make change, make it fast, and move on to a vice presidency in the mainstream of General Electric, that was his plan. As the years dragged on and no promotion materialized, however, the prospect that Kakretz might never leave Knolls loomed ever larger. He became increasingly frustrated and bitter. Kakretz felt he had done an excellent job, for which he hadn't gotten sufficient recognition. He was a dutiful soldier, languishing in the motor pool when what he desperately wanted was a combat command.

Welch wasn't the only master Kakretz had to serve. His direct boss was Russ Noll Jr., head of GE Power Systems, whom Welch had hired to take Schenectady down a notch. Welch had often complained that managers in Schenectady, the birthplace of GE, were preoccupied with the past and too willing to rest on their laurels. Indeed, one of Welch's first actions when he became CEO was to tear down Buildings Ten and Twelve at the main plant in downtown Schenectady, which beginning in 1886 had been the site of the Edison Machine Works and had formed the nucleus around which the Schenectady Works had grown. The decision to raze the buildings was as much symbolic as rational—Welch wanted to send a clear signal that the past was history, and management had better start performing if they wanted a future. Noll continued this practice of threat and intimidation, eliminating thousands of jobs, and his cost-cutting memoranda to Kakretz and the eleven other general managers who reported to him and ran the operating divisions within Power Systems were unrelenting. "Please assure removal of bottled water from each of your components," Noll told his charges in one 1988 memo. "It's an unnecessary expense since there is plenty of city water available for drinking."

In addition to Welch and Noll, Kakretz also had the Navy to contend with. According to Navy tradition, the Naval Nuclear Propulsion Program, of which Knolls was the scientific centerpiece, was the epitome of spit and polish. Although that wasn't really the case and never had been, Kakretz convinced himself and the Office of Naval Reactors, his other CO, that it was. Any embarrassment brought upon Rickover or the "program" would be a threat to Kakretz's career. As a consequence, Knolls, which in accordance with Navy tradition had never been an overly tolerant place, became utterly intolerant of dissent. "Some of us used to think we were in Nazi Germany. You were afraid to speak the truth because the truth got you in trouble," recalls George Fountain, a retired Knolls officer.

Above all, Kakretz demanded conformity. Minimizing embarrassment became a management imperative. Managers who put a lid on problems and did it quietly were part of the "team," and those who brought attention to the problems were enemies. It was Kakretz's demands for conformity that had gotten Jack Shannon demoted. Although Shannon didn't know it at the time, one reason he had been selected in 1982 as head of nuclear safety was that Kakretz, who admired Shannon's distinguished military record, thought he'd be a "team" player. "Jack is a valuable contributor to Knolls. A good man, dependable," Kakretz penciled at the bottom of Shannon's 1984 performance appraisal.

Once in his new position, however, Shannon had aggressively ferreted out problems, one of the biggest of which was asbestos, used to wrap piping and to insulate heating ducts. There were more than six linear miles of asbestos at the lab, much of it in poor condition, and, in some areas, so deteriorated it fell off pipes. Shannon received occasional calls from sobbing secretaries who had found clumps of it on their desks. Shannon was beginning to agitate on the asbestos issue—he had taken his boss, Ted Glasson, and other supervisors on inspection tours, crawling up behind pipes to show them the problem firsthand—and although everyone agreed it was a bad situation, the response was always the same: "Jack, if you think the government is gonna give us money to clean up this mess, you're crazy."

About that same time, another person was also beginning to complain about asbestos, a burly ex-Marine and Vietnam vet by the name of Doug Allen, who had just become president of Local 301 AE of the International Union of Electrical Workers. The union, sister to Local 301 at the Schenectady main plant, had seen a steady exodus of union jobs out of Schenectady as General Electric sought cheaper nonunion wages in such places as South Carolina and Mexico.

Allen's position made him a pariah to Kakretz. In 1986, the same year Welch and Russ Noll had moved GE's gas-turbine manufacturing division and the thirty-five hundred jobs that went with it from Schenectady to South Carolina, Allen began compiling what he called his "death list." He was getting the runaround from management on the asbestos issue, repeatedly filing grievances but getting no action. "Their response was, 'No problem. No immediate hazard.' They just kept stonewalling us," Allen recalls. Finally, after going to the fifth funeral of a fellow employee, he began keeping a running tally of the Knolls rank and file who had died in the line of duty, and the cause of death. Working at Knolls was "just like being in combat," he says. Allen eventually collected more than 150 names on his death list, about half of whom died from some form of cancer, mostly lung or bone. That represented a disproportionate number of the seven hundred members who had paid dues to Local 301 AE since it had begun representing hourly workers at the Knolls Atomic Power Laboratory in 1947.

Shannon's confrontation with Kakretz over asbestos came to a head in the fall of 1985. At the time, Shannon knew nothing of Allen's complaints, but the report Shannon issued on November 26 had a direct bearing on them. Although Kakretz had told Allen that good records were maintained on worker exposure to asbestos, the Shannon report punched holes in that claim—the eighteen-page document cited the lab for dozens of safety deficiencies, including insufficient fire alarm and fire-suppression systems. But the most glaring problem was asbestos. Records on worker exposure either didn't exist or hadn't been kept in accordance with Navy procedures, the report stated.

Shannon hadn't spent twenty years in the Marines, on active duty and in the reserves, for nothing. Rules were rules, and Shannon wasn't about to overlook them just to curry favor with Kakretz. It was this attitude, more than the specific citations in his report, that convinced Kakretz he had to go. On January 10, 1986, Shannon was relieved of his position in a meeting with his boss Jim McHugh, who gave as a reason Shannon's insufficient response to an audit of his work done *after* the November 26 report.

Kakretz may have ditched Shannon, but the asbestos problem wouldn't go away. In November 1986, one year after Shannon's report, a team of Navy inspectors came to the same conclusions as he had, citing "fundamental weaknesses" in worker asbestos protection at the Kesselring site, and four years later, the Department of Energy finally initiated a $30 million program to rid the lab of asbestos, removing forty-two tons of the deadly material from the Kesselring site in 1992 alone. Yet Shannon was never reinstated. The Office of Naval Reactors and the Department of Energy stood behind Kakretz, and his explanation of why he had demoted Shannon.

At first, few people in authority knew much about the Shannon case. By 1988, however, the mass of accumulated deceit was becoming harder to contain, and Frank Bordell's dismissal in the spring of that year was one deceit too many. Even Kakretz's closest allies knew it to be a horrendous miscalculation at the time. To Kakretz, though, Bordell was an insubordinate crackpot whose concern about possible radiation overexposure was not only an outright lie but posed a threat to his career as well as to the reputation of the nuclear Navy. Kakretz believed Bordell would immediately be forgotten, but he was wrong.

Officially, Bordell was terminated on March 24, 1988 for "failure to follow directives and falsification of records." A week later, in an employee newsletter, Kakretz asserted that he took the "strong action" of firing Bordell because the company was determined to maintain "accurate individual exposure records for its employees." Bordell felt it was his concern over the same issue—the accuracy of those records—that led to his dismissal. He feared that employees may have been exposed to higher levels of radiation than their medical records indicated. For that, and his steadfast refusal to back down, he believes, he was fired.

Early in 1987, Bordell had gotten authorization to purchase a computer software program, called INDOS, that automated radiation calculations. That summer, he used INDOS to analyze forty personnel files. He found that seven of them indicated significantly higher exposure levels than had been previously indicated in manual computations. Alarmed, Bordell prepared seven draft reports documenting the discrepancies. Bordell believed that the preliminary calculations showed enough cause for concern to justify the reexamination of an additional fifteen hundred worker files and that a reassessment would show that as many as four hundred workers may have received higher doses of radiation than their medical records indicated. In addition, the federal threshold for radiation exposure may have been exceeded in about twenty cases. After reporting his findings to supervisors, Bordell was told to stop using INDOS to make calculations until formal procedures were in place. He prepared the procedures and submitted them for review in October.

By February 1988, however, no action had been taken on his report, and Bordell was convinced that management intended to ignore his concerns. On February 15, he took a step that Kakretz considered a treasonous act. He wrote a letter to the Department of Energy Inspector General, the same office that Shannon would contact with his complaint a month later, outlining his "serious concerns" that management was willfully violating federal law by failing to report to the department possible internal radiation exposures of employees.

Nine days later, Bordell called the Inspector General's Office to see if they had received the letter. The letter hadn't reached its destination, so Bordell briefly summarized its contents. He also informed Schenectady Naval Reactors several days later that his use of INDOS had revealed possible reportable exposures. At this point, a colleague informed Bordell that his telephone conversations were being monitored. In early March, at the request of his supervisor, Bordell was ordered to turn over all floppy disks pertaining to his INDOS files. On March 8, he discovered that the program had been stripped from his computer menu. He again called the Inspector General's Office, which promised to visit Knolls and investigate in late March or early April. Bordell wouldn't last that long.

On March 16, upon entering the Niskayuna site, he discovered that his security badge was missing. He was immediately escorted to the visitor area conference room, where three GE managers proceeded to recite the charges against him. He was accused of inserting floppy disks and handwritten notes into files without approval, using erroneous INDOS parameters to falsify records, of unnecessarily warning an employee who showed signs of radiation exposure, of continuing to use INDOS to make radiation assessments after being told to cease doing so, of erasing computer records, and of failing to report contamination cases to Knolls management. He was not provided with a written copy of the charges.

Bordell insisted he was innocent. While he did insert handwritten notes into the seven original files highlighting his concerns, Bordell vehemently denied having falsified records. Although Bordell insisted his concerns were valid, Kakretz was in no mood to listen. Bordell was suspended for two weeks without pay, and was told that these were dischargeable offenses. Bordell spoke to the Department of Energy once more before he was officially terminated on March 24. Fourteen months later, in May 1989, he sued GE. The case wended its way through the New York state courts for seven years, with the state's highest court ultimately handing GE a victory.*

The Bordell dismissal went off like a bomb. Kakretz was beside himself. His career was going up in flames. No Naval Reactors facility had ever had negative publicity before. What was worse, workers now openly questioned whether their medical records were phony. On March 30, just six days after the dismissal, Kakretz claimed in a letter to employees that a review of Bordell's results had found them to be in error. Bordell's methodology was flawed, employees were told.

All the frustration Kakretz felt became apparent two months later, on May 26, 1988, a landmark date not just for Kakretz and Knolls but for Welch and GE, too. Kakretz by now saw his struggle with Bordell as nothing less than a holy war, a confrontation between good and evil. The day began with a morning meeting with Shannon, whom Kakretz had once considered a friend. But their encounter that morning, which lasted just five minutes, was anything but friendly. The purpose, instead, was a reprimand. In the two and a half years that had passed since Shannon's first demotion, Kakretz had kept his distance from him. The punishment Kakretz had meted out had effectively undermined Shannon's psyche, and he was despondent over his treatment. But how Shannon felt didn't matter as long as he kept his mouth shut and didn't do anything else that might damage the "program."

A recovering alcoholic, Shannon had baggage of his own that he would want kept quiet. Kakretz also had confidence in Shannon's loyalty to the mili-

---

* In a May 1996 decision, the court, ruling in favor of GE and affirming lower court decisions to dismiss the complaint, said Bordell had not met the conditions of the state whistleblower statute under which he had filed his suit. That statute requires the plaintiff to have been dismissed because of an actual rather than suspected violation of law. Bordell had alleged that as many as seven employees might have been exposed to radiation at levels sufficient to trigger the mandatory Department of Energy reporting requirements. Although the court noted that GE, by firing Bordell, had effectively prevented him from conducting the further investigation that might have corroborated his suspicions, he did not have proof that a violation of law had occurred. Hence, the statute's standard had not been met.

tary and its stiff-upper-lip ethic. In March 1988, however, Kakretz lost all confidence in Shannon when he learned from a Navy mole that his adversary had asked the Department of Energy Inspector General to investigate his case. Kakretz was furious, and he wanted Shannon to know in no uncertain terms that his dissenting activities would no longer be tolerated. Kakretz also suspected that Shannon was providing assistance to Bordell.

"There are things going on at this laboratory that concern you," Kakretz began at their May 26 meeting, as he came out from behind his desk after Shannon had sat down. "I don't expect anything to come of the Bordell situation," the general manager continued, downplaying the case that consumed him.

"I don't know what you're talking about, Al. I'm not involved with Bordell," Shannon replied.

Kakretz couldn't understand how a formerly loyal employee, whom he had trusted and promoted not that long before, could have done this to him. Shannon tried to explain why he had gone to the Department of Energy, but no explanation would suffice. He had done irreparable harm. It was a treasonous act which was a threat to Kakretz's ambition to advance after his time at Knolls. Kakretz then turned to the real reason he had summoned Shannon. "I have here a marginal-performance appraisal on you, Jack, that I agree with."

Shannon hadn't yet seen the document and pushed it aside for review with his boss later that day, but he knew at that moment that Kakretz was beginning to build a phony case against him as documentation for dismissal. The former Marine and ex-fighter had had it. Two and a half years of frustration and anger immediately welled up within him. Shannon moved to a new stage in what had been a grieving process as he mourned the loss of a once successful career. Despondency turned to rage. "No one in this laboratory is going to fuck around with me anymore. I refuse to be lied to by you or anyone," Shannon replied. Kakretz and an assistant who had sat in on the meeting were stunned by Shannon's language and insolence. They were also a little fearful. Shannon had a reputation as a hothead, and he knew how to use his fists.

"No one is trying to fuck around with you, Jack, but your work had better improve," Kakretz replied, summoning up as much calm as he could under the circumstances. On that note it ended. The two men wouldn't meet again. When Kakretz would spy Shannon in the halls, he would turn the other way to avoid him.

On the afternoon of May 26, Kakretz held another meeting with the twenty or so lieutenants who reported to him and who ran Knolls. The meeting began with Kakretz announcing to the group that he had been "born again," and had turned his life over to Jesus Christ. Yet just minutes later, he inexplicably cussed and scolded his charges for not being more diligent and thorough in getting rid of deadwood, as Welch had commanded. Kakretz cited a book he had just read, *People of the Lie*. The book defined evil people as those who were unable to be self-critical. Frank Bordell was just such a person, Kakretz said. He should have been fired years before. He was incompetent and a traitor—to the nation as well as to the Navy and General Electric.

"Bordell is an evil man. He has been an evil man for twenty years, and we are just now finding out about it," Kakretz told his lieutenants, one of whom stopped doodling when he heard his boss invoke the word "evil." The men who heard Kakretz's comments that day were startled at the severity of his words. Not that they weren't used to tirades of one kind or another. Kakretz was not a pleasant man, and he thought nothing of ridiculing subordinates publicly. George Fountain would sometimes occupy himself during meetings keeping count of the times Kakretz swore. The record was seventy-five. But even for Kakretz, his display on May 26 was rare indeed. "I was angry because I knew Frank, and he was not an evil man," recalls Fountain, who attended the meeting.

Kakretz would later deny having called Bordell "evil," as GE sought a dismissal in a defamation suit Bordell had filed against Kakretz and GE. But Judge Loren Brown, of Ballston Spa, New York, didn't buy it. In February 1991, Judge Brown denied the company's petition that would have ended Bordell's defamation claim. Kakretz "has not been candid" in telling the truth about what he said, the judge noted. "Some of those attending the [meeting] remember that Kakretz characterized Bordell as an evil man," Judge Brown wrote. "Notes taken at the [meeting] support the allegation that Kakretz referred to Bordell as evil." In rejecting GE's motion, the judge doubted Kakretz's denials because "uncertainty under oath at the deposition [about what he had said] has become more certain in the affidavit supporting a motion to dismiss. . . . Under the circumstances, what he says . . . lacks credibility."

As explosive as the Bordell incident was, the public was still unaware of the shenanigans at Knolls. Dick Cole's death had gone unnoticed. Doug Allen's complaints about worker exposure to asbestos and radiation hadn't been disclosed. Jack Shannon's demotions were secret. The public didn't know about radioactive waste dumps or fired whistleblowers. As far as the media was concerned, Knolls was a nonstory. Past clippings on the lab, stored in the *Schenectady Gazette*'s morgue, were limited to occasional articles on promotions and ribbon-cutting ceremonies. Knolls was uniformly thought of as a benign, even benevolent, neighbor of New York's Capital district.

That image changed on June 22, 1988. In the end it was a parking lot that altered public perceptions. An article on the front page of the *Gazette* that Wednesday morning disclosed that an unpaved parking lot at Knolls's central office in Niskayuna, adjacent to GE's corporate research and development center, was contaminated with radioactive waste. Knolls employees had parked on the site, on the south shore of the Mohawk River, for twenty years. They were unaware of the radioactivity, which in selected hot spots was nearly three hundred times higher than Knolls's own maximum standards for soil. Both GE and the Department of Energy had long *known* that the lot was radioactive and hadn't bothered to post even a warning sign, much less clean it up.

Although Kakretz at first denied knowing that the area was contaminated, he was forced to recant that statement in a second *Gazette* story the following day. Worse still, Kakretz had sold the 2.2-acre lot to the federal government three months before—on March 29, five days after he had fired Bordell—to shield GE from potential liability. The Department of Energy had quietly agreed to the transaction. The sale of the property, for the price of *one dollar*, might have violated at least two New York state laws prohibiting the transfer of radioactively contaminated land. But the state eventually decided it was unable to pursue the matter because the land was under federal jurisdiction. The state also couldn't order a cleanup.

The saga of the parking lot was big news locally for weeks and rocked Knolls. Mark Hammond, the *Gazette* reporter who broke the story, had been tipped off to it by an anonymous source inside the lab, "Dennis," presumably one of Kakretz's "enemies." Dennis spent several weeks feeling Hammond out on the phone before proposing a meeting. Hammond was told to jog down a bicycle path near the site one Friday morning. He was met by Dennis and two other men, all dressed in khaki camouflage suits. The three men escorted Hammond to the lot. There, with Geiger counters clacking away, they filled several coffee cans with contaminated soil, gave it to Hammond and quickly disappeared.

The parking lot was far from the worst example of contamination at Knolls. That distinction indisputably belonged to the former Separation Process Research Unit, a concrete-entombed but intensely radioactive structure at Niskayuna known to all by its acronym, SPRU. From 1950 to 1954, SPRU's mission was to extract uranium and plutonium from spent atomic fuel. The radiation still inside SPRU, which descends three stories from ground level into the earth, is measured in lethal curies, not the thousands of picocuries found in the parking lot (a picocurie is one-trillionth of a curie).

SPRU's potency is such that it has confounded containment over the years, even after construction in 1954, when the most contaminated areas of the G2 building were sealed in concrete. Just two years later, in 1956, the health physics department discovered "extensive" plutonium in office and lavatory areas adjacent to SPRU. Urine samples taken months later from twenty-four employees who worked in the contaminated areas revealed "no biologically significant deposition of plutonium." But the tests were meaningless, since urinalysis must be performed within days of exposure to detect radiation.

Despite additional cleanups of G2, several audits since 1956 confirmed that the building still wasn't radiation-free. One Naval Reactors audit in 1983 found leakage of contaminated water into G2 office and work areas, radiation that apparently had seeped through fissures and cracks in the concrete. Radioactivity was discovered in lighting fixtures and behind new walls in the restrooms. It had also crept into the drainage system, migrating toward the Mohawk River. "The recent discoveries of contamination . . . represent a real concern to employees who occupy the areas," the report stated. The authors urged that the offices be vacated and that the building be demolished immediately. Neither action was taken.

Although contamination in the parking lot was insignificant compared with SPRU, the public outcry it produced was indeed significant. Since its inception, the Naval Nuclear Propulsion Program had claimed to adhere to the highest safety standards in the nuclear business. It wrapped itself in the Rickover aura of excellence and was an agency supposedly above reproach. But the parking lot incident made the Office of Naval Reactors look more like the Keystone Kops. The lot was contaminated because the dirt used as fill in its construction came from other radioactively tainted sites at Niskayuna, including the so-called "slurry drum area." Drums containing high-level nuclear waste were temporarily stored in this area while awaiting transport for burial elsewhere, and had leaked cesium-137 and strontium-90 into the soil.

Using radioactive dirt as fill for the parking lot was a colossal blunder, but it wasn't the gravest sin. Covering up the lot's radioactivity for twenty years was. Only Kakretz and some of his lieutenants knew the lot was hot. In 1985, the Knolls engineering group, charged with sampling the extent of radioactivity in the parking lot, had sanitized the very top layer of soil so that the radioactivity wouldn't be readily detected. Rather than trying to correct the problem, Kakretz had chosen to conceal it. GE's "behavior in this case leads to the natural question: What else is it hiding?" the *Schenectady Gazette* asked in one editorial. Kakretz and cohort Barry Erickson, manager of Schenectady Naval Reactors, tried desperately to keep the lid on. Responding to New York

State inquiries about the one-dollar land transfer, Erickson wrote in defense of GE: "The Department of Energy does not condone and is not defending the actions of GE . . . in inadvertently placing radioactivity on the subject land. However, the subsequent transfer at no cost to the government of the GE owned land in fact represents a meaningful penalty."

Even the Navy didn't buy it. The parking lot was one mistake too many. Someone had to take the fall. One month after writing the letter, Erickson, who had run the Schenectady office since 1971, was gone. He announced his retirement, effective September 30, 1988.

Worker concern over the situation intensified during the summer of 1988. Aides to several members of Congress, including Senator John Glenn, a frequent and harsh critic of the Department of Energy, were beginning to ask questions. In June, the Government Accountability Project (GAP), a group of public-interest lawyers who befriend government whistleblowers, began its own investigation. On September 8, GAP attorney Tom Carpenter paid his first visit to the area. One week later, on September 15, Kakretz issued a "Security Newsletter, Special Edition," which prohibited any and all statements from employees about Knolls "appearing in newspapers, magazines and books, or made in speeches, on TV, at open meetings, or even in casual conversations." Violators of the policy would be immediately terminated. In accordance with federal law—and Kakretz's own idiosyncratic enforcement of it—employees were warned that they could also face fines of up to $100,000 and could be *imprisoned for life.*

Carpenter deals frequently with whistleblowers and sometimes finds them to be a bit paranoid. In this case, he came to feel that paranoia was justified. Some months later, Carpenter began to suspect that the phone in his Washington office was bugged. He used a pay phone around the block whenever he called people in Schenectady. On one occasion, after placing a call on the pay phone, he returned to his office and discovered that the person he had called had already returned his call. So he returned to the pay phone, only to find two men in business suits cradling the disassembled phone in their hands. They fled.

All the tawdry details of life and death at Knolls were coming to light at exactly the right time for Infact, the activist group that had initiated the boycott against GE to expose and end the company's involvement in the weapons industry. Welch still regarded Infact as merely an irritant. His assessment changed, though, once he had seen *Deadly Deception.* He angrily denounced the film as "malicious" and "full of lies." The film was not just a broadside aimed at General Electric; Infact had also taken direct aim at Welch, who had unwittingly given Infact footage of himself during a public appearance at Harvard University's Kennedy School of Government.

Work-Out by then was in its third year, and tens of thousands of employees had been put through the program. Welch was now selling his vision of worker empowerment and workplace democracy as passionately as he had cut costs a decade earlier. People at Infact had read that Welch would be at the Kennedy School to give a speech. As it turned out, he provided just what the activists wanted. While Welch spoke effusively of GE's commitment to the environment and greater worker welfare, Infact's cameras were rolling. His comments were juxtaposed against grisly scenes of death and destruction in the final cut. It may have been an underhanded technique, but Infact thought that what was at stake justified it. They played for keeps, just as Welch did. They, too, were waging war, applying the same standards of conduct and decency that Welch had throughout his revolution.

It was payback time. Although Doug Allen had read Welch's pronouncements on Work-Out, from his perspective it seemed as if the gap between the Welch rhetoric and the Kakretz reality was best measured in light-years. "I wanted people to know what General Electric was really like, and I wanted Jack Welch to know what was happening in facilities he supposedly managed," Allen says. "I wrote letter after letter complaining about health and safety problems, but no one seemed to care."

It had taken Allen nearly a decade of constant agitation before General Electric and the government had finally faced up to the asbestos problem. In the meantime, Kakretz had meted out punishment against Allen and the union in a variety of ways. Union jobs were lost as Kakretz awarded more and more work to craftsmen not on the company payroll. Other union members, who had had their security clearances challenged and arbitrarily revoked, could no longer work at Knolls. Allen fought for years in some cases to get workers back on the payroll. Allen's role in the film drew approval from some unlikely supporters, including one letter from a GE manager who wrote to compliment him for a job well done. Allen framed the letter, which sits on his desk. Allen also served as an inspiration to filmmaker Debra Chasnoff. After the Infact film crew finished filming Allen, he rose, gave Chasnoff a big bear hug and said to her: "Do something with this, Debra." "Whenever I got frustrated I thought of him and what he said," Chasnoff recalls.

If Welch had truly intended to bring about a "redefined relationship between boss and subordinate," as he claimed was the goal of Work-Out, it wasn't evident in how he dealt with Frank Bordell. In the years following Bordell's dismissal, the company fought hard to keep him from getting his day in court. Twice, it sought unsuccessfully to get the whistleblower's claim dismissed. It also filed suit against Bordell, alleging that he had violated his duty of "good faith and loyalty" to the company by making his concerns public, a claim that was also dismissed. "They have a take-no-prisoners attitude about them. They come right at you," says Bordell's attorney, Ronald Dunn.

As a defendant in the Bordell case, the federal government was not only a party in these actions, it also had to pay for them. Under the 1957 Price-Anderson Act, it is required to reimburse the legal expenses of defense contractors who run Department of Energy weapons facilities. In 1994, the department, under the new "Openness Initiative" of Secretary Hazel O'Leary, disclosed for the first time the cost to taxpayers of defending General Electric, Westinghouse, and other defense contractors against lawsuits like Bordell's. The total bill in the three prior years had been $47 million.

The Work-Out philosophy didn't seem to have any bearing on how Welch dealt with Jack Shannon, either. To the contrary, the contrast between Shannon's fate and that of Kakretz does seem absurd: The employee who tried to do the right thing, the moral thing, was made to suffer for it, while the man who sought to cover up life-threatening wrongdoing settled back into a comfortable retirement. The irony did not escape Shannon, who is still fighting the war he dedicated himself to years ago. As part of that battle, he appears on college campuses to introduce *Deadly Deception*, to condemn his former life, his former employer, and, above all, the government he believes betrayed him, the government that allowed it all to happen. It was the government that closed ranks with GE, refusing to intercede on his behalf while superiors mistreated him. It was the government that disclosed his identity to GE after he brought his complaints to the Department of Energy. And, as Shannon came to learn in the course of a lawsuit he filed—in which he contends that GE and the Department of Energy violated his privacy and related rights under federal law by publicly disclosing information about him*—it was the government that ordered notes taken by Department of Energy personnel who investigated the case to be shredded. According to an anonymous tipster, the shredding was done on the orders of an attorney in the Department of Energy Inspector General's office who was investigating Shannon's claims.

Shannon's distrust of the government was heightened in the summer of 1991, when the General Accounting Office issued its official audit on the Knolls Atomic Power Laboratory. Responding to a request made two years earlier by Congressman Mike Synar, chairman of the House subcommittee on Environ-

---

* The merits of that lawsuit have not been decided. The case was dismissed on various procedural grounds and is now on appeal.

ment, Energy, and Natural Resources, the GAO spent one year examining Knolls. In the end, the report raised more questions than it answered. The GAO gave Knolls a relatively clean bill of health. The Shannon and Bordell cases were not mentioned in the report ("personnel matters," the GAO called them). Neither was the parking lot (it wasn't cited, the GAO claims, because they considered it well documented in the public record). Victor Rezendes, the officer who supervised the report, defends his audit. "Our report is very accurate," he says. But many people disagree, among them Dave Berick, an aide to former Congressman Synar. Berick says he feared the report would be a whitewash when he heard that the Navy was up to its old Rickover-era tricks, taking the GAO auditors out for a sub ride before the report was completed. GAO says it accepted the Navy's invitation for a day trip off the Florida coast aboard the USS *Minneapolis-St. Paul*, a *Los Angeles*-class nuclear attack submarine, because auditors wanted to observe naval procedures at sea. Berick has another interpretation. "Naval Reactors is a very high-powered public relations operation," he says. "They routinely try to win you over, either through persuasion or intimidation." He was so disappointed in the content of the report that the subcommittee didn't release it to the public, as is standard practice; the GAO did. "I just didn't believe it was credible," he says. "I don't feel very good about the way we left this."

In any event, the Department of Energy apparently didn't believe the GAO either. The department has begun the messy process of cleaning up Knolls. So far, it has identified more than two dozen sites at Niskayuna alone for "deactivation," including SPRU, which will require a wholesale demolition, and the parking lot. At the Kesselring site, which isn't even on the cleanup docket yet, two of the original four nuclear reactors have been deactivated, and the two that remain still lack the safety features that Shannon has been complaining about for a decade now.

Shannon's visits to college campuses afford him an opportunity to tell the story that Welch silenced in Decatur, Alabama. The former Marine vents his spleen in forums like the one he attended on a wet, cold night at Penn State. He is still recruiting, only for a different mission. "Maybe your generation can correct what my generation screwed up so badly," he pleads at the conclusion of his talk, his voice choked with emotion. His audience applauds heartily. Several students thank him for coming and commend him for his courage. Afterward, Shannon reflects on his new identity. "I used to wonder what my mission in life was," he says, walking back to his hotel with wife Joan. Shannon holds an umbrella to shield them on the blustery November night. "Maybe this is why God put me here."

His former adversary was not nearly so introspective. Kakretz categori-cally rejected any suggestion that his tenure was less than perfect, and he refused to answer specific questions that, in his view, would only rehash the past: "I don't want to go over all this bullshit again. . . . There's nothing to be gained by doing that." He has since passed away.

For Welch, however, the taint just wouldn't go away. The biggest embar-rassment came on March 30, 1992, Oscar night at the Dorothy Chandler Pavil-ion in Los Angeles. *Deadly Deception* had been nominated for an Academy Award. Debra Chasnoff was accompanied to the ceremonies by Elaine Lamy, Infact's executive director, and Cathy Pillsbury, an Infact volunteer, donor, and heiress to the Pillsbury food fortune. Their red Geo Metro was conspicuous among the white limousines lined up outside the pavilion. When Chasnoff and *Deadly Deception* unexpectedly won the Oscar for best documentary short subject, it was an historic milestone for grassroots activism against cor-porations. Accepting the award from director Spike Lee, Chasnoff used her forty-five seconds of fame to blast GE and Welch. She urged an estimated one billion viewers to join the boycott against the company that "falsely claims it brings good things to life." At that moment, a relatively obscure boycott became a national event.

Although a General Electric spokesman insisted the following day that the adverse publicity had "no impact [on it] at all," that was far from the truth. The telecast gave Infact and its boycott an avalanche of publicity. NBC inad-vertently added to the negative press GE received the next morning, when *Today* show host Bryant Gumbel asked movie critic Gene Shalit about all "the unusual social speeches" on the Oscar show. In his rundown of the night's events, Shalit overlooked the biggest news of all, Chasnoff's acceptance speech. The media picked up on Shalit's flub, which was seen by some as con-firmation that GE, in fact, did influence the network's news.

GE's influence on the media was also confirmed to some in how public television dealt with the question of whether it would air *Deadly Deception.* Although the film won more than a dozen awards and recognitions besides the Oscar—and was selected by the Public Broadcasting Service as one of twelve programs to represent the United States at an international film festival for public television in May 1993—the film was for the most part withheld from the American public. The PBS organization in Washington rejected *Deadly Deception* for national viewing because Infact paid for its production, a supposed violation of the television network's underwriting guidelines. The decision outraged many in the entertainment business and prompted some individual stations, including WNET in New York, to break ranks with PBS and show the film on their own. Hollywood also jumped into the fray. A group calling themselves the Coalition Versus PBS Censorship, whose members included Oliver Stone and Robin Williams, demanded that PBS reverse its decision, which affected not just *Deadly Deception* but another film critical of the nuclear industry, *Building Bombs.* "We are concerned about what rejection of these and many other programs dealing with vital issues implies for the future of public television. We call on PBS to fulfill its responsibilities as a public broadcaster and put these programs on the air," said one Coalition ad that ran in *Variety.* Representatives of the Coalition also met on several occasions with PBS programming chief Jennifer Lawson, who refused to budge.

Perhaps the biggest impact was the influence the film had on Welch. The man who despised negative publicity was now determined to rid himself of Knolls. With the Cold War at an end and the Pentagon pulling back on weapons spending from the unequaled peacetime budgets of the Reagan years, the business of selling arms had lost its luster. The burdens exceeded the financial benefit it provided to Welch. In October 1992, when top chief executives gathered in Hot Springs, Virginia, to golf and schmooze at the annual meeting of the Business Council, Welch approached an old friend, Martin Marietta Chairman Norman Augustine, and asked if he would be interested in buying GE's defense business. A deal was struck over dinner a few weeks later. Welch suggested that the sale include Knolls, even though it wasn't part of the aerospace business that Martin Marietta wanted, and Augustine agreed. Martin Marietta, which subsequently merged with Lockheed, assumed leadership of the armaments industry, a business that for the first time since World War I wouldn't include GE. Once the transaction was concluded in March 1993, Infact called off the boycott, proclaimed victory, and set its sights on the next target—the tobacco industry. The war it had initiated seven years before was finally over.

CHAPTER NINE

GREAT RIVER OF
THE MOUNTAINS

IN THE SPRING OF 1996, while Congress and many state legislatures were backtracking on environmental protection, a book was published that raised troubling new questions about the effect of synthetic chemicals on the environment and human health. The book, *Our Stolen Future*, for the first time summarized the potential dangers of "endocrine disrupters," synthetic chemicals that are believed to interfere with the reproductive hormones of the human body by mimicking estrogen and testosterone. The authors cited animal and human studies linking these chemicals to many insidious forms of damage, including a decline in men's sperm counts; an epidemic of hormonally triggered breast and prostate cancers; neurological disorders in children, such as hyperactivity, reduced intelligence, and violent behavior; and developmental and reproductive problems in wildlife. The book caused a commotion in the scientific and regulatory communities. Vice President Al Gore hailed it as the successor to Rachel Carson's 1962 *Silent Spring.* This "is a critically important book that forces us to ask new questions about the synthetic chemicals that we have spread across this Earth," Gore wrote in the foreword, while *Business Week* called it a "scientific and public relations bombshell" for industry.

The book, which identified fifty-one synthetic chemicals that disrupt the endocrine system, focused on one of the most ubiquitous in the environment, a large chemical family of 209 different compounds known collectively as polychlorinated biphenyls, or PCBs. By adding chlorine atoms to a molecule with two joined hexagonal benzene rings known as a biphenyl, chemical engineers had introduced, in 1929, a concoction of enormous consequence to the early chemical industry. PCBs were among the first of tens of thousands of synthetic chemicals that exist nowhere in nature, and they quickly found their way into a myriad of industrial—and eventually—consumer products. They were used as lubricants, hydraulic fluids, and cutting oils; as an additive in caulking compounds, paints, varnishes, putty, waxes, and pesticides; and as an adhesive in brake linings, tapes, and envelopes. They preserved and protected rubber, made wood and plastics nonflammable, served as a weatherproofing for stucco, and even coated the inside of grain silos.

But it was electrical-equipment manufacturers, chiefly General Electric and Westinghouse in the United States, that made the greatest use of PCB. The new chemical wouldn't catch fire, and made a perfect substitute in electrical products for mineral oil, which was flammable. Beginning in the early 1930s, with the issuance of federal regulations requiring the use of nonflammable cooling compounds in electrical transformers used inside buildings, GE mixed PCB to create a dielectric fluid called Pyranol. The fluid, which filled the metal housings of transformers and capacitors the company made at three plants, two on the Hudson River and one in Pittsfield, Massachusetts, greatly reduced the risk of fire in products that were formerly fire hazards.

Although some evidence of toxic effects in workers began emerging as early as 1936, it wasn't until 1966 that serious questions were raised about the safety of this supposed wonder chemical. A report that year in the British journal *New Scientist* summarized the research of a Swedish chemist who kept encountering what he had eventually identified as PCB wherever he looked—in hair samples from his wife and infant daughter, in wildlife specimens collected thirty years before, in the sea and in the environment. Other health researchers turned up evidence of PCBs accumulating in human body fat and breast milk. Soon it became apparent that PCBs were indeed everywhere—in soil, air, and ocean; in the mud of lakes, rivers, and estuaries; in the body fat of virtually every human being—and that their omnipresence posed a graver threat to human life and the environment than was previously understood. PCBs don't dissolve readily in water. They are "persistent" chemicals, in that they resist the natural processes of decay that would render them harmless. Once ingested, they are drawn by their chemical structure to a human's or animal's fat cells and are virtually impossible to dislodge. Very minute quantities of PCB have been found to interfere and distort hormones, particularly in the embryonic fetus. Often the medical problems that arise out of this chemical interference don't show up until adults who have been exposed to PCBs have children. Toxicologists now believe that the variety of neurological, reproductive, and immune system dysfunctions associated with PCB exposure are more likely to be evident in this second generation. Although biologists disagree over the extent of the threat PCBs pose to human health, there is now renewed concern, so much so that the EPA has expanded its research to better understand how these chemicals disrupt hormones.

But the genie was out of the bottle. Even though the United States banned the manufacture of PCBs in 1976, and other, though not all, industrial countries eventually followed, the chemical industry worldwide (excluding the former Soviet Union) had produced an estimated 3.4 billion pounds of the chemicals in a half century of production, much of which was already loose in the environment and beyond recall. Indeed, as both the federal government and many state governments were soon to discover, outlawing the manufacture of PCBs would be the easy part. Cleaning up the sites they had come to contaminate would be another matter altogether.

GE, over a period of more than thirty years, intentionally discharged into the Hudson River more than one million pounds of PCBs—about thirty pounds a day—from two factories forty miles north of Troy, at Fort Edward and Hudson Falls. The PCBs entered the river mainly via waste water used to wash off the casings of electrical capacitors that were manufactured at the two plants and were submerged in a PCB bath. In 1976, the state of New York, acting with urgency after the federal declaration of the chemical as a public-health menace, attempted to deal with the PCB problem. Abraham Sofaer, a Columbia University law professor who presided over a hearing on the PCB question, judged General Electric guilty of violating state water quality standards: "GE has discharged PCBs in quantities that have breached applicable standards of water quality . . . injured fish, and . . . destroyed the viability of recreational fishing in various parts of the Hudson by rendering its fish dangerous to consume."

The Sofaer hearing did little to resolve the issue—two decades later, the debate still rages over what to do about the Hudson, as GE has successfully forestalled retrieval of PCBs from one of the nation's most majestic waterways—but it was important in another regard: It catapulted Jack Welch in his career. Armed with Sofaer's decision, New York entered into negotiations with GE, judged by Sofaer to be the responsible party. Reg Jones chose Welch to represent the company in the negotiations with the state, a choice that confirmed the import Jones attached to them. Because the Hudson was one of hundreds of sites where GE was potentially liable for expensive environmental remediation, the showdown with New York would set important precedent. Jones was livid over the state's handling of the PCB question, and he had angrily warned then New York Governor Hugh Carey that he would pull all company facilities out of New York if its environmental commissioner, Ogden Reid, forced the two Hudson River plants to go to zero-PCB discharge before Jones thought it feasible.

While Reid, the newly installed commissioner of the New York Department of Environmental Conservation, considered himself a friend of the river, Jones regarded him as a tree-hugging, antibusiness lunatic. Reid had a way of seeking the spotlight, and stirring up controversy. He had been the first New York State official to warn the public, in a very public way, not to eat striped bass from the Hudson. That warning, carried on August 8, 1975 on the front page of the *New York Times*, was the opening salvo in what would become America's longest-running environmental sitcom, in which hapless regulators have tried with no success to compel GE to do the right thing and accept its civic responsibilities. In September 1997, Secretary of the Interior Bruce Babbitt continued the crusade that Reid had begun twenty-two years before. Speaking from a hilltop overlooking the Hudson River, against a backdrop of water, mountains, and sky, Babbitt assailed GE over delays in ridding the river of its chemicals. "The fact is, the sickness of this river today is directly traceable to General Electric," he said. "They have an obligation to join with us as an active partner in the complete restoration of the Hudson River and this valley."

That the Hudson River's PCBs represented a potential public health catastrophe was first confirmed in 1972, when New York State officials began secretly testing the river's fish, spurred by a report in *Sports Illustrated* magazine published two years before. The state testing affirmed what *Sports Illustrated* writer Robert Boyle had uncovered: that fish flesh and eggs had extremely high levels of PCB, concentrations of which were most acute among striped bass, an important commercial fish that ate other species and migrated in large numbers from New Jersey to Cape Cod after spawning in the river. In 1973, the New York environmental agency collected twenty-two stripers from the lower Hudson below the Troy dam, 154 miles from New York City, and found that eighteen had PCB levels in their flesh that exceeded the federal threshold of five parts per million (the legal limit has since been lowered to two ppm). One fish had a reading of 49.63 ppm. But Reid's predecessors, worried about the impact the findings would have on the Hudson River's commercial fishing industry, had chosen to keep this information secret.

To Reid's dismay, he discovered that the state health department had okayed GE's PCB discharge in 1971—the first year in which certification had been required to discharge them into the river—and in 1973 his own agency had issued another permit. Nevertheless, Reid directed his agency to accuse GE of violating state water quality standards and to bring the dumping to an immediate halt. He also ordered the hearing that led to Professor Sofaer's judgment against the company. Reid, however, picked an inopportune time to go after GE—1975, the height of New York City's financial crisis. While Governor Carey was trying to placate the financial community and convince them that New York was a hospitable place to do business, his chief environmental officer was whacking one of the state's most influential corporate citizens. Just four months after Sofaer's decision, Carey, in desperate need of a scape-goat and anxious to mend fences with Jones, demanded—and got—Reid's resignation.

This was the situation when Welch stepped into the ring. With Reid gone, the ambitious, young man from Pittsfield lived up to his reputation as one tough hombre. The state of New York proved no match for Welch, who engineered a settlement, reached in the fall of 1976, that has effectively tied the state's hands ever since. The settlement stated that GE had done nothing wrong, and limited its liability to a mere $3 million, with the state contributing a like amount. To put that number in perspective, current estimates put the cost of cleaning up the river at more than $300 million if a full-scale dredging project is ever undertaken. Welch was not only flinty eyed; he paid attention to the smallest of details, including how GE would pay its portion. After lengthy discussions, the state agreed to accept a wire transfer of the $3 million. Welch didn't want to write a check because he suspected government officials would use it against the company for publicity purposes. "He negotiated hard on that point, and that's when I concluded he was a smart cookie," recalls Lang-don Marsh, who participated in the negotiations, representing the New York Department of Environmental Conservation, where he later served as a deputy commissioner under Governor Mario Cuomo. But Marsh, who dealt with the PCB issue for most of his adult life, has less admiration now for Welch and his tactics: "There is certainly some scientific uncertainty here and legitimate differences over what's best for the river. Having said that, there's absolutely no question that if General Electric had adopted a different atti-tude, this problem would be behind us." Indeed, the Hudson, which to earlier generations symbolized the majesty and wonder of nature, has become a sym-bol of environmental gridlock of truly majestic proportions.

Throughout the 1980s, the debate over what to do with the river—and the extent of the public health problem it posed—was hopelessly deadlocked in an endless procession of claims and counterclaims. As the years passed, scientific evidence of the danger of PCBs mounted. One study by Sandra and Joseph Jacobson, psychologists from Wayne State University in Detroit, had found evidence that babies born to mothers who had eaten two to three meals a month of PCB-tainted fish from the Great Lakes were born sooner, weighed less, and had smaller heads than those whose mother did not eat the fish. The study also found that the greater the amount of PCBs in the umbilical cord blood, the more poorly the child scored on tests assessing neurological development. A subsequent study, published in the *New England Journal of Medicine*, found that children who had been prenatally exposed to PCB in concentrations only slightly higher than those found in the general population exhibited IQ deficits, poor reading comprehension, memory problems, and difficulty paying attention.

As reports continued to pile up—another established that the breast milk of women in Albany and Oswego counties in upstate New York had PCB concentrations approaching unsafe levels—the state of New York applied for a permit to dredge the upper Hudson above Troy to remove the chemicals but was unable to get approval for the site it had chosen for a landfill. In 1983, the river was officially designated one of the nation's worst toxic waste sites when it was placed on the National Priority List of the Comprehensive Environmental Response, Compensation and Liability Act, the so-called Superfund law Congress had passed three years before. Superfund was intended to accelerate remediation of the nation's worst toxic waste sites, and optimists thought the Hudson's designation as a Superfund site and GE's citation as the responsible party would break the regulatory impasse, with the federal government for the first time subsuming what had been up until that point a state-led remediation effort.

The gridlock, though, had only begun. It was the Reagan era, a time when the Environmental Protection Agency was less than zealous in carrying out its role as protector of the environment. A frequent guest at the White House during the Reagan years, Welch had friends in Washington, and it soon became clear that allies like Anne Gorsuch, President Reagan's choice to head the EPA, had no intention of pressing for a quick resolution of the Hudson problem. On the contrary, she was clearly determined to do whatever she could to delay a cleanup of the river. In 1984, a year and a half after Gorsuch had refused to release $20 million that Congress had appropriated to test PCB removal methods in the Hudson, the EPA announced it would not press for removal of the oily chemicals from river sediment, a decision that would be revisited in five years as required under the Superfund law.

In late 1989, when the five years had passed, the political landscape had changed. The stakes in the environmental war had escalated enormously. The number of Superfund sites nationwide had grown to more than one thousand, and GE's potential liabilities had mushroomed. Even though the last of the factories in which GE had made its PCB-laden products had been abandoned in the eighties, the manufacturing legacy still had to be contained. GE was now cited as a responsible party for more than seventy sites under Superfund, more than any other corporation, of which the Hudson was one. The remediation costs had grown to staggering proportions. Worst of all, from Welch's perspective, there were fewer political allies in Washington. The Reagan presidency had given way to that of George Bush, whose choice to head the EPA, William Reilly, was a strong advocate of environmental protection, and hence less swayed by Big Business than his predecessors.

Public opinion was also becoming more pro-environment. Some major corporations were coming around to the idea that society expected more enlightened environmental behavior. Dow Chemical, a company whose name was once synonymous with napalm and Agent Orange, was inviting environmentalists to its headquarters in Midland, Michigan, for meetings with senior managers and board members, and was using environmental goals as one criteria in determining salaries and bonuses. Sun Company, the parent of petroleum refiner Sunoco, became the first major corporation to sign the Ceres principles drawn up by the Coalition for Environmentally Responsible Economies, which promotes an environmental code of conduct for business, and which Welch adamantly opposed.

Welch had chosen a different course. He decided to get more directly involved in an issue he had closely monitored ever since his handling of the negotiations with New York State. In 1990, he expended much energy lobbying New York Governor Mario Cuomo. GE lobbyists in Albany, the state capital, had pulled off a deft legislative maneuver. They had succeeded in attaching a rider to the state budget that would have ceased development funding for a landfill to be sited in the upper Hudson region north of Albany. The landfill was under study as the possible site for PCBs reclaimed from the river should it ever be dredged. While Cuomo was weighing whether to veto the budget to block the landfill funding cutoff, Welch met with the governor to persuade him not to exercise his veto, a tactic that backfired. Cuomo not only vetoed the measure but he also later revealed Welch's persistence on the issue: He "has called me, and lobbied me, about PCBs. I dispute what GE is saying and I said no to his ideas and proposals."

The defeat convinced Welch that he needed more ammunition, particularly in Washington. He hired Stephen Ramsey, the ultimate Washington insider on environmental policy and Superfund guru, to succeed Roger Strelow as GE's vice president for environmental affairs. Welch wanted someone who was tougher, more aggressive, and better connected, more in step with his style of doing business, qualities neither he nor Ben Heineman, GE's general counsel, felt Strelow had. Before joining GE, Ramsey worked for the prestigious law firm of Sidley and Austin, where he wrote a widely distributed memorandum that advised corporate lawyers on how to confound Uncle Sam's efforts to collect the billions owed by polluters under the Superfund law. And before his tenure at Sidley and Austin, Ramsey had served as assistant attorney general for environmental enforcement in the Reagan administration's Justice Department, where he developed the rules for enforcing the Superfund law. Besides being a smart lawyer, Ramsey had excellent connections inside the Beltway with the congressmen and administrators who craft and enforce the nation's environmental law.

Welch hired another former government insider, M. Peter Lanahan, who resigned his post as a deputy commissioner of the New York environmental agency to join GE. Lanahan's duties included waging an aggressive campaign to influence public opinion and convince citizens in the Hudson River Valley that PCBs aren't toxic. One brochure he produced and distributed, "The Hudson River: PCBs, Fact Vs. Fiction," makes the bold claim that the chemical isn't dangerous—despite voluminous scientific evidence to the contrary—citing as evidence two statements from scientists at the Institute for Health Policy Analysis, a probusiness think tank in Washington that GE sponsors (its financial support of the institute wasn't disclosed in the brochure).

Following Welch's credo on the environment means taking the offensive, and people like Lanahan have done just that. Although company representatives portray themselves as good corporate citizens who profess to speak for the larger public good, their actions on the Hudson suggest less altruistic motives. In 1991, for instance, the EPA at the prodding of Scenic Hudson, a river watchdog group, protested a GE quarterly newsletter that Lanahan had founded, *River Watch*, because of what it contended was a misleading title. The new publication, published according to its masthead pledge "to keep the community informed about the PCB situation in the Hudson River," wasn't the problem per se; its subtitle was: *A Report on EPA's Reassessment of the Hudson River*. The federal agency felt the title gave readers the intentional misimpression it was an EPA-sanctioned and -authored publication rather than company commentary. After EPA lodged a formal protest Lanahan backed down and made GE's affiliation with *River Watch* explicit, putting the GE monogram on the masthead.

The company has sought to ply its influence in other ways, some subtle and some not. One of the simplest ways is to swarm the regulatory process by keeping regulators tied up. The protracted controversy over the Hudson has generated hundreds of public hearings. Lanahan and his cohorts understand intimately how government functions, and they also understand how to stall and delay governmental procedures. That's why Welch hired them, many believed. General Electric uses the hearings to deluge the government with commentary, which in turn requires the EPA to spend months responding to what GE has said. Two years after the EPA began the reassessment of the Hudson River in 1989, the agency issued its Phase One report; GE's response to the report was more than six hundred pages long, longer than the EPA document. That reassessment, which was to be completed in two years, has been delayed indefinitely; the EPA acceded to GE's demands that all science in the project be subjected to additional peer review.

Lanahan also has effectively used the Freedom of Information Act to compel state officials to turn over nearly every document they generate. Fulfilling GE's numerous requests has kept many people busy retrieving documents at the New York Department of Environmental Conservation. "While we hardly had the staff to generate the documents, GE had the staff to read and analyze them. I'm sure they pored over every word," says Professor Richard Bopp of Rensselaer Polytechnic Institute. Bopp, arguably the nation's leading expert on the chemistry and sedimentology of the Hudson River, worked at the state environmental agency for a year and a half before returning to academia. He gained substantial insight into the war that's waged on the Hudson by the people who do Welch's bidding and how the minute points can become battlegrounds. Bopp recalls one meeting while he was at the state environmental agency when GE officials interpreted Bopp's data for EPA experts without realizing Bopp was present. Bopp, who grew up in the Bronx and typically dons a New York Yankees baseball cap when he's on the river gathering data, has collected most of the PCB-bearing sediment samples that have been taken from the Hudson in the last twenty odd years. The core sample GE was referring to, 98-6, was his. "I was there to refute their interpretation," Bopp says with a toothy grin. "It was a lot of fun."

Stephen Hamilton is another warrior in the PCB war. As General Electric's manager of environmental science and technology, Hamilton represents the company at many scientific forums. The bulk of his duties, though, have little to do with science. Hamilton recognizes that science will not decide the fate of the Hudson. Politics will, and Hamilton is a polished political operator. He admitted in a sworn deposition taken in one PCB lawsuit that he had personally met *110* times with politicians in the last decade lobbying on PCBs. Some congressmen, such as Gerald Solomon, a conservative Republican from upstate New York and chairman of the powerful House Rules Committee, have been important allies in helping GE successfully fend off a cleanup of the

Hudson. Solomon's letters to constituents on PCBs have borrowed verbatim GE's language in its own handouts. In addition, GE has been a corporate donor to Solomon, who has made numerous attacks on the EPA in conflicts with GE, even though the federal agency can hardly be accused of having pushed a radical pro-environment agenda on the Hudson.

Besides fending off PCB activists and paying business calls on federal and state politicians, Hamilton, a Ph.D. chemist, has tried to head off "bad science"—studies that might heighten the link between workplace cancer and PCBs and hence could prove a financial threat to General Electric. One such mortality study, which emerged in 1990, illustrated the lengths the Welch warriors will go to in defending what they perceive as GE's sovereign interests in the PCB issue. Thomas Sinks and Gregory Steele, two epidemiologists working for the National Institute for Occupational Safety and Health (NIOSH) and the Indiana State Department of Health, respectively, had examined mortality among 3,588 employees at a Westinghouse electrical capacitor factory in Bloomington, Indiana, where PCBs had been used as a dielectric fluid for twenty years, ending in 1977. The study, completed in the fall of 1990 but not yet published, found that thirteen workers had died of malignant melanoma or brain cancer, an alarmingly high death rate that was statistically quite significant. Chris Bailey, the Indiana state health commissioner, felt strongly that the surviving Westinghouse workers should be immediately notified of the study's results. Bailey, NIOSH, and representatives of Westinghouse, GE, and the Monsanto Chemical Company of St. Louis—the three defendants in many PCB lawsuits, Westinghouse and GE for having used PCB-laced fluids in their electrical equipment and Monsanto as the manufacturer of the chemicals—held two private meetings at NIOSH headquarters in Cincinnati in the fall of 1990 to thrash out the issue. NIOSH disagreed with Bailey, as did Hamilton. Asked later in a deposition to recount why he opposed informing the workers, Hamilton said: "I felt that it would raise a lot of concerns, a lot of hysteria, possibly, by misleading people."

What followed was typical of the kind of hardball that passes for business-as-usual at General Electric. Hamilton decided to go straight to the top in Indiana to voice his displeasure, and instructed Everett Murch, GE's chief of government relations with the state, to set up an appointment with the governor's office to discuss the study. Murch, in turn, contacted Philip Bainbridge, a longtime Democratic politician in Indiana, who tried to arrange a private session with Governor Evan Bayh. Bayh asked an aide to meet with the GE contingent, headed by Hamilton, who flew to Indianapolis on a GE corporate jet for the occasion. Although he wasn't an epidemiologist and therefore not best qualified to assess the work of Drs. Sinks and Steele, Hamilton nonetheless asserted that the study was flawed. Its findings were inconsistent with another study GE had commissioned of its own workers at Hudson Falls and Fort Edward that had found no elevated mortality. Hamilton returned to Indiana a second time for a separate meeting with Bailey, who refused to budge and who subsequently revealed the study at a press conference in Bloomington. The following spring, NIOSH sent official notices to all workers who had worked at the factory and been exposed to the chemicals.

When the Bloomington study was disclosed in *Business Week* on August 12, 1991, GE was prepared. A "holding statement" it had distributed internally instructed managers to direct employee and media inquiries to four "independent" scientists who could affirm the negligible health effects of PCBs, all four of whom had at one time or another received financial support for their science from General Electric. But Hamilton and his experts might want to rethink their negligible health assessment: Several additional workers formerly employed at Bloomington have died of brain cancer since the study's 1987 cutoff date.

The PCB war has claimed other victims.

ONE OF THE VICTIMS is Ed Bates. No one at GE ever told him about the potential health hazards of PCBs. Bates is a jovial man, a grandfather in his seventies whose big build and kindly face give him the appearance of a department store Santa Claus. Although he prefers to believe, the evidence notwithstanding, that his superiors simply didn't know PCBs were harmful, his opinion of his former employer has deteriorated in the decade since he has retired. Bates once thought the world of GE. "The GE"—Bates always inserts an article before the letters "GE," like most lifelong residents of Pittsfield, Schenectady, and Erie—"was the knight in shining armor for us. I never would have obtained an education except for the GE." Bates graduated from St. Joseph's High School in Pittsfield in 1939 and a year and a half later, on his nineteenth birthday, won the company's Steinmetz scholarship, enabling him to secure a B.S. in electrical engineering from Union College in Schenectady in 1948. In the intervening years Bates went off to war, navigating a B-29 that was cited in *Ripley's Believe It or Not* for having flipped over in a thermal updraft while bombing Tokyo in April 1945, with the pilots regaining control of the aircraft only a few hundred feet before crashing. He returned home a decorated war hero. For thirty-two years, after his college graduation, while Jack Welch was in Pittsfield selling new plastics, Bates worked in the same town manufacturing electrical transformers (a mainstay product of the old GE that reduced the high-voltage current from the transmission lines into lower voltage) which were filled with Pyranol and PCBs, and which Bates and his buddies built and tested.

The health hazards of synthetic chemicals have been known since the dawn of modern industrial chemistry in the nineteenth century. That is especially true of chlorinated hydrocarbons, the chemical group to which PCBs belong, which includes the pesticide DDT, as well as dioxin, the deadly impurity found in herbicides such as Agent Orange that killed and maimed many Vietnam vets. German chemists in the 1880s were the first to "chlorinate" hydrocarbons—that is, to combine chlorine atoms with those of carbon and hydrogen—and they were also the first to notice a health problem associated with their discovery, a chemically induced form of acne called "chloracne," identified among chemical industry workers in Germany in 1895, and much worse than common acne. Four years later, a Munich doctor published the first of what would be dozens of scientific papers on the hazards of chlorinated hydrocarbons, of which chloracne was believed to be one, but the warnings went largely ignored.

In the 1930s, a decade before GE began dumping PCBs into the Hudson and only several years after Monsanto began manufacturing them in 1929, an increasing number of scientists and physicians became concerned about the health risks of chlorinated hydrocarbons. One of the first warnings came in a paper published in 1936, telling of black workers of the Monsanto-owned Swann Chemical Company in Anniston, Alabama, which made PCBs and supplied them to GE's transformer factories in Pittsfield. The workers had developed horribly disfiguring skin lesions. The paper also suggested biochemical and neurological damage, the same symptoms noted in experiments on laboratory rats in the 1970s, when PCBs finally came under intense scientific scrutiny. The men complained of sexual dysfunction, loss of appetite, and lassitude, though the racially insensitive authors dismissed this last problem as an attribute of "Negroes."

The first documented case linking PCBs to worker sickness at General Electric came just one year later, in September 1937, when Bates was entering his junior year at St. Joseph's High, and Jack Welch was a toddler. The report, in the *Journal of Industrial Hygiene and Toxicology* and authored by Dr. Cecil Drinker of Harvard University Medical School, included a roundtable discussion with one GE manager, F.R. Kaimer, who recounted the awful afflictions that befell workers at the company's electrical wire factory in York, Pennsylvania. Fifty to sixty men suffered from chloracne. "Eight or ten of them were very severely afflicted—horrible specimens as far as their skin condition," Kaimer was quoted in the article. One worker died. Although Kaimer said the company had considered abandoning the chemical that was used to insulate electric wire, no substitute was available. Better hygiene helped ameliorate the problem, Kaimer said, though he expressed concern in the article about possible liver damage among workers stemming from continued contact with the chemicals.

Additional reports about the dangers of chlorinated hydrocarbons followed in scientific and medical journals in the late 1930s and 1940s. GE documents unearthed in one lawsuit filed by the Nevada Power Company against GE, Monsanto, and Westinghouse show that the company was aware of the scientific literature. One 1956 memo, prepared by GE chemist A.L. Bridgman in Pittsfield, listed forty-three published references, dating back to the first citation in 1899, on the physiological hazards of PCBs and other chlorinated hydrocarbons. The report concluded: "It appears to be generally agreed that the following hygienic measures should be taken by personnel working with these materials: (a) regular daily change of work clothes; (b) shower and scrub down of exposed parts of body at the end of the working period; (c) use of a protective skin cream on all exposed body parts; (d) regular periodic cleansing of the work area." The report also recommended pre- and periodic post-employment physical examinations, which GE never provided to Ed Bates or other workers, many of whom had daily contact with PCBs for more than four decades.

PCBs were omnipresent in Building Twelve, the transformer test department, where Bates and his best friend, Charlie Fessenden, worked and which they eventually ran. Wherever Bates went, Fessenden was always nearby. The two were an inseparable pair, a sort of bad cop–good cop team, Ed being an Irish hothead, and Charlie keeping Ed calm and working the system to get things done. The Pittsfield operations processed 140,000 pounds of PCB each week, several thousand pounds of which spilled on the floor, down the drain, and into the Housatonic River, which like the Hudson is off-limits to fishing now. Although the smell of the Pyranol fluid was ghastly, it was a minor irritant compared with other duties that the testing department performed. Workers had daily contact with Pyranol: To test the transformers, they had to plunge unprotected hands, arms, sometimes whole bodies, into large steel cabinets filled with Pyranol fluid. Once the transformers were hooked up and the electricity was humming, the building would be filled with fumes from the

hot Pyranol. There was no protective gear of any kind. The safety and hygiene
measures Bridgman recommended in his 1956 memo were not employed.
There was only one safety precaution, according to the handbook given to
foremen: In the event of eye contact, treat with castor oil. Workers would
periodically "welt out" from their contact with Pyranol, Bates recalls, breaking
out in a reddish rash, which typically resembled multiple mosquito bites.
Bates would send them to the plant physician, whose prescription never varied: He recommended putting them to work someplace else, out of direct contact with Pyranol, until the welts went away, which was usually in a few days.
This platoon system of shuttling healthy workers in and unhealthy ones out
continued the entire time Pyranol was used in the plant.

It wasn't until 1969 that Bates was told of GE's plans to find a substitute
for Pyranol and phase out use of the PCB fluid. Alarm bells had begun to
sound. The first came in 1966, when a scientist named Sören Jensen published
his findings about PCBs in the *New Scientist*. The Danish-born chemist, who
worked at the Institute for Analytical Chemistry at the University of Stock-
holm, was looking for traces of DDT and related insecticides in the wildlife of
his home country, but instead stumbled onto PCBs. It had taken Jensen two
years to identify what was an unknown substance, and his discovery was ominous for several reasons. The PCBs Jensen identified were found in plankton
and in eagles—the bottom and top of the wildlife food chain. They were also
discovered in a country that did not manufacture them. Jensen correctly theo-
rized that the PCBs had come from Germany, where they had been incinerated. Instead of being destroyed, the resilient chemicals had traveled across the
Baltic Sea intact by attaching themselves to airborne dust particles, raindrops,
and snowflakes. Jensen's findings confirmed the fears of many in the scientific community, that PCBs were being absorbed into the ecosystem in large
quantities.

Two years later, in 1968, on the other side of the planet, a second alarm
sounded. At a rice oil factory in western Japan, a machine containing PCBs
sprang a leak, contaminating the rice oil. Thousands of people who used the
oil for cooking became ill. The effects of what came to be known as the
Yusho—rice oil—syndrome included a variety of afflictions: skin eruptions,
swollen eyelids, swollen and painful joints, and general fatigue. One subsequent study identified thirty-three maladies associated with the PCB
exposure. Mothers who had been exposed only fleetingly to the chemical gave
birth to babies of lower-than-average weight and other abnormalities. In the
decades since, *Yusho* victims have shown a significantly higher incidence of

liver cancer, and even today other symptoms persist. Only recently have scientists discovered exactly why so many people got so sick: As the rice oil cooked, the heating of the PCBs altered their chemistry and unleashed a lethal contaminant called polychlorinated dibenzofurans, a cousin of dioxin. The toxicity threshold of furans, as the 135 specific varieties are collectively known in the scientific community, was found in the *Yusho* incident to be one milligram. What that means in layman's terms is frightening testimony to the potential toxicity of PCBs: Ingesting just one milligram of the mutant furans—one 454,000th of a pound—would in most cases cause the person who had swallowed it to break out in skin lesions. Expressed another way, just one ounce of furans would be potent enough to cause chloracne among 28,375 people if the dosage were evenly distributed. The danger of heated PCBs has broad health consequences because they are typically incinerated as a method of destruction. But incineration at temperatures of less than 1,700 degrees Fahrenheit doesn't destroy the PCBs; instead, it can alter them to form furans or dioxin.

Although the *Yusho* and Sweden incidents and the publicity they generated caused GE to seek a substitute for Pyranol, use of the fluid wasn't discontinued in Pittsfield until 1975, one year before the federal prohibition took effect. No new hygiene procedures were put in place in the six years before Pyranol was abandoned. Bates and his coworkers never received the physical exams GE had internally recommended, either in the 1970s or at any time before. Not that the workers were agitating for medical treatment. Pyranol was simply a nuisance that Bates and others had grown to accept. The workers in Pittsfield didn't know that PCBs were harmful, and those who knew at GE hadn't bothered to tell them. As for Bates, he was a defiantly procompany man. The GE was, after all, the GE.

In the late 1970s, however, his blind allegiance began to wane. Many of the workers with whom Ed and Charlie had worked in Building Twelve were dying, many from cancer. At first, Bates thought it was just coincidental, cancer being common among people at his advanced age. But the more cancers he encountered, the more he wondered if they stemmed from the one thing everyone had in common: their place of work. "It seemed like every other week we were going to a wake or funeral," Bates recalls. The high ratio of premature mortality also caught GE's attention. In 1981, one year before Bates retired, the company enlisted David Wegman, then of Harvard University, to do a study of worker mortality in Pittsfield. Wegman had already done a preliminary, unpublished study, released in 1978, which found elevated levels of leukemia and intestinal cancer among Pittsfield workers who had had contact with PCBs. GE had agreed to a followup, and Bates and Fessenden were elated: GE was finally recognizing that there indeed may have been a problem. Two years later, in March 1983, they read in the local Pittsfield paper that the new Wegman study had been completed and results would be released in three months. But publication was delayed on that occasion and five times more before the results were finally announced in January 1990, nine years after the study began.

As the years passed and the study failed to emerge, Bates and Fessenden got suspicious. In 1985, Bates requested that GE provide physical exams to retirees who may have been exposed to hazardous materials. The request was denied. "It is a long-standing general practice in the company not to provide physical examinations to retired employees," Stephen Hamilton, the senior GE official with responsibility for PCBs, wrote in a letter. Bates was undaunted. He and Fessenden began peppering Hamilton with questions about PCBs and the much delayed Wegman study. At one meeting in September 1985, Wegman agreed to provide the pair with mortality data on Building Twelve workers, but three years later, when they finally got information on forty-four deceased colleagues from Building Twelve, the causes of death were misstated. To prove that, Bates and Fessenden retrieved the death certificates of the forty-four men from town halls and city clerk offices throughout western Massachusetts. Confronted with the evidence, which the National Institute of Occupational Safety and Health had confirmed, Wegman acknowledged the error. He attributed it to clerical mistakes and assured Bates it would be corrected. When the final report was released two years later, Wegman handed over his raw data to GE. And GE in turn has refused to provide it to Bates for examination. Hamilton in a deposition taken as part of Nevada Power's lawsuit against GE, Westinghouse, and Monsanto, said the company was obliged to protect the confidentiality of its deceased workers. Bates, who says he was repeatedly assured over the years that he would be given the opportunity to examine the data once the report was released, doesn't buy it. "As much as you hate to say it, I think the stonewalling has been deliberate," he says. All Bates knows for sure is that of the 2,914 white male employees who worked at Pittsfield and qualified for a pension, and who died between January 1, 1969 and December 31, 1984—the study population at first—twelve hundred were excluded from the final mortality tabulation. Their specific identities have been kept under seal. "It's so frustrating," Bates says. "People call me up and say, 'My husband died. Here's his death certificate.' But I can't do anything with it. There's no way you can force the data out."

Meantime, the death toll has continued to mount. In June 1994, the widow of one worker at the Pittsfield transformer factory who died of cancer, and four other retirees, two of whom developed cancer, filed suit against GE and Monsanto, seeking $500 million in damages. Bates knows of another hundred or so workers who have died since the 1984 cutoff date for Wegman's study, among them his dear friend Charlie, of leukemia in February 1992. "Most of the people I worked with are dead," he says. But Fessenden's death is the one he can't forget, the one that still serves as an impetus to Bates and others. Before he died, Fessenden was filmed with Bates in a video that recounts their experiences with PCBs and their fight with GE over the Wegman study. The video, a sort of oral history with the two men on camera for more than an hour responding to an off-camera interviewer's questions, is riveting in its sincerity: the common men fighting the good fight. The three hundred people who viewed it at Berkshire Community College near Pittsfield in November 1992 stood and cheered Bates, and the memory of his deceased pal. The video ends with Bates vowing defiantly: "We're not gonna give up, are we, Charlie." Fessenden firmly responds: "No way."

Whether their valiant stance has had any impact on Jack Welch is doubtful. Rather than being punished for its behavior on PCBs, the company has found a way to profit from it. In the years following the EPA's ban on the chemical, GE started up a new business removing PCBs from the millions of electrical products that contained them. Many utilities and other customers paid GE handsome sums to perform such services. Other utilities, such as Nevada Power, began replacing the old PCB-laden equipment with new gear at their own expense. It has been an enormous task for companies nationwide, so great, in fact, that in 1985 the EPA estimated that 1.6 million capacitors and twenty-one thousand transformers containing PCBs were still in use in the United States. For GE, always quick to seize the business initiative, it represented an environmental misery of enormous market potential. "Is there a PCB accident just waiting to happen in your facility?" GE asked in a 1985 brochure it sent to potential customers.

The threat was real. As the *Yusho* incident showed, the toxicity of PCBs could be greatly magnified when exposed to heat or fire. That was the concern in 1981, when an office tower in Binghamton, New York, had to be evacuated after a basement fire ruptured the transformer and sent smoldering Pyranol fumes, laced with dioxin, up the airvents. Some years later, a ruptured GE transformer spilled fifty gallons of Pyranol in one section of the New York City subway, bringing the entire system to a halt. Not surprisingly, when GE was selling its environmental remediation services to potential customers, it played up the potential danger of PCBs, which of course it plays down when discussing removal of them from the Hudson. "Scores of companies are making unwanted headlines as accidents involving PCB contaminated equipment are impacting corporate images and pocketbooks," GE vice president Clyde Keaton, head of the newly created PCB remediation branch, wrote in a letter accompanying the 1985 brochure. "General Electric offers comprehensive PCB services to aid your staff in solving these problems before they become headaches. We've helped over 1,000 companies successfully manage PCB removal projects in the last five years alone. In fact, we're so confident of our people's ability to manage these projects, we actually assume full liability for the proper and legal handling and disposal of all PCBs and related equipment."

The dirty work of removing the chemicals was left to men like Steve Sandberg, whose story bears an eerie similarity to that of Ed Bates and demonstrates that GE's claims of proper PCB handling and disposal are at best dubious. In April 1989, Sandberg took a job in Anaheim, California, one of nine depots GE ran by then for the reclamation of PCBs. The job held out the promise of considerably more money than he had earned driving a truck for Emery Airfreight and little risk, he thought. His supervisors told him PCBs were "no worse than a teaspoon of salt," Sandberg recalls. To prove it, they showed him a training film, narrated by Walter Cronkite, about the relative safety of PCBs.

Sandberg and the three others who worked with him were very busy. The business was booming, and the phone never stopped ringing as customers sought GE's services. In the two and a half years that he handled PCBs, Sandberg estimates he made four hundred calls on customers in Southern California, cleaning up PCB spills and removing them from equipment. He collected substantial overtime and earned $57,000 one year. The removal process required that Sandberg sometimes lean on and crawl over equipment containing PCBs. Cleaning up spills, which were several inches deep on occasion, when a transformer had ruptured, was also messy. Sometimes he had to get down on his hands and knees to retrieve the oily chemicals. The gloves GE issued to him were canvas, and the protective suit he wore was a kind of throwaway paper that didn't provide sufficient protection. "It would be soaked through in seconds," Sandberg says.

In December 1990, he came down with the skin lesions commonly associated with PCB exposure. Boils broke out on Sandberg's extremities, first his thighs, then his forearms, then his face. They began popping out everywhere, on his hands, even the bottom of his feet. Sandberg, who was still performing many of the same tasks, could hardly move at times because the pain was so intense. He went to several doctors. In July 1991, while in the midst of tests to assess his condition, Sandberg was looking for a purchasing-order book in his boss's office. Instead, he found a folder detailing the possible health side-effects of PCBs. "I was in total shock at what I was reading," he recalls. He confronted his managers for having told him that the chemicals were harmless. From that moment on, he was branded a problem for the Anaheim operation. Sandberg was eventually sent to a toxicologist, who determined that his skin lesions were indeed the result of exposure to chemicals, and he was removed from his cleanup job. He was given a broom and told to sweep the premises, effectively a demotion in that it paid $2 an hour less than his previous position.

On the day Sandberg was removed from his PCB handling job, October 28, 1991, he inadvertently saw a faxed company memorandum on his situation that he wasn't supposed to see. The memo speaks volumes about the damage-control mentality inside GE on the PCB issue. "Stephen Sandberg, the employee in Anaheim who claims to have been poisoned by PCBs, seems to be escalating the situation day by day," Bill Thornton, a GE attorney in Schenectady, wrote to Tim Daly, a manager in the PCB remediation group. "He has made contact with PCB activists in Pittsfield and has copies of correspondence between them and GE." Sandberg may have made a complaint to federal authorities, the memo indicated. In addition, Thornton said, Sandberg may have "stirred up" the employees of a manufacturing company with property adjacent to GE's facility, and might go public with his complaints in either the *Los Angeles Times* or the Anaheim newspaper. "We need to have a plan to deal with the situation rather than stay in a reactive mode," Thornton wrote, a plan for dealing "appropriately" with Sandberg; other employees; the community; federal authorities; and the media. The memo suggested specific experts GE could call upon to refute Sandberg's claims in a meeting with other employees. Public relations was directed to prepare a holding statement for the media "stressing the positive aspects of the work done in the facility." Thornton also recommended that Sandberg be treated with "respect and compassion," and that his complaints and requests be handled in a normal manner.

Ironically, although, contrary to Thornton's suspicions, Sandberg hadn't actually contacted any governmental agencies at the time the memo was written, his reading of it galvanized his resolve to do exactly that. Several weeks later, he contacted the EPA, complaining not just about his own physical condition and GE's treatment of him but about other practices at the Anaheim facility that he believed were improper. In the investigation that followed, the EPA agreed. It found that GE illegally stored reclaimed PCB outdoors in unprotected storage areas for longer periods and in greater volumes than permitted. EPA inspectors found that work areas and soil were also contaminated. The agency temporarily prohibited the Anaheim facility from accepting additional PCB waste and, in March 1993, announced it would seek $353,000 in penalties for the violations of a special federal law regulating the handling and disposal of PCBs. (The matter was subsequently settled, with GE neither admitting nor denying the EPA's allegations, but agreeing to pay $57,000.)

As for Sandberg, who in March 1992 sent a thirty-five-page certified letter to Jack Welch detailing what had happened to him, he has been on medical disability and hasn't worked since April 1992, and has developed an irregular heartbeat that did not exist before his PCB exposure. Although his skin has cleared up, he still has swollen eyelids, wakes up periodically with nightsweats, and is severely lethargic. His blood is contaminated with PCBs. That problem might resolve itself. But the level of contamination in his fatty tissue, which is two hundred times higher than in his bloodstream, probably won't ever diminish. He has seen a psychiatrist for two years to overcome the anxiety he feels about the future. Doctors say his prognosis is uncertain: The PCBs he was exposed to are of the most toxic variety because they had been heated. And his wife has suffered. She was three months pregnant in October 1991 when the extent of Steve's health problems became clear. Doctors were unable to give her assurances that the fetus she carried wouldn't be affected, and rather than take a chance, she decided to terminate the pregnancy.

ANOTHER CASUALTY of PCBs has been Everett Nack, a river rat who says he knows every eddy and every marsh along the Hudson River from Manhattan to Troy. For sixty odd years, ever since he was four years old, he has fished the Hudson, a waterway that for centuries has inspired the imagination of those who have come to know it. The Mohican Indians of James Fenimor Cooper books called the river *Muhheakunnuk*, which means "great waters constantly in motion." To Washington Irving, the Hudson was more than mere water; it was a magical, mysterious place populated by the likes of Ichabod Crane and Rip Van Winkle. Karl Baedeker, the globetrotting German travel guide writer, pronounced the river "grander and more inspiring" than the Rhine. The critic

Henry James, returning home to the Hudson River Valley after years in Europe, was moved by waters he found "perpetually interesting." Even Henry Hudson, whose ship, the *Half Moon*, was repeatedly attacked by Indians on his first and only exploration of the river in 1609, nonetheless found the brilliant fall foliage and majestic scenery captivating. "Great river of the mountains," Hudson dubbed the waterway that would later bear his name.

With the Catskill Mountains to its west and the Taconic Mountains to its east, the Hudson inspires awe. For 315 miles it descends from its source—Lake Tear of the Clouds, a two-acre pond on the southern slope of Mount Marcy, the highest summit in the Adirondacks—to its mouth at the Battery, on the southern tip of Manhattan, linking mountain and metropolitan settings. Nack is drawn to the Hudson in much the same way that the shad and sturgeon he fishes are drawn to it each year to spawn. Fishing the Hudson fulfills in him a biological need. Guiding his eighteen-foot boat out onto the wide river one day, Nack and a party of four ride several miles amid choppy seas before cutting the Mercury outboard motor just above Hyde Park, the resting place of Franklin Delano Roosevelt. To the north, the Catskills loom in a purplish hue, shadowed by fluffy cumulus clouds. Only an occasional convent or monastery on the shore breaks an otherwise endless expanse of trees. It is a scene that evokes a sense of timelessness, one that Henry Hudson first glimpsed on September 15, 1609. In his ship's log, Hudson wrote of the veritable cornucopia of vegetation and wildlife he witnessed: fish, maize, deer, all in prodigious quantities. "The land is the finest for cultivation I ever in my life set foot upon, and it also abounds in trees of every description," Hudson wrote. Nack is not a poetic man—he's an old man of the sea, whose scent is unmistakably that of his profession—but the splendor of the panorama that surrounds him on this fine June day moves the grizzled old fisherman, albeit briefly. "It sure is a beautiful place," he pronounces, before throwing a buoy overboard that will indicate when the encroaching waters are at high tide. He then waits, the pastime of fishermen everywhere.

Nack, wearing red suspenders that accentuate his Lincolnesque lines, was once a full-time commercial fisherman, but PCBs curtailed his career. While the river is in many respects cleaner than it has been in generations, and fish are much more abundant and generally healthier, PCB remains the one nagging trace of chemical that impedes a full recovery of the Hudson, as well as human consumption of the fish. Since 1975, Nack and several hundred other Hudson fishermen have been precluded by New York State from fishing all but two species, shad and Atlantic sturgeon. Moreover, women of child-bearing age and children under fifteen are advised to eat no fish from the Hudson.

Because of the restrictions, Nack has had the bulk of his livelihood eliminated; he figures he's lost more than $1 million in income. The cost for the entire region has been far greater: some $15 million a year in lost revenue for fishermen and other tourism-related businesses.

Although the Mohawk was dredged to rid that river of its radiation, a similar solution has evaded the Hudson. New York State has advocated dredging, a solution steadfastly opposed by Welch, who contends it's unnecessary because the PCBs are degrading naturally on their own. Meanwhile, the chemicals get washed downriver and escape over the Troy dam, several hundred pounds every year, making recovery through dredging or any means impossible.

Until recently, Welch's contention that the river would cleanse itself, and that striped bass would someday again be edible, seemed plausible. Although the average PCB content of striped bass still exceeded the legal threshold of two parts per million, it had declined markedly, from average readings in the high teens in the late 1970s to low single digits a decade later. In the last few years, however, the slow decline suddenly reversed, with average readings in fish jumping by a factor of two to three. General Electric blamed this increase on the leaching into the river of fresh PCBs trapped in the bedrock below the facilities at Hudson Falls and Fort Edward, which evaded a dam and retention system built specifically to keep that from happening. The seepage will stop, the company contends, now that almost all new releases of the chemicals have been found and plugged.

While bureaucrats, technocrats, and businessmen debate the issues and what action to take, much as they have since 1975, Everett Nack burns. Nack isn't so much angry as he is sad over the fate of a magnificent waterway and the fate of many fellow fishermen who have quit fishing the river. "About three-quarters of the guys who used to fish have given it up," Nack says. "Some go on welfare, and some do whatever they can find to do."

Nack has supplemented his fishing income with carpentry work, but a few precious hours are still devoted to fishing. Nack's prey on this day is Atlantic sturgeon, a prehistoric fish that has been taken commercially in the Hudson for centuries. At first a source of cheap meat, sturgeon fishing became more lucrative as the caviar industry flourished. Caviar was as common as cocktail mix in the bars along the Hudson about a century ago, and sturgeon steak was called Albany beef. Today, Atlantic sturgeon is the one species that sustains Nack, and his fishing brethren. The most valuable bounty is the caviar; in a good season, Nack will process 120 pounds of roe, salted according to techniques he learned over years in the trade, which then sells for as much as $100 a pound.

Sturgeon are huge, beastly-looking creatures, up to twelve feet long, and weighing six hundred pounds, as clumsy as the scientific term marine biologists use to describe their habits: anadromous. It is a word that Nack pronounces with difficulty, screwing up his face in odd contours. But the term, applied to fish that live in the sea but return to fresh water to breed, has great significance for him. Because the sturgeon live in the Atlantic ten months of the year, returning to the Hudson every May for just two months while they spawn, they don't ingest the same quantity of PCBs as do other species which spend more time in the river. Hence their unrestricted status. That's good for Nack, because a single female sturgeon and her roe can fetch $3,000 or more at the fish market. On this day, however, he's fishing for the government rather than himself. The sturgeon season officially ended the day before, when Nack's four four-hundred-foot-long nets tethered across the midsection of the river were empty. But as luck would have it, today's catch is a bonanza. In a matter of minutes, Nack and his son Steve draw four massive sturgeon out of the river, each weighing more than two hundred pounds and measuring nine feet long. Nack receives a $250 bounty for each female sturgeon he delivers this day to state officials, who want them for the fish hatchery.

"Goddamn state," Nack curses, hauling the last one, a female, out of the river. His anger is understandable: This was the first time the state had restricted the surgeon season, which under the new rules ended June 15. Were it not for the moratorium, the $1,000 in fish Nack caught that day would have been worth more than $10,000.

Nack's encounter with regulation is a perfect metaphor for the plight of the Hudson: Government regulators have paid excessive attention to often irrelevant details while failing to address an issue fundamental to the very health and survival of the river. It is this bitter irony that Nack can't quite fathom. Nor can he understand the behavior of his other enemy, General Electric. In the summer of 1993, GE settled a suit brought eight years before by aggrieved fishermen on the Hudson and off Long Island, where a separate five-year prohibition on striped-bass fishing was lifted in 1990 for half of the island. The company settled, it said in a statement, to avoid "endless litigation" that it in reality had prolonged. GE established a $7 million fund to compensate "only those [fishermen] who can demonstrate real economic loss." One of those fishermen was Nack, whose demonstrated economic loss was determined by a court-appointed referee to be $5,000. Nack never kept records on

his catch of striped bass, the only species covered under the suit. The prohibition on eels, Nack's chief commercial catch that wasn't included, cost him at
least $50,000 a season.

Although Nack has lived with the calamity of the Hudson River for
twenty years now, it still puzzles him. "GE has done everything it possibly can
to stall off dredging the river," he says. "They just don't have any sense of
shame." About eighty-five miles downriver in Manhattan, Michael "Buzzy"
O'Keeffe also finds the company's behavior reprehensible. A few years ago,
O'Keeffe, proprietor of two popular riverside restaurants in New York City, the
River Cafe and the Water Club, where patrons who order striped bass eat only
the farm-bred variety, was so fed up with the situation he posted signs telling
GE execs to stay away for their "flagrant and pernicious pollution of the Hudson River, spawning grounds of America's Number One game fish, the striped
bass." O'Keeffe, who uses his perch at the River Cafe underneath the Brooklyn
Bridge to fish for striped bass, has been throwing them back longer than he
cares to recall. "The cancer of American industry," he says, his voice full of disdain, "is the bottom line."

By the spring of 1991, Jack Welch was growing more concerned, not about
the health consequences of PCBs, but rather about the potential liabilities that
General Electric might be held responsible for. Estimates of the remediation
costs kept rising. In April, while attending a meeting in Pittsfield of GE Plastics' senior staff, Welch listened as several officers discussed an environmental
remediation study the company had commissioned. Some big numbers were
being tossed around the table. The study presented several alternatives for
removing PCBs from sites in Pittsfield and the nearby Housatonic River, and
the costs associated with each alternative. The more aggressive and thorough
the remediation, the more it cost, with some alternatives totalling in the billions of dollars. Welch suddenly stopped the discussion, and gave the final
word on the approach that should be taken: "On this one, guys, let's just keep
two steps ahead of the law." Years later, the Pittsfield situation would erupt into
a controversy rivaling that of the Hudson, when PCB contamination was
found in soil around homes, and residents learned that the company knew of
the problem as early as the 1980s.*

* After a breakdown in negotiations with General Electric, the U.S. Environmental Protection
  Agency sought Superfund status for the pollution in Pittsfield, and in the adjacent
  Housatonic River. Welch had personally intervened in the negotiations, and had bitterly
  fought the Superfund status, the *Wall Street Journal* reported on April 7, 1998, "which would

Welch's chief concern was what the federal government would compel General Electric to do. For fifteen years GE had managed to exploit every last scintilla of scientific uncertainty to keep New York State at bay, and stave off a dredging of the river. The EPA had been a dependable ally, but now the agency's loyalty was questionable. Not only had William Reilly been appointed administrator of the EPA, but the new head of Region Two, the region that had jurisdiction for the Hudson, was Constantine Sidamon-Eristoff. Descended from Russian aristocracy, Eristoff had been involved in New York city and state government politics during his entire adult life. A patrician who practiced noblesse oblige, he was in the John Lindsay wing of New York's Republican party. In addition to bringing an activist point of view to the job, Eristoff had more than a passing interest in the fate of the Hudson. The Eristoff family estate, in Highland Falls, just north of West Point, had a panoramic view of the river; neighboring estates included those of the Morgan, Rockefeller, Gould, Harriman, Astor, and Vanderbilt families.

Eristoff's early actions confirmed Welch's worst suspicions. When the EPA announced in the fall of 1989, just as Eristoff was taking office, that it intended to reassess the status of the Hudson, Welch had lobbied hard to have GE designated as the scientific overseer of the project. Eristoff was astonished that the company would even propose such a thing. Ever since the sacking of Ogden Reid, a friend of Eristoff's, the PCB issue had been a lightning rod. From the very day he had taken the job as Region Two administrator, Eristoff had been peppered with pleas from friends saying, "Constantine, you have to do something about the PCBs in the Hudson." Groups that advocated aggressive remediation of the river, including Scenic Hudson, regarded General Electric as little more than a felon. When Stephen Ramsey, GE's new vice president for environmental affairs, came on board some months later, he too insisted that GE be designated as scientific overseer of the reassessment. Eristoff turned him down as well. Ramsey demanded a private meeting with Eristoff, who considered such contact inappropriate.

Frustrated by his inability to influence a process that could be key to GE's financial future, Ramsey tried to neutralize Eristoff. Congressman Solomon, a close personal friend of White House Chief of Staff John Sununu, sought to

make the company liable for potentially huge natural-resource damages. GE even suggested it might pull its seven hundred workers out of Pittsfield if the plant is declared a Superfund site." The newspaper reported that as negotiations between the company and EPA continued in Boston, Welch suggested in separate meetings with Pittsfield mayor Gerald Doyle and John DeVillars, EPA's administrator for New England, that if Superfund were invoked, GE might have to move out of the city.

tap that connection and others to call into question Eristoff's credibility. Solomon claimed that Region Two administrators, including Eristoff, had determined to dredge the river even before they began their reassessment. The congressman urged that Region Two be relieved of its duties and that officials in Washington, whom GE had more access to, should take control of the process.

Ramsey also conceived an end run around Eristoff. At Ramsey's request, Welch wrote to EPA Administrator Reilly, requesting a private meeting to discuss GE's perspective on the Hudson River reassessment. When the meeting was convened on June 19, 1991 at Reilly's office in Washington, Welch and Ramsey were in attendance; so was Eristoff, much to their surprise. He had been tipped off to the impending get-together by friends in the agency.

The meeting seems not to have gone according to plan, at least not from Welch's perspective. Reilly departed for Europe after about half an hour, leaving Eristoff in charge. He patiently listened as Welch told him that the river was cleaning itself naturally, and that a process GE had spent millions developing—bioremediation, a method of using microbes to accelerate the natural degradation of PCBs—would prove to be the answer. Above all, Welch was alarmed at Eristoff's plan to include a summary of research on the danger to human health from the consumption of Hudson River fish in a public document the EPA would issue later that summer. GE-sponsored studies showed that the PCBs in the river weren't at all toxic, Welch contended. There were no dangers to human health, he said, and the data that suggested such a connection was flawed and erroneous. Welch knew that the inclusion of this material in the report would be used by environmental activists to promote a dredging of the river. The meeting ended with Eristoff agreeing to reconsider his position, but several weeks later he phoned Welch to inform him that he had decided to keep the data in the report after all.

"I'm disappointed," Welch said. "Does this mean you and Region Two are committed to dredging the Hudson River sediments?" he asked. "No, not at all," Eristoff replied. He said neither he nor the EPA had reached any conclusions, and wouldn't until the reassessment was finished some years thence. "As we discussed at our meeting, science must control this process," Eristoff wrote in a letter to Welch a few days later. "I do not believe it would be appropriate to delay presenting this information to the public. Indeed, inasmuch as the New York State fish advisories and commercial fishing bans remain in effect, information which might permit the public to better understand the risks involved in eating the fish should be made available to it."

Welch needn't have worried. The EPA, bowing to renewed pressure from GE and Congressman Solomon, now says the reassessment won't be completed until the year 2001 at the earliest. Commercial fishing of all but two species is still prohibited on the Hudson, the chemicals still rest on the river bottom, and a cleanup still hasn't begun.

CHAPTER TEN

THE TYRANNY
OF NUMBERS

As THE 1980s CAME TO A CLOSE, Jack Welch, to all appearances, was the most successful and admired CEO of his age. He was widely acclaimed as the man who had revived an American institution, who had wrought dramatic change not just at GE but had also defined the landscape in which change had occurred elsewhere in corporate America, as other CEOs mimicked his tactics. Just as with Henry Ford and his Ford Motor Company, however, there was another side to General Electric that the public had scant knowledge of and the media had paid little attention to. The revolution had sanctioned a tyranny of numbers, in which the numbers—earnings—became the Holy Grail of every GE manager's existence. And that, in turn, had already led GE managers into some ethical lapses, for which the company had been penalized. As the 1990s would unfold, those lapses would become more frequent and celebrated.

Welch recognized the problem, and sought to correct it. In 1989, over the objections of the Corporate Executive Council, a group made up of Welch and the thirteen presidents of GE's businesses (twelve now, with the divestiture of GE Aerospace in 1993), he pushed through a performance evaluation system in which corporate officers, the senior corps of top executives, would be graded on a scale of one to five on how they supported six GE values. "Never bend or wink at the truth, and live within both the spirit and letter of the law" was one; "teamwork depends on trust, mutual understanding, and the shared belief that the individual will be treated fairly in any environment" was another. The values exercise seemed to make sense—who could argue with a policy that seemingly committed the corporation to respect for "individual dignity," or a culture that prized "candor and openness." The problem was that these lofty goals were often at odds with Welch's actions.

While Welch may have wanted to be seen as empowering people and respecting them individually—one of the objectives, after all, of the Work-Out program he had begun in 1988—he was a prisoner of his tendency to demand absolute control. The paradox between the iron-willed Jack Welch and the man who seemed to embrace, not necessarily in what he did but in what he said, a kinder, gentler vision in the spirit of Work-Out, was a dichotomy that would have profound consequences for General Electric. One man who discovered this firsthand was Bob Bowen, whose nineteen-year career as a finance executive came to a quick end in January 1993 because he was too candid in delivering news that did not please Welch. And what happens to managers who deliver bad news is well established—they become targets.

Bowen had been sent to London in the spring of 1992 to fix another European acquisition that had gone awry, Tungsram in Hungary. Made just days after the fall of the Berlin Wall in 1989, the acquisition of Tungsram, which was hailed in the media as another brilliant masterstroke by Welch, did seem propitious: The most visible pillar of communism had been toppled, and the former Soviet bloc would burgeon as free thinking and free markets took root. At the same time, GE Lighting, which had struggled in executing an international strategy, would gain a significant position in Europe to counteract encroachments that Philips and Siemens had made into the U.S. market.

As was true of CGR, however, Tungsram was not what it appeared to be. As a state-owned entity, the company needed modernization badly and had been run by the Communists, who practiced accounting conventions that, needless to say, did not conform to standards in the United States, or anywhere else in the capitalist world. The whole concept of "profit" and "loss" was foreign to Tungsram management. Audits conducted later in accordance with U.S. accounting standards would show that the company had been losing money for more than a decade.

The job of sorting out the financial mess fell to Bowen, who in March 1992 arrived in London as financial chief of GE's European lighting operations, which also included Thorn in the United Kingdom, acquired the year before. Bowen, who had formerly worked in Tokyo in the Medical Systems division, was new to Lighting but had accepted the job, against the advice of friends, because he was seeking another global challenge to round out his experience in Asia. He would also again be working for Chuck Pieper, his boss in Tokyo, who asked Bowen to join him in London. The two had good rapport. They had weathered one scandal in Japan in which people at the Yokogawa Medical Systems division they ran were accused of paying bribes to medical school professors in the sale of medical equipment. During Bowen's four years in Japan, Medical Systems had gone through two chief financial officers in Milwaukee, and another two finance chiefs at CGR.

Bowen was well versed in the accounting techniques that could be employed to enhance a profit-and-loss statement. His investigations at Tungsram, however, revealed a company that was worse off than the relatively favorable picture Lighting president John Opie had conveyed to Welch, so much worse off, in fact, that after only a few weeks on the job, Bowen feared it would be his last at GE. Someone would have to take the fall, and he was low man on the totem pole, and a newcomer to boot. Bowen had no choice: first-round restructuring, prior to his arrival, had been insufficient and additional action was required.

At a meeting in June 1992, Pieper and Bowen made their case to Welch over the strenuous objections of Lighting's senior management. Pieper explained the underlying business performance and the further actions called for. Bowen was there to field the technical questions. What they presented was the hard reality, gruesome though it was: Tungsram appeared headed for a net loss in 1992 in the range of $40 million. Welch would have to advance the company $200 million if it were to survive.

"I'm not giving another dollar" was Welch's response. He had already flushed additional money down the CGR toilet, but Tungsram was too much to take. They would have to tough it out on their own. Six months later, Bowen was invited out to dinner by Pieper, and there, over wine and a linen table-cloth, he was advised that he was being transferred back to the States, with several job opportunities. Bowen understood the underlying message and instead decided to leave GE. Although Pieper hated to do it, someone had to pay the price—and so, unable to save Bowen, he did what most GE managers would have done in similar circumstances: He swallowed hard and executed his orders.* Unfortunately, as news of Bowen's departure from GE sped through GE's close-knit finance organization, it reinforced a message that midlevel managers already understood, that rhetoric was just that, and that candor and openness would not be tolerated. "I almost died when I heard they shot him," says one former colleague. "Here's a guy who stood up, and identified a problem. Why in God's name would they shoot him?"

Why, indeed. Ironically, in March 1993, just two months after Bowen left GE, Welch did exactly what Bowen and Pieper had recommended, authorizing an emergency plan to pump an additional $200 million into Tungsram, which brought GE's total investment in the Hungarian company to $550 million.

---

* Four years later, Pieper himself would leave his post as head of Tungsram.

Bowen's departure demonstrated a fundamental problem within General Electric, one that had manifested itself many times before. Welch could talk all he wanted about values, about doing the right thing, about how executives should stand up and speak out with confidence and assurance when they saw improper or questionable conduct, but Bowen's fate communicated the harsh reality of the GE culture—the bearers of bad news are targeted, even when they are not responsible for what went awry, even when they have simply inherited a bad situation.

Years later, as the transgressions escalated well beyond the practices Bowen had observed, Welch would always claim in public to have been victimized by yet another "rogue" employee, another rotten apple in a very large bin. In truth he believes that jettisoning soldiers, even good people who are trying to do the right thing when things go wrong, is the way warriors, revolutionaries, should conduct their affairs. Total business warfare is an execution-style business, as Welch sees it, and he is the chief executioner.

THEY CALLED IT the "monster chart." It was just a little squiggle of a line, really, between two axes, one horizontal, one vertical, not unlike the millions of charts generated each year inside General Electric. But this chart would have harsh implications for the men who were seeing it for the first time, in October 1992.

The chart was an outgrowth of Welch's tight relationship with the auto industry. In the 1960s, Welch had correctly identified Detroit as a big potential customer for Lexan and Noryl, molded plastics that were beginning to replace steel in cars. In one television commercial, Welch stood behind a Lexan sheet while Detroit Tigers pitcher Denny McLain, who had won thirty games in 1968, threw fastballs at him; of course, the Lexan shielded him. Welch continued to maintain close ties to the auto industry, and to this day meets regularly with the CEOs of the major automakers.

The industry in 1992 was buzzing over the arrival in Detroit of Jose Ignacio Lopez de Arriortua, General Motors's top purchasing executive and cost-cutting messiah. Lopez had gained a tough-guy reputation while working in Spain under Jack Smith, who headed GM's European operations. When Smith, a close acquaintance of Welch's, became CEO, he brought Lopez with him to the United States to shore up GM. Lopez had now caused a stir by compelling parts suppliers to accept double-digit reductions in their prices. Purchasing was a corporate function that seldom got much attention, but Lopez's ferocious approach had made him one of the most feared men in

Detroit. To be "Lopezed" meant to be mangled, to be forcibly coerced into concessions.

General Electric had taken a different approach in its supplier relationships. Throughout the 1980s, it had championed a concept called "partnering," in which suppliers were winnowed to a select few who got the lion's share of the business. GE and its partners would then work together toward the common goal of improving quality, service, and reliability, following a strategy similar to one the Japanese auto industry had executed for years with great success. As far as Lopez was concerned, partnering was much too cozy— purchasing managers were so busy establishing "relationships" that they lost their bargaining leverage when it came time to talk about price. The Lopez technique was as direct as his Basque personality: Send all your suppliers letters, demanding price cuts of 5 percent or more; rebid the contracts of those who refused to go along; and to keep the productivity improvements coming, make the 5 percent reduction an annual event.

By mid-1992, Welch was filled with admiration for Lopez and his approach in dealing with GM's suppliers. During a session at GE's Management Development Institute in Crotonville, New York, he raved about the tough Spaniard, made disparaging comments about the purchasing department, and ordered Gary Reiner, who as head of Welch's business development staff oversaw purchasing, to investigate the situation, and find out if GE was too soft on its suppliers. A member of Reiner's staff found numbers that seemed to support Welch's thesis and suggested an apparent motherlode of potential savings. The heads of purchasing for each of GE's businesses were brought to Fairfield, where Reiner pointed a gun at them in the form of what came to be known among the group as the "monster chart."

The chart got its name because the squiggly line looked like the gaping jaws of a monster. The twelve men understood its significance. As the line ascended from the point where the vertical and horizontal axes intersected, climbing ever further from the horizontal axis with each increment of time, the information it conveyed furrowed many brows. Frank Doyle, GE's executive vice president, who was standing in for Welch that day, later remarked that he really felt for the people in that room, for Reiner was reading a "guilty" verdict, and the consequences of that sentence were clear to all.

If true, the numbers Reiner had crunched suggested an ominous trend. The chart purportedly traced the growing gap between the prices GE paid for its purchased materials and the prices it received for its finished goods. The vertical axis recorded the price inflation differential, the horizontal axis time. Year zero was 1986, and with each successive year, GE paid out progressively more to its suppliers than it took in. By 1991, the cumulative price differential had widened to 16 percent. The ascent of the line from the horizontal axis formed the mouth of the monster. For a company whose annual bill for purchased materials was in the tens of billions of dollars, 16 percent was a number of staggering proportions.

In some businesses, Med Systems for instance, purchased materials represented upwards of 90 percent of its costs. Med Systems had been among the most aggressive in pursuing the outsourcing strategy common throughout GE. Although General Electric was still one of the nation's leading manufacturers, it was not manufacturing in the same sense that Charles Steinmetz would have understood it. What GE today calls manufacturing, Steinmetz would have called mere assembly. The parts are purchased from outside vendors, built to GE specs, then assembled in GE factories with the GE monogram affixed to the final product.

The purchasing managers were dumbfounded and immediately skeptical of the numbers Reiner presented. Because purchased materials represented such a large proportion of total costs, earnings should have dropped significantly if Reiner's 16 percent inflation number were an accurate representation of the truth, but that hadn't happened. GE's earnings had more than doubled from 1986 to 1991. Reiner's numbers defied logic—at Med Systems, there had been price *deflation* on purchased materials of about 3 to 5 percent per year.

"We were all aghast. They couldn't have been right," one participant in the meeting recalls. "Ballistic doesn't even describe the state they were in," says Sylvia Ceravalo, a member of Reiner's staff. "None of them agreed with it."

The purchasing managers questioned Reiner at length about how he arrived at his numbers, and what they really signified. But though the managers clearly didn't believe the information Reiner had presented—and Reiner himself seemed to be backpedaling—they were numbers after all, and in GE numbers take on a life of their own. Welch doesn't like executives who whine. Rather than challenging the numbers, you are expected to accept them, and do something to fix them. Whether they were accurate or not was irrelevant—Welch had already made up his mind that they were. "Once that chart hit the table," another meeting participant recalls, "the GE culture took over to eliminate the gap. We were off to the races." The monster chart was presumed to be accurate because it would allow Welch to advance his "change" agenda.

The gap got eliminated, as well as the people who were judged responsible for it. Welch attended the next meeting of the purchasing managers, and every one subsequent to that. The man who was constantly "reinventing" himself was about to advance a new purchasing philosophy, one that was entirely different from the "partnering" approach that had until then been embraced. His message: Lopez was a hero. General Electric had to get more like General Motors. Tough. Demanding. Unrelenting. It was too soft on suppliers who were taking advantage of GE's generosity.

Welch brought that same message to the business division presidents, who were only too eager to take up the cudgel of supplier reform, and soon were out-lopezing Lopez. J. Richard Stonesifer, head of GE Appliances in Louisville, moved swiftly to get back the 16 percent. In November 1992, just one month after the Reiner session in Fairfield, more than three hundred Appliance division suppliers were summoned to a cavernous ballroom at the Hurstbourne Hotel outside Louisville. There, they got a jolt that left many speechless. Partnering was suddenly passé; in its place was "Target 10," the program Stonesifer and his colleagues unveiled. Starting in 1993, suppliers would be expected to cut their prices 10 percent each year. Although in some instances 10 percent was more than the suppliers made selling to General Electric, the choice was clear: either give up some—all—of your profit margin, or lose GE as a customer. "We see no relief in sight," Stonesifer told the group somberly.

The suppliers, of course, were none too happy. Jim Schepens, a vice president with Citgo Petroleum, which provided a chemical feedstock to GE Plastics, was angry when he received a letter in December 1992 demanding a 7 percent price reduction in the coming year. Schepens wanted to be accommodating, but 7 percent was simply impossible. After haggling over the issue for several weeks, he decided to take his pleas to a higher court—to Welch himself. Schepens didn't know Welch personally, but from what he had read about him, he thought Welch would welcome constructive input from a noncompany source. That, at least, was the conclusion Schepens had drawn from *Control Your Destiny or Someone Else Will*, the book about Welch that had so impressed him he bought copies of it for eight Citgo colleagues. Schepens believed strongly in his cause—he thought the price demands were shortsighted, even unethical, because GE was trying to abrogate a contract that stipulated an agreed-upon price—and he penned a two-page letter expressing his sentiment, showing it beforehand to John Yates, the purchasing manager at GE Plastics. Yates thought the letter was reasonable and expressed a message that he himself wanted conveyed to Welch; he too felt the company was unreasonable in its demands but didn't have the courage to express that opinion directly to Welch.

Days after Schepens mailed the letter, Ron Hall, the CEO of Citgo Petroleum, went to Pittsfield for a meeting with Yates and Gary Rogers, the CEO of GE Plastics who had replaced Glen Hiner. Rogers, who had been called by Welch about the letter while on a trip in China, informed Hall that if Schepens weren't removed from the account, GE Plastics, Citgo's largest customer by a wide margin, would cease buying its supplies from Citgo. Schepens resigned a few weeks later.*

As talk spread within GE about what Welch had supposedly done to Schepens, people in purchasing were increasingly fearful—and disillusioned. "For many years people complained about Jack Welch, and I always defended the guy, but the monster chart was the last straw for me," says Ceravalo, who left GE shortly thereafter. Others were merely concerned with their own survival and were determined to wring even bigger concessions out of their suppliers. In Schenectady, at GE's highly profitable Power Systems division, President David Genever-Watling chose a higher target: 12 percent. The British-born Genever-Watling, whom subordinates nicknamed "Dash" for his hyphenated name as well as his affinity for spiffy clothes and gold cuff links, hadn't climbed the GE latter by pussyfooting around. Before arriving at Schenectady, Genever-Watling had run the Motor division in Fort Wayne, where he had eliminated thousands of jobs and, in addition, even persuaded the survivors to accept reductions of more than 10 percent in their hourly wage.

In Erie, Transportation Systems president Bob Nardelli chose the two-tiered approach: 6 percent the first year, 12 percent the second. Many suppliers were outraged. "One minute it was 'partnering,' the next minute it was, 'We'll break your kneecaps if you don't give us what we want,' " says one supplier who gave Nardelli what he wanted the first year but not the second, and as a result lost business.

Many of the purchasing managers now being asked to wield tire irons were also enraged. In the summer of 1993, Ken Pastewka accepted a $78,000-a-year job in the Erie operation's purchasing department. Pastewka had joined GE out of college in 1979 and had done well for himself. Each successive job

---

* Now retired as CEO of Citgo, Ron Hall says he dismissed Schepens because the letter reflected "very bad business judgment" and was done without his foreknowledge or authorization. "There was nothing wrong with him objecting—it was the way he said it. It was the words and content of that letter. It was written in extremely poor taste."

Hall says he called Welch about the letter, and visited with Rogers, to "apologize for the letter" and to explain that "this was not Citgo's position." Welch, who "appreciated the call, made no demand that Schepens be gotten rid of." Hall says he visited Rogers not because Welch demanded it but because he felt it was the appropriate thing to do under the circumstances.

For his part, Schepens, who negotiated a voluntary termination package with Citgo and has since found new employment, stands by his version of the story. (Ceravalo supports that point of view as well.)

was a better one, as he hopped from Erie to Fairfield and, eventually, to New York City, where he landed at 30 Rockefeller Center in the purchasing department of NBC. After two years of bumping into David Letterman and other NBC celebs in the elevator, Pastewka resigned to take another job outside GE and, two years after that, was recruited to rejoin GE in Erie. Pastewka didn't realize until he returned that the corporate philosophy had changed. The pressure to obtain the price reduction was extreme: meetings to plan strategy began some days at 5 a.m., and ended at midnight, and in between was a day full of anxiety, swallowing packs of Tums and tussling with suppliers, colleagues, and bosses. After just three months, Pastewka had had enough and beat a retreat to his former employer. "You could hire some guy who bags groceries to slap suppliers around," he recalls telling his boss as he exited. "That's not what I signed on for."

Pastewka counts himself among the fortunate; at least he had an employer who was anxious to take him back. Others who weren't so lucky had to scramble to find jobs once the monster had devoured them. Of the twelve men who heard Reiner's fateful words, just two were in their same positions little more than a year later.

Those who live by the sword can also die by it: In the fall of 1994, GM began "Lopezing" GE, refusing to pay the higher prices that Plastics had demanded for its resins. GM went so far as to order its buyers in a memo to "stop all business relationships with GE," a threat that achieved the desired result—about a month later, GE agreed to rescind most of its price increases.

Nor did Lopez turn out to be the hero Welch thought he was. In one of the more celebrated cases of executive intrigue in recent years, General Motors subsequently sued Lopez, claiming that when he and others bolted to Volkswagen, they took confidential GM documents with them, a suit VW eventually settled at significant cost and embarrassment. Moreover, the wisdom of simultaneously demanding lower prices from suppliers who increasingly have greater responsibilities, as companies outsource more of their manufacturing to cut costs, has been called into question. GE discovered as much in 1995, when the introduction of a new washing machine was delayed three weeks by the production problems of a contractor to whom it had farmed out key work.

IN HIS BOOK *The Age of Paradox*, British business school professor Charles Handy relates a conversation he once had with the chairman of a large pharmaceutical company. Explaining the need to remain competitive, the chairman succinctly summed up his company's employment policy: "$\frac{1}{2} \times 2 \times 3$ = P," he said. Deciphered, the code meant his company, in five years' time, would employ half as many people, paying them twice as much as long as they produced three times more. "Competition is healthy, maybe even essential," Handy concluded, "but there has to be more to life than winning or nearly all of us will be losers."

That many of us have been losers has become increasingly apparent as the nineties have unfolded. Handy cited one study by economist David Birch, who found that from 1987 to 1991 big American companies lowered their net payroll by 2.4 million workers, a trend that has accelerated since then. In 1993, the layoffs of major corporations topped six hundred thousand, a count that was greater for one year than at any time during prior years of recession, according to Challenger, Gray & Christmas, a Chicago outplacement firm. For 1994, their tally was 516,000 when American corporations recorded their best profits in years; for 1995 it was 440,000 when profits were even better; and for 1996 and 1997 the totals were 477,000 and 434,000, respectively, when profits were better still (1997's fourth quarter was the highest quarterly count since 1993). But even their figures, which count only the layoffs prominent enough to show up in newspapers around the country, significantly understate how widespread downsizing has become. According to an analysis by the *New York Times* as part of a seven-day series of articles on downsizing that appeared on its front page in March 1996, 3.38 million jobs were lost in the U.S. economy in 1993, the same year Challenger put the number at just 615,000. The *Times* also found in supplemental polling that three-quarters of all households in the United States have had an encounter with layoffs since 1980; one-third of the households had a family member who lost a job, and another 40 percent knew either a relative, friend, or neighbor who had been laid off.

The severity and scope of the downsizing phenomenon represents a significant and historic change in how American businessmen regard layoffs. The rest of corporate America had stolen a page from Jack Welch's playbook. Layoffs were no longer the last gasp of companies applying a tourniquet to keep from bleeding to death, as they were at most corporations in the eighties, General Electric being a notable exception. Now, in the nineties, even CEOs flush with profits were opting to cut employment, typically to make themselves and their companies more profitable.

A good illustration of this is GE's Power Systems division, headquartered in Schenectady, which makes power-generating equipment. In 1986, the business, a GE mainstay for much of this century, was hurting: Demand for electricity was falling precipitously, profit margins were slipping, and GE entertained buyout offers from Siemens and others. After thousands of jobs were eliminated, the market situation had reversed itself; Power Systems generated enormous profits in the early and mid-nineties as utilities in Asia and elsewhere overseas expanded to meet growing demand for electricity. The business was GE's most profitable manufacturing division in 1993 by a wide margin, with pretax profit of more than $1 billion. "Clearly, the profitability of this business is a touch embarrassing," chortled Power Systems president Genever-Watling in a 1993 *Business Week* article. Yet this embarrassment of riches didn't stop him from pushing through the biggest layoffs in Schenectady since the trauma of 1986. GE eliminated eighteen hundred jobs from its Schenectady operation in three successive waves of cutbacks during 1994, a year in which Power Systems's sales rose 7 percent and its profit rose 21 percent.

Layoffs came at a time of "embarrassing" profits because Power Systems had to do better; it always had to do better on the bottom line, even if that meant laying off people, many of them engineers whose brainpower has been the chief reason for GE's global leadership, for more than a century, of the power-generation business. Merely equaling the previous year's huge pretax earnings was unacceptable. The bar had been raised several notches because Welch's reputation as the deliverer of ever higher earnings was at stake, a reputation that was more important to him than the fate of people who would lose their jobs. Indeed, in December 1994, amid signs that the power-generating business wasn't as brisk as it had been, Welch told securities analysts that the division's earnings would nevertheless increase again in 1995, by 10 percent—even as it eliminated another two thousand jobs that year, one thousand of the reductions coming out of Schenectady. Yet even with the savings from the cutbacks, the profit promise was not met: pretax earnings fell to $770 million in 1995, from $1.2 billion the year before.

It goes without saying that just as being inattentive to costs can destroy a business, so, too, can excessive diligence. Both can cause widespread damage to society. The *New York Times*, in its downsizing poll, found that one in ten American adults—about nineteen million people, the combined adult population of New York and New Jersey—said a lost job in their household had precipitated a "major crisis" in their lives. The *Times* didn't spell out what constituted a major crisis, but certainly the experiences of General Electric castoffs qualifies as a proxy for extrapolation: troubles at home in how a spouse and children adapt to the new circumstances; dissolved marriages; unemployment and underemployment; a lack of medical care, perhaps at a time of serious illness; counseling to counteract anger, diminished self-esteem, and heightened anxiety; depletion of savings or retirement money to pay day-to-day bills; alcoholism or, on occasion, suicide.

Downsizing can also catapult businesses into crisis. It has an insidious effect on survivors, too, sapping their morale, undermining their loyalty, destroying their sense of belonging and commitment. The *Times* quoted one formerly gung-ho business analyst at Chase Manhattan, who after ten turbulent years at the bank summed up his feelings this way: "We've all become soldiers. We will obey whatever is said and will not challenge. Since the merger, it's just a nine-to-five job for me." The lean-and-mean approach so fashionable today can hurt companies in countless ways, doing damage not only to people but to the business itself.

One person who can testify to the destructive impact the tyranny of numbers has had on General Electric is Mark Markovitz. A Ph.D. chemist, Markovitz spent his career of thirty-four years improving the design and efficiency of technology that has been the bedrock of General Electric: the electricity-generating turbine. The turbine was a prime example of achievement in the halcyon years when General Electric routinely advanced breakthrough technology. It was developed in the fall of 1896, when inventor Charles Curtis, a tall young man, entered the Schenectady office of Edwin Rice, GE's first technical director, who four years before had hired Steinmetz. GE was already king of the infant electricity industry, with more than nine thousand reciprocating engines in service by that time. Curtis had brought along in his traveling bag blueprints for a new way of generating electricity that he had unsuccessfully tried to peddle in New York City.

What Curtis envisioned was a new kind of machine that would generate electricity from whirling steel blades spinning around the circumference of a wheel at tremendous velocity, thousands of revolutions per minute. Jets of pressurized steam would turn the blades. Examining Curtis's drawings, Rice, who possessed a keen engineering mind, immediately saw the potential. The deal he struck with Curtis would give General Electric huge wealth in the next century. Curtis would be given the best resources and engineering talent of the Schenectady Works to make the turbine practical. In exchange, GE would be allowed to purchase the patent rights if the turbine proved a commercial success.

After two years of failure, Rice's confidence appeared misplaced. The project looked doomed. Curtis, however, refused to quit, and called upon the services of another distinguished engineer, William Emmet, who soon proposed a redesign of the turbine blades. Within a year, Emmet and Curtis had their first functioning steam turbine. Emmet then sold Samuel Insull, a former Edison lab assistant and president of the Commonwealth Edison Company of Chicago, on the steam turbine as a new way of generating electricity at a power station Insull planned to put into operation on Chicago's Fiske Street in the fall of 1903. Insull ordered two five-thousand-kilowatt turbines. As the year 1902 progressed, deadlines came and went. Emmet was having trouble getting the turbine parts correctly machined. In February 1903, the first turbine was still unassembled, and its promised completion date was only a month away. A vote of plant superintendents identified Billy Madigan as the one foreman at the Schenectady Works most likely to complete the work on time. The all-out effort Madigan led to get the turbine up and running by March 7, the date it was successfully tested with Insull on hand, became one of General Electric's most legendary engineering feats.

In the years since, the steam turbine, and the gas version that succeeded it, became mainstays of modern society, generating electricity in concentrations thousands of times more powerful than the first Fiske Street model. A single turbine can now supply the electrical needs of millions of people.

Mark Markovitz continued that tradition of engineering progress. Inside today's giant turbines, the spinning blades generate mechanical energy that is converted to electrical energy by a rotor that turns in the generator. The parts that induce electricity inside the generator have to be well-insulated. The smallest imperfections can cause massive failure. Chemist Markovitz invented a new material several years ago that would provide better insulation and greater reliability. It was a project his supervisors took great interest in. Not only was the performance of the new material vastly superior, but it would also cost about 50 percent less to fabricate. Markovitz was given a staff of two technicians and two engineers to shepherd the new material through extensive reliability testing. But all four of his assistants were either laid off or took early retirement in the spring purge of 1994. Although he eventually finished his project, Markovitz believes the upheaval caused by downsizing has contributed to market share losses Power Systems has suffered in recent years. For instance, in gas turbines, a business GE has virtually owned since its inception in the early 1950s, GE's worldwide market share with manufacturing partners abroad has slipped from the high-50-percent range five years ago to the mid-40-percent now—a huge drop that roughly equals what rivals Westinghouse and Siemens gained over the same period.

Moreover, Markovitz fears that General Electric has lost its cherished edge in technology, and there's plenty of evidence to support that contention.

Utility customers say the upper hand that GE enjoyed for nearly a century has slipped away, and the technology that Westinghouse, Siemens, and ABB Asea Brown Boveri now offer is virtually identical. And in some instances, GE's has been decidedly worse. In the fall of 1994, General Electric began hearing complaints from utility customers that had installed its new F-type turbines, introduced several years before. A turbine at a Florida Power & Light plant near Lake Okeechobee began vibrating so badly that it had to be shut down twice for more than a month each time for repair. At other power plants around the world, cracks were discovered on the seventy-five-ton turbine rotors; several had to be airlifted from sites overseas back to the United States to correct the design flaws that had caused them to crack. It all added up to one of the biggest and most expensive product recalls in the history of the electric-power business, costing GE at least $100 million in transportation, redesign, and repair expenses, while some utilities are seeking damages for the value of the power they would have sold had the turbines functioned properly. It also led Welch to sack Genever-Watling in the spring of 1995, replacing him with Robert Nardelli, the head of Transportation Systems, whom people in Schenectady have nicknamed "Little Jack" with good reason: "Nothing else really will matter if the . . . numbers are not delivered," Nardelli told subordinates at one meeting early in 1996, according to a memo published in the *Schenectady Gazette.*

It's this kind of pressure that Markovitz, who recently took early retirement, finds most objectionable about the GE of Jack Welch. The last of three chemists Power Systems once employed, Markovitz says he understands the need to be efficient, and attentive to costs. But too often managers become fixated on eliminating costs—on satisfying Welch and meeting the profit demands he imposes on them. "It's management by buzzword," Markovitz says. "People chant Jack's slogans—speed, stretch, boundarylessness—without thinking intelligently about what they're doing." More than thirty years with General Electric, fourteen of them with Welch at the helm, have left Markovitz with mixed feelings. "I've been stretched so much I feel like Gumby," Markovitz quips. Then: "All Welch understands is increasing profits. That, and getting rid of people, is what he considers a vision," Markovitz complained bitterly before his retirement. "Good people, tremendous people, have been let go, and it is hurting our business. I'm trying to meet the competition, but his policies aren't helping me. It's crazy, and the craziness has got to stop."

Welch's fixation on cutting costs has damaged other GE businesses as well, like the company's Aircraft Engine division. Established during World

War II as a manufacturer of small engines for propeller-driven aircraft, the division was an outgrowth of FDR's "arsenal for democracy." GE's selection in 1941 by the Army Air Corps to develop the first jet engine gave it early leadership in a field that would revolutionize postwar transport. Less than a year after work began, GE engineers, borrowing upon the turbine concept Curtis had conceived in 1896, successfully adapted the jet engine design of Englishman Frank Whittle to power a small aircraft. On October 2, 1942, the Bell XP-59, equipped with two GE I-A engines, flew in secret for ten minutes above a dry lake bed in California. The jet age was born.

Over the next two decades, under the leadership of Gerhard Neumann, GE Aircraft Engines, headquartered in Evendale, Ohio, grew from obscurity into the nation's leading supplier of jet engines to the United States military. Neumann was a legendary figure, as significant a force in jet engines as Steinmetz had been in the electrification of America. Fiercely independent and a technical genius, Neumann provided leadership in every sense of the word. He built an engineering enterprise that was second to none. Management was homegrown; promotions always came from within. It was an organization that was intensely loyal, and proud of its accomplishments. Performing miracles on a shoestring became its signature. The culture was defiantly self-sufficient. Because of its highly specialized expertise, which very few people in GE understood besides Neumann, and the patriotic nature of its work, the division was given wide latitude and great autonomy. Even during the Cordiner era, when management purges were common throughout GE, Aircraft Engines was left alone.

The division got its biggest boost during the administration of Fred Borch, who succeeded Cordiner as CEO in 1962. The transition from Cordiner to Borch illustrated what the ancient Greeks called *enantiodromia*, the tendency of things to swing toward one extreme and then the opposite in pendulum-like fashion. Borch was in many ways the antithesis of Cordiner. While Cordiner was aloof and autocratic, Borch was friendly, accessible, a consensus manager. In much the same way as the transition from Jones to Welch represented change by design, the board had chosen Borch as a counterbalance to Cordiner. They wanted someone who would be a calming influence and restore GE's reputation, which had been sullied by the "Incredible Electrical" price-fixing conspiracy.

Borch, the former head of GE's lighting business, was steeped in hallowed GE tradition. The Borch years emphasized stability rather than radical change. Borch not only believed in the concept of decentralization that Cordiner had begun, he also practiced it. Line managers were given much greater say in the allocation of corporate resources and more authority over their businesses. But profits did not immediately follow, and by the end of the 1960s the Borch era was maligned inside the company as the "era of profitless prosperity." Borch, however, was a man of vision and of patience, as well. Early on in his administration he had identified three growth industries that he believed GE was positioned to exploit in the years ahead. One industry, computers, was a definite winner, but GE flubbed its effort, and in 1970 sold out to Honeywell. The second industry was nuclear power, which might have succeeded had it not been for Three Mile Island. The third industry was aircraft engines.

Borch gave the go-ahead to move Aircraft Engines away from the safe cost-plus military programs into the more risky market for commercial jets, a market dominated by Pratt & Whitney and one in which GE did not participate. Borch invested hundreds of millions of dollars in GE's development of commercial jet engines in the face of mounting losses. GE invested more than $700 million over a seven-year period before it began to recoup its investment. The decision represented one of the few instances in GE's postwar history in which the company showed patience. The wisdom of Borch's vision wasn't fully vindicated until two decades later, in 1985. That year marked the first time that General Electric surpassed Pratt & Whitney, shipping more commercial-airliner engines than its rival.

By the 1980s, Welch was reaping the windfall from Borch's vision. Aircraft Engines was GE's most profitable and most successful business. In 1987, it employed forty-four thousand, making Aircraft Engines GE's largest business. Although Neumann's successors were accorded the same autonomy he had been given, a policy that had served General Electric well, the tradition of hands-off oversight began to change in the late 1980s. As long as Aircraft Engines continued to contribute megaprofits, Welch left alone the business, and its president, Brian Rowe, who was the only business division president whose tenure predated Welch's selection as CEO. But, a sudden downturn in the aircraft engine business, which hit the military market first, then the commercial market, drew Welch's attention. Rowe recognized the need to cut costs but was reluctant to move as aggressively as Welch wanted. Because of the nature of what Aircraft Engines did, the work tended to be very engineering-intensive. Rowe, an engineer himself who had joined GE during the Neumann era, had fond memories of past engineering triumphs, and he also recognized that cutbacks of the kind Welch wanted were fraught with peril. As profits shrunk, so did Rowe's autonomy.

The disputes between Welch and Rowe simmered through the fall and winter of 1992, with Welch agitating for more layoffs, and Rowe resisting. At the Boca Raton senior management meeting in January 1993, Welch pressed his demands for a faster downsizing of the business. The net profit target had been set at $625 million, and Welch was convinced it wasn't going to be achieved. On January 13, after returning to Fairfield, Welch reiterated his demands in a letter to Rowe.

Though Welch said he had the impression, based on the Boca meeting, that executives at Aircraft Engines now had a more realistic view of the adverse business conditions they faced in 1993, the question was whether Rowe and his team could "translate this realistic assessment into dramatic and radical change fast enough to meet the $625 million net income commitment you have made. We cannot tolerate another miss." Welch said his years of dealing with downsizing had taught him that the best way to quickly communicate "reality" was to attack the "heart" of the business. Engineering was the heart of Aircraft Engines, and taking two thousand people out of that operation would have considerably more impact in conveying the seriousness of the situation than, say, taking "40 people out of 50 different functions." "We must get at major engineering change," Welch urged. He said he would review Rowe's plans to reduce costs in a video conference in three weeks. While the task Rowe faced was enormous and would require "decisive action and great speed," Welch closed by reminding him that his peers in GE would help, and that they were all "counting" on him doing what needed to be done.

In the months that followed, Welch led the attack on Aircraft Engines. Engineers were dumped by the thousands. The victims included Rowe, who was replaced as president by Eugene Murphy, a Welch loyalist. Employment in the division would fall to less than twenty thousand.

The human trauma associated with this bloodletting was severe. Welch had his reductions in force, but at a price. Morale was terrible, and people mourned the passing of the old Neumann culture like a death in the family. Grief was felt by many, including one anonymous Aircraft Engine engineer who was among the victims. "There Is Life After GE," a poem he penned that hung in a lavatory, summed up the feelings of many in the sweltering summer of 1993:

> *When I first started at good ol' GE*
> *Everyone was saying "GE is Me,"*
> *Then, after that we were one big family*
> *Everywhere you looked you saw "GE is We."*

For a while, everything seemed fine
Not many, if any, were in the unemployment line,
GE, they said, was a great place to work
"Come to us, we'll hire you, we've got every perk. . . ."

In one, they got a good friend and even my dad too
And another friend in the next, but it was still too few,
No, GE wasn't finished yet, that had only made three
So another one soon came, and that's when they got me. . . .

All GE cares about is keeping profits high
While we were all asking "How many more, Jack . . . why?"
His answer was "It will only get worse"
By the time Jack's done, not many will survive the GE curse.

So if you get zapped, don't be too sad
It's not whether you work hard, if you are good or bad,
You see, it doesn't matter anymore who is the best
No one, no where, is qualified to pass GE's test. . . .

General Electric was by no means the only aircraft-engine manufacturer that jettisoned people in the early nineties. Faced with a severe plunge in orders, engine makers had no choice but to blast away at costs if they wanted to stay in business. United Technologies, a Hartford, Connecticut–based conglomerate whose products include Carrier air-conditioners, Sikorsky helicopters, and Otis elevators, as well as Pratt & Whitney jet engines, was every bit as hard-boiled as GE, cutting thirty-five thousand jobs since 1990. But in December 1995, United Technologies CEO George David unveiled a new, expensive plan to help workers get reeducated. The company now gives employees time off to attend classes, pays for tuition and books, and even gives those who complete their studies fifty shares of company stock, worth more than $4,000 at current prices. "We're not softhearted," David told *Newsweek*, explaining the rationale for the program. "It's in our interest to have an educated work force." Then again, perhaps David felt he could afford to be generous after Pratt & Whitney bested GE in an important new market, the competition to provide engines for Boeing's new 777 airliner.

While Welch was demanding "major engineering change" and laying off people by the thousands, GE Aircraft Engines was also in the midst of its most daunting engineering challenge in decades. It had begun in the late 1980s, when Boeing began developing the 777, a new aircraft that would fly on just two huge engines, carrying four hundred passengers on hauls of up to seventy-five hundred miles. Engines for the new aircraft would have to be 40 percent more powerful than existing ones, providing enough thrust to lift two Boeing 737s off the ground. With the military market moribund, GE, Pratt & Whitney, and Rolls Royce were desperate for a big score in the new 777 market.

In the 1993 annual report, sent to shareholders in March 1994, Welch proclaimed the GE90, Aircraft Engines' entry in the 777 market, an unqualified success. The GE90 represented a shining example of how speedy the new GE was, of how the company had built a work force with an "absolutely infinite capacity to improve everything," Welch asserted. The GE90 had been designed and built in one-half the normal time, Welch said, by a "boundaryless team." In fact, the new engine had suffered its latest test failure just a few months before shareholders received his letter, a spectacular malfunction high above California's Mojave Desert in which the engine began to disintegrate.

In building the GE90, General Electric had chosen a different course than its competitors. Pratt & Whitney and Rolls Royce took the less risky path of upgrading existing designs for the new high-thrust engine. GE had gambled nearly $2 billion on an all-new design, the first time GE had introduced a commercial jet engine without first working out the bugs in a military predecessor. This had come at a time when Welch, intent on keeping earnings high, slashed the engineering staff by more than one-third through his program of "major engineering change."

In many respects, the engine project was a repeat of the failed refrigerator compressor. Engineers were given a very difficult engineering task and insufficient time in which to do it. Because the development and in-house testing time was so compressed, problems with the engine were not revealed until the very late stage of in-flight testing, when the Federal Aviation Administration (FAA), the government agency that certifies the airworthiness of aircraft, including engines, expects the bugs to have been worked out. But in the case of the GE90, they hadn't been. Four test failures—in May, July, October, and December 1993—preceded the test flight above the Mojave Desert. The latter test could have proven catastrophic had it not been for the pilot's quick decision to shut down the engine, parts of which were later found in the tailpipe. He landed the plane, a 747, on the power of its three other engines. The test was a fitting counterpoint to the first successful test flight, in 1942, not far from the Mojave site.

In the fall of 1994, by which time the engine was supposed to have secured

FAA certification according to GE's accelerated development schedule and six months after Welch's optimistic letter to shareholders, problems were still recurring. Most disturbing to FAA personnel was that the problems were new ones. "Every time they'd go up they had a problem, and it was a different problem," says one observer of the program. To this observer, it appeared that GE lacked the engineering capability to correct the engine's deficiencies. Engineers were working six and seven days a week trying to understand the problems and fix them but, at least once, the engine returned for testing was discovered to have been incorrectly reassembled, which caused additional delay. "There was a lot of rushing around to keep the program on schedule. The pressures on them were tremendous," the observer says.

In May 1995, just four months before a contract deadline to deliver to British Airways the first two of fifteen planes outfitted with the new engine, GE still hadn't obtained government certification. During a test that month, in which a dead bird was fired into the engine to simulate a bird strike, three of the twenty-two fan blades shattered, a failure so severe that it caused the FAA to suspend all certification flights for several months that summer. Pratt & Whitney and Rolls Royce, which hadn't experienced problems with their engines, gleefully seized upon the mishaps, getting big orders from Boeing customers leery of GE engines. Boeing was also losing confidence, as was the FAA. In October, the situation was so grim that the FAA convened a meeting in Seattle, Boeing's headquarters, to evaluate GE's progress on the engine. "There were a lot of people who felt that GE hadn't measured up," recalls one person who participated in the meeting. The lack of quality control, the constant delays, poor design work, unexpected problems cropping up late in the testing—in the opinion of most of the ten or so FAA representatives, the GE90 had been a failure. One lone holdout was all that kept the GE90, a nearly $2 billion investment, from being officially designated by the FAA as a failure, a designation that would have increased a thousandfold the testing required for certification and an action that probably would have led Boeing to terminate the program.

As it was, the financial consequences of the GE90 were profound. The first two planes equipped with the engine were delivered late to British Airways, which triggered contract penalties, and without full FAA sanction, meaning that the planes were not authorized to fly more than one hour's distance from a suitable airport. Although the GE90 finally won FAA certification in October 1996 to fly extended distances over the ocean, British Airways voluntarily suspended trans-Atlantic flights with the new model six months later.

The airline took the action after it twice cancelled flights between London and Boston and Philadelphia because metal in the engine's redesigned gearbox had broken in flight.* As a result, Pratt, which subsequently ran ads trumpeting its full certification for the PW4084 "more than a year ahead of the competition," and Rolls Royce got the lion's share of orders from airlines seeking to equip their 777s with the new, higher thrust engines. In what promises to be a $60 billion market over the next several decades, GE now finds itself in the unusual position of third place in market share. And because of the lower-than-anticipated volume of orders and lower prices, GE took a charge in 1997 of $275 million on the GE90.

THE TYRANNY OF NUMBERS also has a human face. The family of Ivan Winebrenner can attest to that. In many respects, his story is not unique. He was one of the thousands of mill hands, the rank and file who shuffle in and out of the Erie Works each day, as they have since 1910, when General Electric began making locomotives on the shores of Lake Erie. He was also one of the faceless thousands who have lost their jobs. But to the family he left behind—wife Helen, son Kurt, daughter Marilyn—his untimely death was one they will not soon forget.

Helen met her future husband for the first time in June 1972 on a blind date arranged by her Uncle Bill. Ivan had just graduated from high school in Cumberland, Maryland, and was working a construction job with Bill. A photograph of Helen, who lived in Waynesburg, Pennsylvania, across the border from West Virginia, fell out of his wallet one day. Winebrenner retrieved it and was smitten. He kept bugging Bill to arrange a date for him with Helen. They were married a year later, with Helen still in high school.

A year after their marriage they moved to Erie, driving Interstate 79 to the northwest corner of Pennsylvania and carrying everything they owned in the trunk of a Plymouth. When the Winebrenners arrived in Erie on June 2, 1974, jobs were plentiful. Ivan, a gaunt man who stood five foot ten yet weighed just 135 pounds, applied for work at General Electric as soon as he could, and three days later had landed a job.

His first glimpse of the GE Erie Works was like nothing he had ever seen. General Electric was a colossus, a huge compound at the east end of East Lake

* A year later, in March 1998, the *Wall Street Journal* reported that a British Airways 777, equipped with the same GE engines, aborted its takeoff owing to a manufacturing defect in one of the engines.

Road, in a section of town called Lawrence Park. There were dozens of buildings on a tree-lined campus that spanned hundreds of acres. It was a citadel unto itself, sealed from the outside world by a tall fence that encircled a perimeter several miles long. Townsfolk typically referred to GE as "the General Electric," as if they were talking about an institution equivalent to "the church" or "the mob." Inside cavernous buildings, cranes lifted the pieces of two-hundred-ton locomotives like so many Tinkertoys. The sound of train whistles blew all day long and into the night.

At that time, the summer of 1974, the Erie Works was riding the crest of what would turn out to be its high employment watermark. The GE payroll had hit a twenty-year high of 11,376. Although Winebrenner didn't realize it, he was walking into a hotbed of labor activism. General Electric and organized labor had been at loggerheads many times on the shores of Lake Erie. The workers were represented by the United Electrical Workers, a union whose ties to the Communist party had gotten it expelled from the Congress of Industrial Organizations in 1949. Their militant Local 506 ran into the anti-labor passions of Lemuel Boulware, General Electric's labor chieftain in the fifties. John Nelson, the local president, was fired along with several other union officials for refusing to answer questions at public hearings about their alleged ties to the Communist party. The union appealed Nelson's dismissal all the way to the Supreme Court, which in 1956 declined to take up the constitutionality of GE's policy, enforced at many locations besides Erie, of dismissing anyone who invoked the Fifth Amendment. Just one year later, the Democrat-controlled Erie City Council passed a resolution condemning General Electric for its policy of "continual layoffs and removal of operations from the Erie Works." Employment then was ninety-six hundred, a reduction of about half from 1948. The production of household appliances had been transferred to the new Appliance Park in Louisville.

Winebrenner was on the job just two years when he experienced his first strike, a violent walkout after which the courts imposed fines on the union for property damage. Although Winebrenner walked the picket lines until the strike was settled, he didn't like it. He couldn't stand being without a job, having always been a hard worker. Even at the age of twelve, Ivan had been mowing enough lawns that he always had spare cash. His parents borrowed money from him often, and Ivan was proud he had it to lend. Winebrenner had no hobbies and only one passion, antique cars. He seldom spent money on himself, preferring instead to save it. The one exception came in 1990, when Winebrenner asked his wife if he could spend $4,000 to buy a mint-condition 1955 Oldsmobile, a two-tone green monster with big fenders, plush seats, and white sidewall tires. Ivan and his son Kurt built a big barn out back to house their cherished possession, which they washed, polished, and tuned up at odd hours day and night. A self-taught electrician, plumber, auto mechanic, and mason, Winebrenner could tear apart a carburetor or build a stone wall with equal dexterity. He was good with his hands. He spent his free time doing repairs and other handy work. He enjoyed keeping busy.

Winebrenner was also a good father. His first child, Kurt, was born one month after they moved to Erie. Ivan wanted Helen to finish high school and get a nursing degree, which she eventually did. He took a second shift job, working from 4 in the afternoon until 1:30 in the morning. Helen went to school during the day, when he'd be home with Kurt. After finishing his second shift, he'd slump back into his easy chair, feeding Kurt his early morning bottle so Helen could sleep. The second-shift arrangement continued for eight years and gave Winebrenner the opportunity to spend time with his children. He took advantage of it. Marilyn, who was born in 1977, and Kurt spent lots of time alone with their dad. He would take them camping and to the circus. Kurt taught him the same trade skills his dad had taught him. Winebrenner wanted his boy to be self-sufficient.

Winebrenner believed in self-reliance, and practiced it. He was thrifty and hated debt of any kind. When Ivan and Helen borrowed $43,000 to buy their home in the countryside east of Erie, he worked two jobs for a time to retire the mortgage as quickly as possible. Eight years later, in 1986, they owned their home. That year was a turning point in his career at General Electric. After twelve years of continuous work, a time he had rarely called in sick, Winebrenner lost his job for the first time. Carl Schlemmer, then president of Transportation Systems, pared thousands of jobs by cutting deep into the rank and file. Schlemmer, a tough but statesmanlike businessman, had no other choice. A market depression had hurt the locomotive industry. U.S. railroads, which in 1979 bought more than seventeen hundred locomotives, purchased fewer than three hundred in 1987. Costs had to be cut to the bone. Winebrenner was one of thousands of workers who were jettisoned. The strategy worked, at least financially. In 1987, when the market downturn finally hit its nadir, the business earned $34 million, about as much as it had when the troubles began. Erie locomotives managed to eke out a profit every year despite catastrophic business conditions. Welch heaped high praise on Schlemmer and the Erie Works, which, in his oft-repeated phrase, had "changed the wheels while the train was running."

After his furlough from GE, Winebrenner had worked three part-time jobs at once, delivering Domino's pizza, helping a local plumber, and selling insurance. His income didn't match what he had made at GE, but he was supporting the family and helping out Helen, who had gotten her nursing degree and was working at a local hospital. He then got a full-time job at Gannon College in Erie, working as a maintenance man. The pay was only $5.50 an hour, less than half what he made at GE. But Winebrenner loved the work. He got paid to fix things. As a college employee, he also took several night courses tuition-free. His studies included algebra, economics, computer programming, and accounting, and he got As in all but one course.

Then, in 1988, Winebrenner faced a crossroads. Locomotive demand had picked up, and GE was hiring again for the first time in four years. The company accepted more than fourteen hundred applications on the first day, even though there were no immediate job openings. Before it could hire newcomers, GE had to offer work to those who had been laid off and still had recall rights. Winebrenner wasn't sure if he should return, and he talked it over with Helen. GE was a harsher environment than Gannon, but the money and benefits were better. "I want you to do what makes you happy" was the advice she gave her husband. Once Winebrenner had gone back to the Erie Works, the "bumping" began. He would find a job he liked, only to get bumped out of it by someone with more seniority. Winebrenner got bumped five or six times. He eventually landed in a job no one else wanted.

His daily task was one of the worst in Building Six. For eight hours each day, from eleven at night until seven in the morning, Winebrenner would feed thick wire cables into a machine. The company gave him gloves to protect his hands, but Winebrenner didn't wear them because they interfered with the work. Helen would bathe Winebrenner's hands in Epsom salts to soften up the calluses that were so tough he could barely clench his fist. For the first time in his life, Winebrenner hated to go to work. Every night he would go in an hour early to scan a computer, futilely searching for another position in the plant. He applied for dozens of jobs—and was rejected every time. People had bumped him, but he didn't seem able to bump others, even those who had less seniority than he did. As the rejections piled up, Winebrenner became more and more despondent.

His mood and behavior changed. Winebrenner's troubles at work began to affect his marriage, and home life. Always a perfectionist, he no longer kept up with household chores. The lawn went to pot, and repairs around the house didn't get done. This was very unusual behavior for Ivan, who usually attacked repair work with relish. He was angry much of the time, and easily irritated. For the first time in his married life, he began bringing his work home with him. He complained bitterly about how people at GE treated him. "He wasn't happy. There were mornings," Helen recalls, "he'd come home, throw things, and shout, 'You wouldn't believe what they did to me tonight.' "

Winebrenner languished in the wire-pulling job for about two years, feeling trapped. Helen was worried about him. As a nurse, she had dealt with chronically depressed patients, and he showed all the signs, including lethargy and anger. Some days he stayed in bed with the window blinds drawn shut. She was convinced he needed counseling and urged him to go, but he resisted.

He finally escaped the wire-pulling job by quitting. A woman foreman who had seen how the job enraged him took pity on Winebrenner. She had his resignation rescinded and found him another job he liked much better, in Building Eighteen. He worked there about a month and a half when he got notice, on June 10, 1993, that, effective one week later, his employment at General Electric would be terminated. This time, the furlough was final. There would be no recall rights. That same day, before he got the notice, Helen Winebrenner insisted that her husband seek counseling. She threatened to divorce him if he didn't.

The termination of Ivan Winebrenner, who was one of about two hundred workers GE gave "lack of work" notices to that day, was different from the earlier layoff Winebrenner had endured. In 1986, business conditions were bleak. That was not the case in 1993, when GE was recording its best profits in the locomotive business. The business was on a roll, and outsourcing more components would make it even more profitable. In December, CSX Transportation ordered three hundred new locomotives, GE's largest order ever. The jobs of Winebrenner and others were being eliminated as part of GE's corporate strategy of buying locomotive parts rather than making them in-house. On June 12, 1993, two days after receiving his termination notice, Helen Winebrenner discovered her husband's body in their bedroom. He had shot himself in the head, using the same shotgun he had bought to go deer hunting with son Kurt. He was thirty-nine years old.

"It must have been the nurse in me to check for a pulse," she recalls. But it was obvious, from the state of the corpse, that none would be found. Helen vomited for hours afterward. The klieg lights of police cars and television news soon flooded the front lawn of the Winebrenner residence. Kurt, who had just graduated from high school, cleaned up the grisly mess a few days later. In the years following his father's death, he dropped out of college and ran up some large debts; Helen says he's doing better now. At the funeral,

Winebrenner's boss approached the widow to express his condolences. He hated to let Ivan go, he told her, tears welling up in his eyes, but there was nothing else he could do.

Several months later, an engineering supervisor at Erie named Sheldon Potter, who was not Winebrenner's boss but had been moved by news of his suicide, came to exactly the same conclusion, and elected to quit his management job rather than continue the tyranny. "The numbers cause managers to do things that would be seen as totally inhuman in any other context," says Potter, who still carries a laminated plastic card in his wallet, which has a mission statement inscribed on one side and lists "Beliefs" on the other. Belief one: "People, working together, are the source of our strength. They provide our intelligence and determine our reputation and vitality." It was just rhetoric: Potter figures he personally fired at least fifty people during a long career at GE Erie. "People want more security than that place offers."

Meanwhile, the job eliminations kept coming. In September, the union staged a one-day wildcat strike to protest the elimination of 525 jobs. Five finished locomotives were vandalized by unidentified workers who severed electric cables. Anonymous phone callers made death threats against management, which caused the plant gates to be shut one night. Three months later, the union was informed that another 550 jobs were targeted for elimination.

The tyranny of numbers continues. Just two days after Winebrenner's death, Anthony Victor Torrelli, a second member of Local 506 whose employment was also in doubt, killed himself. Torrelli is said to have gone into the plant with a loaded gun, looking for his foreman, before later turning the gun on himself. There have been additional suicides since, but management has turned a blind eye to the problem. "Our union leadership tells us that there is 'great resentment throughout the workforce' over our outsourcing initiative," GE Transportation Systems president Bob Nardelli wrote in a letter prompted not by the suicides but by the union's refusal to accept overtime to protest the policy of outsourcing. Because of the overtime ban, Transportation Systems was failing to deliver its locomotives to customers on time, and workers were jeopardizing future orders, making it necessary "for the company to subcontract even more work to satisfy our production schedule."

Nardelli was perplexed. Why would the union do such a thing? Why would a dying man hasten his death? He couldn't understand what to him was irrational, inexplicable behavior. The necessity of delivering the numbers that Jack Welch demanded had blinded Nardelli to the human dimension of what the company's policies were doing. He wasn't the first GE executive whose heart had been hardened, nor would he be the last. When Nardelli left for his new assignment in Schenectady, he was replaced by David Calhoun, a thirty-eight-year-old newcomer to GE's management elite. Calhoun immediately picked up where Nardelli had left off, announcing late in 1995 that another fifteen hundred jobs would be eliminated. Now the head of GE Lighting, Calhoun, along with Nardelli and others, is considered to be a top contender for the CEO job when Welch retires in two years.

CHAPTER ELEVEN

FROM PATERNALISM TO CANNIBALISM

IT HAD TAKEN the seven men who had preceded Jack Welch as GE's top executive a century to build up the "distinctive set of traditions, values and beliefs" that the seventh man in that lineage, Reg Jones, in 1978 called the "spirit of General Electric." The spirit, according to Jones, had three elements—loyalty, moral integrity, and innovation—and he waxed poetic in applying that metaphor. There could be no argument that loyalty was a pillar of the GE culture, and it remained intact at that time—with the Welch era still three years away, GE was a place of cradle-to-grave employment. Jones's inclusion of moral integrity is more suspect. Considering the company's strong antilabor stance under Lemuel Boulware, or its frequent convictions for price-fixing, it is hard to regard General Electric or the actions of its executives as saintly. The inclusion of innovation is suspect as well, not historically of course—Edison and company had seen to that—but as of the date of Jones's pronouncement. The seventies had not been a particularly inventive period for GE. Among the technology initiatives the company had botched was the mainframe computer business, from which it had withdrawn, and one can imagine that Jones had cited innovation in an effort to rekindle it.

Still, it is useful to look at Jones's three spiritual elements as a landmark of the tenets of General Electric three years before Welch became CEO, as well as a benchmark for how they have fared since. When one does so, it is immediately clear that innovation in the Welch era has come to mean something altogether different from what Edison or even Jones would have understood—it is financial "gamesmanship," rather than technical innovation in an industrial sense. The erosion of GE's inventive spirit, however, has had relatively little immediate adverse effect on its competitive position for several reasons. Unlike IBM, which was dependent on one business and got hit hard earlier in this decade when it was eclipsed in that one business, General Electric's diversity gives it a vast protective cover. Its activities also differ from those of IBM. Welch got out of many of the businesses where the pace of technological innovation is greatest, and hence the competitive risks are greatest—semiconductors, consumer electronics, mobile communications, ceramics. In most of the manufacturing businesses that remain, technological change occurs at a slow rate; the refinements in lightbulb manufacture, for instance, have been largely inconsequential since William Coolidge's discovery of the tungsten filament lamp in 1911. And even in businesses where there is a sudden shift in technology, as occurred in locomotives with the transition from direct to alternating current engines, GE has ample resources simply to buy the technology and catch up when it falls behind.

It was in regard to the other two spiritual elements, loyalty and moral integrity, where the corrosive effects of the Welch revolution were more readily apparent. What Welch had done was to obliterate the implied social contract that had existed at General Electric since the days of Steinmetz. Loyalty not only no longer existed, it was openly ridiculed by Welch himself as an antiquated notion. To get results, Welch and his lieutenants had created a climate of purposeful insecurity, a turbocharged environment in which people were never quite certain they would have a job tomorrow. It was a form of corporate cannibalism, which eventually unleashed a series of scandals that were unprecedented in the history of American business for their variety and scope. More than anything, it was Welch's treatment of GE employees that engendered the cynicism which in turn paved the way for these scandals, blemishing his own reputation and that of General Electric. Rather than being known now for its "moral integrity," GE has become infamous in law enforcement circles as a recidivist.

To many of the people who worked there, the connection between the severity of Welch's demands and the occurrence of repeated scandal was a clear cause and effect, as transparent as glass. "GE has a clear stance—if it's not legal, don't do it. We were inundated with a lot of rhetoric," says Heather Honegger, who until she resigned in 1992 after fourteen years with GE was a fast-track financial manager in one of the company's core manufacturing businesses. "But there was so much pressure to make the numbers that a lot of people were tempted to do things. Either Jack really doesn't know or doesn't want to know the extent to which pressure grinds away at people." One former GE attorney states the case more bluntly: "Nothing the company did [during the Welch era] would surprise me, and I mean nothing. The command was, 'Don't tell me I can't do it, tell me how I can do it.' Those are famous words in the General Electric Company. There isn't a lawyer in GE who hasn't heard the same thing unless he's wearing earmuffs."

GE's repeated violations of the law marked a clear decline in values within the GE "society," which had been put through the most gut-wrenching change in its history. In that regard, General Electric isn't alone. It surely is no coincidence that criminality within GE and throughout American business hit its apex at the very time when the corporate community was most profit-driven and treating its employees with the most egregious disregard. Certainly greed has also contributed to the lawlessness, and there was plenty of that to go around in the latter half of the 1980s. The most vivid display of greed run amuck was the celebrated insider-trading scandal of junk bond king Michael Milken, who in 1987 alone received $550 million in salary and other compensation from Drexel Burnham Lambert, the fifth-largest securities firm in the United States. In March 1989, the government filed a ninety-eight-count felony indictment against Milken on charges of racketeering, conspiracy, mail fraud, and other illegal activities. He went to jail, and Drexel, which paid a record $650 million fine, soon went out of business.

But what of all the corporate criminality against the Pentagon, the infamous $650 toilet seats and other excesses bought at taxpayers' expense? Could personal greed alone explain that? Consider the 108-count indictment returned against General Electric by a federal grand jury in Philadelphia on March 26, 1985, the day Welch's company became the first major defense contractor ever to be indicted on charges of defrauding the government on a defense contract. The indictment stemmed from work GE had done at its Space Systems division in Valley Forge, Pa. (now owned by Martin Marietta), which had won Air Force contracts to make and test the electronic innards of nose cones for Minuteman nuclear missiles.

According to the indictment, to which GE pleaded guilty on May 13, 1985, GE managers had doctored the time cards submitted by hourly workers. The fraud began after a top executive at Fairfield headquarters warned Philadelphia managers that "heads would roll" if they did not stop the cost overruns on the Minuteman contract. The solution they came up with was to charge $800,000 of the Minuteman work to a phony research-and-development project that would be reimbursed by the Pentagon under a separate contract. "The managers feared for their jobs," Ed Zittlau, the assistant U.S. attorney who prosecuted the case, told the *Washington Post*. "From their point of view, the mischarging looked like the lesser of two evils." In this instance, the criminality had nothing to do with personal greed—the managers who doctored the time cards weren't enriching themselves but rather their employer; they thought that cheating was the only way to deliver the numbers that Fairfield wanted, and simultaneously protect their jobs.

Protecting one's job is a phenomenon of relatively recent origin, though it is easy to lose sight of that in today's ruthless environment, where job loss has become so commonplace. In the past, most major corporations, GE included, sought to enlist the loyalty of employees and promote it in ways that seem extraordinary by 1990s standards. The classic American example of this in the twentieth century was IBM, whose history was defined by a man who began his business career keeping books in a butcher shop, who sold pianos, sewing machines, and organs door to door, and whose swift rise to the head of sales at the National Cash Register Company was cut short, at the age of forty, after his conviction in 1913 of conspiracy in restraint of trade, his sentencing to one year in jail, and his dismissal from NCR. For Thomas J. Watson Sr., however, this event produced, in the words of business historian Peter Drucker, "one of the great social innovators in American history."

Born in 1874, the son of a lumber dealer in a rural community near Corning, New York, Watson might have gone to jail along with about thirty other NCR executives had fate not intervened. While their convictions were on appeal, Dayton, Ohio, the home of NCR, was hit by a devastating flood. NCR's president, a driven and flamboyant executive by the name of John H. Patterson, led a brilliant relief effort that, after the appeals court had reversed the lower court's decision, convinced the government to drop further prosecution of its antitrust case. Even before the conviction was reversed, however, Patterson had fired Watson, who was hired the following year, 1914, as general manager of the Computing-Tabulating-Recording Company, the forerunner of IBM.

By 1915, Watson was named president after the appeals court had overturned his conviction, and he began to build an organization that would mirror the one Patterson had established at NCR—with one important exception. The first time Watson spoke to his salesmen he addressed the subject of ethics. "You must not do anything that's in restraint of trade," nor anything that could be "construed by anybody as unfair competition," Watson told his charges. In IBM's "Business Conduct Guidelines," a booklet still distributed to everyone who joins the company, Watson wrote: "Business is being called upon as never before to explain its actions, provide reasons for its decisions and speak out clearly on where it stands on ethical behavior. . . . If there is a single, overriding message in these guidelines, it is that IBM expects every employee to act, in every instance, according to the highest standards of business conduct."

The IBM ethos was rooted in one core, inviolate belief: Watson's respect for the individual. "IBM's total history," Tom Peters and Robert H. Waterman Jr. wrote in their 1982 book, *In Search of Excellence*, "is one of intense people orientation." Watson established clubs to reward the longevity and loyalty he prized and offered memberships in IBM country clubs to all employees for a fee of one dollar a year. While IBM's corporate uniform of white shirt, dark suit, neat hair and shined shoes may have seemed intolerant of individual tastes, Watson treated his employees with dignity and respect, a tradition continued by his son, Thomas Watson Jr., who succeeded his father as CEO. Even throughout the Great Depression, IBM refused to discard people, showing a commitment to its work force that was eventually copied in Japan.

In an essay in *Esquire* magazine in 1983, Drucker sought to put the elder Watson's career and contributions in perspective:

> Watson was actually one year older than Alfred Sloan [the legendary head of General Motors, who served as chairman from 1937 until his retirement at the age of eighty in 1956]. But whereas Sloan in the Twenties created modern management by building General Motors, and with it the modern "big corporation," Watson ten years later and quite independently created the "plant community" that we know to be the successor to Sloan's "big business enterprise" of the Twenties. He created in the Thirties the social organization and the work community of the postindustrial society.
>
> The first ones to see this ... were the Japanese. Again and again I have been laughed at in Japan when I talk about Japan's management embodying Japanese values. "Don't you realize," my Japanese friends say, "that we are simply adapting what IBM has done all along?" And when I ask how come, they always say, "When we started to rebuild Japan in the Fifties, we looked around for the most successful company we could find—it's IBM, isn't it?"

General Electric had paternalistic traditions similar to, though not as deeply embedded as, IBM's; and where IBM had Watson, GE had Charles Proteus Steinmetz. Born in Breslau, Germany, in 1865, two years after Henry Ford, Steinmetz had unique mental powers that were evident early on to classmates in the mathematical society of Breslau who nicknamed him "Proteus," after the Greek sea god who could change shape at will. The name stuck, for it was an apt description. Born deformed, a hunchback with a badly misshapen body, the diminutive Steinmetz seemed to possess a mind so powerful that, to his fellow mathematicians, it was capable of overcoming even physical infirmity. Apparently Steinmetz concurred with the schoolmates' assessment, as he adopted the name "Proteus" as his own on his application for American citizenship (abandoning his given middle names, August Rudolf). An active Socialist and editor for a time of the *People's Voice*, the Socialist publication of Breslau, Steinmetz, who had written one particularly inflammatory editorial critical of the Bismarck government's militaristic tendencies, was forced to flee Germany in 1888 to avoid arrest and imprisonment just as he had completed his university work and his thesis for his doctoral degree, which was never conferred upon him.

Steinmetz studied in Zurich for a year, then, on the spur of the moment, emigrated to the United States in 1889, arriving in New York City on June 1 penniless, handicapped by physical infirmity, and without any knowledge of the English language. Within two weeks he had found employment as a draftsman for Rudolf Eickemeyer of Yonkers, New York, an early pioneer of electrical machinery who put Steinmetz to work in a lab investigating the physical properties of electricity. Within three years, in 1892, Steinmetz's writings on electricity had already attracted a following within the engineering profession, and one admirer, Edwin W. Rice Jr., the top engineer of the newly formed General Electric Company, traveled from Schenectady to Yonkers to meet the man whose "originality and intellectual power had so impressed me."

Over the next thirty-one years, until his sudden death in 1923 at fifty-eight, Steinmetz rendered great service to the electrical engineering profession, and to General Electric. After completing his second year with the company, he was made a consulting engineer, a position he held throughout the rest of his life. His most significant contribution to the march of technology, in addition to more than two hundred patented inventions, was his expression of alternating current in a mathematical formula that allowed engineers to calculate and extend the transmission of high-voltage electrical current over long distances. But Steinmetz's imprint on the early General Electric wasn't limited to theories about electricity; he was also instrumental in shaping the values, ethics, and beliefs that the company would adopt in the twentieth century.

A champion of workers' rights, Steinmetz held true throughout his life to his Socialist credo, but it was socialism with a small "s," a variety that preferred evolution over the revolution advocated by Lenin in czarist Russia, as well as the Wobblies, the American industrial union organized in Chicago in 1905. Too much of a pacifist to condone the violent strikes that the Wobblies staged in the early years of the new century, Steinmetz became an outspoken critic of labor unions, "the most formidable obstacles in bringing about 'industrial cooperation,' " as he said in one speech. Instead, Steinmetz was an unabashed believer in "welfare capitalism," as he called it. "Welfare" didn't carry the negative, post-1960s connotation that it does now, and the men who led General Electric then shared Steinmetz's notion that the corporation could balance the simultaneous goals of protecting the welfare of its workers and achieving an adequate profit. Technocrats, not union bosses, would better solve the grievances of labor, and he envisioned a future society where corporations and the government worked together in a spirit of cooperation, protecting workers against accident, sickness, and old age, regulating working conditions and hours, and developing improved technology to reduce the workday.

In March 1914, just five months after thirteen thousand members of the Metal Trades Alliance staged the longest and largest strike at the Schenectady Works until World War II, Steinmetz wrote a confidential report outlining the elements of welfare capitalism, which was subsequently accepted by the board. The recommendations included lowering to sixty-five the qualifying age for the company's pension, which GE had established in 1913 (Steinmetz also thought the federal government should follow GE's lead and provide a supplemental pension benefit, as was the case in his native Germany; his view foreshadowed by twenty years the eventual Social Security system). Steinmetz championed a concept he called the "wage dividend," a semiannual bonus, equal to 5 percent of a worker's wage, to reward workers for their loyalty, which GE introduced in 1916 and paid, the following year, to nearly twenty-two thousand employees who had more than five years of continuous service.

GE's evolving system of welfare capitalism—administered under the office of the Welfare Department, whose first director was Unitarian minister Albert Clark—was one of the most extensive in American industry. Under Gerald Swope, who became CEO in 1922, welfare capitalism embraced paid vacations; accident, sickness, and death benefits; employee associations and recreational activities; company hospitals; educational courses and tuition reimbursement for continuing education; and cost-of-living increases in addition to hourly wages. The now-popular notions at progressive companies of giving labor a greater say in decision making on the shop floor, through participatory work-teams and shop committees, as well as giving workers more of the fruits of their labor and more ownership, through profit-sharing bonuses and stock dividends, are both concepts that originated with Steinmetz. When hourly workers at the Chrysler Corporation received profit-sharing checks that averaged $8,000 each—their share of the automaker's record profits in 1994, and the greatest profit distribution to the common man in the history of the auto business—they undoubtedly had no idea that Steinmetz had championed their cause eighty years before.

As the GE society became more fraternal, like any fraternity it was guilty of excesses. One tradition, begun under Swope, was an annual meeting for senior management held on Association Island in upstate New York that writer Kurt Vonnegut, who in the 1950s worked in the GE press department in Schenectady, parodied in his novel *Player Piano*. The protagonist of the novel—set against the backdrop of the Ilium Works, America's second-largest industrial plant, which spewed acid fumes and soot over the citizenry of Ilium, New York—was Paul Proteus (i.e., Charles Steinmetz). Vonnegut described a milieu in which top managers (sans Proteus) "spent a week each summer in an orgy of morale building—through team athletics, group sings, bonfires and skyrockets, bawdy entertainment, free whisky and cigars."

But another view of that era is equally valid. While paternalism signified an "orgy of morale building," it also meant that people tended to care for one another. In 1953, when John McLaughlin first joined GE as a young Manufacturing Management program trainee in the Fort Wayne motor business, he needed cash before he got his first paycheck. The training program manager for Fort Wayne, Ralph Woody, lent him the money, and McLaughlin repaid the loan in kind during a long career at GE. After leaving GE in late 1978, McLaughlin sought to reestablish the kind of caring for people that he had known throughout his career and had come to regard as sound business practice. In 1985, he bought a small, specialty motor business in Norwalk, Connecticut, and mortgaged his house a few years later to keep the business afloat. Creditors pitched in to help by extending terms. Fifty jobs were saved and the business survived. Later, though employees had to accept a 15-percent pay cut and a four-day workweek, not a single employee was lost. "No matter what anyone says, loyalty does matter," McLaughlin observes.

The demise of loyalty isn't just the lament of old-timers and has-beens. To Richard Elsberry, it's the essence of what's wrong with American capitalism now. Elsberry, whose thirty-year existence as a briefcase-toting corporate workaholic came to an abrupt end in 1985, when the General Electric News Bureau he worked for was unilaterally abolished, breaks into peals of laughter whenever he reads CEOs like Welch talking about "empowerment," the new corporatespeak. How, he asks, does a person get "empowered" when they're

In 1893, as the new General Electric Company proudly proclaimed that its lamps shone "in the palace of the Mikado as well as in the Opera House of Paris," GE displayed its Tower of Light at the Columbian Exposition in Chicago.

Charles Proteus Steinmetz joined GE in its second year, 1893. His imprint on the company wasn't limited to theories about electricity; he was also instrumental in shaping the values, ethics, and beliefs that GE would adopt in the twentieth century.

By 1928, the year this photograph was taken, more than one million American households had traded their icebox for the Monitor Top refrigerator, a product so unique in its conception that it fundamentally changed the American way of life.

In October 1929, on the fiftieth anniversary of the electric light breakthrough, Thomas Edison, GE's founding father, reenacts his triumphant moment as hundreds of dignitaries look on.

Henry Ford attributed much of his success in the mass production of automobiles to Edison, his friend and camping buddy. Here Ford inspects a GE electric dishwasher and disposal in the first "New American" home in Detroit, circa 1936.

In addition to hosting *General Electric Theater*, Ronald Reagan spent two of the eight years he was under contract to GE on the road, visiting each of the company's more than 130 manufacturing facilities in the United States—including this factory in Schenectady—and addressing all of its 250,000 employees.

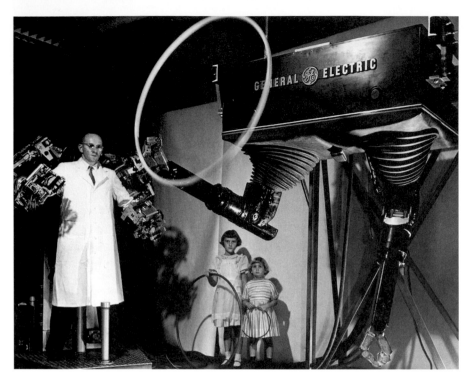

"The House of Magic" turned out inventions in a torrent of creativity, not the least of which was "Handyman," the first robot to simulate the clutching motion of the human hand; here, it demonstrates its dexterity by twirling a Hula Hoop.

Handcuffs barely visible under their coatsleeves, General Electric executives Lewis Burger (left) and William Ginn exit a federal courthouse in Philadelphia in February 1961, after Judge J. Cullen Ganey handed out thirty-day jail sentences to them and others for their part in the antitrust violations of the "Incredible Electrical Conspiracy."

In April 1982, an estimated three thousand pickets—including one with a sign parodying GE's signature slogan—virtually closed down the main GE plant in Schenectady, New York, to protest the company's contracting out of union work, a practice that has become much more common in the years since.

Jack Welch (left) shares a laugh with Thornton Bradshaw, the chairman of RCA, after they announced to the world GE's purchase of RCA for $6.28 billion, the most expensive non-oil acquisition to that date—December 12, 1985— in U.S. history.

Many GE buildings in downtown Schenectady, New York, have been razed during the Welch era, including this steel foundry, which was demolished in the early nineties. Visible in the distant background is the back of the "Meatball," the GE monogram that sits atop the main building.

The arrest of Israeli Brigadier General Rami Dotan, for his role in an illegal attempt to win orders of jet engines for GE, unleashed the first in a succession of great scandals for the company, which pleaded guilty in 1992 to four felonies in the Dotan affair; GE's participation in the bribery-and-kickback scheme was brought to light by a GE whistleblower who sued the company under a statute called the False Claims Act.

In the last twenty years, Schenectady, New York— the city Edison chose in 1886 as the new home for his Edison Machine Works— has lost 22,000 GE jobs, which has made Jack Welch a frequent target of editorial cartoons in the *Schenectady Gazette.*

"Jack Welch's Nightmare on Wall Street"—as *Fortune* magazine called the stunning collapse in 1994 of GE's Kidder, Peabody unit—was triggered, Welch claimed, by the trading abuses of one errant Kidder employee: Joseph Jett. An administrative law judge later sanctioned Jett for books-and-records and other violations but cleared him of securities fraud, the most serious charge against him.

An active and influential behind-the-scenes player in Washington, Jack Welch was a frequent guest at the Reagan White House, as well as a golfing partner of President Clinton's at Farm Neck Country Club in Oak Bluffs, Massachusetts, in the summer of 1997.

In addition to the Hudson River, PCBs leaked by GE plants have contaminated sites in Pittsfield, Massachusetts, including soil excavated from the backyard of this house at 15 Longfellow Avenue; GE has been resisting federal efforts to place PCB remediation of Pittsfield and the nearby Housatonic River under the domain of the Superfund law.

not certain they will continue to have a job? "Jack talks about controlling your own destiny, but how do you do that in a place like GE? I worked damn hard, always gave my best, and it didn't do me any good." Several months after his sudden discharge from the GE "family," when a younger colleague Elsberry had mentored called to get advice on a job offer he had received from GE rival Siemens, Elsberry didn't mince his words—don't be as foolish as I was, he said. Take it. The colleague, Tom Varney, followed his advice and today is part of a growing GE contingent at Siemens, which has seen its sales in the United States double in the last five years.

A third person who laments the passing of paternalism is Mary E. Kuykendall, another white-collar retiree, who spent most of her career in Schenectady touting GE's products and its management through speeches, brochures, and videos. "From a female standpoint," she says, "the 'father knows best' era wasn't the greatest, but it was preferable to the 'date rape' of today." Kuykendall joined GE in 1960, the same year as Jack Welch, "enjoyed the first twenty years and, as a result, worked like hell; in fact, I never had a sick day off." Kuykendall was well regarded by her employer—"two management awards in one year weren't for nothing," her supervisor wrote of her in a 1989 performance appraisal—but she so disliked the style of management Welch brought to Schenectady, and its outcomes, that she quit in 1991 at age fifty-two, and has since written a play, a parody of her experiences in the 1980s, titled *Gold Collars and Resources*; gold collars are the managers who reap money for downsizing the business, resources the victims who get downsized.

Act One opens in the corporate boardroom, where CEO Jack Squat (who, according to the character description, "plays the market, uses his 'resources' as chips and covers himself through rhetoric") and security analyst Ivan ("who buys into the rhetoric because he only looks at the bottom line") celebrate the new record earnings made under the Bold Strokes Vision Program. In Act Two, vice president Hittmann announces the consolidation of eleven U.S. plants into four and the layoff of 75 percent of the workforce of Ilium (borrowing Vonnegut's fictional location), whose actions are covered by a public relations vice president, Alice ("revels in the executive wonderland"), using the "we must be competitive" rhetoric to cover harvesting of the business. Hittmann's stock options are doubled when he extracts tax concessions from the Mayor of Ilium, while Paternal ("general manager of engineering who refuses to believe that engineering is a commodity") and Cartwheel ("general manager of manufacturing who keeps thinking that maybe the greedy and destructive ones will go away if he just keeps working hard") fight a valiant but losing battle to maintain the business. In Act Three, the lights have gone out in the "Electric City," as unemployed resources and former city officials gather in a darkened barroom to lament their fate.

Although Kuykendall's play is a caricature, it also illustrates one important outcome of the revolution that Welch hadn't bargained on—the cynicism and outright anger his actions would engender within General Electric, and the impact that would have in influencing the scandals that were to follow. Some would seek to exorcise their grief through lawsuits or other forms of retaliation, therapy, or perhaps alcohol. Paternalism had given way to cannibalism, and the employee who once felt valued and protected now felt as if Welch regarded him or her as the enemy. And, in a sense, he did. One of the most egregious examples was the case of Vera English.

SITTING IN THE SUNLIT kitchen of her apartment, Vera May English gently rocks an oak rocking chair back and forth in a peaceful metronome-like rhythm, a scene worthy of Norman Rockwell and the very picture of the kindly grandmother that she is. Her attire, pink moccasins, navy blue slacks, and a white blouse with pink pinstripes, is down-home and simple, adorned only by a shell necklace. Her round face and soft features befit an amiable personality, and she sprinkles her conversation with quotations from the Bible and stories from her childhood on a Maine dairy farm. The GE refrigerator in one corner of the kitchen is covered with grandmotherly memorabilia, mostly pictures of her progeny and descendants tacked up with magnets, while in the other corner "Pretty Bird," her caged cockatiel companion, squawks away. A woman of meager financial means, Vera says she tries to live the way Christ commanded, and regularly proffers food and drink to visitors and neighbors in her Mennonite retirement village.

Life wasn't always so peaceful. In her previous existence, as a whistle-blower at a GE nuclear fuel facility, English was the victim of harassment, vandalism, and intimidation in the normally quiet town of Wilmington, North Carolina, where she lived and worked. In the process, English—a woman of grit and determination who began complaining in the late seventies about health and safety violations in the lab where she worked as a technician, and eventually brought them to the attention of the federal government— became an antinuclear heroine to some and a pariah to others. *English v. General Electric Co.* was one of the most celebrated whistleblower cases ever in the nuclear industry, and eventually made its way to the United States Supreme

Court. The unanimous victory English won there set an important precedent for other whistleblowers and made her a national celebrity—actress Meryl Streep, who portrayed nuclear whistleblower Karen Silkwood in the film *Silkwood*, was among the dignitaries who feted English at one ceremony in Washington—but it didn't improve her lot one iota. Instead, English lost her job, her savings, her security, her home and, for a time, nearly her mind.

The first incident of harassment took place on August 20, 1980, when English, a widow at that time living alone, discovered that her home at 74 Holland Drive had been ransacked: Sheets had been pulled from the mattress in the bedroom; photographs of her that had been removed from the family Bible were strewn on the bed; and scattered around one picture were .38 caliber bullets. The case was never solved, and while English to this day believes the vandals were fellow employees from the lab seeking to intimidate her, they didn't succeed—but not for lack of trying. The incident was the first of fourteen that New Hanover County Police investigated between 1980 and 1988, including burglaries, vandalism, obscene phone calls, and, in one instance, gunfire.

The treatment she received from her bosses at General Electric was not much better. Fired from her job in July 1984, English initiated an eight-year legal battle to right the wrongs she had suffered, but she badly underestimated the lengths to which GE would go to win. As other whistleblowers who have fought the company have discovered, court decisions don't always turn on matters of justice but rather on matters of law. There is no doubt that justice was on English's side. The first and only judge to rule on the merits of the case rather than the nuances of the law, Administrative Law Judge Robert J. Brissenden, after listening intently to eleven days of testimony, concluded in an August 1985 decision that Wilmington management had used a trumped-up charge against English as a "pretext for getting rid of an employee who would not stop reporting violations to the Nuclear Regulatory Commission." The judge ordered GE to reinstate her and pay $70,000 in compensatory damages for emotional and psychological distress, a decision the company successfully had overturned years later on procedural grounds. The Nuclear Regulatory Commission also sided with English—though four and a half years after the event. GE paid $24,000 in 1989 for wrongfully terminating English.

More than anything, the case provided enormous insight into the character and behavior of General Electric under Jack Welch, illuminating its quantum shift from paternalism. Though both the NRC and Judge Brissenden had concluded that GE was in the wrong, the company's managers still fought to win, no matter that their foe was a widowed grandmother, a conscientious employee who before her dismissal worked twelve years without incident, no matter that logic would dictate simply settling the case. Had Wilmington management merely accepted Judge Brissenden's initial ruling, they would have saved the company considerable money and ended what became an enormous distraction and embarrassment. GE's legal bill in the English case was around $1 million, according to Travis Payne, English's attorney, considerably more than the $70,000 fine and $73,007.50 in court expenses it was ordered to pay. But logic didn't rule the day; vindication became as important to the men fighting Vera English as it was to her. GE appealed and English appealed in a blizzard of motions, countermotions, and petitions, while verdicts in the case were rendered on eight separate occasions. In the end, GE management convinced themselves that *they* were doing the right thing by meting out punishment against an adversary who was disobedient and deserved what she got.

"We felt sorry for her," says Bertram Wolfe, a retired vice president who supervised the nuclear division that English worked in. But "from our standpoint, she had deliberately tried to hurt the company. It was frankly a matter of principle. She had purposefully gone out of her way to get the lab in trouble. We felt we couldn't accede to a person with that kind of motivation."

English's job was to monitor and control fuel quality, performing the same tasks as Karen Silkwood had at the Kerr-McGee facility in Oklahoma. The GE plant was one of about a half dozen facilities in the United States nuclear industry that processed uranium for use as fuel in commercial nuclear reactors. The quality-control lab was the final checkpoint in a nuclear fuel cycle that began with the mining of uranium ore and ended at Wilmington with the production of enriched uranium, which was fabricated into pellets and loaded into tubes to form fuel rods. The lab was the guardhouse in that process, ensuring that the uranium conformed to specifications set and occasionally monitored by the Nuclear Regulatory Commission. English ran an analyzer that measured whether the uranium was within prescribed tolerances, and if it didn't conform, it would have to be reprocessed, which meant costly delays and lower productivity.

In the early years, English didn't find fault with the lab's commitment to safety and accuracy, but beginning in 1978, after a new manager, Preston Winslow, was named head of the lab, the obsession with productivity led to problems. To meet their production quotas, English suspected her colleagues in the lab were falsifying data and test results, releasing uranium even if it was subpar.* When English complained, Winslow and other male supervisors ridiculed her—"you're doing the work of a supervisor" was the common putdown—but she refused to back off and began complaining about the shoddy work procedures in the lab. The worker who occupied her desk on the shift prior to hers regularly left radioactive contamination behind, a violation of lab and NRC rules, which required that any radioactivity be immediately cleaned up. On one occasion late in 1983, a coworker dumped uranium powder in a nonventilated area of the lab, a violation of NRC regulations. "I could taste it," English recalled during testimony before Judge Brissenden. She immediately reported the incident to Winslow, who then asked the man who had dumped uranium, "Do you smell any powder?" The man said no. "Then Mr. Winslow walked to [within] an inch of my face, smiled and said, 'He didn't smell any uranium,' " English testified.

From the very beginning, English was the odd woman out. She wasn't shy about expressing her opinion, and refused to buckle just because her male bosses didn't like what she said. When friends counseled her not to rock the boat, she would remind them that it was their safety at stake and that employees were duty-bound under the rules of the lab to report safety violations they observed. Yet Winslow and others came to loathe English for her strict attention to the rules, frequent complaints, and what they considered her outright insubordination. In their view, she was a troublemaker, and male coworkers taunted her with expressions like "damn Northerner" and "uppity female." In their opinion, she had no business being in the lab, taking a job that a man should have filled. Good jobs were scarce in Wilmington, which was why GE had come there in 1968. Plentiful labor in a nonunion environment meant that the company would have the bargaining leverage it wanted. The town would achieve some notoriety in the eighties and nineties, with the celebrity of its most famous native son, basketball player Michael Jordan. But when Jordan was growing up there in the sixties, the few jobs that were available—as an auto mechanic, barber, grocery store clerk, or farm hand in the tobacco fields—paid next to nothing.

English was an eager job applicant when GE first came to town. When she was offered a job in the lab in 1972, four years after she had applied, she snapped it up. She had worked briefly for the company twenty-five years earlier in Fort Wayne, as an office clerk, and remembered GE as a fair and generous employer. In Wilmington, her starting salary of $5.35 an hour, the

---

* Winslow, in his testimony before Judge Brissenden, said he never had any indication "that there was any unacceptable release of data" (p. 1882 of the court transcript). When he investigated English's complaints, he found them to be unwarranted.

minimum pay rate at the plant then, was well over twice what she had earned as a medical technician at a local hospital. By the time she was dismissed in July 1984, her pay had risen to $11.82 an hour, an annual salary of $30,486.

The events that led to her dismissal began in August 1982, when English made the first of two confidential complaints to the Nuclear Regulatory Commission, citing problems that her supervisors had ignored: Management paid inadequate attention to proper procedures for controlling radioactive materials; lab supervisors didn't enforce rules that prohibited eating and drinking in the lab, where radioactive materials were handled openly rather than under vented hoods, as was required; workers handled contaminated vials barehanded and dumped containers of uranium carelessly; employees weren't properly "frisking" themselves for contamination with handheld radiation detectors when leaving controlled areas in the lab, as was required—and hence may have carried "hot" residue home on their clothes; inspections by the plant's radiation-safety personnel were rare, perfunctory, and performed by personnel who did not know what to look for; machines to monitor air quality in the lab were placed too high to measure the air employees were breathing. English also discovered that her computer password had been used to alter quality-control test results and release uranium that didn't pass her muster.

Though the NRC investigated English's allegations in September 1982, citing GE for various shortcomings in its lab procedures, many of the problems persisted, particularly the improper use of her computer password. English then took the complaints to her boss's boss, Eugene Lees, chief of quality control at Wilmington. In February 1984, Lees, who the following September was promoted by Jack Welch to succeed James Long as general manager of the Wilmington facility, called English into his office and gave her an ultimatum—she had one week to substantiate her allegations, according to the letter he handed her, which warned that "failure to comply with this instruction will be considered insubordination and will result in severe disciplinary action, up to and including discharge." One week later, English complied with Lees's demands and gave him a six-page document outlining her allegations, a copy of which she also provided to the NRC.

The confrontation between English and Lees came to a head in early March. On Monday, March 5, English came to work to find what had become a familiar sight—radioactive uranium powder and uranyl acid spilled on the top and legs of her worktable. She cleaned it up, as she had dozens of times before. Contamination was also present on Tuesday, Wednesday, and Thursday. Finally, on Friday, March 9, annoyed at the disregard her supervisors had shown for the problem, she left part of the contamination in place, marking it with two pieces of red tape. Two days later, when her supervisor had returned, she showed him the contamination. He promised to have the facility's safety inspectors follow up on her grievances, but on March 16, English was called into a meeting and charged with five violations of plant rules, among them deliberate contamination of a worktable and failure to clean up radioactivity knowing it existed. Her fate had been sealed in a meeting two days earlier in which Lees and four other supervisors decided that English would be removed from the lab and barred from controlled areas of the plant. After the meeting, English was told to turn in her badge and was escorted off the premises, sobbing uncontrollably.

English appealed her removal from the lab. A hearing was held on May 1, 1984, before a panel that consisted of Long, Lees, and Jeff Faucette, the employee-relations manager. English was permitted to have witnesses, and three testified on her behalf. When English was asked if she had anything to say, she began by reciting from memory portions of the first Psalm: "Blessed is the man who does not walk in the counsel of the wicked. . . . He is like a tree planted by streams of water, which yields its fruit in season and whose leaf does not wither. Whatever he does prospers. Not so the wicked! They are like chaff that the wind blows away. Therefore the wicked will not stand in the judgment, nor sinners in the assembly of the righteous. For the Lord watches over the way of the righteous, but the way of the wicked will perish."

Even though the panel decided that four of the five charges were unsubstantiated, the three men upheld her removal from the lab. They concluded that she had "knowingly and intentionally failed to clean up [a] spill of radioactive material," conduct that was "a very serious and significant violation of the Wilmington plant's health and safety standards and procedures," even though the rules hadn't been enforced when English brought the same infractions to their attention. "I deeply regret that this action is necessary," Long wrote after the hearing. English was given temporary work in a warehouse and promised another job, but on July 26, 1984, Thurston Davis, an employee-relations representative and frequent adversary of English's, handed her a termination notice. On the way out, he tweaked her one last time, reprimanding her for wearing sneakers in the warehouse, a violation of safety regulations. When English came to work wearing sneakers the next day, her final day at GE, she was sent home to change into safety shoes.

As turbulent as her employment was, it was relative peace compared with the fireworks that followed. Wilmington management apparently presumed that English, lacking the resources to take on the General Electric Company, would simply go away quietly. She didn't. And although English extracted no monetary gain in the subsequent legal battle, she got some measure of vengeance by laying bare GE's behavior. What made the English case most extraordinary was that the facts were largely undisputed. GE's chief defense was that English was a high-strung, emotional woman whose complaints had little merit, an argument Judge Brissenden rejected. "A review of the NRC findings does not indicate such an innocuous conclusion with reference to GE's record," he wrote. Rather, the extensive discovery proceedings in the case showed the degree to which managers were willing to twist the truth in what became a tangled web of deceit.

After her removal from the lab on March 16 but before her hearing on May 1, and while management was telling English that an investigation into her allegations had found them to be unfounded, the NRC had already informed management several weeks before that there were contamination problems in the lab. The NRC inspection, the direct result of English's written complaints, prompted management to circulate a memo in late February asking employees to be more attentive to safety. In its report, the NRC concluded that managers at the Wilmington facility had ignored safety deficiencies in the lab: "Your staff appeared to adopt a mindset that [repeated instances] of contamination were normal rather than unusual." GE's own internal investigation, conducted in April 1984, before English's final hearing, also concluded that her complaints had substance.

Judge Brissenden's favorable ruling in August 1985 was reversed on January 13, 1987, when Deputy Secretary of Labor Dennis Whitfield disallowed English's complaint because she hadn't filed it within the thirty days required under Section 210 of the Energy Reorganization Act of 1974. Although it had been filed with the Labor Department within thirty days of her final discharge, Whitfield ruled that the statutory clock had begun ticking on May 15, 1984, the date she was given notice on the outcome of her appeal. As a result of that setback, English filed suit. Attorney Travis Payne of Raleigh, North Carolina—her second lawyer, the first one having died—spent the next three years fighting to overturn adverse district and appeals court rulings that had denied English the right to sue GE for intentional infliction of emotional distress. GE had argued that English didn't have that right because federal law superseded state law, which meant that English was precluded from seeking damages for the emotional distress she suffered when GE fired her. A federal court in North Carolina and an appeals court in Virginia agreed with GE, but the Supreme Court didn't. The high court's unanimous, nine-to-zero decision, issued on June 4, 1990, was a remarkable defeat for the company and for the nuclear industry, and gave whistleblowing workers in that industry and many others who had been terminated the right to sue for damages under state law.

"It's a home run for whistleblowers, the most significant ruling affecting whistleblowers in the history of the country," enthused Stephen Kohn, an attorney for the National Whistleblower Center, when the decision was announced. The Supreme Court victory, however, merely gave English the right to sue that she had been denied all along. As it would turn out, winning a claim against GE for intentional infliction of emotional distress was a tall order in North Carolina; Payne, English's attorney, had to prove that GE's conduct had been "extreme and outrageous." In the final appeals court ruling of September 1992 that ended the eight-year struggle, the three-judge panel agreed that "English suffered severe emotional and psychological problems, which apparently arose from her employment at GE." They also agreed that "the essential facts of this case are not in dispute." Still, GE's conduct hadn't met the standard of outrageousness required under the statute. "While GE's conduct may exceed some of the bounds of decency, its conduct simply does not 'go beyond all possible bounds of decency.' . . . In sum, English cannot establish that GE's conduct was *outrageous*, an essential element of a claim for intentional infliction of emotional distress. Therefore, summary judgment in favor of GE is appropriate and was properly granted by the district court."

When Travis Payne called to inform English of the appeals court's final verdict, she was calm, but the events of the last decade have clearly taken their toll. The first psychologist who evaluated English after her dismissal in 1984 found her depression to be so severe that he worried she might attempt suicide, and only recently has English stopped seeing a therapist. "The Lord is my counselor now," she says. She was also rejected in the community that was her home for thirty-two years. One letter from seventeen GE employees, published in the *Wilmington Morning Star* shortly after Judge Brissenden ruled in English's favor, sums up the antipathy many at GE felt toward her. She was perceived as a troublemaker and a potential threat to their jobs, in a community that had few before GE came to town: "The people of Wilmington and General Electric do not owe Vera English any thanks. Her 'whistleblowing' has not helped her fellow employees. . . . We enjoy these jobs and would not do anything to harm the community. . . . Ms. English deserves no thanks and she will get none." The irony is that she does deserve thanks: Current employees acknowledge that the attention she focused on poor lab procedures compelled GE to clean up its act. Even so, Wilmington's safety record isn't the best; as recently as 1991, the plant was on the verge of a major nuclear accident when 330 pounds of uranium were misrouted into a waste storage tank. The NRC immediately sent six specialists to the scene who were able to dissolve the uranium before it went critical and unleashed radiation into the plant.

Despite the tremendous pain she endured, English says she would blow the whistle again. "They made me think I'm crazy, but I'm not," she says, taking off her glasses to wipe away a tear. "I was so naive to believe that Jack Welch would not want this in his company. How stupid I was." She cries easily, but since moving from Wilmington, she is learning to suppress her anger, even overcome it: "Spiritually speaking, I learned many beautiful lessons. How God uses us, for healing and helping others."

In defeating Vera English, General Electric had won a victory, but it had come at a price. More employees had come to distrust the integrity of the system, and at least one, who sold GE jet engines to the Israeli military from an office in Tel Aviv, was so suspicious of his employer that he believed it was incapable of doing the right thing. Vowing not to be destroyed the way English had been, Chester Walsh set a trap to protect himself, simultaneously blowing the whistle on one of the biggest frauds ever committed against the United States government—and enmeshing Jack Welch yet again in another great scandal.

CHAPTER TWELVE

TELLING THE
WHOLE TRUTH

THE ARREST of an Israeli general unleashed the first in a succession of great scandals for GE. On Sunday, October 28, 1990, Israeli police took into custody Rami Dotan, a brigadier general in the Israeli Air Force and a rising star of that nation's military, and three companions, as they were about to board a jet bound for Switzerland. The arrest went virtually unnoticed in the United States, meriting only brief mention in the *Washington Post* the next day, but the news item caught the attention of attorneys at the criminal division of the Justice Department in Washington, who had been tipped off to possible illegal activity by Dotan, the subject of an investigation in his own country for more than a year. Though the details of the case were murky, the criminal division immediately asked the Department of State to cable the U.S. embassy in Israel for more information on Dotan. Although his activities and those of his accomplice, GE executive Herbert Steindler, had been known to many executives inside GE's massive Aircraft Engine division, Jack Welch would later testify that he didn't learn of Dotan's arrest—and the portent it had for him, and General Electric—until December, and by then it was too late to head off the scandal.

One of those in the know was Chester Walsh, a midlevel manager in Aircraft Engines, who eighteen days after the arrest filed a lawsuit against his employer that spelled out in excruciating detail (136 pages of supporting evidence) the illicit relationship between Steindler and Dotan, and the devilishly complicated fraud they had perpetrated against the United States government. The suit, which for the first nine months was sealed at the government's request, invoked the legal concept of *qui tam*, an abbreviation of a Latin phrase meaning "he who sues on behalf of a king as well as himself." *Qui tam* had been codified in U.S. law under an obscure statute, the False Claims Act, which had become a scourge to General Electric, and the source as well of several lawsuits that had been filed against the company by whistleblowing employees.

Enacted in March 1863, several months before the battle of Gettysburg, the law was designed to combat fraud against the Union army, and the profiteering that was rampant then. At Gettysburg, Union soldiers were forced into hand-to-hand and bayonet combat to hold their position when boxes supposed to contain ammunition that had been purchased from private suppliers arrived containing only sawdust. The False Claims Act gave citizens the right to sue on behalf of the government, and provided for a bounty to any person whose claim resulted in restitution to Uncle Sam.

While General Electric executives would later decry such use of the False Claims Act, they had no one to blame but themselves, for GE's contributions to the defense-procurement scandals of the 1980s had persuaded Congress that there needed to be greater financial incentives to potential whistleblowers to combat a systematic looting by defense contractors allied with the Pentagon. The prodding had come from John Phillips, a public-interest lawyer in California, whose Center for Law in the Public Interest, founded in 1971, had stopped oil drilling in Santa Monica Bay, exposed corporate political payoffs, won $400 million in housing subsidies for poor people dislocated by freeway construction—and proved, in the process, that public-interest law needn't be consigned to pro bono work. Phillips was intrigued by the False Claims Act's provisions that gave citizens the right to sue, and tapping into congressional concern about defense-contract abuses, he stitched together a bipartisan coalition that whisked a revised False Claims Act through Congress in just fourteen months. Its revisions gave whistleblowers greater rights, protections, and incentives to ferret out wrongdoing and to press their cases on behalf of the government. President Reagan, who liked its libertarian approach and undoubtedly had no sense of the problems the new False Claims Act would create for his former employer, signed it into law in October 1986.

The amended law was the club that Walsh used to whack GE. Walsh was universally known inside Aircraft Engines as likeable and trustworthy, but that didn't mean he trusted the company that had employed him for twenty-six years. To the contrary, Walsh's experiences, which had been very positive from a career standpoint, had taught him that Aircraft Engines was a rough-and-tumble place. When Walsh, who in Tel Aviv sold jet engines to the Israeli military, first suspected that Dotan and Steindler, a GE executive who outranked Walsh at division headquarters near Cincinnati, were engaged in a fraudulent conspiracy, he kept his suspicions to himself. Instead of reporting it to GE authorities—as the company insists he should have done—Walsh watched the alliance unfold, quietly gathering evidence, and assembling documentation to support his case. In June 1987, while on a visit to Los Angeles, Walsh called on John Phillips, identifying himself as "John Wallace" for the first year and a half. After returning to Israel, he continued to accumulate documents that he took with him to Switzerland, where he had been reassigned, and then to the United States. The documents were ultimately pivotal in the government's case against GE.

GE had outfoxed many whistleblowers before him, but Walsh proved to be a shrewder opponent. A high school dropout, he rose from hardscrabble Quincy, Massachusetts, to become a globe-trotting Mr. Fix-It for GE, accumulating three college degrees along the way. He has street smarts and played his hand with great finesse. Once the scandal broke, in meeting after meeting with government and congressional investigators, the company and an army of attorneys portrayed Walsh as a greedy profiteer, a participant in the crime who intentionally allowed the fraud to spread for years in order to collect a larger bounty. While his nearly $6 million reward may suggest his motives were less than pure, Walsh is a shy, unassuming man who bears no resemblance to GE's portrayal of him as a conniving conspirator and bounty hunter. He has a different explanation of his motives, for which there is also ample evidence.

Walsh had done his homework and knew that his employer often treated whistleblowers harshly. The case of Vera English hadn't been an isolated incident; many people who made public suspected wrongdoing had suffered for it. Walsh insists it wasn't the money he wanted; it was protection. By filing suit under the amended False Claims Act, Walsh would expose the fraud, do the patriotic thing, and, not coincidentally, prevent his superiors from retaliating against him. "Nobody was going to protect me, so I started looking for ways to protect myself," he explains. He concluded that the best defense was a good offense, and the offensive he mounted was a broadside that rocked Welch and GE.

Walsh had researched previous whistleblowers and discovered the case of John Michael Gravitt, a machinist foreman in Aircraft Engines, who in 1982 had stood up during a training session and told thirty colleagues that the company was ripping off Uncle Sam. "The time cards going into supervisors' offices aren't the same ones coming out," Gravitt, a forty-eight-year-old Vietnam vet at that time, declared. A colleague grabbed Gravitt's arm and tried to yank him back to his seat. "He said, 'Shut up, you're going to be fired,' " Gravitt later recalled in congressional testimony, a prediction that proved prophetic.

The profiteering disclosed in the Gravitt *qui tam* suit, which was filed the year following his dismissal in 1984, was GE's alteration of time cards on government jet-engine contracts. Shortly after joining GE in 1980, Gravitt, an ex-Marine who at six foot three and 315 pounds was an intimidating figure, found that he was being subjected to intimidation. Superiors were pressuring him to coax his subordinates to doctor their time cards. By altering the vouchers, managers either billed the government for idle time or transferred billable time from projects that were over budget to projects that were under. Government auditors later concluded that as much as $7.2 million of time was falsely billed to the government, but as Gravitt dug in his heels in opposition to the practice, the pressure on him to participate intensified. At one point he was summoned to his boss' office for what he later called, in an interview with Federal Bureau of Investigation agents, "the 'GE real world speech'—that cheating was something we had to do to keep our jobs." Early in 1983, Gravitt decided to alert senior management. He surreptitiously slipped into the office on weekends, photocopying the altered time cards and, on June 29, 1983, delivering a letter and supporting documents to Brian Rowe, president of the Aircraft Engines division. That same day, he was dismissed from his $35,000-a-year job and was never called back. GE claims Gravitt's termination, of which he had been notified a month before, was part of a broader employment cutback in the business.

Like Vera English, Gravitt set an important precedent for other whistle-blowers but didn't fare so well personally. When lawyers for GE and the Justice Department began to negotiate, they reached a $234,000 civil settlement, and Gravitt, who wasn't permitted to participate in the settlement discussions, was offered a bounty of 10 percent of that amount, take it or leave it. Even more outrageous was the warning Gravitt was given by Vincent Terlep, the top Justice Department attorney in the case, who said that if he didn't accept the settlement, Terlep would "personally see to it that I didn't get a nickel," Gravitt recalls. Terlep later apologized for his comments, while Carl Rubin, the federal judge in the case, rebuked the Justice Department for its handling of the case and rejected the settlement. Finally, in 1989, Gravitt and his attorney, Jim Helmer, a Cincinnati lawyer who had built a lucrative practice from plaintiffs' cases against General Electric, accepted a settlement in which Gravitt and three other GE employees he represented who had also sued their former employer under the False Claims Act shared $770,000. Under the terms of the settlement, Gravitt can't disclose how much of that amount he pocketed but after the payment of taxes and legal costs, he says, "it wasn't all that great."

Walsh was determined to avoid a similar fate. He had been chosen to represent GE in Israel because of his even temperament, unflappable nature, and prior experience in hot spots around the globe, including Vietnam before the fall of Saigon. From the first day he arrived in Tel Aviv on December 28, 1984, Walsh's assignment was to keep Rami Dotan content. It was a task that would clearly put him to the ultimate test.

Dotan, a colonel then, oversaw Israel's ambitious F-16 program, and he awarded tens of millions of dollars in military contracts each year, which meant that he was an important cog in the military procurement wheel. Between 1982 and 1990, the period in which it was Dotan who bought the hardware that kept Israel's elite Air Force fully equipped in the air, the Israeli government ordered $540 million worth of engines, parts, and services directly from GE, and it bought millions more indirectly, purchasing GE equipment from the U.S. government. Dotan had considerable clout, especially because he was considered a national hero whose vast technical knowledge helped Israel maintain air supremacy in the skies of the Middle East. A swarthy man with deep-set eyes and a volcanic temper, Dotan was often intolerable, and Walsh had been forewarned that keeping him content wouldn't be an easy task.

In the clubby world of military procurement, relationships are as important as hardware in clinching a sale. GE had proved as much in its conquest of rival Pratt & Whitney in the military market for jet engines. In the early 1970s, when Pratt had a seemingly insurmountable advantage in the worldwide military market for jet engines, GE salesmen began hearing complaints from Air Force and Navy pilots about flameouts on F-16 and F-14 fighter jets equipped with Pratt engines. By 1978, Pratt, which had been slow to acknowledge the problems and even slower in addressing them, had a full-scale assault on its hands; GE lobbyists had worked the Pentagon overtime and persuaded the top brass to authorize $34.5 million in the coming year's budget to demonstrate a new GE jet engine, initiating a battle between the two companies that was soon dubbed "the great engine war." Six years later, in 1984, both the Navy and the Air Force chose the new GE F110 engine as the power plant for their fighter jets, the same engine that Dotan selected that same year for one hundred F-16s purchased by the Israeli Air Force as part of an air defense program known as Peace Marble Two.

In the United States, certain members of Congress had been particularly helpful in winning the Navy and Air Force's approval, and the GE lobbying office in Washington doled out additional money to senators Thad Cochran (referred to as "a spear carrier" in one 1983 internal GE memo) of Mississippi, Robert Byrd of West Virginia, and Arlen Specter of Pennsylvania. Likewise, Dotan's selection of GE in Israel over Pratt, the contract holder for Peace

Marble One, meant that the favor had to be returned. In exchange for Dotan's selection of GE, Herbert Steindler, GE's top military-jet engine salesman overseas, whom colleagues dubbed "Mr. Israel" because of his extensive experience in the country, convinced his colleagues to use Yoram Ingbir, a Tel Aviv engineer, as GE's subcontractor in Israel for the contract. Ingbir, who had served under Dotan in the military as a jet-engine specialist, had founded Ingbir Engineering, which in the mid-eighties quickly became a major tester of jet engines. That growth, Israeli investigators would later discover, had been the result of kickbacks Ingbir had paid Dotan in exchange for the contracts his firm received. Steindler also arranged for GE to funnel payments to Ingbir through GSK Management Consultants, which operated out of the Matawan, New Jersey, home of Gary S. Klein, an old Army buddy of Steindler's who participated in the fraud. Klein pleaded guilty in May 1993 to money laundering and wire fraud charges.

The scheme Dotan and Steindler hatched was right out of a Ludlum spy thriller. Investigators, who tracked some money the pair embezzled through GSK to the purchase of expensive apartments in Tel Aviv and Rome, eventually unmasked an embezzlement process that was complex and brazen. GSK was paid for thirteen projects and hardware that didn't exist, including $7 million for a facility that was to test the new F-16 engines and a fictitious Hebrew translation of an engine training manual.

The scheme worked like this: Ingbir Engineering, the sole subcontractor for Peace Marble Two, submitted thousands of false vouchers to GE, which in turn billed Israel for Ingbir's work. Israel then billed the United States, following the reimbursement procedures of the $1.8 billion in military aid that the United States provided to Israel each year. The payments GE received were disbursed back to Ingbir through GSK, which permitted the siphoning off of about $11 million that was sent to banks in Belgium and Germany and eventually made its way into Swiss bank accounts held in the name of a Panamanian shell company that Dotan and Steindler controlled. No one in GE, not even Chester Walsh, knew until after Dotan was arrested that the general and Steindler were diverting money into their own personal accounts. The rest of the money that GSK laundered, some $24 million, went back to Israel, where Dotan used it in Oliver North fashion. The general was fighting his own war with the civilian Ministry of Defense, which he considered bureaucratic and obstructionist, and the money permitted him effectively to create his own empire, supporting projects on Israeli military bases as he saw fit without the required authorization of the United States government or his own country's Ministry of Defense.

In his first two years in Tel Aviv, Walsh saw things that seemed suspect, but it wasn't until May 1987 that he realized that activities he had accepted as bad business practice were in fact illegal. That month, after participating in a budget review of the Peace Marble Two program with Dotan and GE program manager George Stringer, Walsh reviewed some contract documents, trying to ascertain the status of each line item, and he soon realized that the company had engaged in the premature and perhaps illegal collection of funds. It had received payment for work that not only hadn't been completed but, in some instances, hadn't even begun. Walsh, though, kept his suspicions to himself, and the following month, while on home leave in Boston, visited the public library to do research on defense contract fraud, and found the name of John Phillips. The following week Walsh entered Phillips's office on West Pico Boulevard in downtown Los Angeles, introduced himself as "John Wallace," and proceeded to tell his story.

At about the same time, Alaric Fine, another GE employee assigned to the Peace Marble project, at Aircraft Engine headquarters in Cincinnati, was also getting suspicious. A West Point grad and born-again Christian, Fine had made repeated inquiries about the status of Test Cell Five, the $7 million facility in which jet engines for the F-16s were supposed to be performance tested. Fine suspected that Yoram Ingbir was not performing work on the test cell, but his attempts to confirm that were being stonewalled, by both Israeli Air Force officials and his bosses in Cincinnati. The documents that swept past his desk raised more and more questions. Finally, in December 1988, Fine traveled to Israel to inspect the test cell for himself and was denied access to the site on security grounds. Amikam Cohen, Dotan's successor as head of the Israeli Air Force's propulsion branch, promised to provide Fine with a photograph of the test cell as well as a letter verifying that certain milestones had been achieved, but all that Fine received was a fuzzy photocopy of some Polaroid photographs and a terse one-page note from Reuven Lior, an Israeli Air Force captain who reported to Cohen. Fine discussed the problem with his boss, Dave McDonald, and got authorization to return to Israel again, a trip he made in February 1989. By that time, Walsh had received the transfer he sought, to Switzerland, and on his way out of Israel had told his replacement about the scheme while taking two cartons of evidence with him.

When Fine arrived back in Israel, he again questioned Cohen, which led to a confrontation—Cohen called Fine a Gestapo agent and insisted that for reasons of security, he couldn't permit him onto the air base to inspect the test cell. Fed up with the lack of support he was getting from his superiors, Fine returned to Cincinnati, prepared a memo outlining his concern that GE was being paid for work it hadn't yet done—in violation of government reimbursement procedures—and asked McDonald to sign the memo and back him up. Though afraid of Steindler, who as GE's in-house expert on Israel carried a lot of clout, McDonald thought a memo might alert upper management to the problem and break the logjam. McDonald agreed to an abbreviated and less accusatory version of Fine's memo, copies of which were sent to Brian Brimelow, the vice president in charge of the engine program, and Ken Bowman, general manager of operations in Cincinnati. Steindler reacted angrily when Fine hand-delivered the memo on March 10, 1989.

"If you're accusing me of doing anything illegal, I don't participate in illegal activities, and I'm not doing anything illegal on this program," Steindler shouted. He phoned two assistants, told them to come to his office immediately, and once they had arrived gave them Fine's letter.

"I'm not involved in the day-to-day matters of the program," Steindler told Fine; that was the responsibility, he said, of his assistants, Charlie Lyons and Al Coutinho, who were instructed by Steindler to resolve the matter.

Weeks later, the matter got resolved all right. McDonald informed Fine that he was being taken off the project and reassigned to another unit within Aircraft Engines because of a "contract scare." On March 17, Rami Dotan had called Bob Turnbull, the top executive in GE's military engine operations, one level removed from Aircraft Engines president Brian Rowe, and had threatened to cancel on the entire Peace Marble Three contract, a $213 million order for seventy-five more F-16 engines, that had been executed in May 1988. Claiming that there had been a security breach, Dotan said that Egypt had obtained a section of the 1988 contract, related to engine modifications, and asserted that Fine was the security leak. He demanded that Fine never come to Israel again. Anxious to do anything to placate Dotan, Turnbull agreed to transfer Fine. Though McDonald assured Fine he wasn't being punished, Fine, who had been assigned to a new project without any prior consultation, was doubtful. Several months later, Fine heard that Al Coutinho, Steindler's assistant, had visited Israel as a result of the memo, and he tracked him down to find out the results of the trip.

Coutinho told Fine that there was no Fifth Test Cell.

Coutinho said that the situation was being resolved and that a deal had been worked out. When Coutinho explained that the Israeli Air Force would receive work equal to the value of the test cell, Fine couldn't believe that management was burying the whole thing. The United States government had been defrauded, and nothing was being done about it. A few months later, in August 1989, Fine ran into Walsh, who was visiting Cincinnati headquarters, and related his conversation with Coutinho. Walsh expressed surprise that GE hadn't returned the money for the Fifth Test Cell and instead had chosen to paper it over by providing replacement items to the Israelis. Coutinho's visit to Israel was the only effort GE made to respond to Fine's memo before Walsh's suit was filed.

As the months passed, however, it became increasingly difficult to contain the deceit. In November 1989, Walsh, who was again visiting Aircraft Engines headquarters, discovered that the Israeli Defense Ministry was beginning to investigate Dotan, following up on a second letter it had received from Opher Pa'il, who formerly bought military supplies for the ministry out of the Israeli mission in New York. Walsh happened to be with Steindler when Danny Kleinman, the Israeli Air Force representative in Cincinnati, showed him a copy of a newspaper article, translated from the Hebrew, that disclosed the Defense Ministry inquiry into possible irregularities in Air Force purchasing and mentioned General Electric. Steindler was visibly upset and, in Israel, so was Dotan. In April 1990, the general paid $50,000 to Master Sergeant Yaakov Frank of the Israeli Air Force to kidnap and kill Pa'il, the suspected informant. About that same time, the Defense Ministry investigation was handed over to the Israeli police.

It was Dotan's arrest on October 28, 1990 that triggered a more contrite attitude on GE's part, and had it not been for Dotan's arrest and Walsh's suit the entire affair would never have come to light. That, at least, was the conclusion of FBI agent Steven Kosky, who began the bureau's investigation of GE four days after Walsh filed his suit on November 15, 1990. When asked two years later during a hearing to evaluate the contribution Walsh had made to the FBI's investigation, Kosky replied: "The government knew absolutely nothing had gone amiss . . . General Electric had taken substantial measures to cover it up for a space of two years. I have no reason to believe that anyone within General Electric would have ever told us besides Mr. Walsh. He brought us the only information we had."

Walsh, who under the terms of his settlement with GE was forced to take early retirement, was naturally regarded as an enemy by General Electric. But strangely, the Bush administration's Justice Department regarded him in a similar fashion, and considered the amended False Claims Act nothing short of unconstitutional. Once the government had settled with GE, Justice Department attorneys turned on Walsh—and their recriminations brought a stern rebuke from presiding judge Carl Rubin, the same judge who had presided over the Gravitt case. Although Walsh had never personally profited from the fraud, he was a "participant," lead government attorney Russell

Kinner argued, because he hadn't revealed his information earlier, and hence deserved less than the 15 percent minimum award, as stipulated under the law, of the $59.5 million the government had recovered. To Judge Rubin, who ultimately approved a reward of just under 20 percent, the attack on Walsh was further confirmation of the department's antipathy toward the False Claims Act and suits initiated by private citizens rather than the government. Rubin was furious at the government's position, and one hearing in his Cincinnati courtroom featured this heated exchange:

> *Rubin:* I am not willing to consider this case in terms of dollars. That's not the issue. The issue is percentage, and that makes a great deal of difference. And whether Mr. Walsh gets enough money to be independently wealthy the rest of his life, again is not before me.
> *Kinner:* . . . we can talk about it on a one-to-ten scale. A ten in the government's view should be reserved for the person who does the most excellent job of bringing the case forward.
> *Rubin:* No, Mr. Kinner. The ten should be reserved for the person who was willing to persevere despite the opposition of the United States. I'm not concerned really with Chester Walsh. I'm concerned with what happens to people who dare to blow the whistle. Where is the aid and comfort that they should be getting from their own government who will benefit? It isn't there. As a matter of policy, you and the Justice Department are opposed to the concept of whistleblowers.
> *Kinner:* Your Honor, I would respectfully disagree—
> *Rubin:* Of course, you disagree. . . . As a matter of fact, Mr. Kinner, I have had more than one whistleblower case. . . . And not in one, not one, did the Justice Department ever give any aid and comfort. You were an antagonist, not a proponent.

Walsh was one of twelve people GE immediately dismissed or unilaterally retired in the aftermath of the Dotan affair, eleven of whom were from the ranks of middle management. Only two corporate officers were disciplined— Bob Turnbull, the man Dotan had called seeking Fine's removal, who retired in November 1992, and Brian Brimelow, who was demoted and retired three years later. Subsequently Turnbull was again on the company payroll as a paid consultant. "GE believes that its employment actions have reemphasized an unmistakable message that lapses in performance which compromise GE's high ethical standards, whether intentional or not, will not be tolerated and will be met by strict discipline," senior vice president Frank Doyle asserted during congressional subcommittee testimony on the Dotan affair. But employees of Aircraft Engines say the message conveyed was that GE operates a two-tier system when it comes to compliance with official corporate policy—the little guys get punished, and the big guys get off. What bothers Chester Walsh most of all is the fate of some colleagues who were unjustly fired and reprimanded, including David McDonald, a twenty-nine-year GE veteran, who was dismissed for what GE termed a "shortfall in compliance culture." Says Walsh of the McDonald dismissal: "He didn't do a goddamn thing wrong. They fired the wrong people. They always do. Upper management never gets hurt."

Even Fine, the one man who more than anyone else had tried to do the right thing, was among those reprimanded. Fine did exactly what Aircraft Engines president Brian Rowe recommended in a memo: If you suspect wrongdoing on a government contract, report it to us before you tell the government. Still employed at Aircraft Engines, Fine refuses to discuss the case, refuses even to answer questions posed to him about the consequences he suffered for having pressed GE to tell the truth about what it had done. "Have you personally suffered any adverse consequence as a result of these events?" Fine was asked during one deposition in October 1992, a question his GE paid counsel instructed him not to answer, an instruction he followed. GE colleagues, though, know what happened. In the aftermath of the company's internal investigation into the Dotan affair, Fine was given a reprimand for not filing the proper forms, had his salary frozen for one year, and, according to investigators who have interviewed him, has expressed concern that his attempts to expose the fraud may have irreparably damaged his career. Paradoxically, he also received a commendation for his actions related to the Fifth Test Cell.

Ultimately, Dotan was tried in Israel, stripped of his rank, and packed off to prison, receiving a thirteen-year sentence that he is now serving. In addition to Herbert Steindler, who was fired by GE in March 1991 and received a seven-year prison sentence after a guilty plea, the United States government indicted one other person, Harold Katz, a dual U.S.-Israeli citizen and former Boston lawyer whose ties to the Israeli underground—and the failure to locate about half of the $11 million that was diverted to Swiss bank accounts—led to speculation that he and Dotan may have been supporting covert Israeli operations. That hypothesis seemed credible, given that it was in Katz's Washington apartment, purchased in 1985, that Israeli agents copied thousands of classified U.S. documents supplied by Jonathan Pollard, a Navy intelligence officer and Israeli spy who was imprisoned for espionage.

According to the settlement GE entered into with the government, the company pleaded guilty to four felonies, including money laundering and violations of the Foreign Corrupt Practices Act. The terms of the settlement actually generated a "profit" for Uncle Sam in that the $75 million that was recovered, including $6 million seized by the Israeli Air Force from Dotan's Swiss bank accounts and returned to the United States, exceeded the $42 million that had been lost. GE paid $59.5 million to settle the Walsh suit and, in addition, paid a $9.5 million fine to settle the criminal complaint that the Justice Department had brought.

It was the third criminal conviction on defense fraud charges for GE since 1985, along with thirteen civil settlements, giving GE the dubious distinction of leading corporate criminal among the Pentagon's one hundred largest defense contractors, ahead of the second-leading offender, Teledyne, which had seven. (Defense-contract fraud was so rampant in GE that in June 1990 the Department of Defense took the unusual step of creating a special office in Philadelphia solely to police and audit GE defense contracts. When the office was disbanded three years later, it had recovered $71 million from more than one hundred contract irregularities, only a handful of which GE had voluntarily disclosed.)

But before the Dotan case could be retired, there was one outstanding detail. Congressman John Dingell insisted that Welch, as CEO of the company at fault, appear before his subcommittee, which was investigating the Dotan affair and other defense industry problems. Welch's testimony, on July 29, 1992, represented a milestone in that he was compelled to acknowledge, for the first time and in a very public forum, that his company had broken the law and to, in effect, accept responsibility for what GE had done.

WELCH WAS no stranger to defense-contract fraud, nor to controversy in his own dealings with the government. The first scandal to receive widespread publicity had come in 1985, when on March 26 Welch learned of GE's indictment on a Minuteman missile contract while watching the evening news. "He went through the roof" is the way one associate describes his reaction that night—and with good reason, for the indictment carried with it swift repercussions for General Electric. Two days after the indictment, Air Force Secretary Verne Orr suspended GE, then the fourth-leading U.S. defense contractor, from doing business with the government, a devastating blow in that Welch suddenly lost the right to sell even lightbulbs to any entity of the federal government, a customer that accounted for nearly one-fifth of GE's revenues at that time. Welch immediately sought to get the suspension lifted, and on April 15 met in Washington with Secretary Orr for a second time. On the basis of statements made during the meetings, Orr repealed most of the suspension two days later.

Three years later, however, another business unit of GE Aerospace, based in Valley Forge, Pennsylvania, was again indicted, this time for overcharging the government $21 million on battlefield computer systems in military vehicles. The government alleged that the cause of the crime was the same as it had been in the Minuteman case—excess pressure from headquarters to get higher profit. Investigators uncovered memos from Fairfield ordering the subsidiary to realize a profit of at least 15 percent on a contract allowing only 8 percent. In addition, the government alleged that Welch and other GE executives hadn't told the whole truth when they met with Secretary Orr and other Air Force representatives when seeking to have the earlier sanctions lifted in 1985. The "misleading and false" statements included failing to disclose a fraudulent practice uncovered in late 1983 by GE auditor Neil Brown that was known as "gross rate protection," under which the company fraudulently billed the government for its overhead expenses on fixed-price contracts. At first, Brown threatened to disclose the practice publicly if the company didn't do so. After assurances that it would be disclosed, Brown was instructed to mark all his audit notes "privileged" and turn them over to in-house counsel, which he did. But the practice he had uncovered wasn't disclosed until two years later, in September 1985, after Welch's meetings with Orr and after the suspension had been lifted.

On September 6, 1985, Welch wrote Orr, who was retiring, to thank him for his "considerate treatment": "Your handling of our situation has been vigorous but fair, and I thought you were straightforward and honest in every dealing." Three years later, United States Attorney Michael Baylson cast doubt on whether the same could be said of Welch, and in a court brief requesting that GE produce certain files that it had withheld on the grounds of attorney-client privilege, Baylson wrote: "Despite the fact that Brown uncovered gross rate protection in 1983, it was not revealed to the government until [September] 1985, and even then it was revealed in what can charitably be characterized as a misleading manner." The government got some of the documents it wanted, which were put in evidence at the trial that ended in February 1990. Based on that evidence, Assistant U.S. Attorney Nicholas Harbist argued in his close that General Electric executives, including Welch, had deceived the Air Force to get the sanctions lifted. Orr, Harbist contended, was told that the Minuteman situation was basically a big mistake, when in reality GE's own internal investigation had revealed the fraud to be much more systematic. The jury agreed with Harbist and found General Electric guilty; two lower-level GE managers were sentenced to jail, and the company paid a $10 million criminal fine and made restitutions to the government of nearly $26 million.

As big as these fraud cases were, they paled in comparison to the Dotan fiasco, which was unnerving Welch as the summer of 1992 approached. GE's relationship with the government, which at that time bought more than $7 billion a year in goods and services from the company, had again been put at risk. Worst of all, although Welch had vowed during his meetings with Secretary Orr in 1985 that such a scandal would not recur—and had hired attorney Zöe Baird the following year to ensure that it didn't—the procedures hadn't been sufficient to prevent a recurrence. Pentagon officials charged with contract enforcement weren't pleased, and on June 1, 1992, they showed the depth of their displeasure when Janet Cook, a feisty attorney charged with enforcing contract integrity for the Defense Department, unilaterally suspended Aircraft Engines from doing any business with the federal government. Although the suspension lasted just five days, the warning was clear and unequivocal—cooperate or you'll be in deep trouble.

Not only did GE's role in the Dotan scandal threaten an immensely important commercial relationship, it was a huge professional embarrassment to Welch, whose reputation was being sullied, this time in a more direct way than in any of the previous scandals. The Dotan affair had shown that integrity was a systemic problem, much more widespread than perhaps even Welch realized, and attempts to cover it up implicated the most senior executives in the Aircraft Engines division. Although Welch and an army of lawyers and public relations specialists sought to pin the blame for the crime on two rogue employees, Herbert Steindler and Chester Walsh, the reality was that dozens of people were culpable. Two years later, in the summer of 1994, when the venerable Kidder, Peabody investment banking house imploded in the most scandalous failure Wall Street had seen since the days of Michael Milken, Welch would again blame the crisis on one rogue employee, bond trader Joseph Jett. But again, though an errant employee may have precipitated a crisis, it was the system Welch had created that had allowed, even encouraged, it to happen. In both cases, moreover, the activities of Steindler and Jett, egregious though they were, provided the kind of income stream that had made superiors very reluctant to ask too many questions. And, in both instances, the people who raised questions, such as Alaric Fine, were either shunted aside or dismissed. Introspection, it seemed, was not encouraged within General Electric.

In the summer of 1992, the last thing Welch wanted to engage in was self-analysis. He had been summoned to testify before Dingell's subcommittee, charged with investigating not just the Dotan affair but the whole system under which military aid had been provided to Israel, a program known formally as Foreign Military Financing (FMF), which paid out more than $3 billion a year to several Middle Eastern allies, including Israel, Egypt, Greece, and Turkey. A cushy subsidy for the U.S. defense industry, this financing was granted to foreign governments with just one stipulation—the aid had to be used for military equipment purchased from U.S. defense contractors. The Dotan scandal had pointed out many shortcomings in FMF, the biggest of which was that the government had never audited it but instead relied on defense contractors and foreign governments to uncover any irregularities.

John Dingell was an eighteen-term Democratic congressman from Michigan whose subcommittee on Oversights and Investigations had been probing defense contract fraud for more than eight years. Known in Washington for the rough treatment he meted out to witnesses who came before his subcommittee, Dingell had skewered Nobel Prize–winning scientists, Navy admirals, and CEOs with equal relish. It was Dingell's subcommittee that had uncovered widespread waste and fraud in Pentagon contracts, including the Air Force's infamous $640 toilet seat. And Michael Deaver, one of President Reagan's top advisers, had gone to jail for perjuring himself at a Dingell hearing. Dingell's reputation for fierce and sometimes sarcastic questioning had inspired a small cottage industry in Washington—the Dingell bar, as it was informally known—lawyers who specialized in counseling witnesses ordered to appear before Dingell's subcommittee.

In Welch, however, Dingell was facing an adversary whose knowledge of Washington and whose connections inside the Beltway were equally formidable. To say that General Electric and its CEOs have been connected to the Washington power grid in this century is to make a gross understatement. Active and influential behind-the-scenes players in Washington, the GE CEOs were virtually an extension of the government during the forty-year period following World War II when the military-industrial complex was at its apogee. They were advisers to presidents, secretaries of defense, admirals, and generals, as well as key players in such initiatives as the New Deal, the Manhattan Project, the War Mobilization Board—and, lest we forget, the employer of Ronald Reagan.

Although Welch probably had no more access to Reagan and his top lieutenants than Reg Jones had had to Jimmy Carter and his, Jones had been squeamish about influencing specific legislation and instead preferred the role of "adviser" on public policy. Welch, on the other hand, was more results-oriented; for him, the Washington connection was a means to an end, and if it didn't yield results it was worthless. The results could be enormous, as had been proven in the tax legislation Congress enacted in 1981. In 1980, General Electric had paid $330 million in federal taxes; in 1981, thanks to the generous investment tax credits contained in legislation that was effectively written by the Carlton Group, a Washington caucus of corporate-tax lobbyists of which GE was a prominent member, the company received a net tax refund of $104 million. The credits proved so generous that GE not only was able to avoid paying any federal corporate taxes between 1981 and 1983—a period in which its net profit exceeded $5 billion—but it also received tax rebates of more than $300 million.

Money helped, and it was dispensed not just to congressmen but to other Washington power brokers as well, including John McLaughlin, host of the televised shouting match *The McLaughlin Group*. General Electric became the sole underwriter of his show, at a cost of $1 million a year, after a 1986 dinner party at the McLaughlins' Virginia home, attended by Mr. and Mrs. Jack Welch (the first Mrs. Welch, who would soon separate from her husband of twenty-seven years), Mr. and Mrs. Charlton Heston, and Nancy and Ronald Reagan. With its sponsorship of *The McLaughlin Group* and other similar issue-oriented programming such as National Public Radio's *Marketplace*, GE would get a forum for promoting its "people helping people" image.

Welch was also assiduous in exhorting GE executives to give more money to the corporate political action committee so that the corporation could engender more goodwill with friends in Congress. GE's PAC contributions to congressional candidates nearly doubled between 1989 and 1992—to $683,350, ranking GE sixth among corporate PACs—an increase that was possible because Welch had expanded the executive pool from which he solicited contributions from one thousand to four thousand.* Sometimes a too-aggressive solicitation of funds brought General Electric embarrassing publicity, such as in 1986 when a memo of NBC president Robert Wright ended up on the front page of the *New York Times*. Wright had told NBC's senior executives: "Employees who earn their living and support their families from the profits of our business must recognize a need to invest some portion of their earnings to ensure that the company is well represented in Washington and that its important issues are clearly placed before Congress. Employ-

---

* The Associated Press reported in March 1998 that GE had spent $4.12 million to lobby the federal government in the first half of 1997. GE was the eighth-biggest spender and fifth-largest among corporations, behind Philip Morris, General Motors, Pfizer, and United Technologies.

ees who elect not to participate in a giving program of this type should question their own dedication to the company and their expectations." The memo caused a firestorm, particularly among executives in the news division, who refused to contribute to the PAC—they considered it a gross violation of NBC's (and every other news organization's) long-standing policy of avoiding even the appearance of political favoritism or affiliations.

In hiring Benjamin W. Heineman Jr., a Washington lawyer whom *The New Republic* had called the possessor of "the best resume in America," Welch had found his legal top gun to exercise clout in the capital. Smart, aggressive, someone who could court influence among both Democrats and Republicans, Heineman, son of a prominent Chicago industrialist and husband of a prominent *Washington Post* reporter, was well versed in the ways of Washington. Indeed, it was a Washington connection—his friendship with Zöe Baird—that had brought Heineman to the attention of Welch. Baird, President Clinton's first choice for attorney general until the disclosure that she had violated the law by hiring illegal immigrants, and Heineman were lawyers whose style was more to the liking of Welch than the taciturn and defensive approach of Walter Schlotterbeck, Heineman's predecessor as general counsel and a thirty-five-year veteran of GE's legal department. Welch wanted attorneys who took the offensive, especially given the mounting legal troubles that were confronting him; he later said he hired Heineman because "I had the best minds in finance and business development and . . . I wanted to have the best legal firm in the corporate world."

With that mandate, Heineman in 1987 began paying top dollar to recruit Washington attorneys who, like him, were welcome on Capitol Hill. In the process, Heineman (whose $2 million annual salary and bonus makes him one of the top-paid corporate general counsels in America) eased out the old-guard left over from the Schlotterbeck era, replacing more than half of the company's 440-lawyer in-house legal department, which would rank among the nation's largest law firms if it were a self-standing entity. Such expertise permits General Electric to do much work in-house for which another corporation would retain outside counsel. The Dotan matter, though, was one of those extraordinary cases that merited outside involvement, and Heineman chose as GE's advocate the Washington law firm of Wilmer, Cutler & Pickering, whose principal was Lloyd Cutler, one of Washington's most prominent attorneys, former White House counsel to Jimmy Carter, and future counsel to President Clinton.

In the summer of 1992, however, Welch's extensive Washington connections weren't helping him one bit. Although Welch had agreed to testify before

Dingell's subcommittee, Judge Carl Rubin knew he had put up fierce resistance and didn't exactly regard it as an act of contrition. Rubin, who had presided over several GE whistleblower suits in his courtroom besides the Dotan case and didn't like the pattern he had seen in those cases, thought the idea of a Welch mea culpa was appropriate given the circumstances; he felt that because of the enormity and scope of the misdeeds—it was, after all, a $42 million fraud, which even by Washington standards was pretty big—someone of stature and rank from the corporation should step forward to publicly accept responsibility. Maybe if Welch had to do the pleading himself, Rubin reasoned, it would head off a future recurrence. Nevertheless, Welch did not want to do the pleading—the situation was humiliating enough, but to admit corporate guilt personally was more than he was willing to endure. The week before the plea was scheduled to be entered, Welch called Dingell at his office in the Rayburn Building in Washington to ask a favor.

"John, you know what they're trying to do to me? Because I'm appearing before you, the judge is saying I should plead," he told Dingell. Welch asked the congressman if he would call the Justice Department and ask them to call off the hounds, in particular one "fuckin' clerk" who was insisting that he plead. When Dingell's aides, who were listening in on the conversation, heard the phrase "fuckin' clerk"—Welch didn't designate him by name—they were stunned at Welch's arrogance because it wasn't a clerk he was referring to but rather Ted Greenberg, a senior attorney in the Justice Department's criminal division. Dingell, who declined to make the call, replied, "That's why you have attorneys," and ended the conversation. The attorneys made one last stab to convince the "fuckin' clerk" and Judge Rubin that someone other than Welch would suffice, and eventually Rubin relented, accepting the guilty plea from Aircraft Engines president Brian Rowe, who stood in Welch's place on July 22, 1992.

There was still the matter of the hearing, which would be held one week later. In the days and weeks before, GE staffers, as well as outside counsel, were doing all they could to ensure it went off smoothly. The hearing had been carefully orchestrated: Dingell would begin with an opening statement, a summary of what the committee had learned about the Dotan affair; individual committee members would follow with statements of their own; Welch would then give his prepared remarks, under oath, followed by the testimony of Frank Doyle, at that time a senior vice president who oversaw GE's Washington and compliance activities; finally, Dingell and the committee members would be free to pose questions to Welch and Doyle. If a gaffe were to occur, it would be here.

The day before the hearing a GE representative called Dennis Wilson, counsel to the Republican committee members, to inquire as to what questions the committee planned to ask. Wilson offered up several likely avenues of inquiry to his caller, including the issue of the special contract policing office that the Pentagon had established in Philadelphia, which Wilson had learned of a few days before from a front-page *Wall Street Journal* story. The caller objected, insisting that was beyond the scope of what General Electric and the committee had agreed to discuss.

"We would like the hearing limited just to Dotan," the caller insisted. Wilson, who was irritated, said no. It wasn't unusual for a corporate representative to inquire about what would be asked, but it was unusual for them to stipulate what they would and wouldn't answer. Wilson, who felt that went beyond the standards of fair conduct, included questions about the Philadelphia remedies unit among the questions he recommended to the committee members. Wilson learned later that after the GE caller received his firm rebuff, some of his colleagues had subsequently called aides to Norman Lent and Thomas Bliley, the two ranking Republicans on the committee, saying they would "prefer" if the questions dealt only with Dotan.

The gravity that Welch attached to the hearing was implicit in the number of handlers he brought with him on the morning of July 29. Although leanness and agility are supposedly the cornerstones of the Welch revolution, the manpower and muscle on display that morning was the very epitome of Big Business. It was standing room only as Welch, Doyle, and several dozen public relations, legal, and investigative specialists exited their limousines, strode past the metal detectors in the front lobby of the Rayburn Office Building, and descended on the imposing chamber where the committee would hold its hearing. Three rows in the middle section of the gallery had been roped off to accommodate the GE contingent, who would soon take their seats behind Welch and Doyle. Sitting among the GE contingent were some of Washington's heaviest hitters, including Cutler, whose attendance underscored the gravity Welch and Heineman attached to the hearing.

At precisely 10 a.m., in Room 2123 of the Rayburn Building, Dingell banged his gavel and brought the proceedings to order. "For over eight years this subcommittee has been investigating the activities of major defense contractors," Dingell began. "Today's hearing addresses corporate wrongdoing involving foreign military assistance programs, in particular the role of the General Electric Company in what has become known as the Dotan affair. . . . What started out innocently as aid to a valued and respected ally seems to have turned into a sordid tale of theft, bribery, money laundering, and attempted kidnapping or murder. Today we will seek to begin to unravel this mystery. We will find out what went wrong at General Electric."

The two hours that followed shed no new information on GE's role in the Dotan affair, the details of what the company knew having already been disclosed to committee investigators in the four months prior to the hearing. What the session did provide, however, was a glimpse into the mind and character of Jack Welch. The man who delivered nine pages of testimony—GE called it a "statement"—was the consummate self-made man, who had long ago overcome the stutter that once disabled his speech. He was slick, polished, and on his best behavior, dropping the phrase "compete like hell" from his prepared remarks, subbing the more sanitized "compete with passion." Welch's considerable political skills were also on display, as was his legendary memory for small details. During a ten-minute intermission, while the congressmen left the chamber to vote, Welch sauntered over to the press table and struck up a conversation with one reporter covering the hearing for the *Washington Post*. "I understand you worked for Mike Harrington," Welch said, dropping the name of a boyhood friend, a former congressman from Massachusetts. The two chatted briefly while Welch joked affably about what a "lousy third baseman" Harrington had been.

Welch summarized for the six congressmen his achievements as the leader of the greatest American corporation: forty consecutive quarters of earnings growth in the 1980s, a $6 billion positive contribution to America's trade balance in 1991, productivity increases of two to three times the national average, and the leading American company in U.S. patents in nine of the last ten years (true at the time, but not so now; GE ranked thirteenth among all patent recipients in 1997, behind eight Japanese corporations and four American, IBM, Motorola, Kodak, and AT&T spinoff Lucent Technologies). What came through loud and clear was his passionate belief in himself and the righteousness of his course. He was indefatigable, able to deliver with great conviction some lines that were so disconnected from reality that they bordered on the surreal: "No one at GE loses a job because of a missed quarter, a missed year or a mistake. That's nonsense and everyone knows it. . . . People get second chances." (Eight months earlier Welch had ended the distinguished seventeen-year career of one GE vice president, Ed Russell, who hadn't even missed a quarter, and had pleaded for a second chance.) Although Welch regretted that the scandal had occurred, he wasn't about to assume personal responsibility. The corporation's ethical lapses weren't his fault; they had nothing to do with him. GE, Welch asserted, had an employee population that would rank with St. Paul or Tampa if it were an American city, which meant that lawlessness was bound to occur despite the corporation's best efforts to police it. The laws of human nature couldn't be repealed. Welch said he was committed to integrity, a word he invoked eight times, but his comments betrayed a higher commitment—to performance.

"Mr. Chairman, we intend to, and must, make this company as competitive as any on earth," Welch said from his seat below Dingell, who was seated on a raised bench at the front of the cavernous chamber. Competition—a word Welch used sixteen times in various forms—was a grand and glorious thing. Drawing an analogy with the Olympics, which NBC was televising at that time from Barcelona, the competitive pressures had driven some athletes to cheat, to take steroids. "What is the solution?" Welch asked rhetorically. "Tell athletes to run slower, jump lower." The 275,000 people who worked for GE at that time—roughly the same number as now—were the Olympians of the business world, and Welch wasn't about to ask them to slow their pace or lower their goals just because a few bad apples were exploiting the system. On the contrary, it would be a terrible mistake to lessen the demands and ask less of your people. "I regret that the system wasn't good enough in this case. But in this company we learn from our mistakes. We take what we learn and then raise the bar of excellence ever higher."

The subcommittee hearing proved more significant for what hadn't been disclosed than what had. Welch and Doyle hadn't told the six congressmen about another scandal that was lurking inside GE's defense business, one that the company was furtively investigating at the time of the testimony that involved not Israel, but Egypt. On March 30, 1992, four months before the congressional hearing, Welch had received an anonymous letter stating that GE officials in Egypt had paid bribes, directly and through a consultant, to Egyptian military officers to win a $125 million radar contract in 1988. The bribes had also given GE access to the confidential bids and specs of a rival American contractor, Westinghouse Electric, that was chasing the same contract. By April 1, Welch had dispatched a team of eight auditors and attorneys to radar headquarters in Syracuse, New York, to investigate; by April 3, the company had hired private investigators to assist with the inquiry; and by April 9, company representatives had gone to Cairo and interrogated the author of the letter. One year later, GE would file a 133-page report with the government summarizing the results of its investigation, which would ultimately end with the settlement of yet another *qui tam* lawsuit and the payment of $5.9 million to the government. The fraud again involved U.S. government funds, paid out under the same Foreign Military Financing program that had come under scrutiny in the Dotan affair, the same program the deficiencies of which the hearing had intended to shed light on. During the question-and-answer portion of the hearing about other abuses of the program beyond Dotan, Welch and Doyle neither were asked about the Egyptian irregularities nor volunteered information about them.

Several weeks passed. When members of Dingell's staff learned in August of the new scandal through an item in a defense industry newsletter, they were furious. "Why didn't you tell us about this during the hearing?" was the question they put to GE's Washington office. "This is Egypt and radar. The other was Israel and jet engines" came the curt reply from a GE representative. "But it's the same program." The Dotan affair was winding down, but now the subcommittee had a new fraud to unravel. In September, subcommittee staffers would for the first time meet the informant who had written Welch the anonymous letter, Zohair Hak, a GE employee who had been stationed in Cairo.

If Welch had forgotten to mention this latest fraud, perhaps it was because he was already embroiled in another scandal, the biggest of his career, which had been brought on by another alleged whistleblower, this time from among the most senior echelon of Welch's inner circle, a GE vice president. The bizarre tale of corporate intrigue involved the secretive De Beers diamond cartel, fugitive diamond merchants, shady international deals, the most prominent trial lawyers in the country—and GE's old nemesis, price-fixing.

CHAPTER THIRTEEN

DIAMONDS AND DIRT

ON JULY 29, 1991, Jack Welch approved a $15,000 raise for Edward J. Russell—the largest raise Russell had ever received in seventeen years at GE—on top of his $190,000 salary as head of GE's Superabrasives division, which manufactured abrasive materials, including man-made diamonds for use in grinding, cutting, drilling, and other industrial procedures. Only a year and a half before that, Welch had given Russell the promotion he had sought ever since joining GE in 1974, naming him a vice president and corporate officer, one of only 127 executives of that rank in the vast GE empire. To Russell, the promotion signified more than elevation to the very top of one of the world's most powerful and select corporations. It meant prestige, status, money, and security, and it represented the fruition of a lifelong ambition for a blue-collar kid who badly wanted a silver spoon. The promotion allowed him to lease any automobile at company expense, and Russell chose a Jaguar. Welch shared in Russell's pride, and wrote him a warm note of praise on the occasion: "I am so pleased for—and proud of—you. This is a hard-earned, well-deserved promotion."

Once Russell had been fired—and once he had retaliated by filing a wrongful termination lawsuit against his former employer—Welch and his attorneys sought to portray Russell as a woefully inadequate manager, who, promotions, praise, and raises notwithstanding, had been fired for poor performance, even though they had little evidence to support that contention. Likewise, Russell and his attorneys would allege that the real reason for his dismissal was that he had run across corporate wrongdoing, including a dozen surreptitious meetings between two alleged conspirators who, the government would later contend, carried out a price-fixing scheme between GE and the De Beers diamond cartel of South Africa. Neither party, however, was telling the absolute truth. Although some very sinister activities had taken place in GE's industrial diamond business, Russell hadn't been fired because of that. Nor had he been fired for poor performance, as United States Magistrate Judge Robert A. Steinberg concluded in his ruling on GE's petition for summary judgment: "Substantial evidence contradicts GE's assertion that Russell's performance was poor. Russell was summarily discharged without any warning or prior disciplinary action or criticism of his performance. Instead, he had received a promotion, a substantial raise and an arguably favorable or at least neutral performance review."

The real reason Russell's career had come to an abrupt end was that Welch had decided it was time for him to go. Russell, on the other hand, could not accept such a capricious and incompassionate end; after all, in his first four years as head of Superabrasives, net income had more than quadrupled, and even though earnings had fallen in his fifth, didn't Welch and the company owe him something after seventeen years of dedicated, exemplary service? Welch obviously didn't think so; managers who couldn't maintain earnings, even in a bad economy, weren't owed anything. At the highest echelons of General Electric, the reality is that careers can end suddenly, sometimes with no warning whatsoever, sometimes for reasons that may seem capricious to the victim.

But if Russell was going to take the fall, he was determined to take Welch and GE with him. In that regard, Russell's case, and his riposte against GE, was a watershed in the corporate revolution of Jack Welch. Hundreds, perhaps thousands, of former General Electric employees who had been fired had retaliated against their employer by filing lawsuits alleging every form of discrimination and wrongdoing imaginable, but never had the code been broken by an executive of such high rank, and never in such a public manner; indeed, because of the spectacular nature of Russell's allegations and the grand jury indictment and trial that followed, his war against GE received coverage like no other wrongful termination suit before or since. The *Wall Street Journal* had front-page coverage on three separate occasions, and there were dozens of stories elsewhere in the *Journal*, and in *Business Week* and the *New York Times*. The Russell case was one of the most closely scrutinized and widely followed business news events of the early nineties.

RUSSELL, a lean, handsome man who stood six feet two inches tall, had risen at 5:30 a.m. on the morning of November 11, 1991, flying from Worthington, Ohio, a suburb of Columbus where GE's Superabrasives division is headquartered, to Albany, New York, and was now driving a rental car slightly more than one hour to his destination, his immediate boss Glen Hiner's office in Pittsfield, Massachusetts. It was a trek that Russell had come to know well during his five-and-a-half-year tenure as head of GE's synthetic diamond business; he had once made the trip eight times in as many weeks. Although he typically found the routine boring, on this morning he welcomed the familiarity of the course, as it allowed him to concentrate on his plans for the next two days. Driving along the hilly contours of Route 20 in western Massachusetts and slipping into a reserved parking lot at the Hilton Hotel in Pittsfield, Russell was deep in thought, fixated on his upcoming budget review with Jack Welch, scheduled for the next day.

When Russell reached Hiner's office, he began to review for Hiner the points he expected to cover in his presentation to Welch. Hiner stopped him. Only five months before, Hiner had written in Russell's annual evaluation that he needed to remain in "his current position, rebuild his team, fix his product line problems and then consider other potential options." But the situation had taken a swift turn for the worse, an about-face so sudden and accompanied by so little warning that Russell had no idea his seventeen-year career at General Electric was about to be terminated.

"That won't be necessary," Hiner said as he handed Russell a letter written on Hiner's stationery as senior vice president, GE Plastics, the business group to which Superabrasives belonged.

As Russell began to read the letter—"To: Edward J. Russell"—the true purpose of his trip became clear. "Dear Ed: Described below are the compensation and benefits arrangements relative to your separation from GE." That one word—*separation*—seemed to leap off the page. The one-page letter, which neatly summarized eight points but gave no reason why Russell was being fired, closed: "If you have any questions, please give Dick Jelinek [Hiner's head of human relations] or me a call. Regards, Glen H. Hiner."

"On what basis are you doing this," Russell demanded, his face flushed, his anger rising.

"Poor performances to Welch in July and September, and problems with customers and peers," Hiner responded calmly.

Three years later, Hiner would tell a jury that dismissing Russell had been emotionally wrenching for him, that firing people was never easy. But on that day, he gave no outward hint of the quandary he said he felt. Hiner was cold and businesslike, Russell would later recall, his demeanor somber, his language deliberate, his manner purposeful.

Although Russell knew Hiner despised him, he could not believe what was happening.

"You've got to be kidding me," Russell protested. "Has Welch approved this?"

"Yes, he has." Actually, as Russell would later discover, Welch had ordered it two months before, in a September 5 fax to Hiner, the day after a meeting in Pittsfield in which Russell "appeared totally out of it," Welch had said in the fax. "Imagine a presentation to you and I and he had *no* numbers and more importantly knew none. I don't want to fool with this fellow much longer but will respect your end of year type timing. . . . Let's discuss this option or others you have. Bottom line has to be Russell has to go!"

Though the decision had been made in September, Welch and Hiner had been careful to conceal their intentions. Russell had had dozens of meetings with Welch over the years, and he knew him to be a man who didn't hold back his feelings, yet in October when Russell had talked to Welch at an officers' meeting not a word of discontent was uttered. They exchanged pleasantries and parted.

"I'd like to talk to Welch about this," Russell pleaded, unaware of the true circumstances.

Hiner didn't seem to be listening. "It is reasonable," Hiner said, breaking through Russell's continued protests, "and final." Russell was escorted to another room, where he sat alone. A driver took the keys to his rented car, and drove him in a limousine to a waiting private jet, which he boarded for his return flight.

IT WAS an ignominious disintegration of Russell's high-level executive career, which had seemed so full of promise for most of its seventeen years. In 1974, when Russell had first joined General Electric as a strategic planner, he was thrilled to be a member of the GE team—and, at the same time, delighted to be leaving ITT Corporation, where he had also worked as a strategic planner. ITT was in the midst of crisis then: In 1972, Congress had investigated an influence-peddling scandal involving company lobbyist Dita Beard (charges that were denied and never proved); and a year later, Anthony Sampson's best-seller, *The Sovereign State of ITT,* described a botched conspiracy with the CIA to block Salvador Allende's 1970 election as president of Chile; Allende was a Marxist who nationalized the company's extensive copper mines and was overthrown in 1973 (ITT initially denied the charges but later admitted, in 1976, that it "might" have sent $350,000 to Chile in 1970 for what it described as "political" purposes). ITT was also laboring under the tyrannical rule of

CEO Harold Geneen, who made hundreds of acquisitions during his eighteen-year tenure, a legendary workaholic who summoned Russell and others to meetings that would begin in the afternoon and occasionally last until midnight.

GE, on the other hand, was a company to be admired, one with a proven track record as a training ground for senior executives as well as *the* place to be for a young, aggressive, up-and-coming strategic planner. Reg Jones, on the advice of management consultants McKinsey & Company, was adding more than two hundred professionals to GE's planning staff, which was charged with identifying those businesses with the greatest potential for growth, and allocating resources accordingly. The new science of strategic planning would be applied with great intellectual rigor, with a heavy emphasis on mathematics and quantitative analysis. Strategic planners sifted through mounds of data, calculated arcane ratios, and plotted them on grids that would tell Jones which businesses were most profitable and most worthy of future investment. It seemed just the place for Russell, who had always felt more comfortable with numbers than people and who had finished all his course work for a Ph.D. in engineering mathematics from Columbia University. His dissertation topic, which was never completed: "Integer solutions to quadratic binary programs." Russell felt that aside from being among the elite of his profession, the money wasn't bad either—the starting salary of $50,000 at GE, not counting the additional perks and stock options, was $15,000 more than he had earned at ITT. "I never dreamed I'd be making that kind of money," recalls Russell, whose thick Long Island accent betrays his working-class roots in Jamaica, New York. "It was a big jump."

It didn't come without a price. Years later, in August 1985, Russell, as an up-and-coming executive in charge of GE's international lighting business, would articulate some of the price for new managerial recruits at GE's boot camp in Crotonville. Be prepared for a rugged work environment, the veteran Russell told the recruits, for GE is a very demanding employer. Russell knew the truth of that statement more fully than he had disclosed—his wife had effectively become a single parent because of all the traveling he did. When Russell had begun, he had made a bargain he didn't understand at the time. If you want to rise and become general managers someday, Russell told his audience, there will be tremendous sacrifices in your personal life; but persevere, it's worth the effort because Jack Welch rewards effort. An ardent disciple of Welch then, Russell hadn't yet experienced the downside of reaching for the brass ring, which for the first time in his career seemed within his grasp. By

1985, Russell, in charge of GE's international lighting business with sales of $280 million and 5,000 employees, was living proof that people with energy and ambition could get ahead at General Electric. Getting ahead meant going the extra mile, talking at Crotonville even if it meant another weekend away from the wife and kids, and pleasing the man whose opinion mattered most, Welch, who once wrote to compliment Russell on the "excellent" job he had done on another occasion at Crotonville.

Russell, though, also lived in fear of "the Chairman," as Hiner called Welch, for he knew that the life expectancy of a GE executive could be perilously short. Just a few months before his address at Crotonville, Russell had made light of his fears in a tabloid newsletter produced for that year's annual planning powwow for the senior execs of international lighting, held in Rome. The newsletter—six pages of camp humor, photographs, and corn-ball captions—captured the pervasive insecurity that managers felt then as they wondered: "Who would be the next victim?" One photograph shows Russell, head tucked in a fetal position, above the caption: "Ed, there's a telephone call for you from Fairfield." Another shows Russell standing before a battering ram, contemplating suicide: "No, no, Ed, wait . . . the call from Fairfield? It wasn't for you after all!!" Still another photograph shows Russell as executioner, standing before a row of sharp iron skewers and saying: "You may be wondering what really happens on a headcount reduction!" There was also a telling photo of Russell, his mouth open wide and about to swallow a date plucked from a champagne glass full of dates: "Jack loves me—Jack loves me not—Jack loves me, etc., etc., etc. . . ."

At that point, Jack loved him, but Russell's wife of fourteen years, Alison, didn't, and in November 1985, just before Welch selected him as the new head of Superabrasives, Russell and his wife divorced. Alison Pfeister remarried, earned a law degree, and now works as an attorney in Akron, Ohio, yet the topic of GE still evokes a spirited response. "Years ago I was too angry to even discuss this," says Pfeister, who will not buy GE products and blames the company for the demise of her marriage. "You talk about bringing good things to life. GE brought shit to our lives."

Her marriage offers a glimpse into the realm of the GE wife, a topic that ironically received much publicity in 1997, not because of Russell's dismissal, but rather the termination of a thirty-one-year marriage between Lorna and Gary Wendt, the head of GE Capital. Mrs. Wendt, who sought an equal share of what her attorneys contended was a $100 million estate, said in court testimony she deserved half after decades of organizing GE dinner parties and trips abroad, giving other "GE wives" tips on shopping and entertaining, and generally being "the ultimate hostess." She was responsible for orchestrating black-tie dinners at their lavish Stamford, Connecticut, home, at which guests such as songwriter Marvin Hamlisch would entertain; for raising two daughters mostly on her own; and for packing and selling houses and giving away pets during frequent relocations.

Pfeister's complaints were similar. Outwardly, things always appeared perfect—that was one of the chief responsibilities of a "GE wife." When she went to Christmas parties or get-togethers thrown by Ed's bosses, "there was an aura of unreality to it all. The woman had this role. Her job was to be the perfect hostess, to further her husband's career, to be perfectly groomed—the nails, the house, the dress. Everything was just so." The reality, though, was different. "There were a lot of women who were bored and lonely. Their husbands were never home when a crisis struck," she says. "That usually resulted in affairs or drinking. Quite a few women were alcoholics." The GE wife also found solace in furs and jewelry—Pfeister recalls one woman, the wife of one of Russell's bosses when he worked at GE Lighting in the early 1980s, whose husband gave her a new fur coat. "She wore it everywhere. She refused to take it off even while she played bridge."

Russell was conscientious, with big ambitions, and in 1976 that ambition took the family to Mexico. He had been laboring in obscurity at corporate headquarters as a strategic planner in consumer products and looking for a way to break out of the pack, to distinguish himself. "There were twenty guys as capable as me, and none of them wanted to go to Mexico," he recalls. Without consulting his wife, he took a job in Monterrey running GE's Mexican lighting business. In the process, Russell took a two-level cut (GE in those days had pay scales similar to the GS rankings in the federal government). Falling back to Level Seventeen, Russell lost some executive benefits, such as stock options, but the gamble paid off in that it caught the attention of Welch, then a young man in a hurry, who as head of the Materials sector was angling to succeed Jones as chief executive against several rivals, including Robert Frederick, Russell's boss. Always on the lookout for aggressive people like himself, Welch, who considered Russell's move to Mexico ballsy, was busy assembling his own corps of shock troops, young swashbucklers who were willing to buck the system and who wanted to win.

The stay in Mexico was a success, at least career-wise. Profits of the Mexican operation surged 400 percent in two years under Russell's leadership, and he was rewarded with a promotion as general manager of GE's international lighting business. But the time in Mexico left scars. When Alison was pregnant and the birth of their third child was imminent, Russell's bosses wanted him to return to Cleveland headquarters. "Ed kept saying, 'I can't come today.' And they kept saying, 'We don't care if your wife is having a baby, get your butt up here,' " she says. The birth was induced, and Russell caught the next flight to Cleveland. "I had the distinct pleasure of having a GE driver take me home from the hospital," says Alison.

As Russell's work load intensified, so did the rewards. In addition to a salary of $190,000 in the year of his termination, he had also accrued incentive compensation for 1991 of $85,000 and drove a green Jaguar with tan leather interior, paid for by GE. At age sixty he would begin collecting an annual pension of $41,784. GE paid his life insurance premium, with a death benefit of more than $750,000, as well as full medical coverage. Russell was eligible to participate in GE's Executive Exchange Plan, allowing him to obtain new GE products every two years at no charge; he retained options to purchase 8,750 shares of GE stock at prices well below market value, thus ensuring him of a handsome profit simply by exercising the options; his account in GE's Savings and Security Program had a value of $170,000; and because he had chosen to defer much of his incentive compensation during his peak earning years, Russell had amassed more than $1 million as part of GE's Deferred Incentive Compensation Plan.

"You get sucked into it one little thing at a time," says a more reflective Russell now. "When you're at the officer level, you start to look at the value of what you have. We all came from blue-collar families. We're not Harvard, Yale, things like that. You just got caught up in it all."

But the sacrifices became increasingly steep, too, as Russell was away on business trips for weeks at a time. When he was home, he was crabby and impatient. Pfeister wrote in a letter that she dreaded bringing up matters about the house, yard, or children when Ed came home because of how tired and irritable he seemed to be. On one occasion, after returning from a trip to China, Russell, to assuage his guilt, surprised his three girls with exotic gifts from the Orient—fans, jewelry, purses, costumes, books, all spread out on the kitchen table. Pfeister, in the letter, compared it to Christmas. But though she and the children were well off financially and well taken care of, the prolonged and frequent absences of their husband and father were too steep a price to pay, exacting a heavy penalty on the family.

The letter closes: "We wives knew what was expected. Our roles were to maintain health and home while our husbands worked relentlessly and tirelessly to further GE's coffers. The price of success—the sacrifice was too great.

I quit the GE crew. I still believe life is more than executive compensation and bonuses."

As a senior executive of General Electric, Glen Hiner had terminated subordinates before, but the Russell dismissal promised to be more acrimonious than most. In part that was because Russell hadn't performed all that poorly—yes, there were grumblings among some subordinates (most of whom Hiner had appointed) about a lack of leadership at Superabrasives, a situation Bradford Smart, a Chicago industrial psychologist and management consultant on retainer with GE, had been called in to evaluate at Hiner's request; and yes, Russell had had two contentious meetings with Welch, one in July and a second in September. Even so, he had been given a positive performance review in June (the basis for the $15,000 raise that Welch had approved); his cash flow and earnings were both on budget; moreover, he hadn't been reprimanded, warned, or even criticized.

Hiner and Russell didn't like each other. Friction between executives was not an uncommon problem in the upper echelons of General Electric. Before being asked to intervene at Superabrasives, Smart had "counseled" twenty-two other GE executives, he later disclosed in a deposition. Russell regarded Hiner as a pampered windbag devoid of scruples, while Hiner considered Russell a gutless wimp who whined incessantly in a schoolmarmish way. Normally Hiner didn't like doing the dirty work of firing people, and would offer kind words of condolence or a chuck under the chin to soften the blow, but dismissing Russell had been cathartic. Hiner felt Russell was getting his just reward for all the grief he had caused him over the years. Little did Hiner know that the grief had only begun.

As Russell returned to Ohio just hours after having been sacked, aboard a GE corporate jet for the last time, he sat motionless. He was still in a state of shock about an hour into the flight, when he grabbed the telephone next to him and dialed his office. His secretary Denise Maurer picked up the phone.

"They shot me. I can't believe it. They shot me."

He kept repeating the words, over and over, shouting at the top of his lungs to be heard above the din of the aircraft. Maurer, an attractive woman who was well connected to the office gossip network, had heard rumors that her boss might be dumped, and while Russell had even dictated a six-page protest memo to Maurer two weeks before, anticipating his "removal as Vice President and General Manager of GE Superabrasives," he had been in denial. Russell assumed he would be given a second chance, and another assignment.

Around 5 p.m., Russell returned to his office—a generous space, decorated with such early American exotica as original Currier & Ives prints, Rookwood pottery, and a Wells Fargo rolltop desk—where he talked out the day's events with Maurer behind closed doors. A driving rainstorm had soaked his trench coat, and his glasses were so covered with water he could hardly see through them. He was still in shock over being fired and dissatisfied with the terms of the financial package he had received, which was substandard, given his years of service and seniority. It was standard procedure within GE to "make the separations as pleasant for everybody as possible," Welch later said, explaining the company's philosophy in a deposition taken in the lawsuit of Jeff Depew. "Most people that see these terminations . . . find them to be extremely generous. We say it's generally in our interest to have our employees work the transitions well, so we err on the side of generosity." In Russell's case, however, GE had cut him off just one year and a few months shy of a pension package that would have allowed him to collect full retirement benefits in less than two years, at age fifty-five. Instead, he had gotten a package in which the retirement benefits wouldn't kick in until age sixty. That six-and-a-half year interval without retirement benefits could be financially ruinous, Russell feared, because he knew that at his age it would be difficult to find another job.

Hiner and Welch were unaware of the memo Russell had prepared, but had they known of its existence and contents they might have treated him with more deference, for the memo spun a tale of corporate intrigue that would launch the government's subsequent investigation of GE and De Beers for price fixing. The memo was venomous—it described Hiner and GE Plastics as, among other things, "the pond scum of American industry." What irked Russell most was the injustice of the situation, that Hiner, whom he considered guilty of indiscretions up to and including an illegal liaison with De Beers, had gone unpunished and had been permitted to fire him no less. Russell vowed to get even; he would not go gently into the good night, as had others whose silence Welch had effectively bought with more lucrative severance deals, nor would he be the good soldier who observed the GE managerial code of conduct that forbade retaliation. The very next day Russell began his search to find a lawyer who would take on General Electric and Jack Welch.

"They'll be sorry they did this to me," Russell told Maurer.

Their conversation was interrupted by a phone call from Brad Smart. Russell was immediately suspicious of Smart's motives. Although Russell thought the work Smart had done that spring had been generally constructive and worthwhile, Smart already knew that Russell had been fired, and he was clearly calling at GE's behest. "GE doesn't need any more age-discrimination suits," Russell recalls Smart saying. The call ended with Smart asking Russell to visit him at his home in suburban Chicago the next week, which Russell agreed to do, thinking that Smart might be able to provide assistance in finding another job, and perhaps shed light on why he had been fired.

Russell busied himself in the eight days before they met searching for an attorney who was willing—and able—to take his case. Some couldn't take the case because their firms already represented GE in other matters, while others were content to take on a wrongful-termination case but got skittish when Russell raised the issue of price-fixing and antitrust allegations. When Russell met Smart on November 19, he still didn't have legal representation, but he was glad to have the opportunity to tell his side of the story. The shock over his dismissal had worn down to a dull ache, and Russell was calm and articulate as he explained why he felt his removal was unwarranted.

The basic problem, as Russell saw it, was a difference with Hiner over what was acceptable behavior, as he had said in his October 30 memo: "The problem has been, is, and will always be fundamental cultural differences with Glen Hiner and GE Plastics." Although Smart had gained some insight into the Hiner-Russell schism during his prior evaluation of Russell, the new details he heard that day suggested that Russell wasn't the crank that Hiner's appointees at Superabrasives had made him out to be in discussions with Smart.

It had been obvious to everyone involved that Hiner and Russell had a very basic conflict. Aggressive, rough-and-tumble GE Plastics conducted its affairs in a manner that was very different from what Russell had experienced before coming to Superabrasives from GE's staid lighting operations. Although Russell was no choir boy, he couldn't believe the kind of behavior and shenanigans that Hiner tolerated at GE Plastics. One Hiner appointee who had come over from Plastics had used company funds to visit prostitutes in Bangkok, where Superabrasives had no customers, and, on another occasion, had taken several drunken colleagues visiting from Worthington to a whorehouse in Munich—an escapade that was charged to his GE expense account. Another Hiner appointee had sexually harassed female associates, had thrown a beer bottle from a moving car in Palm Beach, Florida, and had vomited (from excess drinking) while on a sales call in a Russian government ministry. Convinced he was being sandbagged, with Hiner asserting more control at Superabrasives, Russell continued to protest the improprieties, but disciplinary action was never taken. He was told on several occasions that he didn't understand the importance of "male bonding," and he was openly ridiculed as the "wimp from Worthington."

When it came to following rules, Russell believed in observing the strict letter of the law. GE had a written policy for everything, and Policy 30.3 clearly stated that the company would only reimburse employees for actual, reasonable, and proper expenditures incurred in the conduct of official business. While Russell believed most spending at GE Plastics was unreasonable, Hiner, on the other hand, thought nothing of treating himself to the finest of everything, and had a full-time, personal valet on the payroll, Gregg Bronk. Bronk served Hiner on a private basis as well—he maintained the wine cellar at Hiner's lakeside home in Pittsfield, a cellar stocked with an impressive collection of vintage bottles that Hiner would proudly show to visitors. Hiner's extravagance included having fresh tulips flown in from Holland each day for his room during the 1989 Superabrasives sales meeting in Hawaii.

Russell had only been reporting to Hiner for a few months before he got the first sign that they weren't in sync. In February 1987, Superabrasives held its annual sales get-together in Tucson, Arizona, where they honored "Salesman of the Year" Pheroze Bharucha, who had increased GE's synthetic diamond sales in India from almost nothing to about $5 million in just two years. Bharucha was quiet and polite, a Hindu in his mid-50s who bowed from the waist when introduced, and didn't quite fit Hiner's image of the Rambo-type salesmen at GE Plastics. As Russell escorted Hiner back to his hotel room that night, Hiner questioned his selection of Bharucha. "Looking at all your people," Russell recalls Hiner saying, "he was the last one I would have picked." Just two months later, in April, Hiner, after receiving a positive appraisal of Russell's performance from an emissary he had sent to Worthington to check up on him, delivered a fateful pronouncement. "You're doing a good job, Ed," he told Russell, "but we just don't have any chemistry. You're not my kind of guy." Russell had been in GE long enough to understand the message implicit in Hiner's words: See if you can find a job in another GE division. Russell paid a visit to Jack Peiffer, GE's top personnel officer in Fairfield, but was advised to forget what Hiner had said and get back to work.

That was a huge mistake, for Hiner's verdict had been accurate—their differences were irreconcilable, as were their styles. Hiner was the consummate corporate type, whose climb up the corporate ladder was as much a result of finesse as business acumen. He dressed impeccably, could work a room with the skill of the best politician, and was terrific at projecting sincerity. Russell, on the other hand, was a guy who had succeeded at GE despite his personality, not because of it. A borderline genius who didn't really belong in a big corporation, Russell had a very disciplined and imaginative mind and was constantly throwing out unconventional thoughts, many of which Hiner dismissed as idiotic and goofy ("Goofy" and the "Goofmeister" were nick-names Hiner's clique pinned on Russell). In a corporation where many of the senior executives were, like Welch, loud, aggressive, and extroverted, Russell was introverted and cerebral, a guy who would rather shop for antiques than play golf. (Russell had an extensive antique collection, and he recorded the particulars of every purchase in a log book, which he kept as meticulously as the notebooks he constantly jotted in.) Russell tried desperately to fit in but never was able to. He didn't make friends or mingle easily, disliked chitchat, and seemed out of place at cocktail parties, a setting where Hiner was in his glory.

Superabrasives had long been considered a sleepy backwater within GE. In contrast to Plastics, where people constantly moved out of one job and into another, the employees of Superabrasives tended to stay in the same job a long time and were content doing that. It was a business that mirrored the values of its location at the epicenter of Middle America. This was Main Street, U.S.A., the land of Woody Hayes and Buckeye football. People tended toward the conservative, and the culture was one of caution and secrecy (the secret formula for making diamonds had to remain secret, after all), as opposed to the grand-standing and aggrandizing behavior of Plastics, which was the quintessential sales environment ("shoot first, aim later"). When people from Pittsfield visited Worthington and sought drinking companions for a night out on the town, there were few takers; family responsibilities came first. As far as Plastics executives were concerned, the "wimps of Worthington" weren't their equals and lacked the moxie and stamina of true champions.

They were also seen as wimps in the business arena. In Welch's view, Superabrasives had never exploited its competitive advantages aggressively enough, and as early as 1972, when the diamond-making division was one of several businesses reporting to him, he was plucking people out of Plastics and transferring them to Worthington. "I want you to put some gas into those guys" is the way Bruce Krause, a onetime GE Plastics salesman, recalls Welch's marching orders. "They're just sitting on that money-making machine." Krause went to Worthington, but he couldn't satisfy Welch either—the culture was simply too entrenched. During a trip to Pittsfield several months after having transferred, Krause ran into Welch, seated in a bar with several Plastics cronies, and Welch proceeded to give Krause a critical impromptu performance review in public, a common practice of his in those days.

The industrial-diamond capital of the world, GE's Worthington factory was unlike any other Russell had seen before: a cavernous aircraft hanger filled with presses, from which GE manufactured more than thirty tons of diamonds each year, an output worth hundreds of millions of dollars and roughly equal to all the diamond mined and manufactured everywhere else in the world. The most spectacular sight was found in the sorting room, where the concentration of synthetic crystals was so heavy the floor actually sparkled. The place was kept immaculate, but after decades of diamond-making, glittering diamond grit was everywhere. Workers had to have a second pair of shoes to wear in the facility; if they wore their everyday shoes, the abrasive diamond dust would become imbedded in them and would destroy linoleum or wood floors at home.

Secrecy was key to maintaining the exclusivity and profitability of diamond-making. No unauthorized visitors were allowed inside the production compound, sealed off by two twelve-foot-high fences encircling its perimeter. Between the fences was an unoccupied zone that employees called "No Man's Land," over which guards maintained twenty-four-hour surveillance. All employees leaving the premises were searched, while Xerox machines were held under lock and key to prevent illegal copying and couldn't be used without permission. On two occasions, in the early 1970s, the FBI had called to warn GE that thieves might attempt armed robbery. Brinks trucks were called in to remove the precious inventory temporarily.

The invention of the synthetic diamond had proven to be one of the most significant achievements in GE's illustrious history of technical breakthroughs. For more than three hundred years scientists had experimented with the conversion of carbon to diamonds, but it wasn't until December 1954 that the company's six-man research team—working with presses that simulated the volcanic inferno of the Earth, where Nature naturally manufactures diamonds—were able miraculously to transform graphite, spiked with a catalyst, into tiny tetrahedron diamond crystals. Two months later, in February 1955, C. Guy Suits, director of the GE research lab, proclaimed a "new milestone in man's conquest of matter" before about one hundred assembled reporters in Schenectady. (An embittered Tracy Hall, the physicist who actually made the discovery and felt slighted at not having received special recognition for his achievement, left GE a few months later.)

The De Beers organization of South Africa, which since 1880 had controlled the world diamond industry, immediately sent General Electric a telegram congratulating the research and development lab for its breakthrough, while at the same time reminding the world in a press release that synthetic crystals were not gemstones. Even so, Ernest Oppenheimer, scion of the family that had owned De Beers for most of this century, was understandably concerned, and he had no alternative but to reverse an earlier decision in which he had rejected pursuit of synthetic diamonds. A division of De Beers called Adamant—from the ancient Greek word for diamond—was created to find a process for manufacturing synthetic crystals, and by 1959 De Beers researchers had finally duplicated GE's feat. GE executives learned of De Beers's achievement and urged an end to the patent moratorium imposed by the Eisenhower administration, which had wanted to keep the GE method secret and out of Soviet hands, such was the importance of industrial diamonds for weapons production. In mid-September, GE applied for a patent on its process of diamond synthesis, just weeks before the South Africans did. Litigation ensued as each company claimed the legitimate patent rights to the diamond "invention." In 1960, U.S. Patent No. 2,941,248 gave GE the exclusive right to manufacture diamonds using its high-temperature, high-pressure technology. Because De Beers possessed a worldwide marketing network, the two companies soon decided not to compete against each other but to forge a duopoly, not unlike the arrangement between GE and Westinghouse in the early days of lighting and electricity. The parties settled their suits—with De Beers agreeing to pay patent royalties to GE—and entered into a series of cross-licensing agreements that made it virtually impossible for any other rival to compete in synthetic diamonds. In October 1966, Harry Oppenheimer, Ernest's son and successor as head of De Beers, tried to take the alliance one step further. During a meeting in New York with William Cordier, then GE's top executive in synthetic diamonds, Oppenheimer proposed that the two companies coordinate production. While licensing arrangements are generally permissible under the Sherman Antitrust Act, collusion in restraint of trade is not. To Oppenheimer, whose Anglo American Corporation not only controlled De Beers but 25 percent of the South African economy, the very idea of a law that would prevent businessmen from doing whatever they damn well pleased must have struck him as a peculiar, even quaint, notion. But to Cordier, the executive of a company that only five years before had been raked over by the Justice Department for collusion in electrical equipment, antitrust violations were a very real threat indeed. Not surprisingly, Cordier refused to go along with the scheme.

Man-made diamonds quickly became big business. As techniques were found for bonding the minute crystals together, the commercial uses multiplied—on the cutting edges of products as diverse as tiny dentist drills and oil drilling bits, on abrasive wheels for shaping eyeglasses, on huge saws that cut open asphalt streets. As the business matured, GE's strategy changed, from aggressive research in new technology to vigorous defense of what became old technology. This took the form of litigation against interlopers and, in some instances, industrial spies. One such spy was Chein-Min Sung, a brilliant M.I.T.-educated Ph.D. physicist who worked in Worthington for seven years until 1984, when, frustrated over the company's disinterest in new technology, he quit to join a GE rival. After he had left GE, Sung had passed proprietary information on how to make synthetic diamonds to a South Korean company, Iljin, which was seeking to break the stranglehold that GE and De Beers had on synthetic-diamond manufacture. Russell became suspicious of Sung's activities in 1988, when a member of his staff got a call disclosing that the Norton Company in Massachusetts, where Sung was now head of research, had drawings of a diamond-making die that were identical to GE's. Russell complained about it to Norton officials, but the matter was dropped after they insisted that Norton, which was also a large customer of GE's, had developed the dies on their own.

A year later, however, Sung, under the pseudonym of "Larry King," tried to enlist a Superabrasives employee on behalf of Iljin, which was starting up diamond manufacturing. The Fairfax Group, a private detective agency in the Washington, D.C., area, was hired by GE to investigate the events. GE had used Fairfax several times before, most recently to protect Welch during a visit to Seoul in 1988 while NBC was televising the Summer Olympics. A Fairfax investigator accompanied the GE employee to a June 1989 meeting in New York City with "Larry King." Over the next four months, Sung was under surveillance, his phone calls monitored, his trash examined, and, in September 1989, his home was raided by police. The following year Sung pleaded guilty to transporting stolen trade secrets, serving a sentence of six months home confinement, while Iljin, which claimed it was innocent of any wrongdoing, was enjoined by a federal judge from producing industrial diamonds for a period of seven years.

Although Russell disapproved of some of the tactics GE employed, driving off potential rivals was simply business as usual in synthetic diamonds. Besides, Welch had made it clear that he expected Russell to orchestrate the kind of "quantum leap" turnaround Welch had been seeking there since the early seventies and to achieve sizable profits. Rivals had to be dealt with harshly. But what galvanized Russell most was the open disdain Hiner showed for him and his managerial team. Hiner didn't think Russell and his staff were good enough to be part of Plastics, and he said so when he addressed them for the first time early in 1986. They would have to earn their way onto the A-team.

After Hiner's challenge, Russell began initiatives to develop new products and to find new customers. When Russell arrived in Worthington the year before, the marketing staff was just three people, but it was soon increased to more than thirty, including sales reps in Japan and Europe. Russell also held informational meetings to lift the veil of secrecy that had permeated Superabrasives, sharing financial data with everyone, even hourly employees, an initiative that offended many old-timers but ultimately proved beneficial: the business, which had a $20 million profit goal in 1987, exceeded $30 million in 1987. Sales surged, productivity soared; soon the business was improving dramatically in every statistical measure. By June 1988, Superabrasives was generally regarded as one of the top if not *the* best-performing manufacturing operation in all of General Electric.

At Hiner's operations review in mid-1988, even he commended Russell and his team for their outstanding performance; special T-shirts and coffee mugs had been made to commemorate the occasion, emblazoned with the slogan "Fifty is Nifty," which signified the Superabrasives goal of $50 million in net income. "There was a real sense that we had won our spurs," recalls Gary Weber, Russell's chief of engineering. "Ed brought that business back from the brink," said another former colleague.

By 1989, Superabrasives' net income had reached $70 million while the division had gained market share in the most profitable product segment—concrete-cutting saw diamonds, and the business was winning other accolades, including the Ohio Governor's Award for Quality, presented after a statewide competition in recognition of the best quality procedures, in which Superabrasives bested Honda Motor's operations in Marysville. Hiner wrote in one performance appraisal of Russell: "Excellent overall business perspective on a global basis, style is bright, energetic, committed and communicative." Russell also had achieved noteworthy progress in implementing one of Welch's pet programs, "Work-Out," the new training program for disseminating GE values—every production and management employee in Worthington, thirteen hundred in all, had been through Work-Out.

At the same time, however, there was a rising chorus of dissent over Russell's shortcomings, mainly from people close to Hiner. Complaints about the boss were hardly unique at General Electric, and the complaints about Russell were laughable compared to the tales of despotism Welch had heard over the years about other business leaders. It was money that ultimately did in Russell, who in effect fell victim to the same thing that ended George Bush's presidency—a bad economy. The recession of 1990–91 that propelled Bill Clinton into the White House on James Carville's famous advice ("it's the economy, stupid") also cost Russell his job. Earnings of Superabrasives, which were directly tied to industrial activity, slipped by almost one-third from their

1989 high. Moreover, Russell was not quick in responding to the situation and, from Welch's perspective, he appeared to have no idea of how to reverse it.

Once Russell had been dismissed, however, Welch was disingenuous about why he had been fired. Welch, who was still trying to build enthusiasm for his Work-Out program and the values programming that accompanied it, did not want to say Russell was fired because the earnings had fallen—that would not have been consistent with the new values he was seeking to promote. Instead, on January 6, 1992, in a speech to GE executives at the annual management conclave in Boca Raton, Florida, Welch said one of the reasons for Russell's dismissal was "no '90s values." Yet Professor Todd Jick of the Harvard Business School, who had been hired by Hiner to assess the progress of Work-Out within GE Plastics, had given Russell the highest "values" marks of any manager in GE Plastics and, in a report dated October 29, 1991, cited Superabrasives as "the bellwether for the Work-Out effort due to the early development initiated by general manager, Ed Russell. They have clearly increased openness and empowerment, reduced boundaries of all kinds, and increased team problem solving."

Russell's successes and failures were well known by Brad Smart. During their meeting, Smart listened to him for most of a day and counseled restraint. Russell was obviously angry and hurting, but Smart knew he wasn't a reckless man, and he tried to appeal to Russell's intellect, which was considerable, according to the evaluation Smart had conducted. "Logical, very conscientious, responsible, far above average intelligence, excellent analytic abilities" were the words Smart had used to describe Russell in the report he had prepared. But Smart also knew that GE, from which he had collected as much as $300,000 in consulting fees in one year, had deep pockets and would be a formidable foe, and he advised Russell not to sue GE. They have the best legal team in America, Smart warned Russell; just take the high road, forget it ever happened, get on with your life, and concentrate on finding another job.

Russell didn't heed his advice. In late November he signed an agreement securing legal representation from Jim Helmer, a Cincinnati attorney whom Welch referred to as "the John D. Rockefeller of whistleblowers." Helmer's successful representation of many cases against GE had made him one of Cincinnati's most prominent and wealthy attorneys; his own Jaguar had a license plate that read "TOPGUN," the gift from one satisfied client.

In early December, Russell had his final telephone conversation with Hiner, which ended with Russell telling him, "I'm not accepting what happened." And on a chilly Saturday morning in mid-January 1992, Russell, accompanied by Helmer and Washington attorney Richard Hibey, entered a stately granite building at 1401 H Street in Washington, D.C., not far from the White House. The elevator took them to the sixth floor, where they waited until a secretary came from behind a locked door and ushered them into a well-worn meeting room. Russell had decided to tell his story again, this time to the antitrust division of the United States Department of Justice.

THE STORY RUSSELL TOLD that day was one of corporate intrigue that kept his audience, two antitrust division attorneys, spellbound for six and a half hours. Working from a forty-page chronology that Helmer and Russell—a copious notetaker whose constant jotting had often been a source of amusement to GE colleagues—had prepared, it was a tale straight out of a legal thriller: there were cigars, brandy, and five-star hotels; big-name executives, including De Beers chieftains Nicholas Oppenheimer and Julian Ogilvie Thompson, as well as Viscount Etienne Davignon, one of Europe's most prominent businessmen; diamond merchants furtively swapping confidential information; and, of course, collusion between two companies that together controlled 80 to 90 percent of the worldwide market for industrial diamonds.

In addition to his detailed price-fixing allegations against Hiner, whose meetings with Ogilvie Thompson, Russell alleged, had laid the groundwork for the scheme, Russell also identified two other conspirators: Philippe Liotier, the chief executive of Diamant Boart, a Brussels-based maker of cutting tools that bought man-made diamonds from both GE and De Beers; and Peter Frenz, a German national who headed Superabrasives' European sales. These two men, Russell alleged, served as the crucial conduit for the pricing information that De Beers and GE had swapped to fix diamond prices.

Justice Department prosecutors were impressed that they had a high-level executive making these charges, and the events that followed impressed them even more: GE began initiating price increases for saw, drilling, and cutting diamonds just days after the prosecutors had met with Russell, which were quickly followed by De Beers increases. "Although Russell will likely be viewed [by the jury] as a disgruntled employee with an ax to grind, his allegations regarding the development of the price-fixing plan (written weeks before he was fired), were proved reliable when future events occurred essentially as Russell had predicted," the team of four antitrust attorneys charged with prosecuting the case wrote two years later to antitrust litigation section head Anthony Nanni in the memo that recommended indictment of GE, De Beers, Frenz, and Liotier.

Over the next two months, while the government team shuttled to Ohio to flesh out the details of Russell's story, Welch's decision to send him packing had caused bedlam in Worthington. In late March, Russell's successor as head of Superabrasives, John Blystone, whom Welch had lured back to GE from J. I. Case with a hefty bonus and promises of promotions, realized he was in for a more difficult assignment than he had bargained for when he read the October 30 Russell protest memo that Denise Maurer had prepared but hadn't until then shown to him or anyone else. By that time, the price increases were already in effect, and although Blystone didn't know at that point that Russell had complained to the Justice Department, the allegations contained in the memo clearly signaled big trouble.

"Oh, my God!" Blystone bellowed as he read the memo. "Why didn't you give this to me before?" he demanded of Maurer, who had dismissed it at the time as the torrential outpouring of an angry man. Immediately after Blystone saw the memo, a team of GE attorneys and auditors descended en masse on Worthington, searching and seizing all pertinent documents, including Maurer's private computer files. When Maurer discovered what they had done the next morning, she complained to Blystone. "They don't trust you, Denise," he replied, "but I do." But his trust was short-lived: A little more than a year later, Maurer was forced to resign.

Trust would soon become a most precious and rare commodity. On April 19, 1992, two days before Russell filed his wrongful termination suit, which disclosed for the first time publicly the allegations he had made in private to the Justice Department, Dave Schroeder, the agent heading up the FBI's investigation out of its Columbus office, arranged to tape a telephone call from Russell in the United States to Peter Frenz in Germany. During this call, Russell told Frenz a lie—that he had recorded a previous phone call Frenz had taken from Liotier in Russell's office—which elicited two statements that the government would later allege confirmed Frenz's guilt: one, "I hope you destroyed it," Frenz said, referring to the bogus recording; and the second, "Well, you see the discussion with Liotier was always done in a way that he's our customer."

On April 20, the day after Russell had called Frenz, the FBI descended on Superabrasives' Worthington headquarters with subpoenas that netted some five hundred thousand pages of documents from GE offices throughout the world. Agents started interviewing scores of employees, including Maurer, who a year later would be pressured to resign for what she claimed was Blystone's anger over her cooperation with the FBI.

When news of the suit broke on April 22 in the *Wall Street Journal* and the *New York Times*, Welch, no stranger to controversy, came out fighting. Attending GE's annual shareholders meeting in Florence, South Carolina, that day, he was visibly upset, the *Journal* reported, and denounced Russell's allegations as "pure nonsense." In a letter to GE officers a week later, Welch wrote: "Ed Russell was removed from his job as head of Superabrasives for one simple reason— he was not performing effectively as a GE leader. Any charges by Mr. Russell that I personally was aware of any antitrust or securities law violations are outrageous. I have the utmost confidence in the integrity of . . . Glen Hiner. I also believe [he was] not aware of, or involved in, any such violations. Further- more, I have no knowledge that any company employees engaged in any of these alleged acts."

Although Welch put up a brave front, the gravity of the situation he and his company faced was immediately clear to him. In addition to the Russell suit, the company had been hit with three shareholder derivative suits, alleg- ing that GE and its officers had risked harming the value of GE stock through the illegal acts of company employees; and two customer class-action suits, alleging unspecified damages stemming from the price-fixing. Worst of all, GE's pricing activities were the subject of "a very serious grand jury investiga- tion," J. Robert Kramer II, one of the two attorneys who sat in on the January meeting where Russell had disclosed his allegations, told GE's outside antitrust counsel, William Baer of Arnold & Porter, the same day Russell filed his suit. Baer would later learn that the grand jury proceedings in Columbus were being handled by five experienced, well-regarded attorneys from the antitrust division—a level of staffing that was unusually high and indicated how seriously the government regarded the allegations.

Just how seriously General Electric viewed the situation was communi- cated to Alison Pfeister, Russell's ex-wife, in a phone call she received on June 5, 1992 from Philip Horton, who identified himself as an attorney with Arnold & Porter in Washington, representing GE. Horton said he was calling to find out what kind of person Russell was and "what made him tick." Welch was outraged over Russell's allegations, Horton said, and Russell would "regret that he chose this course." Horton had called at the suggestion of Denise Mau- rer to gain insight into why Russell had filed the lawsuit. Pfeister, who was on relatively good terms with her ex-husband, said Russell's motivation was simple—he filed it because he believed the allegations were true. Why do you think Ed was sacked? Pfeister inquired. Horton explained that GE is a very competitive environment and that while Russell had proven to be an able manager, at the highest levels of the corporation you either produce or are eliminated. Horton said he didn't like digging up dirt on people, but that the stakes in this case were too high, the charges too serious, the potential penalties too severe, to leave any stone unturned. If the allegations were true, Horton said, GE employees could face indictments and jail terms.

The company had thrown an army of lawyers at this case, and, in an unusual arrangement, was covering the legal costs of any GE employees involved on its side. The arrangement allowed Benjamin Heineman, GE's general counsel, to monitor what the Justice Department was doing, as well as what testimony was given to the grand jury, and it also gave the company extraordinary leverage over what people said. Under the provisions of the arrangement, GE could stop paying the legal expenses and demand their money back at any time, for any reason, which could prove financially ruinous to employees below the senior-executive level.

Besides eighteen attorneys from Horton's own firm, Heineman had tapped as the lead defense counsel Dan K. Webb, a rainmaker for Winston & Strawn in Chicago and one of three former U.S. attorneys on GE's defense team, the other two being future White House Counsel Charles Ruff of Covington & Burling, who represented Hiner, and Davis Polk & Wardwell's Robert Fiske, who represented GE's board of directors in the derivative suits. Peter Frenz was represented at GE's expense by heavyweight white-collar specialists Carl Rauh, Robert Bennett—later President Clinton's attorney in the Paula Jones case—and Alan Kriegel of the D.C. office of New York's Skadden, Arps, Slate, Meagher & Flom, while some thirty-five other GE employees were represented by Jenner & Block's Anthony Epstein.

Horton told Pfeister that legal fees in the case were approaching $1 million a month, and that GE would spare no expense to defend itself. Pfeister listened intently for more than an hour and took careful notes. After promising to send Pfeister documents revealing Russell's financial status, Horton concluded the phone call with one final commentary: Russell's complaint was either a lie, self-deception, or the biggest antitrust case in recent history.

Although it evolved into the latter, GE's defense team would put forth herculean effort to convince the Justice Department that the government's star witness in the most significant criminal antitrust investigation the department had mounted since the Carter administration was a pathological liar— Russell "has a track record that clearly establishes that he is not capable of telling the truth," Webb wrote in one September 1993 letter—who had made his claims simply to get back at the company for terminating him. From the outset, the defense team's goal was to convince the Justice Department not to indict the company and, at the same time, eviscerate Russell's civil suit by destroying his credibility. In July 1993, Webb, Bill Baer, and Ronald Stern, GE's Washington, D.C.-based senior counsel for antitrust law and competition policy (and a former colleague of Baer's at Arnold & Porter), took the unusual step of providing the antitrust division with a "white paper" that spelled out what they claimed were twelve lies Russell had told in the six days of depositions Webb had taken for the civil suit.

Justice Department prosecutors, however, weren't persuaded by "the dirty dozen," as the GE defense team called Russell's alleged lies. They felt they had gathered enough evidence, in grand jury testimony and subpoenaed documents, to support an indictment independent of Russell, who was terminated on November 11, *before* the alleged price-fixing had occurred. It was after that date that the Frenz-Liotier connection bourgeoned in private meetings, telephone calls, and faxes in which the two had swapped confidential GE and De Beers pricing information. The prosecutors had also been encouraged by some extraordinary steps taken in the investigation of the case, such as the arrest of one European witness for testimony to the grand jury, and emboldened as well by the arrival that spring of Anne Bingaman, the department's top trustbuster, who had breathed new life into long-dormant antitrust enforcement. Bingaman, a former law professor and antitrust litigator, was encouraging a fired-up staff to look more closely at the business practices of individual companies, and this was a case she clearly wanted to bring to trial, involving as it did high-profile defendants, complicated international schemes, and what litigation chief Anthony Nanni would later call "hard core price fixing." However, because it had been some time since the antitrust division had tried and won litigation so complex, Bingaman in October 1993 retained as lead trial counsel Max Gillam, a veteran West Coast antitrust litigator. Bingaman had worked against Gillam in a major lawsuit years earlier and had been impressed by his ability.

While the defense team's sharing of its "white paper" might have seemed an extraordinary gesture of openness, in that it simultaneously also revealed much of their defense strategy, the prosecution had reasons to question GE's sincerity, and in particular the influence it was exerting over key witnesses. Denise Maurer, who like other GE employees was receiving counsel from a company-paid attorney, was interrogated nine times by GE-retained attorneys, before and after meetings with the Justice Department and depositions; the objective, Maurer later testified, was to influence her testimony: "I was told the government is not my friend, Ed Russell is the enemy, and GE is my employer."

When Maurer revealed that a file Blystone had given her to keep safe from the government document sweep because it contained "personal" information was composed, instead, of business-related documents—including a note Blystone had written, "thru Liotier that De Beers would follow price increase"—the prosecutors in September 1993 summoned Blystone to Washington to give his explanation of the missing file. Magistrate Steinberg also convened a full-day hearing in his Cincinnati courtroom two months later for the questioning of Hiner, Blystone, and others to ascertain why this document and others hadn't been provided to Russell during discovery. That hearing came too late, though, to save Maurer's job. After overhearing Blystone tell his attorney David Towey that "you better get Landis [Maurer's attorney] on the phone and remind him who in the fuck she works for before she screws up our plans," Maurer was informed her services were no longer needed, and she tendered her resignation in June after reaching a severance settlement.

In dealing with Maurer, the defense team had shown its absolute determination to win, but their willingness to play hardball was best evidenced in their treatment of Russell. GE's use of work done by Smart was a case in point. As part of his evaluation of Russell, Smart had prepared two reports: one that described Russell as "very warm, supportive and caring," which had been given to GE, and a second, based on interviews with his more disgruntled subordinates, which hadn't, that characterized Russell as "insecure, paranoid and indecisive." Smart didn't give a copy of the second report to GE until May 5, 1992, *after* Russell had filed his lawsuit; it could not, therefore, have been a factor in Welch's decision to fire him (Welch admitted in his deposition that he didn't even know who Brad Smart was). Nevertheless, GE made extensive use of the second Smart report as support for its contention that Russell had been fired for gross incompetence. Ironically, when GE successfully fought off Russell's attempts to obtain information on the other twenty-two GE executives Smart had consulted, Smart submitted an affidavit supporting GE's position in which he inadvertently pointed out how unfair he had been to Russell: "When an executive chooses to utilize my services, my responsibility is to the executive, and I therefore believe that I must maintain his or her information in strict confidence. . . . Disclosure, for example, of a client's record could prove so embarrassing so as to be literally life-threatening to the individual."

This, however, was a life-and-death struggle. Welch, whose reputation had already been soiled by prior scandal, couldn't afford a guilty verdict for price-fixing, and as the case progressed it was looking graver for General Electric. By December 1993, a draft indictment had already been prepared, and Baer and Webb made the rounds once more at the antitrust division, seeking to prevent presentation of the indictment to the grand jury, meeting first with division staffers, then working their way up the chain of command to litigation chief Nanni, then, in mid-January, to Nanni's superior, Joseph Widmar. Nanni,

Widmar, and Bingaman, each of whom had reviewed the evidence, agreed that this was "a case that can and should be pursued," as the four prosecuting attorneys had written in their January 24 memo recommending indictment, and that the government was justified in bringing a criminal complaint rather than lesser civil charges. The Justice Department refused to back down, and in late January it informed GE that the indictment was set for the middle of February.

On January 14, General Electric had scored a partial victory in the Russell suit, which was scheduled to go to trial in February, when Magistrate Steinberg, who was handling pretrial matters in the case, threw out two of the wrongful discharge counts Russell had brought but decided that the third charge—under an Ohio law protecting whistleblowers—should go to trial. Although Steinberg found "substantial evidence" contradicting GE's claim that Russell had been fired for poor performance and found plausible Russell's allegation that he had been dismissed for protesting GE's relationship with De Beers, Jim Helmer, Russell's attorney, had doubts that he would be able to convince trial Judge Herman Weber (owing to a quirk in the law, there would be no jury if it went to trial) that Russell was a legitimate whistleblower. There were holes not in the substance of Russell's allegations—Helmer had no doubt the price-fixing had occurred—but in Russell's claim that he had been fired because of his protests against it, holes Webb had widened in his extensive questioning of Russell.

One week later, on January 21, Webb called Helmer, whose firm had a lot of money riding on the outcome of the Russell case—Helmer, who was working on contingency, figured he had sunk thirteen thousand hours into it at $200 per hour, for a total exposure of a whopping $2.6 million—to suggest possible terms of surrender. GE would guarantee the $1 million in supplemental pension benefits to which Russell was entitled, as well as medical and insurance benefits worth about $250,000, and would pay a big chunk of Helmer's legal fees if Russell signed an affidavit recanting his claims.

"Jim, I think the language we have been talking about is something along the following lines," Webb told Helmer. "Ed Russell could honestly and truthfully say the following . . ."

The lawsuit, however, had been an epiphany for Russell, whose motivation had changed in the twenty-two months it had progressed through discovery. When he had first made his allegations, Russell's primary motivation was revenge, getting back at Hiner and Welch for what they had done to him. Now, he wanted justice to be done, and he had absolutely no doubt based on the evidence he had seen in that twenty-two months that Frenz and Liotier had fixed prices. On the other hand, the pressure to settle was enormous: Judge Weber wanted a settlement, as did Helmer, whose risk of proceeding with the case far outweighed the potential reward.

Russell continued to waver right up until the end. Welch, hoping to close on a settlement, and Russell were to meet privately in Cincinnati on Wednesday, February 16, the day before the grand jury was scheduled to vote on the indictment. The night before, Russell called Dave Schroeder, informing him of the Welch meeting. Schroeder had recently retired from the FBI, and hence was no longer involved in the case. But fearing that Welch would "buy off" Russell and destroy the government's case, Schroeder got permission to act on behalf of the bureau as a "concerned citizen." He then sought departmental permission to outfit Russell with a hidden recorder to gather possible evidence of obstruction of justice; Bingaman shot the idea down.

The next morning, Russell, accompanied by Helmer, and Welch, accompanied by Webb, met at the nineteenth-floor offices of Dinsmore & Shohl, one of Cincinnati's most prominent and elegantly appointed law firms. For two turbulent hours, Welch and Russell shouted accusations at each other. No agreement was reached. At ten o'clock the four men walked to the federal courthouse to meet with Judge Weber, first Welch and Webb in a private session, then Russell and Helmer. Russell made an impassioned plea that the case be allowed to proceed to trial, but Judge Weber was cleverly maneuvering the parties toward a settlement, which the four reached a few hours later over lunch at the Celestial, a hillside restaurant overlooking Cincinnati. At two o'clock they returned to Dinsmore & Shohl, to inform Judge Weber that they had reached agreement and to prepare documents. At four o'clock GE wired money to Helmer's account in Cincinnati. Russell then signed two documents: one, to be flaunted in public, in which he stated that he had no "personal knowledge" of any crime that GE or any of its employees had committed; and a second, which spelled out the details of the money Helmer had received, which Helmer and Russell agreed never to reveal, and which would remain confidential by order of Judge Weber, who sealed the transcript of the proceedings. As Russell and Helmer left, Webb faxed Russell's first agreement to Bingaman at the Justice Department in Washington, along with an argument that since Russell had withdrawn his lawsuit, and renounced his accusations, Bingaman should withdraw hers.

The defense team was exultant. "The government's chief witness just blew himself up," Ben Heineman said, according to the *Wall Street Journal*. To make sure that top Justice officials read about Russell's apparent capitulation, Joyce Hergenhan, GE's vice president for public relations, called reporters that day at the *Wall Street Journal* and the *Washington Post*, alerting them to the new development.

Armed with Russell's statement, Heineman made one last effort to stave off the indictment. On February 14, Heineman, Welch, Stern, Baer, Webb, and Peter Frenz's three lawyers, Bennett, Rauh, and Kreigel, had had their final meeting with Bingaman and her staff at the Justice Department. Welch had put on an impressive display of his charm and salesmanship, but Bingaman would give no quarter. Calling the case a hard-core violation, she rejected the idea of a civil penalty, and said that the indictment would go forward on a criminal basis. Her best offer was that GE agree to plead guilty to a felony and pay a fine, which Welch unilaterally rejected. Heineman, a close friend to many powerful Democrats, then called on his Washington connections, telephoning a Yale Law School classmate of his, Webster Hubbell, then associate attorney general and Bingaman's boss, one floor above, asking him to hold up the indictment because it would prejudice the coming Russell trial. Hubbell, a "friend of Bill's" and a former law partner of Hillary Clinton's in Little Rock, had previously expressed reservations about the case to both Attorney General Janet Reno and Bingaman. Hubbell, however, was then preoccupied with his own troubles.* He declined to help Heineman.

Now, on February 17, with the Russell trial out of the way, Heineman again asked Hubbell to hold up the indictment; Hubbell declined, and referred him back to Bingaman, who after receiving Webb's fax had called Jim Helmer twice to find out exactly what Russell had agreed to. "Take a message," Helmer had said both times. The Justice Department had never been particularly helpful to Russell, and besides, the champagne celebration he was presiding over with his staff took priority. When Helmer returned Bingaman's call the following morning, she wanted to know what everyone else did: How much had Russell gotten? The morning papers had erroneously reported that Russell had received nothing more than pension and medical coverage; Helmer knew better, but declined to reveal the settlement terms. Helmer assured Bingaman, however, that Russell had not retracted his allegations and that he would testify for the government if there was a trial. That afternoon the grand jury voted and the indictment—against GE, De Beers, Frenz, and Liotier—was approved.

Bingaman then played the same game with Heineman that Helmer had played with her. Heineman had called her that morning after his final plea to

---

* Less than a month later, Hubbell resigned from the Justice Department over billing improprieties at the Rose Law Firm, for which he served a twenty-one-month sentence at a federal prison in Cumberland, Maryland.

Hubbell had failed. When she returned Heineman's call at around 4 p.m. on February 17, it was to inform him that the indictment had been filed minutes before. The feisty Bingaman then issued a statement: "The [antitrust] division will not tolerate . . . sophisticated schemes that are used to fix prices and to disguise criminal activity."

Welch had won a big part of the battle by buying off Russell, but outright victory had eluded him. He fired off a memo of his own: "We will use all the resources of our company to fight these charges, and . . . we will prevail at trial." He was determined not to lose.

CHAPTER FOURTEEN

THE UNITED STATES OF AMERICA V. GENERAL ELECTRIC

THE AMERICAN PEOPLE have long believed in the inherent value of competition, and so has their government, to an extent that makes the United States unique in the world. No culture, no people—not the British, the South Africans, the Japanese, or the Germans—cherishes competition and cutthroat capitalism as much as the citizens of the United States. It is extolled in the pages of the *Wall Street Journal* and in *Forbes* magazine (the "capitalist tool," as its editors call their publication) and in countless how-to business books published each year that promise to reveal the ways that readers can become more competitive. And, ultimately, it is preserved not necessarily by the marketplace but in the laws of our land. The principal legal edifice for promoting competition in the realm of business is the Sherman Antitrust Act, named after Ohio Senator John Sherman, which was landmark legislation when Congress passed it in 1890.

The Sherman Act marked the first time that the federal government had intervened to combat the concentration of economic power in large corporations and in combinations of business concerns. It was, and to a large extent still is, unique in the world, for the idea of seeking to promote competition through vigorous enforcement of antitrust law is a peculiarly American notion, one that other cultures do not embrace. Nearly 80 percent of private industry in South Africa, for instance, is controlled by five superconglomerates. Cartels in some industries, like diamonds, operate openly, while in other industries, like beef and sugar, one or two producers dominate and set prices. The result of this concentration is that the average South African cannot afford goods that the average American takes for granted—steaks, cars, and televisions—because they are so expensive.

Had it not been for antitrust law, the American economy today might resemble South Africa's. Prior to the Sherman Act's passage, various states had enacted similar laws limited to intrastate business, but the phenomenal growth of the "trusts" in the latter half of the twentieth century—Cornelius Vanderbilt in railroading, John D. Rockefeller in oil, Andrew Carnegie in steel, J. Pierpont Morgan in banking—convinced Congress that only the federal government could regulate their growth and preserve competition. The act, which declared every contract, combination, or conspiracy in restraint of interstate commerce or foreign trade an offense punishable by fines and prison sentences, would have greater impact on the conduct and enforcement of American business than any other law. That was not the case at first; the new law's effectiveness was greatly reduced by Supreme Court decisions, such as one handed down in 1922 in which Justice Oliver Wendell Holmes wrote that major league baseball was exempt from antitrust laws on the grounds that "exhibitions of baseball are purely state affairs."

Other businesses were not as fortunate. IBM, for one, was reprimanded repeatedly for alleged collusion and monopolistic practices that the Justice Department's antitrust division challenged three times in lawsuits it filed, in 1933, 1952, and 1969. The net effect of these challenges was minimal; the consent decrees had little impact on Big Blue, which continued its dominance of the early tabulating, sorting, and punch-card machine industry and later in the successor mainframe computer industry. It was ultimately market forces, rather than the enforcement of antitrust law, that reined in IBM, which clung to mainframe computing and was weakened by emergent personal computing technologies offered by Apple and Microsoft, the company Bill Gates founded in 1975, whose licensing agreements with computer makers would themselves become the target of a five-year antitrust investigation. But Microsoft, like IBM before it, was left relatively unfettered under the consent decree brought by Anne Bingaman's antitrust division. It would be left to her successor, Joel Klein, to again take on Microsoft, this time over its control of Web browsers on the Internet.

Telecommunications, on the other hand, was an industry whose very structure had been fundamentally altered by antitrust law. The lawsuit the Justice Department had brought against AT&T that ended with Judge Harold Greene's historic decision, which took effect on January 1, 1984, ordering "Ma Bell" to divest its "babies"—the twenty-two local telephone companies were reorganized into seven regional holding companies—spawned competition the likes of which the telecommunications industry had never before seen, and, for shareholders, was the single greatest engine of wealth creation in this century. Today, shares of AT&T and the regional Bell companies (and their successors) have an aggregate market value of approximately $400 billion—twenty times AT&T's value before the split.

But arguably no American company had been more scarred by the violation of antitrust law than General Electric. The price-fixing and bid-rigging conspiracy of the early 1960s in the electrical-equipment industry was far and away the most widespread and brazen breach of the Sherman Act in this century. When Judge J. Cullen Ganey sentenced the forty-five defendants (eleven of them from General Electric) in his Philadelphia courtroom on a cold winter day in 1961, it was clear that what he called "a shocking indictment of a vast section of our economy" was no overstatement. Although the Justice Department hadn't assembled enough evidence to convict the highest-echelon executives, the men at the top who weren't there that day bore the "real blame," Judge Ganey asserted.

As it was, the scandal had reached well into the executive suite: Three senior GE executives were sent to prison for thirty days each, another twelve were fined and forced to resign, and Robert Paxton, then GE's president, took early retirement amid speculation that he, too, knew about the scheme. It was only the second time in the history of the Sherman Act that a U.S. business executive had been imprisoned for violating antitrust law. (William Ginn, one jailed GE vice president who before he was sent to jail often clashed with organized labor, received a jailhouse gift from James Carey, president of the International Union of Electrical Workers—the board game *Monopoly*.) An angry Ralph Cordiner, who pleaded innocence before a congressional committee charged with investigating the conspiracy, went after the transgressors with a vengeance; some executives were forced to resign even before the grand juries had returned indictments. Worse still, from the company's perspective, was the massive civil litigation that arose out of the criminal indictments, as customers in nineteen electrical product categories sought damages for the excessive prices they had paid as a result of the collusion. The lawsuits threatened to bankrupt GE, for the aggregate size of the claims far exceeded its net worth. By the time all the suits were settled five years later, GE had paid out hundreds of millions of dollars, which the company's lawyers considered a victory.

In the aftermath of the "Incredible Electrical Conspiracy," GE imposed strict codes of conduct to prevent such a scandal from ever occurring again, instituting rules that were tougher than the Sherman Act. Any contact with a competitor, even bumping into, say, a Westinghouse employee in the men's room at a trade show, required that the employee file a "Competitor Contact Form." Three decades later, however, the policies and procedures designed to head off another antitrust scandal had been ignored, and Jack Welch found himself, like Cordiner, having to defend his company against allegations of "hard-core" price-fixing. Complicating matters were two surreptitious meetings between Glen Hiner and De Beers CEO Julian Ogilvie Thompson, encounters that at the very least were problematic for General Electric, Welch conceded when Jim Helmer, Russell's attorney, deposed him on May 11, 1993. Would Welch attend a meeting with a major competitor, with no attorneys present, no minutes, no written agenda, where he had been instructed not to sign the guest register and had been ushered into a private anteroom? Helmer had asked. No, he would not, Welch replied.

Worse still, the meetings had been between two titans of the business world that throughout their respective histories had been dedicated to an ideal that was anathema to the spirit of the Sherman Act—achieving market dominance and maintaining it. Ever since its creation in 1892, General Electric had sought to control the markets in which it competed; indeed, the concept of monopolization had been the very genesis of the company, the reason Charles Coffin had combined the patent rights of his Thomson-Houston Company with those of Edison's General Electric, creating an unassailable monolith in incandescent and arc lighting, electrical distribution, railroad traction, and alternating current motors. A century later, Welch had sharpened the focus with his decree that every GE business had to achieve either a first or second ranking in market share.

De Beers was dedicated, perhaps even more fervently than GE, to the same principle of market dominance. De Beers Consolidated Mines Limited was the invention of the legendary financier Cecil John Rhodes, who in 1880 was granted a British charter to merge his interests with two large mining syndicates in South Africa. Rhodes and the men who succeeded him—Ernest Oppenheimer, his son Harry, and eventually his grandson Nicholas—would dominate the world of diamonds through their control of the De Beers organization, which for more than a century has been the most powerful monopoly in the annals of modern commerce.

Even though De Beers was a South African entity with a significant presence in Switzerland and London, well beyond the territorial domain of United States antitrust law—and therefore not obliged to observe the Sherman Act's admonition against any "combination or conspiracy in restraint of trade"— the government of the United States hadn't been deterred. While collusion and monopolies might have been business as usual in South Africa, those charged with upholding antitrust law in the United States had clung to the notion that even in the diamond trade, competition had to be preserved. On that basis the Justice Department had on three prior occasions investigated De Beers for violations of the Sherman Act, and three times had failed in its attempts, a point that was not lost on Anne Bingaman.

BINGAMAN AND HER COLLEAGUES at the antitrust division knew from the outset that they had a tough case on their hands. "Although we are convinced that the foregoing summary is an accurate depiction of the price-fixing activities of General Electric and De Beers," the next to last page of the twenty-five-page memo recommending indictment read, "we recognize that the conspiracy will be difficult to prove. The price-fixing plan was sophisticated and deliberately designed to be difficult to detect. Frenz and Liotier each have the cover of their positions to explain meetings or communications and all of the illegal meetings and the communications occurred abroad." Still, Bingaman, an experienced trial lawyer who had personally reviewed the evidence at length, was convinced that the government had a strong case.

Her conviction was bolstered by two extraordinary steps the government had taken to gather evidence. The first occurred in April 1993, when James Whitehead had been taken into custody to testify before the grand jury, an unusual arrest orchestrated by Dave Schroeder, the lead FBI agent in charge of the investigation. Schroeder was a pipe-smoking, thirty-year veteran of the FBI nearing retirement, who had been selected by J. Edgar Hoover for his personal office staff early in his career. Schroeder had done countless stakeouts and undercover work but never before had investigated a price-fixing case. What Schroeder lacked in knowledge about diamonds and antitrust law, though, he more than offset with his zeal for "the law." From the very beginning, Schroeder was convinced that the kind of aggressive tactics he had employed in prior criminal investigations—putting GE executives John Blystone and Steve Palovchik under twenty-four-hour surveillance, for instance, or seizing documents quickly rather than employing the broad document requests and protracted negotiations the antitrust division engaged in— would yield results. But the antitrust division called the shots, and while they were experts in tracing complicated events through masses of documents, they had, in Schroeder's view, no grasp of how to run a criminal investigation.

Schroeder had already tried, unsuccessfully, to contact Whitehead, Liotier's successor as head of Diamant Boart in Belgium, sending him a letter via the United States embassy in Brussels asking if he would make himself available for an interview by the FBI. Whitehead did not respond. Monopolies and price-fixing may have been illegal in America, but Whitehead wasn't American and wasn't on U.S. territory, so couldn't be compelled to respond to the letter; inquiries from an American law enforcement agency had no legal standing in Belgium. When Schroeder learned via a GE informant that Whitehead was scheduled to attend the Masters golf tournament in Augusta, Georgia, at General Electric's invitation, he suddenly had the territorial domain he needed to compel cooperation. Schroeder pounced on the opportunity, convincing Jim Clancy, one of the Justice Department attorneys handling the case, to authorize a "material witness complaint," a hardball tactic that the gentlemanly antitrust division was unaccustomed to and hadn't used before. With the necessary paperwork in hand, Schroeder took it to the United States Magistrate in Columbus, with jurisdiction over nearby Worthington, and got a warrant empowering the FBI to take Whitehead into custody on the appointed weekend.

Now they had to locate him among the tens of thousands of people who had descended on Augusta for the Masters—a formidable task, as it turned out. Two FBI agents checked the GE pavilion as well as hotels, motels, and every conceivable overnight accommodation, but Whitehead was nowhere to be found. On Easter Sunday, April 11, 1993, Schroeder was getting jittery; attending his nephew's wedding in Columbus, he spent most of the service glued to a cellular phone in the rear of the church, placing calls to Washington and Georgia. By Sunday evening, the tournament had ended, Whitehead still hadn't been found, and the Justice Department was running out of time.

Schroeder had one last scheme: On Monday morning, he called a secretary at Diamant Boart's facility in South Carolina, pretending to be a friend of Whitehead's who had missed him in Augusta. The secretary didn't know where Whitehead was but promised to relay the message. She did. The phone number Schroeder had given as the number to call was in reality a beeper attached to the agents in Georgia that immediately revealed Whitehead's whereabouts. Several hours later, he was in custody. The agents had tracked him to a chic restaurant in South Carolina, where, waiting outside until he had finished his meal, they handcuffed him, revoked his passport as a material witness to a felony, and put him on a plane for transport to Columbus and the grand jury.

Upon reaching Columbus, and after being arraigned, fingerprinted, and photographed, Whitehead protested his treatment to Schroeder. "You really didn't need to go to all this trouble," he told him. "I would have cooperated if you had asked."

"Did you get our letter?" Schroeder shot back, doing his best imitation of Eliot Ness. "Don't ignore it next time."

Whitehead's testimony yielded one statement that strengthened the government's case. One of the most incriminating documents that the prosecution had unearthed was information that Frenz had received from Liotier detailing De Beers' future pricing that Frenz had sent on to his boss Steve Palovchik, the head of international sales of GE Superabrasives in Worthington (who, in turn, reported to Russell). Such an exchange of information wasn't out of the ordinary and certainly wasn't illegal, GE claimed: what could be more natural than a customer, Liotier, passing information to Frenz, his supplier? But the most damning piece of evidence was what Frenz had written in the cover letter, dated December 16, 1991, to Palovchik: "Liotier of Diamant Boart informed me about planned price increases of De Beers in early 1992. The attached information was given to him confidentially. Please treat the information carefully. . . . Liotier is supporting a price increase and would like to know by December 18, 1991, 18.00 hours European time whether [General Electric Superabrasives] is going to follow."

If Liotier was acting like a normal customer, as GE claimed, then why would he *support* a price increase, which would be contrary to his own best interests as a customer? When asked during his appearance before the grand jury why a synthetic-diamond purchaser would behave in such a way, Whitehead could think of no reason—"you'd have to be a masochist" to do that, he replied, which was exactly what the government wanted him to say.

The second extraordinary event occurred seven months later, in November 1993, when Dave Schroeder and Arnie Celnicker, a Justice Department attorney working on the case, traveled to Brussels to search Liotier's offices at Diamant Boart. The government had been trying, unsuccessfully, to get authorities in Europe to cooperate with the investigation, for obvious reasons—the alleged price-fixing had been arranged by two Europeans, who had met on European soil, beyond the scope of the Sherman Act. At first, European authorities seemed interested in Russell's story—in September 1992, the Justice Department had arranged a meeting at Helmer's office in Cincinnati between Russell and two senior officials from the European Commission in Brussels charged with antitrust enforcement—but their enthusiasm cooled as the case progressed.

Neither Frenz nor Liotier, the alleged conspirators who had exchanged pricing information at least ten times by phone, by fax, and in person, were cooperating with the government's investigation; each had refused the FBI's request that they come to the United States. So if Schroeder were going to obtain documentation for his case, it was clear he needed to go to them. That meant securing the cooperation of either the German or the Belgian government. Schroeder had relayed his requests to the German government through the proper diplomatic channels, but the *Bundeskriminalamt*, the German equivalent of the FBI, had declined to become involved. Finally, in the fall of 1993, the Belgian government agreed to cooperate. Once the appropriate paperwork had been approved, Schroeder and Celnicker had permission to enter Belgium and, under the supervision of the Belgian state police, execute a search and seizure of documents from Diamant Boart's offices. Most important, they would finally have the opportunity to interrogate Liotier, who was scheduled to appear at a hearing in Brussels that the Belgian authorities had sanctioned.

Upon their arrival in Brussels, however, Schroeder and Celnicker discovered that Liotier had left Belgium, returning to his native France, which wasn't cooperating with the antitrust division. Liotier had resigned his position at Société Générale de Belgique, a job he had begun after stepping down as CEO of Diamant Boart in January 1992 in the midst of the alleged price-fixing. Société Générale was Belgium's most influential corporate entity, a conglomerate that encompassed financial and industrial holdings headed by Viscount Etienne Davignon, and that was the indirect owner of Diamant Boart through another Belgian holding company called Sibeka. Liotier's connections to Sibeka, of which he was a director, were crucial to the government's case, because the other principal owner of Sibeka was De Beers Centenary AG of Switzerland, part of the farflung De Beers empire. This was the intricate web of cross stock holdings and interconnections, the government alleged, that enabled Liotier to be the conduit of pricing information between General Electric and De Beers.

But Liotier's secrets would remain his own. The day he was scheduled to appear at the hearing in Brussels, he began a new job at Compagnie Financière de Suez in Paris, majority owner of Société Générale. Their prey had slipped away, and Schroeder and Celnicker were frustrated and angry. The next day, accompanied by two officers from the Belgian state police, they called on Société Générale at their headquarters building in downtown Brussels, armed with a search warrant. When they informed the receptionist why they were there, she informed them that no one was available. "I think it would be a good idea to get someone down here immediately," Jean Marie Secret, the senior Belgian police officer, replied. Schroeder had found a kindred spirit. A few minutes later, Davignon—Belgium's former foreign minister, a onetime EC commissioner, and a powerful man in Brussels—clearly irritated at the strong-arm tactics, came downstairs and escorted the group to his office. He then complained to Schroeder about Whitehead's treatment when he had been arrested in the United States.

"You treated him like a common criminal," Davignon said. Schroeder said, no, quite the contrary. "We waited until he finished his meal." It had been a cordial arrest, as far as arrests go, Schroeder maintained. The sleuths left the premises several hours later after they had finished their search of Liotier's office, and the next day they visited Diamant Boart on the outskirts of Brussels and searched several offices there, including Liotier's. As they were walking out the front door with documents they had seized, two American attorneys stopped Celnicker and Schroeder, demanding to know what had been seized. Before anyone uttered another word, Inspector Secret told the attorneys they were forbidden under Belgian law to ask questions.

"We just want to make sure you are taking these documents according to the rules," one attorney protested. "I told you not to speak and you spoke," Secret replied sternly. "This is Belgium, not the United States." For Schroeder, it was one small victory in a case that had few of them.

The government's case against the alleged conspirators would be a circumstantial one, built on nuances, and the trip to Belgium helped prosecutors assemble more nuance, ultimately convincing the grand jury that GE's claims of innocence were questionable. It may have been circumstantial evidence, but from Bingaman's vantage point it looked convincing. There were many tantalizing questions, which the indictment memo summarized in succinct fashion and which GE, despite the best efforts of some of the most talented defense attorneys in the country, hadn't answered to the department's satisfaction:

Why had De Beers informed its customers in September 1991 that it was not planning to increase prices in 1992—and might even decrease them—only to reverse itself just four months later? If Liotier were merely acting as a customer, as GE contended, why then was he provided with pricing information before any other GE customers and in some cases before GE salespeople? Why didn't Frenz inform Volkmar Murer, the GE salesman in Europe responsible for servicing the Diamant Boart account, or anyone else that he had sent GE's advance pricing information to Liotier? Why did Frenz provide Liotier with pricing data on types of industrial diamonds that Diamant Boart didn't buy in significant quantities? Why had Frenz and Liotier met eight times privately over a four-month period beginning in November 1991—the time during which all of the price increases were announced and took effect—when they had met only twice in the preceding fifteen months? Why hadn't Frenz prepared a single written report on the purpose or outcome of these meetings, as was his typical practice? Why had Frenz suddenly traveled to South Africa for five days in November 1991—he was in Johannesburg on November 11, the day Russell had been fired—against GE policy, and without having a single appointment scheduled for the entire week? And why had Glen Hiner, the head of giant GE Plastics, suddenly taken such an interest in Frenz, a lowly salesman in a business that accounted for just 0.46 percent of GE's total revenue, meeting him repeatedly in 1991 and directly communicating with him, even though they were four levels removed from each other? These were all questions raised by the prosecutors.

Why was Liotier even involved in discussions with Frenz, which continued after Liotier's temporary assignment as head of Diamant Boart had ended on January 1, 1992? This was another prosecution question. If it were a legitimate commercial contact, the appropriate person wasn't Liotier (who nonetheless met with Frenz four times *after* his temporary assignment had ended), but René Lorent, Diamant Boart's purchasing director, who told police that he never saw any GE price documents. As part of their search and seizure mission, the investigators had gone through Lorent's files, and none of the information that Frenz had passed to Liotier was there. It wasn't there, the government inferred and contended at trial, because Liotier had bypassed Lorent and given it directly to De Beers.

The government put forth "herculean efforts," in the words of federal Judge George C. Smith, who presided over the trial, to painstakingly assemble evidence supporting its case in an investigation that spanned two continents over two and a half years. Even so, prosecutors knew they would face many obstacles at trial: key witnesses and documents beyond their reach; Russell had signed an affidavit conceding that he had "no personal knowledge" of price fixing; and everyone else involved—all under the skillful supervision of GE paid counsel—denied any wrongdoing. The government, which had concluded that the evidence against Hiner wasn't strong enough to support an indictment and was unable to extradite Frenz and Liotier, didn't even have a body to put before the jury.

Despite all these obstacles, Bingaman and her colleagues were determined to take the case to trial. They believed unequivocally that GE and De Beers were guilty of "hard-core" price fixing, and guilty as well of sophisticated schemes that had been "crafted to mimic legitimate business behavior," as stated in the indictment memo. Bingaman also wanted to send a clear signal to business that the antitrust torpor of the Reagan and Bush years had ended and that her department was prepared to prosecute to the fullest extent cases involving the conduct of American and foreign companies abroad, which made up 25 percent of the pending grand jury investigations she oversaw. She was further driven, no doubt, by Welch's clear determination to give no quarter and to use any means at his disposal to fight. But perhaps the single greatest element galvanizing the prosecution was that the alleged coconspirator was a company famed for running the worldwide cartel that controlled diamond prices, a company that was so fearful of prosecution, and forfeiture of its assets, that it conducted all business in the United States through intermediaries, a company that had so little regard for U.S. law that it hadn't even bothered to show up at the arraignment, a company whose spokesman in Johannesburg, when asked to explain this nonparticipation in American legal proceedings, claimed as a reason that "we don't do business in the United States," even though the U.S. market is its single largest in the world. This was, after all, no ordinary monopolist; it was De Beers.

BEFORE ONE of the great monopolies of modern times was born—before Madison Avenue convinced the world that "diamonds are forever," creating the demand, and distribution had been brought under the control of a central sales organization, restricting the supply, and before General Electric researchers discovered how to make a synthetic version in the laboratory—the diamond was a relatively obscure crystal of pure carbon, formed in heat and pressure many miles below the ground and brought by volcanic activity to the earth's surface. That volcanic activity had brought a huge quantity of diamond to the surface in South Africa, undiscovered amid the alluvium of the Orange River until 1867, when a fifteen-year-old farm boy by the name of Erasmus Stephanus Jacobs, relaxing under a tree, discovered the first diamond in the area around Kimberley, the future home of the De Beers dynasty. A shimmering pebble some yards away in the muddy riverbank caught Jacobs's eye; he retrieved it and, returning home, gave the white stone to his youngest sister, who placed it among her playthings. The *mooi klip* they called it, Afrikaans for "pretty pebble." A month later, while playing a traditional game called Five Stones, a neighbor, Schalk van Niekerk, so admired the *mooi klip* among the other ordinary river rocks that Mrs. Jacobs gave him the white stone.

Van Niekerk put the stone through various tests and, deeming them inconclusive, sold it for a few pounds to an itinerant trader named Jack O'Reilly, who also wasn't certain if the *mooi klip* had any value. He shopped it around Hope Town, becoming the butt of jokes as every merchant dismissed the specimen as worthless save one, Lorenzo Boyes, who sent the stone to an amateur mineralogist, whose testing established that the "rounded, apparently water-worn river stone" was indeed a genuine diamond measuring $21^1/_4$ carats. Boyes sent out two prospecting parties to the site where the stone had been found, and while both returned empty-handed, he was convinced more diamonds were there. Although professional geologists pooh-poohed the likelihood of additional finds—the geology of the region was thought to be too dissimilar from places where diamonds had been found, such as India and China—in the next year other gemstones were discovered near the Vaal River. The most significant find, a fine white gemstone of 83½ carats named the Star of South Africa, was put on exhibit in Cape Town. Borrowing the Star for presentation to the Cape Assembly, Colonial Secretary Richard Southey boldly predicted: "Gentlemen, this is the rock upon which the future of South Africa will be built."

Ambitious men quickly descended upon Hope Town, and the valley of diamonds at the confluence of the Vaal and Orange Rivers. In 1871, digging began on the farm of Johannes Nicholas De Beer, who had sold his property to a group of investors for a price of 6,000 pounds—several hundred thousand dollars in today's terms. At the same time, an eighteen-year-old named Cecil Rhodes—fifth son of the Rev. Francis Rhodes, vicar of St. Michael's Church in Bishop's Stortford, Hertfordshire, England—landed in South Africa, against the wishes of his parents, and set out on horseback for the diamond fields.

Rhodes's lifelong ambition to attend Oxford had been thwarted by lackluster school marks and insufficient income, but by the time he returned home to England a little more than two years later he had accumulated ample wealth to study at Oxford; his claims in the De Beers mine were already worth almost twice what Johannes De Beer had received for his property. But while at Oxford, Rhodes fell seriously ill with lung disease and, on the advice of a specialist who thought he had no more than six months to live, he returned to sunny South Africa. He lived twenty-eight more years, a time in which he became the most feared and admired white man in nineteenth-century Africa, an "immense and brooding spirit," as his friend Rudyard Kipling called him.

As it would turn out, the abundance of diamonds in South Africa presented a problem for Rhodes and other prominent British financiers who had invested in the early industry. Diamonds were being scooped out of the earth by the ton with steam shovels, and this incredible oversupply threatened to undermine their status as a precious gem, and their price, which depended almost entirely on their scarcity. The major investors realized that they had no alternative but to merge their interests into a single entity that would be powerful enough to control production and, by any means necessary, perpetuate scarcity. The instrument they created in 1880 for this purpose was called De Beers Consolidated Mines Limited, and the man chosen to head De Beers was Cecil Rhodes, appropriately enough since he and his investors now owned a major portion of the De Beers mine.

Rhodes built De Beers into a dynasty that was unrivaled in his lifetime. Building upon an earlier French scheme to monopolize copper, he snapped up from his headquarters in Kimberley every other large diamond mine in South Africa save one—the Kimberley Central mine owned by Barney Barnato, who, like Rhodes, was an English subject who had emigrated to South Africa in 1873. By 1887, Rhodes and Barnato, both in their mid-thirties, controlled the world's two giant diamond mines, and a confrontation between these two enormously ambitious men was inevitable. In the end, Rhodes was the victor, enlisting the support of the most powerful bankers in Europe, who believed that diamond mining would only remain profitable if a monopoly was created that could systematically restrict the supply. They advanced Rhodes the money that enabled him to purchase a controlling interest of the Kimberley Central mine, an acquisition made easier when De Beers dumped its inventory of diamonds, driving down the price of the gemstone as well as of diamond stocks, including Barnato's. By the time Barnato realized what had occurred, Rhodes controlled his company, and Barnato had surrendered.

By 1890, the same year the United States Congress passed the Sherman Act and two years before Charles Coffin engineered the creation of General Electric, Rhodes controlled more than 95 percent of the world's diamond production. To get better balance between supply and demand, he reduced production in Kimberley from three to two million carats a year, which was channeled through a single distribution outlet in London, a syndicate of merchants who sold the diamonds to cutters in Antwerp. With the diamond monopoly firmly established, Rhodes devoted the final years of his life to restoring the British Empire in Africa, organizing a military putsch that challenged Boer settlers in the Transvaal, and colonizing a large portion of central Africa. When he died in 1901 at the age of forty-nine, he was buried on a remote mountaintop in Rhodesia. He had never married, had no heirs—the bulk of his fortune was left to Oxford to pay the tuition of future Rhodes scholars, among them Ben Heineman, GE's general counsel—and his death left a vacuum at De Beers. It was soon filled by another young entrepreneur, Ernest Oppenheimer, who arrived in South Africa the following year.

A member of a Jewish merchant family that was well connected in the diamond world, Oppenheimer was only sixteen years old when he left Friedberg, Germany, and began sorting rough diamonds in the London office of A. Dunkelsbuhler, one of the founders of the syndicate that Rhodes had contracted with in 1893 as the sole distributor of his company's diamond output. Oppenheimer had his heart set on going to the diamond fields, and in 1902 he was sent to South Africa to run Dunkelsbuhler's small office in Kimberley, where he got a thorough education in the inner workings of the syndicate—and gained insight into De Beers' weaknesses.

The men who succeeded Rhodes as leaders of the diamond monopoly believed in their own invincibility, and they scoffed at reports, made public in 1908, of a major find some six hundred miles northwest of Kimberley, just over the South African border in the German colony of Southwest Africa (now Namibia). Oppenheimer later went there to assess for himself the various properties that the Germans called the *Sperrgebiet* (forbidden zone). What he discovered was the richest diamond field in the history of the world, a stretch of beach so strewn with gemstones that the native people could scoop them up with their bare hands.

Although the Germans had broken the De Beers monopoly, the onset of World War I saved the cartel from ruin. Oppenheimer turned the war to his advantage, as he would again twenty-five years later in a second European conflict. He had previously organized a gold-mining company called Anglo American Corporation, which had the financial backing of British and German investors, as well as the American financier J. P. Morgan. With the outbreak of war, the German investors who controlled the Namibian diamond beach were in a state of near panic, fearing their holdings would be expropriated by the British Commonwealth. Oppenheimer offered them a deal they couldn't refuse—their diamonds in exchange for shares in Anglo American. Oppenheimer, who acquired almost all of the German properties, now had the bargaining chip he needed to gain control of De Beers, which feared the huge supply of diamonds under his control. He eventually traded the Namibian mines to De Beers in exchange for a large block of stock, and in 1929 became chairman of the board. Oppenheimer, a naturalized British citizen, was then knighted by the King of England for his services to the Empire.

The Depression was not kind to Oppenheimer—lack of demand drove De Beers's production down from more than two million carats in 1930 to just fourteen thousand carats in 1933—but even more disturbing, diamonds now began turning up all over Africa. In 1930, a De Beers mining engineer warned, "The diamond market is dependent for its smooth function on the maintenance of the illusion in the minds of the general public that the diamond is a rare and valuable stone." A De Beers director agreed, "For goodness sake, keep out of the newspapers and parliament the quantity of diamonds that can be produced and put on the market."

Oppenheimer went to extraordinary lengths to ensure that the scarcity of diamonds wasn't merely an illusion. In the early 1920s, commercial mining was abandoned at America's only diamond mine in southwest Arkansas (Hil-

lary Clinton wore a gemstone from this mine at her husband's first inaugura-
tion) after the principals of the Arkansas Diamond Corporation met in the
New York office of J. P. Morgan with Oppenheimer, who bought the mine and
then shut it down; a Justice Department investigation was unable to determine if the mine had been closed illegally or simply because it was unprofitable. But this supply was a pittance compared with the vast quantity of stones
flooding the market from newly discovered mines in the Belgian Congo. There
was no market for these diamonds because of the Depression, but De Beers
had to continue buying them up, and by 1937 it had built a stockpile of some
forty million carats, a nearly twenty years' supply.

Two events intervened to save Oppenheimer, who, according to one
United States government report, was so despondent he had considered
dumping much of his stockpile into the North Sea to prevent the diamonds
from reaching market in the event his company was forced into liquidation by
creditors. The first was a private treaty Oppenheimer reached with the Belgian
government, which agreed to sell the output from its Forminière mines in the
Congo to De Beers in exchange for his commitment to provide the Belgian
cutting industry with the lion's share of gemstones from his mines. (To further
increase his leverage over the Congo mines, Oppenheimer also bought a large
stake in Sibeka, the Belgian holding company that Philippe Liotier would
become a director of, which owned the Congo mines; Sibeka later acquired a
50 percent stake in De Beers's industrial-diamond manufacturing outside
South Africa.)

The second event was the invention of the diamond grinding wheel. Suddenly, there was another use for diamonds besides as sparkling keepsakes.
Poorly crystallized, subgemstone-quality stones, called bort, could be crushed
into a fine powder, which when impregnated on a grinding wheel made an
ideal abrasive surface in the mass production of automobiles, airplanes, and
machinery. With Europe rearming for war, De Beers had the demand it
needed to dispose profitably of its enormous stockpile.

The significance of industrial diamonds was clear not only to Oppenheimer but to Allied and Axis war planners. The hardest substance known to
man, diamonds were vital to the war effort for the mass production of the
weapons and instruments of war, thus converting civilian industries into a
war machine. The Allies were stockpiling any stones they could obtain, but De
Beers's exclusive control of the entire world supply concerned President Roosevelt, who ordered the War Production Board, at that time headed by Charles
Wilson, on a wartime leave from the GE presidency, to buy from De Beers a
6.5-million-carat supply of nongem-quality diamonds to be kept on U.S. soil.

Oppenheimer refused to relinquish control, calling American fears of a shortage "farcical." FDR searched for a diplomatic solution and tried to enlist the support of Winston Churchill's war cabinet in London to pressure Oppenheimer. The British government, however, was reluctant to press De Beers; an investigation by U.S. intelligence determined why: "The diamond section of the government [which was staffed by former executives of De Beers] and the syndicate seem to be the same." Finally, the United States State Department played its trump card, threatening in a confidential memo, dated April 16, 1942, to stop selling warplanes to the British unless Oppenheimer parted with his precious stockpile. A compromise of sorts was reached, as Oppenheimer agreed to sell the United States one million carats, a fraction of the government's original request.

Germany, meanwhile, seemed to have little trouble obtaining the diamonds needed for its war machine. In November 1943, the OSS (forerunner of the CIA) learned via its agents in Germany that Hitler had only an eight-month supply. The agency investigated the supply pipeline, and an agent code-named Teton reported back from Leopoldville in the Belgian Congo that diamonds from the Forminière mines—the same ones that had been under syndicate control since the treaty Oppenheimer had reached with the Belgian government—were being smuggled in Red Cross parcels via Cairo and Tangiers to the Axis powers at thirty times the official price. The smuggling continued throughout the war; the only thing that would have prevented it was a complete suspension of mining in the Congo, which Oppenheimer steadfastly opposed.

By the end of 1943, the Roosevelt administration, enraged over Oppenheimer's tacit support of the Nazis as well as the cartel's unwillingness to provide larger supplies to the Allies, directed the Justice Department to initiate an antitrust investigation against De Beers. With the assistance of the War Production Board, which still wanted control of the diamond stockpile, and the OSS, the Justice Department gathered a wealth of information that showed how De Beers had exerted its influence globally to monopolize the world diamond market. A 1944 memo to the attorney general concluded, "The United States is paying monopoly prices for an essential material needed in wartime production." If De Beers were an American company, the memo noted, "There would be no question as to [its] having violated the antitrust laws." But even the wartime Justice Department, unencumbered by postwar civil liberties that would later restrict evidence-gathering activities, was hampered by the same lack of jurisdiction that would confound Anne Bingaman's antitrust division. The syndicate sold its diamonds to only a select group of handpicked dealers in the United States; De Beers officials avoided coming to America; all transactions took place in London; and the bank accounts De Beers had in the United States were closed just as the investigation began. The assistant attorney generals who spearheaded the investigation reluctantly concluded that they had little chance of bringing De Beers to justice in the United States, and they abandoned their case in late 1945.

In the early 1970s, the Justice Department thought it had finally found the territorial link it needed to bring De Beers to justice. Acting on complaints it had received from industrial diamond customers who believed they were paying too much for their supplies, the antitrust division investigated a scheme in which De Beers had covertly bought control of several companies in the United States that distributed industrial diamonds. In December 1971, a grand jury was convened, and over the course of the next few years government attorneys interviewed dozens of informants and scrutinized a bewildering maze of some three hundred interlocking companies either partly or fully controlled by Oppenheimer interests, many of them incorporated in Luxembourg, Liechtenstein, Switzerland, and other nations friendly to the Oppenheimer family. The government's case against De Beers seemed airtight. It even found a South African solicitor willing to serve the indictment on De Beers in South Africa who later wrote an affidavit recounting his experience. The De Beers representative tore it up, threw it to the ground, stomped on it— and then threw the lawyer out.

The Justice Department's suit didn't fare much better. Harry Oppenheimer, Ernest's son and successor as head of the cartel, sold off the companies in question, and in the end the antitrust division had to settle for a token victory, a plea bargain on the charge of price-fixing with two small U.S. distributors of diamond grit that had ties to De Beers—in 1975, they pled *nolo contendere* to the charges and paid inconsequential fines.

GIVEN DE BEERS'S HISTORY as one of the leading monopolists of the world—as well as its frequent and bitter battles with the United States government—a prudent businessman might have been wary when meeting with the head of De Beers. This would be especially so for Glen Hiner, since he headed De Beers's only significant rival in synthetic diamonds.

When asked in depositions and during the trial to explain this first meeting in September 1989 (there would be another two years later), Hiner repeated the explanation he had given Ed Russell at the time, one that didn't make sense to Russell. The purpose, Hiner said, was to bring to De Beers's

attention a practice by one of its European distributors that GE considered inappropriate—an Italian company named Escanazi that Russell believed
was paying kickbacks to win Italian customers. Hiner had informed Russell in
August that he intended to take up the issue directly, face-to-face, with Julian
Ogilvie Thompson, the chairman of De Beers. Russell thought it odd that
someone of Hiner's rank would intervene in an issue as trivial as the one
involving Escanazi, and he also couldn't believe that Ogilvie Thompson, one
of the most powerful businessmen on the planet, would want to meet if that
was the sole topic on the agenda.

Knowing how Hiner loved to hobnob with the rich and famous, Russell
assumed he was merely succumbing to the sparkling allure of De Beers. And,
to some extent, who could blame him? After all, the headquarters of the De
Beers syndicate at 17 Charterhouse Street, a modern glass-and-stone structure
in the heart of London's financial district, was a fabled place that welcomed
only the invited. In international business circles De Beers was royalty. Smoking cigars and swilling brandy with the Oppenheimer family was a temptation
Hiner couldn't resist, Russell reasoned. ("Decadence meets sleaze" was
how Russell later characterized the encounters between Hiner and Ogilvie
Thompson.)

As the mecca of the world's diamond industry, 17 Charterhouse was
home to the Central Selling Organization, the organization Rhodes had established in 1893 as the conduit for De Beers's diamonds, and the place where
even today diamond dealers pay their respects every fifth Monday of the year
for an event called a "sight." There, gathered around a long mahogany table on
the fourth floor, the world's wealthiest diamond merchants are quietly handed
cardboard boxes that contain the rough-cut stones they have been allocated
for that period, unglamorous rocks that will be cut and polished into precious
keepsakes for brides throughout the world.

Although merchants have tried over the years to procure their diamonds
outside the syndicate—and countries such as Russia, which mines more than
25 percent of the world's stones, have tried to bypass it—they have learned the
folly of such disloyalty. The diamond godfathers do not view unfriendly acts
kindly, and they have absolute dominion over their business. Such is the
power the syndicate wields that in 1979, when the Central Selling Organization
moved its headquarters up the street from No. 2 to No. 17 Charterhouse Street,
dealers were told to pay their respects, in the form of a cash donation to fur-
nish the new location. More than ten thousand dollars was considered vulgar,
less than five thousand paltry, but money, to be sure, wasn't the point; paying
homage to the Oppenheimer family was. De Beers could certainly afford any

decor it chose, and so could the dealers, thanks largely to De Beers, so if their liege had demanded ten million dollars each, they would out of necessity have had to pay up.

The man Hiner called on in September 1989, Sir Julian Ogilvie Thompson, has a pedigree as world diamond kingpin that is as impeccable as the flawless stones he dispenses. Educated at Oxford as, of course, a Rhodes scholar, he wears Savile Row suits, drinks the finest brandy, and smokes the finest Cuban cigars. Ogilvie Thompson joined Anglo American's London office in 1956 and by 1982 had assumed command of Anglo American and its De Beers unit upon Harry Oppenheimer's retirement, becoming the first person outside the Oppenheimer family to fill that role since Cecil Rhodes.

For Hiner, the son of a coal miner who had grown up dirt-poor in West Virginia, the chance to dine alone with Ogilvie Thompson was an opportunity he simply couldn't pass up, regardless of the risks it might entail. Hiner had expensive tastes, and he loved to entertain customers and friends in opulent ways. Pebble Beach, California, was a favorite hideaway of his; each year, he would rent the entire lodge there for a week, chauffeuring guests in antique Rolls Royce limousines to sumptuous dinners.

Russell, on the other hand, considered any contact with De Beers unwise for two reasons. The first was De Beers's unequivocal position as South Africa's leading corporation. The year before, GE had implemented Policy 20.12, which restricted contact and involvement with South African entities, a policy adopted in conjunction with the board's decision to withdraw from South Africa. General Electric had joined the growing list of American companies that had—in theory at least—protested apartheid, including General Motors, IBM, Coca-Cola, and Warner Communications. The more than thirteen hundred businesses in South Africa that Anglo American controlled accounted for 25 percent of the country's economic output and included the De Beers and Minorco mining companies; First National, the country's biggest bank; Southern Life, one of the biggest insurers; and at least one significant player in every sector of the economy. There could be no denying that Anglo American and De Beers were South African entities, which, if the policy had any real meaning, were supposedly proscribed.

The more important issue that troubled Russell was the antitrust implications that meeting with De Beers raised. In addition to having low tolerance for risk, Russell was a stickler for rules. During his time in Mexico, he had reported a bribe incident to superiors in Cleveland. Bribes were such a commonplace event in Latin America that some superiors thought Russell's report was laughable and questioned his sanity for raising such a fuss. Ironically,

Russell's reputation as a Boy Scout was one of the reasons Welch had chosen him to head Superabrasives upon the discovery of some bookkeeping hanky-panky there. Russell brought his zeal for policies and procedures to Worthington. He felt his subordinates needed to be educated about the diamond cartel—who De Beers was, how they behaved, what they did in the marketplace to maintain dominance—and one of his first acts was to distribute copies of a book, *The Diamond Invention*, a history of the De Beers cartel by Edward Jay Epstein.

What was normal concern on Russell's part over the meeting between Hiner and Ogilvie Thompson, however, became alarm when Russell learned that Hiner intended to meet with Ogilvie Thompson without any attorneys present. The two men who together controlled upward of 80 percent of the world's synthetic diamond business would be meeting and dining alone, without a written agenda, without attorneys, without minutes, nothing to verify what was said. Russell considered that in itself prima facie violation of Policy 20.5, "twenty-five" as it was known inside GE, the policy crafted after the "Incredible Electrical Conspiracy" under which company personnel were supposed to avoid in their conduct even the appearance of impropriety. "No employee shall attend or remain present," the policy read, "at any surreptitious meeting of competitors." Hiner's meeting was clearly surreptitious—it was being held in private on De Beers's own property—and it was clearly a meeting of competitors.

Even if nothing untoward took place, a private meeting between Hiner and Ogilvie Thompson would give customers and law enforcement agencies a very real appearance of impropriety.* On the basis of all this, Russell questioned Hiner's plans, though in a way that probably only galvanized Hiner's resolve. "Do you know who these guys are?" Russell recalls asking, in the schoolmarmish tone that Hiner had come to resent. "Don't worry, Ed, I know how to handle myself."

In March 1990, six months after their initial meeting, Hiner and Ogilvie Thompson exchanged letters (neither of which was produced by GE; Russell saved a copy of the letter Hiner received, despite instructions that he "toss" it). In November, a second meeting was scheduled but cancelled at the last minute for reasons that the Justice Department was unable to ascertain.

---

* Eventually Welch was forced to concede this in his deposition before trial; the defense team viewed it as very problematic. The outcome of the case "was not a sure thing," one attorney on the defense team told the *American Lawyer*. "The case had this atmosphere—where people are going to meetings and smoking cigars at fancy hotels in London and stuff—that we knew there may have been jurors out there that would nail us."

Also in November 1990, Hiner initiated communications with Peter Frenz, the European sales manager, contacts that Hiner's own secretary, Louise Koval, later characterized as "extraordinary" because they violated the chain of command, which was as follows: Frenz, last on the totem pole, who reported to Steve Palovchik, who reported to Russell, who reported to Hiner, who reported to Welch. Hiner had contacted Frenz, without informing either Russell or Palovchik, to plan a meeting in Brussels, which took place on February 12, 1991, between Hiner, Etienne Davignon, Frenz, and Philippe Liotier, the last two, of course, the indicted parties who, the government alleged, carried out the price-fixing. Although the defense team contended that the purpose of the meeting was merely social, that claim was undercut by communication exchanged between Frenz and Hiner beforehand, including one memo in which Frenz spelled out the details of the corporate connections between Davignon, chairman of Société Générale; Liotier, a director of Sibeka, which was 54 percent owned by Société Générale; and De Beers, which owned 20 percent of Sibeka.

During the trial, Russell testified that this meeting had established the mechanism for the price-fixing. Several days after the meeting, Russell testified, he received an electronic-mail message in which Frenz wrote that he and Liotier had agreed to handle a "special project" at Hiner's request. Russell called Frenz to inquire what he was referring to and was told that Hiner had suggested to Davignon that Frenz and Liotier could work together to help "stabilize prices," testimony that was ruled admissible over GE's vigorous objection.

The lack of price discipline was a much-discussed topic within General Electric. Be it aircraft engines, refrigerators, lightbulbs, or medical diagnostic equipment, customers were increasingly price-sensitive. But the situation in synthetic diamonds was particularly puzzling to Welch and Hiner, a business that was, after all, an oligopoly of the most concentrated sort. The more than 80-percent share of the world business that GE and De Beers together controlled was a remarkable hegemony for modern capitalism—by contrast, GE and Whirlpool, the two top refrigerator makers, together controlled less than half of just the United States market. Yet despite near absolute dominance in synthetic diamonds, the two top players seemed not only unable to raise prices, they couldn't even maintain them. That partly was a reflection of the changing dynamics of the industry; as more newcomers jumped into the fray, particularly in Asia and Europe, this tail increasingly wagged the pricing dog of GE and De Beers. But GE's inability to assert control in the pricing realm was also a reflection, Hiner and Welch were convinced, of Russell's lack of leadership. Indeed, it was a meeting in Fairfield with Welch, on July 11, 1991, that was the beginning of the end for Russell, a meeting in which he told Welch and Hiner that overall he anticipated a 3 percent price *decline* in each of the next three or four years. Not long thereafter, Russell was out of the loop, price increases were suddenly in the works, and the Frenz-Liotier connection was in high gear.

Hiner's relationship with Ogilvie Thompson also got cozier in the months that followed. On July 22, 1991, eleven days after Russell had issued his forecast of falling prices, Hiner floated the idea of direct cooperation with De Beers in a meeting in Pittsfield with Russell and his staff, specifically suggesting the possibility of exchanging technical information. Once the meeting had ended and Hiner had left, the six people who stayed behind, including Russell, openly questioned what plausible reason Hiner might have for wanting to meet with De Beers. The very idea of technical exchange seemed ludicrous. When asked some fourteen months later to summarize the sentiment expressed that day, Mark Sneeringer of Russell's staff gave the following recollection when he was asked to "generally describe what happened in the informal discussion after Mr. Hiner left":

"Opinions were expressed that meeting with De Beers was not a good idea."

When he was asked if there was a reason stated as to why it was not a good idea, he said:

"The reasons that I remember were that there had been no such meetings with De Beers in the past, there was a potential problem of customers getting a misperception as far as what the meeting meant, and there was a strong opinion that telling De Beers the state of our technology would give them a competitive advantage which they might capitalize on to cause us harm in the marketplace."

The next day, Hiner, who was insistent on pursuing his idea of a technical exchange, called Russell and instructed him to prepare a briefing paper of technical topics that could be discussed with De Beers. Russell suspected that the technical exchange was merely an excuse to follow up on the pricing issues that had been raised during the Davignon luncheon in Brussels. The agenda Hiner was proposing made no sense to Russell. Hiner had virtually no knowledge of synthetic-diamond technology and had shown little prior interest in it. Only once, for a total of five minutes, had he toured the diamond manufacturing facilities in Worthington. Although Hiner's plans to meet De Beers concerned him, Russell felt powerless to do anything about it. And on several occasions he confided his concerns about his own fate to his secretary, Denise

Maurer, who grew tired of listening to him. "I asked him on more than one occasion, 'Why don't you just do something about it?' 'I can't,' he'd say. 'Why?' 'They would fire me. My life would be ruined.' "

The best protest Russell could muster under the circumstances was contained, he claimed, in the briefing paper. Written by Mark Sneeringer, the contents and fate of the briefing paper became a major subplot in a case filled with intrigue and deception. Suspicious of Hiner's motives and feeling powerless to do anything about his meeting with De Beers, Russell instructed Sneeringer to include in the briefing paper a warning about the potential antitrust ramifications of such a meeting. When Russell delivered the paper to Hiner in Pittsfield on September 3, 1991—the day before they met with Welch, and two days before Welch ordered Russell's termination—Russell testified that he pointed at the antitrust warning and said: "This is what concerns us," to which he said Hiner replied, "The Chairman knows what I'm doing, okay?"

That comment, which Hiner denied having made, upped the stakes for Welch, because it suggested that Welch may have decided to fire Russell not for poor performance—Welch's contention, for which there was little supporting evidence—but instead because Russell was a whistleblower, which in fact Russell never had been. However, the briefing paper did contain an antitrust warning—watered down after several revisions—and the fact that the draft of it hadn't been turned over initially by GE, and that the final paper was missing, strengthened Russell's whistleblower claim, and left Magistrate Steinberg suspicious about what had happened to it.

"Did you destroy the [briefing paper]?" Steinberg inquired of Hiner during a hearing in his Cincinnati courtroom on November 23, 1993.

"No, I did not."

"Did you cause anyone else to destroy the [briefing paper]?" Steinberg asked, glaring at Hiner from the bench.

"No, I did not."

Although Hiner acknowledged having received the briefing paper, he couldn't recall looking at it prior to or during his second meeting in London with Ogilvie Thompson on September 20—another meeting in which no attorneys were present—even though the stated purpose of the meeting was to discuss technical issues with which he was admittedly unfamiliar. The witness who followed Hiner that day, his secretary Louise Koval (who gave Hiner a warm embrace before the hearing began), testified she had found the file she had prepared for Hiner's London trip but that the briefing paper was inexplicably missing.

Steinberg concluded that there was enough legitimate dispute over the material facts surrounding the briefing paper to merit sending the whistleblower portion of Russell's claims to a jury. "This man deserves his day in court," he pronounced at the conclusion of the hearing. That decision gave Jim Helmer, Russell's attorney, the lever he needed to extract a settlement that was favorable to him and his client but threatened the Justice Department's criminal case.

HELMER WAS MORE SKILLED in his handling of the civil case than the government was in its criminal prosecution, which commenced in a Columbus courtroom on October 25, 1994.

The trial was effectively over before it began. Galvanized by Welch's resolve to win—Welch was briefed at the conclusion of every trial day—Dan Webb led a team of about a dozen lawyers from several firms, supported by about a dozen more in Chicago and Washington. Working out of an office in Columbus, the defense trial team was an ad hoc law firm, typically beginning their day around 7:30 a.m. and ending it well after midnight. Virtually all of them had been involved in the case from the start—a distinct advantage over their chief adversary, Max Gillam, who had been brought in by Bingaman only a year before—and they had thorough knowledge of the federal rules of evidence, which greatly influenced the outcome of the trial.

Even before the trial began, for instance, the defense team convinced Judge Smith in pretrial arguments to delay testimony of the prosecution's first three witnesses. These witnesses, whose testimony was later excluded altogether, were critical to the government's case. One witness was a Harvard Business School professor, an expert on the De Beers diamond cartel, who was supposed to spell out for the jury De Beers's history of market collusion, as well as corporate connections between De Beers and Diamant Boart, to establish the government's contention that Liotier was effectively working for De Beers. The other two witnesses were the Belgian police officers, Inspector Secret and his assistant, whose report on their search and seizure of documents in Belgium was held up by litigation Diamant Boart had initiated in Belgium and whose testimony was ruled inadmissible.

With many important witnesses excluded at the start, the government was forced to rely on Russell more heavily than it might have wanted to. As it turned out, Russell wasn't silenced by the terms of his settlement with GE—Gillam got him to repeat the claims he had made in his civil suit—but he might as well have been. Webb, a skilled court orator who gained fame during the Iran-contra prosecution for his questioning of Oliver North, as well as former President Ronald Reagan, who years before had named Webb U.S. Attorney for the Northern District of Illinois, rattled Russell in three days of cross-examination. Russell came off looking vindictive.

GE was also aided by the government's poor presentation of the case—Gillam looked clumsy and unsure, compared with the smooth Webb, misspeaking many times and often referring to documents in evidence books that were either missing or misplaced—and by certain witnesses whose testimony was different from what they had told the grand jury. James Whitehead, the Diamant Boart executive who had been arrested after attending the Masters golf tournament and who had told the grand jury that only a "masochist" would support a price increase, voluntarily returned to the United States to tell the jury several previously forgotten reasons why his company would do that. Asked to explain the discrepancy in his prior testimony, Whitehead replied: "Well, you arrested me, you imprisoned me, and you put me on a late night plane. I didn't arrive here until early in the morning, and I got no sleep that night. So, my recollection possibly wasn't at its best." Another Diamant Boart official, Carl Roemmele, who had previously told the grand jury that he hadn't gotten advance word of GE's price move, also changed his testimony. When the government had seemingly impeached Roemmele's credibility, he was able to produce a memo he claimed had been written at the time that proved he had gotten advance word—conveniently faxed, in midtrial, by Diamant Boart, which had steadfastly refused to respond to Justice Department subpoenas throughout the government's investigation. Even the one witness that the government had granted immunity to in exchange for his testimony, Steve Palovchik, who spent more time on the stand than anyone other than Russell, apparently was less convincing than he had been before the grand jury. When Denise Maurer, a friend of Palovchik's, read newspaper accounts of what he had said, she called him and accused him of wimping out. Palovchik, a tall man with square shoulders and an athletic build, replied: "The government totally botched it up." Better lawyers could have gotten the truth out of him, he said. After finishing the conversation, Maurer called Justice Department attorney Celnicker and pleaded with him to put Palovchik back on the stand.

"I appreciate your call," Celnicker said, "but this is almost over. Just forget about it."

In the end, it was a rout—and a bizarre culmination to one of the oddest cases in the annals of antitrust law. At 3:45 p.m. on Monday, December 5, Judge Smith called for a break in the defense's case, which had begun the week before, and asked that Gillam and three other counsel at the prosecution table come to his quarters. There, he informed them that he had decided to grant GE's motion for a judgment of acquittal. The judge had determined that even viewing all evidence in a light most favorable to the prosecution, the government had failed to prove the most crucial element of its case—that Liotier had acted on behalf of De Beers when he passed De Beers' sensitive pricing information onto GE. The prosecution team was shocked; acquittal motions are rarely granted, and they can't be appealed if rendered in midtrial. Immediately afterward, Judge Smith, in the privacy of his chambers, asked those jurors who would have voted for conviction to raise their hands. Only three did. He felt vindicated.

Thus ended the biggest, highest-profile antitrust case that the Justice Department had brought in more than a decade, with the antitrust division more than living up to its reputation of losing the few cases they do take to trial. It was a huge setback for Bingaman, whose efforts to revive antitrust enforcement and establish a bolder and more aggressive agenda had been torpedoed. About a month after the trial had ended, Bingaman's rival in antitrust enforcement, Robert Pitofsky, chairman of the Federal Trade Commission, hired one of the men who had defeated her, William Baer of Arnold & Porter, as his top antitrust enforcer at the FTC.

Although Gillam was gracious in defeat—he stopped and shook Webb's hand—he remains convinced to this day that Judge Smith erred badly. "This judge was not an evidence rocket scientist," Gillam told the *American Lawyer* a week later. "Almost every ruling he made excluding evidence, and that includes the Rule 29 [acquittal] ruling, was wrong. I like Smith as a man—I just think he was terribly wrong in this case. . . . There's no doubt in my mind that this case had to be brought and that GE is guilty as hell."

Judge Smith, who issued a mountain of written rulings and orders in the case, ninety-one in all, remains equally convinced that the government simply didn't prove that the indicted parties had conspired to fix prices. "You've got connections, innuendo, and things happening, but you also have legitimate reasons for them meeting and exchanging information," he said three days later. "They may have done this for all I know, but we're dealing with what came out in the courtroom."

Russell—the "village idiot," as John Blystone referred to him during a chance encounter several weeks later with FBI agent Schroeder at the Columbus Mall—heard the news via a fax from his wife, Shirley, to his hotel in Beijing, where he was buying lightbulb companies for Sylvania. GE had won, but the reaction at Superabrasives headquarters was surprisingly subdued. There was no open celebration like the one that had followed Russell's capitulation when he had signed his affidavit the February before. Perhaps it was subdued because even in victory, the participants could plainly see the wages of war. Jack Welch's decision that Russell had "to go" had had stunning consequences for GE Superabrasives, and for the entire corporation—not the least of which was the money GE had spent defending itself (a sum considerably more than the maximum $10 million fine it would have paid in the event of a guilty verdict). GE's reputation had been besmirched, and the attentions of its executives had been diverted for three years. But of course Welch *could* claim vindication and victory.

CHAPTER FIFTEEN

————————

THE RECKONING

WITH JUDGE SMITH'S DECISION and after thirteen turbulent but, from Wall Street's perspective, hugely successful years at the helm of General Electric, after fifty-one consecutive quarters of earnings gains, after increasing the value of GE's stock from $12 billion in 1981 to $90 billion early in 1994 and making the company the most valuable and arguably most powerful in the United States, Jack Welch at the age of fifty-eight had earned, by most measures, the right to universal acclaim. He was still receiving adulation as America's most rapacious chief executive—"a lion" of the "corporate jungle," Ken Auletta, the respected chronicler of the broadcasting industry, called him in one *New Yorker* piece on NBC. But, like Sisyphus, Welch seemed unable to reach his mountaintop. The misadventure at GE kept blemishing his otherwise outstanding financial achievements.

There was a certain irony in it all. As the stock went ever higher, the scandals reached a crescendo as well, each one worse than the one that had preceded it, as if Welch were a figure in a Shakespearean tragedy. In the 1980s, there had been the refrigerator fiasco, the whistleblower lawsuits, and the Philadelphia Pentagon fraud cases, one ending in a guilty plea, the other a conviction. All were problematic, to be sure, but in each instance, the business media and investors shrugged. As the years passed, however, the misadventures became more noticeable. In 1992, there was Infact's Oscar-winning portrayal of GE's nuclear activities culminating with Debra Chasnoff's exhortation to "boycott GE," and, just four months later, the settlement of the Dotan affair, with Welch giving his mea culpa of sorts (live on C-Span, no less) to John Dingell's subcommittee. In 1993 came the succession of calamities at NBC—the rigged truck crash on the news-magazine show *Dateline* and the loss of David Letterman to CBS. And in 1994, of course, the diamond caper, which, despite the end result, had created a huge wave of bad publicity.

The biggest and most costly scandal of all, in terms of financial and job losses, was yet to come. This scandal, which began to unfold in the spring of 1994, involved GE's Kidder, Peabody securities firm, and it caught Welch completely off guard. His first warning that something was amiss came when Michael Carpenter, his onetime strategic planner in the mid-'80s whom he had installed in 1989 as head of troubled Kidder, approached him in April at Fairfield headquarters and confided that he was having a reconciliation problem. Although Carpenter said he didn't believe there would be any impact on the bottom line, three days later he reversed that assessment—and said the impact could be as great as $350 million. A horde of GE auditors and investigators descended on Kidder's headquarters at 10 Hanover Square in lower Manhattan, one block from Wall Street. What they found was disastrous.

The Kidder debacle, which began with accusations leveled by the firm against a thirty-six-year-old bond trader by the name of Orlando Joseph Jett, ultimately cost GE $1.2 billion in 1994, before Kidder was liquidated and its remains sold to rival PaineWebber. The entire dizzying implosion occurred in the space of just six months, one of the most sudden and catastrophic failures in the history of Wall Street, eclipsing even the spectacular fall of Michael Milken's Drexel Burnham Lambert, which survived for more than three years before the junk-bond scandal sank it in 1990.

To his credit, Welch doesn't dally in a crisis. By early summer, just two months after Carpenter had uttered his fateful warning, Welch had sacked him, along with much of Kidder's senior management, replacing them with trusted lieutenants from Fairfield. He had taken the public relations offensive, appearing on NBC cable-TV airwaves (CNBC) to disseminate a favorable version of events and calm unnerved investors. And by July, Welch was even able to make light of the situation. During an awards ceremony at the Metropolitan Club in New York, Welch, as the 1993 "Chief Executive of the Year" (as determined by *Chief Executive* magazine) passed the mantle to the 1994 winner, Bill Gates, CEO of Microsoft. After being introduced as one of America's great assets, Welch smiled and took the podium.

"A year ago, I was selected as the chief executive of the year for my vision, my brilliance, my leadership and my genius," he said, "for acquiring a brokerage firm called Kidder, Peabody eight years ago." Then he quipped, "That 1986 acquisition has helped journalists through the summer doldrums and improved my concentration on the golf course. When I'm standing over a ten-foot putt on the green, my golfing partners inevitably ask me, 'Jack, how's Joe Jett doing?' "

By singling out Jett, even in jest, Welch was delivering what had become by midsummer the GE mantra: Jett did it, Jett did it, Jett did it. . . . But only six months before, Jett, whom colleagues at Kidder had dubbed the "human piranha" for his voraciousness in pursuing profits, had been held up at GE's annual management retreat in Boca Raton as the very model of the "take no prisoners" approach to business that Welch had preached time and again since his landmark speech at the Pierre Hotel in December 1981.

Now that calamity had struck once again, now that another GE employee had run amuck, Welch was singing a very different tune to the media. He was shocked, just shocked, over what had occurred. "This violates everything we believe in and stand for," he said in a statement released immediately following Kidder's disclosure of the Jett affair. Welch also portrayed himself as the victim: He was "damn mad, both at the violation and its impact," which had broken a ten-year "string of 'no [earnings] surprises,' " ended by yet another errant employee who, like other miscreants before him, had crossed the line in his pursuit of profit, willfully and wrongfully taking advantage of his employer for personal gain. Of course, that portrayal contained an element of truth: Jett had engaged in trading that was akin to a pyramid scheme, cleverly taking advantage of a glitch in Kidder's accounting system and extending his settlement dates on government bonds, offsetting the settlements as they came due by buying bigger and bigger forward positions that progressively inflated his earnings. In the process, Jett tallied $350 million in phony profits in just twenty-eight months before the lid finally blew off.*

Then again, as much as Welch tried to pin the catastrophe on one individual, it also became increasingly clear as the scandal unfolded that he, too, deserved blame. Welch had sanctioned the recognition of Jett as Kidder, Peabody's outstanding employee for 1993, its "Man of the Year," while approving the $9 million bonus he had received just months before the scandal broke. In awarding compensation greater than his own, Welch had failed to ask one elementary question: How could Jett have possibly achieved trading profits of $150 million in 1993 from swapping bonds with the Federal Reserve, one of the world's most efficient and lowest-margin markets, when the previ-

---

* Jett maintains he is innocent. He claims that he was using—not abusing—Kidder's computer system and that he conducted his trades openly, even disclosing them to internal auditors. But in July 1998, Carol Fox Foelak, an administrative law judge for the SEC, ruled that Jett knew Kidder did not understand the source of his bond-trading profits, and when his activities were discovered, he "denied wrongdoing and gave misleading and conflicting explanations." Thus, Jett exhibited an "intent to defraud" Kidder, for which, in addition to books-and-records violations, he was barred from the securities business, fined $200,000, and ordered to repay $8.2 million in bonuses. Jett, who was cleared of fraud, the most serious charge against him, has appealed.

ous full-year earnings record had been only $20 million? In addition, as was the case with Ed Russell's dismissal, Welch had made poor personnel decisions, entrusting the management of Kidder to two friends, neither of whom had ever worked on Wall Street, much less run a firm of Kidder's size and scope. The first was Silas Cathcart, a veteran GE director and one of Welch's biggest admirers on the board; the second, Mike Carpenter, who succeeded Cathcart, ran the firm for four of his five years without the required securities license, and it was his pursuit of profits—and desire to please Welch, his mentor—that set the stage for the cataclysm that was to follow.

But perhaps most important, it was Welch who established the business creed to which everyone at Kidder subscribed. "The tone set by top management—the corporate environment or culture within which financial reporting occurs—is the most important factor contributing to the integrity of the financial reporting process," the Securities and Exchange Commission concluded after a three-year investigation of an accounting fraud unrelated to General Electric, words that apply as well to what occurred at Kidder, Peabody. According to the Welch creed followed so assiduously by Carpenter, profits were essential, and the imperative of achieving them as quickly and expediently as possible ultimately ruined Kidder. As GE's own inquiry into the Jett affair concluded—a report authored by Gary Lynch, a securities lawyer at Davis Polk & Wardwell and former chief of enforcement at the SEC—it was Jett's enormous contributions to the bottom line that made his superiors reluctant to ask questions. "As his profitability increased," the report observed, "skepticism about Jett's activities was often dismissed or unspoken." Yet with or without the shenanigans of one errant bond trader, the fact remains that Kidder was troubled long before Jett ever walked through its doors.

It seems improbable now, given all the gunslinging that brought down Kidder and the magnitude of the troubles it endured in its final years, but for most of its existence venerable Kidder, Peabody was anything but a Wall Street gunslinger. One of America's oldest investment banks, the firm had been founded by Henry Kidder and Francis Peabody in Boston in 1865, at the end of the Civil War. The firm raised capital for the railroad boom and was an early subscriber to one of Thomas Edison's earliest inventions, a rudimentary stock-quotation service. In 1929, Kidder, Peabody was devastated by the stock market crash, and two years later Albert Hamilton Gordon, a young bond trader at Goldman, Sachs, put up $100,000 to acquire the firm along with two partners, who moved it from Boston to Wall Street.

The modern Kidder, Peabody soon took on the personality of its principal owner. Gordon, the son of a wealthy Boston leather merchant and a graduate of Harvard College and Business School, was a Brahmin of impeccable bearing, a physical-fitness fanatic, parsimonious, conservative. His firm was a stalwart of establishment respectability and the rarefied world of old money, dominated by WASP men whose discreet ways cultivated a blue-chip clientele, including United States Steel and American Telephone & Telegraph. But in the hierarchy of Wall Street, Kidder, Peabody remained a second-tier firm, behind the likes of Salomon Brothers, Morgan Stanley, Merrill Lynch, First Boston, and Goldman, Sachs. It had only one legitimate star, Martin Siegel, a 1980s rainmaker who could command huge fees and retainers.

Siegel had joined the firm in 1971 at the age of twenty-three, precisely because it was filled with older men. Fresh out of Harvard Business School, the first Jew Kidder had hired in corporate finance, Siegel saw opportunity aplenty there. By 1977, before his thirtieth birthday, he was a director (the second-youngest in the firm's history, after Al Gordon) and an acknowledged expert in one specialty niche of the emerging merger and acquisition field: takeover defense. He conceived brilliant but controversial tactics, such as the golden parachute, which endeared him to many corporate managers fearful of hostile takeovers. Hundreds of corporations paid six-figure retainers just to have Siegel and his expertise on hand in the event a predator began snapping up their shares. Siegel was one of Wall Street's hottest properties—a "heartthrob," *Business Week* called him, a reference to his movie-star looks—and Kidder rode along on his coattails.

But the M&A game that Siegel had so skillfully navigated and propelled was a two-edged sword for Kidder and many other small, thinly capitalized firms on Wall Street. By the mid-1980s, the securities business was being overtaken by the very forces it had unleashed. Firms like Kidder had by tradition cherished their legacies of independence and private ownership, but those values were increasingly difficult to retain, given the financial realities of that era. To be a serious player, you needed heft—capital—to go along with expertise, the kind of heft that newcomers like Drexel Burnham Lambert had. The Drexel leviathan had already stolen away some of Kidder's top, young prospects.

The crushing blow came in January 1986, when Siegel, who had privately come to the conclusion that Kidder couldn't survive on its own, informed Al Gordon that he, too, was jumping ship to join Drexel. The taciturn Gordon's only comment: "All good things must come to an end." He was referring as much to the firm as he was to its star, for without Siegel the firm could only compete on the basis of capital, and its capital was precariously low. Even Gordon had recently come around to the view that Kidder should be sold, persuaded in part by a liquidity crisis in late 1985. Carrying a record inventory of municipal bonds and other securities, Kidder had pushed itself into a highly leveraged position, which meant it was nearing noncompliance with minimum capital requirements required by the SEC. Faced with the prospect of being unable to meet end-of-year cash demands, Richard Stewart, the chief financial officer, spent New Year's Eve trying to line up short-term bridge loans. Not until 10 p.m. did he finally assemble a syndicate of foreign and U.S. investors willing to come to the rescue.

The crisis underscored themes that Fred Joseph, Drexel's chief executive officer, had stressed in his courting of Siegel. Drexel had the capital that Kidder sorely lacked, and Wall Street was clearly moving toward a situation in which the dominant dealmakers would soon be a handful of capital-rich firms. It was only a matter of time, Joseph argued, before Drexel began chipping away at Siegel's blue-chip clientele. Although they didn't jump ship, other Kidder principals saw the same lurking threat that had caused Siegel to leave. Some partners, such as Max Chapman, Siegel's chief rival in the next generation of leadership, favored selling a minority stake to a foreign investor, perhaps the Japanese. Gordon had broached the possibility of a capital infusion with his successor as chief executive, Ralph DeNunzio, who wanted Kidder to stay independent and had bolstered his position by shrewdly conferring stock over the years on his own allies.

With Siegel's departure, however, the calculus swiftly changed. As word of his defection spread throughout the ranks, a crisis atmosphere settled over Kidder. When John Gordon, Al's son, learned of the news from his father, he caught an immediate flight back from San Francisco to attend an executive meeting the next day. The younger Gordon later threatened to leave Kidder unless his father compelled DeNunzio to seek new sources of capital, while other Wall Street firms were moving in the same direction: In late January, Morgan Stanley, for generations the very model of the elite private investment bank, had decided to sell shares to the public.

At the same time, Robert Wright, a buddy of Welch's from their days together at GE Plastics and chief executive of GE's huge financial services division, was keeping close tabs on Wall Street. Wright, who had been growing financial services' earnings at a fast clip, desperately wanted to be a player in the lucrative securities business and had sought unsuccessfully for three years to buy a position in it. While big companies like Sears, American Express, Travelers, and Prudential snapped up Wall Street firms, Wright's overtures to several targets, including Goldman, Sachs; Morgan; Drexel; and Bear, Stearns, went for naught. Upon learning of Kidder's quest for capital, Wright arranged a meeting between DeNunzio, Welch, and Lawrence Bossidy, then GE's vice chairman, in early April in Fairfield. Within a few weeks, in late April, a tearful DeNunzio convened Kidder, Peabody's directors and announced that General Electric had agreed to pay $600 million for 80-percent ownership (GE bought the remaining 20 percent in 1990, when it advanced Kidder an additional $550 million to offset a portfolio of problem securities). Although the sale brought Gordon, DeNunzio, and others considerable sums—GE had paid a very steep premium, and Gordon alone received more than $40 million for his shares—it also represented the end of an era. The Kidder they had known was now irrevocably gone, but not even they could have imagined how quickly it would disintegrate.

The elements of that disintegration were evident even in small events that had preceded the sale. Kidder had clung to its paternalistic traditions long after they had gone out of fashion on most of Wall Street. The Kidder "family" was just that (one reason Siegel's departure to Drexel had stung so much). Indeed, in the final hours of negotiations between Wright and DeNunzio, as the two struggled to reach terms that would close the deal, DeNunzio excused himself to attend the Sunday afternoon christening of a Kidder executive's child.

While there were obvious cultural differences between the prima donnas of Wall Street and the organization men of GE, General Electric had had years of experience running commercial lending and leasing activities. What could be so difficult or different about Wall Street? After all, who knew more about management than GE, the company that had virtually invented it? Just digest a few facts and figures specific to the securities business, put the managers and managerial systems in place to run it, and—*voilà*—the deals would pour forth like lightbulbs from an assembly line. In preparing for his first meeting with DeNunzio, Wright had spent the weekend before cramming himself full with financial data on the securities industry—"as much as I could inhale at once," Wright told the *New York Times*—as if one big gulp was all he needed.

Thus began a grim lesson for Welch and his colleagues, who learned the disastrous consequences of entering a business they didn't fully understand, a lesson many other corporations had learned before—and have learned since. In reality, the dynamics of Wall Street are fundamentally different from the asset-driven businesses General Electric knows well, businesses where the competition is by definition circumscribed and GE has the clout that comes from being a big fish in a small pond. In the river of Wall Street, on the other hand, even a piranha can quickly become prey. It is talent-, rather than asset-, driven; people are the competitive edge rather than bricks and mortar. When Siegel departed for Drexel, a large percentage of Kidder's profits departed with him. The superstars tend to be temperamental; they expect to be well treated, well rewarded, and given wide latitude. The securities business is also one where perception can quickly become reality, especially in a crisis—and that, too, was a lesson GE learned just ten months after agreeing to purchase Kidder.

On May 12, 1986, with the ink barely dry on that agreement and Siegel just settling into his new job as cohead of M&A at Drexel, the great insider-trading scandal broke. At 2 p.m. that afternoon, Gary Lynch, the SEC enforcement chief, called Drexel CEO Fred Joseph and, in a ten-minute conversation, revealed that the government planned within a matter of minutes to charge Drexel investment banker Dennis Levine as the ringleader of a group of merger specialists who were illegally swapping inside information. Levine, arrested later that day, was the first of four players who were the core of the ring. By September, the second, Ivan Boesky, an arbitrageur at his own firm in New York, had surrendered to federal authorities and become an undercover agent for the Department of Justice. Boesky fingered the infamous Michael Milken as well as Siegel, whose friendship with Boesky had ended in 1982. Siegel had leaked Boesky advance information on a defense technique, dubbed "PacMan" after the then popular video game, that Siegel's client Martin Marietta planned to employ in fending off Bendix Corporation's hostile takeover. Boesky, who made $120,000 on his Bendix position, paid Siegel $150,000 in $100 bills for the information, a premium that would ensure his "insights" on future deals.

Although he had been caught, Siegel didn't go quietly. In addition to pleading guilty to two counts of insider-trading infractions, he turned government informant and fingered two former Kidder colleagues, arbitrageurs Timothy Tabor, who had already left the firm, and Richard Wigton, who on February 12, 1987, was led away from Kidder's executive offices in handcuffs by federal marshals. The arrests rocked Kidder and alarmed Welch, who learned of Wigton's arrest just moments after it had occurred, when a secretary burst into an executive dining room at Fairfield with the news. A swat team of GE investigators was dispatched to audit Kidder's books, while Joseph Handros, GE's deputy general counsel, was put in charge of the case. Two days later, with Handros in attendance, Kidder officials and a phalanx of attorneys, including lead outside counsel Sullivan & Cromwell, met their accusers: Gary Lynch, accompanied by four representatives from the Justice Department, most notably Rudolph Giuliani, then head of the Manhattan U.S. Attorney's office and future New York City mayor.

The meeting did not go well. Kidder's attorneys took a combative approach, belittling Siegel's reliability and questioning the strength of the government's case, which outraged Giuliani and his colleagues. After reviewing additional government information that went beyond Siegel's allegations—about a stock-parking scheme allegedly involving others in the firm—Charles Carberry, an assistant U.S. attorney in Giuliani's office, said bluntly: "We're going to indict you." A flurry of recriminations and countercharges followed. The Kidder team then stormed out of the room, leaving Lynch, Giuliani, and their assistants stunned.

When Handros reported back on the outcome of the meeting, Lawrence Bossidy, then a GE vice chairman, and Welch were immediately concerned. An indictment against Kidder could level the firm, all but wiping out GE's $600 million investment. At that moment Bossidy and Welch decided to take direct control not just of the case but of the entire firm, which up until that point had operated somewhat autonomously. Sullivan & Cromwell was dismissed, and, in a follow-up meeting with Giuliani, Bossidy adopted a conciliatory tone, acknowledging "serious problems" at the firm and offering concrete steps to remedy the situation. Kidder's top management, including DeNunzio, president Jack Roche, and chief counsel Robert Krantz, would be swept away; the firm would abandon arbitrage trading altogether; and it would work out an appropriate settlement with the SEC (which wound up to be a payment by Kidder of $25.3 million). Giuliani was pleased. And when indictments were handed down in early April against Tabor and Wigton, Kidder was not among the indicted parties. Giuliani even went so far as to praise GE as a "responsible corporate citizen" at a subsequent press conference.

But Bossidy's fast work turned out to be a Pyrrhic victory. Although GE staved off the indictment, its handling of the situation drove a wedge between Kidder, Peabody people and their new bosses. As part of the settlement, GE had thrown Wigton to the wolves, suspending him without pay and stopping payment of his attorney's fees, which angered many at Kidder who believed, fervently, that "Wiggs" was innocent of any wrongdoing.

In May, the government, faced with the prospect of a trial it was unprepared to try, asked in a stunning about-face that its indictments of Tabor and Wigton be dismissed. The next day Bossidy and Welch carried out their pledge to the prosecutors, ousting DeNunzio, Roche, and Krantz and installing as chairman Silas Cathcart, the GE director and former CEO of Illinois Tool Works, whose appointment elicited a sardonic response from one anonymous

Kidder official, made famous in the *Wall Street Journal*: "I was thinking just the other day that what we need around here is a good tool-and-die man." Anger within Kidder grew.

The dispute over the fate of Wigton reached its apex when Max Chapman, a fierce Kidder loyalist who had been named chief operating officer after DeNunzio's ouster, told the press that Wigton would be returning to the firm. GE then issued its own statement, correcting what Chapman had said: While Wigton's salary would be restored and his legal fees paid, he would not be reinstated.

The events of the spring of 1987 shattered any lingering notions of collegiality at Kidder, Peabody, which had lost its independence and much of its character and had been transformed into an organization that veterans of the firm barely recognized. A virtual parade of people left, including Al Gordon's son John. Some were angry about paltry bonuses; others groused about a lack of strategic direction and Cathcart's inexperience, while still others were fired. In the aftermath of the stock market crash in the fall of 1987, fifteen hundred people lost their jobs. By the end of 1988, with Kidder drifting aimlessly and its best people leaving, Welch had come to the conclusion that Kidder needed new leadership.

Among the five finalists for the job were three officials from other Wall Street firms, Max Chapman, and the only candidate who had no prior Wall Street experience, Michael Carpenter. Welch chose Carpenter, a loyalist and his former strategic planner; Chapman, one of the last vestiges of the old Kidder, quit. The disintegration of Kidder, Peabody continued.

THE FINAL EPISODE in that disintegration was written by Joe Jett. But how did Jett do it? Even with Nicholas Leeson's escapades in mind—Leeson's losses of $1.3 billion in futures trading brought down Britain's venerable Barings Bank in 1995—it is hard to understand how Jett could have hidden $350 million in faked profits for a period of more than two years, before any superior began to get suspicious. And it is difficult to fathom how Jett's subterfuge could succeed at any deception, since GE had already endured one scandal. The auditors who had pored over Kidder's books in the aftermath of the Siegel escapade had found many things they didn't like. Kidder had been run in loose fashion, like the family business it aspired to be; there were no systems and controls, which was why Bossidy had acknowledged "serious problems" and had been so willing to accommodate Giuliani. But the systems and controls had been put in place by the time Carpenter arrived in January 1989, when the firm was deemed to be squeaky clean. So how could Jett have succeeded?

The answer lies in the environment in which Jett played out his amazing trades. The environment Carpenter in part inherited and in part created was one of high turnover and low morale, of unlicensed and uninformed executives, of high-risk gambles in the bond markets. It was, in short, a perfect hothouse for growing calamity, the kind of place where a person of Jett's inexperience—he had *no* prior background in government bond trading—could, in just twenty months, be running Kidder's entire government bond operation, supervising twenty other traders and himself subject to very lackadaisical supervision.

Just how lax the supervision was is illustrated by the firm's inattentiveness to such important details as having its top officers appropriately registered and licensed. When Carpenter arrived in 1989, point one of his stated "six point plan" for revitalizing Kidder was to reestablish the firm's total commitment to integrity, words that sounded good (especially given Welch's frequent statements on the topic). But as it turned out, "total commitment to integrity" was no more than window dressing. Surprisingly, not everyone at Kidder had the proper registrations. That some were brokering without a license may seem like small potatoes—and in light of all that went wrong at Kidder, it was—but it is akin to practicing law without having passed the bar exam. Moreover, since Carpenter himself was one of the principals who was unlicensed for most of his time at Kidder, it represents a lapse that takes on greater significance in light of what occurred.

Carpenter, British-born, Harvard Business School–trained, is, like Welch, a chemical engineer. After a stint at Britain's Imperial Chemical Industries, he had emigrated to the United States seeking a more lively business climate, quite typical of the kind of executives who find favor with Welch. Smart, articulate, with an uncanny ability to say what people wanted to hear, he was, in a word, "smooth," and his career as a consultant for nine years with Boston Consulting Group, before joining GE in 1983, had helped him hone the skills that Welch much admired. That Carpenter knew next to nothing about the securities business mattered little to Welch, who had a long track record of handing businesses over to executives he trusted but who had no background in that business. Inexperience sometimes led to catastrophe, which if given a second chance the executive could in time overcome. Carpenter's crisis, on the other hand, was so severe he didn't get a second chance. "Where Carpenter fell down was in not understanding the business well enough to run it," one former colleague asserts.

It was Carpenter's performance while doing work for GE as a BCG consultant that had led Welch to offer him a job repeatedly. Only Vincenzo Morelli, the former BCG consultant who had worked on Carpenter's planning staff during the days leading up to the RCA acquisition, had presentation skills that rivaled Carpenter's. "He was one of the most articulate people I'd ever met," one former member of Kidder's management committee recalls. But Carpenter could also be one of the most sycophantic, the executive adds, a tendency that was particularly evident in his relationship with Welch. "He bragged all the time about Jack. 'Jack's depending on me to turn this around,' that kind of thing. He wanted everyone to know how close he was to Jack."

Because of their special relationship, Welch permitted Carpenter to circumvent the normal chain of command. Kidder was a subsidiary of GE Capital Corporation, the financial services unit, which meant that technically Carpenter should have reported to GECC President Gary Wendt, who had been Carpenter's boss before his arrival at Kidder. But Carpenter and Wendt despised each other, and instead of compelling civility between the two for the good of their respective organizations, Welch allowed Carpenter to report to him rather than to Wendt, which opened a Pandora's box. Besides undermining potential "synergy" between the two financial organizations, which had been the original rationale for buying Kidder, the unusual reporting relationship took Wendt, as skilled an evaluator of balance sheets as existed within GE, out of the loop as a gatekeeper of Carpenter, who needed much more oversight than he received.

The odd reporting relationship also amplified Carpenter's "hero worship" of Welch. Carpenter didn't want to let Welch down for obvious and not-so-obvious reasons. The obvious was that his career could come to a very abrupt halt unless he pleased him, and that meant generating the high-powered profit growth that Welch expects of every GE business. But Carpenter's desire to please went way beyond the simple ambitions of a forty-one-year-old executive on a very fast track. Like many of the young men in Welch's court, he was in awe of him.

By 1989, however, pleasing Welch was no simple task. Kidder was an absolute mess. Hobbled by mass defections, it had virtually no income stream and lousy morale. Moreover, speculation was rampant, on Wall Street and within the firm, that Welch planned to sell the firm as soon as Carpenter made the numbers respectable. But Kidder's biggest problem was the mediocrity of its businesses. It had closed down its only truly successful trading operation, risk arbitrage, as part of its settlement with the SEC, and while its retail brokerage name was well known, it had high expenses and many unproductive brokers. Investment banking earned money, but because of the plethora of dealmakers it had lost, the firm was a second-class player in the M&A field, which itself had fallen on hard times in the aftermath of Siegel's confessions and the insider-trading scandal.

Undaunted, Carpenter vowed to return Kidder to prominence as a great investment bank, and he spent money lavishly at first to achieve that goal, recruiting Scott Newquist, a onetime mergers and acquisitions star at Morgan Stanley, to restore Kidder's M&A practice. Newquist in turn hired back many of the M&A specialists Kidder had lost, but as Carpenter soon discovered, it took time to reestablish a lost franchise, and time was definitely in short supply. Welch had already soured on the securities business: He wanted earnings restored as quickly as possible, and a buyer found in short order, former senior executives recall; Carpenter, who told colleagues he only expected to be at Kidder two years, was anxious to satisfy Welch's wishes.

Quickly, the vision of carefully building strategic niches devolved into the standard GE formula—cut, cut, chop, chop, which came in the form of a GE-style initiative that Carpenter called the "Profit Improvement Committee," a gang of three who knew little about the securities business. In a sense, however, knowledge would have impaired one's obedience to the task at hand. "I had no argument with taking out cost, but there was no thought behind what the appropriate reduction in a particular department might have been," recalls one senior executive, who was told to eliminate unilaterally 20 percent of his staff. "Carpenter gave the committee numbers and the committee gave them to us. It was an exercise, not a solution, just a game so he could tell Jack there was a Profit Improvement Committee, and what a great job it was doing bringing about profit improvements."

Another former senior executive, who had been recruited only months before to build up Kidder's expertise in a particular specialty, recalls a presentation he gave to Charles Sheehan, a veteran GE executive installed at Kidder in 1987 to strengthen the firm's accounting controls whom Carpenter had asked to run the brokerage division. About halfway through the presentation of charts and graphs, which the staff had spent months preparing and which showed how Kidder stacked up against its rivals, Sheehan asked, "How much did those boards cost?" "That said it all," says the executive, who left shortly thereafter.

One department, though, was exempt from the axe: the Fixed Income division, which would play an increasingly important role in providing the income stream Carpenter desperately needed. He had concluded that Fixed Income, which traded and underwrote bonds of all kinds as well as other, esoteric debt instruments, was the quickest and easiest route to profits, and he set out to catapult the firm into a dominant position in one niche of the fixed-income arena, that of mortgage-backed securities.

There was potential reward in that strategy but also great risk. In the mortgage-backed business, Wall Street firms made much of their money by underwriting securities created by pooling home mortgages, which are packaged into bonds and sold to investors. Aggressive participants in this market must be willing to hold large inventories of securities that don't sell and, as with any inventory, there is cost associated with carrying it. A clothing retailer might stock up on what he believes to be a hot line of spring fashions, only to discover that the consumer didn't respond favorably and that he's stuck with unsold inventory; in the same way, the risks in carrying bond inventory can be equally capricious. In an environment of falling interest rates, holding a big bond inventory can be advantageous as the bonds gain in value, but conversely, when interest rates rise, that same inventory can lose value.

Carpenter knew those risks, but he also knew that if Kidder were willing to accept much higher inventories of mortgage-backed securities than other firms, it could grab a bigger share of the underwritings. He figured that hedging strategies could shield the inventory from some of the risk and that in the hands of his best traders the inventory might even become the source of significant trading profits. And he also had, as the head of Fixed Income, Edward Cerullo, an experienced trader who was eager to work with him in executing a more aggressive growth strategy.

The most noteworthy thing that can be said of Cerullo, besides the fact that he was Joe Jett's boss, was that he knew how to survive. The trauma at Kidder may have chased away many folks, but not Cerullo, whose star ascended amid the chaos or, perhaps, because of it. His greatest talent was the ability to "ride the tide" and forge alliances with the appropriate people, in this case Carpenter. Cerullo didn't wow people with his brilliance, as a Martin Siegel had, nor did he exhibit the leadership and *gravitas* of a Max Chapman, a tough ex-Marine, former football player at the University of North Carolina, and Cerullo's mentor in the fixed-income department. Cerullo, a onetime high school math teacher and part-time schoolbus driver in suburban Philadelphia, had two great passions—his disdain for cigarette and cigar smoke and his desire to accumulate great wealth, of which the latter was hardly a mark of distinction on Wall Street. Few people would have predicted in 1979, when Cerullo joined Kidder, that within ten years he would be one of the highest-ranking executives at the firm. But then, few people would have foreseen the exodus of executive talent that permitted Cerullo's ascendance to occur.

Carpenter gave Cerullo carte blanche in running Fixed Income, and Cerullo, running what amounted to a fiefdom several blocks away from the Hanover Square headquarters, turned the 760 traders in that division loose, unleashing a produce-or-perish culture. For the first few years the strategy of pumping up mortgage-backed bonds seemed to work fine. The Cerullo-Carpenter partnership seemed a model of profitable cooperation: Cerullo built the business, supposedly keeping track of his traders, while Carpenter ran interference for Cerullo, keeping his critics—and there were many—at bay. Kidder became the top underwriter of mortgage-backed securities on Wall Street, with more than twice the market share of its leading rival. Headed by superstar bond trader Michael Vranos, the mortgage group, one of twelve trading desks within Fixed Income, generated more than two-thirds of Kidder's profits in its final years. Cerullo and Vranos made a fortune—the former's bonus was $20 million in 1993, while the latter's totaled $15 million—and Carpenter looked like a genius. Unprofitable in 1989 and 1990, Kidder suddenly was posting earnings that pleased Welch, zooming from $119 million in 1991 to $439 million in 1993. Although some problems continued to attract media attention—in particular one lawsuit filed in 1992 by the Equal Employment Opportunity Commission, in which the federal agency charged that the firm, in its zeal to cut costs, carried out a policy of widespread age discrimination, firing management-level employees over the age of forty, while retaining and hiring younger people—Carpenter's accomplishments and the comeback he had seemingly orchestrated won very favorable press.

The comeback, however, turned out to be tainted. One of the earliest indications that Cerullo and company may have been too zealous in their pursuit of profit came in 1991, when Linda LaPrade, a Kidder vice president, filed suit against Cerullo, claiming that her former boss had pressured her to inflate bids for government security allotments. As manager of the New Issue Agency desk, part of the Fixed Income division, LaPrade would bid for Kidder's allotment of Treasury bonds, which traditionally had been a meager 1 percent. Cerullo wanted to amass a larger share. Beginning in the summer of 1989, she says, he demanded that LaPrade overstate the number of customer orders, threatening her with termination if she didn't comply. She also claimed that when the SEC inquired about that practice two years later, as part of a crackdown on preorder inflating throughout Wall Street, Melvin Mullin, Cerullo's deputy, who would later emerge as a key figure in the Jett scandal, demanded that LaPrade sign an SEC questionnaire denying that Kidder had inflated its bids. According to LaPrade, when she refused, various Kidder officials, Cerullo among them, claimed in a series of letters to the SEC that LaPrade was the sole instigator of the practice, and as a result had been terminated.*

But the LaPrade episode was small change, compared with the vigorous debate that senior management was engaged in at that time. Each Monday, the Inventory Committee, a group of seven senior executives, including Cerullo and Carpenter, would meet to discuss the topic that had brought rancor to the group: the enormous growth in Kidder's leverage. The strategy of pursuing aggressive profits in mortgage-backed bonds had greatly boosted the firm's bond inventory, shoveling more debt onto an already bloated balance sheet. Every week, the inventory went up, as did anxiety among some members of the Inventory Committee. Among the most anxious was Richard O'Donnell, the chief financial officer, who was adamant that the leverage was getting out of hand. By April 1993, Kidder's assets had begun exceeding $80 billion on a regular basis, which O'Donnell, who had to bridge the larger long-term positions with short-term borrowings, considered too high. By the end of August, it had ballooned to $99 billion, up to $20 billion in just two months. Cerullo was piling more and more bonds onto a tiny equity base, which meant significant danger if the securities weren't sufficiently hedged with interest-rate futures or some other offsetting security.

"This conversation happened every week for two years," recalls one participant in the meetings. "Everyone kept saying, 'Gee, all this inventory building up, isn't this a problem?' And Cerullo would say, 'Don't worry, it's hedged.' And we'd say, 'Hedged against what? Interest rates? The stock market?' We never got a straight answer. Carpenter would fold every time. I knew enough to know what I didn't know, but Mike didn't have a clue how a trading operation was supposed to operate." The implausibility and insufficiency of the answers coming from Cerullo eventually fueled a kind of gallows humor among disgruntled members of the Inventory Committee. The dissidents banded together and sent Cerullo a coffee mug with the inscription, "I have CRS," which stood for "Can't Remember Shit."

Even Welch was buffaloed. During the periodic operations reviews of Kidder, Peabody, when Welch would leaf through the requisite looseleaf binders and methodically interrogate his subjects, he relied heavily on Bossidy, his top deputy, who had run GE's financial services unit in the 1970s and whose understanding of a financial organization's balance sheets was profound. But Bossidy had left in 1991 to become CEO of Allied-Signal, and

---

* LaPrade's claims are pending in arbitration.

Welch's knowledge of financial nuance wasn't as great. Early in 1992, during a post-Bossidy operations review in Fairfield, Welch began to take up with Carpenter and his staff the same line of questioning that had stymied the Inventory Committee for two years. "All this inventory building up, isn't this a problem?" he asked. "We are a hundred percent certain that the inventory is marked correctly, and it's a hundred percent hedged," came Cerullo's reply. Welch didn't pursue the matter further.

As it turned out, however, the inventory wasn't fully hedged. And as with a small boat caught amid squalling seas, that meant big trouble as Kidder headed into turbulent bond markets in the spring and summer of 1994. Although O'Donnell had managed to convince Carpenter that the leverage needed to come down, he was still at odds with Cerullo, who wanted to continue expanding the activities of the Fixed Income division, which accounted for 90 percent of Kidder's $72 billion balance sheet at year-end 1993. Even though the number was lower than it had been, Kidder was dangerously leveraged: every $1 of its equity was supporting $93 of assets, compared with average leverage for the industry of $1 to $27. What's more, even though the firm's inventory of mortgage-backed bonds had been reduced by $6 billion, it still had a whopping $16 billion on its books. But Kidder probably could have survived had it not been for Cerullo's greatest mistake: his blind allegiance to Joe Jett.

IF MELVIN MULLIN, Cerullo's assistant, had done a thorough background check on Orlando Joseph Jett before recommending his hiring, he would have discovered a young man who was clearly a bad risk. Jett had washed out at three jobs, two of them on Wall Street, before landing at Kidder; ironically, the only job of the three that he hadn't lost had been at GE itself.

Jett had grown up in Wickliffe, Ohio, a mostly white suburb east of Cleveland, the youngest of three children and one of the top students in his public high school. After gaining acceptance to the prestigious Massachusetts Institute of Technology and graduating from there in 1983 with a degree in chemical engineering, Jett pursued a career in that field at GE Plastics' plant in Selkirk, New York. GE thought it had found a star in Jett—a black engineer from MIT who was ambitious and smart, sprinkling his conversation with quotations from Nietzsche, Byron, and Plato—but the young engineer soon proved a disappointment, showing surprisingly little aptitude for chemical engineering given his MIT credentials. Jett also seemed to be at odds with himself, and struggling to find his identity. He returned from one vacation in

England with a phony British accent, but after being transferred from the research building to the manufacturing floor, traded his BMW for a Jeep and asked colleagues to address him as "Joseph," rather than "Or-LAHN-do," following the Spanish pronunciation he had previously insisted upon.

"Joseph" would give him acceptance in a white world that "Orlando" could never have, Jett explained. "I just discovered that people did not call back Orlando Joseph Jett, but when I used 'Joseph,' I would get a call back almost immediately," he told Ed Bradley of *60 Minutes*, during an interview that aired in February 1995.

The butt of numerous jokes and clearly not on a fast track, Jett left GE after two years, in 1985, to enroll at Harvard Business School, where he was dismissed from a part-time job in the library, following accusations that he had falsely listed time he hadn't worked. After finishing his course work at Harvard, he spent two undistinguished years at Morgan Stanley trading mortgage-backed bonds, a job he lost in a round of layoffs. He was fired from his next position at First Boston, also as a mortgage-backed trader, for poor performance. Jett's career had taken such a turn for the worse that he had pretty much given up on the idea of landing another trading job on Wall Street; he later told his friend Alphonse "Buddy" Fletcher Jr. that he figured he would have to settle for a position as a computer consultant.

But Jett, a frequent and outspoken critic of affirmative action during his days at Harvard, applied for a job at Kidder at exactly the right moment. The firm, which had one of the worst records of minority hiring and promotion on Wall Street and was under pressure from GE to do better, was in the midst of a celebrated race ruckus. Fletcher, a highly successful stock trader, had accused Kidder of withholding half of his multimillion-dollar bonus because he was black. A few months later, in June 1991, Fletcher filed suit against Kidder, the same month Jett's resumé found its way from the Human Resources department to Cerullo's Fixed Income division. Much to Jett's surprise, Mullin, then head of the government bond desk, offered him a lucrative job trading Treasury securities, even though he had no background in that specialty. Jett accepted, though, he later confided to Fletcher, he was somewhat perplexed, as was his father. The mystery of how Jett had landed such a plum job was cleared up, for the father at least, when he read a newspaper article about the Fletcher case; he sent the clipping on to his son.

But no matter how he had gotten the job, Jett was determined not to wash out again. He usually arrived before 7:30 a.m., the first one in, and rarely left before 7 p.m., the last one out. Despite his best efforts, however, Jett didn't seem to be catching on; colleagues whispered that he wasn't up to the task.

Kidder gave him no formal training in executing trades with the United States Treasury; rather, he was expected to learn via osmosis, by watching the other traders around him and by asking questions of Mullin, his supervisor. Clearly disappointed in Jett's early performance, Mullin awarded him a meager—for Wall Street—$5,000 bonus for 1991 and wrote in a year-end review that Jett had had "a slower start than anticipated" but "seem[ed] to be improving." Yet within six months, Jett had miraculously become a star, and in a June 15, 1992, memo to Cerullo, Mullin recommended that he receive a substantial raise:

> Performance in 1992 has been outstanding. . . . Profitability in STRIPS [for Separate Trading of Registered Interest and Principal of Securities, the type of Treasury securities Jett was trading] at this time is $8.4 million. This profit level substantially exceeds that of 1991, and on an annualized basis far exceeds our best ever performance in STRIPS. . . . The level of profitability has been consistent with no month under $1 million; profits have come from intelligent trading activity and close attention to detail. Joseph has worked diligently to become one of the best STRIPS traders in the business.

In April, two months before the memo was written, Jett had phoned Fletcher, who since leaving Kidder had founded his own investment firm, and asked to meet him at the Coffee Shop, a trendy Manhattan restaurant. There, over drinks, Jett revealed that two colleagues had accused him of "mismarking," inflating the prices of securities he held, which was illegal. Jett ascribed the accusations to racism or perhaps jealousy over his recent success, which stemmed from what he described as a "yield curve" trading strategy, a way of betting millions on small interest-rate changes he successfully predicted would occur. Although it sounded implausible and highly speculative to Fletcher, Jett insisted the trades were fully hedged and that his system was foolproof. "It sounded nonsensical, but listening to him preach it really seemed like he believed in what he was doing," Fletcher recalls.

In reality, Jett's newfound success resulted not from improved trading but from forward transactions he had begun in November 1991, when his status at Kidder was most uncertain. It is entirely possible that his earliest trades were simply the product of a flawed accounting system, which erroneously booked profits on trades it shouldn't have, and his own inexperience. But as the trades grew in number and size—$3.6 *trillion* worth over twenty-eight months, with nearly half of that transacted in the first quarter of 1994 alone—

it would prove to be too systematic a practice, too well orchestrated, and too clear in its intent, for Jett to claim it was all a misunderstanding.

Quite the contrary, the scheme revealed a very sophisticated understanding of government-bond markets, which run according to strict rules and procedures. To facilitate the trading of Treasury bonds, which can be divided into separate principal and interest components that trade separately, the Federal Reserve Bank of New York makes even exchanges of whole bonds for "strips," the interest component, and vice versa. These trades with the Fed are cash-neutral, in much the same way that a bank would exchange four quarters for a dollar. What Jett discovered was that by entering into forward trades with the Fed, to be settled as far off as ninety days later, and continually rolling the transactions over as the settlement dates came due, Kidder's accounting system would book a "profit" on the exchange—the differential between the current price of the bonds and their forward price. The Lynch investigation concluded that Mullin and Cerullo were unaware of what Jett was doing and failed to uncover it because they didn't monitor his trades closely enough. Jett, on the other hand, would later maintain his innocence, claiming that both men knew exactly what he was doing, and in fact had ordered him to do it to inflate Kidder's earnings.

In any event, it was quite clear to many people on Wall Street that Jett was racking up profits in 1992 and 1993 on a scale that had never been achieved before in the prosaic and marginally profitable field of government-bond trading. For 1993, Jett's phantom trades represented 27 percent of the Fixed Income division's profits, up from 6 percent in 1992. And as his results got more astounding with each passing quarter, Jett attracted more notoriety—and more support from Mullin and Cerullo, who kowtowed to their superstar trader. Rather than questioning his activities, they promoted Jett, awarding him Mullin's job in February 1993 as head of the government trading desk, a position Mullin had vacated to establish a new trading desk in Fixed Income.

In a situation reminiscent of the Dotan affair, in which Herbert Steindler was able to deflect questions about his illicit relationship with General Dotan, Jett was persuasive as well, abetted—like Steindler—by the enormous profits his activities seemingly contributed to GE's bottom line. In one instance, in April 1992, Jett was able to convince Cerullo to dismiss Hugh Bush, a trader who had challenged the accuracy of Jett's pricing marks, after Jett provided Cerullo with a tape of a phone call that proved Bush had been job-hunting. In a second instance one year later, Jett berated Charles Fiumefreddo, manager of trading accounting, for finding in Jett's ledger about $1 billion in trades entered for forward settlement of up to four months. David Bernstein, Cerullo's aide, was called in to mediate the dispute and, after reviewing the situation, sided with Jett.

While there were many other missed opportunities, when questions about Jett's activities either weren't asked or weren't pursued, people throughout Wall Street were asking plenty of questions about his amazing trades. How was he doing it? Jett had, quite literally, become a legend in his own time. When rival bond traders at other firms tried to replicate his trades, they appeared to be highly unprofitable. Yet each month, word would filter back that Jett had achieved new record earnings. The traders who worked with him were also perplexed. Jett maintained a record of his trades in a large red diary he kept on his desk, which he told subordinates they were never to touch. What was in that diary? fellow traders wondered. He must have discovered some sort of "black box," a system for beating the Fed at its own game. "No one could believe it. He seemed like an idiot. These guys tell me they spent half their time spinning theories on how Jett was making his money," says attorney Jeffrey Liddle, who represents three clients who worked on the government trading desk.

The fascination of Jett's coworkers was so great that when Bernstein informed them in June 1993 that the firm was installing a new accounting system which would have the effect of lowering bonuses on the government desk, they didn't quibble. "The response wasn't, 'We won't cooperate.' The response was, 'Now we can figure out what Jett does,' " Liddle says. The traders were stunned—and more than a little suspicious—when they were informed that Jett would keep a private, and separate, accounting system. But this accounting change, which took effect in September, caused a marked increase in the volume of Jett's forward trades.

In the fall, after a meeting with Welch to review the pool of available money for bonuses in 1993, Carpenter submitted a list of employees who would receive payouts in excess of $1 million, along with a dossier on each individual explaining their activities, which Welch reviewed the weekend before a final meeting with Carpenter. At the top of the list were Cerullo and Kidder's two superstar traders, Michael Vranos and Jett. Welch approved the $9 million bonus to Jett and sanctioned Carpenter's selection of him as Kidder's "Man of the Year."

But just weeks after that award was conferred, Jett's reputation unraveled. His trading positions had grown enormously; he had booked profits of $36 million in January and $30 million in February, more than double his reported profits for all of 1992, and Bernstein and Cerullo were concerned. In early March, after seeking out ledgers to quantify Jett's forward positions and studying the information at home over a weekend, Bernstein informed Cerullo that Jett had *$89 billion* in outstanding forward positions. Although Cerullo confronted Jett at that time and found his explanations to be wholly inadequate, he held out hope that the profit-and-loss distortion arising out of these transactions would be minimal, and didn't reveal their existence to colleagues until three weeks later.

By mid-March, traders had their first hint that something was amiss. Kidder auditors began roaming the trading floor, and Bernstein, seated in his glass-enclosed office adjacent to the trading floor, spent hours burrowed beneath thick stacks of records. His subsequent analysis concluded that the possible distortion from Jett's trades could be as great as $300 million, and he phoned Cerullo on vacation in Colorado to give him the bad news. At that point, Cerullo called Carpenter, who had the same problem telling Welch that Cerullo had had with him. He waited two weeks before issuing his ominous warning that they were having a reconciliation problem. In the meantime, Jett was repeatedly questioned while the auditing and analytics staff searched desperately for credits associated with the forward positions. There were none, and on Friday, April 15, 1994, Kidder experts concluded that Jett had rung up about $85 million in losses from his legitimate trades and $350 million of fake profit from his phantom ones. Two days later, Kidder stunned the financial world by disclosing the scheme and its $350 million charge, as well as the dismissal of Jett, who failed to show for one last meeting with Cerullo on Saturday morning.

Carpenter had immediate problems on his hands, not the least of which was the liquidation of Jett's enormous government-bond holdings. As it turned out, however, the Jett affair was the least of his troubles. In the months that followed, other Kidder traders were dismissed for trading irregularities. But the most intractable problem Carpenter faced wasn't linked to any individual; it was the big growling bear market that had developed in mortgage-backed bonds. As early as February, when interest rates had begun to spike as the Fed sought to combat inflation, Kidder had begun having trouble financing its huge mortgage inventory. Assets had ballooned to $106 billion, of which increasingly illiquid mortgage-backeds represented a hefty $16 billion.

The mortgage-bond market was in paralysis, and Kidder, as the biggest holder of inventory on Wall Street, found it couldn't even get a fix on the value of its holdings because there were no buyers. Kidder faced a situation not unlike that of the final days of Drexel: It was holding a huge inventory of bonds—in Drexel's case, it had been junk bonds—for which there were virtually no buyers. Jett would later claim that in early April, during one of the most difficult periods in the mortgage-market plunge, Bernstein and Cerullo ordered him to unload government bonds because the firm was in violation of net-capital rules and it couldn't find any buyers for mortgage bonds.

The meltdown in the mortgage market forced one important customer of Kidder's, Askin Capital Management, into bankruptcy. Although Carpenter tried to put a positive spin on Kidder's situation—"the basic underlying performance and earnings power of the organization is still very strong," he told the *Wall Street Journal* in an interview that fateful Sunday when he had revealed the Jett hit—the market would be the final arbiter of Kidder's fate, and it was already giving a clear thumbs-down.

Welch, relying on the sugar-coated assessments that Carpenter had provided to him, badly underestimated the severity of the situation Kidder faced. In early May, in a meeting with about a hundred anxious securities analysts and institutional investors, he assured them that the firm would be modestly profitable in the second quarter and that management had "gone through the Kidder portfolio and there were no more shoes to drop." But losses for the quarter eventually totaled $29 million, and Kidder was soon on life support, receiving capital infusions of $550 million between April and June—$200 million of it from GE.

Finally, in late June, Welch, vowing to rebuild Kidder into a "strong firm," relieved its CEO for the third time in seven years, ousting Carpenter and replacing him with Dennis Dammerman, GE's chief financial officer, and Denis Nayden, a troubleshooter and top executive from GE Capital, both of whom had no practical experience on Wall Street. Even if they had, it's doubtful it would have helped, for the situation was much more desperate than anyone could have imagined. The turmoil, which was undercutting morale and triggering defections, was aggravated by constant press leaks.

By late summer, the situation was grave. Losses had continued to pile up throughout the summer—they were more than $400 million for the year through September, excluding the Jett writeoff—as the mortgage market proved intractable and new business slowed to a standstill. Welch faced an unpleasant choice: either pump huge sums of money into a rescue plan that had no certainty of succeeding—on the order of $500 million—or swallow his pride and sell whatever was salable to any buyer willing to buy it. He chose the latter, and in October, GE announced that it had agreed to sell what was left of Kidder—$50 billion of customer assets (excluding what remained of the troubled mortgage-bond inventory, which GE had already transferred to another company affiliate) and its brokerage network and investment banking operations—to PaineWebber; GE received PaineWebber stock in exchange.*

When the sale was revealed to Kidder's senior management, Al Gordon, the retired patriarch of the firm who at age ninety-three still maintained an office at 10 Hanover Square, summed up the feelings of all with one pithy sentence. "I feel like I'm reading my own obituary," he said, and walked out of the room.

FOR SO MANY, Kidder's ownership by GE had been disastrous: for the more than five thousand people who had lost their jobs during the eight years GE owned the firm; for Jett, who is contesting SEC administrative sanctions fining him $200,000 and barring him from the securities industry for life; for Mullin, who settled with the SEC by paying a $25,000 fine and agreeing not to work in the securities industry for three months; for Cerullo, who settled with the SEC by paying a $50,000 fine and agreeing not to work in the securities industry for one year; for Carpenter, whose GE career came to an abrupt end; for GE stockholders, who took a bath on their investment in Kidder; and even for Jack Welch.

Welch did not suffer monetarily; that's not the way CEO compensation works in corporate America. Although GE shares lost value in 1994, directors rewarded Welch handsomely for his handling of the Kidder crisis, increasing his 1994 salary and bonus about 8 percent to $4.35 million and also conferring stock rights on an additional 320,000 shares (adding to his treasure chest of unexercised stock options, which were worth $107 million at the end of 1996 and will be worth considerably more if Welch and his successor can keep the stock climbing in the years ahead). The board's compensation committee, headed by Silas Cathcart of "tool-and-die" fame, cited Welch's "decisive management of operational and strategic issues, including the difficulties which arose at Kidder, Peabody," and praised "his drive to reinforce a culture of integrity."

No, it was Welch's prestige that suffered. While there had been many opportunities to question whether the common assessment of Welch as the greatest CEO of his era was justified—whether Welch was good for America,

---

* That stock holding has done very well in the years since. GE's 23 percent stake in PaineWebber was worth $1.65 billion, the *Wall Street Journal* reported on May 14, 1998, thanks to the rally the bull market had spawned in brokerage stocks.

whether he was good for GE—the media by and large until now had chosen to perpetuate his myth as as dominant a figure as ever existed on the American business scene. He continued to be lionized in the press and at business schools, even as evidence of his poor decisions and recklessness—and GE's illegalities—mounted. But Kidder was too catastrophic a failure to ignore. What's more, the scandal hadn't occurred in Erie or Schenectady, Columbus or Evendale, Pittsfield or Nela Park, isolated enclaves where only the local paper reported on GE's transgressions. This scandal had occurred on Wall Street, America's financial epicenter, a place where so much of what happened profoundly affected the rest of the nation.

In the fall of 1994, the major media turned on Welch with a vengeance. No longer was he "the most admired corporate manager in America"; no longer would Wall Street accord him the benefit of the doubt. *Time,* under the headline "Jack In The Box," referred to him as the "embattled chairman of General Electric," while *Newsweek* the same week began its story: "You can hear the sound of the pedestal cracking." Even *Fortune,* which had done more than any other publication to elevate Welch to management sainthood, took some heavy shots at their former hero in a cover story proclaiming, "Jack Welch's Nightmare on Wall Street: Like it or not, the scandals at Kidder, Peabody were brought on by GE's management." "The problems at Kidder may have less to do with the fired few," wrote *Fortune* associate editor Terence Pare, "than with the business creed to which they subscribed, a creed whose prophet is the charismatic Welch."

It was the moral bankruptcy of that creed that the Kidder fiasco had most forcefully exposed. Jett himself was a disciple of that creed; his message, when he spoke in January 1994 at the annual retreat in Boca Raton, was a paean to the profit-at-all-costs mentality, how important it was to succeed and to make money. But now there could be no denying that just making money was a hollow, soulless pursuit; that Welch and his managers too often were fixated on that goal; and that there had been, as a result, terrible consequences.

CHAPTER SIXTEEN

THE SOUL OF
A NEW MACHINE

Work is, by its very nature, about violence—to the spirit as well as to the body. . . . It is about a search, too, for daily meaning as well as daily bread, for recognition as well as cash, for astonishment rather than torpor; in short, for a sort of life rather than a Monday through Friday sort of dying.

From the introduction to *Working*, by Studs Terkel

DO BUSINESSES NEED a soul to succeed, a sense of purpose beyond just making money? Do people need more than "daily bread"—the modern, corporate equivalent might be profit-sharing, bonuses, and stock options—to prosper in their endeavors, to achieve to the fullest extent of their God-given abilities? These kinds of questions asked by Studs Terkel in his 1972 bestseller—and raised as well in Tracy Kidder's book on the birth of a new computer, from which the title for this chapter is taken—may strike many American businessmen as wholly inappropriate and irrelevant to capitalism in the 1990s. Capitalism is not about spirituality, about a relationship with anything divine, about doing to others as you would have them do unto you, this school of thought would argue; quite the contrary, it's the antithesis of anything godly. It's about doing harm to the other guy before he harms you; it is business as war. One recent management book of this genre featured Attila the Hun as an example of how businessmen ought to behave. "For most people and organizations," writes business consultant Donald G. Krause in his book, *The Art of War for Executives*, "today's battlefields are not physical places that can be located on a map. Today's battles occur within the minds of those who comprise the constituents of an organization. . . . [They] are information battles because information determines both perception and opinion. Those who use information weapons effectively, both to attack and to defend, will win. Those who do not will lose."

The book, which summarizes the military principles of the ancient Chinese warrior Sun Tzu and applies them to modern business, advocates the "profit-at-any-cost" philosophy. It's old wine in a new bottle. The question of what business owes society seemed to be settled in the four prosperous decades immediately following World War II. Most CEO's accepted the notion that they had responsibilities to employees, communities, and the public at large, as well as to customers and shareholders, and that it was their duty to maintain an equitable and working balance among the claims of these various groups. Even so, the tension between money and morality has always been a part of American capitalism. Thomas Jefferson was complaining that "money, not morality, is the principle of commercial nations" within a generation of our country's founding, while Woodrow Wilson sadly observed a century later that "we are all caught in a great economic system, which is heartless." The struggle between numbers and values, between pragmatism and idealism, between the ordinary and the visionary, has been played out many times in the history of American business, in boardrooms, executive suites, labor halls, even the courts.

Shareholders of the Ford Motor Company once sued Henry Ford to prevent him from lowering the price of the Model T, which fell by 58 percent from 1908 to 1916, and which Ford did as much out of a sense of idealism as pragmatism, while the Wall Street Journal accused Ford of "economic blunders if not crimes." "I don't believe we should make such an awful profit on our cars. A reasonable profit is right, but not too much," Ford said. "I hold this because it enables a larger number of people to buy and enjoy the use of a car and because it gives a larger number of men employment at good wages. Those are the two aims I have in life." Poppycock, the Journal's editors fumed. Ford, a naive farmboy, was injecting "spiritual principles into [capitalism] where they do not belong," and pursuing "the most foolish thing ever attempted in the industrial world," a policy that would soon "return to plague him and the industry he represents as well as organized society."

History shows that Ford, not the Wall Street Journal, was right. The Ford Motor Company and society ultimately benefited from Henry's strict adherence to what the Journal derisively called his "spiritual principles." Likewise, David Packard, who with his partner William Hewlett started the Hewlett-Packard Company in 1939 in a Palo Alto garage that is now a designated California landmark, was a spiritual idealist who had a vision of H-P conducting its affairs to generate wealth for his shareholders but also do something of value for society. "I want to discuss *why* a company exists in the first place," Packard told employees in 1960, three years after H-P had sold stock to the public. "In other words, why are we here? I think many people assume, wrongly, that a company exists simply to make money. While this is an important result of a company's existence, we have to go deeper and find the real reasons for our being. As we investigate this, we inevitably come to the conclusion that a group of people get together and exist as an institution that we call a company so they are able to accomplish something collectively that they could not accomplish separately—they make a contribution to society, a phrase which sounds trite but is fundamental."

When Packard died in March 1996 at eighty-three, he left the bulk of his vast estate, mostly Hewlett-Packard stock, to the foundation he and his wife had founded in 1964. With assets that now exceed $9 billion, the David and Lucile Packard Foundation is the nation's third-largest philanthropic organization, behind only the Lilly and Ford foundations.

What have been the fundamental values of General Electric during the Welch era? No doubt it is the corporate equivalent of a machine, and a new one at that, but does his GE have a soul, a sense of purpose beyond just making money? And what of the "spirit of General Electric" that was bequeathed to Welch in 1981, that "distinctive set of traditions, values and beliefs" that Reg Jones had invoked on the hundredth anniversary of the founding of the Edison General Electric Company? Before taking up these questions—and their significance for American business and for American society—it's important to set the scene with three encounters that have particular poignancy.

Scene one, the maquiladora border region on the Mexican side of the Rio Grande.

Although it hasn't quite been the giant sucking sound Ross Perot predicted, there's little doubt that more and more manufacturing jobs are migrating to Mexico's *maquiladora* region close to the U.S. border. Wages now average about $1.80 per hour in the region, where an estimated work force of more than seven hundred-fifty thousand are employed, a population expected to reach nearly one million by the year 2000.

In the summer of 1993, it seemed important to see firsthand how these people live, and judge Perot's statement that cattle in the United States lived better than the working poor of the *maquiladora*. He wasn't exaggerating. GE, one of the largest employers along the Mexican border, had refused my request for a tour of company facilities and communities there, but the Roman Catholic Church, which polices the activities of U.S. multinationals in the region, was only too happy to oblige. My escort in the territory in and around Ciudad Acuña, across from Del Rio, Texas, was Leslie Gates, a recent Yale University graduate and newcomer to Mexico, who had taken up residence south of the border as a church-supported representative in the region.

Life in the *maquiladora* was a process of adjustment for Gates but perhaps most nettlesome were the roads. "They've been building this road since I got here," she remarked, steering her beat-up Toyota to the left, then to the right, swerving to avoid ditches. It was a hopeless task, as hopeless as trying to find shade from the midday sun. The potholes in the dirt road alongside GE's low-lying factory were as omnipresent as the stench of human feces that covered the *colonia* under the scorching sun like a heavy blanket. There was no running water, no electricity, no sanitation of any kind; the only toilets were outhouses.

The car came to a jostled, stagecoach-like halt inside the cooperative community of tumbleweed and barefoot children where hundreds of GE families lived, a Mexican equivalent of what we once called, in the United States, "company towns." Gates greeted several people by name and strode to the home of one woman who, like her neighbors, lived in a shanty built from the leftover waste of the products she made. Shipping pallets served as the frame for her house, sheathed in cardboard that bore the familiar GE monogram.

The woman welcomed Gates at the doorway (without a door) with a broad smile and a warm embrace, offered me a cup of Coca-Cola, then told her life story, which sounded jarringly similar to those of the dozen or so GE workers I had already met at four locations up and down the Rio Grande. The wages were by American and even Mexican standards poor (GE pays about half as much as Ford Motor); the productivity required of them was great; they claimed that they often performed menial tasks that they thought exposed them to industrial chemicals; and they said that their Mexican bosses didn't always treat them fairly (one woman in Reynosa, several hundred miles southeast of Acuña, claimed her three-months-pregnant sister had had a miscarriage on a GE assembly line one night but was refused medical attention until the night shift had ended).

But the woman in this shanty offered one detail I hadn't heard before. There was a packet of GE home electrical accessories atop her clothes cupboard, the same three-prong adapters and extension cords made at the plant, and found at countless retail outlets across the United States. "Where'd that come from?" she was asked. It was a Christmas gift that GE gave to employees, she replied—a gift that served to underscore the incongruity of her plight: electrical devices in a makeshift shelter with dirt floors and without electricity.

Scene two, Erie, Pennsylvania.

Erie is a metaphor for the modern American malaise, which might be summed up as follows: If we're doing so well as a nation, then why do we feel so lousy? By many measures, the United States economy and American business are more competitive than they've ever been. Corporate profits are at record levels, and so is productivity. Unemployment and inflation are both unusually low. The Dow Jones industrial average rose more than 30 percent in 1995 and continued its upward climb through 1997. The economy has been expanding for seven consecutive years. In industry after industry, where only a decade ago the United States was being trounced—autos, machine tools, computer chips—American business has come roaring back. Yet, at the same time, poll after poll has shown that the American people feel greater unease and frustration, more anxiety and less satisfaction with life, than they've ever felt before. What gives?

As we have discovered as a nation in the last ten years or so, the price of beating the competition has been bitterly high: wave after wave of downsizing layoffs, wage increases limited or forgone, replacement of full-time workers by part-timers or temporary hired hands, outsourcing of activities and hardware that corporations once did in-house. Victory means that companies like GE are prospering, but at a high cost. And no GE community illustrates this better than Erie, home to GE Transportation Systems, which, according to the numbers at least, is doing better than ever. Indeed, Robert Nardelli, who doubled the transportation unit's sales to $1.5 billion in the three years he was there, is no doubt doing better: Jack Welch chose him in the spring of 1995 to head the bigger and more prestigious Power Systems division in Schenectady.

In Erie, however, success is seldom accompanied by celebration. Although the business is doing the best in its history, with orders in hand for hundreds of new locomotives, employees feel *less* secure because jobs continue to be eliminated. When I first visited Erie in the fall of 1993, I was stunned by how deep the resentment ran. I had never encountered a business where morale was worse, and the people I met were so bitter that it was difficult to understand what kept their anger under control. Union meetings were angry affairs; workers denounced their leadership for not being more militant, for not standing up to the company, even though there was little if anything the union could do but capitulate.

Hard-core unionists weren't the only people who felt frustrated. Through a contact I had made with a church support group, where white- and blue-collar GE employees would gather together to talk out their frustrations, I visited the home one November night of Greg August, a white-collar office worker whose malaise had all the symptoms of battle fatigue. August was once so dedicated to the company that his children jokingly called him "Mister GE." When his daughter Colleen married a union man, it caused a deep rift in the family because August, stridently antiunion, couldn't keep his gung-ho company attitudes to himself. August worked in purchasing, putting in twelve-hour days, six days a week, even working Christmas on occasion when manufacturing said they needed him to pick up special delivery parts and supplies at the train depot. He also summarily fired subordinates the company ordered him to dismiss. But several years ago, he had fallen victim and been laid off. He was immediately recalled, but the experience had changed him. Unquestioned loyalty became deep anger over the incessant demands the company made of its employees. His mood that November night was dour, as he ran through a litany of horrid occurrences: people he had known who had lost jobs, had killed themselves, or lost control in other ways.

"No matter how hard you try, it's never good enough," he said. The demands of his own job had caused his hair to fall out, the result, his physician determined, of job-related stress. "I've come to a point where I just don't give a shit what they do—there's no future in this business for me or anyone."

Perhaps August had overstated the case. Then again, he wasn't alone in the anger he felt. In the months that followed, several workers sought me out to talk about their individual circumstances. What struck me in these conversations, and others that had preceded them, was that a lot more had been lost in Erie than jobs. It seemed as if the most basic of societal values had been lost. "It used to be that you wanted to go to work and do the job for them," said Mike Gieza, another battle-weary veteran of the General Electric wars, "but it's not that way anymore."

Scene three, New York City.

The view from the executive suite is stunning, and what a suite it was—at 30 Rockefeller Plaza, the home of the NBC television network in midtown Manhattan. GE executives at this level live in a rarefied world worthy of *Bonfire of the Vanities*; one member of this elite club is said to have once quipped that a GE executive's idea of hardship is riding in a limo rather than a helicopter. At this level, the stock options, bonuses, and other perks keep rolling in as long as the earnings flow onward and upward. So it was not surprising that my meeting in the fall of 1992 with Michael Gartner, president of NBC News, wasn't exactly revelatory. His five years at the helm of NBC News hadn't been the stuff of legend—he had been blamed for bungling the *Today Show* transition from Jane Pauley to Deborah Norville, naming the alleged rape victim in the William Kennedy Smith trial, and serving up the grisly tabloid TV of *I Witness Video*, and he had just ended a nasty scrape with the disgruntled Arthur Kent, NBC's erstwhile "Scud Stud" correspondent.* But Gartner had succeeded in the one realm that mattered to Welch: the bottom line. When Gartner arrived, the news division was losing $60 million a year. He cut news bureaus, eliminated jobs, endured the wrath of critics who said he cared less about news than about profits, "cleared out a lot of the underbrush," as Welch later characterized it.

It was an arrangement that Gartner, a respected newspaper journalist who had no background in broadcast news prior to joining NBC, insisted he found very satisfying. Squeezing me in between appointments with his boss, Bob Wright, and Bryant Gumbel, Gartner, who always wears bow ties, enthused profusely about GE and Jack Welch. On GE: "They demand that you be good in your job; they provide the resources to allow you to be. They provide financing. They reward good ideas. They stay totally out of the journalism of the place." Gartner liked everything about Welch: his vision, his decisiveness, his leadership, his impatience, his humor, his charm, his charisma, his interest in news, even his stutter. "He makes you feel like you wish you had a stammer," Gartner said.

It was almost an hour before Gartner let down his guard and offered up one trenchant, almost prophetic comment. "You're well liked when you're succeeding. I have no doubt that if this place were in a ditch, they'd get rid of me. I don't have any delusions about that."

"You're well liked when you're succeeding." In that one simple sentence Gartner had hit on something quite profound. If you weren't succeeding, however success was defined, then you weren't well liked. And because you weren't well liked, your existence might be in jeopardy. You were defined not on any individual basis but by what you delivered. And because there was no

* Kent sued NBC for breach of his employment contract, a suit the network settled before trial by paying Kent an undisclosed sum and retracting certain statements made about him in the dispute.

guarantee that you would always continue to deliver, nothing was guaranteed, at least in the working world. Those were the words of a person at the top of the pyramid, which leads me to a paradoxical conclusion: *The head of an organization as important and influential as NBC News felt as insecure, perhaps more so, as someone at the bottom.* Gartner's statement is an appropriate summation of the pervasive anxiety of our age, where no one feels secure, maybe not even Jack Welch.

In any event, Gartner undoubtedly had no idea how prescient his observation had been. Less than six months later, after Jane Pauley and Stone Phillips issued an on-air apology to viewers of *Dateline* and to General Motors for rigging the explosion of GM pickup trucks, Gartner was out of a job. Someone had to be sacrificed, and Gartner was most vulnerable, even though he had "cleared out the underbrush" and Welch had praised his handling of the crisis at a meeting of NBC managers the day after the apology (which was issued on Gartner's own initiative).

So much for job security at GE, where Welch proved once again what all GE executives already know—that outcomes matter more than people.

THAT, TOO OFTEN, is the zeitgeist of our age; what has occurred at General Electric during the Welch era is by no means unique but quite representative of the values (or lack thereof) of corporate America. Welch took a lethargic, bureaucratic company and made it into a predator—creating America's most "valuable" corporation, one that was quick to pounce on opportunities, voracious in its pursuit of profit, as nimble as any in the jungle—but the greatest tragedy of the Welch era is the hollowness of purpose that GE has exhibited. The goal has always been, ever since the Pierre Hotel speech, that GE be No. 1 in every market it competes in, but toward what end? It is winning for the sake of winning. A higher purpose, a sense of service toward communities, people, or humankind—none of this was ever sincerely articulated or instilled. There have been, to be sure, contributions to charity—$60 million worth to New York State alone in the last five years, as Welch noted in one recent letter to Governor George Pataki. But even philanthropy comes at a price. In this instance, Welch said that in light of GE's generosity and long history of good corporate citizenship in New York, he could not understand why the state was supporting a review of the Hudson River under the Natural Resources Damages provisions of the federal Superfund law, which could hold GE liable not only for ridding the river of PCBs but also for damage done by their presence to the entire environment of the Hudson River valley.* Welch asked the governor to hold off initiating the review and, barring that, not to single out GE in any release announcing commencement of the process to the news media. Pataki complied with the latter request but not the former.

What has been acted out at General Electric over the last seventeen years is a metaphor for a vast American morality play. This drama has as its thematic focus the most omnipresent yet paradoxically most unexamined social phenomena of the 1980s and 1990s: our lack of compassion and sensitivity, our outright cruelty to one another.

When Cleveland Browns owner Art Modell announced in the fall of 1995 that he was moving the team to Baltimore to take advantage of a lucrative offer made to him by the city and state, sports commentators nationwide were apoplectic over Modell's act. Yet listening to NBC sportscaster Bob Costas one day as he condemned Modell's "corporate greed," one couldn't help but be struck by the irony. When Welch decided to close a factory in Hickory, North Carolina, and move it to Mexico, as he did recently, throwing more than one thousand workers on the street, no one beat their breast on national television (and certainly not on NBC) condemning Welch for his greed. Somehow, we have collectively come to believe that it is not right for Modell to be greedy—professional football provides public entertainment and, as such, is considered a kind of public trust—but it is perfectly fine for Welch to be. How often does a CEO sacrifice anything! When PepsiCo Chairman Roger Enrico announced in March 1998 that he would give up his $900,000 salary to fund scholarships for the children of lower-paid Pepsi employees, his gesture received the attention it did because the public has not come to expect that sort of behavior from our business leaders. CEOs, after all, are supposed to be greedy, not sacrificial, and the greedier they are the better it is for stockholders.

That is unsophisticated and dangerous thinking. Profits are important, but they must be measured in terms of the social consequences.

In our rush to "reengineer" and to extol the virtues of being "competitive," we have forgotten that there is more to achieving success in business than just racking up steady earnings gains and making the shareholders

---

* Congress has been debating for several years now changes in the Superfund legislation, and GE, according to press reports, has been generally acknowledged as one of the most aggressive corporate lobbyists in the debate. Limiting the scope of potential liabilities under the Natural Resources Damages provisions is an issue the company has championed.

wealthier. Of course, this would strike the reengineering crowd as soppy, sentimental thinking. "The idea that if I come to work, and I work hard, and I play
by the rules, then I'll have a job forever—hooey," Michael Hammer, a management consultant and author of the best-selling bible of corporate reengineering, said in one *Washington Post* article that recounted the agony of eight
hundred workers who had been jettisoned at a factory in Elkhart, Indiana
("dislocated," in the parlance of corporatespeak, as if they had merely collectively turned an ankle). Hammer continued: "That's a naive fiction we were
able to indulge during an unprecedented and unreplicated period of economic growth."

There is little doubt that the past is past, that there are new competitive
realities in the 1990s, that capital and jobs are more mobile and global, that
technology is changing how we define work, and that we as a society must
adjust and become more competitive to keep pace—who but a Luddite can
argue against progress, the most cherished of American ideals? But if Hammer
is right, are we really progressing? In reality, we may have already taken a giant
step backward and paid too steep a price in our quest to become the most productive and competitive economy on the planet. The evidence that we are is
too overwhelming to ignore; our current direction represents, as Tom Clancy
might say, a clear and present danger to American society.

There is a price, whether it shows up on GE's balance sheet or not. Parents pulling their children out of college, marriages breaking up, people losing
their homes and cars, in some instances even their lives. Ultimately, society
bears the cost, and the cost is not just physical but psychological. Every time a
large company announces a major layoff, people feel less secure. There's a
spiritual element to this as well. When Pope John Paul II writes in his *Evan-
gelium Vitae* of a growing "culture of death," in which people are valued only
for their material worth or usefulness, and are tossed aside when they become
a hindrance to those who have power over them, one can't help but see the
obvious parallels to the world of big business and the current state of the
American psyche.

What is fueling the growth of the militia movement, and the "angry white
male" syndrome we've read so much about since the tragic bombing in Oklahoma City? Who are these angry white males and what's fueling their anger? I
don't have any definitive answers, but an event that occurred in Meadville,
Pennsylvania, two months before the federal building in Oklahoma City was
blown apart, offers some insight, I think, into the psychology of people who
Pope John Paul II might call the "dispossessed" of our age.

Meadville, in the northwestern corner of Pennsylvania about thirty miles south of Erie, is a classic middle-American college town. At its geographic center is the "diamond," a leafy town square of war memorials, surrounded on all four sides by stately columned buildings of Greek Revival and Federalist architecture. For generations it was a city that prospered, making a smooth transition more than a century ago from the agricultural to the industrial age, as the interests of the railroaders and the town fathers intersected to bring factories upon which a man might build his life. There was prosperity—two movie houses downtown, a newspaper that was fat, locally owned, and put out several editions—and civic pride, Meadville being the home of Talon, the country's first and leading zipper manufacturer. But the wealth gradually dissipated as the descendants of the factory owners sold their legacy to corporations, managed by men who were instructed to lift their eyes no higher than the bottom line.

Today, although there's a Wal-Mart on the outskirts of town, the factories and downtown stores are mostly gone. So, too, are the manufacturing jobs that supported whole families, and gone with them the faith in the future they represented. When the last vestiges of Talon left in 1994 for cheaper labor and sunnier climes in the South, an era in Meadville's history ended. To some extent, then, it is not surprising that frustrated, angry men would turn out one snowy February night to hear Mark Koernke, one of the chief spokesmen for this country's growing militia movement, who was little known before the Oklahoma City bombing. But *one thousand* of them did; I can't imagine a thousand people turning out for any event in Meadville, except perhaps the summertime Crawford County fair.

No doubt some were passionate "gun people"; Meadville is in a mostly rural area where hunting remains a way of life. No doubt some were military castoffs, tax evaders, survivalists, misanthropes, anti-Semites, or white supremacists. But some who heard Koernke's message of hatred and distrust were another type of dispossessed—conservative, patriotic, God-fearing men who once voted for Ronald Reagan and once believed in the rules but now think they no longer apply. They are men who search for meaning in a world that has passed them by and doesn't care about their welfare.

Lest this is seen as an overly dramatic rendering of the American psyche, consider an earlier question: If we're doing so well as a nation, then why do we feel so lousy? The answer is that we're not doing so well. We have sacrificed stability in our relentless pursuit of efficiency and profit. One need look no further than GE to get some sense of the price that we have paid: GE today does three times the business it did in 1980, with half the workforce. Its profits are way up, as they are elsewhere in American industry—the average return on equity of the Standard & Poor's 500 companies exceeded 20 percent in 1997, the highest level of corporate profitability in the postwar era—but at what price? This economic recovery is the first in the postwar period in which wages were still falling in the fifth year of the recovery.

For many people, these are the absolute best of economic times. And many employers treat their employees fairly and equitably. But as rich as this country is in GNP, it is poor in social tranquillity. Many are angry about lay-offs continuing amid what are supposedly good times, which strikes them as mean and arbitrary; many are angry that their bosses pay only lip service to the notion of valuing employees and have gotten fat raises while those at the bottom haven't; many are angry because they work without benefits or work two and three jobs because one doesn't pay enough; many are angry that people are working harder, generating more goods and services more effi-ciently, but are reaping fewer of the benefits; many are angry that the value of loyalty has gone down. And even though corporate downsizing appears occa-sionally to have finally run its course, the next wave in the cycle is always just beginning. Even to those who are employed, the threat of downsizing seems omnipresent.

PART OF OUR ANGER stems from the fact that there was a different ethos before the "age of cannibalism." In the era that preceded this one, "the age of paternalism," CEOs believed that their purpose wasn't simply to make share-holders wealthier; it was their duty, indeed their obligation, to serve other constituencies, and to grade themselves on how well they did that. Their legacy wasn't just what they did during their time in office; it was what they bequeathed to the generation that followed. There was exploitation, in that era and in earlier periods, which gave rise to employment laws and unions. But for forty years, up until a decade ago, the typical American CEO sought to balance the claims of various interest groups. Shareholders were one constituency, to be sure, but so were employees and communities, which were deemed at least as important, and in many instances more so, than the stockholders.

Thomas Watson Jr., whose father was the defining force of IBM for four decades, expressed the noblesse oblige of that age when he said, in 1962, that "beliefs must always come before policies, practices and goals." In 1935, when Robert W. Johnson Jr., son of the man who founded Johnson & Johnson, first penned the company's "credo," he committed the world's largest maker of health-care products to a similar ideology—"enlightened self-interest," he called it—that put service to customers first, service to employees and to management second and third, service to communities fourth, and service to stockholders last. "When these things have been done," he wrote, "the stockholders should receive a fair return."

George W. Merck, the son of the founder of the Merck pharmaceutical firm, articulated the same ideals in 1950 when he said: "I want to . . . express the principles which we in our company have endeavored to live up to. . . . Here is how it sums up: We try to remember that medicine is for the patient. It is not for the profits. The profits follow, and if we have remembered that, they have never failed to appear. The better we have remembered it, the larger they have been." When the research lab that Merck had founded in Rahway, New Jersey, commercially developed the first penicillin during World War II, he agreed to make information on its production available to rival companies to ensure that sufficient supplies of the new medicine were produced to meet the war needs.

Is it any wonder that Merck, three CEOs later, after it had spent four years developing the drug Mectizan that cured a parasitic disease called river blindness, established an advisory committee in 1987 which distributes the tablets for free to rural villages throughout Africa? Or that Merck, in 1995, gave $20 million to increase the number of black university students who pursue science careers, the largest corporate gift ever to the United Negro College Fund? A cynic would say that if a company ever did such things, an investor would simply put his money elsewhere. Well, in the case of Merck, the reverse has happened. In fact, the company that gained the most market value in 1995— the stock judged by investors to be the most worthy of their dollars—was Merck, not General Electric.

Asked why Merck had pursued the development of a drug for which there were likely to be no paying customers, Merck CEO P. Roy Vagelos explained that to have abandoned development of the product would have demoralized Merck scientists who had dedicated their lives to preserving and improving human life. Vagelos also noted that sometimes altruism pays unforeseen dividends. For instance, Merck is the largest U.S. drugmaker in Japan today, the result, Vagelos believed, of its decision after World War II to introduce tuberculosis-fighting streptomycin in that country, even though it made no money doing it. "The long-term consequences of [such actions] are not always clear, but somehow I think they always pay off," he concluded.

In the era of paternalism, laying off people was considered an extreme measure, to be taken only in the most dire of circumstances, often as a last resort before padlocking the front gate. Even the robber barons of yesteryear subscribed to the notion that jobs and their creation was the most important aim of capitalism and that maintaining employment was a socially responsible, laudable goal worthy of the "captains of industry." In other words, in the prevailing ethic of that time, laying off workers was seen as a sign of business failure, and Wall Street shunned those shares. Contrast that with today's environment, where the more draconian a company's behavior, the more likely it will win the market's favor.

When Mobil Corporation announced earnings of $626 million for the first quarter of 1995—a reversal of a $145 million loss a year earlier—and a week later disclosed plans to eliminate forty-seven hundred jobs, almost 10 percent of its workforce, employees were understandably perplexed. "It just doesn't make a whole lot of sense," said one refinery worker, quoted in the *Wall Street Journal.* "You could see them cutting back personnel and doing different things to get out of a bind, but just to make more profit, I just don't understand." He may not have, but Wall Street certainly did: Investors bid up Mobil shares to a fifty-two-week high.

What changed in the intervening twenty years, so that an event that once would have been viewed in negative terms is now viewed positively? It's hard to imagine that laying off people is any less a repudiation of a company's business conduct now than it was then. What changed, however, was our *response* to it, how we view it, which is largely shaped by the culture we live in, and the values of that culture. At the beginning of the recent recession in Japan, the worst in that country since the modern economy was born after the war, the chairman of Toyota wrote a letter to all of his employees saying, "Under no circumstances will we fire anybody." Toyota still hasn't, though many other Japanese corporations have. Generally speaking, however, Japanese and German corporations still do not engage in downsizing to the degree and harshness of their U.S. counterparts. All the support that the Japanese businessman gets—from the government, from the financial community, from his workers, from his social circle, from society—depends on his behaving according to an accepted convention of business etiquette, and it remains a convention that still discourages layoffs. In America, our expectations and cultural priorities are different. Here, stability is seen as having relatively little value. We as a society have come to believe, mistakenly, that laying off people is what progressive, forward-thinking companies do. The fact that the welfare of people is no longer a consideration in the minds of investors reflects what is perhaps the most far-reaching paradigm shift of the last decade in corporate America, and Jack Welch's actions were instrumental in leading that shift. After all, if the nation's most admired, most successful CEO jettisoned people in staggering numbers, then why shouldn't we?

Fortunately, there is cause for hope. When the baseball strike in 1994 cost Pinnacle Brands $40 million in lost trading-card business, the company challenged its workers to come up with new products and cost-cutting ideas; they did, and sales jumped 80 percent in two years. No jobs were lost. When Deluxe Corporation announced in January 1996 that it would close twenty-six of its forty-one check-printing plants in the United States, the new CEO John A. Blanchard III elected to stretch the shutdowns out over two years and quadrupled company payments for education, to as much as $7,500 per worker annually. When Malden Mills's factory in Lawrence, Massachusetts, burned down in 1995, owner Aaron Feuerstein elected to keep the fourteen hundred workers on the payroll until it was rebuilt. "What right do I have to destroy a major city just to get a few more dollars in the bank that I won't spend before I die?" Feuerstein said when asked to explain his decision. "The money would only go to my children and spoil them." The company was back in business, with a new plant, in 1997.

Not every big company in American subscribes to the notion of people as expendable. Hallmark Cards, the Kansas City greeting card company, has a practice of eschewing layoffs, yet that hasn't prevented it from achieving high profits and, at the same time, extracting higher productivity and efficiency from its workforce in the slow-growth, stiffly competitive greeting card industry. Jobs are eliminated, but people aren't. They are retrained, and given new skills, which are put to use elsewhere in the company. Although advances in printing technology have made many jobs obsolete, because of Hallmark's ironclad commitment to retraining, a camera operator who once made color separations photographically, for instance, can acquire the skills needed to make the transition to computer scanners.

Occasionally an injury may prevent someone from performing his manufacturing job. Such was the case for Greg Hetzler, whose injured elbow left him unable to perform his duties as a "scrapper," which involved using a rubber mallet to hammer cards out of large litho sheets. Hetzler went on Hallmark's "surplus-placement program," and was soon placed in a new position in computer services. "I've talked to people outside Hallmark," Hetzler says, "and they tell me that at other companies, in my situation you'd be gone. Hallmark didn't do that. The company has been good to me."

Hallmark does this not only out of a sense of social responsibility, which has been its way since 1910, but also because it believes deeply that people are its most valuable resource. Laying off people is a short-term response to business conditions, which should be considered in a long-term context, CEO Irv Hockaday contends. Managing for the long haul means investing in people and protecting them from sometimes cyclical, changing markets. "I believe there are two qualities that enable companies to be successful," says Hockaday, the first nonmember of the Hall family to hold the top job at Hallmark, "a commitment to excellence and a recognition of the value of people to an organization. You can't have one without the other."

As a privately held company, Hallmark can probably do that more easily than most. But a few publicly held companies have found that a more benevolent philosophy can work. Cooper Tire & Rubber Company of Findlay, Ohio, 125 miles west of Akron, is a case in point. Even though the tire industry has not been a secure place in the last decade, Cooper, the ninth-largest tire maker in the world, proves that a business needn't be No. 1 to succeed and prosper. Employment has risen 37 percent in the last five years. Cooper's remarkable 6,800 percent stock appreciation in the 1980s testifies to its results, which are the envy not only of its industry but of manufacturers worldwide.

Like Hallmark, Cooper has found ways to energize its workforce and keep sales growing so layoffs are unneeded. One way it provides incentive is by sharing the wealth. Many of Cooper's 10,500 employees are wealthy, and not just those who work in the executive suite (which hardly qualifies as a suite; the executive offices feature linoleum floors, shabby furniture, and threadbare carpets). An employee who joined the company in 1965, making just $7,000 a year then and more than $40,000 now, today would own one hundred thousand shares of Cooper stock, worth several million dollars, had he faithfully invested 6 percent of his salary in stock purchases matched by the company. There are many people who have done just that. Cooper takes its egalitarian philosophy seriously and has capped the salaries of senior executives to maintain a uniform spread between employees at the highest rung of the corporation and the lowest. Such salary caps are rare elsewhere in American industry. In fact, the average CEO's salary in the United States is now forty-eight times greater than the average worker's, compared with a disparity of thirteen times in Japan and nine times in Germany.

Another reason for hope is that the myth of the successful corporation existing solely to maximize profits is finally being critiqued and given a more thoughtful examination. *Built to Last: Successful Habits of Visionary Companies,* published in 1994, examined eighteen pairs of companies in common industries, seeking to answer the question: What made one "visionary," the other mediocre? Why did Motorola and Walt Disney flourish, while Zenith and Columbia faltered? What were the elements of sustained success, generation after generation? The conclusion of authors Jerry Porras and James Collins, two Stanford University business school professors, confirms what

Reg Jones had sensed in 1978: that a company's "spirit" was indeed one of its most valuable assets.

Wall Street isn't comfortable thinking about spiritual issues—it's hard to assign a value to such things—but what Porras and Collins concluded was that the truly great companies have a sense of purpose and being, a "spirit" if you will, that elevates their endeavors above the pedestrian goal of merely making money. I would concur wholeheartedly. In my nineteen years of studying American, Japanese, and German businesses—eleven of them on the staff of the *Wall Street Journal*—I can say unequivocally that I have yet to see an instance where that wasn't the case. People need to believe in the value of their work, and they need to feel that their employer values them. The visionary companies understand this. They have a core ideology that nurtures people, and they adhere to it. They are "clock builders," the authors assert, rather than "time tellers." They understand that a company must exist for a purpose and that its raison d'être must be more than the sum of its net income statements.

One businessman who understood this very well was Max De Pree, the now retired CEO of office-furniture maker Herman Miller and the author of a 1989 bestseller, *Leadership Is an Art*. Under De Pree's stewardship, Herman Miller, founded in Zeeland, Michigan, by his father in 1923, became one of America's most financially successful and admired companies. A hundred dollars invested in Herman Miller stock in 1975 had grown to nearly $5,000 by 1986, one of the best performances of any Fortune 500 company during that period. Moreover, a 1988 *Fortune* poll picked Herman Miller as one of the nation's ten most-admired companies, and one of the top four in the quality of its products. But when De Pree retired, what struck him about the card he received from his colleagues was that not one person mentioned anything he or the company had achieved during his time as CEO. What they all talked about was what he had meant to them, which led De Pree to this conclusion: Your achievements in business won't be remembered, but your legacy—the lives you touched, the lessons you taught—will be.

In Peter Drucker's seminal study of General Motors, *Concept of the Corporation*, he found much to admire in the career of Alfred P. Sloan Jr., father of the modern GM who snatched the U.S. auto market away from a stumbling Henry Ford. From 1924 to 1940, General Motors's market share rose from 19 percent to 48 percent, an increase largely attributable to Sloan's organizational plan, the most famous in the history of American business, which GM directors approved in 1920. But while Sloan built an organizational infrastructure surpassing any other in corporate America, a design that remains largely intact to this day, his vision was too pragmatic and cold. GM had no soul, as exemplified in Sloan's own book, *My Years with General Motors,* which Drucker described as "perhaps the most impersonal memoir ever written." "Sloan's book . . . knows only one dimension: that of managing a business so that it can produce effectively, provide jobs, create markets and sales, and generate profits. Business in the community; business as a life rather than a livelihood; business as a neighbor—these are all absent in Sloan's world."

They are increasingly absent in our world as well, which makes one wonder about the future of capitalism. Are we headed for a new dark age, as economist Lester Thurow predicts? If there is no guiding ideology other than avarice, no sense of purpose other than enriching the shareholders, will the system unwind under the weight of its own moral decay? Would incentives that encouraged companies to become more sensitive to the needs of other stakeholders prevent that from happening? One of the more intriguing proposals in this regard was put forward by Jeff Bingaman, a Democratic senator from New Mexico. Companies that met the seven criteria as an "A-Corp." would receive more favorable tax treatment; speedier federal-agency reviews; exemptions from certain regulatory requirements, and preference when competing for U.S. government contracts. In addition, to encourage more patience on the part of investors, Bingaman's plan would impose a small tax on the sale of securities that occur within two years of purchase, using the proceeds to pay for a huge education and training tax cut for America's working families.

VISIONARY COMPANIES UNDERSTAND that it is in their own best interest to behave responsibly rather than have it legislated upon them. Unfortunately, there are relatively few visionary companies in America right now. Most succumb to the expediency of Wall Street's demands.

In *Built to Last,* General Electric was identified as visionary. Certainly compared to Westinghouse, it was; and certainly throughout most of its history, it was. But it is not today. Ultimately, history will judge Jack Welch as the quintessential CEO of the late twentieth century, symptomatic of our times, no more, no less. He will be seen as an executive who made the trains run on time, who did one thing and did it well in the context of the times but never embraced a bolder vision, never achieved the greatness that could have been his. The fact that he was lionized in his time will matter little to future generations and likely will be seen as indicative of how cutthroat and vicious an era it was, a time when there was virtually no vision in the mainstream of American business. Money is always what matters most to Welch, that and running the most profitable corporation on the planet. History, I believe, will judge him harshly for that.

The visionary companies of our era will be the Motorolas and Intels, the Microsofts and the Hewlett-Packards, companies that were able to create whole new businesses instead of just squeezing the lemon until it had no more juice.

History will eventually set the Welch record straight. Above all, he will be held responsible for GE's multiple misadventures: transgressions in which entire businesses were destroyed and thousands of people lost their jobs. Business historians will come to understand the anxiety and insecurity Welch instilled and how that contributed to a make-money-at-all-costs mentality that was a perfect hothouse for growing calamity. They will wonder why the CEO and his legion of defenders never conceded the obvious—that amid the celebrated GE culture, something was desperately wrong, that in some ways it was dysfunctional, a company whose "distinctive set of traditions, values and beliefs" had been torn apart, leaving only a void. Those historians will wonder why Welch was never held accountable, why the tough questions were never asked, why shareholders and directors looked the other way.

They will wonder why GE was hailed as such a success, when it was unable to grow anything new, other than financial services, and while growth in its core manufacturing businesses was at best anemic. They will wonder why acquisitions such as RCA were ever undertaken when the intent was merely to dismantle what was bought as quickly as possible. They will wonder why a company that owed its very existence to technology lowered its research and development spending 19 percent, in real terms, in the 1990s, even while it continued to post record profits; why it didn't invest more with an eye on the future. They will wonder if multiple-business conglomerates make sense in a world of escalating complexity.

But what they will judge Welch most harshly for will be his inability to let up and let go, for GE will never be the same after he departs. Historians will come to realize that the dominant leader is all too often more liability than asset. They will wonder why the board didn't compel him to choose a successor earlier, and how a corporation with such rich traditions and history as GE ever became so dependent on the personality of one man.

Early in 1995, Welch was interviewed by Marshall Loeb, the onetime editor of *Fortune* and for many years a Welch devotee. Throughout his life Welch had often dispensed his mother's aphorism that people should control their destiny, but on this occasion he didn't appear to control his own. Welch "looked wan," Loeb wrote, having just returned from a trip to Asia with a debilitating parasite. Shortly after the interview, he had angioplasty to unclog a coronary artery and, when that didn't take, heart-bypass surgery at Massachusetts General Hospital, which sidelined him for several months and sparked a cascade of speculation in the business press about who might succeed him and whether the company was properly prepared for such a portentous event.

Welch has always taken encounters with the media seriously, and the session with his old friend Loeb was introspective, at times revealingly so. When Loeb asked if the restructuring going on in the American economy might not be alienating people, and if corporations had responsibilities to anything or anyone besides their shareholders, Welch replied: "I think that's a helluva question. A proper balance between shareholders, employees and communities is what we all try to achieve. But it is a tough balancing act. . . . In our society, whether we like it or not, we have to satisfy shareholders." At another point, Welch talked about his favorite business, GE Plastics, which "had an up year [in 1994], something like ten percent," which he considered a "poor" performance. "They should have been up thirty percent to forty percent."

Finally, Welch was asked about what qualities he looked for in managers. Apparently, he didn't recall what he had just said about GE Plastics, that 10 percent was simply not good enough. "Early in my career," he replied, "there was way too much focus on making the number, on delivering the goods."

The great deliverer of earnings had acknowledged what critics already knew to be his fatal flaw, one that was demonstrated in his rejection of a mere 10 percent return. Maybe, just maybe, he wanted too much. Maybe he was his own worst enemy. Maybe he had pushed too hard.

A NOTE ON SOURCES

When John Winthrop Hammond wrote *Men and Volts: The Story of General Electric* more than a half century ago, the story then was one of invention, and the material to write that book came largely from scientists and engineers, the industrial pioneers who built the magnificent machines that gave rise to the American Century. Unfortunately, America has changed since then. The modern writer who sits down to cite his source material for *The Story of General Electric*, circa 1998, might be tempted to call it *Men and Law*, for much of the primary source material nowadays comes from the courts.

In the interest of space, I have cited specific sources for my information in the notes that follow rather than attempt to list all of them here. General Electric and its adversaries have been very litigious. Thus, there's a veritable treasure trove of court-generated documents— depositions, affidavits, transcripts, court orders and opinions, exhibits—on which I have been fortunate to draw.

Investigatory bodies have also provided a great wealth of material. Among the documents that I counted as indispensable were the Justice Department memorandum recommending indictment of General Electric and De Beers on price-fixing charges; the Government Accountability Project's report on the Knolls Atomic Power Laboratory; the notes of congressional investigators looking into the Dotan affair; and the "Report of Inquiry Into False Trading Profits at Kidder, Peabody."

Private correspondence was another category of primary material on which I was able to draw. Several letters of Jack Welch's—to Dennis Dammerman (May 16, 1984), to Verne Orr (September 6, 1985), and to Brian Rowe (January 13, 1993)—were invaluable, as were Alison Pfeister's letter to the author and the private correspondence of Richard Cole.

I have also drawn on interviews with approximately 320 people and have tried to identify as many as possible.

All the dialogue and thoughts attributed to people in the book are real, based on either documents or interviews, or both. Each time a person is speaking, I have tried to indicate the source in a note, unless it is repetitious in the same chapter.

As indicated in the notes, I have benefited greatly from the work of many scholars and writers. General Electric generates a lot of newspaper and magazine coverage, and I have noted the articles from which I have drawn. The coverage of one newspaper, the *Schenectady Gazette*, was a cut above and deserves special mention.

General Electric is one of the most studied corporations in America, and several works were especially valuable and need mention. Two memoirs of ex–General Electric employees that I found very useful were James R. Burnside, *The Selling of General Electric* (Schenectady, New York: High Peaks Press, 1990) and John T. Broderick, *Forty Years with General Electric* (Albany, New York: Fort Orange Press, 1929). On the history of GE, the aforementioned *Men and Volts: The Story of General Electric* (Philadelphia: J.B. Lippincott, 1941) is a classic that I heartily recommend to anyone who has an interest in the history of industry and manufacturing. Tom Lewis, *Empire of the Air: The Men Who Made Radio* (New York: HarperCollins, 1991), is the definitive work on the history of radio, as well as a pleasure to read. Also in the "good read" category are three books that I found indispensable: Robert H. Boyle, *The Hudson River: A Natural and Unnatural History* (New York: W.W. Norton, 1979), David Gelernter, *1939: The Lost World of the Fair* (New York: The Free Press, 1995), and Ken Auletta, *Three Blind Mice: How the TV Networks Lost Their Way* (New York: Random House, 1991). On the evolution of business ethics, Peter Baida, *Poor Richard's Legacy: American Business Values from Benjamin Franklin to Michael Milken* (New York: William Morrow, 1990), served as a constant guide. One subject that I perhaps overresearched, in part because the reading material was so good and the subject so fascinating, is De Beers. Edward Jay Epstein, *The Diamond Invention* (London: Hutchinson & Co., 1982), and Stefan Kanfer, *The Last Empire: De Beers, Diamonds, and the World* (New York: Farrar Straus Giroux, 1993), are invaluable to anyone with an interest in the world-famous diamond cartel and its monopolistic practices.

Because I did not have direct access to Welch, I drew on two books that did: Robert Slater, *The New GE: How Jack Welch Revived an American Institution* (Homewood, Illinois: Richard D. Irwin, 1993), and Noel M. Tichy and Stratford Sherman, *Control Your Destiny or Someone Else Will* (New York: Doubleday, 1993). Although I don't think either gives a complete and accurate picture of GE in the Welch era—the former is too superficial, while the latter is too sycophantic—they do provide useful information.

No reading syllabus on General Electric would be complete without some mention of Thomas Edison. Two of the best treatments of the man and his life are Matthew Josephson, *Edison: A Biography* (New York: McGraw-Hill, 1959), and Neil Baldwin, *Edison: Inventing the Century* (New York: Hyperion, 1995). They should be required reading in every business school in America.

NOTES

PROLOGUE

3 THE CASE OF JEFF DEPEW: Recounted to the author by Jeffrey S. Depew. The account of events described in the prologue is Depew's own.

4 DEPEW'S SALARY: Cited in the lawsuit Depew filed in U.S. District Court, District of Connecticut, May 18, 1993, p. 3.

  "SUCCESS IN THIS ASSIGNMENT": Letter to Jeffrey S. Depew from Stephen Rabinowitz, August 22, 1990, part of the court record.

6 WELCH HAD STUDIOUSLY AVOIDED: Welch's negotiations with Bradshaw received extensive coverage in the press at that time; see also Robert Slater, *The New GE: How Jack Welch Revived an American Institution* (Homewood, Illinois: Richard D. Irwin, 1993), p. xv; and Noel M. Tichy and Stratford Sherman, *Control Your Destiny or Someone Else Will* (New York: Doubleday, 1993), p. 122.

  "WE CAN DO THIS FASTER": Depew's recollection of what Welch said.

9 "I NEVER WANT": The author interviewed Depew on two occasions in April 1994, and the quotations attributed to Welch come from Depew's recollection of the event in the second of those interviews. The quotations attributed to McNerney also come from this second interview.

  In a May 24, 1996 affidavit, Depew swore to the following: "I observed that he [Welch] became very upset when he discussed what had happened with Mitsubishi, saying that he 'did not want to see any more fiascos' such as what had occurred with Mitsubishi, and I realized that Welch would need someone involved in the negotiations to take the blame for that failure. When McNerney called me on March 6, 1992, to inform me that my position would be eliminated as a result of a reorganization of ED&C and I discovered that I was the only executive to lose my job as a result of the 'reorganization,' I realized I was the scapegoat."

  When asked on October 26, 1993 in a deposition to recount comments about the reason for his dismissal made to him by John Arrington, the head of personnel for

ED&C, Depew testified that Arrington said the following: "He said that Jack [Welch] at this point had a burning desire for the Far East, that it was his intent on determining who should be in there, and what skills were required to succeed there. And then he said that in my exposure to Welch that I had not gotten a ringing endorsement from him in Boca Raton at the operating manager's meeting, which probably raised questions in McNerney's mind, and he assumed that there was subsequent discussions between Welch and McNerney regarding what should be done and by whom" (Depew deposition, pp. 101–02). The decision to fire Depew had been McNerney's, though, not Welch's, Depew testified Arrington as having said.

9	THE JUDGE'S RULING: In granting GE's motion for summary judgment on September 18, 1997, U.S. District Judge Janet Bond Arterton dismissed four of the counts in the complaint because the plaintiff had not demonstrated that the smaller severance package he had received violated the Employee Retirement Income Security Act. The fifth count, that the defendants had breached an oral contract with the plaintiff, was dismissed because the alleged violation was of Connecticut common law and hence should be decided by a state rather than federal court.

In her summary of facts, Judge Arterton noted that Depew had faxed a letter to McNerney on September 7, 1992, detailing the discrepancies between the severance he had been told he would receive and the one GE had informed him of on September 2. On the letter, a subordinate of McNerney's had written "committed—now taking away" (the judge's ruling, p. 3). "In September of 1992," the judge's ruling states on pp. 3–4, Depew "received a communication from Peter Mondani, Arrington's assistant in ED&C's Human Resources Department, informing him that GE's policies regarding benefits under the Executive Deferred Salary Plan and Stock Option Plan had changed since the time of the original agreement and GE was no longer able to offer [him] what had been agreed to in March of 1992."

11	A 1,155 PERCENT INCREASE: The increase is cited in "Size Matters," *Fortune,* April 28, 1997, pp. 200–01. General Electric was the top-ranked gainer among Fortune 500 companies over the fifteen-year period, as measured in dollars, its market value having gained $155.9 billion, ahead of Coca-Cola ($143.7 billion), Intel ($112.2 billion), and Merck ($101.3 billion). GE's percentage increase ranked eighteenth among the top twenty-five gainers in dollars. The top five gainers percentage-wise were: Nationsbank Corp. (15,033 percent), Intel (11,220 percent), Fannie Mae (8,100 percent), Chase Manhattan (5,300 percent), and Wal-Mart Stores (4,969 percent).

HUNDREDS OF THOUSANDS OF JOBS: The net job loss, derived by comparing average employment for 1980, as stated in GE's 10K filing with the Securities and Exchange Commission for that year (402,000), with its 1997 filing (276,000), is 128,000. That comparison, however, understates the number of lost jobs because it also includes jobs gained in businesses GE bought. In Tichy and Sherman, *Control Your Destiny,* p. 8, the authors estimate that GE added, between 1981 and the early 1990s, 150,000 people through companies it had acquired. Approximately 300,000 people had left GE during the period: 170,000 through layoffs and another 135,000 who were employed in businesses GE sold. That 300,000 figure is without a doubt higher now.

12	ABOUT FIVE HUNDRED PEOPLE: The *Wall Street Journal* ran a news brief on September 2, 1993, which said that 454 people were losing their jobs with the close of GE's compressor plant in Columbia, Tennessee. GE was cited as the source for this information. The five-hundred-people count includes this number, as well as a rough estimate of how many individuals had previously lost employment in management, which GE, to the author's best knowledge, never disclosed.

13 MORE INSTANCES OF PENTAGON FRAUD: "Defense Procurement Fraud: Information on Plea Agreements and Settlements," a report of the U.S. General Accounting Office, Washington, D.C., September 1992, appendices I–II.

14 "LET'S NOT KID OURSELVES": Quoted in "GE May Try to Sell Kidder After Debacle," *Wall Street Journal,* April 19, 1994.

15 SHARES WELCH OWNS: The appreciation and value of Welch's shares were reported on the *New York Times* news service on March 12, 1997; the report further noted that more than $56 million of these shares are in accounts on which Welch has yet to pay income taxes, one of several forms of tax deferral made available to corporate executives under federal law. The $107 million estimate on the value of unexercised stock options is found in "Executive Pay," *Business Week,* April 21, 1997, p. 66.
"PEOPLE AT GE DON'T": Author interview.

16 "DON'T WE HAVE": Quoted in "Bobbing and Weaving on the Issue of Layoffs," *New York Times,* May 18, 1996; the Hastings quotation comes from the same story, a report on President Clinton's Corporate Citizen Conference.
"WHAT I'M CONCERNED ABOUT": Quoted in "Selling Entire Stock!: Capitalism Is Giddy With Triumph; Is It Possible to Overdo It?," *Wall Street Journal,* May 14, 1998.
IS IT ANY WONDER: Support for this statement is found in "The Ties That Lead to Prosperity," *Business Week,* December 15, 1997, pp. 153–55; the article cites National Opinion Research Center data. The percentage of Americans polled who answered yes, that "most people can be trusted," has fallen from 44 percent in 1976 to 33 percent in 1996. The Conference Board survey was also reported in *Business Week,* "Taking Stock of the '90s," February 9, 1998, p. 30.

17 "NO ONE SHOULD": Quoted in "Captains Courteous; Era of the Brutal Boss May Be Giving Way to a New Sensitivity at the Top," *Washington Post,* August 31, 1997.
ONE RECENT SURVEY: The two surveys were cited in "The Downside of Downsizing," *Business Week,* April 28, 1997, p. 26.

18 "BE A GREAT LISTENER": Quoted in "Captains Courteous," *Washington Post,* August 31, 1997.

19 ACCORDING TO THE SURVEY: Conducted by International Survey Research, the survey and Greenspan's comments are found in "Job Insecurity of Workers Is a Big Factor in Fed Policy," *New York Times,* February 27, 1997.
"WE'RE EDGING BACK": Quoted in "Captains Courteous," *Washington Post,* August 31, 1997.
PRESIDENT CLINTON: Quoted in "Clinton Prods Executives to 'Do the Right Thing,' " *New York Times,* May 17, 1996.
"MONEY, POWER, FAME": Quoted in "The Gospel According to Dr. Mark," *Business Week,* May 19, 1997, p. 61.

CHAPTER ONE
MADE IN AMERICA

21 EARLY LABORATORY HISTORY: Matthew Josephson, *Edison: A Biography* (New York: McGraw-Hill, 1959), p. 133.
"ELECTRIC LIGHT PROBLEM": Slater, *The New GE*, p. 2.
"TWENTY EARNEST MEN": Josephson, *Edison*, p. 134.

22 "INVENTION FACTORY": Josephson, *Edison*, p. 137.
"WE'VE GOT TO": Quoted in "The Man Who Found the Universe in a Light Bulb," *American Heritage of Invention & Technology*, Winter 1998, p. 30.
"INTEREST IS AN INVENTION OF SATAN": Quoted in "Edison: What Made the Lightbulbs Go On?" *Business Week*, February 20, 1995, p. 17.
"THERE IS NO SIMILAR INSTITUTION": From a letter dated November 14, 1887, taken from Edison's notebooks, which are preserved at the Edison Laboratory, West Orange, New Jersey.
"THE RESEARCH LABORATORY": Quoted in "Edison's Greatest Invention," *Wall Street Journal*, July 13, 1992.
"A BUSINESS OUT OF INVENTION": Quoted in Josephson, *Edison*, p. 137.
EARLY EDISON HISTORY: Three of the best accounts of Edison's early years (and the events leading up to the formation of General Electric) are by Josephson, *Edison;* John Winthrop Hammond, *Men and Volts: The Story of General Electric* (Philadelphia: J.B. Lippincott, 1941); and Neil Baldwin, *Edison: Inventing the Century* (New York: Hyperion, 1995).

23 "AN UNBROKEN LINE": Hall of History, *The General Electric Story: A Photo History*, vol. 4 (Schenectady, New York: The Hall of History Foundation, 1980), p. 76.
"THE ELECTRIC DECADE," "THE MOST SPIRITUAL": Baldwin, *Edison*, pp. 230–31.
"ELECTRICITY LIGHTS OUR CITY": Quoted in Tom Lewis, *Empire of the Air: The Men Who Made Radio* (New York: HarperCollins, 1991), p. 2.

24 EDISON BEHELD DEVICES: Josephson, *Edison*, p. 466.

25 "IS NOT A MANUFACTURER": John T. Broderick, *Forty Years with General Electric* (Albany, New York: Fort Orange Press, 1929), p. 79.
EVEN IN THE PANAMA CANAL: Hammond, *Men and Volts*, pp. 356–58.

26 "ONE MEASURE OF GE'S VAST DIVERSIFICATION": "The Overhaul of General Electric," *Fortune*, December 1955, p. 116.
"THAT FACTORY OF THE FUTURE": Quoted in Slater, *The New GE*, p. 12.
"RONALD AND NANCY REAGAN": A photograph of the Reagans in their "all-electric home" is found in Infact, *Bringing GE to Light: How General Electric Shapes Nuclear Weapons Policies for Profits* (Philadelphia: New Society Publishers, 1990), p. 48.
VISITING EACH OF THE COMPANY'S: Lou Cannon, *Reagan* (New York: Putnam, 1982), p. 93.
EARLY HISTORY OF RADIO: Lewis, *Empire of the Air*, pp. 72–73; also Hammond, *Men and Volts*, pp. 350–51.

28 AGREED TO PAY $4 MILLION: Lewis, *Empire of the Air*, p. 141.
BOWING TO PRESSURE FROM ROOSEVELT: Lewis, *Empire of the Air*, p. 142.

29 METHODICALLY TESTED: Baldwin, *Edison*, p. 112.

"HAVING GOOD FUN TODAY?": James R. Burnside, *The Selling of General Electric* (Schenectady, New York: High Peaks Press, 1990), p. 46.

THE CONQUEST OF TUNGSTEN: Coolidge's development of the tungsten-filament light bulb is told by Hammond in *Men and Volts*, pp. 333–39.

SAVED THE NATION $200 MILLION: Hammond, *Men and Volts*, p. 339.

30 ONE MOLECULE OF AIR: Hammond, *Men and Volts*, p. 352.

IT WAS A UNIQUE TIME: A unique account of the time is by David Gelernter, *1939: The Lost World of the Fair* (New York: The Free Press, 1995).

VISITORS GAPED: Gelernter, *1939*, p. 45.

NEW GADGETS WERE ON DISPLAY: Gelernter, *1939*, p. 271.

IN A GE ADVERTISEMENT: The ad appeared in *Current History*, June 1939, p. 4.

31 "I THINK, WITHOUT QUESTION": "A Conversation with Roberto Goizueta and Jack Welch," *Fortune*, December 11, 1995, p. 102.

32 IN THE PROCESS, SCHENECTADY: The tally of lost jobs was derived by comparing employment totals in 1978–79 and the spring of 1996, as reported in the local newspapers of the seven cities cited. For Evendale, the base was 1987, its year of peak employment; for Pittsfield, the base was 1975. The 1,850 jobs that Lockheed Martin still maintains in Pittsfield (until 1993 a GE Aerospace business) were, for the purposes of this comparison, counted in GE's favor.

33 GE HAS EITHER CLOSED: Ninety-eight fewer plants was derived by comparing GE's own figures, as stated in the company's 10K filings for the years 1980 (228 manufacturing sites) and 1997 (130).

34 "THE JOB OF INDUSTRY": "Villains? Heck no. We're Like Doctors," *Newsweek*, February 26, 1996, p. 48.

DID NOT MOVE FAST ENOUGH: Welch has made this statement many times, including in "A Conversation with Roberto Goizueta and Jack Welch," *Fortune*, December 11, 1995, p. 98.

ABOUT 10 PERCENT LESS: The number was derived by comparing GE's 1995 sales of goods, $33.2 billion (as stated in its 10K filing), equivalent to $17.8 billion in 1980 dollars. GE's sales in 1980 were $25 billion, of which 81 percent, or about $20 billion, was from the sale of goods, according to Tichy and Sherman, *Control Your Destiny*, p. 15. Another analysis points out the same lack of growth in manufacturing. For the five years through 1992, according to the consulting firm of Stern Stewart & Company (which developed the concept of "economic value added"), GE lost $503 million of economic value in its manufacturing businesses; a $1.7 billion gain from financial services gave the entire corporation a positive EVA of $1.1 billion for the period. EVA measures the wealth managers have created or lost for shareholders in running a business. The analysis is found in "GE Monkeys With Its Money Machine," *Fortune*, February 21, 1994, p. 81.

35 FEWER THAN HALF: "A Search for Answers to Avoid the Layoffs," *New York Times*, March 9, 1996.

"THE CONVENTIONAL ECONOMIC WISDOM": Robert H. Waterman Jr., *What America Does Right: Learning from Companies That Put People First* (New York: W.W. Norton, 1994), p. 25.

MOTOROLA'S ORIGINS: Kevin Maney, *Megamedia Shakeout: The Inside Story of the*

Leaders and the Losers in the Exploding Communications Industry (New York: John Wiley & Sons, 1995), p. 295.

35 THE NUMBERS TELL: Spending for plant and equipment and research and development come from a comparison of the two companies' annual reports.

36 AN 85 PERCENT SHARE: Maney, *Megamedia Shakeout,* p. 292.

37 BETTER PARENTS: "Motorola's School for Parents," *Business Week,* August 21, 1995, p. 6.
IN 1975: Robert Levering and Milton Moskowitz, *The 100 Best Companies to Work for in America* (New York: Penguin Books, 1993), p. 321.
MOTOROLA UNIVERSITY: Levering and Moskowitz, *The 100 Best Companies to Work for in America,* p. 321.
SIX SIGMA QUALITY: Levering and Moskowitz, *The 100 Best Companies to Work for in America,* p. 319.
ITS DEFECT RATE PER MILLION OF TWENTY-THREE THOUSAND: Cited in "GE Puts Emphasis on Fewer Defects; 'Six Sigma' Plan Could Become CEO's Legacy," *Cleveland Plain Dealer,* January 18, 1998.

38 GE REINVESTS: "R&D Scoreboard," *Business Week,* June 27, 1994, pp. 78–103; updated with data from *R&D* magazine, October 1997.
GE HIT ITS PEAK: James C. Abegglen, *Kaisha: The Japanese Corporation* (New York: Basic Books, 1985), p. 124.
THE TOP U.S. PATENT RECIPIENT: According to patents tracked by IFI/Plenum Data Corporation of Wilmington, North Carolina.
THE LATEST GENERATION: "Siemens to Build $1.18 Billion Plant for D-Ram Chips," *Wall Street Journal,* December 27, 1993.

39 "UNTHINKABLE": Quoted in "Trimming Down: In the New Mergers, Conglomerates Are Out, Being No. 1 Is In," *Wall Street Journal,* December 31, 1997.
"ONE OF THE MOST COMPETITIVE": Siemens Corporate Mission Statement, adopted May 1990, p. 3.

40 THE DYNAMIC GE MANAGER: The GE Values Statement, circa 1992, is found in Tichy and Sherman, *Control Your Destiny,* p. 343.
THE COMPANY THOMAS EDISON BEGAN: Aircraft Engines, Appliances, Power Generation, Materials, and Technical Products and Services accounted for 37 percent of GE's consolidated revenues in 1997; financial services was 44 percent.

41 ONLY ZENITH: "Zenith to Sell a Controlling Stake to LG, Korean Giant," *New York Times,* July 18, 1995.
"LUDICROUS, ABSOLUTELY LUDICROUS": Slater, *The New GE,* p. 198.
IT SHOULD NOT BE PERMITTED: Senator Hollings's objections to the sale of the Westinghouse unit to Siemens were made in a letter to Treasury Secretary Robert Rubin, reported in the *Pittsburgh Post-Gazette,* November 22, 1997. GE's Industrial and Power Systems division, which competes against Siemens, has a significant manufacturing presence in Greenville, South Carolina, the state Hollings, the ranking Democrat on the Senate Commerce Committee, represents.
HITACHI STUCK IT OUT: "Inside Hitachi," *Business Week,* Sept. 28, 1992, p. 100.

42 "THE HOLY PLACE": The phrase guides used during a tour of the museum by the author in July 1993.
"THOUGH WE CANNOT LIVE": Pamphlet from the Hitachi Central Research Laboratory, printed in Japan, November 1991.

42   ABOUT 6 PERCENT: "Inside Hitachi," *Business Week,* p. 94.
"WE HAVE ROOTS": Speech by Reginald H. Jones, reprinted in the GE Jubilee section of the *Berkshire Eagle,* October 7, 1978.

43   "THE MOST IMPORTANT SINGLE FACTOR": Quoted in Peter Baida, *Poor Richard's Legacy: American Business Values from Benjamin Franklin to Michael Milken* (New York: William Morrow, 1990), p. 296.
"CLEAR YOUR MIND": Quoted in Baida, *Poor Richard's Legacy,* p. 336.

44   10.8 MILLION AMERICANS: Baida, *Poor Richard's Legacy,* p. 331.

44–5 KEEPING PEOPLE ON THE PAYROLL: Hallmark Cards company newsletter, August 14, 1991.

45   COOPER TIRE & RUBBER: "Now Hear This, Jack Welch!" *Fortune,* April 6, 1992, p. 94.
LEVI STRAUSS: Waterman, *What America Does Right,* p. 301.
DOUBLED THE PERCENTAGE OF WOMEN: "Managing by Values," *Business Week,* August 1, 1994, p. 49.
"BY FAR THE BEST": Quoted in "At Levi Strauss, A Big Cutback, With Largess," *New York Times,* November 4, 1997.
HAGIOGRAPHY: The following are reviews of *Control Your Destiny or Someone Else Will.* From the *Toronto Star,* March 7, 1993: "In 1984, Jack Welch, chairman of U.S. giant General Electric Co., was named by *Fortune* magazine as America's toughest boss. Those less kind called him 'Neutron Jack'—a reference to the fact that Welch's decisions seemed to vaporize employees and leave 'only the buildings standing.' As you read *Control Your Destiny,* however, Welch sheds his image of brute and takes on an aura of managerial sainthood. . . . The style at times is too effusive in praise of Welch. Tichy is a respected academic, but he is also a consultant to GE and so he is both careful and forgiving in his criticisms of Welch." From the *Financial Times,* January 21, 1993: "Tichy can speak with authority about GE, since he has had a ring-side seat at the Welch transition, both as a long-time consultant to the company and as head of its executive training school for two years. But this hardly makes him an impartial observer. . . . The book is marred by being too reverential, devoting remarkably little space to the weak spots in Welch's record." From the *Dallas Morning News,* March 14, 1993: "As for [the Tichy-Sherman] book, it has no pretense to objectivity. . . . From the picture of Jack Welch on the cover to the significant space given over to his direct quotes inside, it's CEO megalomania all the way."

CHAPTER TWO
PASSING THE BATON

46   JONES'S BACKGROUND: Recounted in Slater, *The New GE,* pp. 18–19; also Richard T. Pascale, *Managing on the Edge: How the Smartest Companies Use Conflict to Stay Ahead* (New York: Simon & Schuster, 1990), pp. 196–97.
"A LEGEND WITH A LIVE WIRE": Quoted in "General Electric: Strategic Position, 1981," Harvard Business School Case Study 381–174, p. 1.

47   PECULIAR HABITS: Welch's gum-, ice-, and nail-chewing habits are covered in Tichy and Sherman, *Control Your Destiny,* p. 9; and in Slater, *The New GE,* p. 47.
CUSSED LIKE A LONGSHOREMAN: Welch's use of salty language was recounted to

the author in dozens of interviews with people who have worked closely with him; see also Tichy and Sherman, *Control Your Destiny*, p. 43.

47 HE WAS THE ATYPICAL CEO: A portrait of the typical CEO is found in David L. Kurtz, Louis E. Boone, and C. Patrick Fleenor, *CEO: Who Gets to the Top in America* (East Lansing, Michigan: Michigan State University Press, 1989), p. 1.

LIKE BOTH HENRY FORD: Kurtz, Boone, and Fleenor, *CEO*, p. xviii.

WELCH'S RELATIONSHIP WITH HIS MOTHER: It comes up often in interviews he grants; for his own words of what his mother meant to him, see Tichy and Sherman, *Control Your Destiny*, p. 47.

WELCH QUIT CATHOLICISM: Tichy and Sherman, *Control Your Destiny*, p. 48.

PITIED HIS PASSIVE FATHER: The characterization of John Welch Sr., as "passive" is Welch's own in Tichy and Sherman, *Control Your Destiny*, p. 46. The story of his being snubbed for the ROTC scholarship is recounted in Slater, *The New GE*, pp. 30–31, and in many articles since.

48 "ALWAYS HAD MY NOSE PRESSED": Tichy and Sherman, *Control Your Destiny*, p. 46.

"TO MAKE A MILLION": "Roberto Goizueta and Jack Welch: The Wealth Builders," *Fortune*, December 11, 1995, p. 83.

HIS AGGRESSIVE PLAY, ON ANOTHER OCCASION: Author interview.

49 "IT WAS JACK WELCH PLASTICS": Charles Carson was interviewed by the author.

THE COMPANY WELCH INHERITED: The situation Welch faced when he took over as CEO is described in Harvard Business School Case Study 381–174; also "Trying to Bring GE to Life," *Fortune*, January 25, 1982, pp. 51–58.

"PROBABLY NO SINGLE COMPANY": Quoted in Tichy and Sherman, *Control Your Destiny*, p. 27.

JONES AT BETHLEHEM: The author covered Bethlehem Steel for the *Wall Street Journal* while Jones was a director there.

50 "U.S. BUSINESS FINDS ITSELF": Jones's letter is quoted in Tichy and Sherman, *Control Your Destiny*, p. 28.

HISTORY OF THE CORDINER ERA: Pascale, *Managing on the Edge*, pp. 183–88; also Ronald G. Greenwood, *Managerial Decentralization: A Study of the General Electric Philosophy* (Lexington, Massachusetts: D.C. Health and Company, 1974), pp. 13–27.

A RIVAL EXPLOIT THE INVENTION: Burnside, *The Selling of General Electric*, p. 15.

51 AT HIS FIRST BOARD MEETING: "The Overhaul of General Electric," *Fortune*, p. 115.

"FOR A MAN TO GET HIS ARMS": Tichy and Sherman, *Control Your Destiny*, p. 37.

52 "IF MANAGEMENT IS DOING ITS JOB": Pascale, *Managing on the Edge*, p. 187.

"A MINIMUM OF SUPERVISION": Tichy and Sherman, *Control Your Destiny*, p. 37.

EVERY DEPARTMENT GENERAL MANAGER: Pascale, *Managing on the Edge*, p. 185.

53 "THE INCREDIBLE ELECTRICAL CONSPIRACY": *Fortune* dubbed it so in its April 1961 issue; the article was reprinted in the February 11, 1980 issue, p. 174.

THE TWENTY INDICTMENTS: As part of the Philadelphia litigation, according to documents provided to the author by the U.S. Department of Justice, the government brought suit against the indicted parties in twenty separate product categories; General Electric was a defendant in eighteen of them. In six of the cases GE pleaded guilty, and in twelve it pleaded nolo contendre. It paid a fine to settle each of its eighteen pleas, paying a total of $427,500, out of $1,924,500 collected by the government from all defendants. Seven executives from all the defendant companies served thirty-day sentences, and twenty-three others had their sentences suspended. Three of the seven executives who went to jail were employed by General Electric: William S. Ginn, Lewis J. Burger, and George L. Burens. Ginn pleaded guilty in one case and nolo contendre in another and paid fines of $12,500; Burger pleaded guilty and paid a $2,000 fine; Burens pleaded guilty and paid a $4,000 fine. GE was the leader in fines paid, executives jailed, and executives indicted.

54   "CHOIR PRACTICE": Burnside, *The Selling of General Electric,* p. 84.

"SURE, COLLUSION WAS ILLEGAL": "The Incredible Electrical Conspiracy," *Fortune,* p. 175.

55   HE NEVER ATTENDED ANOTHER MEETING: Baldwin, *Edison,* p. 228.

A MUCKRAKING MAGAZINE: *Electricity's* allegations are summarized in a speech entitled, "Charles A. Coffin: Pioneer Genius of the General Electric Company," p. 13. The speech was delivered by GE President Charles E. Wilson on April 25, 1946 at the Hotel Pierre in New York City to the Newcomen Society of England.

56   RIVAL INVENTORS: Pascale, *Managing on the Edge,* p. 180.

"GENEROUS ELECTRIC": The oft-repeated phrase of GE retirees from the era before Welch.

GENEROUS IT WAS: Pascale, *Managing on the Edge,* p. 182.

"EXCESSIVE COMPETITION": Tichy and Sherman, *Control Your Destiny,* p. 35.

DOMINANCE AROUND THE GLOBE: Pascale, *Managing on the Edge,* p. 181.

57   SUED GE THIRTEEN TIMES: According to documents provided to the author by the U.S. Department of Justice's Antitrust division, the outcome of the thirteen cases was as follows: GE was found guilty in one case and paid a $20,000 fine; the government won litigated judgments in two cases; GE pleaded nolo contendre in three cases and paid fines totaling $30,000; and GE accepted consent decrees in six cases in which it agreed to cease activities asserted as illegal by the government. The one case (over Sherman Act violations in tungsten carbide patents, tools, and dies) in which there was a favorable outcome was a suit brought in 1940, postponed indefinitely in 1942 because of the war, and dismissed on the government's motion in 1949.

WELCH WAS DOMINEERING: Welch's behavior and personality traits were recounted to the author in many interviews with contemporaries of his from that time.

"MOST TALKATIVE": "The Wealth Builders," *Fortune,* p. 83.

58   WELCH WAS VACILLATING: The description of his near-departure from GE was related to the author in an interview with Reuben Gutoff.

PLASTICS FORMED FROM IT: The history of PPO and Noryl was recounted to the author in interviews with Gutoff, Charlie Reed, and others involved in the discovery.

59   CATASTROPHIC EXPLOSION: Charles Reed characterized the explosion as such in an interview with the author. In addition, two articles in *Fortune* make reference to this incident, as follows: "At General Electric, Jack Welch bombed early on. A pilot plastics plant that he managed blew up in 1966, and he was held accountable for design flaws," (May 1, 1995); "In 1966, testing a new manufacturing process, he blew up a pilot plant" (March 27, 1989).

WELCH'S FEUD WITH STANLEY GAULT: Gault declined to be interviewed; the feud was related by people who were their contemporaries, including Reuben Gutoff, Welch's boss at the time.

60   "ALL OF THE TOP MANAGERS": Tom Morton was interviewed by the author.

60   ONE COLLEAGUE REMEMBERS: Author interview.

"DINK": The phrase was recalled by Welch's contemporaries from that time who were interviewed by the author; it also appears in Tichy and Sherman, *Control Your Destiny,* p. 30.

ONE VISITOR TO PITTSFIELD: The visitor was a GE manager at that time.

61   "JACK DOESN'T ALLOW": Author interview.

THE MORE HE WOULD STAMMER: Welch's stutter while he cursed was the subject of much behind-the-back ridicule, associates who worked with him then recall.

"JACK ALWAYS TOOK CARE": John Thoma was interviewed by the author.

A VERY DEFINITE CULTURE: The culture was described to the author in interviews with more than thirty current employees or people who worked at GE Plastics during that time.

62   ACCOMPLISHING HIS OBJECTIVES: The account comes from John McLaughlin, who was interviewed by the author.

"YOU'LL NEVER BUY IT": McLaughlin's recollection of what Welch said.

62–3 CAUSED A COMMOTION: The story was recounted by Alison Pfeister, who was interviewed by the author, and her then husband Ed Russell, who witnessed the events.

63   "HE BEHAVED AS IF": Pfeister's recollection of what occurred.

"IMPROVEMENT IN HANDLING": Quoted in Tichy and Sherman, *Control Your Destiny,* p. 43; the same page has Welch's colleagues from that time calling him a "wild man." The "wild man" characterization is repeated by Robert Wright in Slater, *The New GE,* p. 50.

SEARCH FOR HIS SUCCESSOR: The process Jones orchestrated to select his successor is recounted in Richard F. Vancil, *Passing the Baton: Managing the Process of CEO Succession* (Boston: Harvard Business School Press, 1987). The book was excerpted in the January 4, 1988 issue of *Fortune,* "How Companies Pick New CEOs," p. 74.

64   OUTSPOKEN OPPONENTS OF WELCH: Dance and Parker both declined to be interviewed; their opposition to Welch, as well as Dance's support of Gault and Parker's of Burlingame, was related to the author by people involved in the selection process. In Tichy and Sherman, *Control Your Destiny,* p. 57, the authors acknowledge that Parker and Dance "favored candidates" other than Welch.

"REG JONES WAS A VERY STRAIGHT MAN": Author interview.

SEVERAL TECHNOLOGY INITIATIVES: The L-7 project was characterized in Slater, *The New GE,* as a "fiasco" (p. 47). As for the Halarc lamp, its failure was described in the Harvard Business School's Case Study 9-385-315.

65   "WHY, ME, OF COURSE": Quoted in Slater, *The New GE,* p. 48

THREE OR FOUR OF THE CONTENDERS: "How Companies Pick New CEOs," *Fortune,* p. 76.

THE COMPROMISE: "How Companies Pick New CEOs," *Fortune,* p. 76.

CHAPTER THREE
TOTAL WAR

67   ONE DAY: Welch's use of the letter was first noted in "Trying to Bring GE to Life," *Fortune,* January 25, 1982, p. 53. The letter, written by Kevin Peppard, director of business development for Bendix Heavy Vehicle Systems in Elyria, Ohio, appeared in the November 30, 1981 edition of *Fortune,* p. 17.
     A SPEECH HE GAVE: A copy of the speech was obtained by the author from the archive of one former employee.

68   AN INVESTOR WHO IN 1971: The statistics on the performance of GE shares were quoted in "Trying to Bring GE to Life," *Fortune,* p. 51.
     "TAKE A LOOK": From an interview with former strategic planner Greg Vereschagin.
     "IF I COULD": "John F. Welch Presentation to Financial Community Representatives," Hotel Pierre, New York City, December 8, 1981, pp. 9–10.

69   "WHERE WE ARE NOT": "John F. Welch Presentation to Financial Community Representatives," p. 12.
     "THIS CONTAINS THINGS": From the cover letter that accompanied distribution of the speech, dated December 21, 1981, from T.M. (Sam) Egbert to all members of the now defunct News Bureau, part of the Advertising and Sales Promotion department, also defunct, formerly of Norwalk, Connecticut.

70   "WHAT THE HELL": Welch's testy reaction is summarized in Tichy and Sherman, *Control Your Destiny,* p. 60.
     THREE INTERLOCKING CIRCLES: There's no doubt that Welch issued a "fix, sell, or close" edict, but there are people who doubt that the strategy of three interlocking circles evolved as neatly, from his own hand, as is portrayed in Tichy and Sherman, *Control Your Destiny,* p. 89. A da Vinci–like drawing of the three interlocking circles first appeared in "General Electric—Going with the Winners," *Forbes,* March 26, 1984, p. 106, two years after Tichy and Sherman say Welch originally scribbled them. For the purposes of this narrative, the author has accepted Welch's (i.e., Tichy and Sherman's) version of the evolution of this concept.
     ONE FOUR-PANEL CARTOON: The cartoon strip was described to the author by people in Schenectady who recalled having seen it.

71   RALPH KETCHUM: Ketchum declined to be interviewed; the story of his dismissal— and how colleagues felt about it—was related to the author by people he interviewed who worked at GE Lighting at that time.
     TOM THORSEN: Thorsen declined to be interviewed; the circumstances of his departure from GE are to this day informed speculation, based on the suppositions of people he worked with, whom the author interviewed. The assertion that Thorsen's clash with Welch was over the degree of autonomy Finance would have is based on these interviews, as well as the text of a letter, dated May 16, 1984, that Welch sent to Thorsen's successor, Dennis Dammerman, a copy of which was obtained by the author. The tone and substance of the letter suggests that Welch wanted to assert greater control over Finance while at the same time giving his spin on how Thorsen and others had come to misinterpret statements he had made about Finance.

72   "THERE IS NO PLACE": Welch letter to Dammerman, May 16, 1984.
     WELCH WOULD CAST: Corroboration for this statement is found in the lawsuit filed

by Jeffrey S. Depew, according to David M. Cohen, his attorney. Additional support is found in "Combative Chief," *Wall Street Journal*, August 4, 1988.

72　HE CONSOLIDATED: Tichy and Sherman, *Control Your Destiny*, pp. 69, 75.
FIRST WELCH HAD TO PERSUADE: Welch's showdown with the town fathers of Crotonville was related to the author by people familiar with it.

73　"SCROTUMVILLE": The nickname nonbelievers use in referring to Crotonville.
U.S. COMPANIES NOW LOSE: Statistics are quoted in "Loyalty? Now There's a Notion," *Business Week*, March, 18, 1996, pp. 20–21, a review of Frederick F. Reichheld, *The Loyalty Effect: The Hidden Force Behind Growth, Profits, and Lasting Value* (Boston: Harvard Business School Press, 1996).
"IT IS MANAGEMENT'S": Quoted in "Loyalty? Now There's a Notion," *Business Week*.
"THERE ARE THREE GREAT EXPERIENCES": Burnside, *The Selling of General Electric*, p. xiii.
"SOLID CITIZENS": A phrase that kept cropping up in dozens of interviews with GE old-timers.

74　"PEOPLE WHO TREAT PEOPLE POORLY": Author interview.
A NONSENSICAL CONCEPT: Welch's antipathy toward the word "loyalty" was mentioned by several GE executives interviewed by the author and is supported in his own words. "Loyalty to a company, it's nonsense," Welch was quoted as having said in "Combative Chief," *Wall Street Journal*, August 4, 1988.
WELCH HATED THE MAIL: In Tichy and Sherman, *Control Your Destiny*, the authors acknowledge Welch's sensitivity to the mail he received at that time and assert that he "personally answered letters of complaint from laid-off employees, and directly intervened in cases of injustice that came to his attention," p. 78. The copy of one letter he wrote to the wife of an executive the company had terminated is reprinted on p. 276.
THE "NEUTRON JACK" MONIKER: The nickname, which originated in *Newsweek*, "had no redeeming features," Welch said in the November 30, 1992 issue of *Newsweek*, p. 63. "None. I hated it; I still hate it."

75　"CAMPAIGN AGAINST LOYALTY": So dubbed by people at the Fairfield headquarters.
"FRANK MADE IT QUITE CLEAR": Author interview.
"SPEED, SIMPLICITY, SELF-CONFIDENCE": The phrase received prominence in the late eighties, in particular in Welch's April 26, 1989 address to GE shareholders at the annual meeting in Greenville, South Carolina, and in "Speed, Simplicity, Self-Confidence: An Interview With Jack Welch," *Harvard Business Review*, September–October 1989, pp. 112–120.
"WE HAVE TO PERMEATE": "John F. Welch Presentation to Financial Community Representatives," p. 14.

76　"JACK HAD THIS IDEA": Richard Sim was interviewed by the author.
"IT WAS A FOOLISH THING": Author interview.
"IT WAS IDIOTIC": Other people who worked at Med Systems at that time also recall hearing of a fat person who was hidden whenever Welch came to town.

77　"HE'S A CLASSIC MAN'S MAN": Bud Rukeyser was interviewed by the author.
BROADCASTING WAS A BUSINESS: The philosophical split between Rukeyser and Grant Tinker, on one side, and Welch and Wright, on the other, is dealt with at length in Ken Auletta, *Three Blind Mice: How the TV Networks Lost Their Way* (New York: Random House, 1991), pp. 391–413.

77 IN A SURVEY: Auletta, *Three Blind Mice*, p. 479.

78 "I DON'T BELIEVE": Rukeyser's recollection of what Welch said to him.

"WE WALKED INTO": Kent's speech, given on January 21, 1998, was printed in *The Commonwealth*, February 23, 1998, p. 4.

79 "MAYBE A MINUTE": "The Peacock Preens Again," *New York Times*, April 14, 1996.

80 "CESSPOOL": Welch invoked the phrase often as a characterization of Consumer Electronics and Major Appliances, former executives of those businesses recall; the phrase appears as well in Tichy and Sherman, *Control Your Destiny*, p. 83.

WITNESSING ONE BROWBEATING: James West was interviewed by the author; the executive is deceased and his widow did not return the author's phone calls seeking information on the circumstances of her husband's death.

81 HIS TRIP TO TYLER, TEXAS: The details of this trip were conveyed to the author by a person who accompanied Welch.

"THIS IS A PRODUCT": The person's recollection of what Welch said.

THE "MEATBALL": Burnside, *The Selling of General Electric*, p. 38.

A MAN ON A MISSION: John Harnden was interviewed by the author.

CHAPTER FOUR
THE BIG SWING

83 "ACCORDING TO FORMER EMPLOYEES": Quoted in Tichy and Sherman, *Control Your Destiny*, p. 86.

84 ONE SUCH LOYALIST: Kevin Sharer was interviewed by the author.

85 "I KNOW A LOT OF GUYS": Sharer's recollection of what Welch said to him on the occasion of their first meeting.

RICKOVER HAD A POLICY: The background on Rickover came from interviews with Sharer, as well as other officers at GE's Knolls Atomic Power Laboratory who had served there under the Admiral. In addition, the author credits Norman Polmar and Thomas B. Allen, *Rickover* (New York: Simon & Schuster, 1982), upon which he relied extensively in subsequent chapters.

"JACK CAN BE INTIMIDATING": Sharer interview.

TWO PACE-SETTING TRENDS: The author covered both U.S. Steel and Gulf Oil as a reporter during that time in the Pittsburgh bureau of the *Wall Street Journal*.

86 THE MORE THAN ONE HUNDRED OPERATIONS: An exact count is problematic; Tichy and Sherman, *Control Your Destiny*, p. 9, say Welch sold 125 businesses in his first four years.

"TAKING A SWING": Quoted in the appendix of Harvard Business School Case Study 9-385-315, "General Electric, 1984."

87 HIS HANDPICKED TEAM: Of the team, the author interviewed, in addition to Sharer, Greg Vereschagin and Vincenzo Morelli; only Mike Carpenter declined to be interviewed.

WELCH WASN'T PARTICULARLY CONCERNED: The team's consensus impression.

88 IDEAS FOR POSSIBLE ACQUISITIONS: Welch was very involved in the team's activities, the team members recall.

88 A FEW VERY SERIOUSLY: GE's interest in Raychem and E Systems, which was not reported at the time, is Vereschagin's recollection.

89 "I DON'T THINK I'VE MOVED": His comment, made to students of the Harvard Business School during a meeting there, is in Slater, *The New GE*, p. 117.

89–90 HAD BEGUN BREAKFASTING REGULARLY: Welch's meetings with Rohatyn are dealt with at length in the prologue of Slater, *The New GE*, as well as in chapter 8 of the same book.

90 "THIS IS GOING TO BE ONE": Slater, *The New GE*, p. 120.
"WE HAVE JUST SEEN": Rohatyn's speech was quoted in "Felix and Alan: Now That's an Odd Couple," *Business Week*, February 19, 1996, p. 35.

91 HE HAD EMIGRATED: Background on Sarnoff's early life comes from Lewis, *Empire of the Air*, pp. 89–118.
"YOU ARE THE BRAVEST MAN": Quoted in Lewis, *Empire of the Air*, p. 359.

92 "NOW WE ADD RADIO SIGHT": Quoted in Lewis, *Empire of the Air*, p. 275; the historic significance of Sarnoff's speech is also addressed in Gelernter, *1939*, pp. 167–68.
REVEALED HE HADN'T FILED: Lewis, *Empire of the Air*, p. 360; the epilogue, pp. 359–62, deals with RCA's calamitous decline in the years following Sarnoff's departure.

93 "GIVES US THE FINANCIAL CAPACITY": Quoted in Lewis, *Empire of the Air*, p. 361.
"AN EXCELLENT OPPORTUNITY": Quoted in Slater, *The New GE*, pp. 119–20.
"THE TOUGHEST JOB IN GE": Quoted in "GE's Gamble on American-Made TVs," *Fortune*, July 6, 1987, p. 51.
TO ACCEPT THREE CONDITIONS: The conditions under which Miller accepted the job are summarized in "General Electric—Consumer Electronics Group," Harvard Business School Case Study 9-389-048, 1988, p. 15.

94 IN THE MONTHS THAT FOLLOWED: The description of what Miller did to resurrect RCA comes from the Harvard Business School Case Study, as well as "GE's Gamble on American-Made TVs," *Fortune*.

95 AN ITALIAN NATIONAL: The author interviewed Vincenzo Morelli, as well as several colleagues who worked with him at GE.

96 ARRANGED A SERIES OF MEETINGS: Morelli is the source of information about this meeting.
ALL OF A HALF HOUR: The estimate of the length of the negotiation with Gomez is Welch's own in Tichy and Sherman, *Control Your Destiny*, p. 181; on the same page, Welch aide Paolo Fresco characterizes the swap as "a masterstroke," which has to be one of the boldest mischaracterizations of a business deal in the annals of American business.
"WE DIDN'T NEED": Tichy and Sherman, *Control Your Destiny*, pp. 188–89.
FELT THEY HAD BEEN MISLED: Author interviews. Slater, *The New GE*, p. xvii, says Welch promised not to sell any part of RCA without giving the business a careful look first.
IN THE SPAN OF: The numbers are quoted in Auletta, *Three Blind Mice*, p. 392.

97 WHO LISTENED QUIETLY: Miller's reaction to news of the deal that Welch had struck is summarized in the Harvard Business School case study, p. 16.
"THE CHANCE OF A LIFETIME": Quoted in "General Electric to Sell Consumer-Electronics Lines to Thomson SA for Its Medical Gear Business," *Wall Street Journal*, July 23, 1987.

97   "YOU'RE THE YOUNGEST": Morelli's recollection of what Welch said to him.

98   HOW UNFAVORABLE: The description of events at CGR comes from Morelli and other people at the company then.

99   "THAT'S PRETTY IMPRESSIVE": Morelli's recollection of what occurred; another person who sat in on the meeting recalled the exchange.
"I HAVE NO IDEA": Participants in the meeting recall Trani as having said this.
"VINCENZO, HOW COULD YOU GIVE": What Welch is recalled to have said, according to people present at that time.

100 "COULDN'T WE HAVE DONE THIS": Morelli's recollection of what he said to Trani.
AFTER AN HOUR-LONG DIATRIBE: Morelli's estimate of the length of their encounter.
IN 1991, IT WAS SUED: The count of the number of people who died comes from "GE Unit, Technician to Pay $3.7 Million Over Faulty X-Rays," *Wall Street Journal,* April 7, 1993.
HE WOULD POUND TABLES: Welch's table-pounding was described to the author by one CGR employee who accompanied him to one meeting.

101 "I CAN'T UNDERSTAND WHY": Author interview.
"CAN ANYONE TELL ME": Author interview.
ADDED TWO HUNDRED PEOPLE: "Is It Payoff Time at Thomson?" *Business Week,* November 20, 1995, p. 114.

CHAPTER FIVE
A CULT OF PERSONALITY

103 BACKGROUND ON HENRY FORD: Taken from Baida, *Poor Richard's Legacy,* pp. 190–211.

104 "THE WAY TO MAKE AUTOMOBILES": Baida, *Poor Richard's Legacy,* pp. 195–96.
"OUR OWN SALES DEPEND": Baida, *Poor Richard's Legacy,* p. 198.
"MORE OR LESS BUNK": Baida, *Poor Richard's Legacy,* p. 200.

105 "FIRST CAME THE ELIMINATION": Quoted in Baida, *Poor Richard's Legacy,* p. 202.
"THE LARGEST PRIVATE": Quoted in Baida, *Poor Richard's Legacy,* p. 207.

106 "YOU'VE GOT TO BE": Quoted in "Talking Management with Chairman Welch," *Washington Post,* March 23, 1997.
ONE GE BOARD MEMBER DEMURRED: According to one person who was privy to the board's deliberations on the day they considered the acquisition.

107 "WOULD YOU FUCK A CUSTOMER": The story was told to the author by the husband of the woman who had been propositioned.
"KATANGA": The Katanga story was recalled by several people who had worked at GE Plastics, as were the serial vandalism and incidents of sexual harassment.

107–8 HEAVED A GRAND PIANO: The author confirmed it with people who saw it happen.

108 "YOU BETTER BEHAVE HERE": Author interview.
"THERE WAS A RAPPORT": Author interview.

109 "I DIDN'T EVEN KNOW": The author interviewed Rebecca Deitz; Uwe Wascher declined to be interviewed.
HE INSISTED THAT SHE LEAVE: Deitz related the story of her boss's demand that she

leave the hospital and drive back; two colleagues who worked with her at that time corroborated her account.

109   SEXUAL HARASSMENT: Besides Deitz, the author spoke with other women who made similar allegations.

"I CAN SEE YOUR NIPPLES": Deitz's recollection of the comments certain men made to her.

"FORCE FUCK": It was by no means an obscure phrase; several people the author interviewed had knowledge of it.

A MIDWESTERN COMPANY: The author covered Borg-Warner as a business reporter in Chicago in the late seventies.

111   INVARIABLY, MERGERS DON'T WORK: "The Case Against Mergers," *Business Week,* October 30, 1995, pp. 122–30.

THE STRATEGIC PLANNERS: According to people on Hiner's staff; Hiner declined to be interviewed.

112   CHANGED HIS DEMEANOR: This was not subtle but commonly noted among people on Hiner's staff.

HINER CONVINCED HIMSELF: Most observers view Hiner as the impetus behind the deal. One person on his staff explained his motivation in acquiring Borg-Warner.

THE AUCTION THAT FOLLOWED: The specifics of the bidding between Exxon and GE were not reported at the time; they were disclosed to the author by sources on the Borg-Warner side.

113   "THERE WERE SOME PRETTY BIG": Author interview.

114   "I COULDN'T BELIEVE WHAT I HAD HEARD": Richard Smith was interviewed by the author.

"INCOME PLAYS": Smith's description of financial gimmickry.

"YOU'VE GOT FIVE MINUTES": The quotation comes from Borg-Warner people who went through the process.

115   MORE THAN $50 MILLION BELOW: The numbers cited here come from internal GE documents obtained by the author.

"NET INCOME ISN'T THE ONLY": Quoted in "Bottom-Line Guy: A Brutal Negotiator, GE Capital's Wendt Builds a Conglomerate," *Wall Street Journal,* November 2, 1994.

116   MOST OF THE GOODWILL: This information comes from accountants familiar with the tax treatment of the merger.

"MIDNIGHT FLIGHT": One consultant to Electrical Distribution & Control has work notes documenting the flight, which were provided to the author; in addition, two ED&C employees the author interviewed were familiar with the incident.

117   WHEN RUSSELL LEARNED: The author interviewed Edward Russell about the Asahi transaction; his description of events was the same as told to several federal investigatory agencies, including the Defense Logistics Agency, according to notes the author obtained of that interview. In addition, the author verified Russell's description of the transaction with two GE executives, one in corporate accounting at Fairfield headquarters, the other a department manager at Superabrasives.

WROTE A TWO-PAGE LETTER: The letter, dated December 26, 1989, was from T. Chonan, General Manager, Third Plastics Division of Mitsui & Co., to Dennis C. Daigneault, Director-Finance, GE Plastics Pacific, Tokyo.

118   "THERE MUST HAVE BEEN": Author interview.

118 RECORDED A 44 PERCENT: Statement is found in General Electric's 10-K filing with the Securities and Exchange Commission, for the fiscal year ended December 31, 1989, p. 36.

WELCH SINGLED OUT PLASTICS: As part of his lawsuit against GE, Edward Russell, a former vice president, prepared a chronology of events during his employment there; Welch's rebuke of Plastics' performance at the March 1990 Corporate Executive Council meeting is cited on p. 33 of Russell's chronology; it was also verified independently by others familiar with the meeting.

119 THE LAST TWO YEARS: The numbers cited in this paragraph come from notes Russell took as a member of Hiner's staff and appear in his chronology.

AFTER RECEIVING HIS TERMINATION NOTICE: The author interviewed Jan Vestergaard.

"YOU FUCKIN' GUYS": In addition to Russell, one other member of Hiner's staff recalled Welch as having uttered the expletive. As a general remark, Welch's use of profanity is one of the most frequently mentioned aspects of the man. In Slater, *The New GE,* the author has four quotations in which Welch swears (pp. 79, 137, 166, and 174).

"HE LOOKED LIKE HE WAS": Author interview.

120 "YOU'RE FUCKIN' CRAZY": Several people in attendance recalled Hiner's assertion and Welch's response.

"VERY ROUGH": Hiner declined to be interviewed; the response attributed to him is Russell's recollection of what Hiner said to him. They were alone at the time.

HAD ALREADY BEGUN LOOKING: Hiner so testified in the government antitrust suit against GE.

CHAPTER SIX
THE DEATH OF THOMAS EDISON

122 OVER THE TEN-YEAR PERIOD: The statistics are found in "Competitiveness Index 1994," a report of the Council on Competitiveness, pp. 19–20.

REAL SPENDING DECLINED: These statistics are found in "Basic Research Is Losing Out As Companies Stress Results," *New York Times,* October 8, 1996.

ACCORDING TO ONE SURVEY: The survey, published in *Fortune,* was cited in "The R&D Dilemma: The High Cost of Cutting Back," *HBS Bulletin,* April 1993, p. 34.

123 "A DECADE FROM NOW": Quoted in Slater, *The New GE,* p. 67.

PAID $103 MILLION: The payment is found in "GE, in Patent Suit, To Pay $103 million," *New York Times,* July 1, 1997.

"NEARLY HALF OF THIS INVESTMENT": "General Electric Dedicates R&D Center," PR Newswire, October 4, 1982.

124 GARY CARLSON: Carlson's predictions are cited in "GE Names Head of Ceramics Unit," *New York Times,* November 18, 1983.

THE MOST SPECTACULAR FAILURE: The story of the failure of the rotary compressor, "Chilling Tale: GE Refrigerator Woes Illustrate the Hazards in Changing a Product," was first published under the author's byline in the *Wall Street Journal,* May 7, 1990.

125 A PRODUCT SO UNIQUE: Information on the background and development of the Monitor Top is taken from three articles archived at the Hall of History, Schenectady,

New York: "Refrigeration," "Boom and Bust, 1920–39," and "Our Friends Call It 'The House of Magic.' "

126 THE DEADLINE THAT HAD BEEN IMPOSED: The author wrote a story about the rotary compressor for the *Wall Street Journal*, which appeared May 7, 1990. Several days after publication of the story, he received a three-page letter, dated the day of its publication, from a "confidential source," saying that the story hadn't gone far enough. It reads in part: "In your article of May 7th on the GE refrigerator woes, you state that the full story of GE's compressor fiasco has never been told. It appears to us that it still hasn't; hence, we would like to induce you to publish a sequel that positions the total situation a bit more accurately or with greater precision. . . . Why do we say that you have still not revealed the full story? Simply because you tell the 'how' and not the 'why' all this occurred. . . . Why did all this occur? . . . It is clear in our view that this responsibility lies at the feet of Jack Welch, who produced all this pressure that caused all these individuals to act erratically due to fear for their well-being. Any number of the individuals on the attached list will confirm this if you can get them to lay it on the line. Some should willingly do this and we have asterisked them to hopefully assist your further inquiry, if you feel, as we do, that the 'why' should be answered and the responsibility fixed." The author subsequently interviewed nine of the thirty executives named in the appendix. There was agreement among them that Welch had set the deadline for completion of the project; that because of that deadline the time-tested manner of introducing a new product more gradually had been abandoned; and that these two factors, in conjunction, caused the failure.

127 THE COMPRESSORS WEREN'T PERFORMING WELL: The *Journal* story quoted technician Paul Schank, one of the people who did the limited compressor testing that was done, who had found evidence of excessive wear and heat in the compressor. Schank's supervisors "discounted the findings and apparently didn't relay them up the chain of command," the story said. Evidence that the compressor was defective— evidence presented to management *before* the refrigerator was put into mass production— was not followed up on, because of the tight deadlines Welch had set and the pressure to get the job done within those deadlines.
"THE PRESSURE TO GET THIS PROJECT DONE": The author interviewed Robert Derman as part of his research for the *Wall Street Journal* article.
"IT WOULD HAVE TAKEN": Author interview.

128 "ON THAT ONE": Author interview of the person who heard Welch make this remark, at the video filming.
IT DIDN'T EVEN PLACE: "The Great Refrigerator Race," *Business Week,* July 15, 1993, pp. 78–81.

129 A "WILD SWING": Quoted in "Are We Eating Our Seed Corn?" *New York Times,* May 13, 1990.
"EATING YOUR OWN MOTHER": The author heard Roderick use this expression to describe share repurchases on many occasions while covering U.S. Steel.
ACTUALLY, WELCH HAD SAID: "GE Shares Lag Market Badly, Despite Plethora of Positives from Perplexed Welch's Efforts," *Wall Street Journal,* May 16, 1988.
"MY REAL DEEP SADNESS": Quoted in Slater, *The New GE,* p. 120.

130 WELCH ADDRESSED A MEETING: The meeting was described in "Combative Chief:

GE Chairman Welch, Though Much Praised, Starts to Draw Critics," *Wall Street Journal,* August 4, 1988.

130 "WE ARE $4 BILLION BEHIND EXXON": Quoted in "Will GE Topple IBM's Crown As the Stock-Market's Value King?" *Wall Street Journal,* July 23, 1990.

"I'D SAY FOR THE GOOD PEOPLE": Quoted in Auletta, *Three Blind Mice,* p. 326.

131 "YOU'RE KILLING ALL THE STOCKS": The author interviewed Larry Grossman; his exchange with Welch was also reported in the *Columbia Journalism Review.*

"WE'RE NOT SURE WHY THIS IS THE CASE": Quoted in "GE Wants to Bring Another Good Thing to Life: Its Shares," *Wall Street Journal,* March 7, 1989.

132 HENRY FORD'S FIRST ATTEMPT: Baida, *Poor Richard's Legacy,* p. 193.

135 "HE SAID THAT WELCH": Drickamer's comments were made to Wentorf, who related them to the author in an interview.

ROLAND SCHMITT: He declined to comment on his departure from GE.

136 THE AXE FELL HARD: The author interviewed Joe Wirth.

137 "THERE WAS MORE": Quoted in "The Man Who Found the Universe in a Light Bulb," *American Heritage of Invention & Technology,* Winter 1998, p. 33.

"THEY SAID, 'WE DON'T HAVE ANY INTEREST' ": The author interviewed Hay.

"PAPER LOCOMOTIVE": "Head of Steam: GE Locomotive Unit, Long an Also-Ran, Overtakes Rival GM," *Wall Street Journal,* September 3, 1993.

138 "GENERAL ELECTRIC HAS CHANGED ITS ORIENTATION": The author interviewed Tom Johnson.

"IT PROVIDED US": "Jobs, Job Training Lost in GE Changes," *Erie Daily Times,* December 7, 1993.

139 "WE FEEL THAT WE CAN GROW": Quoted in *Business Week,* 1993 Enterprise section, p. 215.

140 HIS SECOND STOCK BUYBACK IN FIVE YEARS: "Quarterly Dividend Up 12% and Stock Buyback Is Raised," *New York Times,* December 16, 1995.

CHAPTER SEVEN
DEADLY DECEPTION I

142 "THE LEGACY OF PROBLEMS": Michael Jordan was interviewed by the author.

"THE OCEAN APPROACHES TO OUR COUNTRY": Quoted in Polmar and Allen, *Rickover,* p. 115.

143 "I AM A CREATURE OF CONGRESS": Quoted in Polmar and Allen, *Rickover,* p. 208.

MORE THAN 150 TIMES: Polmar and Allen, *Rickover,* p. 224.

SECOND ONLY TO J. EDGAR HOOVER: Polmar and Allen, *Rickover,* p. 214.

A CONGRESSIONAL GOLD MEDAL: Polmar and Allen, *Rickover,* p. 218.

144 HELD THE FIRST CONGRESSIONAL: Polmar and Allen, *Rickover,* p. 207.

SIGNS ALONG THE ROAD: The author visited the site as part of his research.

A REPORT ISSUED IN NOVEMBER 1988: The New York State report is summarized in "Cleanup or Coverup? Confidential Briefing Paper Concerning the Knolls Atomic Power Lab," Government Accountability Project, Washington, D.C., July 21, 1989, pp. 37–47.

144   ONE OF WHOM RECALLED CLEANING UP: "Cleanup or Coverup?" p. 46.

145   "YOU JUST WASHED YOURSELF OFF": Quoted in "Cleanup or Coverup?" p. 46.

AN ASSESSMENT BY GENERAL ELECTRIC: The assessment, known as the Knapp Report—after Bruce F. Knapp, the manager of Radiation Controls and Health at the Knolls Atomic Power Laboratory, who authored it—is a detailed survey of Knolls's history and radiological status. The author obtained a copy of the report and interviewed one member of the review team who assisted Knapp in its preparation. The report clearly establishes that there was residual radiation at the Peek Street site post-1955.

HAD BEEN USED AS A FOOD WAREHOUSE: "Cleanup or Coverup?" pp. 39–40.

AS RECENTLY AS FEBRUARY 1993: "Quiet Cleanup of Radioactive Wastes Under Way at Peek Street Facility," *Schenectady Gazette*, February 19, 1993.

APPEARED BEFORE THE SUBCOMMITTEE: The author obtained a copy of their joint statement, made before the subcommittee on Research and Development of the Joint Committee on Atomic Energy, March 19, 1959.

"WE HAVE NO CONFIDENCE": Suarez and Hoffman statement, p. 1.

146   "I DO NOT BELIEVE": Quoted in Polmar and Allen, *Rickover*, p. 213.

"THE MOST VALUABLE": Quoted in Polmar and Allen, *Rickover*, p. 181.

"CITIZEN ATOM": Burnside, *The Selling of General Electric*, p. 62–72.

147   HIS FATHER WOULD BOIL: The author interviewed Jack Shannon.

SHANNON'S DOSIMETER WAS TAKEN AWAY: Besides Shannon himself, the author interviewed approximately ten of his colleagues, who corroborated this story and others.

148   GEORGE FOUNTAIN: The author interviewed Fountain, who was Manieri's supervisor at the time the discharge occurred. Manieri told Fountain what he had done. Manieri, on his deathbed, also told Frank Bordell, who was interviewed by the author.

149   THE HIGHLY RADIOACTIVE HUNK OF METAL: A 1982 photograph of the reactor vessel, in transit via railcar from Ballston Spa, New York, to the National Engineering Laboratory in Idaho, was reprinted in the *Schenectady Gazette*, March 22, 1989.

HE DISCOVERED THAT KNOLLS: The estimate of 389 tons of buried hazardous wastes is found as well in "Twin Sites Served as Toxic Dumps," *Schenectady Gazette*, March 21, 1989.

SHANNON'S CAREER SUDDENLY TOOK: The author has reviewed hundreds of pages of documents supporting Shannon's contentions, in which his story never wavered. It was consistent with his testimony, on November 16, 1989, before the House Committee on Education and Labor, Subcommittee on Labor-Management Relations. In addition, the author interviewed numerous people who were familiar with the circumstances of Shannon's demotion, including Bob Stater and George Fountain, and found that their stories corroborated Shannon's, which is summarized as well in the Government Accountability Project report, "Cleanup or Coverup?" pp. 19–23. The Department of Energy Inspector General, John C. Layton, also investigated Shannon's case. In a memorandum, dated September 7, 1990, Layton found "procedural deficiencies" in how Shannon's superiors had dealt with him and his complaints. "We found that KAPL [Knolls Atomic Power Laboratory] officials did not always strictly adhere to KAPL personnel policies and procedures," Layton concluded. In Layton's view, however, the evidence did not reach the legal threshold of outright "discrimination."

149 "THE WHOLE THING WAS SUCH A FARCE": The author interviewed Stater.

"THEY DIDN'T MAKE ANY EFFORT": The author interviewed Fountain.

150 "A PERSON OF UNQUESTIONED HONESTY": Bruce F. Knapp, performance appraisal of Jack Shannon, May 21, 1979. "Shannon is a person of good moral character and reputation," Knapp wrote.

SUPERIORS AT KNOLLS HAD FALSIFIED: Shannon made that claim in his suit against General Electric and the Department of Energy and in testimony he gave on November 16, 1989, to the House Committee on Education and Labor, Subcommittee on Labor-Management Relations. "Since my disclosures to the Inspector General," Shannon said, according to the transcript of his remarks, "I have been the subject of continuous retaliation and harassment. For instance, I have received three unsatisfactory performance appraisals within the last year, been threatened with loss of salary, been requested to see a psychologist by my manager and been denied opportunities to interview for open positions. Additionally, my former managers placed false and derogatory information in my personnel security file maintained by the Office of Personnel Management, without my knowledge."

151 "WHY HAS THE GENERAL ELECTRIC COMPANY": Shannon's recollection of what he said to Welch.

"YOU CAN'T BELIEVE THAT!": Tichy and Sherman, *Control Your Destiny,* p. 81.

153 REMOVING RADIOACTIVE WASTE: "America's Nuclear Secrets," *Newsweek,* December 27, 1993, pp. 14–20.

"MORE THAN ONCE": The author interviewed Clayton Crandall.

ONE MEMO DESCRIBED AN EXPERIMENT: "America's Nuclear Secrets," p. 17.

"TOO MANY OF THESE EXPERIMENTS": "America's Nuclear Secrets," pp. 14–15.

154 THOSE EIGHTEEN SUBJECTS: The settlement figures on the plutonium experiments were disclosed in "U.S. Pays for Radiation Tests," *Miami Herald,* October 25, 1996.

IT WAS BARBARISM HIS COMPANY: GE's participation in the use of prisoners for radiation experiments was reported in the *Seattle Times* on December 31, 1993, under the headline, "Hanford memo suggests more illegal testing." According to the article: "The [Newton] memo, marked 'strictly private,' was written four months after General Electric Co., the main contractor at Hanford, and Seattle's Pacific Northwest Research Foundation began irradiating the testicles of inmates at the state prison in Walla Walla and at prison facilities in Oregon. Those studies, aimed at determining the effects of radiation on human reproductive organs, were concluded in 1971 and have been well publicized. In both cases the inmates were paid volunteers, and there is no indication that the studies were illegal. But [Battelle spokesman Jerry] Holloway said the timing of the 1963 memo suggests that, at the time the prisoner experiments were approved, other questions had arisen about previous human studies." A copy of the Newton memo was given to the author by Tom Carpenter, an attorney with the Government Accountability Project, who until his transfer to GAP's office in Seattle had investigated Knolls.

"I HEREBY AGREE": Quoted in "America's Nuclear Secrets," p. 15.

"THE RECORDS ON THE PAST EXPERIMENTS": Quoted in the memorandum of C.E. Newton Jr., manager of Composite Dose Studies & Records, to A.R. Keene, manager of Radiation Protection, December 12, 1963, which was obtained by the author. The existence of the memo was disclosed in "Hanford Memo Suggests More Illegal Testing," *Seattle Times,* December 31, 1993.

156 IN FAVOR OF A RESOLUTION: The author obtained a copy of the resolution, described in "Nuclear Weapons Production at the General Electric Company," United Methodist Book of Resolutions, pp. 433–34.

157 IT WAS AN ODD SPECTACLE: The encounter was described to the author by Sister Susan Mika.
THE FILM, MADE IN NINE MONTHS: The author interviewed Debra Chasnoff. Additional information on her background was found in "Bringing Bad Things to Light," *Washington Post,* April 23, 1992.

158 THE ONCOLOGY OF COLE'S CANCER: The author interviewed Dr. Martin.

159 "I'M GONNA BE A BIG SHOT": Don Cole was interviewed by the author; his recollection of what his brother said.
"THIS COUNTRY IS THE BEST ONE AROUND": Quoted in "Man Persists With High Hope," *Hartford Courant,* April 25, 1976.
"TO SET THE RECORD STRAIGHT": An affidavit by Richard F. Cole, April 4, 1976.
"IN THE NEARLY NINE YEARS": Cole affidavit.

160 "AS I ACQUIRED": Cole affidavit.

161 "DIDN'T GET A BLOODY PENNY": The author interviewed Joe Thompson.
"WAS THE HARDEST THING I EVER HAD TO DO": Quoted in a letter from Richard Cole to his brother Don, dated March 5, 1976.
"SINCERE REGRET": Quoted in a letter from President Gerald Ford to Richard Cole, dated June 18, 1976.

162 HIS ACADEMIC CREDENTIALS: The author interviewed Frank Bordell. His credentials are summarized in his lawsuits against General Electric, which also name Albert E. Kakretz and Richard Winslow as defendants.

163 CONTRIBUTING TO HIS SUSPICIONS: The work histories of Manieri and Phoenix are reviewed and summarized in "Cleanup or Coverup?" pp. 33–36.

CHAPTER EIGHT
DEADLY DECEPTION II

164 "HOW WILL YOU KNOW": Author interview.

165 DEMING BELIEVED: The author interviewed Deming while a reporter at the *Wall Street Journal.*
"ULTIMATELY WE'RE TALKING ABOUT": Quoted in Tichy and Sherman, *Control Your Destiny,* p. 203.
"GE'S CHAIRMAN IS PUSHING IDEAS": Headline from the cover story of "Inside the Mind of Jack Welch," *Fortune,* March 27, 1989.
"BECAUSE IT STRIKES RIGHT AT THE HEART": Quoted in Slater, *The New GE,* p. 222.

166 NONE WAS A MORE DEVOTED DISCIPLE: Kakretz's behavior and managerial style were described to the author by many subordinates who worked for him at KAPL.
SURPASS EACH OTHER IN MEANNESS: The author interviewed about a dozen people who had worked at Knolls under Kakretz, now deceased, and the opinions expressed about him were universal. The comments of George Fountain were typical. He described Kakretz as "arrogant," "dictatorial," "insensitive to people's feelings," "a kick

ass kind of guy," "very intimidating," "almost like the mafia," a person who would "ridicule people and embarrass them in front of others."

168 PRACTICE OF THREAT AND INTIMIDATION: The author had numerous conversations with Mary Kuykendall, who worked in public relations for Noll during the period in question and who characterized his management in that manner.

"PLEASE ASSURE REMOVAL": A copy of the memo, dated October 11, 1988, was obtained by the author.

"SOME OF US USED TO THINK": The author interviewed Fountain.

"JACK IS A VALUABLE CONTRIBUTOR": Kakretz comments from Shannon's 1984 performance appraisal, a copy of which was obtained by the author.

A BURLY EX-MARINE: The author interviewed Doug Allen.

"THEIR RESPONSE WAS": Allen's recollection of what he was told.

DEATH LIST: Allen provided a copy of his "death list" to the author. As of its date, March 30, 1988, it lists 140 hourly workers, and forty-one salaried.

170 A TEAM OF NAVY INSPECTORS: The phrase "fundamental weaknesses" is the Navy's own and appears on p. 2 of the cover letter that precedes the "Report of Board of Investigation on the Possible Exposure to Asbestos of Personnel at the Kesselring Site," dated November 19, 1986, a copy of which was obtained by the author. The memo was written by D.J. Hamilla, chairman, Board of Investigation, to B.M. Erickson, manager, Schenectady Office of Naval Reactors.

AN INSUBORDINATE CRACKPOT: Kakretz declined to be interviewed and has since passed away. The author's assessment of his state of mind is based on numerous interviews with people who knew Kakretz and worked with him, as well as a review of court documents filed as part of Frank Bordell's suit against GE and Kakretz. That lawsuit established that Kakretz felt enough animosity toward Bordell to have referred to him, in a meeting with managers two months later, as an "evil man." In addition, Kakretz clearly felt that Bordell had been insubordinate, since "unauthorized" (though unspecified) activity was the chief reason cited for Bordell's dismissal, according to the official company statement on the matter, issued March 30, 1988.

"FAILURE TO FOLLOW": Quoted in "Bordell 'Whistleblower' Case Tore Open a Pandora's Box of Radiation Riddles," *Schenectady Gazette*, March 23, 1989.

171 SHOWED ENOUGH CAUSE: Bordell's explanation for what he did, and why he did it, is found in his lawsuit against General Electric, filed in the Supreme Court of the State of New York, County of Saratoga, No. 45-1-89-0918.

AT THIS POINT: Government Accountability Project (GAP) report, "Clean Up or Cover Up?" July 21, 1989, p. 13.

173 "THERE ARE THINGS GOING ON": Shannon's recollection of what Kakretz said to him; Kakretz declined to be interviewed.

"I HAVE HERE": Shannon's recollection of what Kakretz said to him.

THE MEETING BEGAN: The events of May 26, 1988 have been dealt with extensively in the courts.

174 "BORDELL IS AN EVIL MAN": Though Kakretz disputed having said that, it was the conclusion of Judge Loren Brown, in denying a GE petition for summary judgment on February 7, 1991, that his statements "lack[ed] credibility."

"HAS NOT BEEN CANDID": Judge Brown's decision, p. 3.

175 AN ARTICLE ON THE FRONT PAGE: "Parking Lot at Knolls Lab Contaminated at

Least 20 Years by Nuclear Waste," *Schenectady Gazette,* June 22, 1988.

175 THE SALE OF THE PROPERTY: The sale of the parking lot is covered in "Cleanup or Coverup?" pp. 50–52.

THE SAGA OF THE PARKING LOT: The author interviewed Mark Hammond. In addition, the author obtained an internal GE report, an assessment of the radiation in the parking lot, conducted in 1984. The report, prepared by R.E. Zawadzki, clearly shows that the Office of Naval Reactors and the Department of Energy knew of the contamination at least four years prior to the property's sale for one dollar. In a follow-up letter, dated August 26, 1985, M.N. Ross, manager, Laboratory Support Services, advised Schenectady Naval Reactors: "The soil contamination is extensive and includes several areas with surface radioactivity levels ten to sixty times the normal background level."

There is no dispute among any of the parties that the parking lot in question was indeed contaminated and that the property was sold in March 1988 to the Department of Energy for one dollar. The New York State Labor Department subsequently investigated the transaction and found six violations of state labor law (reported in the *Schenectady Gazette* on August 6, 1988). "In the end, the State of New York decided that it was unable to pursue the violations since jurisdiction over the land had been transferred into federal hands," is the explanation given for why New York didn't pursue the matter, according to the Government Accountability Project's report on the Knolls Atomic Power Laboratory (pp. 51–52). The public record in this matter clearly establishes that the site was contaminated; that GE and DOE (and Kakretz) knew it was contaminated; and that it was sold in the unusual manner it was to shield GE from potential liability. As to whether there was a cover-up of the lot's radioactive status, the record clearly shows that Kakretz, GE, and DOE were aware of this problem for at least four years before the property was sold. The definitive assessment of the parking lot's status was conducted in 1984, based on the results of 468 soil core samples taken to assay the radioactivity. One source familiar with the report contends that after this report was made, Kakretz ordered the sanitizing layer of soil because he did not want to correct the larger problem, which would have required digging up the entire lot and brought attention to a situation of which only a select few were aware.

HE WAS MET BY DENNIS: The description of events is Hammond's.

SEPARATION PROCESS RESEARCH UNIT: The history of this facility, and its extensive contamination, is discussed in "Cleanup or Coverup?" pp. 24–32.

176 "THE RECENT DISCOVERIES": Quoted in "KAPL's Radioactive Waste Lingers; Awaiting Final Cleanup and Grave," *Schenectady Gazette,* March 21, 1989.

"WHAT ELSE IS IT HIDING?" "Negligence at Knolls," *Schenectady Gazette* editorial, June 23, 1988.

177 ERICKSON WROTE: Letter, B.M. Erickson, manager, Schenectady Naval Reactors, to Dr. Francis Bradley, New York State Department of Labor, p. 2, August 22, 1988.

"SECURITY NEWSLETTER, SPECIAL EDITION": The author has a copy of the newsletter.

SOME MONTHS LATER: The story was told to the author by Tom Carpenter during an interview.

"MALICIOUS" AND "FULL OF LIES": Welch's comments were made in a Q&A interview published in *Newsweek,* November 30, 1992 (pp. 62–63):

"Q: When Letterman made fun of you, you used the tape inside GE to discuss GE's excessive bureaucracy. Have insiders screened 'Deadly Deception'?

"Welch: No. Because it's all nonsense. It's malicious . . . full of lies. . . ."

178 "WHENEVER I GOT FRUSTRATED": The author interviewed Chasnoff.

179 "THEY HAVE A TAKE-NO-PRISONERS ATTITUDE": The author interviewed Ronald Dunn.

THE TOTAL BILL: "Energy Department Paid Out $47 Million for Firms' Legal Fees," *Wall Street Journal,* January 5, 1994.

ACCORDING TO AN ANONYMOUS TIPSTER: The call was taken on September 6, 1991, by Donald Aplin, the managing attorney for the Government Accountability Project in Washington, D.C. Aplin stated in a sworn affidavit, given November 12, 1992, that "the caller refused to give his name. The caller had a male-sounding voice. I took notes of the call. A copy of the notes are attached to this affidavit. My notes of the call itself state the following: . . . Caller said: 'I just got word about the Shannon stuff, the Westinghouse [*sic*] case, that Michael Connolly [*sic*] has ordered those papers shredded today. Ray Millikin has a copy of everything still, he works for FCC. He won't come forward freely, he wants to be subpoenaed. He has everything, and knows everything.' " Michael Conley says that the Inspector General's files eventually may have been discarded in the normal course of things, but that to his knowledge no relevant information was destroyed.

180 "OUR REPORT IS VERY ACCURATE": The author interviewed Victor Rezendes. In addition, the author reviewed the August 1991 GAO report, "Environmental, Health, and Safety Practices at Naval Reactors Facilities," and found it to be a remarkably superficial and deficient review of the situation at KAPL.

"THEY ROUTINELY TRY TO WIN YOU OVER": The author interviewed Dave Berick.

"MAYBE YOUR GENERATION": The author attended Shannon's presentation at Penn State, on November 11, 1992.

181 "I DON'T WANT TO GO OVER": The author had a brief telephone conversation with Kakretz, during which he made this remark.

"FALSELY CLAIMS IT BRINGS": Quoted in Slater, *The New GE,* pp. 243–44.

"THE UNUSUAL SOCIAL SPEECHES": Quoted in "Boycott Blackout," *Entertainment Weekly,* April 17, 1992, p. 10. On another occasion, according to the article, "At NBC, a Question of Censorship," in the December 2, 1989 edition of the *Washington Post,* NBC News officials deleted three sentences critical of network owner General Electric from a report on the *Today* show. The report, produced by WMAQ-TV in Chicago, was on the use of bogus and substandard materials in American industry.

182 "WE ARE CONCERNED": The ad appeared in *Variety,* January 6, 1993.

WELCH APPROACHED AN OLD FRIEND: "This Deal Could Send Martin Marietta Into Orbit," *Business Week,* December 7, 1992, p. 35.

CHAPTER NINE
GREAT RIVER OF THE MOUNTAINS

183 "IS A CRITICALLY IMPORTANT BOOK": Quoted in Theo Colborn, Dianne Dumanoski and John Peterson Myers, *Our Stolen Future* (New York: Penguin Group, 1996), p. vii.

"SCIENTIFIC AND PUBLIC RELATIONS BOMBSHELL": Quoted in "From Silent Spring to Barren Spring," *Business Week,* March 18, 1996, p. 42.

184 AS EARLY AS 1936: Colborn, Dumanoski, and Myers, *Our Stolen Future,* p. 90. The author's own review of the scientific literature found research on the toxic effects of PCBs as early as 1936, and on the toxic effects of the chemical group to which PCBs belong, chlorinated hydrocarbons, as early as 1899.

A REPORT THAT YEAR: Jensen's findings are summarized in Colborn, Dumanoski and Myers, *Our Stolen Future,* p. 90.

VERY MINUTE QUANTITIES: The medical problems associated with exposure to PCBs are addressed at length in *Our Stolen Future;* they also have been the subject of a number of recent studies, one of which was reported in "Report Links PCB Exposure With Children's Development," *New York Times,* September 12, 1996. The article summarized a report in *The New England Journal of Medicine* in which Drs. Joseph L. Jacobson and Sandra W. Jacobson, psychologists at Wayne State University in Detroit, found that exposure before birth to relatively small amounts of PCBs can result in long-lasting deficits in a child's intellectual development.

185 AN ESTIMATED 3.4 BILLION POUNDS: The estimate is found throughout the literature on PCBs and is repeated in Colborn, Dumanoski, and Myers, *Our Stolen Future,* p. 91.

"GE HAS DISCHARGED PCBs IN QUANTITIES": Quoted in "For the Hudson, Bad News and Good," *New York Times Magazine,* October 24, 1976.

HE HAD ANGRILY WARNED: Jones's threat was reported in "For the Hudson, Bad News and Good," *New York Times Magazine.*

186 "THE FACT IS": Quoted in "Babbitt Assails G.E. Over Delay in Ridding Hudson of Chemicals," *New York Times,* September 26, 1997.

SPURRED BY A REPORT: The *Sports Illustrated* article, "Poison Roams Our Coastal Seas," was published on October 26, 1970, by writer Robert H. Boyle. Boyle, one of the foremost experts on the Hudson River, authored *The Hudson River: A Natural and Unnatural History* (New York: W.W. Norton, 1979), a wonderful book on the river's flora and fauna, in which he also reviews his involvement in the PCB question. What he discovered about the PCB levels of Hudson River fish–and disclosed in *Sports Illustrated*–is found on pp. 297–99 of his book. The author's rendering of the early chronology of the PCB question is taken from "For the Hudson, Bad News and Good"; from Boyle's account in the epilogue of *The Hudson River;* and from Karen E. Limburg, "PCBs in the Hudson," in *The Hudson River Ecosystem.*

187 "HE NEGOTIATED HARD ON THAT POINT": The author interviewed Langdon Marsh when he was a deputy commissioner for the New York Department of Environmental Conservation, a post he vacated when Governor Cuomo wasn't reelected.

ONE STUDY BY SANDRA AND JOSEPH JACOBSON: The study and its findings are summarized in Colborn, Dumanoski, and Myers, *Our Stolen Future,* p. 190.

188 THE BREAST MILK OF WOMEN: The federal report is cited in "The Hudson Can't Heal Itself," October 11, 1992, part two of a four-part series on the PCB problem that appeared on the *Poughkeepsie Journal's* editorial page on four consecutive Sundays, October 4 through October 25, 1992.

189 SOME MAJOR CORPORATIONS: The activities of Dow and Sun were described in "Who Scores Best on the Environment," *Fortune*, July 26, 1993, pp. 106–114. The article ranked General Electric among "The 10 Laggards."

HE "HAS CALLED ME, AND LOBBIED ME": Cuomo's comments were quoted in "Hudson River Must Be Cleansed," *Poughkeepsie Journal*, September 29, 1991.

190 MEMORANDUM THAT ADVISED: Ramsey's activities as a corporate attorney and advocate of probusiness environmental policies are discussed in "Citizen GE: How Multinationals like General Electric Have Seized Power in the United States," *Rolling Stone*, April 16, 1992, p. 66: "Heineman hired a former colleague from Sidley and Austin, Stephen D. Ramsey, who had previously served as assistant attorney general for environmental enforcement in the Reagan administration. At Justice, Ramsey developed rules for enforcing the Superfund law. . . . At Sidley and Austin, Ramsey looked for ways to stymie the Superfund law, writing a widely distributed memorandum that told corporate lawyers how to confound the government's efforts to collect the billions owed by polluters under the statute." The article was excerpted from a book by William Greider, *Who Will Tell the People?: The Betrayal of American Democracy* (New York: Simon & Schuster, 1992).

WELCH HIRED ANOTHER: Lanahan's activities were described to the author by people familiar with them; he declined to be interviewed.

191 THAT'S WHY WELCH HIRED THEM: Because Welch declined to be interviewed, the author cannot know for certain what his intent was in hiring Lanahan (who has left GE). But it was the opinion of people the author interviewed on this issue that Lanahan was hired because Welch wanted someone who knew government procedure intimately—and who knew how to forestall the process. People who expressed this view were, among others: Cara Lee, of Scenic Hudson, an environmental advocacy group; Langdon Marsh, deputy commissioner of the New York Department of Environmental Conservation; several members of EPA's Region 2 office in New York City; Professor Richard Bopp of Rensselaer Polytechnic Institute; Constantine Sidamon-Eristoff, former EPA administrator of Region 2; and Everett Nack, a commercial fisherman.

"WHILE WE HARDLY HAD THE STAFF": The author interviewed Richard Bopp.

MET 110 TIMES WITH POLITICIANS: The estimate is Hamilton's own, found on p. 268 of the deposition he gave on March 2, 1993 in Trumbull, Connecticut. He was deposed as part of a lawsuit, filed in the U.S. District Court for the District of Nevada, by the Nevada Power Company against Monsanto Company, Westinghouse Electric Corporation, and the General Electric Company, Case Number CV-S-89-555-LDG-LRL.

192 CORPORATE DONOR TO SOLOMON: The General Electric Company Political Action Committee gave the candidate $5,850 in the 1991–92 reporting period, as reported by the Federal Election Commission. The only higher corporate donors were the PACs of professional associations.

HAS TRIED TO HEAD OFF "BAD SCIENCE": The phrase is Hamilton's own, taken from his deposition. When asked why he had visited with the governor's aides in Indiana, Hamilton said he felt "concern" that the study's finding of elevated levels of brain cancer "would raise a lot of concerns, a lot of hysteria, possibly, by misleading people …" (p. 314). ". . . I wanted them [the aides] to understand that there were other scientific issues related to this study that had not been properly addressed, and that should they make further public announcements, they would not make the same kind of announcement that I thought was flawed" (p. 318).

192 ONE SUCH MORTALITY STUDY: The circumstances of Hamilton's intervention in the Indiana study are described by Hamilton in his deposition, pp. 304–36.

"I FELT THAT IT WOULD RAISE": The statement comes from Hamilton's deposition.

WHAT FOLLOWED WAS TYPICAL: The author interviewed several people involved in the study, who recounted the circumstances of its public dissemination.

193 A "HOLDING STATEMENT": A copy of the holding statement, as well as the August 15, 1991, cover memo written by Dr. Ralph R. Boericke, was submitted into the court record as part of the Nevada Power lawsuit.

SEVERAL ADDITIONAL WORKERS: According to people familiar with the Bloomington facility.

ONE OF THE VICTIMS: The author interviewed Ed Bates.

194 FOUR YEARS LATER: The 1899 paper is cited in GE's own review of the scientific literature, which was described in "The Physiological Hazards of Pyranol Components," March 27, 1956, by A. L. Bridgman, of the Analytical Chemistry department in Pittsfield, Massachusetts. The document was placed into the public record as part of the Nevada Power lawsuit.

ONE OF THE FIRST WARNINGS: The paper is referenced in "The Problem of Possible Systemic Effects from Certain Chlorinated Hydrocarbons," *The Journal of Industrial Hygiene and Toxicology,* September 1937.

195 "EIGHT OR TEN OF THEM": "The Problem of Possible Systemic Effects from Certain Chlorinated Hydrocarbons," p. 303.

"IT APPEARS TO BE GENERALLY AGREED": Bridgman memo, p. 2.

WORKERS HAD DAILY CONTACT: The description of operations in Building Twelve comes from Bates.

196 THE FIRST CAME IN 1966: Jensen's discoveries are summarized in Colborn, Dumanoski, and Myers, *Our Stolen Future,* p. 90.

197 ONE OUNCE OF FURANS: The estimates on the toxicity of furans come from the Hamilton deposition, p. 71.

"IT SEEMED LIKE EVERY OTHER WEEK": Bates was interviewed by the author.

198 "IT IS A LONG-STANDING GENERAL PRACTICE": Letter, Stephen B. Hamilton Jr., to Edward L. Bates Jr., July 26, 1985; a copy of the letter was sent to Jack Welch.

THE CAUSES OF DEATH WERE MISSTATED: Wegman didn't return phone calls seeking comment. The description of events comes from Ed Bates, who was interviewed on numerous occasions by the author. Wegman acknowledged the error in a letter, dated February 12, 1988, that was sent to Stephen Hamilton of GE and to Sherwood Guernsey, a representative in the Massachusetts state house who assisted Bates. The letter was also sent to Bates, who provided a copy to the author. It reads in part: "It has been correctly noted that a number of the causes of death were incorrect." Wegman attributed the mistake to a clerical error and apologized for it.

TWELVE HUNDRED WERE EXCLUDED: A total of 1,714 subjects were included in the study, out of an identified employee population of 2,914 white males who had earned pension rights, whose last place of work was the GE Pittsfield plant, and who died between January 1, 1969 and December 31, 1984. Exclusions were made, Dr. Wegman wrote in the executive summary of the study, "for inadequate or absent work history records and appropriate exclusions for selection of control subjects."

199   IN JUNE 1994, THE WIDOW: "Former GE Workers Sue Over Exposure to PCBs, Other Toxic Chemicals," Associated Press, June 21, 1994.

THE VIDEO: The author reviewed a copy of the video.

"IS THERE A PCB ACCIDENT": Taken from GE's advertising literature for its PCB Service Program.

OFFICE TOWER IN BINGHAMTON: The office tower is pictured in GE's advertising literature.

200   "SCORES OF COMPANIES ARE MAKING": From the June 4, 1985 form letter of Clyde D. Keaton, vice president and general manger, Domestic Apparatus & Engineering Services division, Schenectady, New York.

MEN LIKE STEVE SANDBERG: He was interviewed by the author. Sandberg's story was also recounted in "U.S. Agency Seeks $353,000 Fine From GE," *Los Angeles Times,* March 10, 1993.

201   "STEPHEN SANDBERG, THE EMPLOYEE IN ANAHEIM": From the memorandum of Bill Thornton to Tim Daly, dated October 29, 1991.

202   AS FOR SANDBERG: The information about Sandberg's medical condition comes from Sandberg, who conveyed it to the author in an interview. He made the same statements to the *Los Angeles Times.*

"GREAT WATERS": Quoted in Boyle, *The Hudson River,* p. 21.

"GRANDER AND MORE INSPIRING": Quoted in Boyle, *The Hudson River,* p. 17.

203   "PERPETUALLY INTERESTING": Quoted in Boyle, *The Hudson River,* p. 17.

"GREAT RIVER OF THE MOUNTAINS": The phrase is recorded in Hudson's log from his 1609 expedition of the river, an entry made on October 4 as he was preparing to return to Holland; it is quoted in Boyle, *The Hudson River,* p. 33.

GUIDING HIS EIGHTEEN-FOOT BOAT: The author interviewed Everett Nack and accompanied him one day while he fished for Atlantic sturgeon.

"THE LAND IS THE FINEST": Hudson's entry in his log on September 18, 1609; quoted in Boyle, *The Hudson River,* p. 31.

204   THE SLOW DECLINE SUDDENLY REVERSED: The new discharge was disclosed in a news release by the New York State Department of Environmental Conservation on June 24, 1994.

205   "ENDLESS LITIGATION": Quoted in "GE to Establish a $7 Million Fund to Settle PCB Suit," *Wall Street Journal,* August 16, 1993.

206   "THE CANCER OF AMERICAN INDUSTRY": The author interviewed Buzzy O'Keeffe; his signs advising GE execs to stay away were reported in "GE Go Home," *New York Post,* October 8, 1993.

"ON THIS ONE, GUYS": The account of what Welch said is found on p. 46 of the written chronology of Ed Russell, a former General Electric vice president. The chronology was provided to the Justice Department in connection with his allegation of price-fixing in the industrial-diamond business. Russell was present at the meeting, which occurred on or about April 17, 1991, at a so-called Session C (manpower planning), when he heard the comments attributed to Welch.

206 THE PITTSFIELD SITUATION: It was reported upon in "Chemical Reaction," *Wall Street Journal,* December 4, 1997, including allegations under investigation by the Massachusetts attorney general that GE covered up internal memos that might have revealed the presence of PCBs on the property in question earlier.

207 WELCH HAD LOBBIED HARD: Four EPA officials were the sources of this information, including Constantine Sidamon-Eristoff, whom the author interviewed in July 1994.

"CONSTANTINE, YOU HAVE TO DO": The author interviewed Constantine Sidamon-Eristoff; the description of events comes from Sidamon-Eristoff, as well as EPA staffers familiar with the situation.

RAMSEY TRIED: EPA officials, including Sidamon-Eristoff, made this assertion. The author sought to interview Ramsey, but the request was rejected by the company.

208 "I'M DISAPPOINTED": The comments attributed to Welch are Sidamon-Eristoff's recollection of what he said.

"AS WE DISCUSSED": Letter, Constantine Sidamon-Eristoff, administrator, Region II, U.S. Environmental Protection Agency, to Jack Welch, July 15, 1991.

CHAPTER TEN
THE TYRANNY OF NUMBERS

210 A PERFORMANCE EVALUATION SYSTEM: Pascale, *Managing on the Edge,* p. 211.

211 YOKOGAWA: The scandal was widely reported in the Japanese media.

212 "I'M NOT GIVING": Bob Bowen's recollection of what Welch said.

"I ALMOST DIED": Author interview.

213 "ROGUE" EMPLOYEE: The phrase has been used to categorize former employees who have been dismissed, the company contends, for ethical breaches; it was used most forcefully in the campaign against Joe Jett, the bond trader who, according to GE, single-handedly brought down Kidder, Peabody.

THE "MONSTER CHART": The story of the "monster chart" was related to the author by people in the purchasing department and was corroborated by Sylvia Ceravalo, a member of Reiner's staff.

IN ONE TELEVISION COMMERCIAL: Slater, *The New GE,* p. 37.

UNDER JACK SMITH: The author covered Jack Smith in Europe while a correspondent in Germany for the *Wall Street Journal.*

214 "PARTNERING": The concept was explained to the author by people in purchasing who had put it into practice.

FRANK DOYLE: His comment was made within earshot of several purchasing people, who related it to the author.

215 "WE WERE ALL AGHAST": Author interview.

"BALLISTIC DOESN'T EVEN DESCRIBE": The author interviewed Sylvia Ceravalo.

"ONCE THAT CHART HIT THE TABLE": Author interview.

216 THERE, THEY GOT A JOLT: Stonesifer's presentation at the Hurstbourne Hotel was recorded in a videotape made by GE, which was passed to *Business Week* via a supplier who attended the meeting. The videotape was the basis for its article, "Cut Costs or

Else," March 22, 1993, pp. 28–29, which explains "Target 10" but failed to put it in the broader context of the "monster chart."

216 "WE SEE NO RELIEF": Quoted in "Cut Costs or Else," *Business Week.*

217 IF SCHEPENS WEREN'T REMOVED: This assertion came from Jim Schepens, whom the author interviewed in May 1994.

"ONE MINUTE IT WAS 'PARTNERING' ": Author interview.

218 "YOU COULD HIRE": The author interviewed Ken Pastewka.

"STOP ALL BUSINESS RELATIONSHIPS": The memo was quoted in "GM Hits at GE, Threatens Boycott over Price Hike for Plastic," *Detroit Free Press,* November, 16, 1994.

WAS DELAYED THREE WEEKS: "Has Outsourcing Gone Too Far?" *Business Week,* April 1, 1996, p. 27.

219 HIS COMPANY'S EMPLOYMENT POLICY: Charles Handy, *The Age of Paradox* (Boston: Harvard Business School Press, 1994), p. 3.

"COMPETITION IS HEALTHY": Handy, *The Age of Paradox,* p. 6.

3.38 MILLION JOBS WERE LOST: "On the Battlefields of Business, Millions of Casualties," *New York Times,* March 3, 1996.

220 "CLEARLY, THE PROFITABILITY": Quoted in "A Big Offshore Surge for GE's Juice Factory," *Business Week,* June 21, 1993, p. 72.

WELCH TOLD SECURITIES ANALYSTS: His prediction of a 10 percent gain was reported on the Bloomberg Business wire on February 28, 1995, under the headline, "GE Power Systems Plans to Cut More Jobs as Sales Slow."

221 "WE'VE ALL BECOME SOLDIERS": Quoted in "The Company as Family, No More," *New York Times,* March 4, 1996.

WHAT CURTIS ENVISIONED: The description of the encounter between Curtis and Rice is taken from Hammond, *Men and Volts,* pp. 275–84.

222 CHEMIST MARKOVITZ: The author interviewed Mark Markovitz.

GE'S WORLDWIDE MARKET SHARE: The market share estimates were obtained from industry sources.

223 IT ALL ADDED UP: The problems with cracking rotors and other defects were recounted in "Power Ranger: GE Taps Trains Chief In Effort to Shore Up Troubled Energy Unit," *Wall Street Journal,* May 6, 1996.

"NOTHING ELSE REALLY WILL MATTER": Quoted in "Power Ranger," *Wall Street Journal.*

"IT'S MANAGEMENT BY BUZZWORD": The author interviewed Markovitz.

224 NEUMANN WAS A LEGENDARY FIGURE: Neumann's exploits are chronicled in his autobiography, *Herman the German* (New York: William Morrow & Company, 1984); the culture of the Aircraft Engine division is also described in Pascale, *Managing on the Edge,* pp. 194–95.

226 "TRANSLATE THIS REALISTIC": Letter, to Brian H. Rowe from Jack Welch, January 13, 1993.

"THERE IS LIFE AFTER GE": A copy of the poem was sent to the author.

227 "WE'RE NOT SOFTHEARTED": Quoted in "The Hit Men," *Newsweek,* February 26, 1996, p. 47.

228 IN FACT, THE NEW ENGINE: The problems of the GE90 received extensive coverage in the business media, for instance in the *Wall Street Journal*'s story, "General Electric's New Jet Engine Pushes Technology," April 4, 1994.

229   "EVERY TIME THEY'D GO UP": Author interview.
      A FAILURE SO SEVERE: GE's failure on the bird-strike test was reported in "Jet Lag:
      Engine Troubles Put GE Behind in Race to Power New 777s," *Wall Street Journal*, July 12,
      1995.
      THE FAA CONVENED A MEETING: A person who participated in the meeting
      described to the author what occurred.
      "THERE WERE A LOT OF PEOPLE": This quotation comes from an official with the
      Federal Aviation Administration who sat in on the meetings in which the GE90 was
      evaluated; the author interviewed him in April 1996. In addition, according to a report
      in the *Wall Street Journal* on January 13, 1997, the FAA report "cited sloppy GE manufac-
      turing as a reason for delaying permission for extended flights by the plane over water."
230   THE AIRLINE TOOK THE ACTION: The suspension of trans-Atlantic flights was
      described in "Atlantic Flights by 777 Jet Are Discontinued," *New York Times*, March 14,
      1997.
      IVAN WINEBRENNER: His story was recounted to the author by his widow, Helen
      Winebrenner, who was interviewed on several occasions, in person in November 1993
      and in follow-up conversations in spring 1994.
231   JOHN NELSON WAS FIRED: Nelson was suspended and discharged under a GE policy
      issued in 1953 under which the company immediately suspended any employee who
      refused to testify, under oath, when questioned about their ties to the Communist party.
      Nelson refused to answer the questions of one Senator Butler, an antilabor legislator
      whose committee was investigating alleged labor affiliations with the Communists. Nel-
      son died at the age of forty, a few years after his dismissal, according to press reports
      from that time.
      COUNCIL PASSED A RESOLUTION: The resolution was reported in the *Erie Times-
      News*, July 26, 1957.
234   HE HAD SHOT HIMSELF: The obituary, printed in the *Erie Daily Times* on June 14,
      1993, did not call the death a suicide. The author learned of the suicide through conver-
      sations with people who had worked with Ivan and who knew that he had shot himself.
235   "THE NUMBERS CAUSE MANAGERS": The author interviewed Sheldon Potter.
      ANTHONY VICTOR TORRELLI: The author had a telephone conversation with
      Torrelli's mother, who confirmed his suicide.
      "OUR UNION LEADERSHIP": Letter, from Robert L. Nardelli, president and CEO, GE
      Transportation Systems, to his "fellow employees," July 7, 1994.
236   ANOTHER FIFTEEN HUNDRED JOBS: "Transportation Unit May Cut As Many As
      1,500 Jobs," *New York Times*, October 10, 1995.

CHAPTER ELEVEN
FROM PATERNALISM TO CANNIBALISM

238   "GE HAS A CLEAR STANCE": The author interviewed Heather Honegger.
      "NOTHING THE COMPANY DID": Author interview.
239   THE 108-COUNT INDICTMENT: "Federal Jury Charges $800,000 Fraud by GE," *New
      York Times*, March 27, 1985.

239   "THE MANAGERS FEARED": Quoted in "Israeli Military Aid Scandal Jolts GE," *Washington Post,* July 20, 1992.

240   "ONE OF THE GREAT SOCIAL INNOVATORS": Quoted in Baida, *Poor Richard's Legacy,* p. 297.
THE SON OF A LUMBER DEALER: The background on Thomas Watson Sr. comes from Baida, *Poor Richard's Legacy,* pp. 295–98.
"YOU MUST NOT DO ANYTHING": Baida, *Poor Richard's Legacy,* p. 298.
"BUSINESS IS BEING CALLED UPON": Baida, *Poor Richard's Legacy,* p. 298.

241   "IBM'S TOTAL HISTORY": Quoted in Baida, *Poor Richard's Legacy,* p. 305.
"WATSON WAS ACTUALLY": Quoted in Baida, *Poor Richard's Legacy,* p. 301.
CHARLES PROTEUS STEINMETZ: Information on his background comes from several GE publications archived at the Hall of History, Schenectady, New York.

243   "THE MOST FORMIDABLE OBSTACLES": Quoted in Ronald R. Kline, *Steinmetz: Engineer and Socialist* (Baltimore: Johns Hopkins University Press, 1992), p. 248.
"WAGE DIVIDEND": Kline, *Steinmetz,* p. 247.
UNITARIAN MINISTER ALBERT CLARK: The reverend's activities are described in Kline, *Steinmetz,* p. 247.

244   "NO MATTER WHAT": The author interviewed John McLaughlin.

245   "JACK TALKS ABOUT": The author interviewed Richard Elsberry, who wrote about the demise of his corporate career in the *New York Times Magazine,* "Set Free," January 4, 1987.
"FROM A FEMALE STANDPOINT": The author interviewed Mary Kuykendall.
GOLD COLLARS AND RESOURCES: The author obtained a copy of the play.

246   VERA MAY ENGLISH: The author spent two days with English at her retirement village in Virginia. In addition to English, the author interviewed several of her coworkers, who corroborated her story.

247   THE FIRST INCIDENT: The English case was covered extensively in North Carolina. The date of this first incident comes from "Mrs. English Takes on GE," *The Independent,* May 24, 1985.
FOURTEEN: The number comes from official incident reports that were filed with the New Hanover County Police department and were reviewed by the author.
"PRETEXT FOR GETTING RID": From the Decision and Order of Robert J. Brissenden, Administrative Law Judge, U.S. Department of Labor, issued on August 1, 1985, Case Number 85-ERA-002, p. 10.
ALSO SIDED WITH ENGLISH: According to the judgment, which was entered on March 13, 1989, the NRC determined that a violation of its regulations had occurred. A Severity Level II penalty was imposed, Hugh L. Thompson, Jr., Deputy Executive Director for Nuclear Materials Safety, Safeguards, and Operations Support, wrote, "because plant management was involved in discriminat[ing]" against English. "Acts of discrimination against an employee who raises safety concerns or who communicates with the NRC will not be tolerated."

248   "WE FELT SORRY FOR HER": The author interviewed Bertram Wolfe.
FALSIFYING DATA AND TEST RESULTS: English's claims are laid out in a seven-page report she prepared, "Allegations of Violations to Company Practices and Procedures in Chemet Laboratory," dated February 21, 1984. The report, which was sent to Eugene

Lees, Winslow's boss, along with a cover letter, lists her specific complaints in great detail and alleges that management was aware of these procedural deficiencies and falsifications yet failed to do anything to correct the situation. The ongoing nature of the violations, particularly contamination in the Chemet lab, caused the Nuclear Regulatory Commission to later observe: "Your routine surveys, as well as special surveys performed at the request of the NRC, indicated that some areas were repeatedly contaminated above your administrative action level. In some cases, you cleaned the specific area as required by license condition without attempting to identify the cause or to take specific action to prevent a recurrence. Your staff appeared to adopt a mindset that these levels of contamination in the lab were normal rather than unusual." In addition, the author interviewed on several occasions one lab employee, still in the employ of GE, who corroborated English's claims. He said that as a result of her allegations, deficient lab procedures were uncovered and changes were made.

249 "I COULD TASTE IT": Quoted in "Ex-GE Worker Weeps on Stand," *Wilmington Morning Star,* March 26, 1985.

"DO YOU SMELL ANY POWDER?": Quoted in "Ex-GE Worker Weeps on Stand" *Wilmington Morning Star.*

250 THE EVENTS: "The essential facts of [the English] case are not in dispute," the U.S. Court of Appeals for the Fourth Circuit concluded in its decision, published September 28, 1992. The facts as presented in this account are taken from the court record of her case, filed in U.S. District Court for the Eastern District of North Carolina, Number 87-31-CIV-7-D.

251 A HEARING WAS HELD: The account of events is English's own.

"KNOWINGLY AND INTENTIONALLY": From the letter of James A. Long to Vera English, May 15, 1984, p. 1.

"I DEEPLY REGRET": Long letter, p. 2.

252 "A REVIEW OF THE NRC FINDINGS": Judge Brissenden's Decision and Order, pp. 8–9.

"YOUR STAFF APPEARED": Quoted in "Plaintiff's Brief in Response to Summary Judgment," July 22, 1991, p. 12.

OWN INTERNAL INVESTIGATION: The Wieczorek investigation, so called for the GE employee who conducted it, initially concluded that all four of English's allegations "were found to be valid," according to documents GE provided to the plaintiff as part of the lawsuit. But in the final version of that report the conclusion was weakened to read that the four violations "were found, for the most part, to have substance." When the author contacted Wieczorek in an attempt to interview him, he refused to answer any questions about his findings, or the English case in general.

253 "IT'S A HOME RUN": Quoted in "Long Fight Ends in Victory for N.C. Whistleblower," *USA Today,* June 5, 1990.

"ENGLISH SUFFERED SEVERE": Appeals court decision, September 28, 1992, p. 11.

"WHILE GE'S CONDUCT": Appeals court decision, September 28, 1992, pp. 13–15.

"THE PEOPLE OF WILMINGTON": Quoted in "Mrs. English Deserves No Thanks from GE," *Wilmington Morning Star,* August 17, 1985.

MAJOR NUCLEAR ACCIDENT: "NRC Heads to GE Plant that Processes Uranium," *Wall Street Journal,* May 31, 1991.

CHAPTER TWELVE
TELLING THE WHOLE TRUTH

255   WENT VIRTUALLY UNNOTICED: "Israeli General Arrested," *Washington Post,* October 29, 1990.

HE DIDN'T LEARN: Welch so testified, under oath, in the "Hearing on the Roles of General Electric and the Department of Defense in the Illegal Diversion of Tens of Millions of Dollars in Foreign Military Assistance to Israel," U.S. House of Representatives, Committee on Energy and Commerce, Subcommittee on Oversight and Investigations, July 29, 1992, p. 39 of the official transcript.

256   CONTAINING ONLY SAWDUST: This historical tidbit is taken from the order of Judge Carl B. Rubin in Case Number C-1-90-792, *United States of America v. General Electric,* December 4, 1992, p. 2; in a footnote, the judge cites *The Gettysburg Campaign* as a source.

PHILLIPS WAS INTRIGUED: The background on John Phillips comes from "Honesty Pays Off: John Phillips Fosters a Growing Industry of Whistleblowing," *Wall Street Journal,* January 11, 1995.

257   "JOHN WALLACE": The author interviewed Chester Walsh.

A HIGH SCHOOL DROPOUT: The background on Walsh comes from a variety of sources, including his interview with the author and "Portrait of a Whistleblower," *Miami Herald,* January 17, 1993.

"NOBODY WAS GOING TO PROTECT ME": Walsh made the comment in his interview with the author.

"THE TIME CARDS": Quoted in "Bounty Hunter: Ex-Foreman May Win Millions for His Tale About Cheating at GE," *Wall Street Journal,* June 23, 1988. In addition, the author interviewed Gravitt, as well as his attorney, Jim Helmer.

258   THE WARNING GRAVITT WAS GIVEN: That was Gravitt's contention when he was interviewed by the author. Jim Helmer, Gravitt's attorney who was in the room when the remark was made, says he considered Terlep's remarks a threat. Terlep told U.S. District Judge Carl B. Rubin the following, according to the transcript of a status conference in the case held on November 26, 1985 (p. 10): "First of all, your Honor, I would like to straighten something out about what Mr. Helmer has called a threat. The conversation he refers to was with me. I certainly didn't consider anything in my conversation a threat. The conversation with Mr. Helmer was made in the spirit of trying to settle this matter. I presented alternatives to Mr. Helmer and I presented alternatives as to what the Department of Justice had decided to do in this instance. . . . If Mr. Helmer took whatever I said as a threat, I apologize personally to him. It certainly wasn't meant as a threat by the Department of Justice."

259   DOTAN HAD CONSIDERABLE CLOUT: The background on Dotan's activities in the Israeli military was taken from a variety of sources, including the interview with Walsh as well as with U.S. investigators. In addition, the author credits "The Money Trail: U.S. Firms Are Linked to an Israeli General at Heart of a Scandal," *Wall Street Journal,* January 20, 1992.

TO AUTHORIZE $34.5 MILLION: GE's clever lobbying campaign, in which it bested Pratt & Whitney, is revealed in "Bringing Good Things to GE," *Washington Post,* April 13, 1985, from which the figure comes.

259   "A SPEAR CARRIER": Quoted in "GE Files Offer Rare View of What PACs Seek to Buy on Capitol Hill," *Washington Post,* June 1, 1993. Sen. Robert Byrd received an additional $2,000 for his PAC, and additional (but unspecified) money was recommended for Senators Cochran and Specter, according to the article, based on internal GE memos unearthed in a lawsuit filed in 1986 by the late Philip M. Stern, who founded Citizens Against PACs.

260   INGBIR, WHO SERVED UNDER DOTAN: Ingbir's relationship with Dotan was the subject of extensive coverage in the Israeli press, including "Yoram Ingbir's Engines Empire," *Ha-Aretz,* November 1, 1990.

    THE SCHEME: The substance of how the scheme worked was revealed in "The Money Trail," and summarized by U.S. Representative John Dingell, Chairman of the House Subcommittee on Oversight and Investigations, in his opening statement during the July 29, 1992 hearing.

261   WALSH SAW THINGS: The details of Walsh's involvement were revealed in two days of testimony before Judge Rubin on November 2–3, 1992. The transcript from that testimony was reviewed by the author, and it is incorporated in the description of events.

    FINE TRAVELED TO ISRAEL: The details of Fine's involvement were revealed in a sworn deposition, taken on October 23 and 27, 1992, in connection with Walsh's civil suit against General Electric. The transcript from that testimony was reviewed by the author, and it is incorporated in the description of events. Fine declined the author's request for an interview.

262   "IF YOU'RE ACCUSING ME": Fine's recollection of what Steindler said to him, as recorded in his deposition, p. 323.

    COUTINHO SAID THAT THE SITUATION: Fine's deposition reads as follows (p. 331 of the transcript):

> Q: Did anything ever come of your memo, Fine 17 and 18?
>
> *Fine:* Other than my being removed from the program?
>
> Q: Other than your being removed from the program.
>
> *Fine:* Yes.
>
> Q: What else happened?
>
> *Fine:* Al Coutinho was asked to go on an upcoming trip to Israel to look into the situation.
>
> Q: Did he?
>
> *Fine:* Yes.
>
> Q: Did he resolve the concerns?
>
> *Fine:* It depends on how you define "resolve the concerns."
>
> Q: Did he make things right in Israel?
>
> *Fine:* In my mind, no.
>
> Q: What did he do?
>
> *Fine:* He informed me that there was no test cell and that reportedly the Israeli Air Force would get substance of equal value for the dollars associated with the test cell.
>
> Q: Up until that point, had you any understanding that Israel was going to get something else in exchange for the test cell?
>
> *Fine:* No.

Q: Why wasn't that a satisfactory resolution of the matter to you?

Fine: Because that's not what their contract called for.

Q: Did GE investigate the concerns you raised in your memo at the time?

Fine: Could you specify what time period, please?

Q: In 1989, did GE investigate the concerns you raised in your March 10, 1989 memo?

Fine: Other than that trip Al Coutinho made to Israel, I am not aware of anything else that GE did to investigate my concerns.

263   STEINDLER WAS VISIBLY UPSET: Walsh so testified in the hearing before Judge Rubin, November 3, 1992, p. 68 of the official transcript.

THE GENERAL PAID $50,000: Dotan pled guilty to having given $50,000 to an assistant, Sgt. Major Yaakov Frank, in April 1990 to arrange the killing, kidnapping, maiming, or threatening of Pa'il. This fact was also mentioned by Congressmen Dingell in opening remarks at the public hearing on his subcommittee's investigation into the Dotan affair (July 29, 1992, p. 6 of the official transcript).

"THE GOVERNMENT KNEW": Agent Kosky's deposition was given *in camera* and held under seal. The contents (on pp. 88–89 of the transcript) were disclosed in Judge Rubin's December 4, 1992, order, p. 5.

264   "I AM NOT WILLING": The exchange occurred on November 3, 1992 and is recorded on pp. 72–74 of the transcript of proceedings.

TURNBULL WAS AGAIN: According to people at GE Aircraft Engines, as well as Brian Brimelow, who was interviewed by the author.

"GE BELIEVES": From the transcript of the Dingell hearing, July 29, 1992, p. 33.

265   "HE DIDN'T DO": Walsh made the remark to the author in their interview.

"HAVE YOU PERSONALLY SUFFERED": The question was put to him in his deposition, and he declined to answer it.

THAT HYPOTHESIS: Initially, Katz had agreed to be interviewed by the author, but later he declined. The link between Katz and Pollard was raised by Dingell during the hearing, as well as in "The Money Trail."

266   THE THIRD CRIMINAL CONVICTION: The tally comes from "Defense Procurement Fraud: Information on Plea Agreements and Settlements," a report of the U.S. General Accounting Office, September 1992.

IT HAD RECOVERED: The author obtained, through a Freedom of Information Act filing, the report of the "Office of Counsel, Philadelphia Remedies Unit," a branch of the Defense Contract Management Command, District Mid-Atlantic. The Philadelphia Remedies Unit was officially created on June 1, 1990. As of December 31, 1991, the unit had under its jurisdiction 149 open matters, 82 of which were classified as criminal cases under active investigation by the Defense Criminal Investigative Office. The $71 million recovery estimate comes from the report.

"HE WENT THROUGH THE ROOF": Author interview.

267   HADN'T TOLD THE WHOLE TRUTH: The substance of the government's case is outlined in "Government's Reply to Defendant General Electric's Response to Motion for Production of Records," criminal Case Number 88-515, filed in the U.S. District Court for the Eastern District of Pennsylvania. The phrase "misleading and false" is the government's, from p. 1 of the introduction which reads as follows: "The GE records reveal

that misleading and false statements were made by GE to Air Force authorities, including the Secretary of the Air Force, in 1985 in an effort to mitigate administrative sanctions following a previous indictment of the company." When the author interviewed on September 30, 1993 Nicholas C. Harbist, the Assistant U.S. Attorney who helped prosecute the case and did the closing argument, asking him for the identities of the GE executives who made the "false and misleading" statements, he named Welch. Welch, he said, was in the meetings, and had met face-to-face with Secretary Orr, at which time the "false and misleading" information was conveyed.

267 AFTER WELCH'S MEETINGS: The allegation is found on pp. 9–10 of the "Government's Reply." In addition, the author interviewed special agent Robert Koons, who investigated the case, and Assistant U.S. Attorney Nicholas C. Harbist, who prosecuted it.

"CONSIDERATE TREATMENT": The letter, from Welch to "Dear Verne" (Air Force Secretary Orr) and dated September 6, 1985, was obtained by the author through a Freedom of Information Act request, filed with the Department of the Air Force.

HARBIST ARGUED IN HIS CLOSE: The author interviewed Harbist.

268 TWO LOWER-LEVEL GE MANAGERS: They were James Badolato, GE/MATSCO's subcontracts manger, and his boss, Gerald A. Leo, both of whom were imprisoned, and both of whom declined the author's request for an interview.

THE SUSPENSION: Cook outlines the reasons for the suspension, and its rescinding, in a June 5, 1992 letter to the General Electric Aircraft Engines Group, obtained through a Freedom of Information Act request. "The decision to terminate the suspension is . . . based upon information presented since the suspension to DLA [Defense Logistics Agency] by GEAE and General Electric Co., the corporate parent of GE," Cook wrote. "The information outlines certain steps that GEAE has taken since the suspension was imposed that indicate that continued suspension of GEAE is not necessary at this time to protect the Government's interest."

AN ERRANT EMPLOYEE: During administrative proceedings held by the Securities and Exchange Commission in the summer of 1996, the SEC argued that Jett was a cunning flimflam artist. Jett contended that he conducted his trades openly—even disclosing them to Kidder's internal auditors—and that his superiors were not only aware of what he was doing but encouraged it because of the seemingly enormous income it provided.

269 THE DINGELL BAR: The phrase was used in "The Anatomy of a Scandal," *Pittsburgh Post-Gazette*, December 27, 1994. The series detailed Dingell's involvement in another investigation his committee had delved into: the alleged research improprieties of Dr. Bernard Fisher, a world-renowned cancer researcher at the University of Pittsburgh, who has since been exonerated.

270 GENEROUS INVESTMENT TAX CREDITS: GE's use or, according to critics, abuse, of the investment tax credits, enacted in the first year of the Reagan administration, received extensive press coverage in the mid-eighties, including in "Bringing Good Things to GE," *Washington Post*. It is reviewed as well in Slater, *The New GE*, pp. 109–110.

THE SOLE UNDERWRITER: The gathering was reported in "The Devil in John McLaughlin," *Esquire*, November 1992, p. 69, and was confirmed by one of the participants.

NEARLY DOUBLED: "GE Files Offer Rare View of What PACs Seek to Buy on Capitol Hill," *Washington Post*.

270 "EMPLOYEES WHO EARN": Quoted in Auletta, *Three Blind Mice*, pp. 223–24.

271 "THE BEST RESUME": Quoted in "Ben Heineman's In-House Revolution," *The American Lawyer*, September 1989.

"I HAD THE BEST": Quoted in "Ben Heineman's In-House Revolution," *The American Lawyer*.

272 "JOHN, YOU KNOW": The conversation was related to the author by aides to Congressman Dingell, who listened in as it took place.

"FUCKIN' CLERK": Their recollection of what Welch said; the author also spoke with Ted Greenberg, the Justice Department attorney about whom Welch had spoken, who confirmed that reports of Welch's remark had gotten back to him.

"THAT'S WHY YOU HAVE": The remark attributed to Dingell is what his aides recall him as having said.

273 "WE WOULD LIKE": The author interviewed Dennis Wilson; the remark is his recollection of what the caller said to him.

THE GRAVITY: The author was in the press gallery on the day of the hearing, July 29, 1992.

"FOR OVER EIGHT YEARS": Dingell's remarks are recorded in the official transcript of the proceedings, p. 3.

274 A "STATEMENT": Welch read from a "statement," while Doyle's prepared text, distributed by the company, was described as a "testimony," even though both men were under oath.

"I UNDERSTAND YOU WORKED": The remark was overheard by the author, who was seated near Steven Pearlstein, the reporter covering the hearing for the *Washington Post*.

"NO ONE AT GE": Welch's comment is recorded on p. 18 of the official transcript.

275 "MR. CHAIRMAN, WE INTEND": Transcript, p. 16.

"WHAT IS THE SOLUTION?": Transcript, p. 16.

"I REGRET": Transcript, p. 19.

ON MARCH 30, 1992: The date was later established by congressional investigators. In addition, the author interviewed Hak, whose anonymous letter was acknowledged to have been received by Welch on March 30 in GE's own voluntary disclosure on the case, the "Report of the General Electric Company to the United States Government in Connection with the Department of Defense Voluntary Disclosure File Number 252," which General Electric submitted to the government on April 23, 1993. The March 30 date is noted on p. 7 of that report.

THE BRIBES: The sequence of events, as well as GE's access to Westinghouse's confidential bid, is described in the aforementioned report, a copy of which was obtained by the author.

276 NEITHER WERE ASKED . . . NOR VOLUNTEERED: There were two questions posed by Representative Eckart that could be construed as giving either Doyle or Welch the opportunity to disclose the Egyptian situation. "Do you think the FMF program as it is currently structured is ripe, then, for this kind of abuse?" Eckart asked (p. 54, official transcript). And: "Have you examined to what extent, if any, there were potentials for similar abuses . . . similar schemes . . ." (p. 55).

"WHY DIDN'T YOU TELL US": From an interview with a member of Dingell's staff.

"THIS IS EGYPT": Author interview.

NEW FRAUD TO UNRAVEL: The Hak case was settled in October 1993 when Martin

Marietta, which had purchased the radar business from GE, paid $6.7 million to the U.S. government to resolve the civil claims.

CHAPTER THIRTEEN
DIAMONDS AND DIRT

277   THE LARGEST RAISE: The inconsistencies in Welch's claim are reviewed in Magistrate Steinberg's "Order and Report and Recommendation," Case Number C-1-92-343, U.S. District Court, Southern District of Ohio, January 14, 1994, p. 11. The specifics on Russell's raise and salary are part of the court record.

   "I AM SO PLEASED": Quoted in "End of the Road: Firing of Executive Gives Rare Glimpse of Intrigue Inside GE," *Wall Street Journal,* November 23, 1993.

278   WELCH HAD DECIDED: Russell contended that he was fired because he objected to increasingly cozy relations between his boss, Glen Hiner, and executives at the De Beers diamond cartel. GE contended that Russell was fired for poor performance. For the purposes of this narrative, the author has accepted Welch's claim that, fed up with Russell's deficiencies as a leader, he decided on September 5, 1991 that Russell "has to go." The author has reservations about this version of events, however. As Judge Steinberg pointed out in his January 14, 1994, order, "There is scant documentation evidencing Russell's poor work performance as alleged by GE," p. 11. But Russell's portrait of himself as a whistleblower (in contrast to people who truly were, such as Jack Shannon, Frank Bordell, Vera English, Chester Walsh, and others, whose stories the reader has already had a chance to evaluate) is also flawed. Because the author has doubts about the versions of events related by both GE's principal actors in this case and Russell, he has tried to stick to the facts of the case and render a portrait that is consistent with the evidence as presented in court. After four years of tracking the many twists and turns of this case—studying thousands of pages of documents, reviewing depositions and testimony, interviewing dozens of witnesses, including one government agent who investigated the case as it unfolded—there is just one truth that the author believes unequivocally: that General Electric and De Beers did indeed collude with each other to fix the price of industrial diamonds. The government's case was ultimately undermined by court rulings excluding crucial evidence, by witnesses who changed or retracted statements, and by poor presentation of the case, which would have been very incriminating in the hands of more capable prosecution. Simply put, the government was outlawyered by the opposition.

   HAD RISEN AT 5:30 A.M.: The author logged more than one hundred hours of interviews with Edward Russell, over a period of several years. The description of his routine that morning comes from one interview conducted in 1992.

279   ONLY FIVE MONTHS BEFORE: Hiner's letter is part of the court record.

   "THAT WON'T BE NECESSARY": The author sought to interview Hiner, posing a request in person on one occasion; he refused to discuss any aspects of the case. The quotation attributed to him is Russell's recollection of what Hiner said to him. The sequence of events as described here is confirmed in the court record and in both men's testimony during the criminal trial.

   "IF YOU HAVE ANY QUESTIONS": From the letter of Glen Hiner, Senior Vice President, GE Plastics, to Edward J. Russell, November 11, 1991, a copy of which was obtained by the author.

279 THREE YEARS LATER: Hiner so testified during the criminal trial in Columbus, Ohio.

280 "YOU'VE GOT TO BE KIDDING": Russell's recollection of what he said.

"IMAGINE A PRESENTATION": A portion of this September 5 fax was quoted in "End of the Road," *Wall Street Journal.* The full text was disclosed as part of the court record.

ITT'S ADMISSION: Cited in "Harold S. Geneen, 87, Dies; Nurtured ITT," *New York Times,* November 23, 1997.

281 HIS DISSERTATION TOPIC: Details about Russell's early career were described to the author by Russell.

282 THE "EXCELLENT" JOB: Welch's note was described to the author by Russell.

THE NEWSLETTER: A copy of it was provided to the author by Russell's first wife, Alison J. Pfeister.

"I WAS TOO ANGRY": The author interviewed Alison Pfeister.

283 "THE ULTIMATE HOSTESS": Quoted in "CEO's Divorce Dissects Job of 'Corporate Wife,' " *Wall Street Journal,* December 6, 1996.

"THERE WERE TWENTY GUYS": Remark was made to the author in the course of one interview with Russell.

MOVE TO MEXICO BALLSY: The author interviewed several of Russell's colleagues from that time, and based on those interviews, believes that Russell's assertion is accurate.

284 "ED KEPT SAYING": Russell recollects the comment, made by Pfeister, and concurs with her description of events regarding the birth of their child.

SO DID THE REWARDS: The specifics of Russell's financial situation were described in the affidavit of Harbig D. Garbedian, a GE employee; a copy of it was sent by GE counsel to Russell's ex-wife.

"WE WIVES KNEW": Letter from Alison Pfeister to the author, September 22, 1992, p. 4.

285 TWENTY-TWO OTHER GE EXECUTIVES: The disclosure, made in a deposition taken on June 14, 1993, was later picked up in the press, including several *Wall Street Journal* articles.

HAD BEEN CATHARTIC: The author interviewed several executives close to Hiner, including one member of his staff who was sent to Columbus on a "fishing expedition" to evaluate Russell. Everyone interviewed agreed that Hiner had an intense dislike of Russell, and that in firing him he would have purged ill will he had felt for a long time.

"THEY SHOT ME": The author interviewed Denise Maurer, and both she and Russell recall the conversation.

SIX-PAGE PROTEST MEMO: The author obtained a copy of the memo, to "Fellow GE Associates," dated October 30, 1991.

286 "MAKE THE SEPARATIONS": Welch's comments are taken from the transcript of his deposition in the Depew case, given October 31, 1995, p. 37.

"POND SCUM": Russell memo, p. 1.

"THEY'LL BE SORRY": Maurer's recollection of what Russell said; Russell doesn't recall having said it.

"GE DOESN'T NEED": Russell's recollection of what Smart said; Smart declined the author's invitation to be interviewed.

287 SOME COULDN'T TAKE THE CASE: A common occurrence when people going up

against GE seek legal representation; many of the nation's leading law firms already do work for GE and hence are "conflicted out."

287 WHEN RUSSELL MET SMART: In addition to Russell's statements as to this meeting, he constructed a chronology of events as they occurred, a copy of which was obtained by the author. Russell's notes on the November 19 meeting appear on p. 63 of that chronology.

"THE PROBLEM HAS BEEN": Russell memo, p. 1.

ONE HINER APPOINTEE: All these allegations are found in the memo Ed Russell wrote two weeks before his dismissal on November 11, 1991. And they were all subsequently alleged in depositions taken by Russell's attorneys as part of his wrongful termination suit against GE.

"WIMP FROM WORTHINGTON": A commonly used phrase, known to many people at Superabrasives and GE Plastics; it appeared in a November 23, 1993, headline in the *Wall Street Journal.*

288 A WRITTEN POLICY: The author obtained a copy of GE's written policy.

HINER'S EXTRAVAGANCE: The tulip tale was confirmed by Denise Maurer, who had arranged for their placement on several occasions.

"LOOKING AT ALL YOUR PEOPLE": The comment that Russell recalls Hiner having made to him.

RUSSELL PAID A VISIT: People on Hiner's staff confirmed Russell's visit to Peiffer.

289 "I WANT YOU TO PUT": The author interviewed Bruce Krause.

THE INDUSTRIAL-DIAMOND CAPITAL: The contents and appearance of the Worthington factory were described to the author by Russell and others who had visited it over the years. In addition, it was described on National Public Radio's *Morning Edition* by Robert Hazen, a researcher at the Carnegie Institution of Washington, D.C., who has written about the scientific discoveries that led to the industrial-diamond business. Hazen was interviewed on January 25, 1994, and the author obtained a copy of the transcript.

290 THE INVENTION OF THE SYNTHETIC DIAMOND: The author interviewed three of the six people who made the discovery: Tracy Hall, Francis Bundy, and Robert Wentorf.

"NEW MILESTONE": The comment, by C. Guy Suits, director of the GE Research Lab, is found in an article he wrote and presented to the American Chemical Society, "The Synthesis of Diamond: A Case History in Modern Science," November 3, 1960, p. 3.

AN EMBITTERED: The story of Hall's falling out with the other members of the research team is a book in itself. Suffice it to say that the American Chemical Society finally credited Hall some thirty years later as the rightful inventor of synthetic diamond.

A TELEGRAM: Edward Jay Epstein, *The Diamond Invention* (London: Hutchinson & Co., 1982), p. 145. Background on the history of De Beers in chapters 12 and 13 comes mainly from this book and another, Stefan Kanfer, *The Last Empire: De Beers, Diamonds, and the World* (New York: Farrar Straus Giroux, 1993).

291 TO FORGE A DUOPOLY: The elements of the duopoly are described in Epstein, *The Diamond Invention*, p. 147.

IN OCTOBER 1966: Harry Oppenheimer's proposal is found in Edward Jay Epstein's *The Diamond Invention*, p. 148. In his footnotes, Epstein cites Justice Department documents he obtained through a Freedom of Information Act filing as the source of information on this meeting and Oppenheimer's proposal.

292   ONE SUCH SPY: The story of Sung's theft—and GE's subsequent lawsuit against Iljin—was covered extensively in the news media. One of the first articles was "Spy Story: How Secret GE Recipe for Making Diamonds May Have Been Stolen," *Wall Street Journal,* February 28, 1990. In addition, the description of events related to Sung comes from Ed Russell.

TO PROTECT WELCH: Russell recalls being told this when he inquired about other work Fairfax had done for GE.

RUSSELL BEGAN INITIATIVES: There are many people who speak highly of the work Russell did in the first few years after his arrival at Superabrasives. A typical comment is that of Gordon T. Collier, who in a seven-page unsolicited affidavit said: "Russell was a very good, normal, intelligent, principled, open individual, capable of good managerial activities. He was approachable. . . ."

293   THE BEST-PERFORMING: Several people, including one on Hiner's staff, characterized it as such.

"THERE WAS A REAL SENSE": The author interviewed Gary Weber.

"EXCELLENT OVERALL": Hiner's performance appraisal is part of the court record. In a later review, dated June 26, 1991 and cited by Magistrate Steinberg in his January 14, 1994 order (p. 10), Hiner wrote: "excellent workforce strategies," "both good as a business planner and in the execution of those plans," "good listener and accepts advice." The review concluded with this recommendation: "Ed needs to remain on his current position, rebuild his team, fix his product line problems and then consider other potential options."

NOTEWORTHY PROGRESS: Russell's progress was praised effusively in Professor Todd Jick's report.

294   WELCH WAS DISINGENUOUS: The contradictions among Welch's and GE's explanations for why Russell had been fired are discussed at length in Judge Steinberg's order and were the basis for his decision that the case should proceed to trial. "As we stated at the December 1, 1993 hearing," the judge wrote (p. 12), "the timing of the discharge decision, in conjunction with the lack of documentation regarding Russell's alleged poor performance, the inconsistent reasons given for his discharge, and the unusual circumstance of discharging a highly placed executive without warning or prior discipline, constitute sufficient evidence to require a trier of fact to determine whether or not Russell was discharged for a legitimate reason or for his alleged whistle blowing activity."

"THE BELLWETHER": The report of Professor Jick, "Workout Status and Recommendations for Self-Sufficiency," was submitted into the court record; his comments are found on p. 4 of that report.

"LOGICAL, VERY CONSCIENTIOUS": The comments are taken from Smart's "Developmental Plan," p. 1, which was sent to Russell on April 29, 1991.

"I'M NOT ACCEPTING": Russell's recollection of what he said to Hiner.

295   A FORTY-PAGE CHRONOLOGY: The author obtained a copy of that chronology.

BIG-NAME EXECUTIVES: Liotier and Frenz were named in the indictment, as were General Electric and De Beers; Nicholas Oppenheimer, Ogilvie Thompson, and Davignon were not. However, the Justice Department memo recommending indictment of

GE, De Beers, Frenz, and Liotier (dated January 24, 1994) maintains that Oppenheimer, Ogilvie Thompson, Davignon, and Hiner as well, even though not named in the indictment, were instrumental in establishing the working relationship that made the scheme possible.

295 "ALTHOUGH RUSSELL": Memorandum, from David A. Blotner, Arnold C. Celnicker, Joelle A. Moreno, and James T. Clancy, to Anthony V. Nanni, Chief, Litigation I Section, "Industrial Diamonds Grand Jury Investigation—Recommendation to Indict General Electric, De Beers, Peter Frenz and Philippe Liotier," January 24, 1994, p. 1. The author obtained a copy of the twenty-five-page memo, which summarizes the Justice Department's evidence, including the witnesses it expected to call at trial, as well as its strategy for prosecuting the case.

296 "OH, MY GOD!": The description of what John Blystone said comes from Denise Maurer, whom the author interviewed on several occasions. The same exclamation is recorded in the unpublished manuscript of Bruce Dunnington, who gave the author a copy for review. Dunnington, a former executive in the diamond industry turned writer, also investigated the case, and witnessed the trial. Blystone was among the executives the author requested to interview on April 22, 1993, in a memo hand-delivered to Dan Webb, GE's counsel. That request was later denied.

DURING THIS CALL: The sequence of events is established in the court record.

"I HOPE YOU DESTROYED": Both of Frenz's comments are established in the court record.

297 "PURE NONSENSE": Quoted in "GE Launches Internal Probe Into Charges," *Wall Street Journal*, April 23, 1992, which also reported that Welch was "visibly irritated."

"ED RUSSELL WAS REMOVED": Letter, to GE Officers from John F. Welch, April 29, 1992.

"A VERY SERIOUS": Quoted in "GE Crushes the Trustbusters," *The American Lawyer*, January-February 1995, p. 58.

"WHAT MADE HIM TICK": The phrase is found on p. 2 of the affidavit filed October 27, 1992 by Alison J. Pfeister, based on her phone conversation on June 5, 1992 with Philip W. Horton. Exhibit A of the affidavit is the letter Horton sent to Pfeister afterward, thanking her for talking to him. What Horton didn't realize was that Pfeister disliked GE more than her ex-husband.

"REGRET THAT HE CHOSE": Pfeister affidavit, p. 3.

298 COULD FACE INDICTMENTS: Pfeister affidavit, p. 5.

AN UNUSUAL ARRANGEMENT: Russell's attorneys established the terms of GE's indemnification in the course of their lawsuit. It was established that GE had entered into written agreements with all eighty-three of its case-in-chief witnesses that it listed for trial, including even individuals not in its employ, such as psychologist Brad Smart. The author obtained copies of eleven of the indemnification agreements (including the one signed by Smart) all of which have the same provisions and conditions. Under point 4 (a) (p. 3), the Smart letter states: "GE, in its sole discretion, at any time and for any reason, may cease to advance legal expenses on behalf of your client." And under 4 (d): "A decision by GE to cease advancing legal expenses does not relieve your client of the obligation to repay GE for its advancement of legal expenses pursuant to the terms of the undertaking entered into by your client." The agreements require, as a stipulation for expense reimbursement, that the party's attorney submit *monthly* to GE "at a minimum . . . a description of the work performed during the month, the names of each lawyer and paralegal working on the matter during the month, the amount of time spent by each lawyer and paralegal, the hourly rate of each lawyer and paralegal, and an itemized list of direct charges." By this process, GE was able to effectively remind each of its witnesses monthly what his total legal indebtedness was to GE, the accused.

298 $1 MILLION A MONTH: Pfeister affidavit, p. 2.

THE BIGGEST ANTITRUST CASE: Pfeister affidavit, p. 7.

"HAS A TRACK RECORD": Assertion was made in a September 24, 1993 letter from Dan Webb to the author's attorney, Roslyn Litman.

299 "THE DIRTY DOZEN": Taken from a quotation by Ben Heineman in "GE Crushes the Trustbusters," *The American Lawyer*, p. 59.

"HARD CORE PRICE FIXING": Quoted in "End of the Road," *Wall Street Journal.*

BINGAMAN HAD WORKED: The background on Bingaman, and her relationship with Gillam, comes from "GE Crushes the Trustbusters," and "At Justice, the Taming of a Whirlwind," *New York Times*, October 22, 1995.

"I WAS TOLD": This quotation is taken from Maurer's interviews with the author.

300 "THRU LIOTIER THAT DE BEERS": The author obtained a copy of Blystone's hand-written note, dated February 29, 1992, from which this quotation is taken.

CONVENED A FULL-DAY HEARING: The author was in the courtroom for that hearing and obtained a transcript of it.

"YOU BETTER GET LANDIS": This statement is part of the court record and was confirmed for the author in interviews with Maurer.

SMART DIDN'T GIVE: Magistrate Steinberg drew the same conclusion in his January 14, 1994 order: "There were two reports prepared by Smart regarding Russell: a "discouraging" April 16, 1991 report and a "positive, upbeat" April 29, 1991 report. Smart did not forward the April 16, 1991 negative report to GE until May 5, 1992, well after plaintiff's discharge. It could not, therefore, have factored into Welch's decision-making process," p. 10.

"WHEN AN EXECUTIVE": Smart's statement was made in his affidavit, which is part of the court record.

301 "A CASE THAT CAN": Indictment memo, p. 24.

HELMER FIGURED: Those were the numbers Helmer disclosed to Russell.

"JIM, I THINK": A portion of the conversation, which took place on January 21, 1994, was taped, and a transcript of that portion was obtained by the author.

THE LAWSUIT, HOWEVER: The author had several telephone conversations during this period with Russell, in which he revealed his conflicted mental state; he was in a quandary over what to do.

302 THE NIGHT BEFORE: A description of Schroeder's attempt to get a wire on Russell is in "Fatal Flaws: How the Federal Case Against GE, De Beers Collapsed So Quickly," *Wall Street Journal*, December 28, 1994. It was also confirmed to the author in interviews with both Russell and Schroeder.

NO AGREEMENT WAS REACHED: The sequence and description of events in the final days before and after the settlement of Russell's suit is taken from interviews with the principals, and from two published articles: "GE Crushes the Trustbusters," *The American Lawyer*, and "Multifaceted Case: Price-Fixing Charges Put GE and De Beers Under Tough Scrutiny," *Wall Street Journal*, February 22, 1994.

302 "PERSONAL KNOWLEDGE": The author was provided with a copy of the Russell affidavit; the phrase "personal knowledge" was "direct knowledge" at an earlier point in the negotiations between Webb and Helmer.

303 HEINEMAN THEN CALLED ON: Heineman's appeal to Webster Hubbell was reported in "Multifaceted Case," *Wall Street Journal,* February 22, 1994.

304 "THE [ANTITRUST] DIVISION": Quoted in "Multifaceted Case," *Wall Street Journal.*
"WE WILL USE": Quoted in "Multifaceted Case," *Wall Street Journal.*

CHAPTER FOURTEEN
THE UNITED STATES OF AMERICA V. GENERAL ELECTRIC

305 NEARLY 80 PERCENT: Estimate comes from "Keeping Corporate Score: In South Africa It's Even Hard to Find the Players," *New York Times,* March 2, 1996.

306 "EXHIBITIONS OF BASEBALL": Quoted in John Helyar, *Lords of the Realm: The Real History of Baseball* (New York: Villard, 1994), p. 10.
THREE TIMES IN LAWSUITS: Baida, *Poor Richard's Legacy,* pp. 301–03.

307 "A SHOCKING INDICTMENT": Quoted in "The Incredible Electrical Conspiracy," *Fortune,* February 11, 1980, p. 174.
THE BOARD GAME *MONOPOLY*: The author had heard of this story in Schenectady and Pittsfield, and confirmed it in an interview with William Bywater, past president of the International Union of Electrical Workers, who knew Carey.
GE HAD PAID OUT: "Pittsfield and the Antitrust Cases," *Berkshire Eagle,* October 7, 1978.
"COMPETITOR CONTACT FORM": Executives the author interviewed from both General Electric and Westinghouse recalled the forms.

308 NO, HE WOULD NOT: Welch's deposition was for a time held under seal; his comment was disclosed to the author in a memo, written May 12, 1993 by Russell and sent to Helmer and the author, which reviewed what Welch had said.

309 "ALTHOUGH WE ARE CONVINCED": Indictment memo, p. 24.
DAVE SCHROEDER: The author interviewed him on several occasions.

310 MOST OF THE SERVICE: The description of events was recounted to the author by Schroeder.
"YOU REALLY DIDN'T NEED": Schroeder's recollection of what Whitehead said.

311 "LIOTIER OF DIAMANT BOART": From the fax of Peter Frenz to Steve Palovchik, December 16, 1991; the fax is cited in the indictment memo, p. 15.
"YOU'D HAVE TO BE A MASOCHIST": Whitehead's comment was revealed during the trial.

312 COMPANY CALLED SIBEKA: The interrelationships among Société Générale, Sibeka, De Beers Centenary, and Diamant Boart are shown in a diagram in the indictment memo, p. 6.
"I THINK IT WOULD BE": Schroeder's recollection of what Secret said.

313 "YOU TREATED HIM": Schroeder's recollection of what Davignon said.
"WE JUST WANT TO": The encounter and dialogue was related to the author by Schroeder, who was present at the time.
TANTALIZING QUESTIONS: The questions are summarized in the indictment memo.

314 "HERCULEAN EFFORTS": Phrase comes from the Opinion and Order of Judge George C. Smith, for the Southern District of Ohio, Eastern Division, December 5, 1994, p. 31. "CRAFTED TO MIMIC": Indictment memo, p. 24.

315 "WE DON'T DO BUSINESS": Quoted in "Multifaceted Case," *Wall Street Journal.*
A SHIMMERING PEBBLE: The story of Erasmus Jacobs's remarkable discovery is told in Kanfer, *The Last Empire,* p. 16.
"ROUNDED, APPARENTLY": Quoted in Kanfer, *The Last Empire,* p. 24.

316 "GENTLEMEN, THIS IS": Quoted in Kanfer, *The Last Empire,* p. 27.
CECIL RHODES: His upbringing and early life are dealt with in Kanfer, *The Last Empire,* pp. 58–66.
"IMMENSE AND BROODING": Quoted in Kanfer, *The Last Empire,* p. 58; the quotation is taken from a memorial poem Kipling penned on the occasion of Rhodes's funeral.

317 BARNATO HAD SURRENDERED: Rhodes's scheme to bankrupt Barnato is told in Kanfer, *The Last Empire,* pp. 102–06, and in Epstein, *The Diamond Invention,* pp. 64–67.

318 ANGLO AMERICAN CORPORATION: The description of Oppenheimer's maneuverings comes from Epstein, *The Diamond Invention,* pp. 72–75.

319 A PRIVATE TREATY: Epstein, *The Diamond Invention,* p. 79.

320 "FARCICAL": Quoted in Epstein, *The Diamond Invention,* p. 81.
"THE DIAMOND SECTION": Quoted in Epstein, *The Diamond Invention,* p. 81.
CODE-NAMED TETON: Epstein, *The Diamond Invention,* p. 85.
"THE UNITED STATES IS PAYING": Quoted in Epstein, *The Diamond Invention,* p. 84.

321 A GRAND JURY WAS CONVENED: Epstein, *The Diamond Invention,* p. 181.
THEY PLED: Epstein, *The Diamond Invention,* p. 187.

322 "DECADENCE MEETS SLEAZE": Russell's "Fellow GE Associates" memo, p. 5.
A "SIGHT": It is described in Kanfer, *The Last Empire,* pp. 3–4.
TO PAY THEIR RESPECTS: Kanfer, *The Last Empire,* p. 4.

323 SIR JULIAN: The background on Ogilvie Thompson comes mainly from Kanfer, *The Last Empire,* pp. 345–47.

324 HANKY-PANKY: The impropriety, in which the Internal Revenue Service audited two sets of books kept by Superabrasives, resulting in about a $7 million net income reversal over three years, was confirmed to the author by GE personnel who investigated the matter. In addition, a summary of the activities is found in Ed Russell's chronology of events (p. 6), a copy of which was given to the Justice Department and was obtained by the author. It is substantiated in one document (GE RU1-000037) provided to Russell in the discovery of his lawsuit.
"NO EMPLOYEE SHALL ATTEND": The author obtained a copy of Policy 20.5; the cited sentence is found under "Participation in Trade Associations and Other Meetings with Competitors," section (a), subheading (1).
APPEARANCE OF IMPROPRIETY: From conversations the author has had with Justice Department officials who investigated and prosecuted the case, it is clear they considered Hiner's contact with Ogilvie Thompson highly suspect, and in and of itself prima facie evidence that a crime had been committed. The meetings "establish[ed] a working relationship between GES [General Electric Superabrasives] and De Beers," according to the indictment memo (p. 3), which from the prosecution's point of view had paved the way for the Frenz-Liotier connection.

324   "DO YOU KNOW WHO": The exchange is Russell's recollection of what he said, and Hiner's reply.

"TOSS" IT: Hiner wrote a letter to Ogilvie Thompson on March 6, 1990, which was not produced by General Electric. "The only reason that we are aware of its existence," the indictment memo reads in a footnote on p. 3, "is that it is referenced in the March 22 responding letter to Hiner from Ogilvie Thompson. The March 22 letter was also not produced by General Electric, but was retained and provided to us by Russell despite Hiner's instructions to Russell that he 'toss' it." The author obtained a copy of the March 22 letter.

326   HINER FLOATED THE IDEA: Sneeringer so testified in a sworn deposition given September 21, 1992 as part of Russell's lawsuit:

Q: "What did Mr. Hiner say concerning De Beers?"

Sneeringer: "Mr. Hiner raised the possibility of a technical exchange between GE and De Beers." (p. 118 of the official transcript)

"OPINIONS WERE EXPRESSED": Sneeringer deposition, September 21, 1992, p. 152 of the transcript.

327   "I ASKED HIM": Maurer's recollection of her exchanges with Russell.

"THIS IS WHAT CONCERNS": Russell's recollection of what he said; Hiner didn't recall the exchange, nor did he recall in court testimony that the briefing paper contained an antitrust warning.

"DID YOU DESTROY": The exchange is found on p. 13 of the transcript of proceedings before Judge Steinberg, November 23, 1993.

328   "THIS MAN DESERVES": Magistrate Steinberg's statement, from the transcript of proceedings.

THE TRIAL WAS EFFECTIVELY OVER: In addition to interviews with the principal players, the author's summary of the trial is taken chiefly from the following sources: daily stories published in the *Columbus Dispatch*, the *New York Times*, and the *Wall Street Journal*; "Fatal Flaws," *Wall Street Journal*; "GE Crushes the Trustbusters," *The American Lawyer;* and the unpublished manuscript of Bruce Dunnington, who sat through the trial and briefed the author on the proceedings as they occurred.

329   LOOKING VINDICTIVE: Several jurors thought so.

"WELL, YOU ARRESTED ME": Quoted in "Fatal Flaw," *Wall Street Journal.*

APPARENTLY WAS LESS CONVINCING: That was the conclusion of several people familiar with his testimony, including Denise Maurer, whom the author interviewed on several occasions, and whose comments to that effect are found in the unpublished manuscript of Bruce Dinnington, a onetime executive in the diamond industry turned writer who sat through the entire court proceeding in Columbus. Palovchik's testimony is also discussed in *The American Lawyer* piece on the case, "GE Crushes the Trustbusters," January–February 1995.

"THE GOVERNMENT TOTALLY": Maurer's recollection of what Palovchik said.

"I APPRECIATE YOUR CALL": Maurer's recollection of what Celnicker said.

330   "THIS JUDGE WAS NOT": Quoted in "GE Crushes the Trustbusters," *The American Lawyer,* p. 66.

"YOU'VE GOT CONNECTIONS": The author interviewed Judge Smith.

THE "VILLAGE IDIOT": Blystone's characterization of Russell was made to Dave

Schroeder, the lead FBI agent in the case, whom the author interviewed on many occasions.

CHAPTER FIFTEEN
THE RECKONING

332 "A LION": "The Race for a Global Network," *The New Yorker,* March 6, 1995, p. 53.

333 HIS FIRST WARNING: Welch's admission that he was unaware is found in "GE May Try to Sell Kidder After Debacle," *Wall Street Journal,* April 19, 1994.

"A YEAR AGO": Quoted in "Laughing at GE's Expense: Honored Leader Jokes About Trading Scandal," *New York Times,* July 14, 1994.

334 "HUMAN PIRANHA": The author interviewed several of Jett's colleagues, who confirmed the nickname, as well as his celebrity at the Boca Raton meeting.

"THIS VIOLATES EVERYTHING": Quoted in "Kidder Discloses Scam in Bonds, Fires Top Trader," *Wall Street Journal,* April 18, 1994.

ONLY $20 MILLION: This figure, which was reported in the press, was confirmed in interviews with traders who worked on Kidder, Peabody's government-bond desk.

335 WITHOUT THE REQUIRED: That Carpenter did not have a license to manage a brokerage firm was first reported in the *New York Times;* *Fortune* followed it up and ran an entire story on the subject in its September 5, 1994 issue (p. 42), "Was Carpenter Brokering Without a License?"

"THE TONE SET BY TOP": The SEC report, on an accounting fraud at Chambers Development Company that was revealed in March 1992, was quoted in "A Look at How the SEC Disposed of Chambers's Claims," *Pittsburgh Post-Gazette,* May 14, 1995.

"AS HIS PROFITABILITY INCREASED": "Report of Inquiry Into False Trading Profits at Kidder, Peabody & Co. Incorporated," prepared by the law firm of Davis Polk & Wardwell, August 4, 1994, p. 19.

MOST OF ITS EXISTENCE: The background and history of Kidder, Peabody comes from interviews the author conducted with former Kidder, Peabody principals, and from James B. Stewart, *Den of Thieves* (New York: Simon & Schuster, 1991).

AN EARLY SUBSCRIBER: Baldwin, *Edison,* p. 48.

336 THE FIRST JEW: Stewart, *Den of Thieves,* p. 22.

"HEARTTHROB": Quoted in Stewart, *Den of Thieves,* p. 28.

"ALL GOOD THINGS": Albert Gordon declined the author's request for an interview. He is quoted in Stewart, *Den of Thieves,* p. 214.

337 LIQUIDITY CRISIS: Richard Stewart's desperate search for capital is recounted in *Den of Thieves.*

CAUGHT AN IMMEDIATE FLIGHT: Stewart, *Den of Thieves,* p. 214.

DESPERATELY WANTED: The strategic planners in Mike Carpenter's group, who were interviewed by the author, had knowledge of Wright's desire to expand.

338 WRIGHT ARRANGED A MEETING: The encounter, and events that followed, are recounted in "Kidder's Road to Acquisition," *New York Times,* May 5, 1986.

CHRISTENING: "Kidder's Road to Acquisition," *New York Times.*

"AS MUCH AS": Quoted in "Kidder's Road to Acquisition," *New York Times.*

339 THE ARRESTS ROCKED KIDDER: Welch's reaction to Wigton's arrest was first disclosed in "Damage Control: How GE and Kidder Managed to Ward Off an Impending Disaster," *Wall Street Journal*, June 8, 1987, and was later recounted in *Den of Thieves*.

340 "WE'RE GOING TO INDICT": Quoted in Stewart, *Den of Thieves*, p. 336.

"RESPONSIBLE CORPORATE": Quoted in "Damage Control," *Wall Street Journal*.

341 "I WAS THINKING": The anonymous Kidder official was quoted in "GE Drops Two Kidder Executives in Latest Insider-Trading Fallout," *Wall Street Journal*, May 15, 1987.

342 SURPRISINGLY, NOT EVERYONE: A cover story in *Fortune* ("Jack Welch's Nightmare on Wall Street," September 5, 1994) makes this point: "Carpenter was not the only one at Kidder without a license. Charles V. Sheehan, who ran retail sales under Carpenter from 1989 to 1991, was not licensed for that position. Sheehan, a former GE manager, failed to meet the most basic requirement of a broker: He never took the Series 7 exam. And a recent report in the *Wall Street Journal* raises questions about the licensing of one of Kidder's traders."

CARPENTER: Carpenter was among forty executives the author requested to interview in a memo, dated April 23, 1993, hand-delivered by the author's attorney, Roslyn Litman, to Dan Webb, GE's counsel. General Electric declined the invitation. The author also subsequently spoke to Carpenter on the phone after he had left Kidder in 1994 and again conveyed his desire to interview him; Carpenter declined. The background on Carpenter comes from interviews with his colleagues and subordinates at General Electric and Kidder.

"WHERE CARPENTER FELL": Author interview; the comment is a typical assessment of Carpenter's shortcomings as the head of Kidder, Peabody.

"HE WAS ONE OF THE MOST": Author interview.

DESPISED EACH OTHER: The Carpenter-Wendt animosity was first brought to the author's attention by a former senior Kidder executive. His assertion was subsequently substantiated in the June 14, 1993 deposition of Brad Smart, the industrial psychologist involved in the Russell case who admitted under oath that he had done work for GE in seeking to improve relations between Carpenter and Wendt. Smart's activities in executive disputes (including the Wendt-Carpenter conflict) were also the subject, later, of a front-page story in the *Wall Street Journal*.

344 "I HAD NO ARGUMENT": Author interview.

"HOW MUCH DID": Author interview.

345 IT COULD GRAB: Carpenter's strategy was explained to the author by people who were at Kidder at the time and had knowledge of it. In addition, it is reviewed in many post-mortems written about Kidder after the bond scandal surfaced, including "Jack Welch's Nightmare on Wall Street," *Fortune*, September 5, 1994, pp. 40–48; and "Bond Epic: How Kidder, a Tiger in April, Found Itself the Prey by December," *Wall Street Journal*, December 29, 1994. The ascendance of the Fixed Income Division is also examined in the Davis Polk & Wardwell report.

346 THE EARLIEST INDICATIONS: LaPrade's allegations are set forth in her complaint. The *Wall Street Journal* reported on May 2, 1994: "Linda LaPrade, a former Kidder vice president, sued Kidder in 1991 claiming that Mr. Cerullo pressured her to inflate bids for government 'agency' securities, telling her 'profits and performance were most important,' and threatening her with termination if she didn't comply, according to her

lawsuit." Neither Cerullo nor Mullin returned phone calls seeking comment on her allegations.

347 AMONG THE MOST ANXIOUS: According to one person who regularly attended the Inventory Committee meetings.

BY APRIL 1993: The balance sheet figures come from the Davis Polk & Wardwell report, p. 59, which states in a footnote on that page: "Throughout much of 1993, Cerullo and O'Donnell were at odds over the size of Kidder's balance sheet."

"THIS CONVERSATION": Author interview.

"I HAVE CRS": Author interview.

348 "ALL THIS INVENTORY": The remarks attributed to Welch and Cerullo are what one person who heard the exchange recalls them as having said.

DANGEROUSLY LEVERAGED: The numbers are cited in "Jack Welch's Nightmare on Wall Street," *Fortune*, p. 43.

JETT HAD WASHED OUT: The background on Jett comes from interviews with coworkers and subordinates at Kidder, as well as "Jett's Passage: How a Kidder Trader Stumbled Upward Before Scandal Struck," *Wall Street Journal*, June 3, 1994.

349 "I JUST DISCOVERED": The quotation comes from the transcript of the *60 Minutes* broadcast, "Did He, or Didn't He?" February 19, 1995, p. 9.

HE HAD FALSELY LISTED TIME: The *Wall Street Journal* reported June 3, 1994: "While at the business school, Mr. Jett was fired from his part-time job at the computer-services center in the business-school library. Two former colleagues recall that his dismissal was the result of accusations that he falsified time sheets, listing hours he hadn't worked.... Mr. Sard [Jett's spokesman] acknowledges that Mr. Jett was fired from his job, but denies that he falsified time sheets or claimed racism. Instead, he was fired because he took off an hour from work for a job interview...."

HAVE TO SETTLE: The author interviewed Fletcher.

HE SENT THE CLIPPING: This account comes from Fletcher, who learned of it in a conversation with Jett.

350 "A SLOWER START": Mullin's comments are taken from a footnote in the Davis Polk & Wardwell report, p. 48.

"PERFORMANCE IN 1992": From the same report, p. 50.

JETT HAD PHONED FLETCHER: Their meeting, which was reported in "Jett's Passage," *Wall Street Journal*, was confirmed to the author by Fletcher.

"IT SOUNDED NONSENSICAL": Fletcher interview.

BUT FROM FORWARD TRANSACTIONS: The description of Jett's trading activities comes principally from the Davis Polk & Wardwell report and from newspaper and magazine accounts.

351 REPRESENTED 27 PERCENT: The numbers come from the official report of inquiry, p. 52.

TO DISMISS HUGH BUSH: The incident is reported in a footnote (p. 49) of the official report of inquiry, but Bush's identity was not revealed. The author established the identity through interviews with Kidder traders who worked with Bush at that time. Bush declined to comment on the incident.

IN A SECOND INSTANCE: Reported in the Davis Polk & Wardwell inquiry, pp. 55–58.

352 "NO ONE COULD": The author interviewed Jeffrey Liddle.

352   "THE RESPONSE WASN'T": Liddle interview.
      THIS ACCOUNTING CHANGE: Inquiry report, p. 45.
      WHICH WELCH REVIEWED: According to one person familiar with the bonus review
      procedure.
353   UNTIL THREE WEEKS LATER: The chronology of events comes from the Davis Polk
      & Wardwell report, which chastises Cerullo (p. 79) for his delay in informing the appro-
      priate people at Kidder. "Cerullo made no mention to O'Donnell [the chief financial
      officer] of Jett's forward positions or any concerns Cerullo may have had about them.
      Indeed, although he found Jett's explanations unsatisfactory, Cerullo failed to advise
      accounting, finance or legal personnel of Jett's massive forward positions until the end
      of March."
354   ASKIN CAPITAL MANAGEMENT: The bankruptcy reorganization filing (under
      Chapter 11 of the federal bankruptcy code) of three investment funds run by Askin
      Capital Management was reported in the *New York Times* on April 8, 1994.
      "THE BASIC UNDERLYING": Quoted in "Kidder Discloses Scam in Bonds, Fires Top
      Trader," *Wall Street Journal.*
      "GONE THROUGH THE KIDDER": Quoted in "The Ax Falls: GE's Mr. Welch Ousts
      Kidder's Chairman, Names Financial Aides," *Wall Street Journal,* June 23, 1994.
      "STRONG FIRM": Quoted in "The Axe Falls," *Wall Street Journal.*
355   "I FEEL LIKE": The quotation, related to the author by one person present in the room
      when it was said, was confirmed by John Gordon, Al Gordon's son.
      FOR CERULLO: "SEC Charges Former Trader for Kidder With Fraud," *New York Times,*
      January 10, 1996.
      "DECISIVE MANAGEMENT": The statement, from General Electric's annual proxy
      filed with the Securities and Exchange Commission, was carried on the Bloomberg
      Business News wire on March 7, 1995, under the headline, "GE Raised Welch's Bonus
      and Salary to $4.35 Million in 1994."
356   "JACK IN THE BOX": The headline appeared in the October 3, 1994 issue of *Time,* p. 56.
      "YOU CAN HEAR": "Scratches in the Teflon," *Newsweek,* October 3, 1994, p. 50.
      "THE PROBLEMS AT KIDDER": "Jack Welch's Nightmare on Wall Street," *Fortune,*
      pp. 40–41.

CHAPTER SIXTEEN
THE SOUL OF A NEW MACHINE

357   "WORK IS, BY ITS VERY": Studs Terkel, *Working: People Talk about What They Do All
      Day, and How They Feel About What They Do* (New York: Pantheon Books, 1974).
      ATTILA THE HUN: The book is cited in "New Book on Jesus, Corporate Manager Non-
      pareil," *New York Times,* March 16, 1996. Its title was not given.
      "FOR MOST PEOPLE": Donald G. Krause, *The Art of War for Executives* (New York:
      Perigee, 1995), pp. 6–7.
358   "MONEY, NOT MORALITY": Quoted in "Does America Still Work?" *Harper's,* May
      1996, p. 35.
      "WE ARE ALL CAUGHT": Quoted in "Does America Still Work?" *Harper's,* p. 35.
      ONCE SUED HENRY FORD: Baida, *Poor Richard's Legacy,* p. 201.

358   "ECONOMIC BLUNDERS": Quoted in Jerry Porras and James Collins, *Built to Last: Successful Habits of Visionary Companies* (New York: HarperBusiness, 1994), p. 53.
     "I DON'T BELIEVE": Quoted in Porras and Collins, *Built to Last,* p. 53.

359   "I WANT TO DISCUSS": Quoted in Porras and Collins, *Built to Last,* p. 56.
     WHEN PACKARD DIED: "With Fortune Built, Packard Heirs Look to Build a Legacy," *New York Times,* May 6, 1996.

360   "THEY'VE BEEN BUILDING": The author interviewed Leslie Gates during a visit to Mexico in July 1993.
     THE WAGES WERE POOR: In July 1993, the author traveled to Mexico and with the assistance of Roman Catholic missionaries, interviewed at length several Mexicans who worked at different GE locations along the *maquiladora.* The assertion that GE pays about half of what Ford pays was derived through a comparison of wage scales provided by the Catholic missionaries and social agencies that track such things in the United States (the electrical industry in general is one of the lowest-paying employers in Mexico, while the auto industry is one of the highest, attributable in part to the higher skills required for auto as against lightbulb assembly). Concern over possible exposure to industrial chemicals was a topic that came up frequently. One worker, Jacobo Ramirez Monrreal, speculated that a cleaning agent he used might be making him woozy, and causing others to faint. As for the worker who alleged the miscarriage, that came directly from the woman, whom the author interviewed through an interpreter. The woman—she would not give her name, but she was the sister of another GE worker, Maria Luisa Alba Lopez, who first mentioned the incident—described it in detail.

362   "NO MATTER HOW HARD": The author interviewed Greg August during a visit to Erie in November 1993.
     "IT USED TO BE": The author interviewed Mike Gieza.

363   "CLEARED OUT A LOT": Quoted in "The Peacock Preens Again," *New York Times,* April 14, 1996.
     "THEY DEMAND THAT YOU": The author interviewed Michael Gartner during a visit to New York City in October 1992.

365   WELCH ASKED THE GOVERNOR: The author obtained a copy of the letter, from Welch to Pataki, dated June 23, 1997.

366   "THE IDEA THAT": Quoted in "New Industrial Era Finds Workers Fighting to Regain Jobs," *Washington Post,* November 29, 1993.

367   KOERNKE'S MESSAGE OF HATRED AND DISTRUST: Mark Koernke's speech on February 4, 1995—to a crowd in Meadville, Pennsylvania, estimated at more than one thousand people—was characterized this way in the *Pittsburgh Post-Gazette* (on February 12, 1995): "For 3$\frac{1}{2}$ hours, Mark Koernke sketched a bizarre tableau of conspiracy and betrayal—an impending one-world government that he believes has spirited foreign troops into the United States where they fly about in mysterious black helicopters awaiting the signal to take over the country and take resisters to awaiting detention camps. The enemy, as Koernke sees it, is a new world order run by a group of international governments and financial interests he theorizes have been at work for 50 years.... Many of the listeners, according to those who attended, already wore caps with military insignias. Welcome to Armageddon."

368   THIS ECONOMIC RECOVERY: "Worker Earnings Post Rise of 2.7%, Lowest on Record," *New York Times,* November 1, 1995.

368 "ENLIGHTENED SELF-INTEREST": Quoted in Porras and Collins, *Built to Last*, p. 58.

369 "I WANT TO": Quoted in Porras and Collins, *Built to Last*, p. 48.

THE DRUG MECTIZAN: Levering and Moskowitz, *The 100 Best Companies to Work for in America*, p. 278.

"THE LONG-TERM CONSEQUENCES": Quoted in Porras and Collins, *Built to Last*, p. 47.

370 "IT JUST DOESN'T MAKE": Quoted in "Thanks, Goodbye: Amid Record Profits, Companies Continue to Lay Off Employees," *Wall Street Journal*, May 4, 1995.

"UNDER NO CIRCUMSTANCES": Quoted in "Does America Still Work?" *Harper's*, p. 43.

371 WHEN THE BASEBALL STRIKE: "Writing a New Social Contract," *Business Week*, March 11, 1996, p. 60.

WHEN DELUXE: "Writing a New Social Contract," *Business Week*, p. 61.

"WHAT RIGHT DO I HAVE": Quoted in "The Hit Men," *Newsweek*, February 26, 1996, pp. 47–48.

"I'VE TALKED TO PEOPLE": Quoted in "Alternative Employment Opportunities Show Hallmark's Long-Term Commitment to Employees," *Noon News*, a publication of Hallmark Cards Inc., November 23, 1992.

372 "I BELIEVE THERE ARE": Quoted in "Excellence, People Help Us Overcome Challenges," *Noon News*, May 8, 1991.

COOPER'S REMARKABLE: The stock appreciation numbers are found in "Now Hear This, Jack Welch!" *Fortune*, April 6, 1992, p. 94. The description of Cooper comes from a visit the author made to the company while on assignment for the *Wall Street Journal*.

THE AVERAGE CEO'S SALARY: The wage-disparity numbers are found in "Does America Still Work?" *Harper's*, p. 46, which cites as a source Graef S. Crystal, *In Search of Excess: The Overcompensation of American Executives* (New York: W.W. Norton, 1991).

373 HERMAN MILLER: The background on Herman Miller comes from the foreword of *Leadership is an Art* (New York: Doubleday, 1989).

374 "SLOAN'S BOOK": Quoted in Porras and Collins, *Built to Last*, p. 54.

AN "A-CORP.": The idea is spelled out in "Does America Still Work?" *Harper's*, p. 45.

376 "I THINK THAT'S": Quoted in "Jack Welch Lets Fly on Budgets, Bonuses, and Buddy Boards," *Fortune*, May 29, 1995, p. 147.

"THEY SHOULD HAVE BEEN UP": Quoted in "Jack Welch Lets Fly on Budgets, Bonuses, and Buddy Boards," *Fortune*, p. 145.

"EARLY IN MY CAREER": Quoted in "Jack Welch Lets Fly on Budgets, Bonuses, and Buddy Boards," *Fortune*, p. 146.

ACKNOWLEDGMENTS

Writing a book "is the closest a guy can come to having a baby," my good friend and mentor, the novelist Alfred Kern, observed in a recent letter. "Our pregnancies can last one hell of a long time, can they not?" They can indeed. And when the pregnancy drags on past its due date, as often occurs in literary endeavors, it is friendship—and faith—that keeps a writer from growing weary and losing heart. In that regard I consider myself a man most fortunate, for there were many people who befriended me, and prayed for me, in the course of writing this book. They include Rev. John Eby, Laurel Tessmer, Rev. Terry Timm, and Rev. Richard Wolling; the aforementioned Al Kern, whose letters were a source of encouragement at the times when I needed it most; and David Bear, Bill Furedy, Doron Levin, Dick Staaf, and Joe Williams, whose wise counsel and brotherly support were truly cherished.

It would be impossible to list all those who have given me help or information in the last six years. I have cited in the notes many of the more than three hundred people who spoke with me, often repeatedly, as interview subjects, and who generously provided their time as well as insights on the General Electric Company. They know who they are, and my debt to them is great.

Certain debts must be acknowledged specifically. *In Columbus, Ohio:* Dave Shroeder was a tireless, huge ally who spent many hours explaining the intricacies of the federal government's case against GE for price-fixing in synthetic diamonds, and who came to my defense when detractors sought to discredit me. Ed Russell gave me unparalleled access, in hundreds of hours of face-to-face meetings and telephone conversations, and unparalleled information not just on the diamond case but on the culture and history of GE in general. Denise Maurer candidly provided many details of the varied and complicated subplots of the diamond case. Paul Martins, of Cincinnati, guided me through the tortuous pathways of that case, explaining many legal nuances. Bruce Dunnington kept me abreast of developments in the Columbus courtroom as the trial unfolded; I also thank him for sharing his own manuscript.

In Schenectady, New York: Words cannot express my gratitude to Jack Shannon. He is one of the most courageous men I have known, a man of true conviction whose assistance was immeasurable, and whose determination was inspirational. John Harnden generously provided his observations, as well as a stack of books, which gave insight into the grandeur and glory of the "invention factory." Mark Markovitz spoke out with courage and conviction. The staff of the Hall of Electrical History were helpful, generous with their time, and exceedingly honest. Mary Kuykendall was tireless in her willingness to pass on information on the latest happenings in the former "Electric City." I am also grateful to many reporters in the newsroom of the *Schenectady Gazette*, for reporting on GE without fear or favor, for answering inquiries, and for returning frequent phone calls.

In Washington: Tom Carpenter, of the Government Accountability Project, provided many documents and devoted many hours explaining GE's management of Knolls and of Hanford. Scott Armstrong, of Taxpayers Against Fraud, was helpful in providing information on the various defense-contract scandals, as were Rich Hynes, Zie Hak, and Chester Walsh.

In the Hudson River Valley: I am grateful to Cara Lee, for introducing me to a network of people who care deeply about the river and its survival for future generations. Included among them were two people who gave me assistance above and beyond: Dr. Richard Bopp, who personally guided me to strategically important PCB sites on the river, and whose love of geology and the New York Yankees I share; and Everett Nack, who treated me to the most splendid time this or any other writer could have, the day we went fishing for sturgeon.

In Pittsfield, Massachusetts: Ed Bates is one of the kindliest gentlemen I have had the pleasure of knowing, and I am deeply grateful for the effort he put forth in explaining his own involvement in the PCB controversy, as well as leading me to other concerned parties. *In Connecticut:* John McLaughlin is a kind and gentle soul, and I thank him for opening many doors for me. *In Boston:* Phil McGovern was an uncompromising ally and a trusted friend. *In Mexico:* I wish to thank Leslie Gates and Kelly Poff for serving as interpreters and tour guides in the *maquiladora*, and my thanks go as well to the Roman Catholic Church for the important work it does there, and for the assistance its representatives provided to me. I am also deeply grateful to Siemens, Hitachi, and Toshiba for the access they granted me to their respective research facilities in Germany and Japan, and to their executives overseas.

This project would not have gotten started without the enthusiastic support it received at its inception from colleagues at the *Wall Street Journal*, including Carol Hymowitz, Ed Pound, and managing editor Paul Steiger, who graciously granted me a leave of absence to work on the book, and in addition provided wise advice. I wish to thank my editors at the *Pittsburgh Post-Gazette*: John Craig, one of America's great newspaper editors, and managing editor Madelyn Ross. I am deeply grateful for the support I have received from colleagues at the *PG*, many of whom brought GE-related material to my attention, and for research assistance provided by Steve Karlinchak, Andrés Martinez, and Caroline Abels, whose ferreting out of court documents in Connecticut saved me vast quantities of time. I also wish to thank court clerks in locales too numerous to mention, and public and newspaper librarians in the following cities: Cincinnati, Columbus, Erie, Fort Wayne, Louisville, Schenectady; and Pittsfield, Lynn, and Salem, Massachusetts.

My agent, Ed Novak, looked after business and more; he helped refine my thoughts, he put pencil to paper, he was a confidant and trusted ally. I am deeply indebted to Jonathan Segal, my editor, who believed in this project and held firm despite gale-force winds; without his unceasing support, this book would not have been published. Jon dispensed patience and firmness in equal measure as required. I am grateful, too, for the title he contributed, and for the many hours he toiled shaping the content of the manuscript and polishing its words. My lawyer, Roslyn Litman, wrote some great letters at some crucial junctures. She was a tiger, but with style and grace.

I want to thank my children, Brendan, Cara, and Erin, who endured the distractions of their father far too long. And from my heart, I want to thank my wife, Louise, who demonstrated more patience and fortitude than should be demanded of any woman in several lifetimes. Above all, I want to thank God, for this is a project that has been—and will continue to be—in His hands.

T.F.O'B.

INDEX

Thomas F. O'Boyle has been writing about business and management issues since 1979. He covered U.S., European, and Asian industrial corporations for eleven years at the *Wall Street Journal*, including a four-year assignment as the *Journal*'s correspondent in Germany. Mr. O'Boyle was named business editor of the *Pittsburgh Post-Gazette* in 1994, where he is currently an assistant managing editor. He lives with his wife and three children near Pittsburgh.

A NOTE ON THE TYPE

This book was set in Minion, a typeface produced by the Adobe Corporation specifically for the Macintosh personal computer, and released in 1990. Designed by Robert Slimbach, Minion combines the classic characteristics of old style faces with the full complement of weights required for modern typesetting.

Composed by Creative Graphics, Allentown, Pennsylvania
Printed and bound by Quebecor Printing,
Martinsburg, West Virginia
Designed by Robert C. Olsson